Learning at a Distance
A World Perspective

Edited by

John S. Daniel
Martha A. Stroud
John R. Thompson

374
.4
L438

Athabasca University / International Council for Correspondence Education

Edmonton, 1982

The text of this book is set in Frutiger typeface and composed on a Linotron 202 linked to a computerized text processing system.

Every effort has been taken to ensure that these materials comply with the requirements of copyright clearances and appropriate credits.

Cover Photography: Bob Zebic
Visual Designer: Bob Robertson

© Athabasca University / International Council for Correspondence Education, 1982
ISBN 0-919737-00-5

Table of Contents

Preface 5

International Trends

Paper 1
Introduction 7

Paper 2
Trends in the Use of Audio-Visual Media in Distance Education Systems
Tony Bates 8

Paper 3
Distance Teaching North and South
Hilary Perraton 16

Paper 4
Correspondence Teaching: Second Choice or Second Class?
Giampaolo Bonani 19

Paper 5
Individualizing Support Services
David Sewart 27

Paper 6
Recent Research in Distance Learning
Dan O. Coldeway 29

Paper 7
Teaching Models for Designing Courses Creatively
John A. Bååth 37

Paper 8
From New Delhi to Vancouver: Trends in Distance Education
Desmond J. Keegan 40

Paper 9
Adult Education: A Perspective for the Eighties
James A. Draper 43

Paper 10
A Study of Two Self-Study Youth Centres
Ben K. Gitau 47

Learning at a Distance and National Development

Paper 11
Introduction 52

Paper 12
The Inevitability of Distance Education in Africa
Joe K. Ansere 53

Paper 13
Distance Education in Developing Countries: The Need for Central Planning
Bakhshish Singh 61

Paper 14
Problems of Distance Education in Developing Countries
Ruddar Datt 63

Paper 15
The Status of Correspondence Education in India: A Survey
Arun K. Gupta 65

Paper 16
Distance Education Without Hardware
Gunvant B. Shah 67

Paper 17
Some Problems with Printed Materials in Basic Adult Education
Eloísa Trillo 68

Paper 18
The Fires of Distance Education in Latin America
Paul S. Anderson 70

Paper 19
The Capricorn Interuniversity Program: An Example of International Cooperation in Distance Education
Luis Nicolini 72

Paper 20
Using Distance Education to Train Business and Government Personnel
Andrew H. Joseph & Susana B. De Milanesi 73

Paper 21
National Policies for Distance Education
Kenneth Noyau 75

Paper 22
Conflict in Distance Education
Barry Hutchinson 76

Paper 23
Correspondence Education: Private Enterprise and Public Responsibility
Erling Ljoså 77

Paper 24
Continuing Education by Distance Study
Otto Peters 79

Paper 25
The Reform of Adult Education in French-Canada: An Expanded Role for Home Study
John S. Daniel 81

Paper 26
Elementary Education of Children at a Distance
John Penberthy 82

Table of Contents

The Process of Learning at a Distance: Recent Research and Developments

Paper 27
Introduction 86

Paper 28
The Adult Learners: Who Are They, Why and Where do They Learn?
Ignacy Waniewicz 87

Paper 29
What Does Educational Psychology Tell Us about the Adult Learner at a Distance?
Dan O. Coldeway 90

Paper 30
Designing Interesting Courses
Alvin Finkel 94

Paper 31
Orientations to Studies, Approaches to Texts: A Relational View of Study Skills Applied to Distance Learning
Ference Marton & Lennart Svensson 97

Paper 32
Understanding the Distance Learner as a Whole Person
Alistair Morgan & Elizabeth Taylor & Graham Gibbs 103

Paper 33
Individual and Group Work in Distance Studies: Which Process for What Purpose?
Klaus Müller 106

Paper 34
Content Analysis for Course Design
Marg Penney 107

Paper 35
The Readability of Study Materials: Recent Research in New Zealand
Nola Holmes 109

Paper 36
Attrition: A Case Study
Douglas G. Shale 113

Paper 37
Reducing the Drop-Out Rate in Advanced Courses
Alan Woodley 118

Paper 38
The Drop-Out Problem and What To Do About It
Torstein Rekkedal 118

Paper 39
Correspondence vs. On-Campus Courses: Some Evaluative Comparisons
Earl R. Misanchuk 122

Paper 40
Liaison Between the School System and the Correspondence Branch
Chet Tesarowski 124

Paper 41
Characteristics and Attitudes of Correspondence Students
Christopher K. Knapper & Mary Ann Wasylycia-Coe 125

Paper 42
How Different is the Distance Student?
F.R. Jevons 126

Paper 43
Student Achievement as a Function of Student Time: A Comparative Analysis
V.J. White & J.C. Taylor 128

Paper 44
The Cost-Effectiveness of Distance Teaching for School Equivalency
François Orivel & Dean T. Jamison 133

Student Support and Regional Services

Paper 45
Introduction 134

Paper 46
The Role of the Correspondence Tutor
Roger Lewis 135

Paper 47
Student Support: How Much is Enough?
Kevin C. Smith & Ian W. Small 137

Paper 48
Industrialized Counselling
Helmut Fritsch 140

Paper 49
Studying at Home
Louise Singer 141

Paper 50
Training Telephone Tutors
Bente Roed Cochran & Alan Meech 143

Paper 51
Student Support at a Crossroads
Simon Caron 145

Paper 52
Study Circles
Heikki Kirkinen 149

Paper 53
Student Support Services in Continuing Education
A. Roger Mills & Alan W. Tait 151

Paper 54
Mobile Learning Centres in an Open Learning System
Don Salter 154

Paper 55
The Role of Regional Centres
Denys Meakin 157

Paper 56
Local Support for the Local Learner
Mike Walker 159

Paper 57
FlexiStudy
Richard Freeman 162

Policy-Making and Management

Paper 58
Introduction 166

Paper 59
Plan to Reality: The Netherlands Open University
Ruud de Moor 168

Paper 60
Plan to Reality: The Japan University of the Air
Takashi Sakamoto 171

Paper 61
Plan to Reality: The Open Learning Institute
Ian Mugridge 174

Paper 62
Resource Allocation in the Australian Two-Mode University
Patrick Guiton 176

Paper 63
Distance Education by Cooperation
Hjalmar Rande 179

Paper 64
A Cooperative Model for Distance Studies
Karlheinz Rebel 180

Paper 65
From Realities to Plans
Douglas G. Crawford & Gail C. Crawford 182

Paper 66
Comparative Models of Distance Education: Institutional Design and Management
Geoffrey Potter 185

Paper 67
How Can the Conventional University Serve the Distance Learner?
Herbert Mainusch 187

Paper 68
The Neglected Role of Disciplinary Research in the Distance University
Stephen Griew 188

Paper 69
Managing the Course Development Process
Jack Foks 191

Paper 70
Updating the Course Team
Roger Bédard 193

Paper 71
Systems Approaches in Distance Education
Charles R. Shobe 195

Paper 72
Responding to Economic Austerity: Can Economic Models of Distance Teaching Help Us?
Greville Rumble 199

Paper 73
The Administrator's Task: Conventional and Distance Education Compared
Pierre DeCelles & Clément Marquis 201

Paper 74
Standards for Independent Study: The American Experience in Higher Education
Susan S. Burcaw 202

Paper 75
Accreditation: A Workable Option
D.W. Holbrook 204

Paper 76
How Does the Public See Us?
David M. Young 206

Paper 77
The Use of Media in Public Relations and Advertising for Correspondence Courses
Marcia Brock 213

Paper 78
How Can Regional Associations Be Useful? The Example of ASPESA
Ian McD. Mitchell 215

Paper 79
A Regional Basis for an International Organization for Distance Education
Jerry Grimwade 217

Diverse Subjects, Diverse Approaches

Paper 80
Introduction 218

Paper 81
Learning to Learn
Kathleen Forsythe 219

Paper 82
Increasing Student Involvement, Minimizing Teacher Dominance: The Assessment and Practice of Writing Improvement
Alister Cumming & Ronald Mackay 222

Paper 83
Read and Write Better
Brenda Howell 227

Paper 84
Tell Me How to Write
Janet Jenkins 227

Paper 85
Learning Spanish at a Distance
Doris T. Stephens 230

Paper 86
Teaching University French from a Distance: The Student Population Examined
Dominique A.M.X. Abrioux 232

Paper 87
Learning French at a Distance: The Student's Perspective
Muriel H.L. Stringer 236

Paper 88
Teaching Languages Through Broadcasting
Sheila Innes 239

Paper 89
Distance Education for the In-Service Training of Teachers
A.M. Nashif 241

Paper 90
Uses of Case Studies in Self-Learning Texts
Graham H. Weaver 245

Paper 91
The Training of Teachers of Second Languages at a Distance
Réal G. Boulianne 245

Paper 92
Music in Distance Education: Possibilities and Limitations
Bernt J. Ottem 247

Table of Contents

Paper 93
Business Education: Our Major Challenge
J. Grant Loudon 250

Paper 94
Affective Education at a Distance: An Extensive Experiment
Louise Marchand 251

Paper 95
The Future of Teaching Technological Subjects at a Distance
John H. Horlock 252

Paper 96
Providing Continuing Education for Special Professional Groups
Ralph C. Smith 255

Paper 97
Distance Study at the Post-Graduate Level
Börje Holmberg 258

Paper 98
Open Access Study
Keith C. Sullivan 261

The Contribution of Media and Technology to Learning at a Distance

Paper 99
Introduction 263

Paper 100
Three Ways of Providing Computer-Assisted Learning at a Distance and Their Probable Impacts on Various Classes of Clients
Gary M. Boyd 265

Paper 101
Distance Education and the Information Revolution
John C. Madden 268

Paper 102
Reflections on the Use of Media in Distance Education
Horst Dichanz 271

Paper 103
Television in Distance Education
Wolfgang Schimeck 272

Paper 104
Student Perceptions of Media in French University Distance Education Systems
Robert Lefranc 273

Paper 105
Academic Equivalency of Credit Courses by Teleconference
G. Barry Ellis & Robert S. Chapman 276

Paper 106
The Contribution of Broadcasting to Adult and Continuing Education
Neil H. Barnes 278

Paper 107
Multi-Media Methods for Adult Basic Education
Anthony R. Kaye 281

Paper 108
The TVOntario Academy
Ignacy Waniewicz 285

Paper 109
Videodisc and Videotex: New Media for Distance Education
Susan G. D'Antoni 287

Paper 110
Using Videotex in Distance Education
Paul Hurly & Denis Hlynka 291

Paper 111
Videodiscs: Will Laser Technology Help Light the Way for Learning at a Distance?
R. Ruggles & D.E. Blackmore 292

Paper 112
The Contribution of Data Processing to Student Administration at the Open University
H. Zvi Friedman 292

Paper 113
Towards the Integrated Use of the Computer in Distance Education
Kari Lampikoski 296

Paper 114
Increasing Completion Rates with Computer-Assisted Lessons
C. Alex Phillips & Roger G. Young 298

Paper 115
Tutoring by CYCLOPS
David McConnell 299

Paper 116
Reaching Learners Through Telecommunications
Raymond J. Lewis 300

Paper 117
Text Processing: The Revolution in Word Manipulation
Don W. Cowper & John R. Thompson 301

Paper 118
Experimental Research on Computer-Assisted Distance Education
John A. Bååth 303

Appendix

Distance Education - Musical Revue
Ross Paul 306

Glossary of Terms 308

Bibliography 310

Notes on the Contributors 318

Author Index 325

Subject Index 329

Preface

Learning at a distance is becoming an increasingly common form of education in many countries of the world. The growth of institutions that provide instruction at a distance has been accompanied by the development of a body of knowledge about the principles and procedures that can make this form of learning a successful and satisfying experience for students. Without starting a debate about whether this body of knowledge should be designated an academic discipline, it is easy to find signs of its new maturity as a field of study. Terminology has become more precise, an important example being the consensus that has emerged in the last few years around the definition and use of the term *distance education* to describe the field as a whole. Scholarly communication has been facilitated by new publications, notably the journal *Distance Education* launched in 1980 by the Australia and South Pacific External Studies Association, and already the possessor of an international readership. The South American bulletin *ED-DIS*, published in Portugese and Spanish, is of even more recent vintage, and the British Open University now maintains a document centre that monitors developments all over the world.

As these examples imply, academic communication about distance education is highly international in nature, which gives a special importance to world conferences and regional gatherings. The last world conference of the International Council for Correspondence Education (ICCE), held in New Delhi in 1978, was followed a year later by the Conference on the Education of Adults at a Distance (CEAD) convened by the British Open University to celebrate its first ten years of existence. At the final session of CEAD a proposal to create a new international association for individuals and institutions active in distance education provoked a lively debate. The final consensus was against the proposal, largely on the grounds that it would be more appropriate to encourage ICCE, a body already forty years old, to fill the role by expanding its membership and interests and improving the quality and effectiveness of its activities.

This book is part of the response of ICCE to that challenge. It constitutes the basic document of the Vancouver world conference on *Learning at a Distance* in 1982. This book describes the state of the art of distance education in the early 1980s. It was planned by the program committee of ICCE consisting of Giampaolo Bonani (Italy), Adrea Fineza (Philippines), Bill Fowler (United States), Janet Jenkins (United Kingdom), Desmond Keegan (Australia), Erling Ljoså (Norway), Vijaya Mulay (India), Regino Cordero Romo (Spain), David Sewart (United Kingdom), Keeneth Tsekoa (Lesotho), Chester Zelaya Goodman (Costa Rica), Audrey Campbell, Susan Fleming, Martha Stroud, and John Daniel (Canada).

The committee used a version of the Delphi technique to map out the field of distance education, identify topics of special interest, and choose contributors to write about them. The original plan called for about fifty articles. In the event the announcement of the project aroused such interest that after careful selection the book still includes papers or abstracts from over 120 authors representing some 25 countries. We regret that no papers were forthcoming from the communist world but with that exception the international coverage is good.

A theme of international dimensions common to many papers is the prospect of distance education becoming a major shaping force in societies all over the world. To judge from several contributors distance education seems to be approaching a crossroads where it will either stride towards its full potential in the mainstream of the social, cultural, and economic activities of virtually every nation of the world, or toddle along on the periphery where it has been since its beginnings. As evidence is cited not only the rapid growth and changes in communications technologies but also the pressure of economics in developed and developing nations alike to extend education to previously neglected or poorly served segments of society. (This often comes under the rubric of *lifelong learning* for industralized nations and *basic education*—or simply *literacy*—for nations of the third world. Whatever the more distant future holds, the next decade or two seems destined to become increasingly active for distance educators and their political hosts throughout the world.

The papers were prepared for publication by the editorial team. Space limitations obliged us to shorten most articles and, in cases of late submission or duplication of topic, to include abstracts only. We are grateful to all the authors for permission to edit or abstract their papers and we apologize if at any point we have inadvertently modified the sense of the original. Our overriding aim has been to help the reader and for this reason we have provided introductions to the major sections of the book. Naturally, many papers touch on the themes of several sections but we hope the subject index will make it easy to find all references to a particular topic.

The project would have proved impossible without the help of many colleagues. It is a pleasure to acknowledge the support received from our own institutions and from the University of British Columbia and the Open Learning Institute. For their contribution at the editorial stage we are especially grateful to Elizabeth Gardham and Lan Tsang of Concordia University, Peter Krueger and Sam Smith of the

Preface

University of Calgary, and Barbara Spronk of Athabasca University.

The physical production of the book was carried out using the integrated text processing and photocomposition facility at Athabasca University. We are particularly indebted to Don Cowper and Wendy Edmondson for making the system work so well for us.

Finally, we thank the contributors for writing such interesting papers. Working with these papers has been a rewarding experience. We have learned much about distance education and we hope that readers of the book will share the sense of newfound knowledge we gained in putting it together.

John S. Daniel
Martha A. Stroud
John R. Thompson

International Trends

Introduction
Paper 1

The nine articles in this first section of *Learning at a Distance: A World Perspective* have been chosen because they highlight important trends. Many of these trends are explored in greater detail in the subsequent sections, each of which explores a particular facet of distance education.

The opportunities for learning at a distance have expanded rapidly since 1960. Perraton (paper 3) reports the creation of twenty distance learning projects in Africa in fifteen years and the tripling of the number of correspondence institutions in Australia in less than a decade. He also observes a dramatic growth in the literature of distance education, which is evidence, according to Keegan (paper 8), of the buoyancy of distance teaching institutions and the increasing volume of research and scholarship in the field. This rapid development, and the extreme diversity of the institutions involved, leads Keegan to attempt to define distance education more precisely in terms of its fundamental distinguishing characteristics. Sewart (paper 5), however, warns against overstressing the distinctiveness of learning at a distance. Although the production of course materials does resemble an industrial process, the mediation required between student and materials places distance study firmly on a continuum with other forms of education: "A mass-produced package of 'knowledge' cannot be fitted to a student as a mass-produced nut can be fitted to a bolt".

The possibilities of learning at a distance are of particular interest to developing countries for, as Draper (paper 9) points out, social and community action depend on individual learning. Formal and non-formal learning are both important and psychological distance can be as significant as the barriers of geography and time. People must be helped both to anticipate the future and to participate in making it. To contribute most effectively to the process distance education must provide new curricula. Both Perraton (paper 3) and Gitau (paper 10) warn developing countries that they miss a great opportunity if they use learning at a distance simply to make the old colonial curriculum available more widely. Bonani (paper 4) joins Gitau in urging the unique role of correspondence study in helping drop-outs from the conventional systems of primary and secondary education to obtain fulfilment through employment.

Learning at a distance has taken a diversity of forms in different countries. Keegan (paper 8) distinguishes four basic models for providing education at a distance while Bonani (paper 4) examines the political principles that determine how it is organized in different countries around the world. He urges greater awareness of the essential complementarity of public and private institutions. Perraton (paper 3) looks at the successes of systems in the "three worlds" and notes that distance learning has made the biggest contribution in the developing world, partly because many leaders in these countries are sympathetic to the non-traditional methods through which they often received their own education. In the communist world the integration of distance education with employment is especially close and notable successes in the industrialized western world are the high quality of learning materials and the comprehensiveness of some student support systems.

Student support is a recurrent theme throughout the book. In this section Bååth (paper 7) claims that tutors can play a key role in clarifying comprehension and linking course content to the student's existing framework of knowledge and experience. Establishing this linkage is vital if meaningful verbal learning rather than rote learning is to be achieved. Sewart (paper 5) points out that since institutions can have little direct control over tutor-student interactions they should pay particular attention to selecting and training tutors and providing them with up to date information on their students. All the same, Gitau (paper 10) and Coldeway (paper 6) sound cautionary notes about tutoring. Gitau warns that too much tutoring can re-create the unhealthy dependence on the teacher that it is one of the virtues of correspondence education to avoid. Coldeway, basing himself on a literature review and his own research, argues that distance education has created too much mythology around the tutoring function. There is a wide gap between the reality of the student-tutor relationship and institutional rhetoric on the subject. This is a particular symptom of the general weakness of research on learning at a distance until very recently and Coldeway hopes that future writing will give increasing importance to rigourous studies with properly defined variables and boundaries. He would also like to see a more subtle measure of institutional success and student satisfaction than the drop-out rate. While this may be desirable both Sewart (paper 5) and Perraton (paper 3) imply that the embarrassment of high drop-out rates is a useful goad that should not be blunted by complex rationalizations.

Paper 1

The use of audio-visual media is an important element of the transformation of correspondence education into distance education. Bates (paper 2) provides a fascinating review of the changing role of media. He records a clear trend away from broadcasting in distance education. Perraton (paper 3) finds this trend disquieting and argues that the world's massive educational needs require recourse to the mass media. Draper (paper 9) hopes that radio will have a major educational role in the developing world.

In the context of the trend away from TV broadcasting Bates (paper 2) examines the characteristics and applications of videodiscs, video and audio cassettes, telephones, videotex, and computers. He concludes that audio-visual media are currently underused in distance learning—partly because few of the staff of educational institutions have training in media. The move from broadcasting to student-controlled media should provide opportunities for conventional institutions to do more teaching at a distance, although the lack of trained staff will likely be an even bigger obstacle in their case.

In looking to the future, the authors each identify relationships of special importance to distance education. Bates would like to see closer and more equal partnerships with broadcasting agencies and Perraton fears that some distance learning projects will merely produce pale copies of an inadequate conventional system of education. Recognition of the substantial role of private institutions is important to Bonani, and Sewart emphasizes the essential unity of all forms of learning. Closer awareness of the value of educational research and instructional theory is urged by Coldeway and Bååth respectively. Finally, Keegan, Draper, and Gitau emphasize that learning at a distance will help provide a better future for millions of people if it can maintain a dynamic relationship with changing patterns of employment, leisure, and work.

Paper 2

Trends in the Use of Audio-Visual Media in Distance Education Systems

New media may produce a move away from large distance education systems towards more local initiatives based on conventional institutions.

The main trends

It is easier to set out what I think are the main trends than it is to justify my views, so let me start with what normally might be considered conclusions:

- There is a clear movement *away* from using broadcasting by distance learning systems.

- The range of audio-visual media suitable for distance education is rapidly increasing.

- The educational potential of audio-visual media still tends to be under-exploited by distance learning systems.

The evidence

It is impossible for one person to be familiar with trends in every distance learning system. However, in 1980 I was commissioned by the International Institute of Educational Planning in Paris to carry out a survey of the use of audio-visual media in 12 distance learning systems, deliberately chosen to provide a variety of distance learning institutions known to use audio-visual media (see Table 1). In other words, the sample was deliberately biased towards those already using audio-visual media, as the survey was part of a study designed to identify the main planning and management needs of distance learning institutions using audio-visual media (Bates, 1981).

My evidence is based primarily on the data provided by the 12 institutions through a specially designed postal questionnaire, and from discussions at a workshop in Paris attended by representatives of each of the 12 institutions. This evidence is also supplemented by my experience of working on distance projects in Norway, Thailand, Iran, and the Philippines.

Table 1: The 12 distance learning institutions in the survey

Institution	Country	Type of Distance Learning Institution*
		(see Bates, 1981 for full discussion).*
1. Educational Television Foundation of Maranhão	Brazil	Media-based formal school system
2. College of the Air	Mauritius	Independent d.l.i. teaching to external formal qualifications or syllabuses
3. Distance Learning Centre	Lesotho	
4. Allama Iqbal Open University	Pakistan	
5. Athabasca University	Canada	
6. Everyman's University	Israel	Autonomous credit-giving multi-media system established solely for distance learners
7. National Radio and Television University for Teachers	Poland	
8. Open University	United Kingdom	
9. Sri Lankan Institute of Distance Education	Sri Lanka	
10. Universidad Estatal a Distancia	Costa Rica	
11. Norwegian Institute of Distance Education	Norway	Cooperative multi-media systems, involving several autonomous organizations
12. Institute of Adult Education	Tanzania	Autonomous multi-media systems, non-credit giving

The move from broadcasting

The move from broadcasting is not recent, but goes back to the original shift from "A University of the Air" to the creation of "An Open University". The original Planning Committee of the Open University soon realized that the amount of learning materials required to meet the needs of a full range of degree courses would be too great to cover by broadcasting alone. However, I was surprised to find that while 9 of the 12 institutions used broadcast television, and 10 used radio, apart from the Open University and ETV Maranhão (which is a schools system) only one broadcast more than 10 hours a week of television, and none broadcast more than five hours a week of radio. The Open University in the UK with 35 hours a week of television, and 24 hours a week of radio, was clearly very different from the other 11 institutions. In only 3 of the 12 institutions (ETV Maranhão; NURT, Poland; and Mauritius College of the Air) was television the main medium. In all the others, print was the main medium.

Why is it that broadcast television and radio services, with their glamour and appeal, their ability to reach mass audiences, their many years of experience in educational broadcasting, and their often formidable political influence, appear to be playing so small a role in the development of distance learning systems? The survey provided some suggestions, none of which is likely to come as a surprise.

Firstly, in most countries, the broadcasting service is provided by an organization—a national broadcasting organization, commercial stations, or a government department—separate from the distance learning system. Eleven of the 12 institutions were dependent on a separate broadcast organization for the production and distribution of at least some of their broadcast material. Despite the high costs, the problems of recruitment, and the difficulty of fully using expensive facilities, most institutions wanted their own television production facilities. The main reason was their perceived lack of control over production material. Satisfactory cooperation between broadcast organizations and educational institutions seems difficult to achieve in most countries. It has obviously proved hard for others to find a model equivalent to the unique cooperative partnership between the Open University and the BBC.

The second major problem was getting adequate transmission facilities. Most institutions were dissatisfied with the *quality* of the times available, particularly for broadcasts aimed at adults. However, I have some sympathy for the broadcasting organizations here. Since none of the institutions had more than 10,000 students following any single course, this was the maximum target audience for what were often national transmissions. Many transmissions—especially at the Open University—are aimed at fewer than 500 students. It is not surprising that broadcasting organizations are unwilling to make available peak viewing or listening times to such small, specialist audiences. *Serious* teaching, even in distance education systems, is rarely aimed at *mass* audiences, in broadcasting terms.

Perhaps more surprising was the difficulty in several countries of *accessing* the target audience through broadcasting. While it is perhaps to be expected that in Tanzania, radio can reach only about 45% of the population, I was surprised to find that Athabasca University had real problems in getting television programs to students because of the complexities and limitations of the cable TV system in the province.

Cost, however, did *not* seem to be a major reason why broadcasting was not heavily used. Many institutions in any case do not have to pay the "real" cost of broadcasting, and when they do, it is sometimes separately paid for by their governments. None of the 7 institutions that provided cost information used more than 20% of its total budget on broadcasting.

I believe that the *main* reason why broadcasting is not used more by distance learning institutions is because of academic distrust. Those responsible for the academic content of courses in the 12 institutions rarely had received any training in the use of audio-visual media. Few of the institutions were able to specify why television, for instance, should be used instead of print. There is a lack of an educational theory that can provide clear guidelines as to the unique advantages of television or radio over print or face-to-face teaching. I shall be returning to this issue later, but most teachers and educators are unable or unwilling to see the *educational* (as distinct from the *distributional*) advantages of television and radio. Little has been done in the last 10 years to remove this distrust. Indeed, in some institutions, closer exposure to broadcasting and broadcasters has increased this distrust.

A wider range of media

There are two distinct trends emerging here. The *number* of different audio-visual media suitable for distance education is increasing rapidly, offering more choice, and more difficult decisions regarding the selection and integration of media. Secondly, the *boundaries* between different media are breaking down, again causing difficulties for distance learning systems, this time regarding management and production. I will discuss below some of the new developments in audio-visual media that are affecting—or will very soon affect—distance education systems.

Video cassettes and videodiscs

Six of the 9 systems in the IIEP survey using television now offer a video cassette service to students. In all cases, this is mainly a back up to transmitted programs—in other words, each program is broadcast at least once, and some programs are also available on cassette for use at local centres. Currently, though, market penetration is not yet sufficient, even in the more prosperous countries, for distance education systems to be able to assume that a majority of potential students will have video cassette machines in their own homes. Indeed, it is likely to be several more years before this situation occurs—if ever—although for certain specialist courses, like postgraduate training for doctors, or in-service training for teachers, availability of cassette machines is already high in North America, Japan, and Western Europe.

Video cassettes are used in most courses to back up transmission, rather than as the main system of distribution, because broadcasting (or cable) penetration is generally more extensive. However, the use of cassettes merely to distribute programs made as broadcasts means that the full educational potential of video cassettes is not yet being fully exploited. This potential will become clearer when I discuss audio cassettes, but video material produced right from the beginning for use only on cassette (or disc, for that matter) requires a very different style of production and can serve a different range of teaching functions from broadcast television. Where distance education systems depend heavily on students attending local centres, video cassettes can more easily be used specifically as video cassettes. Group use of video cassettes enables students to draw out much more from the programs than if they are watching in isolation; programs used individually by students on cassettes lend themselves much more to the teaching of skills.

Video cassette use is certain to increase. Costs will continue to drop, particularly with the availability now of a 1/4" video cassette system. More importantly, production for distribution on cassette will free distance education systems from their dependence on broadcast organizations for television production. In-house production or the use of small video production companies becomes feasible. While this will give more flexibility on costs, and perhaps more control over program material for distance education systems, there could be a loss of range and quality in programming that would reduce the range of educational functions that can be met by television.

Therefore the judgement of whether to use video cassettes *instead* of broadcasting will remain a difficult decision for several more years for some institutions. For distance education systems, like the Open University, with large numbers of programs and students, transmission costs can still be lower than video cassette distribution costs. The main advantage of broadcasting is its ability to reach into every home, and cassettes will not be able to do that for a long time, if ever.

The difficulty of writing a paper a year before publication is nowhere better illustrated than when discussing videodiscs. In Britain, at the time of writing, we are still awaiting the launch of any videodisc system. In terms of hardware, discs appear to have advantages over cassettes: freeze-frame, a rapid and accurate search, large single frame storage capacity, slow and speeded-up motion, and lower machine cost. The value, however, of videodiscs for distance education will depend crucially on three factors: the speed and extent of domestic market penetration of any single system compared with video cassettes; the unit cost of producing discs in relatively small production runs per program; and further developments in cassette and television distribution technologies. There is evidence for instance that the next range of cassette machines will incorporate several of the technical features currently unique to discs, such as freeze-frame and fast search. The high cost of copying discs currently makes them economical only for very large runs. Many institutions, however, want small runs, perhaps 1000 to 5000 copies at the most for home use, even less for local centre use. Cassette use also makes it possible to despatch video material through *transmission* (perhaps at night) using automatic recording devices activated by coding signals. Thus a single student requires only one or two cassettes for all his programming, instead of several discs. In a system with 50,000 students and perhaps 1000 programs, this could give significant cost advantages to cassettes over discs.

All this, however, is speculation. I do not expect discs to be in widespread use in distance education within the next five years. I do expect video cassette use to expand substantially over the next five years. Anyone wanting to speculate on these two media beyond that time scale is either very brave or very foolish.

Cable and satellite TV

Satellite and cable TV should provide more channels and hence more and better transmission times for the minority broadcasting required by distance teaching systems. However, satellites are not significantly different in structure or function from terrestrially transmitted broadcasts, unlike programs made for use on cassettes or discs. Moreover, terrestrial transmissions may still be better at reaching the kind of target audiences often given priority by distance education systems. Rural communities are often not well served by cable.

Athabasca University shows how difficult it is to provide systematic and comprehensive coverage for its students via cable. Memorial University, Newfoundland, provides general educational programming via cable for the population of St. John's, but its distance education courses have to use video cassettes for the outreach centres in the rest of the province.

Satellite TV will give better rural coverage, and a uniform national or at least regional service, but, like cable systems, commercial and financial structuring could well result in satellite TV being received by only the more wealthy sectors of society. Furthermore, it is likely in Western Europe that the maximum number of television channels available to any single country via satellite will be five, so increased access to peak times for distance education systems is by no means certain via satellites. Government regulations will be crucial, and distance education systems will need a strong lobby to ensure their interests are protected if they wish to use cable or satellite.

Audio cassettes

Video cassettes, videodiscs, and satellite TV are "exciting" technologies and arouse great interest in educational circles, but in my own institution, the greatest media development during its 12 years of existence has been the humble audio cassette. In 1981, there will be 68 courses using 184 audio cassette productions, equivalent in playing time to 588 radio programs. In 1977, hardly any OU course used program material created specially for cassette use.

In the production year 1981/82, 164 radio programs and 234 cassette programs will be made, so the OU is now already making more material for use on cassettes than on radio. Furthermore, over a third (38%) of the students who listen to radio programs hear them on recordings. I was therefore surprised to see that only 5 of the 12 institutions in the IIEP survey used audio cassettes. The main difficulty for developing countries was the lack of cassette machines in student homes and the difficulty of physically distributing cassettes. At the OU, over 87% of students had access to audio cassette machines, and it is no more expensive for the OU to purchase and copy cassettes, and to mail them to students with their other materials, than it is to pay for radio transmission times for courses with fewer than 500 students.

There are several reasons why audio cassettes are so popular now at the Open University. The academics like them, because they feel they have more control over their use, and can integrate cassettes more tightly into course design. Cassettes can be used in a variety of ways—for mastery learning, for commenting on diagrams, charts, tables or text, for backing up or commenting on other media (cassettes have been found extremely useful for analysis of linked television programs), as resource material (bringing recordings of real-life situations, conversations, interviews, etc., which are then analysed), or for specialist lectures that explore the wider significance of the course subject. The use of two channels—sound and vision—in a controlled and integrated way, through the combined use of cassette and print or "media", is a very powerful teaching medium.

Students like audio cassettes. In a majority of courses, they are ranked as the most useful component after the correspondence texts. In a few courses, they have been ranked as the *most* useful component of the course. The features that appeal to students are their convenience (they can use cassettes whenever they wish to study), the control students have over them (they can play parts of the cassette as many or as few times as they need), and their informality. Students frequently comment that cassettes are like having a personal tutorial with the course author in the student's own room, a quality that appears to be lacking in radio programs, however skilfully they are made. Cassettes have a production style and process very different from that of radio programs.

I therefore see audio cassettes integrated with correspondence material as a major area for development in distance education: they are cheap, easy to control and make, convenient for students, and above all, educationally effective. (For further discussion see Durbridge, 1981).

Telephone teaching

Telephone teaching is used extensively in 4 of the 12 institutions and is proving to be popular with both tutors and students. There are, nevertheless, still many problems. Several institutions did not have a telephone system widespread enough or reliable enough to be useful (e.g., Tanzania). Even where there is good national coverage, line quality is often a problem. In some countries (e.g., Norway), telephone teaching is prohibitively expensive because of problems of distance. It is also clear that special skills from tutors, and discipline from students, are required, particularly for teleconferencing. This again is an area where careful costing is necessary, particularly since telephone charges can easily be "lost" in other budgets, but nevertheless contribute a real cost to the institution.

However, if distance education systems wish to provide a wide range of courses to students who are often scattered or isolated, telephone tuition is the only practical way of providing two-way, interactive tutorials. For instance, at the Open University, in one region covering a population of around 4 million, there are over 100 courses with fewer than 50 students. The most that such a region can afford to provide in the way of face-to-face tuition is one or two day schools on a Saturday. Even then, many of the students will have to travel over 100 miles to attend. Telephone tuition in such circumstances is not a poor alternative to face-to-face teaching; the alternative is no direct tuition at all.

There is still great resistance to telephone teaching. At the Open University, each region is responsible for its own tutorial arrangements. In 1981, one region scheduled over 200 hours of telephone tuition. Several other regions scheduled none. Such differences cannot be explained solely in terms of geography. There seem to be four main problems: technical problems; lack of visuals; costs; user resistance.

Line quality and connection is still a problem in many countries. Lines from rural locations in particular (ironically, the areas that benefit most from telephone tuition) can be poor. Poor operator performance can wreck group telephone tutorials via conference call systems. Distance learning systems can overcome this by installing conference bridging equipment in area offices, providing their own operators, and renting dedicated lines from local centres to the headquarters (as at Wisconsin). However, the latter solution does not help the home-based student. Nevertheless, despite the technical difficulties, there are enough examples of successful tuition by telephone to suggest that well prepared, well trained tutors supported by committed administrators, will usually succeed. But it is still very hard work. (See Robinson, 1979).

The lack of visual support can be overcome by use of systems such as CYCLOPS, developed at the Open University. This allows tutors and students to use a light-pen to write or draw on an ordinary TV screen. The picture is converted digitally to a second signal and sent down a standard telephone line, where it is decoded and appears on the TV screen at the other end of the line. Pre-prepared visual material (stored on audio cassettes) can also be sent down the line. This low-cost system is being used in 1981 and 1982 on 20 courses in 15 centres in one of the OU's regions. Again, while the system works well technically, it requires tutors, students, and telephone operators to be carefully trained. (See McConnell and Sharples, 1981).

While costs depend very much on geographical factors and phone company pricing policies, a general problem arises from the fact that students usually pay their own costs of travel to face-to-face tuition, while distance education systems tend to pay the telephone charges for telephone tuition. Thus telephone teaching tends to *reduce* student costs, but *increase* institutional costs.

The main problem, however, still seems to be human factors. Telephone teaching requires administrative and financial procedures that are not always understood by administrators who are geared to providing face-to-face support. Tutors need to change their tutorial methods if telephone tuition is to be successful. More structure and preparation are required. Some students, particularly the more elderly, at least in Britain, often regard the telephone as an instrument to be used only in emergencies. They even worry about the cost to the University—it is considered (quite often wrongly) to be much more expensive than face-to-face tuition. Training of administrators, tutors and students, is crucial for successful use.

I think, therefore, that more and more distance education systems will use telephone teaching, but it will spread slowly, and will meet considerable resistance.

Viewdata and teletext

Developments using the standard television screen for the display of textual and graphical information will also have important implications for distance education systems. There are two different kinds of system: those that use spare transmission capacity to broadcast textual information (such as Ceefax and Oracle in Britain), which I shall describe as "teletext"; and those that connect the television set with the telephone system (Prestel, Telidon, Optel, etc.), which I shall call "viewdata systems".

The main use of teletext is for instant news-type services: stockmarket prices; weather forecasts;

news summaries. Teletext services are currently limited by the number of pages available, (at the moment about 800). Capacity is determined by the memory store of the microprocessor in the TV receiver, which decodes the signal. Linking of independent but compatible, larger-capacity microprocessors, in the form of domestic computers, to standard television sets will allow for greater capacity in the future, but even then it is unlikely that teletext will be of great use to distance learning systems. The main limitation of teletext, apart from capacity, is the lack of interaction. There is little the user can do but search for material that is being transmitted. Publicity and advertising seems to be the most likely function of teletext for distance education systems.

Viewdata systems appear to have more educational potential. By combining the telephone with the television set, the user has access to a potentially limitless source of information and computing power. Quite apart from the powerful central computer system provided by national telecommunications systems for viewdata, it is in theory possible to access other powerful mainframe computers, provided the owners of such systems are willing to be accessed and have compatible software. Furthermore, organizations can set up their own viewdata computer systems, so that all the telephone company is providing is the line for carriage. Thus the Open University is experimenting with its own viewdata system, called Optel. The aim eventually is to enable staff, students, and tutors, to communicate from anywhere in Britain. While such developments must be compatible with the "national" viewdata system in terms of connections and display of material on the screen, variations on methods of accessing or of searching for information can be independently developed. Thus, because of the limitations of the current branching system used by Prestel, the Open University is experimenting with a keyword system for accessing information. (See Bacsich, 1981).

Viewdata is clearly a major new technology, which is still in a very early stage, so it is difficult to predict its potential for distance education systems. Much will depend on the speed and extent of the domestic market penetration, and above all on costs, particularly of telephone charges and the preparation of software. However, viewdata systems do have the potential for rapid updating of information (particularly useful for professional training and development) and for computer-aided instruction. My own belief, though, is that it will eventually be more useful for administrative purposes, providing students or potential students with information about courses and course regulations, tutors with student records, and for providing changes or alterations in supplementary materials for courses.

Domestic computers

The rapid development of microprocessors will make powerful but cheap computing facilities a realistic possibility for many homes in the more prosperous countries. Already some Open University courses provide students with a cheap microprocessor as a home experiment kit. Quite apart from the value of using computers for students to learn about computing, microcomputer systems can be linked to a standard TV set and aid instruction, using cassettes or discs mailed to students.

The major problem is not hardware costs, but the costs of preparing and writing computer programs, and the problems of compatibility between different domestic computer systems. Because of the special skills and the time required to develop effective computer-aided instruction, the target number of students must be large. There is a danger then of centralizing learning through the eventual domination of two or three major systems (such as PLATO); in that event, it will be cheaper for many distance education systems to buy programs.

For this reason, I suggest that the greater flexibility of systems such as CYCLOPS and telephone teaching where no computing skills are required of tutors or course designers, where direct interaction between tutor and student is still possible, and where individual teachers or institutions feel they still have control over teaching content and methods, may eventually be more important for distance education than home-based computer-aided instruction. I suspect that many of the educational functions of computer-aided learning can be done more easily, conveniently, and cheaply through a combination of audio cassettes and print.

Looking to the future

Only a few years ago most distance education systems relied almost entirely on correspondence teaching backed up by face-to-face tuition in groups, or they relied on broadcast series backed up by a textbook and possibly some face-to-face tuition. Now the range and combination of media available is suddenly bewildering. Nevertheless, it is possible to pick out some features that enable us to estimate what will be most useful over the next five years, accepting that varying socioeconomic and geographic factors will result in differences in what will be more important to one system rather than another.

The first feature is accessibility. What media are likely to be available—or can be provided economically—in most students' homes over the next few years? Accessibility will also be influenced by the extent to which a distance education system is dependent on the use of local centres—more expensive equipment can be provided in local centres, where shared use is possible—but I am more concerned here with home-based learning. The second is convenience. Can the student use the medium when and where it suits him, and without extra training? The third is academic control. How easy is it for the teacher to design and prepare the material himself? How much training will be required? The fourth feature is the extent to which the medium provides a "human" touch—to what extent can the learner relate to the tutor or teacher through the medium? And lastly, what is available *now* that can be used?

Using these criteria, print materials, audio cassettes and possibly telephone teaching still look the best immediate bets. Within five to ten years, the next most promising developments appear to me to be video cassettes and viewdata systems. But it would be wrong to suggest that one should look to just *one* medium. Choice is clearly increasing, but even existing audio-visual media are under-exploited. New media will not be adopted unless we look a little more closely at the reasons for the third trend—the under-exploitation of audio-visual media—and what needs to be done to improve their use.

The under-exploitation of audio-visual media

It was clear from the IIEP survey that existing audio-visual media were not being used as much as they could, and that when used, they were not always successful. The reasons for this cannot be understood without first answering a more fundamental question: do distance education systems *need* audio-visual media? Just because the technology is there, do we *have* to use it?

In some ways, it is hard not to use it. Teaching takes place in the wider context of people's lives. They use television and the telephone for reasons other than learning, and often distance education systems need to use technology to access their students in the first place. But the main reason why I believe it is important to use a wide range of media, including audio-visual media, is that different media serve different educational functions. Thus using a media broadens the range and effectiveness of distance education.

There is clearly no satisfactory single "theory" that tells educators which media to use in which situations. Nevertheless, the increasing range of media does make it a little easier to see what are the main educational differences between media in distance learning situations, and hence to spot some of the unique educational characteristics associated with each medium. Here I can only briefly give examples of what I mean (see Bates, 1981a for a fuller treatment).

Broadcast television (including cable and satellite) or radio is still the easiest way of reaching adult learners or potential learners at a distance. Its main advantage is its accessibility—it reaches every home—and it can be entertaining and attractive. It is therefore important for recruitment and motivation. It can also make available to the learner educational resources that would be difficult to provide in any other way—such as film of overseas countries, ingenious and expensive graphics, access to world leaders in politics and education, etc. Broadcast programs can provide an overview of subject matter dealt with in more detail in texts. Because of the high costs of such activities, they can be justified only if the target audience is large, and follow-up is generally required.

Perhaps broadcasting's greatest value then is as part of "campaigns": adult literacy, raising awareness of social issues, etc.

Print material is more useful for providing content where a good deal of ground needs to be covered or where the subject matter needs to be dealt with in depth, or where certain skills (analytical, mathematical, conceptual) need to be developed. Like broadcasting, print can reach into every home if there is a decent postal service.

Video cassettes can assist the application of the more abstract and analytical ideas covered in print to the more concrete and complex real world. Students can be asked to understand how these abstract concepts explain real-world situations and the limitations of such concepts through video. Video can provide models or bridges to understanding, by giving concrete examples or visual models of abstract ideas. Broadcast television can also do this, but video is more suitable because of the increased control and repetition available to the student.

Audio cassettes allow for mastery learning, explanation and discussion of graphical, tabular, and printed conceptual material, practice in problem-solving, and exercises in mathematical processes. Audio cassettes can be used for providing resource material, such as discussions, interviews, case-study material, language use, for analysis by students, and for step-by-step analysis and discussion by the unit author.

Telephone tuition (and CYCLOPS) enable individual problems to be dealt with directly by a tutor, and can provide seminars and tutorials where interpersonal and interactive communications can take place between students and tutor, and students and students. Telephone tutorials can provide guidance on assessment, feedback on progress, diagnostic analysis of problems, and a broadening or a linking up of core teaching materials.

Viewdata provides the opportunity for computer-assisted or programmed learning and enables material to be corrected or updated quickly and cheaply. It can also cut down on administrative mailings and provide easier access to administrative information and student records.

There is no super-medium. Each can serve different functions. Thus media do not differ as much in their suitability for dealing with different *content* but do differ in their suitability for dealing with different *learning skills* or *teaching approaches*. Each medium therefore *enriches* or *adds to* the educational process. The logical consequence of this is not to select but one or two "super-media", but to use a range of media in a planned and integrated manner so that a variety of educational functions and approaches can be offered.

It is perhaps easier now to see why audio-visual media in particular still tend to be under-exploited in distance education systems. Conventional education—the route through which most teachers in distance education systems have progressed—is dominated by face-to-face tuition and print. Few teachers fully understand the unique characteristics and limitations of audio-visual media. In Britain and many other countries, university academic staff receive no training in teaching methods. School teachers rarely, if ever, receive training in the use of the kind of audio-visual media available to distance education systems. Perhaps more surprisingly, none of the 12 distance education systems in the IIEP survey provided any systematic in-house training for its academic staff. Furthermore, understanding of media is little helped by the professionalization of media production—television is left to the producers to get on with; selection of media is the job of the educational technologist.

However, new developments in media are making nonsense of these professional boundaries. Some media—telephone tuition, for instance—do not need a specialist producer, although the teacher does need to develop additional skills; others, like CYCLOPS and viewdata, would be helped by specialist graphic designers or computer programmers, but are not dependent on such help (and the same would apply to production help for audio cassettes—useful, but not essential). However, teachers do need *training* to make the most of these media, first to raise their awareness of their potential, and secondly to make sure that the media are used effectively and competently.

It therefore seems to me essential that, given the rapid developments in media, each distance education system now needs a unit to monitor and develop appropriate media and train academic staff.

There seems also to be a major implication for broadcasting organizations. I have seen a trend in recent years towards more cooperative projects between broadcasting organizations and other agencies concerned with continuing and adult education (correspondence schools, workers' educational associations, etc.). However, broadcasters, even in these cooperative projects, have often been reluctant to give up their autonomy. Programs tend to be proposed on a "take-it-or-leave-it" basis, and other agencies are often invited to participate only when a program series has been decided. The development of new media, particularly video cassettes, could lead to two quite opposite developments. Distance education systems will become less dependent on broadcasting organizations and will therefore be less willing to be treated as minor partners. This could result in broadcasting organizations becoming *more* isolated and running their *own* series with little use of other media, or (as I would hope) broadcasters could get down to a more equal partnership as one of several agencies working together to provide integrated, multi-media courses.

Lastly, I see the possibility of a move *away* from large, national distance education systems and projects towards more local initiatives based on local, conventional education institutions. The new media provide local institutions with the opportunity to develop their own off-campus programs at reasonable costs, and with enrolments of full-time students steadily dropping in a number of countries, this may be an important lifeline for a number of institutions. However, if training is still inadequate in national distance education systems, at least they are deliberately structured and organized for distance education. I have my doubts about whether conventional educational institutions, particularly at a higher education level, will be able to make the structural and career development changes that would be necessary for successful distance teaching.

Tony Bates
The Open University
United Kingdom

References

Bacsich, P. (1981) *The Open University Viewdata System.* Milton Keynes: Open University (mimeo).

Bates, A.W. (1981) *The Planning and Management of Audio-Visual Media in Distance Learning Institutions.* Paris: Unesco.

Bates, A.W. (1981a) The unique educational characteristics of television and some consequences for teaching and learning. Submitted to: *Journal of Educational Television and Other Media.* 1981.

Durbridge, N. (1981) *Audio-Cassettes in Higher Education.* Milton Keynes: Open University (mimeo).

McConnell, D. and **Sharples**, M. (1981) *Distance Teaching by CYCLOPS: Tutor Handbook.* Nottingham: Open University.

Robinson, B. (1979) *Telephone Teaching: A Handbook for Tutors.* Nottingham: Open University.

Paper 3

Distance Teaching North and South

Assessing the achievements of distance education means balancing successes against failures.

What has distance education achieved in the last 20 years? The literature has certainly grown. I could find only half a dozen titles when I started looking in 1964; now I expect to hear, any day, that someone has started a distance education abstracts service. Dismal thought. Institutions have grown dramatically, if not as fast as the literature. Between 1960 and 1975, for example, over 20 distance teaching institutions were set up in Africa. Between 1972 and 1980 the number of correspondence institutions in Australia listed in the Commonwealth directory grew from 15 to 46. To assess where we have got to, and where we may go, it is convenient to look separately at the rich countries of the west (the first world), at the Soviet bloc (the second world) and at the poor countries of the south (the third world). We start with the success stories.

The first and second worlds

I'd pick out three major successes in the west: the quality of teaching materials, the sophistication of support services, and the ability to offer formal education at a distance at cut prices.

The Open University set a new visual standard with its very first courses, and has maintained it since. Correspondence education no longer conjured up images of yellowing cyclostyled pages of blurred typescript once their courses came off the press. Of course not everything has been as glossy. But, in terms of educational structure as well as appearance, we now have courses of a quality undreamt of in education of a generation ago.

We now have, too, a whole range of support services to go with the printed texts. If you want witnesses, read the columns of self-analysis by tutors and counsellors in *Teaching at a Distance*. Or look at the materials developed for training tutors at Murdoch University. Or consider the Swedish sophistication of CADE, where a computer can give a better answer to a student than a human tutor.

As for costs, once again the Open University gives us solid evidence that distance teaching can be cheaper than orthodox: Leslie Wagner has demonstrated that it costs less to produce a graduate through that university than through orthodox ones (Wagner, 1972, 1977 and 1980). In Germany, in South Korea, in Japan, distance-teaching projects at secondary and tertiary levels seem to have yielded similar results (Young et al, 1980: 66). Distance teaching can sometimes give us formal education at cut price.

Moving east, the Soviet Union has taken distance teaching seriously for longer than many countries, with its principal correspondence college, the All-Union External Polytechnic Institute, going back over 50 years. The peculiar strength of distance teaching there lies in its integration with work. As students study on their correspondence courses so, it appears, they are gradually promoted to better jobs. Their practical work is often done at their place of employment. They get paid study leave once a year to attend residential courses and take their examinations. And in Leningrad, I was told that the best factory managers regard the education of their employees in the same way as a parent does that of his children. It may sound paternalist, but it's not a sentiment I've heard elsewhere about correspondence students.

The third world

Distance teaching has been taken more seriously in the south than in the north. That is the most striking difference between the two. In the west, it has been used mainly to help small minorities of students beyond the reach of ordinary schools and colleges; from a national point of view the minorities were never particularly important. In the east, distance teaching has been more important: Stalin chose it as a way of increasing the production of the technicians and technologists needed for Soviet society between the wars. But it was never at the centre of the educational system. In the south, it has come far nearer that centre, and has been used, for example, for the vital task of training teachers in a dozen or more countries. In Tanzania distance education using radio campaigns has played a central role in adult education, teaching people about political issues, about health, and about the environment. In a number of countries in Africa, distance teaching has been used on a scale that is proportionately far greater than in Europe or North America.

There are, perhaps, two reasons for this. The first is, simply, that in the 1960s newly independent states were desperate to expand their educational systems at an unprecedented rate and had to use unorthodox methods to do so. Second, many of the small, educated elites who had struggled to get an education during the colonial period had used unorthodox methods to do so and remained sympathetic to them.

In the third world, too, we find distance teaching institutions developing curricula specifically for adults. The important experience here is that of the radio schools, like Radio Santa Maria in the Dominican Republic, ACPO in Columbia and ACPH in Honduras. They had succeeded not just in offering an alternative route to formal school-style qualification, but in developing a new sort of education based on the real interests and concerns of rural adults (see White 1976a, White 1976b and the extensive literature on ACPO).

What have we done?

We can summarize these achievements briefly. Distance educators in different countries have:

- developed high quality teaching materials
- worked out sophisticated ways of tutoring students at a distance
- sometimes taught people more cheaply than the traditional educational system
- tied education to work in industry
- used correspondence and radio for jobs of central importance like the training of primary school teachers
- developed curricula specifically for adults.

But, sadly, these achievements are piecemeal: you won't find all of them in any one place. And if we are to take a cold look at distance teaching's future they should be seen against distance teaching's failures.

What haven't we done?

We can distinguish between the internal measures of the success or failure of distance teaching, as indicated by examination or completion rates and costs, and external measures that concern themselves with education's effect on society. The internal evidence, on completion rates for example, is not particularly encouraging. Even with all its sophistication, only about half of the Open University's students achieve their degrees. And their results are better than many others: around a quarter of those who launch themselves on courses of basic education through the radio schools in the Canary Islands and in the Dominican Republic complete their courses (see Perraton 1981 for a summary of the evidence). Such comparisons are invidious; it is a far harder life to be peasant farmer than to be a typical Open University student in Britain. But it is difficult to be satisfied with an educational system in which half or more of the students don't get what they want.

The evidence on costs is mixed. Table 1 summarizes the evidence on projects where comparable information is available and where comparisons with the cost of orthodox teaching are possible. It establishes that there are circumstances in which distance teaching will prove cheaper than the alternative. It does not always do so, and it is rare for it to work out at less than half the cost of the alternative.

My guess is that we may be able to improve the success and retention rates, but we are less likely to reduce costs. We have made little headway on three issues that would go high on my agenda for distance education's next few years.

Integration

The first is about shifting the boundaries between education, work, and leisure. Although distance teaching has expanded opportunities for study in many countries, it has done so not by creating an alternative kind of education, but by turning thousands of homes into miniature schools. With what appears to be structural unemployment, with 80 years of concern about urban alienation behind us, with the microprocessor offering to change the location of work, much distance teaching in the west remains in a very 19th-century mould of education for self-improvement. Samuel Smiles would have approved. The east and the south give us some hints of an alternative pattern—the Soviet Union with its close links between work and home study, and the radio schools of Latin America with their attempt to develop an alternative curriculum for adults. For the most part, though, there is a missed opportunity for a kind of education that is not based on schools or colleges.

Alternative education

The second failure is perhaps contained within the first. It confronts most starkly those countries of the south that are now beginning to achieve universal primary education. Many are looking for a less costly form of secondary education, and quite a number have seen distance teaching techniques as a way of providing alternative secondary schools. But, most often, these have merely linked correspondence and broadcasting with attendance at supervised study centres. This is the pattern, for example, in Malawi and Zambia and it is the pattern that was being considered for the Open School of India. Gradually, the study centres can be improved with better buildings, more equipment, some training for their supervisors and so on. But with each improvement the study centre looks more like a school, albeit less well endowed than the proper schools, and, typically, teaching those students who failed to get into a proper school. The challenge here is in curriculum and in organization: to find a pattern of education at a distance, which is relatively cheap, and which provides an alternative secondary education. For, in many countries, the needs of primary school leavers are beginning to pose the most severe social problems that will not be solved by a rash of fourth-class schools offering a pale carbon copy of the standard academic curriculum.

Broadcasting

The third failure concerns the relation between education and broadcasting. Traditionally, they are

Table 1: Costs and success rates of some distance teaching institutions

Country and Institution	Level of education	Annual enrolment at time of study	Annual cost per student in US (1978)	Measures of success: measure used	rate	Comparison between costs of distance teaching and costs of orthodox education
Brazil IRDEB	Secondary	8 000	67[1]	Examination passes	37%	D/t is probably more expensive
Canary Islands ECCA (radio school)	Upper primary/ lower secondary	23 000	64[2]	Number promoted to next class after 6-months study	72-75%	D/t is cheaper
Colombia ACPO (radio school)	Primary equivalent	70 000	34[2]	Number taking end-of-course examination	53-56% (1962-66) 22-26% (1967-68)	D/t is cheaper
Dominican Republic RSM (radio school)	Primary equivalent	20 000	30[2]	Number taking examination for promotion to next stage	56-69%	D/t is cheaper
Kenya Correspondence Course Unit	Teacher training	340-2 900	325[1]	Teachers promoted as a result of course	90%	D/t is more expensive
Malawi Malawi Correspondence College	Secondary	3 800	160[1]	Examination passes: as proportion of enrolments as proportion of exam entrants	13% 21%	Cost per successful student dearer than for day schools but cheaper than for boarding schools
South Korea Air Correspondence High School	Secondary	20 000	68[1]	Examination passes	46%	D/t is cheaper
United Kingdom Open University	Tertiary	56 500-62 500	1177[3]	Graduates as proportion of: final registration provisional registration[4]	54% 44%	D/t is cheaper

Notes

[1] These costs are summarised in Perraton (1979)
[2] These costs are summarised in Perraton (1981)
[3] Wagner (1980), taking his 1976-79 figure of 1976 £500 as 1978 US $1177
[4] Figures are for graduations up to 1979 for the OU's first cohort of students (cf. Vice-Chancellor's Reports 1971 and 1979)

uncomfortable bedfellows. The ordinary school repeats the same lessons, year in, year out, for each new cohort of students. Repetition is of the essence. Broadcasting, in contrast, glories in its fleetingness, and the good broadcaster is always seeking novelty. The failure to articulate the relationship between the two means that, in Australia and New Zealand, for example, colleges that pioneered the linking of broadcasting and correspondence in the 1930s no longer have access to broadcasting time. In Britain, ten years after the Open University, links between broadcasts and other supporting agencies remain sporadic and improvised. In many countries where education has access to a broadcasting channel it is to one with a small audience, or a low-power transmitter, or at an awkward time. And yet, if we are to do something about the first and second of my issues, educators need access to broadcasting as a means of reaching audiences they might otherwise never meet. Using video cassettes or other bits of gadgetry cannot put education into the public view, and into the public domain, in the same way.

The agenda for 1984

There is, of course, a link between my three issues. All are about relationships. And the solutions to all of them will demand new relationships between distance education and orthodox education, based in schools and colleges. But I see no instant solutions. The aim of this paper is merely to suggest items that belong on our agenda for the next few years. I'd end simply by arguing for this kind of agenda, posing this kind of question. The evidence on the internal efficiency of distance teaching is only just good enough for us to pose them. But if we don't do that, if we don't focus on questions about the role of education in society, then distance teaching will rightly remain on the periphery, until it disappears into the limbo of dead educational gimmicks. I hope that isn't where it really belongs.

Hilary Perraton
International Extension College
United Kingdom

References

Perraton, H. (1981) *Basic Education and Mass Media* (mimeo) (unpublished report to the World Bank, IEC Cambridge)
Perraton, H. ed. (1979) *Alternative Routes to Formal Education: Distance Teaching for School Equivalency* (World Bank, mimeo) (also John Hopkins University Press, forthcoming)
Wagner, L. (1972) The economics of the Open University. *Higher Education* 1, 2, 158-183.
Wagner, L. (1977) The economics of the Open University revisited. *Higher Education* 6, 3, 359-381.
Wagner, L. (1980) Costs and effectiveness of distance learning at the post-secondary level. In Unesco (1980) *The Economics of New Educational Media* vol. 2 Paris: Unesco.
White, R. (1976a) *An Alternative Pattern of Basic Education: Radio Santa Maria*. Paris: Unesco.
White, R. (1976b) *Mass Communications and the Popular Promotion Strategy of Rural Development in Honduras*. Stanford: Institute for Communication Research.
Young, M. et al. (1980) *Distance Teaching for the Third World: The Lion and the Clockwork Mouse*. London: Routledge and Kegan Paul.

Correspondence Teaching: Second Choice or Second Class?

Recuperating drop-outs requires commitment from educators and politicans alike.

Introduction

The principal aim of this paper is to stimulate people involved in distance education—particularly correspondence education—to give some much needed consideration to the following questions:

a. Can correspondence education contribute to solving the problem of dropping out at the secondary level, and to the more general problem of providing pre-university scholastic preparation to people unable to obtain it in the classroom?

b. What organizational and pedagogical conditions are necessary to achieve this objective?

If we look at the impressive growth of literature on distance teaching, we realize most of it refers to the university level (Mackenzie et al, 1977), although correspondence education, television, and radio have also been used for qualification or diplomas at the secondary level. However, research on this level has been incomplete and sporadic and does not give immediate and clear answers to the two questions we are considering.

Correspondence teaching and secondary education

We can cite a few examples of the use of correspondence teaching at the secondary level (Sarramona, 1975): in 1910, in Australia, the first wide distribution of correspondence courses was sponsored by government for elementary students in isolated regions. This program was later extended to secondary and technical study and to adult learning (Harris and Williams, 1977): in the United States secondary correspondence courses were developed at the beginning of the century in order: a) to allow young people who had finished elementary school in areas where secondary schools did not exist to continue their studies; b) to allow secondary school students to study subjects their local schools did not offer.

These are efforts directed at allowing young people to continue their studies without interruption. Relatively different in its aims is another well known effort—that of the French "Centre National de Télé-Enseignement", created as a result of the outbreak of World War Two. Students of secondary and technical schools were removed to more secure areas where they had to be reached by correspondence. This service was later extended to elementary schools and to courses at the university level (Pagney, 1977).

Systems of teaching technical courses at the secondary level also appeared in other countries. In New Zealand thousands of apprentices and students in the commercial and industrial sector have enrolled in the Technical Correspondence Institute (Fakes, 1973). In Holland a system of teaching technical and general subjects has been developed by private schools. In Poland the training of extramural technicians is made possible through correspondence courses by the Polytechnic Institute, which also makes extensive use of television (Stone, 1977). In other socialist countries—beginning with the Soviet Union and East Germany—secondary-level correspondence education is the norm for technical and professional preparation by those not accepted at the selective higher institutions (Mackenzie et al, 1977; Shapovalenko, 1963).

These experiences and many others are the result of the basic principle of the right of everyone to an education, which justifies, in all countries of the world, the advent of mass education.

Correspondence education, in this sense, is one of the instruments of the so-called "parallel school". It compensates for some deficiencies of formal educational systems that cannot accommodate everybody.

Furthermore, distance learning—not only by correspondence but also by means of multi-media—is spreading above all in the emerging nations of Africa, Asia, and Latin America (Brodolini, 1979).

In a certain sense it is widening the formal educational system, keeping its content and structure, but liberating it from the physical limitation requiring co-presence of teacher and student.

Correspondence learning as an alternative

In industrialized nations, other educational phenomena of interest to correspondence education are developing. The main one is the continuing education of adults (Council of Europe, 1978), which is transforming all of our traditional concepts on education, breaking down the fixed scheme of "time-for-school" and "time-for-work" that characterized the passage from adolescence to maturity.

No less important are the problems of falling-behind-in or dropping-out-of school—closely linked to the problems of scholastic and social selection.

Education in industrialized countries tends to value the timing of the acquisition of technical or professional competence—a process that occurs in a determined amount of time (the school year) as a result of pedagogical causes (teachers, didactical means). The student who does not succeed in acquiring the required competence in the given amount of time—according to the final verdict of the teacher—receives a negative judgement (failure, probation).

With the spread of mass education the accumulation of negative judgements, which leads to delay in finishing studies, is itself a problem and is considered an indication of low productivity or inefficiency of the educational system (Trivellato, 1979a). To students who fall behind we have to add the drop-outs, whether for scholastic reasons or for reasons outside the school such as socioeconomic factors (Trivellato, 1979b). Dropping out of school is the most dramatic indication of the inefficiency of the traditional school system.

The age for compulsory school attendance varies, but it is universally accepted that a person should attend until the age of 16 and it is desirable that he complete secondary school (until the age of 18 or 19). Thus the government tries to find ways of keeping young people in school to that age, either setting up itself or allowing private institutions to set up alternatives to formal education. However, the objective is never completely reached: the school system continues to lose a good number of students (Jencks, 1972). The victims of these "failures" are not indisposed to study for the rest of their lives simply because they find themselves in contrast to scholastic institutions.

The offer of an opportunity to "recuperate" is often accepted favorably, especially on two conditions: a) if it allows the person to shorten the time it takes to acquire the qualifications he was not able to obtain in school; b) if it allows him to study while he works. In this context, correspondence education is seen as an alternative, a second chance at success (Husen, 1974).

The case of Italy

When analysing education from a social point of view we must not over-emphasize the possibility of lessening the inequalities in education by purely educational means (Bowles and Gintis, 1976): those measures that make a "learning society" more just and democratic far exceed the putting into effect of the "right to study". Nevertheless, it is a principal duty of politicians and educators to fully develop instruments that reduce educational discrimination. There is no doubt that the Mediterranean European countries represent an important test for this problem: economic difficulties cause a high percentage of drop-outs because of the premature entry into the work force of adolescents who must contribute to the family budget, together with an insufficient organization of public education institutions.

Among these countries Italy stands out. It has a dichotomous economy—an industrialized North and a South in constant crisis. For this reason it affords a useful reference for comparing an advanced area with an underdeveloped one (Bonani, 1978).

In Italy during 1975-76 almost all of the students enrolled in the first grade at 5 or 6 years of age finished elementary school. However, at the end of the cycle, at least 5% had repeated one or two years and 1% had dropped out.

As the level advances the number of drop-outs increases. The success rate drops to 90% in junior high (11-13 years of age): 5% interrupt their studies and 9% repeat some grades.

At the secondary level (14-18 years of age) the success rate drops to 80%; drop-outs reach 9% (concentrated mainly in the first year of study (16.2%)).

Table 1 illustrates the situation with regard to falling behind and dropping out (Gatullo, 1976).

Table 1: Rates of regularity, falling behind, and lack of attendence of 100 students of the same age

age	attend school regularly	are behind in school	don't attend school or dropped out
6	99.8	-	0.2
8	87.4	12.1	0.5
11	72.7	24.2	3.1
13	55.7	33.1	11.2
16	26.6	19.6	53.8
18	15.2	12.6	72.2

At the age of 13 almost half the student population has already dropped out or is at risk. At the age of 16 more than half is already in the job market (explicit or hidden): at this age only one-fourth of Italian adolescents are studying regularly. This means that about 6 million young people have undergone an educational trauma.

This data becomes more negative if we break it down between North and South. For example, at 13 years of age in the North there are 63 "regular" students out of 100, as opposed to only 45 in the South; but more important there are only 3.5 drop-outs in the North as opposed to almost 20 in the South. We find that at 13 years of age 2 males drop out as opposed to 5 females in the North and 14 males as opposed to 26 females in the South. Of the upper classes 99% of children from 6-13 years of age attend school against 88% from the working class. One hundred percent of children from the same age group of parents with degrees go to school as opposed to 84% of children of literate parents without degrees.

What does this data mean for correspondence schools in Italy? It can be used as a means of predicting some of the important characteristics of the potential market for alternative education.

In countries like Italy, in fact, where a higher living standard makes parents more willing to pay to educate their children (Dei and Rossi, 1978), there is a great probability that after a period of reflection (that might coincide with another attempt to enter the formal school system), the young "drop-out" will try another way of obtaining a scholastic diploma or its equivalent, even though this will no longer be free as is formal state education. The Italian examination system compels everyone wanting a "valid" certificate to try for a state certificate. If preparation is done outside state institutions, the candidate is considered "private".

The offer of scholastic recuperation

If this is the mechanism behind dropping out, we must ask what kind of distance teaching institution can take over the alternatives. Each country will obviously decide on the basis of its political and cultural realities. A recent study by the National Centre of Sociology of Social Legislation in Brussels classified organizations for distance teaching in three categories (Weinstock, 1978):

— *liberal* systems, in which correspondence teaching is a private and commercial initiative (even if with some public financing). Germany, Belgium, Great Britain, the United States, Italy, Spain, Portugal and France are in this category.

— *systems in which private institutions play a public role,* in which centres for teaching by correspondence, although private, offer a more generalized service for common interest (the Scandinavian countries and Holland).

— *socialist* systems, in which there is a state monopoly on all efforts (all the countries of East Europe).

The problem of drop-outs at the secondary level is a relevant common problem. It would seem opportune that even in a "liberal" society the state engage as much in recuperating drop-outs by offering them correspondence study as it does in financing other forms of "residential" recuperation. But this is not the situation. The example of the British Open University, which is financed publicly but is a formal private institution, is not adopted in other contexts except in the case of analogous efforts on the university level. Only in the Scandinavian and Dutch systems do we find total or partial reimbursement of fees. Here we have an extension of benefits of the welfare state, which makes the northern countries that much more affluent in terms of social services.

In countries like Italy and Spain, however, we find total "ignorance" on the part of the state. Recuperating correspondence students in private schools must pay for all of their education—although the fees are lower than those of equivalent schools requiring attendance (Karow, 1979). Although the mentality of public administration is evolving, the principle behind this "ignorance" of the state requires the complete separation of public and private interests (Sarramona, 1975). Apparently the same principle is behind the French and German systems where if the state decides to take part in scholastic recuperation by distance means, it establishes its own institituions (Telekolleg, CNTE) and cannot conceive of the possibility of financing the studies of individual students in private institutions (Karow and Storm, 1977).

Some quantitive estimates

Recuperation on the secondary level through correspondence education is possible in all European countries although in different ways. But what percentage of the requests for this recuperation are met through these channels?

It is impossible to answer this question, for two reasons:

1. the uncertainty about the number of drop-outs from the various scholastic systems (Gozzer, 1977)

2. the uncertainty about the number of people enrolled in public or private correspondence schools and about the number among them following scholastic courses (Karow, 1977).

Only from a strictly indicative point of view we can remember that Unesco (Faure, 1974) numbered those enrolled in secondary schools in Europe (10-18 years) at 27,944,000 at the beginning of the 1970s. We can reasonably conjecture that at least 15% of this population is destined not to complete secondary school. Every eight years we would have (4,191,600 × 8) = 33,532,800 drop-outs. According to estimates by the German BIBB (Karow, 1977) in the same countries the number of people enrolled in correspondence schools every year totaled 5,000,000 at the beginning of the 1970s.

We can estimate that approximately 20% are in scholastic courses (1,000,000) and that about 20% of these (200,000) will drop out every year. The courses in question are always given in "compressed" form—estimated at five-eighths of the time required for residential schools.

Drop-outs produced by the scholastic system every year (eight-year cycle)
4,191,600 (A)

Students enrolled in correspondence courses of a scholastic nature every year (equivalent cycle - five years)
800,00 (B)

Percentage of drop-outs interested in correspondence education

$$(B) \times 8/5 \div (A) \times 100 = 30.5\%$$

We see that the percentage is low, but not to be underestimated. Without giving too much credence to these statistics, which are completely lacking in definitive statistical bases, we can nevertheless realize that there could be a *significant contribution by distance education* to the democratization of teaching in European countries, regardless of whether the systems are public or private.

To analyse the situation in Italy we must point out that faced with almost 350,000 drop-outs every year, correspondence schools enrol almost 50,000 students in scholastic courses annually. If we subtract from these the people who do not finish (25%) we have the following estimate of "recuperation" of drop-outs on the secondary level:

$$(37,500 \times 8/5 \div 350,000) \times 100 = 17.1\%$$

This is a percentage, as we see, not to be underestimated.

Characteristics of correspondence drop-outs

After attempting to answer the first of the two questions we began with, we will try to analyse the elements behind the second question.

First we must examine which kind of drop-outs enrol in correspondence schools in search of recuperation.

Research in this area is not complete, but we can give some fundamental indications (Cropley, 1977; Bonani, 1979). In anagraphical terms we usually find: adult students between 18 and 25 years of age, female more than male (with significant percentage fluctuations between 65 and 50 for the former) (Holmberg, 1977; Erdos, 1976). Up to 50% are married (Van Eck and Houtkoop, 1979).

We find a prevalence of young people from non-urban areas, with low but not drastically low economic status (middle-low class, most working unsteadily). (These surveys are usually done by private institutions.)

Usually, 50% interrupted their studies at the end of elementary school or the beginning of junior high without trauma, because of personal or family decisions. The others were forced to leave against their will for health or economic reasons. We know very little about the general cultural conditions of the students or their interests outside their correspondence studies.

A varying percentage have already taken correspondence courses. Thus there is a tendency to repeat the experience of distance learning (Van Eck and Houtkoop, 1979).

A knowledge of the characteristics of those drop-outs is most useful for the institution in which they enrol (Redmond, 1977). This is confirmed by research done by the Open University, Lund University, and the Universidad Abierta in Spain.

Italy has recently begun research in this area. Accademia has begun giving analytical questionnaires to its students, assuming a distinction between those in scholastic courses (40% of 30,000 yearly enrolments) and those in professional or cultural enrichment courses (Bonani and Sauda, 1980). The resulting picture partly confirms the description given above. From a rational sample of 1353 students in 1978, the situation and attitudes of 517 people are presented in Table 2.

Table 2: Characteristics and attitudes of Accademia students

	Percentage
Enrolled in junior high-school	37.7
enrolled in secondary school	62.3
North Italy	53.5
Centre	19.3
South	27.2
Males	35.2
Females	64.8

Age

Up to 20 years of age	20.2
20-25	24.8
25-30	31.5
over 30	4.5
(no data)	19.0
attended school regularly (until interruption)	91.8
attended school irregularly	8.2
Interrupted studies	57.0

reason for interruption

- economic	73.7
- family	9.9
- scholastic (failure-dissatisfaction)	10.1
- health	1.7
- lack of facilities	2.7
- other	1.9

Reasons for enrolling in correspondence school (possible multiple-choice)

- to acquire specific cultural preparation	41.5
- to improve job possibilities	47.4
- to get ahead in present job	23.6
- for hobby	13.0

Work while studying?

- no	28.8
- yes	71.2

Satisfied with present job while studying?

- yes, do not wish to change	22.2
- yes, but wishes to change	15.3
- little satisfied	2.1
- no, but does not wish to change	—
- no, wishes to change	31.6

It would be superfluous to give detailed analysis of this data. It is only important to note the relevant number of people who interrupted their studies for economic reasons and also the noticeable number of students who are working. Also interesting is the number of people who return to scholastic study without having immediate employment objectives. For our purposes it is of value to note the phenomena that led 10% of the students to leave school "for scholastic reasons".

Reasons for returning to school

The correspondence student is usually motivated to learn, through free choice and for economic or career rewards (Entwistle et al, 1974).

Nevertheless, the incentive to advance is not sufficient to overcome "fear of failure", which, according to researchers (Barratt-Brown, 1976), characterizes the alternative study experience and which is certainly related to previous failure in the formal system (Richardson, 1975).

The correspondence school thus has the job of compensating not only for past failure but also for the insecurity that that failure caused (Redmond, 1977).

Summing up these observations, we must face the fact that there are many personal conditions and characteristics of students that the school must "keep under control". A synthesis is given in Table 3 (Kennedy and Powell, 1976).

Table 3: Characteristics and conditions that can influence students in correspondence schools

characteristics (slow change)

a. motivation
b. state of maturity
c. educational background
d. personality
e. ability
f. educational self-esteem

conditions (rapid change)

a. occupation (changed, new job, temporary job)
b. relations with family and peers
c. health
d. economic conditions
e. support from the institute

If we read this table keeping in mind that the student could be an effective scholastic drop-out (who has had to interrupt his studies against his will) the "characteristics" column becomes particularly important.

The experience of correspondence schools shows us that adults whose studying is integrated with work and family life have a much better chance of obtaining intellectual satisfaction (McClusky, 1970). This "interiorization" of study in day-to-day life happens more frequently and completely in the person who decides to study in order to change the trend of his past educational experience. Even a "weak educational background", therefore, can be a condition for greater "security in one's studies" by correspondence, on the condition that it is taken into consideration by the individual as a condition to be overcome (Watts, 1979).

We wish to suggest, through this observation, that the psychological and human condition of the scholastic drop-out can be *taken advantage of* to provide successful distance learning if the institution studies its students and establishes individual relationships with them.

Conditions for recuperation

This leads us to what one can do to give the scholastic drop-out a real chance in correspondence schools. If the first condition for success is that the school *know the student,* the second is that it *establish an individual relationship with him.*

It is not our intention in this paper to enter into the subject of individual relationships; anyone active in distance learning is aware of the numerous aspects of this problem.

We wish only to underline the most useful aspects in meeting the demands of a drop-out.

The first aspect is the human one: for the person who has suffered failure, more than for a generic correspondence student, an adequate counselling service is fundamental both at the beginning and throughout the course of study (Nicholson, 1977). We would emphasize the moment the student is welcomed by the school, at which time he must feel that *his* problem has been understood as something specific and important (Sewart, 1979). This is true whether the institution works only by correspondence (Daniel and Marquis, 1979; Menal, 1977) or has a tutoring, face-to-face service throughout its territory. In the latter, individualization is made easier if the tutor has those human and professional characteristics that allow him to be accepted as a valid guide in the studies of the student and, in a certain sense, in his life (Gibbs and Durbridge, 1976; Harris, 1975). From the first encounter—which is necessarily of a general nature and which could be defined as pre-inductive, (Sewart, 1979)—a program of study and a series of objectives for the induction period must be worked out. This can be facilitated if there are specific didactical instruments:

- study units that bring all the students to the same level, mainly consisting of formative tests

- preparatory micro-courses in basic subjects (mathematics, languages, graphic expression) that permit verification of the students' level of preparation (Freeman, 1975).

It is important that there be no suggestion of an "examination" during this phase. In the case of negative results during the initial phase there should be remediation. An alternative would be to intensify the student-tutor relationship, which is not practical even for institutions combining distance learning with face-to-face service, given the high number of students who use this facility.

A third condition is a good relationship between the student and the study material. In the traditional school the relationship the drop-out student had with his texts might have been critical: textbooks in formal schools are complex and are written with the idea that they will be *mediated* by the teacher.

Texts for correspondence schools must have a highly motivating dialogue structure (Anderson, 1979). It is also necessary that the material allow effective self-regulation of studying time (Davies, 1976/77), and that the student not be asked to work too hard nor to acquire abilities too elevated or sophisticated to be learned by correspondence (Davies, 1979).

Studies show that learning *only* by correspondence, especially in the case of "recuperation" courses, has fewer motivating elements than a mixed teaching structure (correspondence education plus face-to-face contact) (McDonald and Knights, 1979):

the production of high-quality teaching materials is thus limited but can be integrated, especially in publicly oriented systems, with the creation of tutorial centres.

Accademia, although a private institution, has vast resources in this area: throughout Italy it has 53 tutorial centers that are open Saturdays and Sundays to give support and counselling.

These centres play a major role for students of scholastic courses. Nearly 80% of students who attend are enrolled in secondary courses at Accademia. The work of the tutor in these centres is divided into three stages:

- introductory stage: getting students to know the school, the services of the centres, and above all techniques of correspondence study

- stage of initiation into individual subjects: by appointment, the student is given brief periods of guidance in difficult material

- control stage: the student makes use of the tutor only if he confronts specific difficulty. In this advanced stage the telephone is heavily used.

The centres also have the very important function of preparing the student for a successful state examination, foreseen for all scholastic courses (although not all students enrol with this objective in mind).

An end to scholastic failure

It is useless to deny that one of the motivations of drop-outs who enrol in correspondence study is the hope of ceasing to be drop-outs in the future.

The success of the school in granting (or in obtaining from other institutions) diplomas, certificates, qualifications that are publicly valid, or in any case usable in the job market, is therefore one of the avenues of success from the student's point of view. Aside from everything that has been written about the validity of correspondence education, much of the effect on recent enrolments is the practical usefulness for the student—both in final examinations and in using the competence acquired in the job market.

Preparing adequately for examinations outside the institute is a critical moment for private institutions, who have at stake their own pedagogical reputation as well as the scholastic future of the student. Although different schools act in different ways, I wish to point out the relevant experience of private institutions such as Accademia.

The task of the school is not only that of giving a valid formative base to the student and of overcoming his anxiety, there is also much to do on the bureaucratic level (finding the public school where the examination can be taken, presenting documents and study programs of the student, etc.). Above all there is the extremely difficult task of getting the state examiners who will judge him to recognize the specific preparation he has received through distance education.

At this point, factors come into play involving the reputation of correspondence education, the mentality of the teacher-examiner (more or less traditionalist), and the ability of the tutor in charge of the official relationship with the school at which the examination is taken.

It is not necessary to emphasize these aspects, which are obviously overcome at an institutional level if the correspondence school is of public origin. They need to be called to attention because in order to free the student from the condition of scholastic drop-out we must realize that we are not dealing with theoretical or psychological facts but those of a social nature such as public approval in acquiring what in Italy is referred to as "the piece of paper".

Some goals for Mediterranean correspondence schools

We observed at the beginning of this paper that the problem of dropping out is accentuated in countries that are less developed and whose educational systems are less well equipped. There is no doubt, if the official data is correct, that all the Mediterranean countries with the exception of France are in this group. Scholastic evasion is linked to other social factors that imply "abnormal" mobility of the population: internal migration from south to north or from rural areas to large urban centres; emigration to more industrialized central European countries. Correspondence education is one instrument able to adapt itself to the educational needs arising from these situations. Perhaps the Mediterranean countries such as Italy, Spain, and even Yugoslavia, in which correspondence education is developed, can further direct this function to other countries, mailing courses in their mother tongue to emigrants who desire scholastic and technical qualifications and "following" those students who have to move within the country for reasons of employment. Among these people scholastic drop-outs are no doubt numerous.

There is no lack of examples in this area both of a public and a commercial nature: French, Dutch, and English schools that give courses for students who have gone abroad; Spanish schools that have set up branches in Latin America; the spreading of courses given by Italian schools to central European countries through specialized agencies—all these are efforts to be observed and studied. Distance teaching has unexpected potential, some of which, perhaps, is still to be discovered.

Giampaolo Bonani
Istituto Teologico per Corrispondenza
Italy

References

Anderson, N. (1979) *Strategies and Applications for Correspondence Course Development.* Rome: Accademia (EHSC Autumn Workshop).

Barratt-Brown, J. (1976) Courses for disadvantaged adults. *Teaching at a Distance* 6.

Bonani, G. (1978) *The Slow Demise of the Work Ethic.* Rome: Society of International Development.

Bonani, G. (1979) *L'Insegnamento per Corrispondenza e il suo Pubblic.* Rome: Accademia.

Bonani, G. Sauda E. (1980) *Gli studenti della Scuola Accademia.* Rome: CISID.

Bowles, S. Gintis, H. (1976) *Schooling in Capitalist America.* New York: Basic Books.

Council of Europe (1978) *Permanent Education-Final Report.* Strasbourg.

Cropley, A. (1977) *Lifelong Education.* New York: Pergamon Press.

Daniel, J. Marquis C. (1979) Interaction and independence: getting the mixture right. *Teaching at a Distance.* 14.

Davies, E. (1976/1977) The role of self-paced study in undergraduate science teaching. *British Journal of Educational Technology.* 7, 3 / 8, 2.

Davies, W. (1979) Open learning or open access? *British Journal of Educational Technology.* 10, 2.

Dei, M. Rossi M. (1978) *Sociologia Della Scuola Italiana.* Bologna: Il Mulino.

Entwistle, N. Thompson, J. and Wilson, J. (1974) Motivation and study habits. *Higher Education.* 3,4.

Erdos, R. (1976) *La Mise en Place d'une Institution d'enseignement par Correspondance.* Paris: Unesco.

Fakes, J. (ed) (1973) *Technical Education at a Distance.* Cambridge: IEC.

Faure, E. (ed.) (1974) *Apprendre a Etre.* Paris.

Fondazione Brodolini (1979) *L'Insegnamento a Distanza.* (Research Report: mimeo) Rome.

Freeman, R. (1975) Preparatory studies and adult education. *Teaching at a Distance.* 4, 31-44.

Gattullo, M. (1976) *L'Andamento della Selezione Scolastica.* Bologna: Il Mulino.

Gibbs, G. Durbridge, N. (1976) Characteristics of the Open University Tutors. *Teaching at a Distance.* 6, 96-102 and 7, 7-22.

Gozzer, G. (1977) *La Scolarizzazione di Massa.* Rome: Accademia.

Harris, W. Williams, J. (1977) *A Handbook on Distance Education.* Manchester: Department of Adult Education.

Harris, W. (1975) *The Distance Tutor.* Manchester: Department of Adult Education.

Holmberg, B. (1977) *Distance Education.* London: Kogan Page.

Husen, T. (1974) *Talent, Equality and Meritocracy,* The Hague: Martinus Nijhoff.

Jencks, C. (1972) *Inequality.* New York: Harper-Colophon.

Karow, W. Storm, U. (1977) *Wie kann Fernunterricht zur Verbesserung der Beruflichen Bildung Beitragen?* Berlin: BIBB.

Karow, W. (1977) *Privaten Fernunterricht in 16 Ländern. Übersicht und Vergleich.* Berlin: BIBB.

Karow, W. (1979) *A Survey of 16 Countries' Private Correspondence Education.* Rome: Atti Convegno Accademia.

Kennedy, D. Powell, R. (1976) Student progress and withdrawal. *Teaching at a Distance.* 7, 61-75.

Mackenzie, N. Postgate, R. Scupham, J. (1977) *Open Learning.* Paris: Unesco Press.

McClusky, H. (1970) *An Approach to the Differential Psychology of the Adult Potential.* Washington: Adult Education Association.

McDonald, R. Knights, S. (1979) Returning to study: the mature-age student. *Programmed Learning and Educational Technology.* 16, 2.

Menal, J. (1977) *La Relacion Alumno-Tutor en al Enseñanza para Correspondencia.* Copenhagen: CEC.

Nicholson, N. (1977) Counselling the adult learner at the Open University. *Teaching at a Distance.* 8.

Pagney, B. (1977) *L'Enseignement à Distance et la Formation Professionelle.* Berlin: BIBB.

Redmond, M. (1977) Aspects of adult learning. *Teaching at a Distance* 8.

Richardson, M. (1975) Who are preparatory studies for? *Teaching at a Distance.* 4, 35-37.

Sarramona, J. (1975) *La Enseñanza a Distancia.* Barcelona: CEAC.

Sewart, D. (1976) A new look at the preparation of Open University students. *Teaching at a Distance.* 15.

Shapovalenko, G. (1963) *Polytechnical Education in the USSR.* Paris: Unesco.

Stone, G. (1977) The television agricultural high school - Poland. In Mackenzie et al (1977).

Trivellato, U. (1979a) Instruzione ed economia. In *Quindicinale di Note e Commenti.* Rome: CENSIS.

Trivellato, U. (1979b) *Sociologia Della Scuola Secondaria.* Rome: Accademia.

Van Eck, E. Houtkoop, W. (1979) *Educational Careers of Participants in Correspondence Courses at General Secondary School Level.* Amsterdam: Kohnstamm Instituut.

Watts, G. (1979) Personal counselling at the Open University. *Teaching at a Distance.* 15.

Weinstock, N. (1978) *Les Cours par Correspondance du Secteur Privé en Belique.* Brussels: Centre National de Sociologie du Droit Social.

Individualizing Support Services

The richness and variety of the Open University's student support system sustains and supports students at a level comparable to that of conventional university systems.

In the popular conception of distance education, two characteristics are regularly noted, namely that it is relatively new and that it is generically different from traditional education. Thus, distance education is widely viewed as being entirely separate from traditional education, a view based not only on the notion that its teaching methods are different but also on perceptions of its students. This view permeates the whole structure and funding of the genre—with the notable exception of "external studies" in Australia where on-campus and off-campus students are often taught the same course and many on-campus students are part time.

The purpose of this paper is to cast doubt on the theory of distance education as a discrete teaching methodology and to show that it can offer a service to students at least as rich and at least as individualized as the traditional system.

Because there are examples of the use of written material for educational purposes almost from the beginnings of written records, it is not teaching at a distance that is new but rather the growth and popularity of distance teaching institutions, particularly in the last decade. This growth has occurred *pari passu* with the development of technologies and processes, and its characteristics, releasing the student from the traditional confinement of time and space and admitting of part-time study. These have proven attractive in an increasingly complex society, where change is rapid, where a need for updating knowledge and for continuing education is now generally accepted, and where, in any case, a more extensive education is becoming the *sine qua non* for the maintenance of a position in the society's workforce.

Distance education is an industrialized form of teaching in that it employs the technologies of the 20th century (see Peters, 1965 and 1973). But the analogy should not be carried too far. Our conception of the industrial process is of one that produces an unvarying product in large quantities and, therefore, at low cost. Such a product is acceptable and has been proven successful when it is as simple as a pencil or as complex as a motor car. It would be wrong, however, to think of distance education—or at least successful distance education—in these terms.

Most distance teaching systems use a package of attractively presented self-instructional materials the basis of which is almost invariably print, although audio and video material now often plays an important role. A great deal of time and effort is put into producing this package. This production is the major—sometimes perhaps the only—basis for economic calculations of cost-effectiveness and it therefore dominates distance education. The production of a standard package through a quasi-industrial process in no way guarantees learning on the part of a student. A mass-produced package of "knowledge" cannot be fitted to a student as a mass-produced nut can be fitted to a bolt. Each student brings his own frame of reference. For an adult student this may be a very rigid framework and into it must be placed new concepts that are possibly quite outside and even alien to his previous experience. An excessive concentration on the teaching package is the industrialized and institution-based approach to teaching at a distance and it is characterized by the very use of the word "teaching".

What is required for successful learning is a student-based approach, which is inherently more difficult since students are infinitely variable. The student-based approach does not require the abandonment of the mass-produced standard package; it requires mediation between the unified package and the diverse student base.

Such mediation cannot be built into the package itself. While the package may successfully incorporate the basic subject matter, it does not admit of the almost infinite variation of advice and support that has been part of the role of the face-to-face teacher. The academic content of the course is a common requirement for all the students and the cost benefits of the industrialized form of production are here applicable. The interpretation of the course is ever a variable and needs an individual approach which mass production cannot offer, but which requires the mediation of a teacher (see Sewart, 1981).

Learning at a distance is different from conventional learning. Immediate feedback is almost entirely absent as is the class session that allows students to estimate their success in relation to their peers. The vast majority of students cannot succeed in a course through self-instructional materials alone. Beyond the package of materials, there is a need for individualized advice, support, interpretation, and mediation capable of meeting the diverse needs of the students. The success of a distance education system rests upon a correct balance between the teaching package and the advisory and mediating function.

In our complex society the gulf between the system and the individual is filled by intermediaries such as social workers, doctors, and teachers. They are the employees of the system, but their primary concern is not for the system itself, but rather for the individual. They seek to represent individual needs in a professional way to such an extent that they force the system to recognize these needs and adapt to meet them. In distance education, no less than in conventional teaching, this intermediary function is taken on by the tutor or counsellor. However, in distance education this function is more important because of the physical separation of student and institution and the impersonal teaching package.

This requirement for mediation might seem to contradict the feasibility of distance education. If that is the case, the fault lies in the popular and overly simplistic definition of distance education.

If we consider the variety of teaching and learning processes as points on a hypothetical scale, we might place at one end a continuous face-to-face dialogue between one teacher and one student, in which the teacher represents the sole source of knowledge and provides the mediating function. Further along could be found a conventional primary school and even further is the secondary school in which the teacher is no longer the sole source of knowledge, being challenged, for example, by the printed word as well as the student's peer group. Much further along comes traditional university education, in which the teacher has been largely supplanted as the fountain of knowledge by books and other materials. At the end of the scale comes the independent student learning solely from materials by himself. On this scale the Open University with its individual support system would appear very close to conventional institutions of higher education. Thus it is wrong for us to see distance education as a discrete genre. The mediating function and the academic content might appear to be separate but the separation of these functions is more perceived than real. Physical separation does not deny the integration of these functions.

The successful integration of the functions is the touchstone of success for distance education. The success of the Open University is popularly seen as its teaching package, the attractively produced printed materials integrated with audio and video presentations. It is almost certainly correct to assert that it is not this package alone, but rather the package with the integrated mediation through tutors and counsellors that has brought about the success of the Open University. There are several institutions now producing packages of a comparable standard. Few also have the mediating function—although the importance of this seems to be increasingly recognized—and therefore few approach the success rate of the Open University.

If we look at this mediating function in the Open University, we find that when a student commences his studies he is assigned to a tutor-counsellor at one of 260 local study centres in the United Kingdom. Tutor-counsellors will normally be responsible for all tuition and counselling of the students in their foundation year. They will be available on a fairly regular basis for face-to-face contact and this contact will be extremely varied, ranging from strictly academic matters to the broader educational context. Contact is also maintained by correspondence and telephone. In addition, tutor-counsellors are responsible for marking and commenting on assignments. After the students have moved on from the foundation course to post-foundation courses, tuition becomes the province of the specialist course tutor whose central activity will be correspondence teaching but who may also meet students in tutorials or contact them individually by telephone or letter. However, tutor-counsellors continue to provide stability and continuity since the student's original tutor-counsellor retains his role as adviser throughout the student's educational career. Thus, there is a continuous educational support that cuts across disciplines and across faculties and remains constant for the student from initial registration until graduation.

It is this individual and long standing relationship that breaks down the isolation of the home-based student through the provision of sympathetic help in planning a beneficial work pattern in a highly complex system. This continuity is the basis of the individualized service to students (see Clennell et al, 1977).

The personal relationship formed between students and tutor-counsellors is beyond the ability of the Open University to influence extensively once it has begun. The University must rely on the staff to adopt the approach they think best. However, the Open University does control the relationship between itself and the tutor-counsellor. It can provide the most up to date information on the student's progress, and it can also use the intermediary's assessment of a student to determine its formal response to a student. There has therefore arisen between the Open University and its tutor-counsellors a complex two-way information flow. On the one hand the tutor-counsellor is mediating on behalf of the student when the student requires certain special services; on the other hand the institution is keeping the mediator up to date on the student's formal status.

It would be appropriate to stress the efforts of the Open University to set standards for its mediators both through careful selection and through briefing and training. Tutors and counsellors are not selected on the basis of research and publications or administrative abilities. They are selected for their abilities and interest in the mediating or teaching function peculiar to the Open University. This stress on the mediation function is unique in higher education in the United Kingdom, and possibly in the world. It is possible because of the separation of course production and teaching that allows the University to appoint staff who are most suited and most interested in one of these discrete activities.

Some of the 260 study centres are also used for tutorial contact for post-foundation courses, but here the provision is less extensive, probably consisting of between three and six tutorials each year in a small selection of these study centres, normally in the larger urban areas. Study centres can offer facilities for laboratory instruction beyond that which is possible through the provision of home experimental kits, and most study centres house a terminal linked to a mainframe computer—an important element in an increasing number of courses. In addition, study centres can provide a locus for student interaction ranging from academic study groups to purely social activities.

Students do not use study centres as often as the Open University makes them available and attendance at tutorials fluctuates widely. However, we are also aware that students do not always read every word of the course units or even every course unit; that some do not read the set books; that some omit the radio and television broadcasts entirely; and that some make little or no use of home experimental kits.

The richness and variety of the standard package allows students to study through a variety of media. The richness and variety of the mediating system involving tutor-counsellors, tutors, study centres, correspondence contacts, telephone contacts, etc. sustains and supports the students in their learning. Students may choose the provisions that best suit their own circumstances and they can be helped in making this choice by an experienced tutor-counsellor. Thus, for some students who do not take advantage of the variety of support services, their educational experience will come very close on the scale to pure (sic) distance teaching; for others who make the most extensive use of what is offered, these support services might come quite close to the other extreme on the scale. For most, however, the support services will offer no less an individualized provision than the conventional institutions of higher education in the United Kingdom, and possibly a great deal more.

David Sewart
Open University
United Kingdom

References

Clennell, S. Peters, J. and Sewart, D. (1977) *Teaching for the Open University*.

Peters, Otto. (1965) Der Fernunterricht, Materialen zur Diskussion einer neuen Unterrichtsform, Weinheim.

Peters, Otto. (1973) Die didaktische Struktur des Fernunterrichts, Untersuchungen zu einer industrialisierten Form des Lehrens und Lernens, Weinheim.

Sewart, D. (1978) Continuity of concern for students in a system of learning at a distance. Hagen: *ZIFF Papiere* 22.

Sewart, D. (1980) Creating an information base for an individualised support system in distance education. *Distance Education*, 1, 2.

Sewart, D. (1981) Distance teaching: a contradiction in terms. *Teaching at a Distance*, 19.

Recent Research in Distance Learning

Since the careful manipulation of variables and the clean analysis of well gathered data are still rare, true research constitutes only a small part of the impressive literature of distance learning.

Introduction

A review of the literature of distance learning suggests that imprecise definition of boundaries and variables has limited the usefulness of research in this area. Published papers on distance learning fall into five categories:

— position papers that discuss the phenomenon from the authors' perspective with little attempt to define terms and variables

— descriptions of practice at a particular institution

— papers reporting general research findings using variables that are so broad and loosely defined (e.g., tutoring versus non-tutoring) that replication would be practically impossible

— research studies with precisely defined variables (e.g., a particular approach to tutoring) that could be replicated—although they rarely are

— research that applies to distance learning although not conducted with this application in mind.

The last is potentially the largest category of all.

Paper 6

The role of research in distance learning

Various authors (Peters, 1971; Bååth, 1978; Holmberg, 1977; Ljoså, 1978) have noted that educational researchers have paid scant attention to distance learning. Some of the factors limiting the role of research in this area are:

- educational researchers are rarely present during the design of distance learning systems

- there is no clear paradigm for research in distance learning and it is difficult to attract funds to develop one

- there have been no consumer groups or publication outlets for such research (although this is changing)

- some institutions are averse to defining boundaries and variables clearly since practitioners work with macro-level variables (e.g., tutoring) and fear that breaking them down into components will complicate the phenomenon

- educational researchers often ask questions of no practical, or even theoretical relevance. The tendency to ask "What happens when you try this?" diverts them from the more important issue of "How do you make this happen?" (Geis, 1980)

- researchers in distance learning test variables that are really classes of variables (e.g., comparisons of distance and classroom learning). The results are impossible to replicate and of dubious utility anyway.

Although educational research may and should contribute significantly to distance learning as it matures and expands across institutions, these problems hinder any review of the literature.

Previous reviews of distance learning research

A review by Childs (1971) presented at the Paris World Conference of ICCE in 1969 provides an excellent summary of findings up to 1968. The key areas attracting the attention of researchers were completion rates, the reaction of students to correspondence study, student characteristics, the methodology of correspondence study, student achievement, and comparisons of correspondence with other instructional methods. The work on these topics was disparate in quality and quantity with little precisely defined research. Childs also examined research, such as that of Dubin and Taveggia (1968) on teaching methods, that had implications for distance learning although not conducted with that application in mind.

A slightly more recent review by Mathieson (1971) contains a larger number of references and an excellent annotated bibliography. It reported on the history of correspondence study and recent trends and discussed methods in terms of self-directed learning. The literature review concentrated on achievement and completion by learners and concluded:

> These findings add weight to the importance of motivational level and goal clarity in correspondence completion. Indeed, it seems clear from these studies that one direction in which research ought to be pushed is on the motivational structure of the correspondence student and discovering methods to reinforce motivation toward completion. This problem might be handled through several means: 1) an added emphasis on the counselling and guidance process in correspondence study; 2) extending the idea of supervised correspondence study into the group correspondence concept with appropriate mobile facilities; and 3) redesigning the curriculum methodology to take extra advantage of contemporary learning theory.

It is clear from Mathieson's review that before 1971 a database for making decisions about learner completion did not exist. Indeed, it is doubtful whether it was even legitimate to prescribe avenues for future research from this base.

The remainder of this paper reviews some more recent research in the light of a recent two-year project conducted at Athabasca University called REDEAL (Research and Evaluation of Distance Education for the Adult Learner) (Project REDEAL, 1980).

The basis for research into distance learning

Rather than being designed within a particular theoretical framework, most research on distance learning attempts to find solutions to perceived problems. While approval for this approach from administrators and sponsors may be easier to obtain, the results are rarely generalizable.

REDEAL began by establishing a three-part analytical base that attempted to bridge the gap between the need for practical information and the desire to contribute to a comprehensive theoretical framework.

An initial aim, since Athabasca University has a significant attrition problem, was to provide information applicable to the improvement of learner motivation. Instead of proceeding by trial and error we considered three sources of information: research on learner management models, research on learner treatment, and the relationship of this research to problems facing Athabasca University. First, the problem of motivation and management was analysed in terms of relevant recent research in higher education. This revealed that only Keller's Personalized System of Instruction (PSI) (Keller, 1968), which showed superior effectiveness on various dimensions, had a consistent record of improved learner performance (Kulik, Kulik and Colin, 1979). Moreover, PSI had been used in a range of settings (Toft, 1975), it could be linked to a theoretical base, and its variables could be specified and controlled. Second, assuming interaction between learner differences and treatments, it seemed that recent work by educational researchers on learner x treatment interaction (Cronbach and Snow, 1977; Snow, 1977) was relevant to distance learning from both practical and theoretical perspectives. Since aptitude, the principal student characteristic considered in that research, is largely irrelevant in studies of distance learning, a major goal of REDEAL was to determine learner attributes important in the interaction between learners and treatments. Third, the project had to consider key issues facing Athabasca University. Although some of these fell naturally into the previous two categories, others were more idiosyncratic (e.g., attrition measurement, the effect of group seminars, the skills required of telephone tutors).

Relevant recent research

The Personalized System of Instruction

The PSI has four basic features (Keller, 1968).

- reliance on the written word for instruction
- self-pacing by students
- students must perform at a specified criterion to demonstrate mastery
- use of proctors (tutors) to help students and give them feedback.

PSI produces higher achievement and course ratings than other instructional methods (Kulik, Kulik and Colin, 1979). Its application has been researched at the primary and secondary levels (Wilson, 1978; Creaner and Dubé, 1978), in paraprofessional training (Fawcett et al, 1976; Petrusa, 1978), and on a university campus with continuous enrolment (Toft, 1975). There are obvious similarities between PSI and distance learning (Northcott, 1975), and Elton (1980) has suggested that since PSI "provides a microcosm of an open university system", some common problems could best be investigated in the context of the Keller plan.

Despite the parallels between PSI and distance learning many distance courses either do not combine the elements of PSI in a systematic manner or leave out essential features (e.g., frequent assessment, immediate feedback, clear objectives and a match between objectives and assessment, systematic integration of the tutoring function). The course selected for investigation by the REDEAL team was no exception. Before this introductory accounting course could serve as the basis for an investigation of the variables in the PSI model it had to be brought up to an "acceptable instructional baseline" by rewriting objectives and assessment items and breaking the content into units for feedback purposes.

Since the type and immediacy of feedback appeared to have a direct effect on learner motivation we decided to investigate a variety of feedback models in the context of PSI. Comparison between immediate and delayed feedback and between telephone and mail feedback were combined. Student's choices of feedback modes and their patterns of behaviour in each were examined in order to shed light on completion/attrition. The costs of each mode were identified. Naturally it was necessary, in order to conduct the experiment, to modify certain aspects of the University's instructional system (e.g., tutor role, grading policy, record-keeping).

Results showed that the PSI phone version produced higher completion rates while there were minimal differences between PSI mail (delayed feedback) and instructional baseline (self-feedback) versions. There were no differences in examination performance for any version. When given a choice students opted clearly for the PSI phone version and this version increased the numbers completing early units of the course. In later units of the course, however, differences in completion rates were minimal. The PSI phone method is only slightly more costly than the others when total course costs are considered.

This work, though limited in scope and generality, suggests that further work on PSI in distance learning is important. Bringing PSI and distance learning together will require modifications to institutional policies and procedures, which adminstrators should be prepared to make given the proven record of PSI in other settings.

Tutoring

Whether he interacts with students by mail, by phone, or in person the tutor is regarded as an important part of the communication network in most distance education systems (Holmberg, 1974) and has received considerable attention in the literature. In fact, despite all the testimonials to the importance of tutors (Graff, 1965); Harper, 1971; Knowles, 1966) research into their activities and functions is rare and experimental studies of the characteristics and effects of different types of tutoring are almost non-existent.

Harris (1975) found that the majority of tutors in correspondence colleges are part-timers although some institutions prefer to use full-timers or a combination of the two (Graff, Saxe and Ostlyngen, 1966). Reports of tutor functions (Harris, 1975; Peters, 1971) are consistent with a survey in which Bååth (1976) asked distance institutions to rank order 12 activities. Feedback and motivational functions were important and tutors were expected to provide personal, encouraging comments as well as standard feedback on assignments. The distance learning tutor clearly has a multiple function (teacher, administrator, counsellor, facilitator, motivator, record-keeper) different from that of the classroom teacher.

Stein (1960) reported a direct relationship between tutor personality and learner success although this conclusion was based only on a change of tutors in a single course. However, Grahm (1969) found that students ranked the instructional and motivational value of written tests, self-tests, and assignments above that of tutors' feedback and comments. In Britain, Glatter and Weddell (1971) found that, according to students, tutors were not good at identifying and explaining problems and often took little personal interest. Bååth and Wångdahl (1976) also showed that the conventional view of tutor effectiveness may be overstated. They failed to confirm the hypothesis that extensive feedback and increased personal and supporting comments would increase student achievement and decrease withdrawal rates. Although tutoring may be one of the most difficult areas to research the effort is important because of the apparent disparity between the intended and the actual results of tutors' work.

REDEAL looked at two aspects of the tutor function. First, it tried to identify the essential skills required, their impact on learner performance, and how to impart them to tutors. Second, it examined the effects of an incentive system to encourage greater tutor involvement with students. In a preliminary study, which tracked the activities of students for several months, very shocking results were obtained. Tutors were not making regular contact with most students and even when they did, relatively little of the exchange was related to the course or to administrative matters.

A possible explanation for this poor showing was the system of payment based on a simple head count of the students assigned to each tutor. We thought this system might actually encourage tutors to ignore difficult students and provide little information to the University on student progress. REDEAL therefore conducted an experiment with a stratified remuneration system that paid tutors for providing information on student progress and gave them a bonus when a student completed a credit. This system was compared with the head count system and a second control group of tutors who provided, without additional pay, information on non-completing students (Coldeway, 1980a).

This scheme did not enhance credit completion although the experimental tutors provided ten times more information on those who had fallen behind than did the volunteer group. The experimental tutors assured us that since it would increase their pay dramatically, they were doing all they could to keep students progressing. They were, however, incapable of improving the completion rate.

Another REDEAL project attempted to examine the use of peer tutors since the literature shows such tutors to be effective in both PSI (Johnson, 1975) and conventional higher education (Schreve et al, 1976; Beck, 1978; Kersteins, 1976; Patterson, 1976; Hays, 1978). The advantages of peer tutors are that they know the course well from having taken it themselves (Coldeway and Schiller, 1974) and identify readily with the role and problems of the student. They may also work for lower wages, for credit, or even for the experience, and often report learning more about the subject through tutoring than they learned when they took the course.

In the event, the extensive study of peer tutoring we had hoped to conduct was scaled down to a more limited project for reasons that are as interesting as the results themselves. The larger study was blocked by academic staff members who feared that peer tutoring would undermine the credibility of the institution, hurt the self-image of regular tutors, and give the administration an excuse to use cheap labour. The results of the limited study suggested peer tutoring can be effective in distance education. Peer tutors could perform the duties of regular tutors and their students did as well in the course. Institutional resistance, rather than considerations of tutoring skills and student performance, is the main obstacle to the extension of peer-tutoring (Coldeway, 1980b).

Since the literature is full of references to the importance of the interpersonal relationship between student and teacher (Aspy, 1969; Brown and Copeland, 1979; Knowles, 1975) REDEAL also attempted to determine the effects of training tutors in interpersonal skills. This tutor skills program (Williams, 1980a) had the following purposes:

- to design a workshop to train tutors in the interpersonal skills needed to tutor adults effectively by phone

- to train a group of volunteer tutors through the workshop

- to measure changes in verbal interaction with students that may result from training

- to determine the effect of tutor training on student progress.

A workshop was designed with the help of Carkuff Associates (Williams, 1980b) that did teach the desired skills. Analysis of recordings of the tutors' subsequent interactions with students showed they were using the skills, although not at the level thought important by the experts. While time pressures meant that data on student performance was sparse, such results as there were indicated that students performed better when their tutors had received training in interpersonal skills.

This project (Williams, 1980a) reveals the need for an extensive analysis of tutor skills in distance learning. The tutorial function is complex and future research should begin by assigning relative weights to tutoring skills, including content expertise and interpersonal skills. Present research shows that interpersonal skills can be increased significantly.

Face-to-face contact

Comparisons of distance learning and instruction in person go back more than fifty years (Zeigel, 1924; Larson, 1929; 1936). More recently the literature on face-to-face contact with distance learners has been reviewed by Wångdahl (1977). She reports a widespread belief that group contact can play a humanizing, motivating, and instructional role in a distance learning system. Harrington (1977) related high failure and withdrawal rates to student loneliness, and Athabasca University staff rated group contact among the five most important research issues (Peruniak et al, 1980). Although the seminar has been the most widely researched form of group contact

(Gaff, 1976; Gall and Gall, 1976; McKeachie, 1975; Wångdahl, 1977) it is not yet clear whether seminars help the distance learner.

The REDEAL research on seminars attempted to discover how they could be introduced in a continuous enrolment system, how many students would find them of value, and what the reinforcing effects would be (Peruniak, 1980). The problems of arranging seminars did not prove insurmountable. Although students do attend seminars without compulsion and without the attraction of specific credit for the activity, there is little evidence that they come for social reasons. It did appear that seminar groups had higher completion rates on the first credit of the course (experiments were conducted in two courses) but the data do not allow this phenomenon to be attributed solely to seminars.

This is a complex area. The literature suggests seminars are related more to institutional values and specific course content than to their effect on student performance. For this reason it is difficult to transfer the results of research from one institution to another.

Pacing

Letting learners progress at their own pace has been widely urged (Bloom, 1968; Flammer, 1971; Keller, 1968). However, self-pacing often leads students to withdraw or procrastinate (Born and Whelan, 1973; Glick and Semb, 1978). Procrastination leads to inferior academic performance or eventual withdrawal (Henneberry, 1976; Lloyd and Knutzen, 1969; Schwartz, 1976). Although most of these results were obtained in conventional educational settings, similar data are reported for self-paced home study courses. Harrington (1977) reported drop-out rates over 90% and Donehower (1968) found a completion range from 19-64% across 56 institutions, also noting that the probability of course completion related significantly to submission of the first assignment. Lack of time and poor time management explain many withdrawals (Carp et al, 1973; Bradley and Lehman, 1975).

Such results have led many to urge the importance of instructional management (Tosti and Wilson, 1972), scheduling and time management (MacKenzie et al, 1968; Anderson and Tippy, 1971). Unfortunately, computer-managed systems for this purpose (Dick and Gallagher, 1972; Merrill, 1974) have limited applicability in distance learning.

The REDEAL project analysed the results of an experiment conducted at Athabasca University in 1978 that gave students the option of having a computer-generated study schedule (Spencer, 1980b). Most students opted for one of these personal schedules, which suggested appropriate assignment/examination dates within the maximum time allowed for the course. However, students did not like the schedules and few used them. Although the experiment was not sufficiently systematic to be generalizable it is clear that simply making a schedule available is not enough for distance learners.

Two other REDEAL studies examined the effects of pacing. In the first an instructor met regularly with students in an isolated community while they progressed through a course designed for self-study (Spencer et al, 1980). This format, known as a paced-package course, had a higher completion rate and was less costly than the regular self-paced format used by the other students in the course.

The second study (Crawford, 1980) compared completion rates in an identical course offered at Athabasca University and at North Island College on a self-paced basis and at the Open Learning Institute where the semester system fixed the starting date and the dates of examinations. The results indicated higher completion rates in the paced format at the Open Learning Institute, in conformity with the results of the paced-package study.

Although it is clear that more rigid pacing increases completion rates a caveat is in order. A system of fixed entry and deadline dates may prevent some students from enrolling, thereby reducing the openness of the institution. Before moving to paced systems, institutions should carefully explore other methods of learner management and self-management.

Completion rates

The literature on distance learning seems clear on one issue. Although attrition rates are not simple to measure and compare they are generally very high, both in absolute terms and in comparison to traditional institutions (Pantages et al, 1978). The results of Harrington (1977) and Donehower (1968) were mentioned above and Bradley and Lehman (1975) found that 43% of the students at Empire State College withdrew.

Two common methods of measuring completions are in use:

Total Enrolment Formula

$$\% \text{ Completion rate} = \frac{\text{Course completions} \times 100}{\text{total enrolment}}$$

National University Extension Association (NUEA) Formula

$$\% \text{ Completion rate} = \frac{\text{course completion} \times 100}{\text{total enrolment} - \text{total non-starts}}$$

Unless there are no non-starts the NUEA formula will always give a higher completion rate. However, the notion of non-starts deserves attention.

Orton (1977) defined non-starters as those who cancelled their registration before submitting assignments. This has the advantage that the student himself determines his non-start status; but it assumes that all courses have assignments monitored by the institution. The time interval between enrolment and first measurable assignment is a critical variable. The length of this period differs widely for students at, say, the UK Open University and students at most

North American institutions.

Further measurement problems arise in institutions that let the learner pace himself. It is difficult to know how long to wait before calculating the completion rate. Bradley and Lehman (1975) showed one third of the students to be still enrolled but not completed after a year and Shale (1980) noted a similar trend. Coldeway et al (1980) observed that students who completed usually took longer than the time allotted for course completion at Athabasca University.

In the light of these considerations, and because it was not practical to wait long enough to determine the status of all students in a cohort, REDEAL opted to take statistical snapshots of attrition/completion at particular stages. It also investigated the use of course completion prediction formulae for course revision and planning purposes (Coldeway and Spencer, 1980b). One variable used was the student's rate of progress since academic staff often commented that students who work steadily tend to complete.

A rate function was calculated for six courses at particular stages (9 months for a 12-month course and 5 months for a 6-month course). Students were classified as potential completers if their rate of progress matched the rate function. To determine the predictive validity of the classification, completion data was collected long after most learners should have completed the course.

The results were most encouraging. The reliability coefficient of predictive validity for the rate function was 89.7%, indicating that the rate function was an excellent predictor of course completion.

Although the drop-out phenomenon in adult education is of concern (Boshier, 1978) it would be wrong for research to focus on ways to reduce attrition. Understanding students' needs and whether they are being met is more important. One day better definitions and measurement of learner success and satisfaction will doubtless replace the present rather crude measures of completion/attrition.

Learner x treatment interaction

Since a concern for individual differences appeals to many educators the work of Cronbach and Snow (1977) has led to a growing interest in "Aptitude-Treatment Interaction Effects". There has, however, been confusion over the practical use of the idea (Snow, 1977) and over appropriate measures for aptitude (Tobias, 1976). The approach involves looking at the effects of instructional treatments on sub-groups of different aptitude levels. Since the acquisition of standardized aptitude data goes against the grain of the openness often espoused by distance education systems, researchers must find measures of individual differences that are not specifically aptitude scores (Crawford, 1977).

The REDEAL team quickly concluded there were, in fact, six potential interactions represented by the possible pairs of four variables:

- learner characteristics
- course structure and design
- treatment effect
- learner performance

The interaction between learner characteristics and the course materials is likely to be very important, as is that between learner characteristics and treatment effects. (By "treatment" is meant the learner management and motivational scheme, which is usually quite distinct from the course package).

Although learner performance is usually considered a dependent variable REDEAL included it in the model as a main effect after finding that various patterns of learner performance influence other dependent variables—including future learner performance. Even if performance is probably best seen as a component of learner characteristics it may be useful to separate it out in order to highlight its effect.

Finally, the interaction between treatment effect and course structure and design may have great relevance to distance learning. The present work on PSI (Spencer, 1980a) underscores the importance of considering the delivery model when the course materials are being designed.

Two REDEAL studies (Coldeway and Spencer, 1980a; Coldeway et al, 1980) attempted to gather information about potential interactive effects. The first involved monitoring the behaviour of 38 randomly selected students for several months. Each week these students submitted a form describing their activity in the course and their interaction with the institution. A computer file of the performance of these students and their demographic characteristics was also generated. The results supported the importance of interactive effects in distance learning. They showed that although the students and their problems were heterogeneous on many dimensions they were not being treated differentially to any significant degree. But it was clear that course events (e.g., examinations, tutor contact) had an effect on learners and that early behaviour in the course influenced the potential impact of other variables later on.

The second study used the computer to look at interactions between learner characteristics and learner performance for over 550 students. The interactions appear to be important although the results did not allow us to pinpoint major predictors of success. However, in conformity with the previous REDEAL work it was clear that success at one stage made the students more likely to be successful at a second stage—in the same or a subsequent course.

Conclusion

The literature on distance learning reflects a genuine commitment to the expansion of educational opportunity worldwide. The work accomplished is impressive although only a small proportion of it qualifies as research. This review has summarized some of this research. We are painfully aware that not all important work has been cited and that some key pieces of research have been missed. Several areas of distance learning research and development were not included such as counselling, materials design, course evaluation, curriculum development, institutional management, technological applications, experiential learning, and cost-effectiveness analysis.

While we have been critical of the lack of systematic research in distance learning we observe that such activity is becoming more important and widespread. However, the careful manipulation of variables and the clean analysis of well gathered data are still rare. There is much to be learned about research into distance learning and still more about distance learning itself.

Dan O. Coldeway
Athabasca University
Canada

References

Anderson, T.H. and Tippy, P.H. (1971) An exploratory study of correspondence students. *ERIC Report Number 70960.*

Aspy, D. (1969) The relationshop between teacher functioning and facilitated dimensions and student performance on intellectual indices. *Florida Journal of Educational Research.*

Bååth, J.A. and Wangdahl, A. (1976) The tutor as an agent of motivation in correspondence Education. *Pedagogical Reports.* University of Lund: Department of Education.

Bååth, J.A. (1976) Postal contacts and some other means of two-way communication: practices and opinions at a number of European correspondence schools. *Pedagogical Reports.* Number 5. University of Lund: Department of Education.

Bååth, J.A. (1978) Research in development work correspondence education. *ICCE Newsletter.* 8, 4, 9-15.

Beck, P. (1978) Peer tutoring at a community college: training and using peer tutors. *College English.* 40, 437-439.

Bloom, B.S. (1968) Learning for mastering. *Evaluation comment number 1.*

Born, D.G. and Whelan, P. (1973) Some descriptive characteristics of student performance in PSI in lecture courses. *Psychological Record.* 23, 145-152.

Boshier, R. (1978) Relationship between motives for participation in and drop-out from adult education. *Psychological Reports.* 43, 23-26.

Bradley, A.P. and Lehman, T. (1975) Attrition at a non-traditional Institute. Saratoga Springs: State University of New York, Empire State College.

Brown, M.A. and Copeland, H. G. (1979) *Attracting Able Instructors of Adults.* Jossey Bass.

Carp, A. Peterson, R. and Roelfs, P. (1973) Learning Interests and Experiences of Adult American. Berkeley, California: Educational Testing Services.

Childs, G.D. (1971) Recent Research Developments in Correspondence Instruction. In *The Changing World of Correspondence Study: International Readings.* MacKenzie and Christensen (eds.) University Park: Pennsylvania State University Press.

Coldeway, D.O. (1980a) An Examination of Tutor Management Strategies for use in Distance Education. *REDEAL Research Report #2. Project REDEAL* Athabasca University.

Coldeway, D.O. (1980b) Exploring the Effects of Peer Tutoring in Distance Education. *REDEAL Research report #3. Project REDEAL.* Athabasca University.

Coldeway, D.O. and Schiller, W.J. (1974) Training Proctors for the Personalized System of Instruction. In R.S. Ruskin and S.F. Bono (eds). *Proceedings of First National Conference on Personalized Instruction in Higher Education.* Washington, D.C.: Centre for Personalized Instruction, Georgetown University.

Coldeway, D.O. and Spencer, R. (1980a) Distance Education: Interaction between Learner Attributes and Learner Course Performance. *REDEAL Research Report #9.* **Project REDEAL.** Athabasca University.

Coldeway, D.O. and Spencer, R.E. (1980b) The Measurement of Attrition and Completion in Distance Learning Courses. *REDEAL Technical Report #8. Project REDEAL.* Athabasca University.

Coldeway, D.O., McKrury, K. and Spencer, R. (1980) Distance Education from the Learner's Perspective: The Results of Individual Learner Tracking at Athabasca University. *REDEAL Research Report #10. Project REDEAL.* Athabasca University.

Crawford, G. (1980) Student Completion Rates under Three Different Pacing Conditions. *REDEAL Technical Report #11. Project REDEAL.* Athabasca University.

Crawford, J. (1977) Interactions of learner characteristics with a difficulty level of instruction. Paper presented at the annual meeting of American Education Research Association, New York.

Creaner, R.C. and Dubé, N.S. (1978) Administration of Personalized Instruction Programs in the Middle School. In J.G. Sherman, R.S. Ruskin, and R.M. Lazer (eds.). *Personalized Instruction in Education Today: Selected Papers from the Third and Fourth National Conferences on Personalized Instruction.* San Francisco: San Francisco Press.

Cronbach, L. and Snow, R. (1977) *Aptitudes and Instructional Methods.* New York: Urbanton Publishers.

Dick, W. and Gallagher, P. (1972) Systems concepts in computer-managed instruction: an implementation and validation study. *Educational Technology.* 12, 33-39.

Donehower, J.M. (1968) Variables Associated with Correspondence Study Enrolments at the University of Nevada, 1963-1965. unpublished Master's thesis.

Dubin, R. and Taveggia, T. (1968) The Teaching Learning Paradox. Center for the Advanced Study of Education Administration, University of Oregon, Eugene, Oregon.

Duby, P.B. and Giltrow, D.R. (1978) Predicting student withdrawals in open learning courses. *Educational Technology.* February, 43-47.

Elton, L.R.B. (1980) Can the Keller Plan help in our understanding of the problems of distance learning. *Journal of Personalized Instruction.* 4, 2, 94-99.

Essex, D.L. And Anderson, T.H. (1972) Some Correlates of Success in Correspondence Study. *ERIC Report Number 70952.* 1972.

Fawcett, S.B. Matthews, M.R. Fletcher, R.K. Morrow, R. and Stokes, T.F. (1976) Personalized instruction in the community: teaching helping skills to low-income neighborhood residents. *Journal of Personalized Instruction.* 2, 86-90.

Flammer, G.H. (1971) Learning as the constant and time as the variable. *Engineering Education.* 61, 511-514.

Gaff, J.G. (1975) *Faculty Renewal.* San Francisco: Jossey-Bass.

Gall, M.D. and Gall, J.P. (1976) The discussion method. In N.L. Gage (ed.). *The Psychology of Teaching Methods.* The 75th Yearbook of the National Society for the Study of Education. Chicago: University of Chicago Press.

Geis, G.L. (1980) Research: Use, Abuse and Refuse. Paper Presented at the Annual Meeting of the American Educational Research Association in Boston, April 8th, 1980.

Glatter, R. and Wedell, E.G. (1971) *Study by Correspondence.* London: Longmans.

Glick, D.M. and Semb, G. (1978) Effects of pacing contingencies on personalized instruction. a review of the evidence. *Journal of Personalized Instruction.* 3, 36-42.

Graff, K. (1965) Exercises and tests in correspondence education. *Home Study Review.* 6, 1, 22-29.

Graff, K. Saxe, B. and Ostlyngen, E. (1966) Correspondence education in Europe today. In *CEC Yearbook.* Lincoln: CEC. 42-77.

Grahm, A. (1969) *What Students Think of Assignments in Correspondence Education.* Malmo: Hermods.

Granholm, G.W. And Ljoså, E. (1977) ICCE Research Survey 1976. *ICCE Newsletter.* 7, 4, 3-30.

Grant, D.A. (1962) Testing the null hypothesis and the strategy and tactics of investigating theoretical models. *Psychological Review.* 69, 1, 54-61.

Harper, W.R. (1971) A system of correspondence. In Mackenzie, O. and Christensen, E.L. (eds.) *The Changing World of Correspondence Study.* University Park: Pennsylvania State University Press. 7-13.

Harrington, F.A. (1977) *The Future of Adult Education.* San Francisco: Jossey Bass Publishing.

Harris, W.J.A. (1975) *The Distance Tutor.* Bournemouth: Department of Adult Education, University of Manchester.

Hays, R.A. (1978) Implementation of a Peer Tutoring Program. Introductory Practicum, Nova University.

Henneberry, J.K. (1976) Initial progress rates as related to performance in a personalized system of instruction. *Teaching of Psychology.* 3, 178-181.

Holmberg, B. (1974) *Distance Education.* Malmo: Hermods.

Holmberg, B. (1977) *Distance Education: Survey and Bibliography.* London: Kogan Page.

Hornik, R.C. (1976) Useful evaluation designs for evaluating the impact of distance learning systems: methodology. *Educational Broadcasting International.* 9, 6-10.

Johnson, K.R. (1975) An Evaluative Reiview of the Proctor Compnent of Personalized Instruction. Paper presented at the American Psychological Association, New Orleans, 1975.

Keller, F.S. (1968) Goodbye teacher. *Journal of Applied Behavior Analysis.* 1, 78-89.

Kelly, H. (1963) From the editor's notebook. *Home Study Review.* 4, 3, 1-3; 43-49.

Kersteins, G. (1976) Report on the Peer Tutoring Program: 1973-1975 School Years. El Camino College, Torrence, California.

Knowles, M. (1975) *Self-Directed Learning: A Guide for Learners and Teachers.* Chicago: Associated Press, Follett Publishing Company.

Knowles, M.J. (1966) The Role of the Instructor in Correspondence Study. In Wedemeyer, C. (ed.) 100-106.

Kulik, J.A. Kulik, C.C. and Colin, P.A. (1979) Meta-analysis of outcome studies of Keller's Personalized System of Instruction. *American Psychologist.* 34, 307-318.

Larson, A. (1936) Comparative quality of work done by students in residence in correspondence work. *Journal of Educational Research.* 25, 105-109.

Larson, A. (1929) A Study of the Relative Ability and Achievement of Class Extension Correspondence and Residence Students at the University of Kentucky. University of Kentucky, Lexington, Master's Thesis.

Lewis, R. (1975) The place of face-to-face tuition in the Open University system. *Teaching at a Distance.* 3, 26-31.

Ljoså, E. (1978) Trends and priorities in distance education research. *ICCE Newsletter.* 8, 4, 4-8.

Lloyd, K.E. and Knutzen, N.J. (1969) A self-paced program undergraduate course in experimental analysis of behavior. *Journal of Applied Behavior Analysis.* , 2, 125-133.

MacIntosh, N. and Morrison, V. (1968) Student demand progress and withdrawal: the Open University's first four years. *Higher Education Review.* 7, 37-66.

MacKenzie, O. Christensen, E.L. and Rigby, P.H. (1968) *Correspondence Instruction in the United States.* New York: McGraw-Hill.

Malley, J.I. Brown, A.P. and Williams, J.W. (1976) Drop-outs from external studies: a case study of the investigation process. *Epistolodidaktika.* 2, 170-179.

Mathieson, D.E. (1971) Correspondence Study: A Summary Review of the Research and Development Literature. ERIC Clearinghouse on Adult Education. Syracruse University, New York, March 1971.

McKeachie, W.J. (1975) *Teaching Tips.* Lexington: D.C. Heath.

Merrill, P.F. (1974) Computer-Managed Instruction at Florida State University, In H.E. Mitzell (ed.) An Examination of the Short-Range Potential of Computer-Managed Instruction. Conference Proceedings, November 6-8, 1974. National Institute of Education.

Monstain, B.R. (1974) Students who desire independent study: some distinguishing characteristics. *College Student Journal.* 8, 85-92.

Northcott, P. (1975) The Keller Plan in external studies. *ASPESA Newsletter.* 2, 4.

Orton, L.J. (1977) Completion and non-starts rates in correspondence courses. *Canadian Journal of University Continuing Education.* 4.

Page, E.B. (1958) Teacher comments and student performance: a seventy-four classroom experiment in school motivation. *Journal of Educational Psychology.* 49, 1, 173-181.

Pantages, T.J. and Creedon, C.F. (1978) Studies of college attrition: 1950 to 1975. *Review of Education Research.* 48, 1, 49-101.

Patterson, R.T. (1976) Planning and Implementing a Peer Tutoring Approach to Individualized Instruction to Improve Reading Achievement. *Max II Report.* Nova University.

Peruniak, G. (1980) Seminars as an Instructional Strategy in Distance Education. *REDEAL Research Report #6. Project REDEAL.* Athabasca University.

Project REDEAL, (1980) Athabasca University.

Peruniak, G., Spencer, R.E. and Coldeway, D.O. (1980) Interface of the Host Institution, Athabasca University. *REDEAL Technical Report #6. Project REDEAL.* Athabasca University.

Peters, O. (1971) Theoretical aspects of correspondence instruction. In Mackenzie, O.and Christensen, E.L. (eds.) *The Changing World of Correspondence Study.* University Park: Pennsylvania State University Press. 223-228.

Petrusa, E.R. (1978) Opthalmoscopy: a self-paced unit for physician assistants. In J.G. Sherman, R.S. Ruskin and M.R. Lazer (eds.). *Personalized Instruction Education Today: Selected Papers for the Third and Fourth National Conferences on Personalized Instruction.* San Francisco, San Francisco Press.

Savins, D. Pfeiffer, J.W. and Ragsdale, J.P. (1972) Effective letters and postcards of encouragement on the submission of lessons in correspondence study. *Journal of Experimental Education.* 41, 87-90.

Schreve, B. Majer, K. and Hedges, L. (1976) The OASIS Peer Tutoring Program: A Model for Academic Support. LaJolla, California. University of California, San Diego.

Schwartz, G.E. (1976) What is doing the teaching in PSI courses? In L.E. Fraley and E.A. Vargas (eds.). *Behavior Research and Technology in Higher Education.* Gainsville, Florida: University of Florida, Society for Behavioral Technology and Engineering. 35-40.

Shale, D. (1980) Course completion rates. Edmonton: Athabasca University, Office of Institutional Studies. August 1980.

Sjogren, D.D. (1963) The influence of varied teacher behavior on performance in correspondence study. *Journal of Experimental Education.* 32, 81-83.

Smith, P.J. (1976) Some factors contributing to the rate of student withdrawal from part-time correspondence courses. *Epistolodidaktika.* 1, 26-33.

Snow, R.E. (1977) Individual differences and instructional theory. *Educational Researcher.* 6, 11-15.

Spencer, R.E. (1980a) Investigating the Use of the Personalized System of Instruction in Distance Education. *REDEAL Research Report #1. Project REDEAL.* Athabasca University.

Spencer, R.E. (1980b) The Effects of Computer-Generated schedules on the Performance of Athabasca University Learners. *REDEAL Research Report #5. Project REDEAL.* Athabasca University.

Spencer, R.E. Peruniak, G. and Coldeway, D.O. (1980) A Comparison between Pace-Package and Home-Study Courses with Respect to Completion Data. *REDEAL Research Report #11. Project REDEAL.* Athabasca University.

Stein, L.S. (1960) Design of a correspondence course. *Adult Education.* 10, 161-166.

Tobias, S. (1976) Achievement treatment interactions. *Review of Educational Research.* 46, 61-74.

Toft, R. (1975) College TV: A New Approach. In J.M. Johnston (ed.). *Research and Technology in College and University Teaching.* Gainsville, Florida: Department of Psychology, University of Florida.

Tosti, D. and Wilson, S. (1972) *Learning is Getting Easier.* San Raphael: Individual Learning Systems.

Tough, A. (1978) Major learning efforts: recent research and future directions. *Adult Education.* 28, 4, 250-263.

Wangdahi, A. (1977) Types of Face-to-Face Contact in Combination with Correspondence Education. A Survey of the literature. *Pedagogical Report Number 10.* Lund, Sweden: University of Lund, Department of Education.

Wedemeyer, C. (1974) Theory of Learning By Correspondence - Some Theoretical Propostions. Keynote Address to the N.H.S.C. Conference in South Bend, Indiana, October 7th, 1974.

White, M.A. (1976) Reflections on research into higher education by external study in Asutralia. *Epistolodidaktika.* 2.

Wiedhaup, C.J.J. (1976) Dutch research on correspondence education: KISO Project. *Epistolodidaktika.* 1.

Williams, E. and Holloway, S. and Hammond, S. (1975) Student reactions to tutoring by telephone in Britain's Open University. *Educational Technology.* 15, 42-46.

Williams, V. (1980a) Research and Evaluation of Tutor Skills Training Project. *REDEAL Research report #4. Project REDEAL.* Athabasca University.

Williams, V. (1980b) Communications Skills Workshop for Tutors: The Manual. *REDEAL Technical Report #7. Project REDEAL.* Athabasca University.

Wilson, J.A. (1978) Johnny Gets Personalized. In J.G. Sherman, R.S. Ruskin and M.R. Lazer (eds.). *Personalized Instruction Education Today: Selected Papers for the Third and Fourth National Conferences on Personalized Instruction.* San Francisco: San Francisco Press.

Wilson, W.R. and Miller, H. (1964) A note on the inconclusiveness of accepting the null hypothesis. *Psychological Review.* 1, 3, 238-242.

Ziegel, W.H. (1924) The Relation of Extra-Mural Study to Residents Enrolment and Scholastic Standing. George Peabody College for Teachers, Nashville, Tennessee. Ph.D. thesis.

Teaching Models for Designing Courses Creatively
There is nothing as practical as a good model.

One way of developing distance education for the future would appear to be through deliberate application of relevant educational theories or models. The famous psychologist Kurt Lewin once wrote: "There is nothing as practical as a good theory." In this context, the term "model" could easily be substituted for "theory".

In this paper I will confine myself to some general teaching models of potential relevance to distance education. The paper is based on my book *Correspondence Education in the Light of a Number of Contemporary Teaching Models.* One of the limitations of the study reported in this book should be mentioned: all of the selected teaching models are psychologically oriented, and teaching is also influenced by non-psychologically factors—social, economic, and political above all. The present study does not deal with models of this type.

Teaching models

These are the teaching models dealt with in my study:

— Skinner's behaviour control model

— Rothkopf's model for written instruction

— Ausubel's advance organizer model

— Egan's structural communication model

— Bruner's discovery learning model

— Rogers' model for "facilitation of learning"

— Gagné's general teaching model

While models represent various theoretical approaches to learning, they also reflect different views on teaching or, in other words, control of the students' learning.

Skinner advocates an extreme form of behaviourism. To him, learning equals acquiring new behaviour. Behaviour is seen exclusively as responses to stimuli in the organism's environment. Therefore, teaching must mean an extremely strict control of the learner's environment.

Rothkopf represents a considerably modified variety of behaviourism. Actually, his main concept, *mathemagenic activities,* refers to all student activities aimed at learning—not only external behaviour but also processes within the individual. In his model for written instruction, Rothkopf, in contrast to Skinner, does not advocate elaborate teaching programs, but recommends short study guides to textbooks, etc. The aim of such study guides should be to facilitate and control the students' mathemagenic activities.

Ausubel adopts a cognitivistic view of learning. Later on, I will outline his model in more detail.

To a greater degree than Ausubel, Bruner views

human learning as an active, even creative process. He thinks that *discovery learning* as an educational method would best agree with man's search for knowledge. We would not be told the essential concepts and principles, but be challenged by a problem-oriented approach to find them ourselves.

Egan's model incorporates ideas from Bruner and Ausubel. The most distinct feature of this model is a technique called *structural communication* that aims to promote a high level of understanding and even creativity.

Rogers advocates an extremely student-centred approach to learning. The student should have complete freedom to learn whenever he wants, and in whatever way he wants.

Gagné's model may be the most general of them all. In the latest development of his model (1977), Gagné has adopted an information-processing view of learning. Earlier versions of the model have been applied to correspondence education in several contexts, not least in the Scandinavian countries (e.g., Ahlm, 1972; Bååth, 1979; Lampikoski and Mantere, 1976; *Veiledning for brevskolelaerere,* 1977). In all these cases, the emphasis has been on one isolated part of the Gagné model—the analysis of various teaching functions.

The space available does not permit a full account of my investigations, but I will outline in more detail one of the models and make suggestions as to how distance education could be analysed and developed on the basis of this model. I have chosen Ausubel's advance organizer model.

Ausubel's advance organizer model

View of learning

David Ausubel makes a clear distinction between two kinds of verbal learning: meaningful verbal learning and rote learning. He maintains that most of the learning principles found by traditional learning psychology are relevant to rote learning but not to meaningful verbal learning. For instance, techniques like small learning steps, distributed practice, and repetition have considerably less effect on meaningful than on rote learning (Ausubel, 1963: 186-212).

Ausubel also distinguishes between discovery learning and reception learning. According to him, discovery learning (where the learner has an opportunity to discover principles on his own) is important in solving several everyday problems, but has a strictly limited value in education contexts (Ausubel, 1963: 17). With few exceptions, the use of discovery methods leads to a waste of time and resources. Consequently, meaningful reception learning, where the student acquires knowledge with the aid of well structured oral or written presentation, is the subvariety of learning to which Ausubel devotes himself almost exclusively.

According to Ausubel's "subsumption theory of meaningful verbal learning and retention", meaningful knowledge emerges through a process by which the new material is incorporated within an individual's cognitive structure. As a rule, this is achieved by subsuming the new material under more general ideas or concepts in the existing structure.

View of teaching

Ausubel attaches extreme importance to the connecting of new material with the student's previous knowledge and cognitive structure. How could this be done in the best way? By using *advance organizers,* Ausubel (1963, 1968) tells us.

An advance organizer is an introduction designed to bridge the distance between what the student already knows and what he needs to know in order to assimilate the new material successfully. Advance organizers are different from introductory overviews as well as summaries (Ausubel, 1963: 214). In contrast to summaries, advance organizers should be given before the learning material, since Ausubel maintains it is essential that they influence learning in a proactive way. Moreover, both introductory overviews and summaries are usually written at the same level of abstraction as the learning material, while advance organizers should be devised at a higher level of "abstraction, generality, and inclusiveness".

Advance organizers can be divided into two major forms: expository organizers are aimed at facilitating the structuring and meaningful acquisition of completely new material, primarily by anchoring it in more inclusive concepts and principles in cognitive structure.

Comparative organizers are more common and of greater use. They are used when a new learning task contains partially known material, and their purpose is to point out similarities and differences between the new learning material and previously learned, related material.

The advance organizer idea is based on two general principles regarding how learners' cognitive structures are optimally affected through teaching—irrespective of subject matter. One is called the principle of progressive differentiation; the other the principle of integrative reconciliation.

The principle of progressive differentiation (Ausubel, 1963: 79-80; 1968: 152-155) in teaching material implies that the most general and inclusive ideas should be introduced at the beginning of the instruction. After that, the subject matter is gradually structured down to the specific details. In other words, Ausubel's model implies that teaching normally proceeds from the abstract to the concrete.

The principle of integrative reconciliation (Ausubel, 1963: 80-81; 1968: 155-158) means that "water-tight bulkheads" should never be built in between different parts of learning material. The teacher (or writer) should instead endeavour to demonstrate how various concepts and principles are related to each other.

Before proceeding to a new area, students should have adequately mastered the previous material. This is a consequence of the two principles of progressive differentiation and integrative reconciliation. The consolidation of the material studied just before is facilitated through reviews, repetition, and exercises—not necessarily with explicit feedback. Thus, the purpose of these measures is not only to further the retaining of the material just learned but, to a high degree, also *to facilitate the integration of the subsequent material into the cognitive structures of the students.*

Ausbel's model applied to correspondence education

In Ausubel's model, the pedagogical process is comparatively strictly teacher-controlled, and the model does not require simultaneous communication between teacher and student. These two conditions make the model well suited to "pure" correspondence education.

Teaching material

Actually, the application of the model could be comparatively straightforward. In correspondence course materials one should start with the most inclusive concepts and principles and then proceed by progressive differentiation (more or less strictly realized) and integrative reconciliation to the most specific application. Each new chapter—or at least each new study unit—should be introduced by means of an organizer with the purpose of relating the new material to previously studied material and other relevant knowledge. The relations should be pointed out by means of subsumption or comparison.

Extreme care must be attached to conceptually clear texts and logical organization of the material. Each study unit should contain reviews, exercises, and other measures aimed at consolidating the previously learned material and—above all—at promoting transfer of learning to subsequent study units.

Postal two-way communication

When we apply the advance organizer model to correspondence education, the start of a course appears to present a particular problem. The question is how to design the first advance organizer. Does a correspondence educator have sufficient knowledge, not only about the target group's average level of knowledge, but also about each student's capacity to relate the introductory material to his cognitive structure?

Here, the correspondence tutor may have an essential task: to adapt the beginning of the course as far as possible to each student's specific starting position. Such an attempt would probably imply contacts between tutor and student before the student submits his first assignments. These initial contacts could be based on a test of previous knowledge and/or other data before the start of the course.

Generally, the primary task of the assignments and of the correspondence tutor should be to promote consolidation of material already studied. In his comments the tutor must strive for conceptual clarity and logical cogency in order to further "the stability, clarity and organization of...subject-matter knowledge" (Ausubel, 1963: 76).

Simultaneous contacts

Individual telephone tutoring is a practical means of helping students at the beginning of the course.

Telephone contacts during the course should be used to promote students' comprehension of the material. The telephone tutor ought to concentrate on comprehension of essential concepts and principles and the relations between parts of the material.

Probably the ideal means of serving these two purposes would be face-to-face contacts between tutor and student.

General results

After this short presentation of one of the teaching models and its possible application to correspondence education, I would now like to indicate a few general results of the study.

All the models—Skinner's, Rothkopf's, Ausubel's, Egan's, Bruner's, Rogers', and Gagné's—are applicable to correspondence teaching, but not every model can be applied naturally and smoothly. This is related to the views of the goals that teaching/learning should have and to how strictly controlled the students' work towards these goals ought to be. *The stricter the control towards fixed cognitive goals, the easier the application of the model to correspondence education.*

With some simplification, it would be possible to arrange all of the models except Gagné's—starting with Skinner's and ending with Rogers'—on a sliding scale with regard to the ease with which they can be applied to correspondence education. Skinner's and Rothkopf's models seem to be easiest to use, but neither Ausubel's or Egan's provides any fundamental problems. Bruner's model demands more student-initiated activities and dialogue, and is therefore more difficult to apply. In Rogers' model, the initiative is entirely with the student himself. Here, supplementing simultaneous contact by telephone or face-to-face appears more justified than in any of the other models. Models with stricter control of fixed goals also seem to imply a greater emphasis on the teaching material than on two-way communication.

Concluding comments

Finally, a few words on the practical use of a models approach.

Which model to choose? That must depend on a number of factors:

- one's basic view of learning (and, with that, maybe also one's basic view of man)
- the variety of goals of the teaching planned

However, knowledge of the students—personality, cognitive aptitudes, etc., as well as preference with regard to studying—could also be

Paper 7

considered when choosing a teaching model. For example, a model implying strict control would not be suitable for highly autonomous students (cf. Moore, 1977). In addition, economic constraints must always be considered.

In applying teaching models one should be prepared to combine or modify various models (cf. Joyce and Weil, 1972: 384; Mathis and McGaghie, 1974: 49-50) whenever this appears justified. Pedagogical phenomena are "man-made": they do not yield scientific laws (Gowin, 1972). We can therefore never find out *the* best method or *the* teaching model that is most appropriate in all contexts. Nevertheless, each of us can try out, experiment, search for what is most suitable to his own teaching situation.

John A. Bååth
LiberHermods
Sweden

References

Ahlm, M. (1972) Telephone instruction in correspondence education. *Epistolodaktika* 2, 49-64.

Ausubel, D.P. (1963) *The Psychology of Meaningful Verbal Learning*. New York: Grune & Stratton.

Ausubel, D.P. (1968) *Educational Psychology: A Cognitive View*. New York: Holt, Rinehart & Winston.

Gagné, R.M. (1977) *The Conditions of Learning*. (3rd ed.) New York: Holt, Rinehart & Winston.

Gowin, B. (1972) Is education research distinctive? In Thomas, L.G. (ed.) (1972)*Philosophical Redirection of Education Research*. Chicago, Ill.: The University of Chicago Press. pp. 9-25

Joyce, B. and Weil, M. (1972) *Models of Teaching*. Englewood Cliffs, N.J.: Prentice-Hall.

Lampikoski, K. and Mantere, P. (1976) *Didactic Principles as Tools in Analysing and Developing a Guidance System for Distance Education*. Helsinki: The Institute of Marketing.

Mathis, B.C. and McGaghie, W.G. (1974) From theories for learning to theories for teaching. In Stiles, L.J. (ed.) (1974) *Theories for Teaching*. New York: Dodd, Mead & Company. pp. 30-50

Moore, M.G. (1977) A model of independent study. *Epistolodidaktika* 1, 6-40.

Veiledning for Brevskolelaerere (1977) Oslo: Brevskoleradet.

Paper 8

From New Delhi to Vancouver: Trends in Distance Education

Recent trends in distance education point to continuing fragility but with hope for greater stability in the future.

Assessments of distance education in the last decade were generally favourable. Daniel and Stroud (1981: 201), for instance, write of the "great leap forward" of the 1970s. The world of distance education will gather at Vancouver in 1982 as it did at New Delhi in 1978. It is an appropriate time for taking stock. Not all the signs are favourable.

Taking the New Delhi conference as a point of focus for the decade of the 1970s and Vancouver as an entry to the 1980s, this paper attempts to delineate trends in distance education.

Definition

One hundred and fifty participants from 39 nations walked the corridors of the Ashoka Hotel in 1978. They represented well the farrago that is distance education: open universities and schools of the air; TV and radio projects; government-sponsored institutions prohibited by statute from charging fees alongside profit-making colleges; literacy and rural improvement projects; computer-based instruction and instruction based on mimeographed notes.

With such a variety of programs and institutional types engaged in this field, a prerequisite for any study of trends is to define precisely what one means by *distance education*. *Distance education* is a generic term that includes the range of teaching/learning strategies referred to as "correspondence education/study" at the further education level in the United Kingdom; "home study" at the further education level and "independent study" at the higher education level in the United States; "external studies" at all levels in Australia; and "distance teaching" or "teaching at a distance" by the Open University of the United Kingdom. In French it is referred to as *télé-*

enseignement/formation à distance;
Fernstudium/Fernunterricht in German; *educación a distancia* in Spanish; and *teleducação* in Portuguese.

Six characteristics of distance education programs are:

- the separation of teacher and learner
- the influence of an educational organization that distinguishes it from private study
- the use of technical media, usually print, to unite teacher and learner
- the provision of two-way communication so that the student may benefit from or initiate dialogue, which distinguishes it from other uses of educational technology
- the teaching of people mainly as individuals and rarely in groups, with the possibility of occasional meetings for both didactic and socialization purposes
- the elements of a more industrialized form of education in which activities like job scheduling, warehousing, postal and media dispatch are characteristic functions.

(Keegan, 1980)

Models

When examined from the focus of this conference on learning at a distance, institutions teaching at a distance can be classified in four main groups. Institutions that only develop distance teaching materials or only examine distance students are not considered here.

The correspondence school model

The learner depends almost entirely on postal contact with the institution.

The correspondence schools send learning materials by post to the student. The student studies the materials and posts assignments back to the institution where they are marked, commented on, and posted back to the student. The student studies the comments, completes the next assignment, and the process is repeated.

The multi-media system

The learner has at his disposal a wide range of learning media and (often voluntary) face-to-face sessions.

In a system similar to that of the Open University of the United Kingdom the link between learning materials and student learning is assured by as coherent a structure as possible. The student is supported by a wide range of activities in an effort to achieve a satisfactory educational experience and prevent avoidable drop-out.

The consultation model

The learner must attend face-to-face sessions in addition to studying at home.

This model is noteworthy because the correspondence element is reduced to a minimum and the emphasis is placed on regular attendance at seminars (consultations). Once the learning materials are developed and distributed to the students, the system relies heavily on private study, with motivation, clarification, and evaluation of learning provided by the seminars. An example of this model is *Fernstudium* in the German Democratic Republic.

The integrated mode

The distance learners are kept parallel with a group of on-campus students and their progress is monitored against the on-campus students.

External and internal teaching are integrated. The same staff teach and assess both sets of students, who are enrolled in the same courses, take the same examinations, and qualify for the same degrees and diplomas.

New Delhi: From Cinderella to competitor

Distance education entered the seventies as the Cinderella of the educational spectrum: the opprobrium for malpractice by the few still tainted the field as a whole. By the time of the New Delhi conference distance institutions were, in many areas, competing successfully for what were already diminishing cohorts of students.

The decade was dominated by the success of the Open University. Over 400,000 undergraduate students applied to study in the years 1971-1980. Currently, 70,000 are enrolled, and 40,000 have already graduated with their B.A. (Open) degree. The Open University's penetration of all levels of British academic and political life, together with its claim that the degrees it offered were as valid as those of its conventional counterparts, brought it stability within the decade.

Less spectacular, but no less stable, was the march of the Centre National de Télé-enseignement, founded in 1939, to its 200,000th annual enrolment from 104 countries in programs ranging from primary schooling to *agrégation* and in subjects as diverse as art, Chinese, and music.

Vancouver 1982: Ten propositions

The effort to delineate trends in a sector of education may range from professional judgement to personal wish-fulfilment. In order to suggest validity for the judgements presented here, I have offered illustrations of each tendency with the understanding that readers will substitute their own examples and modify accordingly their acceptance of, or dissent from, the trend identified.

1. Buoyancy

The published papers of the 11th ICCE conference at New Delhi (Wentworth, 1978), of the Open University conference on the education of adults at a distance in 1979, and the preliminary interest in the 12th ICCE conference at Vancouver give evidence of confidence and buoyancy. This is noteworthy in an atmosphere of financial cutbacks for education by many governments and fears of falling enrolments in developed countries, some of which are now failing to achieve zero population growth. The proceedings of these conferences suggest that the distance institutions (or the distance sections of composite institutions) feel that their share of annual cohorts of students is not diminishing.

2. Fragility

The innate conservatism of educators means that non-traditional forms of education are characterized by fragility. Distance education ranks amongst the non-traditional forms. Stable support for the non-traditional in education can be achieved only by a fundamental change in political opinion within a country.

The 1980s began inauspiciously. The *Edmonton Journal* of Thursday, 13 March, 1980 showed Mayor Herman Leicht rejoicing at the move of Athabasca University from Edmonton to Athabasca, a settlement 145 km nearer the North Pole. News followed swiftly that Courses by Newspaper of the University of California at San Diego was running into funding difficulties; that the external studies department of the Royal Melbourne Institute of Technology was under threat from the dean of the face-to-face faculties; that the Télé-université in Quebec was placed in trusteeship.

3. From further education to higher education

The 1970s saw the development of a higher education sector in an area that had largely been dominated by further education institutions. Further education (technical and vocationally orientated colleges) provision was maintained but rapid development both qualitatively and quantitatively was experienced in the higher education sector. In Australia five universities and thirty-nine colleges of advanced education taught at a distance in 1981; in 1970 there were three universities and half a dozen colleges.

4. From privately sponsored to publicly supported

The 1970s witnessed the growth of publicly supported institutions and their growing influence in a field previously characterized by privately sponsored schools. The new open universities are examples. It is ironical that in the period between New Delhi and Vancouver, when consumer protection legislation in a number of countries tended to reduce the viability of some traditional operators in correspondence education, electronics manufacturers emerged as new competitors for enrolments in the distance education field. Control Data Education Company—owner of PLATO—is the best known.

5. From developed to developing countries

Distance education began in the industrial cities of 19th-century England, Germany, Scandinavia, and the United States. Mainly in Australia and Canada does it belie its urban origins and embrace vast distances. In the last two decades swift developments have brought successful local foundations in developing countries (Young et al, 1980). A more forceful role nationally and internationally was signalled by the reformulation of the African Association for Correspondence Education at Addis Ababa in 1979 (Hakemulder, 1979) and the holding of a regional symposium on distance teaching in Asia at Penang in 1981.

6. Autonomous multi-media systems

In the 1960s there were distance universities only in South Africa and the USSR (Peters, 1965: 115). The trend towards the founding of open universities has been one of the most distinctive of the 1970s (Kaye and Rumble, 1981) in both developed and developing countries. The Open University of the United Kingdom enrolled its first students in 1971. It was quickly followed by new foundations in Spain (1973); Pakistan (1975); Athabasca in Canada as an open university (1975); Hagen in the Federal Republic of Germany (1975); Israel (1976); UNA in Venezuela (1977); UNED in Costa Rica (1978); Iran (1978); Sri Lanka (1980). An eleventh, in the Netherlands, has been approved but delayed by financial considerations.

7. Print and non-print materials

The 1970s began with high hopes for universities of the air. Success was limited (Karow, 1979: 3) and most institutions remained print-based. In 1980 Bates of the Open University concluded that "television and radio in particular are proving to be of less significance in teaching systems or more difficult to use successfully than was originally expected." (Bates, 1980)

The period from New Delhi to Vancouver produced a rapid development of new communications technology, ranging from microcomputers to satellites, each of which was put forward as an asset to education at a distance. An ever-growing series of monographs, especially from the Institute of Educational Technology at the Open University, assessed critically the quality and quantity of learning achieved from existing non-print media.

8. From Peters to Pagney—developing a theoretical basis

The comparative and theoretical investigation of Peters in the 1960s and 1970s led to the postulation of two forms of education: "conventional face-to-face education" and "distance education" (Peters, 1973: 310). Administrators of conventional systems, and many distance educators who feel safer under the shade of the conventional umbrella, tend to view distance education as a fringe form of normal education and back away from the radicalness of Peters' position.

At the European Home Study Council conference at Bled, Yugoslavia in May, 1980 Pagney (1980) advanced the theory that there are two forms of "normal" education: conventional education and distance education. If this proposal were accepted it would signal an important development: those who assign revenue from public funds need to make provision for both forms of education.

9. Distance education as a discipline

The 1970s began with calls from scholars like Otto Peters, Michael G. Moore and John A. Bååth for a new conceptual framework for distance education. The call went largely unheeded. Distance educators complained of the inadequacy of staffing and funding formulas derived from a conventional educational administration, but did little to create a theoretical basis for a cohesive alternative system.

Between New Delhi and Vancouver there were signs of a nascent discipline of distance education and of efforts to establish the techniques and procedures that constitute the body of knowledge known as distance education. The term *distance education* emerged as a generic term in English; professional training for the field was proposed from a number of centres; the Deutsches Institut für Fernstudien at Tübingen continued its publication of four series of research monographs; an international journal *Distance Education* was published from Australia; Kaye and Rumble's *Distance Teaching for Higher and Adult Education* provided an analytical framework for research.

10. Lifelong learning

The Vancouver conference comes at a time when it is necessary to reassess the fragility of the non-traditional in education in the light of the achievements of distance education in the decade just completed.

But the context in the 1980s will be different.

The acceptance of a philosophy of lifelong education for the working adult will lead to questioning of the elimination from recurrent education, by the timetabling of lectures, of precisely those adults who contribute to the Gross National Product during the course of their studies. Other queries will be raised on the necessity of adults joining a learning group to receive education. Some will argue from this that distance education is a normal, or even necessary, form of provision.

Desmond J. Keegan
Open College of Further Education
Australia

References

Bates, A. (1980) *The Planning and Management of Audio-Visual Media in Distance Learning Institutions.* Paris: I.I.E.P.
Daniel, J. and Stroud, M. (1981) Distance education: a reassessment for the 1980s. *Distance Education* 2, 2, 201-220.
Hakemulder, J. (ed.) (1979) *Distance Education for Development.* Bonn: German Foundation for International Development.
Karow, W. (1979) How to find the right work in distance education. *Epistolodidaktika* 2, 3-9.
Kaye, A. and Rumble, G. (1981) *Distance Teaching for Higher and Adult Education.* London: Croom Helm.
Keegan, D. (1980) On defining distance education. *Distance Education* 1, 1, 13-26.
Pagney, B. (1980) Quels advantages l'enseignement à distance peut-il offrir à l'enseignement formel? E.H.S.C. Conferences proceedings. (mimeograph)
Peters, O. (1965) *Der Fernunterricht. Materialien zur Diskussion einer neuen Unterrichtsform.* Weinheim: Beltz.
Peters, O. (1973) *Die didaktische Struktur des Fernunterrichts. Untersuchungen zu einer industrialisierten Form des Lehrens und Lernens.* Weinheim: Beltz.
Wentworth, R. (ed.) (1978-79) *Correspondence Education: Dynamic and Diversified.* London: Tuition House.
Young, M. Perraton, H. Jenkins, J. and Dodds, T. (1980). Distance Teaching for the Third World. The Lion and the Clockwork Mouse. London: Routledge and Kegan Paul.

Adult Education: A Perspective for the Eighties

Paper 9

The eighties will see enormous improvement in distance education if we approach the opportunities with the proper perspectives.

Introduction

The present form of adult education is linked to the future in the way that *being* is linked to *becoming*. The challenge to create a desired future is not less an act of faith and determination than the present towards which we once strived.

Learning at a distance has two terms requiring clarification. *Learning* implies both formal and non-formal learning. Non-formal education is the predominant form of learning among most adults. *Distance* must be viewed as geographical as well as psychological and both types contribute to isolation. Both create distance between learning resources and learners. Whatever the cause or condition of isolation, it will influence the motivation to learn as well as the mode and frequency of the delivery of educational services.

Any discussion on adult education must focus on the Third World, where most of humanity resides.

Goals and realities

There are a number of realities that need to be stated. For instance, in many developed countries, "our colleges and universities can never again be described as exclusively the province of the young" (Harrington, 1979: XI). As Harrington points out, the adult education revolution is barely underway. One assumes that it will not only continue but gain momentum as average populations become older, and will influence formal as well as non-formal educational programs.

Another reality is that advanced technology does not automatically improve instruction. One must not be duped by the mystique of technology without understanding its limitations: technology is secondary to the message it is programmed to deliver. The electronic culture will increasingly touch upon the lives of men and women. Attempting to humanize man through communication technology is a worthy goal, but it can be dehumanizing as well. Technology must be applied with appropriate care. "Appropriateness" is determined by the cultural and geographical context and the learning goals to be achieved.

During the last two decades, developing countries achieved substantial progress in education at all levels. Traditional methods were somewhat modified and there has been an increase in local management.

> As a result, education systems have become better structured and have extended their reach to areas previously unserved. Serious attempts have also been made to improve the quantitative efficiency and the quality of education systems, and to make them more relevant to indigenous life and culture and to the different needs of regional populations within a country.
> (World Bank, 1980: 8)

The World Bank report goes on to say that rates of literacy have substantially increased. However, about one-third of the children of primary school age in developing countries are not enrolled in school and only 9% of those in the 18 to 23 year age group are attending school.

Adult education has invariably been linked to community development. Most community and social action is really an act of individual learning, of changing attitudes, of acquiring skills, including those of communication, and of gaining information and knowledge. Self-help and self-reliance seldom take place without a voluntary act of learning. The constraints to innovative learning are often the same that constrain participation. The book *No Limits to Learning: Bridging the Human Gap* (1979: 24-29) makes the point that all societies must enhance learning in order to close the gap between the world's growing complexity and our capacity to cope with it. The authors describe two concepts they believe constitute the main features of innovative learning: *anticipation*, which is the capacity to face new, possibly unprecedented situations (the ability to deal with the future); and *participation*, which is a social activity attempting to increase involvement at all levels.

Paralleling the fact that we face more issues and problems than ever before, there is also the reality that we have more resources available to us. We have the know-how to deal with the increasing number of problems faced today, and distance education can help provide the knowledge to deal with them. The way we perceive the issues will determine the way we tackle them.

Finally, any perspective on the future of adult education is based on the assumptions one makes about human nature and the ability of people to learn.

Program trends for the eighties

Radio

The eighties have unlimited possibilities for learning, including the delivery and content of distance education. One might assume that radio will continue to be a focus for much of this learning. Throughout a large portion of the world, there is now approximately one radio for every 20 people. In many countries, special radio programs are being produced by farm broadcasters for rural listeners, and there are many examples of radio listening groups. Many of these attempt to initiate development from below, involving individuals and their communities with a goal of bringing about a new social order characterized by greater human dignity. Many of these programs include the interaction and combination of broadcasting, print material, and discussion/listening groups. Already there exists the Developing Countries Farm Radio Network. Although it has no broadcasting of its own, it has a potential audience of nearly 100 million people around the world, and this figure is likely to increase substantially.

Other media

One challenge of the eighties is to continue to be innovative in the use of radio. In addition, other media innovations will increasingly make use of satellites and microcomputer-based systems in bringing television to remote areas, and combinations of cable TV, the electronic blackboard, fiber optics, and the telephone. One such innovation is Telidon, which is a Canadian video system that converts a simple television set into a powerful information and educational tool. The eighties are likely to see a more creative use of TV as an educational device, taking into account cultural, linguistic, and institutional differences.

Adult illiteracy

Another great challenge will be to deal successfully with the deplorable adult illiteracy rate in the world, including illiteracy in many so-called developed countries. Even for countries that have undertaken literacy programs, the lack of follow-up and continuing reading material became self-defeating. Lessons have been learned in this regard. Continuing support of the neoliterate can include a combination of print material with other forms of distance learning, including radio.

Participation

Increased participation is one way of improving the effectiveness of distance programs. For instance, in the early seventies, the participation rate in further education in Alberta was low. The Alberta Commission on Educational Planning generated a report called "A Choice of Futures", which envisaged the creation of a life-long learning system for the province. In three years, a process involving hundreds of citizens devised and implemented a policy based on a number of philosophical ideas including: (1) the "Client First" principle, in order to serve all the people in the province; (2) the "Varied Perspective" principle, whereby "people in many agencies, pursuing different disciplines, holding different philosophical perspectives about education, must be involved in continuing education programming in a given community"; (3) the "Systematic Communications" principle, in which various autonomous agencies communicate systematically with each other; (4) the "Maintenance of Flexibility" principle, retaining adaptable and flexible faculties. Implementation of these principles has resulted in the creation of a number of local Further Education Councils in the province (Falkenberg, 1976: 36-37).

Another Canadian experiment is the Memorial University community learning centres project in Newfoundland and Labrador. This project works with rural communities, with a strong oral tradition, which were experiencing rapid change resulting from new technology, mass formal education, and accelerated centralization of the population (all conditions similar to many developing countries). Using a community education approach, traditional and non-credit courses were made available, as well as video tapes on a wide range of topics. Access was also achieved through public broadcast television and intra-community communications, information sharing, and education. Other technology was made available as well, including audio cassettes, telephone, written publications and, in some cases, 16 mm film equipment. A monthly newsletter is also circulated among all the centres. All these attempt to stimulate community discussion, using local animators and a community forum approach. This project shows how a participatory multi-media approach to distance education can be achieved (Lee, 1976: 31-33).

Innovations in developing countries

During the first two decades following World War Two, the dominant model for development from the industrialized west has been critically examined and alternative and more indigenous forms of development are being sought. Some of the most innovative adult non-formal education programs are occurring in developing countries. Much can be learned from China, Cuba, Nicaragua, and Tanzania about literacy programs. Increasingly, western industrialized countries will likely look to the lesser industrialized countries for innovations, and this should have a humbling effect.

Needs assessment

The assessment of needs is likely to be done with more care and accuracy. The questions that one asks invariably determine the answers one receives. For example, asking "What courses would you be interested in taking?" implies that learning cannot occur outside courses. More accurately, one can ask "What things would you like to learn about?" followed by an analysis as to whether or not the institution asking the question can deliver the required learning.

Basic world problems

Greater priorities need to be given in the eighties to solving the basic problems of the world, broadening the definition of development, and dealing with poverty and its manifestations of malnutrition, disease, squalor, and illiteracy. Fresh drinking water for the world by 1990 is a universal slogan. Comprehensive and integrative approaches need to be used in linking learning and development.

A variety of perspectives

A number of final points reflect the perspectives of the eighties.

- Whereas distance learning has been traditionally thought of as an individual enterprise, it will increasingly involve groups learning together, creating a support system. Distance learning is therefore likely to be interactive and reactive. It will also include more two-way communication between the learning resource and the learner.

- Linked to the above, there may be greater sharing of resources, for instance, inter-library loans, and inter-agency cooperation.

- Two interesting phenomena may characterize the eighties. On the one hand will be the role of education in increasing nationalistic feelings. On the other hand, distance learning has a potentially important role to perform in bringing about greater global and international feelings, understanding, and respect. One method is to introduce non-western materials into social science and humanities programs, attempting to eliminate parochial traditions, and establish a broad, multi-cultural world view.

- Traditional institutions are likely to become more involved with problem-solving and community service, working directly with people in community settings, linking research and action. Research, evaluation, and training in the area of literacy training are things that the universities can potentially do well (Draper, 1973: 27-35).

- On a world-wide basis, whereas the focus of educational programs will increasingly be on the disadvantaged adult, distance learning will continue to serve an expanding clientele, including business, labour, and other community groups. Already, distance learning programs have been applied to needs in the work place, including basic job training, as well as improving technical and managerial skills.

- It seems important to take what various programs and institutions have learned from working in rural areas and adapt these to urban settings, extrapolating basic principles, including the use of media.

- Many countries have a tradition of using volunteers in learning/educational settings. It seems that the eighties will see an increase in the use of such volunteers, realizing that they need to be trained. The volunteer should be given respect and not exploited as has sometimes been the case.

- Those involved in adult education have sometimes been politically naive. The fact is that the act of education frequently raises social and political consciousness. Educational programs are sometimes perceived to challenge policy and unfortunately many governments have a low level of tolerance for such activity. However, political education is not to be confused with the attempt to have people become better informed. For instance, the extension division of Memorial University has developed and implemented an intensive series of study-discussion programs related to the impact of newly discovered oil fields.

- In some societies, and certainly in many professions, leisure is minimal. Distance learning needs to understand and accommodate this. The concept of life-long learning is nonetheless a truism.

- Learning is often perceived narrowly to include the acquisition of subject matter and/or skills. Each of these, though, is accompanied by attitudes and feelings. How does distance education account for these? A knowledge of learning theory seems essential.

- Research and evaluation are sometimes viewed as unnecessary activities. The eighties, however, are likely to see more appropriate activities of this kind, with a view to improving program efficiency and effectiveness.

Concluding comments

The United Nations Conference on Science and Technology for Development, held in 1979, has referred to telecommunications as one of the five main subject areas of science and technology (Butler, 1979: 144). The introduction of new technologies to the developing nations of the world is essential and every effort is to be made to ensure that these technologies are appropriately used.

Frank Feather states that:

> You cannot cope with the new world using values and leadership styles of the industrial era. The Post-Industrial Age will be characterized by decision-makers who set policy based more on intuition and creative insights generated by a more active right-brain.
> (1980: 7)

He then goes on to present a comparative table of industrialism (left-brain) and post-industrialism (right-brain), as each relates to the human, global, and managerial perspectives.

The overall conclusion of the First Global Conference on the Future, held in 1980 in Toronto, is that:

> The myriad of global problems (energy, poverty, food, environmental degradation, etc.) cannot be solved either individually or by direct application. Rather we can only continue to tinker with these vital issues. The real solution is to develop a higher level of global understanding. Through a common global mind will come co-operative efforts essential to address the world problems in the 1980s.
> (Feather and Mayur, 1980: 4)

In any discussion about perspectives in the eighties, one must reflect on the freedom to choose. Sadly, the truth is that the freedom of many people in the world is nonexistent or limited.

> Some people at present are in social situations which enable them to "colonize" the future. Through their actions in the present, they significantly limit other peoples' choices and chances in the future. In contrast, most poeple are formally ignorant of the future; we tend to be uneducated about the future, have unexamined ideas about it, and have few institutionalized ways of clarifying and acting upon our future hopes and fears. Indeed, vast areas of social and human behaviour are structurally shortsighted, if not wholly hindsighted.
> (OECA, 1975: 6)

One does not have to be a futurist to know what one wants, or what one believes or values. One perspective on the eighties is that distance learning will expand the horizons and choices of a greater number of people, and bring us closer, through this decade, to freedom, peace, and justice.

James A. Draper
Ontario Institute for Studies in Education
Canada

References

Botkin, J.W. Elmandjra, M. and Malitza, M. (1979) *No Limits to Learning: Bridging the Human Gap.* (A report to the Club of Rome). Toronto: Pergamon Press.

Butler, R.E. (1979) World communication network. *Transactional Perspectives.* 5, 3, 114.

Draper, J.A. (1973) Universities and the challenge of an illiterate population: A research question. *New Frontiers in Education.* 3, 1, 27-35.

Falkenberg, E. (1976) Journey of a thousand miles. *Learning* 1, 1.

Feather, F. (ed.) (1980) *Through the '80s: Thinking Globally, Acting Locally.* Washington, D.C.: World Future Society.

Feather, F. and Mayur, R. (1980) The co-optimistic solution. *Futures Focus.* 1, 1.

Harrington, F.H. (1979) *The Future of Adult Education.* Washington, D.C.: Jossey-Bass Publishers.

Lee, G.E. (1976) An experiment in communications and adult education for Newfoundland and Labrador. *Learning.* 1, 1.

The Ontario Educational Communications Authority (OECA) (1975) *Alternative Futures and the Role of the Media.* (Workshop 2) Toronto: OECA.

World Bank (1980) *Education: Sector Policy Paper.* Washington, D.C.: World Bank.

A Study of Two Self-Study Youth Centres

Results obtained at two self-study centres point out the possibilities for major improvements in the Kenyan educational system.

Introduction

Kenya's twin problem of growing primary school drop-outs and youth unemployment has been the subject of extensive studies. In 1966, for example, a conference convened at Kericho in western Kenya to work out specific solutions led to more comprehensive studies by the National Christian Council of Kenya (NCCK). In a brief paper titled "After School What?", NCCK (1965) came up with ideas that established the first village polytechnic. The Village Polytechnic Programme was in 1974 taken up by the government of Kenya and launched as a sectoral part of the Special Rural Development Programme. Further studies by a team of experts from the International Labour Office (1972) suggested that the problem did not lie in the number of primary school leavers but in the structure of education. We shall examine that view after noting the following statistics.

While Kenya's population is rising at a rate of about 3.5% (i.e., some 300,000-400,000 persons a year) the output from the primary education system is about 300,000 a year with only 100,000 absorbed by all government secondary schools, self-help schools, private schools, village polytechnics, and all employment sectors. There is thus an annual addition of 200,000 youths to the swollen ranks of the unemployed. The cumulative growth of unemployed primary school leavers since 1963 stands at over 1.5 million (Mungai, 1976).

This problem is aggravated by the fact that over half of Kenya's population is under 15 years of age. The 1979 census shows that of the total population of 15.5 million, 8.5 million are under 15.

The problem defined

Since the majority of these drop-outs have had some education, there should be more effective channelling of youth into productive activities. It is difficult for the country to sustain its development when such a large proportion of its youth is without any productive work. The immediate problem is therefore to find ways of dealing with development using education as the primary tool (Mungai, 1976).

This view is wholly congruent with that of the 1972 ILO team. In its view, Kenya's primary education system produced leavers for an economy that was increasingly unable to provide jobs. The ILO team reported:

> The problem of youth employment does not lie so much in the numbers of primary-school leavers. It lies much more in the whole philosophy of education, which mentally prepares the pupils for formal, non-rural employment in the context of an economy which has failed to generate enough employment opportunities of this sort; and in the foreseeable future this will continue to be so, unless there are fundamental changes both inside the school and outside.

(ILO, 1972: 237)

This, of course, means that there has to be very close integration of education and community life, particularly in rural areas.

Village-level experimental efforts to redress the situation

Two projects described here are bold efforts to redress the "primary school leavers' syndrome" at the village level. If the projects are replicable they can form the first step in providing realistic and environmentally based education throughout the nation.

The Muguga Project

The first project was a community effort pioneered by a local animateur who is also a leading Kenyan educator: Professor Joseph Maina Mungai of the University of Nairobi. In 1976 Professor Mungai and the community of Muguga formulated a proposal for a comprehensive education centre comprised of pre-primary, primary, secondary, vocational, continuing, and adult education sections.

In late 1976 and early 1977 the secondary education component was launched. This involved a self-study class of primary school leavers and drop-outs using a classroom at the local primary school. The main element of instruction was correspondence materials developed by the Correspondence Course Unit, Kenya's only public correspondence institution.

Forty-six students were registered in seven subjects: mathematics, English, history, physical science, geography, biology, and Kiswahili. The students were provided with study materials and relevant textbooks produced by the Correspondence Course Unit. They were to study for the Kenya Junior Secondary Examination. They would also receive counselling and tutoring from the animateur and from tutors provided by the Correspondence Course Unit.

The students studied through 1977, 1978, and 1979. There was a drop-out of between 30% and 40%. Of the twenty who attempted the Secondary Examination in November 1979, 90% passed in at least one subject. Their performance was better than that of many students from conventional schools in the area.

The Kirigu Project

Following the success of the Muguga Project, a second project was initiated at the Kirigu Primary School, Dagoretti Location—a peri-urban area in the Nairobi Extra-Provincial District. The project began in February 1980, again largely through the efforts of Professor Joseph Mungai. To date there are 31 registered students with a regular attendance of 25 students. They are enrolled in the same subjects offered in the Muguga Project, with the addition of agriculture. The aim of the latter is to integrate theoretical studies with vocational training. There are six part-time counsellors who help students with both instructional and personal problems. In order to overcome their feeling of isolation and rejection, the students require about ten hours of counselling a week at first. As they mature, they need only two hours a week or less.

An assessment of the projects

These projects, Muguga in particular, have proved that out-of-school youth can be provided with a good secondary education through correspondence studies—at lower cost than traditional methods. This form of education also makes youth self-reliant, realistic in setting their goals, and more disciplined in their approach to problems. In addition, correspondence study youths are more likely to change their values and become more productive.

These studies also highlight a number of challenges; it is argued, for example, that the high drop-out rate was caused by the lack of full-time teachers. Furthermore, primary school leavers are usually 12 to 14 years old, an age at which self-study is difficult. Therefore, students require concentrated counselling for not less than six months. Another problem is peer influence: youths not attending school were persuading attending students to give up their studies. Students felt humiliated at being in the same building with primary school children.

Parental attitudes had a strong influence on students. Some parents, cynical about this form of education, counselled their children against it. There is also evidence that too much assistance from animateurs and the Correspondence Course Unit made the project appear suspect and led the parents and children to demand better terms. A "school" mentality led to a problem when parents and children repeatedly asked to have students wear school uniforms to conform with conventional students.

The Kirigu project, which is still in existence, has a particular problem: the attempt to "vocationalize" the curriculum, which is nullified by the examination system. The agricultural course, however, will form the basis for helping rural children to see the value of integrating their studies with the realities of their environment.

There are additional problems. Most Kenyans have absolute faith in the merits of government-aided national secondary schooling (with government-aided self-help schooling as a second choice and private schools as a poor third choice). This dominance of the formal school system in the minds of Kenyans is complete. After all, didn't successful Kenyans benefit from a western, institutionalized, capital-intensive education? Admittedly they did, but there are new dimensions they did not encounter.

The population growth rate has changed: primary school leavers have increased by as much as 500 to 1000%; the economy is strained by supporting this unplanned increase; the formal employment sector has not expanded; rural-to-urban migration is proliferating; the cost of formal education has soared to 33% of annual government expenditure on training; and the cost of energy is rising rapidly in the face of greater demand for basic needs.

In spite of all these changes, Kenyans remain committed to the formal education system. We saw evidence of this thinking in both projects.

What is required is a comprehensive program of adult education to make Kenyans aware of the important principles underlying self-study at this stage of Kenya's development. Kenyans must come to accept the fact that 95% of all primary school leavers will live and work in rural areas. Kenyans must understand the need to integrate education and occupations, remembering, for example, that in traditional African societies there was a direct connection between adult roles and childhood activities: children would perform actual adult agricultural and craft work. These values must be inculcated in Kenyans who will otherwise continue to nurture false hopes that create frustration and a sense of rejection.

To begin with, Kenyans must understand that formal high schools provide only one form of education. Most parents know they possess plenty of knowledge, but do not realize their knowledge constitutes genuine, if informal, education. The task is not to replace the traditional school system, but to reform rigidly dogmatic Kenyan attitudes by introducing the notion that there are viable alternatives. These alternatives, incidentally, need the formal school system as much as the formal system needs them.

Self-study centres and rural development

Our experiments included an agricultural course to form the basis for vocational training in the future. This goal can be attained only if these projects continue to be "coated" with elements of the formal school system until a "take-off" stage is reached. The "take-off" stage will be reached when certain rigid attitudes have been sufficiently changed. At that time, non-formal approaches will not require the kind of nurturing we are giving our two projects.

We introduced a course in agriculture as well as a course in home science. At first students resented these courses. But after they were included in the courses students had to sit for public examination, they became readily accepted.

Table 1: Academic curriculum and vocationed skills

Secondary School Curriculum	adaptation for a farming career/vocation	adaptation for a small-scale artisanry in motor mechanics	adaptation for housewife work
Language	-letter writing -comprehension of instructional manuals -writing reports and keeping records of production, etc.	-letter writing -comprehension of instructional manuals -writing reports on repair projects	-letter writing -comprehension of recipes/health manuals -writing reports on health or housing problems, etc.
Social Studies	-civics -village development -cooperative principles -agricultural economics -population education	-civics -trade union organization -economics -business management -population education	-child development -civics -cooperatives -population education
Maths	-farm budgeting -pricing -produce recording -mechanical and construction design -stock-keeping	-mechanical drawing and calculation -budgeting -pricing -stock-keeping, etc.	-home-budgeting -calculation of dietary combinations, etc.
Science	-animal husbandry -soil science -plant biology -basic mechanics, etc.	-mechanics -motor combustion principles -electricity -metalwork, etc.	-health and childcare -human biology -nutrition -hygiene -home repair hints, etc.
School	-cooperative -farmers union -village organizations	-trade unions -town clubs, etc.	-cooperatives -women's clubs/associations, etc.

We carried integration a step further by using nearby small-holder farms for demonstrations. A correspondence lesson on livestock was supported by visits to farms with animals. This is the first stage of integrating education with local economic realities. It is difficult because students require assurance that the examination-oriented curriculum will remain intact. During this stage we teach the academic curriculum while incorporating vocational skills and positive attitudes. The example in Table 1 is a rough illustration of the pattern that will emerge when this stage has been fully implemented. It is patterned on a scheme (Dodds, 1976) we found appropriate.

By means of curricula linking vocational and social realities to learning, it will be possible to provide students with the essential knowledge and skills taught in the formal system without divorcing education from environment. It will also be possible to provide a learning opportunity to youths who cannot attend formal secondary school.

Student motivation and discipline

We have found that in spite of constraints it is possible to motivate students. The major cause of low motivation is a sense of rejection, isolation, and low prestige accompanying failure to attend a formal high school. Other factors are a lack of self-discipline and private-study techniques.

Because of the high value attached to formal schooling, these students have a sense of rejection that sometimes leads to hostility. We have used tutor-counsellors to help them with pedagogic issues and also with developing an identity. We have, for instance, used examples of prominent, well educated Kenyans and successful local people who studied on their own to illustrate that private study does not necessarily mean inferior education. The students take a long time to accept this view, but gradually come around.

We have found that bringing correspondence students together in a study centre boosts their morale. It tends to counteract their sense of isolation. Radio support programs also introduce a "personal touch". We have not, however, succeeded in dispelling the sense of low prestige that comes from being housed in a primary school. In spite of our active discouragement, students constantly ask for school uniforms.

Counselling has been an integral part of these experiments. Students are unwilling to become self-disciplined and self-reliant. They keep asking for a class prefect, a penal system (e.g., corporal punishment), and in general for a reversion to a school system of aversive control. Most parents do not believe their children can be trained to be self-disciplined.

It is a gradual and painstaking process for students to see the significance of self-discipline. One method that has succeeded is linking a lesson in, say, health science to a problem like personal hygiene. When students see the connection, it becomes easier to get them to sweep the classroom or wash their clothes.

Tutoring

Another problem has been that students treat tutors as teachers rather than as counsellors. We have found that too much face-to-face counselling nullifies the very objectives of the experiment. Therefore, tutoring sessions are becoming increasingly advisory rather than tutorial. Tutors give necessary pedagogical assistance but avoid assuming excessively instructional roles. The ultimate goal is to surrender the task of learning the students. Thus group work is emphasized, but with care to avoid having some students become dependent on others.

Tutor-marked assignments and study techniques

Students have tended to downgrade tutor-marked exercises, and we have had to press them hard to do the assignments themselves and use the counselling sessions only for especially difficult problems. A related area is training students to study on their own. In the past, tutors used only verbal training methods, mainly because students could not understand written notes. But as they progress, students can comprehend manuals on private study, and the Correspondence Course Unit has produced its first comprehensive manual of that kind.

Student newsletter

Another method for improving study techniques as well as counteracting feelings of isolation is a student newsletter. The first was produced about two years ago, although at that time little attention was given to the self-study centres. In future, more coverage will be given to these experiments in the form of feature articles on self-study, problem columns, student commentaries, student success in public examinations, etc.

Tutors' comments on written assignments

Assignments are corrected with the purpose of increasing the students' sense of achievement, mainly through positive, encouraging personal comments.

Replicability

We have gathered a lot of experience from our two self-study centres, but it is a requirement of research to carry a study to the end before deciding to proceed with the project, abandon it, or adjust it. We would say that the projects are successful in the areas they are located. Therefore, we would recommend that if there is to be replication, special attention should be given to environment. The Muguga and Kirigu centres have the advantage of being near the Correspondence Course Unit. Being near the city of Nairobi means that communication has been prompt and direct, and students have access to urban sophistication. Students have also benefited from the animation of leading personalities. Urban proximity does not, however, nullify the possibility of replication. Rather, we are giving pointers that will be of use in conducting similar experiments.

Summary

There will be no chance in the near future for Kenya to provide enough places for formal secondary education. A parallel secondary system must be developed through distance education. Correspondence courses linked with self-study provide the ideal approach. Successful replication of our efforts will depend on how much attention is given to the unique qualities of the location. Finally, we believe that the effort of launching these experiments is no mean achievement.

Ben K. Gitau
University of Nairobi
Kenya

References

Dodds, T. (1976) Educational alternatives by distance teaching. Paper reproduced at Adult Studies Centre, University of Nairobi. (mimeo)

International Labour Office. (1972) *Employment,* incomes and equality: a strategy for increasing employment in Kenya. (4th ed., 1977) Geneva: ILO.

Maturi, I.B. (n.d.) The role of the tutor in distance education. Nairobi: University of Nairobi. (offset)

Mungai, J.M. (1976) Proposal for establishment of Muguga-wa-Gatonye Comprehensive Educational Centre. University of Nairobi. (mimeo)

National Christian Council of Kenya. (1965) *After school what?* Nairobi: NCCK.

Thitu, P.N. (1980) Analytical and evaluation study of Muguga-wa-Gatonye distance education pilot project. Diploma dissertation, University of Nairobi.

Learning at a Distance and National Development

Paper 11
Introduction

The contribution of education to national development could conveniently be measured by the degree to which a nation's social, cultural, and economic aspirations are served by its educational system. Considering this measure with respect to distance education, the difference between potential and reality is one of the striking themes of this section. This is not to say that the only tone is one of frustration, and in fact Ljoså (paper 23) and Penberthy (paper 26) point to a solid history of achievement in distance education in cooperation between private and public sectors. Nevertheless, contributors who deal with the role of distance education and national development do tend to stress the gulf between what could be done and what is actually being done. Here perhaps more than elsewhere we are introduced to the conflicts that inevitably arise when education mixes with politics.

Extreme examples of this kind of conflict are related by Trillo (paper 17) from El Salvador, Rhodesia, and Peru where political changes disrupted or effectively destroyed projects that educators had spent much time in preparing. Education in industrialized nations is not immune to political problems either, as Daniel (paper 25) shows in reporting on the "chaotic situation" produced in the province of Quebec by a combination of lack of government policy and competition among educational institutions. It is of course in developing nations that these problems are most intense.

Ansere (paper 12) offers a thorough analysis of education in Ghana, emphasizing the discrimination inherent in the traditional system, which acts as a "sorting machine" preventing a large proportion of the population from obtaining appropriate levels of education. Distance education, Ansere argues, can make education much more accessible—more democratic since it does not, like traditional education, restrict access because of geography, ability to pay, or job requirements.

Ansere's view of traditional education is shared to some degree by a number of contributors including Bonani (paper 4), Gitau (paper 10), Singh (paper 13), Datt (paper 14), Gupta (paper 15), and Peters (paper 24). Bonani concludes that since only one quarter of Italian youths are studying regularly at the age of sixteen, the traditional system is not functioning well. Gitau reports even more disturbing statistics from Kenya and finds that a major obstacle to gaining support for distance education is the widespread view among Kenyans that a traditional education is the only legitimate one. (Anderson (paper 18) relates a similar problem in Brazil where Brazilians from all classes are skeptical about the legitimacy of distance education.) Singh, Datt, and Gupta echo each other in stating that although the traditional universities in India were given the opportunity to develop distance education, they have not done an adequate job—partly because of financial problems but also because of lack of effort and, Singh claims, their attitude that distance education is second class education (and distance educators are second class educators). Peters takes a less aggressive position in describing the foundation of the Fernuniversität in West Germany, but he makes it clear that one primary reason for establishing a university dedicated solely to distance education is that the traditional system inherently provides insufficient access to education.

The Fernuniversität seems to be a response that would be welcome elsewhere since one frequently stated problem is the lack of a central agency or central control over distance education. Singh (paper 13) and Datt (paper 14), call for the establishment of either a state institute or a distance education university to take control of distance education in India and Noyau (paper 21) argues that no nation can have a successful distance education system in the absence of some form of state involvement. The example of Quebec mentioned earlier corroborates this argument.

State involvement does not necessarily mean that there is no role for private enterprise. Norway (Ljoså, paper 23) has evolved a healthy working relationship between private and public sectors, and the history of distance education of children related by Penberthy (paper 26) contains important contributions from the private sector. Shah (paper 16) relates successful private ventures in India and Bonani (paper 4) and Joseph and De Milanesi (paper 20) demonstrate that the experience of private enterprise has valuable lessons for distance educators everywhere and that private operations like Accademia in Italy and ULSA in South America are often willing to try innovative approaches.

Whatever the merits of state involvement, distance institutions are profiting by cooperating with each other. PIUTEC, an organization dedicated strictly to this purpose, was established in South America (Nicolini, paper 19). PIUTEC was formed to exchange staff and information and to establish a documentation and a research centre to be shared by universities in five nations. Anderson (paper 18) describes more broadly based inter-institutional cooperation in South America. The National Extension College in the United Kingdom has carried the theme of cooperation so far as to have all teaching and support services offered by local institutions (Freeman, paper 57).

Different forms of cooperation are found elsewhere. The Netherlands Open University was founded on the basis of cooperation with industry and trade unions to set up its programs (de Moor, paper 59). In Norway there has been a wide range of cooperative activity between distance education institutes and industry, government, school boards, and voluntary groups (Ljoså, paper 23).

Besides the problems involved with printed materials such as cost, availability of texts (Ansere, paper 12) inadequate reading levels among students and lack of common terminology (Trillo, paper 17) there is the issue of high technology—especially in developing nations. Draper (paper 9) sounds an optimistic note, but Hutchinson (paper 22) and Shah (paper 16) are cautionary. Hutchinson shows with an example from Hong Kong that the use of television has to be matched to the social milieu to achieve the desired results. Shah claims that costly television and radio cannot compete with print in India.

One of the most disturbing notes in papers on national development is the emphasis on human wastage—usually represented in terms of the number of drop-outs. The figures given by Ansere (paper 12), Bonani (paper 4), and Gitau (paper 10) paint a grim picture of national development in some nations: many thousands of youths are denied the opportunity either to develop their own potential or to contribute fully to the social, cultural, and economic life of their nation because they cannot continue their education to an appropriate level. If distance education is given the chance to fulfil what many see as its true potential, it will be in this area that it makes its essential contribution.

The Inevitability of Distance Education in Africa

Conventional education cannot meet the needs of Ghana and distance education is the only alternative.

Introduction

All new nations especially those in Africa have pledged themselves to rapidly develop their economies, to democratise their political system and to offer social justice to all their peoples—in a word, to improve the standards of living of the people. These aims require among other things the broadening of education opportunities for their fulfillment. So far, African nations have largely depended upon the conventional education system for the achievement of these goals, and have devoted increasing amounts of their wealth towards that end. The returns, however, have not been commensurate with the expenditures.

Authorities such as Coombs (1968), Jolly (1969), and A'Aeth (1975), to name a few, have described this situation as an education crisis or an educational dilemma. All have agreed that the formal education system alone could not possibly solve the problem and that some other system of education should be employed in addition. Some like Illich (1970) and Reimer (1972) in exasperation have advocated the abolition of the formal school system, but it is the opinion of the writer that this approach is too extreme.

The burden of this paper is to demonstrate how deficient the conventional education system in Ghana has been and how advantageous it would be to use distance education to meet the ever increasing needs of the people for education and training. We will first explain the experiment we in Ghana have made in distance education, identify the areas in which the conventional education system in Ghana has failed, explain the advantages of distance education, and give indications as to possible areas of expansion in the programme.

The Ghana distance education experiment

Ghana made its official debut in distance education in November, 1970 when the Correspondence Education Unit was established by the Institute of Adult Education, University of Ghana. This was when the programme was officially launched and the first set of students registered.

Before that time the idea of running distance education programmes in the country had been discussed both in government circles and within the university. For a full account of how the programme started, readers are advised to look at the article by the present writer in the December 1979 issue of the *Kenya Journal of Adult Education* (Ansere, 1979).

There were, of course, previous distance education programmes in Ghana. Well before the question of the establishment of the distance education programme was raised many educated people were taking correspondence courses from overseas correspondence schools, mostly for university degrees before 1948 when Ghana established its first university. Although some of these overseas correspondence schools continue to offer courses to Ghanaians, the scale is greatly reduced. This is as a result of the establishment by the University of Ghana of the two programmes of correspondence education for General Certificate of Education courses and the Part-Time Degree Programme that offers face-to-face learning for working people who cannot leave their jobs and homes to study.

Ghana had four main reasons for establishing the distance education programme. By far the most important was to increase the opportunities people had for secondary education. For many people, the programme was the only alternative they had for secondary education.

The second reason was that the overseas correspondence courses were for the most part irrelevant to the needs of the newly emergent nation. The third reason was to relieve the Institute of Adult Education of some of the heavy burden it carried in running secondary education courses in the evenings for large numbers of middle school leavers who could not be absorbed by the traditional secondary schools. The running of the evening class programme for CGE courses took about 75% of the resources of the Institute.

Although it was not mentioned in any official publication, it would appear that the possible saving of foreign resources was one other reason why the Government became interested in local distance education programmes. As much as $37,000 (Ansere, 1979) was spent by the state in helping Ghanian citizens procure course materials from overseas correspondence institutions.

The Ghanian distance education programme started small and has had a modest rate of development. The course mix and the media mix have been kept small and simple. We started off with only 2 GCE courses, English language and mathematics, and gradually added more subjects till now we have a complement of 7 courses: English language, mathematics, economics, government, history of West Africa, bible knowledge and principles of accounts. These are offered at the ordinary level only. We have not yet mounted any science courses nor have we introduced advanced level courses.

Up to now, the printed correspondence lesson forms the only medium of instruction. That is probably why we have stuck to the name "Correspondence Education Unit". This makes the Ghana programme one of the least sophisticated applications of education technology in the world.

We have, however, been experimenting with the integration of correspondence study with face-to-face meetings at the Accra Workers' College.

Our programme was built onto an existing adult education organisation, the Institute of Adult Education, which had existed since 1948, and had developed a wide network. This made the programme relatively easy to establish and to manage. The building was already there complete with printing and typing machines and the staff were simply drafted from the other programmes of the Institute. The resource commitment was thus relatively small, and it was easy to handle the initial student demand.

Lessons are written not by a team of writers but by single writers. After a course is written, however, it is subjected to rigorous editing by a team consisting of the course writer as the subject specialist and a number of staff members from the Institute, one of whom is the chairman of the Editorial Board.

Keeping the programme on a modest scale has given us time to reflect and to experiment, and we have been able to grapple with certain knotty problems. Six years after we completed all 7 courses the economy of the country started weakening, and foreign resources became very difficult to obtain. Consequently we could not import the necessary textbooks. The prices of the few books that could be obtained locally were so high that students could not afford them. In 1975 we were forced to abandon the courses based on textbooks and in their place write what we call "self-contained courses". This was at a time when we had thousands of students in our system, which meant that we had to produce the new courses quickly.

However quickly we tried to write the new courses we have been unable to complete them, mainly because of printing hold-ups. Most of the lessons have been written, edited, and typed, but they have not been printed because our machines had become too old to work. And when the machines become operative, paper and other printing materials vanish from the local market. We have been inundated with a spate of uncomplimentary letters from students, and we have become increasingly incapable of doing anything about the situation. The ideal position would have been to continue with the old courses in spite of the lack of textbooks while we got on with the production of the new courses.

Another problem is incessant delays in the mailing service, which was reasonably good when we started the programme. But as a result of economic stagnation and the consequent deterioration in labour morale, it has become very slow and irregular.

This situation brings to the fore the importance of poor countries starting programmes on a modest scale. Even with our small scale of operation, we are finding it difficult. We certainly would have found it harder if the programme had been bigger in terms of the range of courses offered, the media used, the resources committed, and the number of students. It was probably fortunate that we did not obtain foreign aid in the initial organisation of the programme. (We sought but failed to obtain assistance from the Ford, Rockefeller, and Dag Hammarskjold Foundations as well as the University of Wisconsin.) If we had had foreign assistance, the programme might have been organised on a scale too large to manage in the face of the difficulties enumerated above. Externally aided projects may be successful at the beginning, but when external support ends the programme almost invariably turns into a white elephant for the host country.

Defects of the formal education system

The formal educational system has many defects, but the ones that interest us here are its low absorptive capacity, its high cost and its inability to develop the country's manpower.

In 1961 African states including Ghana pledged themselves to provide by 1980:

a. universal, compulsory, and free primary education to all children of school age

b. secondary education to 30% of the children who complete primary school

c. higher education, mostly in Africa itself, to 20% of those who complete secondary education.

These promises were made in Addis Ababa at a conference organised by Unesco for African States (Unesco, 1961). There was another conference at Tananarive in 1962, also sponsored by Unesco, at which African governments were enjoined to enrol 60% of their higher education students in the various branches of scientific and technical education (Unesco, 1962).

The year 1980 has past, and African states are nowhere near the achievement of most of these goals. See Table 1 for achievements to 1966.

The targets set for the first and the second levels of education could not be attained by 1965/66; only the target for the third level of education was reached, and in fact exceeded in many countries. The inability of African states to meet these targets was recognised as early as March, 1962 by African Ministers of Education at a conference in Paris.

What is the position in Ghana? In 1960/61 when the Addis Ababa conference was held, the proportion of children in the compulsory age group between 6 and 14 years regularly attending* primary and middle schools in Ghana was 42.9% By 1970 the proportion had increased to 62.5% (Population Census of Ghana, 1972: XXIV). Compared with other African countries, Ghana's performance is quite impressive, but universal primary education is far from complete realisation.

We might get a fuller appreciation of the problem by looking at absolute figures given in Table 2.

* By regular attendance is meant attendance at an educational institution at least four hours a day receiving general education in which the emphasis is not on vocational training. This definition, according to demographers, excludes private tuition, correspondence study, night schools, and trade schools. Arabic schools that teach only the Koran are excluded, but those offering school subjects in addition are included.

Table 1: Educational targets and attainment in Africa

	1st level Education	2nd level Education	3rd level Education
Proportion of enrolment to relevant age group for the year 1960-61	36	3	0.2
Target figures set for 1965-66	47	6	0.4
Figures observed for 1965-66	44	5	0.4

Source: (Jolly, 1969: 9)

Table 2: Proportion of children aged 6-14 years who went to school in 1970

Total number of children in the compulsory school age group.	No. of children in the compulsory school age group who were in regular school attendance.	No. of children in the compulsory school age group who were not in regular school attendance
2,128,152	1,330,235	797,917

Source: (Population Census of Ghana, 1972: xx)

Close to 800,000 children who should have gone to school in 1970 did not do so. If we add children who had passed the compulsory age and who missed the chance to go to school in previous years, the number would be larger. In 1970 there were 593,696 persons in the next age group, that is 15-24 years, who had never been to regular school, and as many as 2,400,149 people 25 and over had also not been to school. As many as 3,791,762 persons in the country remained deprived of basic education in the year 1970. This represents 43.2% of the total population of 8,559,313.

These figures are more staggering if we take account of the incidence of wastage in the first cycle schools. Not every child who is admitted remains in school till the end of the cycle. Out of the 199,263 pupils who started the six-year primary school in 1968/69, as many as a third dropped out. In the same year, some 130,969 pupils began the four-year middle school cycle, and by the end 39,393 (30%) had dropped out.

No full-scale research has been done on the causes of drop-outs in Ghana. The only research that has come to the notice of the writer is conducted by Kiram Campbell-Platt (undated), of the National Council on Women and Development and F.O. Akuffo (undated), tutor at Asamankese Secondary School. There are also references to the topic in the works of Bleek (1975), Smock (1975), and Robertson (undated). The formal school system is unable to keep the children in the system; it is not that the children are unable to remain in the schools. As it is presently structured, it is irrelevant to life in rural areas where the majority of the school children live, and it cannot give the children the knowledge and skills they need in the urban areas where many migrate after schooling.

Another area in which the formal school system fails is at the secondary level. As Table 3 shows, only a very small fraction of pupils who complete middle schools enter secondary schools.

Table 3: Proportion of middle school leavers entering secondary schools

School Year	Middle School Leavers	Admission into Secondary School Form One	Percentage of Middle School Leavers Entering Secondary Schools
1966/67	51,266	4946	9.7
1967/68	53,961	6370	11.8
1968/69	60,235	6207	10.3
1969/70	62,857	7157	11.4
1970/71	67,655	7800	11.5
1971/72	72,225	7950	11.0
1972/73	62,529	7784	11.2
		Average	11.0

Source: (Ghana Manpower Statistics, Education and Manpower Development in Ghana, 1975: 4)

Table 4: Number of children who passed the Common Entrance Examination but got no admission into Secondary Schools 1967-1974

Year	No. of Candidates	Passes	% of (c) of (b)	No. of passes who gained admission to secondary schools	% of (e) of (c)	No. of passes who were denied places in Secondary schools	% of (g) of (c)
(a)	(b)	(c)	(d)	(e)	(f)	(g)	
1967/68	49,385	14,283	28.9	9,510	66.6	4,773	33.4
1968/69	61,162	17,348	28.4	10,654	61.4	6,694	38.6
1969/70	69,968	14,973	21.4	12,133	81.0	2,840	19.0
1970/71	75,888	15,646	20.6	13,059	83.5	2,587	16.5
1971/72	75,890	18,738	24.7	14,249	76.0	4,489	24.0
1972/73	96,309	17,129	17.8	15,039	87.3	2,090	12.7
1973/74	79,080	21,389	27.1	16,439	77.0	4,950	23.0
Average		17,072		13,012		4,060	24.0

Source: (Ghana Education Statistics, Digest of Educational Statistics, 1976: 127)

With an average of only 11% of the middle school leavers entering secondary schools more and more children are denied secondary education each year.

We will get a better picture when we compare the number of children who qualify for secondary schools by passing the Common Entrance Examination with the number of such children who actually get admitted. The figures in Table 3 do not give the whole picture because not every child who completes middle school both wants and can afford secondary school. Many enter the teacher training colleges and technical and vocational courses while some enter the labour force. Some females, especially repeaters, marry.

Table 4 shows the number of children who declare their desire and prove their capacity by passing the Common Entrance Examination and who nonetheless are denied places.

While an average of 17,000 children pass the Common Entrance Examination every year, only 13,000 are admitted. Thus 24% who pass the examination to enter secondary schools do not obtain places.

In the report on the Common Entrance Examination conducted in 1980, the Registrar of the West African Examinations Council commented,

> In view of the very limited available places in secondary/technical schools, one wonders whether it is prudent to go on accepting unlimited number of candidate entries, when 20% of the candidates would gain admission to secondary/technical schools.
> (Reports on Examinations, 1980: folio 4)

The Registrar obviously was taking a line of least resistance. His implication that entries should be limited is undemocratic. A more acceptable method would be to find ways of admitting all those who pass the examination. Once such way now being considered by the Government is to turn the secondary boarding schools into day schools. Another much cheaper and more innovative way is to offer secondary education by distance education. Unfortunately not much has been done about this option.

As in the first cycle of education, a proportion of the pupils drop out before they reach the end of the cycle. In 1967/68, a total of 8904 pupils entered secondary schools but by the end of the five-year period, 954 (11%) had dropped out.

Not everyone who completes the General Certificate of Education Examination continues into the third cycle of education. Some take jobs in the public sector. Others with superior qualifications naturally continue their education and prepare for what is called the "Advanced Level General Certificate of Education", usually in four subjects. With passes in the four subjects, the person applies to one of the three universities.

It would have been instructive to present statistics showing how many qualified people are denied admission by the universities, but these statistics are not available. We can, however, quote Dr. D.A. Bekoe, Vice-Chancellor of the University of Ghana, speaking at a matriculation address.

> ...it is not everybody who wants to study at the university who succeeds in getting the chance. There must be many of your own friends who unlike you, could not get in. For the Arts courses we could offer places to much less that 50% of those who qualified, and for the science-based courses, we could admit only about 50% of those who qualified.
> (Bekoe, 1980: 2)

Thus it could be that only half of those who want to enter university and qualify to do so are admitted. Table 5 gives us an idea of the absolute numbers involved.

Table 5: Advanced Level GCE Passes, 1977-80

Year	Number
1977	1589
1978	1720
1979	1644
1980	1763
Average:	1679

Source: (Ghana Education Statistics, Digest of Educational Statistics, 1976: 129)

Although not everyone who obtains the Advanced Level GCE qualification desires to go to the university, most apply.

The formal school system acts at every stage as a sorting machine, selecting small proportions of its clientele for entrance into successive levels while dumping the vast majority by the wayside. This is the surest way of creating an educationally frustrated society.

The cost advantages of distance education

It has been proved beyond doubt that nonformal education costs much less than formal education. This has been attested to in the studies of Coombs (1968), Ahmed (1975), and Jolly (1969) for nonformal education generally and Rumble (1976), Kaye (1973), Laidlaw and Layard (1974), and Wagner (1977) for distance education in particular. To see whether this is true of the Ghanian situation, the writer compared costs at the Correspondence Education Unit in running the GCE Ordinary level programme with the costs at the Achimota Secondary School (a conventional secondary school) in running a similar programme. The results are given in Table 6.

Each system has a greater proportion of its total costs (i.e., capital costs plus recurrent costs) in the form of capital costs. Also, the proportion of capital costs to total costs is slightly greater in the correspondence programme. The proportion would have been greater if both the subject mix and the media mix had been greater. If the Institute had offered science courses, for example, there would have been increased capital costs for science kits and part-time laboratory attendance. Radio and television would also have resulted in more capital expenditures.

It is the relatively large proportion of capital or fixed costs to total costs that encourages distance education institutions to want to increase student numbers, for the greater the number of students, the lower will be the average cost per student.

Costs of plant and machinery take a larger share of the total at the Correspondence Education Unit than at the Achimota Secondary School. Costs of buildings and furniture are large in the conventional school because of the necessity for classsrooms and dormitories for students, and housing and offices for staff.

Not only are capital costs in conventional education larger than recurrent costs, but the level of capital costs is directly related to changes in student numbers. In order to cater to more students fixed assets have to be increased. In contrast, capital expenditures are not closely related to changes in student numbers in distance education.

Recurrent costs for serving 1336 students in the Achimota Secondary School are greater in absolute terms than the recurrent costs incurred in serving about three times the number in the distance education system. Looking at the recurrent costs in terms of averages, the ratio per student is 59:1. If we include the value of the output lost to the economy as a result of able-bodied individuals withdrawing from active employment in order to devote themselves full-time to studies, the ratio would be greater still.

Table 6: Comparative costs of distance and formal education

Type of Cost	Correspondence Education Unit, Legon ¢	Achimota Secondary School ¢
A. Capital Costs		
1. Buildings	222,318.20	24,178,400.00
2. Furniture and Fittings	24,762.75	1,199,320.00
3. Plant and Machinery, eg. printing machines duplicating machines and typewriters	930,050.50	173,580,00
4. Motor Vehicles	50,000.00	186,800.00
Total	1,227,131.45 (86%)	25,738,100.00 (82%)
B. Recurrent Costs per annum		
1. Salaries and Allowances	135,217.00 (65%)	4,722,607.76 (86%)
2. Utility Services e.g. water, electricity and consevancy	2,000.00	600,000.00
3. Motor Running Expenses	2,400.00	57,632.45
4. Maintenance Repairs and Renewals	2,500.00	66,994.96
5. Telephone Charges	3,000.00	24,000.00
6. Postage and Telegrams	18,000.00	4,000.00
7. Printing Materials and Stationery	43,683.00	23,614.63
8. Science Materials	0.00	17,038.00
Grand Total	206,800.00 (14%) ¢1,433,931.45	5,515,837.00 (16%) ¢31,253,987.00
Number of effective students	2984	1336
Average Recurrent Cost per effective Student	¢69.03	¢4,128.00

Source: (The files of the Institute of Adult Education (Accounts office) and the Achimota Secondary School (Bursar's Office))

Some Achimota pupils, especially the seniors, would be eligible to enter the labour force if they were not pursuing full-time studies.

In both cases manpower constitutes the largest single item in recurrent expenditures, but the share of manpower costs in the formal system is greater than in the distance programme.

The proportion of the costs of manpower to the toal recurrent costs in the Achimota Secondary School is 86% as against 65% in the distance education programme. This is to be expected since the formal school system depends very heavily on personal teaching while distance education is heavily dependent upon the written lesson.

It should be mentioned that we have so far been considering the gross average recurrent costs of the two institutions and not their net or actual average recurrent costs. To arrive at the net recurrent costs, we have to net out revenue derived from fees paid by the students. If we do this, the net average recurrent costs of each one of the two programmes would be correspondingly lower.

Manpower development

Another area in which conventional education has failed is the area of manpower development. Evidence for this can be found in the levels of literacy among the country's labour force as depicted in Table 7.

Despite great efforts to expand education and training, the labour force still remains largely uneducated and untrained. As much as 72.2% of the labour force have had no schooling at all. And among the remaining 28% the majority have very low education.

What is more serious is that the educational attainment of high-level manpower, that is, the professional, administrative and managerial grades, is very low. Only about 11% of this class of workers have high-level education; the majority of them have up to only secondary school education.

One would, of course, expect the low-level manpower not be highly educated, but the proportion of these workers who have no education whatsoever is too large for a country like Ghana that is desirous of carrying out rapid socioeconomic development and is anxious to raise the standard of living.

We can gain additional information about the weakness of the formal education system by looking at the number and quality of teachers the system has produced. The Accelerated Development Plan for Education launched in 1951 resulted in a great expansion in the enrolment of children in the first cycle schools. This expansion in the level of enrolment was accompanied by an increase in the number but not the quality of teachers (see Table 8).

Table 7: Educational attainment of Ghanian workforce (1970)

None	Primary and Arabic	Middle	Secondary	Teacher Training	Commercial Technical	University
All Occupations						
72.2	7.9	16.2	0.6	0.9	0.8	0.4
Professional Technical and Related Workers						
9.3	1.4	38.1	14.9	25.1	3.8	7.4
Administrative and Managerial Workers						
18.3	3.9	35.2	20.6	1.5	5.4	14.8
Clerical and Related Workers, Government Executive Officials						
2.9	0.6	66.1	18.2	0.4	10.9	10.0
Sales Workers						
77.9	8.1	12.7	0.9	0.0	0.3	0.1
Agriculture Animal Husbandry and Forestry Workers, Fishermen and Hunters						
84.8	7.7	7.4	0.1	0.0	0.0	0.0
Production and Related Workers, Transport Equipment Operators and Labourers						
57.7	10.8	29.7	0.9	0.0	0.9	0.0
Service Workers						
52.8	6.6	36.9	2.6	0.1	1.0	0.1

Source: (Demographic and Social Statistics Division, Central Bureau of Statistics.)

Table 8: Number of teachers in primary and middle schools, 1974/75 - 1978/79

School Year	Total Number	Number Trained	Number Untrained
1974/75	52,161	44,005 (84.3%)	8,156 (15.7%)
1977/78	67,181	45,620 (69.4%)	21,561 (30.6%)
1978/79	72,726	46,248 (63.6%)	26,478 (36.4%)

Source: (Ghana Education Statistics, Digest of Educational Statistics, 1974/75: 34; 1977/78: 2; 1978/79: 1A)

There has been a great increase in the number of teachers but the proportion of trained teachers has fallen over the years. In other words, the more teachers there are, the larger the proportion of the untrained.

Universal primary education, which previous governments have tried to achieve and the present government enjoined in Article 10 of the Constitution of the 3rd Republic of Ghana to provide by 1992, can only come about if there are sufficient trained teachers. The figures in Table 8 indicate that the formal school system cannot produce trained teachers in sufficient quantity and that some other method should be found to train teachers quickly and cheaply. Distance education is the best method. It has the advantage of producing trained teachers quickly and cheaply, but also the teachers need not withdraw from the classroom while being trained.

Conclusion and recommendations

From the foregoing discussion, it is clear that the formal school system has proved inadequate to the tasks given to it. It has failed to provide universal primary education for the children of compulsory school-going age; it has failed to absorb all the persons who qualify for second and third cycle education; its nature and structure have helped to drive away some of the people who were admitted into the schools; and it has failed to train sufficient numbers of the country's workforce.

It has been said that if half of the children of primary school age are denied education (as is virtually the case in Ghana), and if the population is rising at the rate of 3% per year (as is also the case with Ghana), the country will have to treble its educational provision at the primary level to have all its children of compulsory school age actually in school within a decade. That is obviously beyond the ability of the formal school system.

Evidently some other system should be employed to meet this great educational need. This other system is nonformal education, of which distance education is a part. This is not to suggest that distance education should replace formal education; they should complement each other.

Far too many African countries have put too much emphasis on formal education, and far too few have considered nonformal education. It is paradoxical that it is developed countries with well developed educational systems that have shown more interest in employing innovative educational technologies. Developing countries with their limited resources should be more interested in cost-effective educational technologies.

Of all the advantages of distance education the most important are the provision of wider access to education and the savings in time and money it offers. Other merits include flexibility in enabling the person to learn at his own pace, place and time. The fact that people can study anywhere augurs well for rural development. One of the reasons why middle school leavers desert the rural areas for the urban areas is the lack of educational facilities in the former. If the middle school leavers resident in the rural areas can obtain education through correspondence study, they may stay in the rural areas and help develop the areas. Perhaps of more significance is the fact that under distance education, the learner develops a sense of maturity. This is made possible by the discipline he had to impose upon himself in order to succeed in learning and his ability to choose between competing claims on his time and energy.

There is no limit to the number and types of educational programmes that can be offered by means of distance education. It has been successfully used in Australia for primary education, and for functional education in Niger, Senegal, and India through radio clubs. The Mauritius College of the Air programme and the Institute of Adult Education Correspondence Education programme in Ghana are examples of distance education being used for secondary education. In Ivory Coast distance education is used for in-service training and for reaching illiterate rural populations. The British Open University programmes, the Zambian Correspondence Education programmes and the Nigerian Correspondence and Open Studies Unit (COSU) of the University of Lagos (to name but a few) have proved that university degrees whether Arts or Science can be done by distance education. In the USSR university students are obligated to undertake half of their degree courses by distance education and half by classroom study.

We in Ghana have distance education programmes for secondary education and agricultural extension for farmers through the radio farm forums: we should use the system for many other programmes such as nonformal education programmes, teacher training and university degrees in management and administration. In choosing programmes we should be guided by the criteria of "investment" education and not so much by "consumption" education. In other words, we should offer the type of education that will enable the recipients to use it directly to improve their productivity on the farms and in the factories and offices.

Joe K. Ansere
University of Ghana
Ghana

References

A'Aeth, R.A. (1975) *Education and Development in the Third World.* Saxon House, pp. 10-14.

Ahmed, M. (1975) *The Economics of Nonformal Education: Resources, Costs and Benefits,* New York: Praeger Publishers.

Akuffo, F.O. High wastage in women's education: the case of the rural elementary school girls. (unpublished and undated).

Ansere, J.K. (1979) The development of correspondence education in Ghana. *Kenya Journal of Adult Education.* 7, 3, 12-18.

Bekoe, D.A. (1980) Vice-Chancellor's Address at Matriculation, 8/11/80, p.2.

Bleek, W. (1975) *Sexual Relationships and Birth Control in Ghana: A Case Study of a Rural Town.* University of Amsterdam, Holland.

Campbell-Platt, K. Drop-out rates among girls and boys at the primary, middle and secondary levels of education in selected schools in Accra. Research Paper, National Council on Women and Development (unpublished and undated).

Coombs, P.H. (1968) *The World Education Crisis: A Systems Analysis.* London: Oxford University Press.

Ghana Education Statistics, Digest of Education Statistics (1976) (pre-university) 1974/75, Accra: Government Printer.

Ghana Education Statistics, Digest of Educational Statistics (pre-university), 1974/75, 34; 1977/78, 2; 1978/79, 1A.

Ghana Manpower Statistics, Education and Manpower Development in Ghana. (1975) Accra: Ministry of Economic Planning. February, 1975. (mimeo)

Illich, I. (1970) *De-Schooling Society.* New York: Harper and Row.

Jolly, R. (1969) *Planning Education for African Development.* East African Publishing House.

Kaye, A.R. (1973) The design and evaluation of science courses at the Open University. *Instructional Science.* 2.

Laidlaw, B and Layard, R. (1974) Traditional versus Open University teaching methods, a cost comparison. *Higher Education* 3.

Population Census of Ghana, 1970 (1972) Statistics of Localities and Enumeration Areas. Accra: Census Office. vol. II, June, 1972.

Reimer, E. (1972) *School is Dead: Alternatives in Education.* New York: Doubleday.

Reports on Examinations (1980) Registrar, West African Examinations Council. Ghana National Committee, Item 7 of the Agenda for the 20th meeting held 16-17 December, 1980, folio 4.

Robertson, C. The nature and effects of differential access to education in Ga society. *Africa.* 47, 2, 208-219.

Rumble, G.W.S.V. (1976) The Economics of the Open University of the United Kingdom. The Open University Academic Planning Office, June, 1976.

Smock, A. (1975) Development and the education of woman: the case of Ghana. International Division Meeting on Support of Education, Ford Foundation.

Unesco (1961) Conference of African States on the Development of Education in Africa. Addis Ababa, 15-25 May, 1961, Final Report, p.v.

Unesco (1962) The Development of Higher Education in Africa. Report of the Conference held at Tananarive, 3-12 September, 1962, p. 61.

Wagner, L. (1977) The economics of the Open University revisited. *Higher Education.* 6, 359-381.

Distance Education in Developing Countries: The Need for Central Planning

Paper 13

Developing nations should seriously consider establishing a central institute to organize distance education in their countries.

Introduction

In most developing countries, the demand for education has consistently run ahead of resources. Traditional classroom methods could meet the demand when higher education was the monopoly of the elite and the prosperous. However, with the passage of time and awakening among the masses, the elitist concept had to be discarded in the face of the modern social objective to democratize education by extending educational opportunity to all sections of society.

Formal education could not achieve this objective unless it was made very extensive—a heavy cost no developing country could afford. Another constraint to the formal system is that it can admit only full-time students and cannot satisfy the aspirations of millions of working men and women who want further education. This is true even in highly developed countries. It is, therefore, absolutely necessary for developing nations to think of alternatives. Distance education seems to be the solution. It has been successful in a number of developed countries, and is now being adopted in developing countries with encouraging results.

The advantages of distance education

Distance education has a great sociological justification as it can help not only in extending education but also in equalizing educational opportunities. It can carry education to varied and dispersed student populations, even in remote rural areas, and it can provide instruction at all levels.

If distance education institutions can ensure proper organization of instruction and motivate learners to evolve a careful study program, it can prove a much more effective alternative. It can provide vocational education, even to teachers and thereby speed up the expansion of education in the backward sections of society.

Distance education offers a vast scope for innovations in teaching methods, greater variety of subjects, interdisciplinary options, as well as qualitative improvements. There is a strange fallacy among some academicians that technical and science subjects cannot be offered by distance education. They are probably not aware of the tremendous success achieved by polytechnics in Russia that offer full-fledged engineering and technical courses as well as refresher courses for top engineers. Technical universities and institutes in the United States are also teaching technical courses at a distance.

Developing nations could therefore find this system eminently suited to their needs, and far more economical than the formal system.

Requirements for success

Success depends largely on organization, particularly in developing nations.

A major consideration of developing nations is economics. This was stretched a little too far in India where distance institutions were expected to be almost wholly self-financing. They were given block grants for a 5-year period, and then expected to fend for themselves. What is amazing is that while they were expected to absorb about 25% of the total enrolment for higher education, they were given less than 5% of the total budget. This is irrational. Without adequate continuing grants, distance institutions will deteriorate into substandard coaching academies.

Because of revisions to pay scales and rising costs of materials and printing, but no proportional increases in student fees, almost all distance institutions in India with enrolment up to 10,000 students are now in deficit.

There are, however, needless wastes, the most glaring being the unnecessary duplication of course materials. There has been no effort to produce common course materials. In addition to financial savings, cooperative production would encourage the pooling of a broad range of talents and produce courses that were both better planned and more academically sound.

When the Ministry of Education and the University Grants Commission thought of starting correspondence courses in India they sent three delegations to the USSR. They reported that the two outstanding features there were a common syllabus for all correspondence institutes and a centralized system of course production. This ensured quality course materials (which could be supplemented locally) and an economic saving. It is a pity that the autonomy of universities has not enabled us to introduce these features in India.

A central institute

The main reason for this failing is the absence of an effective central agency for distance education. It is time developing countries gave serious thought to this matter. Such an agency could:

- undertake research on distance education
- bring about collaboration among various distance institutes on such matters as preparing course materials, running study centres, conducting personal contact programs, and producing radio and TV programs
- publish a journal on distance education to exchange expertise, information, and research
- arrange in-service training for staff
- offer courses relevant to national needs, thereby serving as a model to other institutes.

This central institute, which should be a university, should supervise distance education throughout the country and ensure appropriate academic standards. Various distance education institutes could continue to function as departments of their universities, but they would be obliged to follow the directives of the central institute. Alternatively, we could assign all distance education matters to the central institute, and affiliate all other distance institutes to it. The syllabus would be prescribed by the central institute, which would also be responsible for examinations.

Distance education in India is presently more or less an extension of the traditional system, and the important objective of offering vocational and interdisciplinary courses at a distance has been completely ignored. A central institute could carry out a comprehensive survey of educational needs and offer more relevant courses. This would not only make education more meaningful but would also help increase productivity and efficiency, thereby furthering national objectives.

Conclusion

The control of universities over distance education in India has given it credibility, but it has also restricted its growth. Academics generally consider distance education an encroachment in their domain—a second-rate education—and they look upon distance educators as second-rate teachers. And since university teachers dominate academic bodies, innovations suggested by distance education institutes are often turned down.

If we give serious thought to these problems we shall have to think of establishing a central agency to ensure proper development of distance education in consonance with national development.

Bakhshish Singh
Punjabi University
India

Problems of Distance Education in Developing Countries

Paper 14

The characteristics of students in developing countries may require unique approaches to distance education.

The problems facing distance education in developing countries like India are different from those in developed nations, mainly because of different student characteristics.

The characteristics of correspondence students presented in this paper represent statistics on correspondence students at the University of Delhi for the 1970-1980 year.

1. Economic background

More than one-fourth of the students are from the poorer sections of the population (having an annual family income of less than Rs. 5000 (US$ 641)). Nearly two-thirds are from families with an income less than Rs. 10,000 (US$ 1282)—i.e., the poor and the lower middle classes. Only one-third are from the middle and upper classes.
(See Table 1)

2. Employment status

The fact that 46.3% of undergraduates were employed while only 28.5% of graduates were employed shows that the desired termination of education after the first degree is a myth. The truth is that correspondence directorates are nothing but extensions of university departments—created only to accommodate their overflow. The demand for increased education is a consequence of unemployment.
(See Table 2)

3. Marriage and employment

Unmarried unemployed (males and females) account for about 78% of enrolments in the B.Com.(Pass). The predominance of this group is largely explained by two factors. First, unable to get a job, these young men and women try to improve their qualifications to stand at the head of the queue of job seekers; and, second, for women, it is a kind of waiting time before marriage.

The second group of significance is the unmarried employed males and females. Both feel a kind of dissatisfaction with their present status, and try to improve their qualifications to get a better job. However, the number of married females (both employed and unemployed) is insignificant. This may be explained by the higher social security of married Indian women. Besides, the burden of married life in Indian society leaves little extra time for women. For women, the more social and economic security, the lower the desire to improve academic qualifications.
(See Table 3)

4. Finance

An important reason for a large number of drop-outs, ranging from 35-40%, is the inability of students to pay the fees. Financial assistance in the form of exemption from tuition fees or stipends is less available to students taking correspondence courses than to those attending on campus. This problem is aggravated by the fact that the average correspondence student is poorer than the average campus-based student.

5. Urbanization

Corrrespondence education has remained highly urbanized. In a country like India, where 22 universities were running correspondence courses during 1979-80, a network of library-cum-study centres could not be established in more than 40 towns. In a country with 2910 towns and 550,000 villages, this is a very meagre expansion of facilities, and correspondence courses have therefore failed to penetrate the remote and rural areas. Students from rural areas are not able to use the libraries at the headquarters or travel to participate in contact pro-

Table 1: Family income of the students of correspondence courses in Delhi University (1979-80)

Income	No. of students in sample	Percent of total
Up to Rs. 5000 (US $641)	215	27.4
Rs. 5000 - 10000 (US $641 - 1282)	312	39.8
Rs. 10000 and above (US $1282 and above)	257	32.8
Total	784	100.0

Table 2: Proportion of employed and unemployed correspondence students at Delhi University, 1979-80.

	Distribution of students		
	Employed	Unemployed	Total
Undergraduates			
B.A.	1744	1720	3464
B. Com.	1815	2406	4221
Sub-total	3559	4126	7685
% of total	(46.3)	(53.7)	(100.0)
Post-graduates	191	479	670
	(28.5)	(71.5)	(100.0)
Total	3750	4605	8355
% of total	(44.9)	(55.1)	(100.0)

Table 3: Sexual and marital status of students in M.A. and B. Com. (Pass)

	M.A.		B. Com. (Pass)	
	Number	Percentage	Number	Percentage
Females	423	(71.8)	159	(17.1)
Unmarried unemployed	316	(53.6)	144	(15.5)
Unmarried employed	43	(7.3)	10	(1.1)
Married unemployed	41	(7.0)	4	(0.4)
Married employed	23	(3.9)	1	(0.1)
Males	166	(28.2)	769	(82.9)
Unmarried unemployed	79	(13.4)	581	(62.6)
Unmarried employed	37	(6.3)	134	(14.4)
Married unemployed	3	(0.5)	4	(0.4)
Married employed	47	(8.0)	50	(5.4)
Total	589	100.0	928	100.0

grams. Thus the drop-out rate among rural students is very high.

6. Program development

There has been very little effort by universities in developing countries to promote continuing education through distance methods. Eighty-eight percent of India's correspondence students were enrolled in traditional programs, while professional programs accounted for barely 12%.

Some directorates have started LL.B./B.G.L. courses, but unfortunately, the Bar Council of India has not accredited these courses. Science education through correspondence is negligible, requiring expensive experimental kits, laboratories, etc. In the absence of a university dedicated to correspondence education exclusively, the task has been left to the traditional universities, which have their own problems to deal with. Consequently, distance education in India has suffered. It must be improved. For this purpose, new courses have to be designed for the needs of our society. More specifically, courses must be linked to job requirements. They may be short-duration diploma courses to develop the "continuing" aspect of education.

Conclusion

Efforts must be made to help the poorer sections of society improve their academic qualifications. Fee exemptions and travel assistance are required to enable poorer and rural students to take courses and make full use such centralized services as libraries and contact programs. Along with these efforts there is a need to develop more vocational courses that will allow people to find useful employment. Last, but not least, every developing country should set up a university exclusively devoted to the development of correspondence education. This task should not be left to the traditional universities who have neither the time nor the proclivity to develop correspondence education techniques.

Ruddar Datt
University of Delhi
India

The Status of Correspondence Education in India: A Survey

Paper 15

A survey of correspondence institutions in India indicates the need for many changes.

Introduction

The post-independence era in India has witnessed unprecedented expansion, including the area of education. The system enrols over 100 million students, employs over 4 million teachers, and spends 100 million rupees (2.5 billion US dollars) each year. It is preparing to enrol an additional 100 million in the next 10 years and has launched a massive adult literacy campaign to make half of India's 250 million illiterate adults educated and self-reliant within that time. While formal education predominates, non-formal methods are gaining momentum (statistics from the Ministry of Education for 1980 establish enrolments in government-managed correspondence institutions at 89,237). Growing demand for continuing education along with pressure to equalize educational opportunities accounts for the establishment of a network of correspondence institutions. This has resulted in a good deal of expansion, diversity, duplication, confusion, and malpractice.

But if correspondence education is to become a worthwhile alternative to formal education, its status needs to be empirically established and critically analysed. This is especially true since correspondence education is not restricted to the universities or government bodies. Further, there are no specific regulations or policies governing correspondence education institutions. Still in their infancy, such institutions are isolated not only from the mainstream of education but also from each other—there is little exchange of ideas, innovations, or research.

During the Eleventh World Conference of ICCE in New Delhi, the National Council for Correspondence Education of India presented some basic facts on correspondence institutions in India. The information was incomplete because many institutions had not supplied data, and the data was restricted to universities. Nothing was revealed about the mechanics of developing and operating correspondence courses, funding patterns, instructional and evaluation techniques, or problems facing correspondence education. The principal investigator suggested the need for a comprehensive survey. It is fitting that the results of such a survey be presented to the Twelfth World Conference of ICCE.

Design

A 20-page questionnaire was mailed to nearly 150 institutions including universities, state departments of education, school boards, autonomous and statutory bodies, and private institutions. One section of the questionnaire was reserved for responses on general questions such as follow-up and evaluation of correspondence courses, research programs, strategies for publicizing and advertising courses, problems faced, and the activities desired in a proposed agency for the coordination of correspondence institutions.

Despite many reminders as well as appeals to the ICCE and NCCE Presidents, the questionnaires were slow in returning. With some exceptions, private institutions were not interested in divulging details.

Results

While the final results are likely to take some time to analyse, the following preliminary observations can be made.

1. The majority of correspondence institutions in India began in the 1970s. Most were established as constituents of universities, state boards of education, or by the private sector and offer undergraduate and graduate degrees, with an emphasis on graduate courses. Private institutions differ in functioning mainly as coaching institutions for the various university and competitive examinations. Vocational courses are provided mainly by the private sector through courses that are, by and large, unrecognized.

2. The duration of courses varies from 3 months to 3 years, with an average of 1 year. Enrolment varies greatly, ranging from 25 to 6302, and declines over a three-year period. The language of instruction is mainly English, followed by Hindi. Regional languages can be found in some language and some undergraduate courses.

3. Admission to correspondence courses in government institutions is permitted to take place at the same time as admission to formal courses in the same institution (i.e., in May/June/July). Private institutions are more open, allowing registrations throughout the year, especially in shorter courses.

4. In statutory bodies and university-managed institutions correspondence examinations are the same examinations taken by students in regular courses. Thus correspondence students are not accommodated by examination procedures suiting their special needs.

5. The pass percentage of students in correspondence courses ranges from a low of 4% to a high of 100% with the average being 40%. Thus there is a good deal of waste in correspondence courses, which are expected to attract the more highly motivated and achievement-oriented student.

6. The institutes of correspondence education spend a significant amount of their budget on administration while academic staff are, by and large, neglected.

7. There is much duplication of courses for the same degree in a particular state or region. This has thinned the student population and has wasted meagre financial resources. At the same time, wide variations in fee structure are found for the same course offered by different institutions in the same region.

8. Most government institutes have to share their buildings with other departments and have no facilities such as reading rooms, hostels, seminar rooms, teacher rooms, auditoriums, or laboratories for correspondence pupils.

9. Course materials are usually planned by experts; are reviewed (though seldom revised) from time to time; are introduced, usually through a personal letter; are written in essay format in the third person (indicating lack of involvement) in an unattractive, mimeographed form. Books for further reading are suggested and sometimes sent. Lessons are sent regularly—usually once a month by ordinary post.

10. Most courses are prepared by one person and therefore incorporate the subjective view of a single individual.

11. Lessons are generally reviewed only when there is a change in syllabus. Use of audio cassettes and radio broadcasts is limited.

12. Student assignments are sent in once or twice a month. Most are based on essay questions. Answers are sent back with the corrections, and model answers are sometimes included. Thought-provoking assignments involving field work are rare. Little credit is given to assignments and there is no organized feedback available to teachers or administrators.

13. Many institutes have been unable to afford contact programs. Those that can hold them once a year, for a period between 1 to 14 days, preferably during vacation to encourage attendance. Activities centre on lectures. Attendance varies from 20-60% of students enrolled. One reason for this low attendance may be that these programs do not give students extra credit.

14. Most facilities available to students are in the mode of fee payment (in easy installments) and consist of guidance services and library facilities.

15. Among the major problems cited are lack of students and funds, and lack of encouragement from the state government. Private institutes face the additional problem of lack of recognition. Correspondence education would be strengthened by government grants and concessions for items such as student travel, postage, and advertising.

16. Most institutions rated their performance as average, thereby suggesting they are not very satisfied with their accomplishments.
17. There is a consensus regarding the establishment of a council for the control and improvement of correspondence education.
18. Regular follow-up, periodical reviews, research, and innovations in correspondence centres are almost non-existent. Some private institutes, however, are experimenting with innovative techniques.
19. Correspondence educators lack formal training. Furthermore, they consider themselves inferior to their counterparts in the formal system.

Summary

In view of the present conditions facing correspondence institutes, the future of distance education in India does not seem promising. There is a need to have a second look at the system, to recognize its limitations and to establish a more meaningful relationship with the changing needs of society. The range of courses has been quite restricted. There is an urgent need for decentralization and diversification and course materials need to be practically oriented for different target groups. Moreover, a technology for distance education needs to be evolved to suit our circumstances. This would go a long way in giving it a distinct entity without reducing its effectiveness.

Arun K. Gupta
Model Institute of Education and Research
India

Distance Education without Hardware
(Abstract)

The potential of distance education is vital to a developing country like India where, even after massive expansion of the conventional school system there is still, for every school or college student, another young person who cannot receive formal education. Since television and radio are costly and their effectiveness cannot be taken for granted, the solution for developing countries lies in distance education without hardware, otherwise known as correspondence education.

India has used correspondence education successfully in many fields. In-service correspondence-cum-contact courses have enabled many teachers to adapt to a new curriculum or to obtain a B. Ed. degree. A new institute has been established to meet the personnel needs of the banking industry through a series of programmed learning texts. Similar texts for the life insurance industry have been published (in English and ten Indian languages) in over one hundred thousand copies and 12,000 agents have been trained. Rashtriya Chemicals and Fertilizers Ltd. has been a leader in applying this approach in industry and the programmed materials of its training institute have proved effective for technicians, operators, engineers, and managers. Gujarat Agricultural University alone reaches over 5000 farmers with courses on a number of topics. This is but a partial list of the growing volume of distance education being conducted in India without hardware.

Gunvant B. Shah
South Gujarat University
India

Paper 17

Some Problems with Printed Materials in Basic Adult Education

Distance educators in developing countries face obstacles in the areas of finance, language, culture, and politics when they use print.

> Developing countries around the world face common critical educational problems: shortages of schools, trained teachers and administrators, as well as irrelevant or nonexistent textbooks and instructional materials.
> (Searle et al, 1976: xiii)

During the last decade, there has been a lot of emphasis on mass media to cope with these problems, based on the idea that transferring the educational task from teachers to materials takes advantage of economies of scale (Adams, 1971: 241).

Educational projects in many underdeveloped countries have used radio and television, but little has been reported about printed materials. Perhaps the most celebrated use of programmed instruction occurred in Rhodesia in the early sixties. Schramm (1973: 243), reporting on Rhodesia and projects in Europe, concludes: "the results... leave little doubt that programmed instruction works as well in developing regions as in economically more advanced countries."

One of the most successful uses of printed materials for distance education in Latin America is that of Mexico's Accelerated Primary and Open High School, which began in 1974. The school uses self-instructional printed material supported by TV broadcasts and tutorial guidance. Although the project has not been thoroughly evaluated, "it is possible to talk about the efficiency of the materials and the increasing number of people that accredit their studies through this system" (Alegria, 1978: 41). Following these positive experiences and those of the well known Open University in the United Kingdom, there was a complusive interest among developing countries in improving adult education through self-instructional printed materials. Unfortunately, most of the projects counted more on the enthusiasm of its defenders than on technical knowledge, and failed from the very beginning. Some were suddenly stopped because of political changes, others suffered the effects of the economic crisis. Those succeeding in the first stage of producing materials soon discovered other problems related to their distribution and use.

But we can learn, even from unsuccessful experiences. From our own and from similar projects we have identified four of the problems common to developing countries using printed materials in distance education: finance, language, culture, and politics.

Finance

As Jack McBride (1975:3) of the University of Mid-America claims, the development of high quality open learning courseware is expensive. For underdeveloped countries this may be the greatest problem. Basic printing standards may be unattainable, not because of ignorance, but because of a lack of resources (Contreras, 1972: 21). Authors may be unable to use drawings or photographs because they are too expensive or require too much space. Even the choice of authors will be affected: the pay is low and the best are hard to attract. Finally, there will not be enough money to pay for the expensive process of pilot-testing and re-writing the materials.

Language

One of the most difficult problems is language. Kinsela (1980: 3), in a study of indigenous students in developing countries from the South East area, reports on the problems caused by the absence of a technical vocabulary in local dialects. The solution there was communication English courses for Polynesians and special technical English assignments for those whose standard of literacy was not high enough to cope with technical work.

The problem of language is especially acute given that while printing costs decrease with volume, distance education involves many cases of indigenous students in different regions speaking different languages within the borders of one country. The New Zealand Technical Correspondence Institute therefore advises that a distance project can be successful only where there is a common teaching language (Kinsela, 1980: 6).

Culture

The cultural background of the target population for printed materials has to be considered from the beginning of the project. One of the main problems here is knowing the user's reading habits, reading preferences and reading level.

In a pilot project in 1977 our students had very poor reading habits. Most of them never read a book; about 40% read a newspaper once or twice a week; and only 10% regularly read some kind of literature (religious booklets, sports magazines, etc.).

Asheim (1953: 454-461) reports that research throughout the world shows that adults choose in the first place material that is at hand; from this they select the easiest to read and only then do they choose what interests them. Spaulding (1952: 91), in a study of adults with low reading levels in rural Mexico and Costa Rica, reports that they preferred recreational readings first, materials related to health second, and material on home economics third.

Although these investigations were published almost thirty years ago, we have no information about similar work undertaken recently. We consider that printed material cannot be used in basic adult education unless there is a previous stage of development of reading habits and an awareness of the adult's reading skills and preferences. We agree with Kinsela (1980: 7) when he states that "the teaching organization must be staffed by writers and markers with a good working knowledge of the indigenous language, customs and problems."

Politics

Political changes are unpredictable in developing countries and educational programs are always affected by these sudden changes.

A report from El Salvador indicates that the Universidad Centroamericana "Siméon Cañas" has been working since 1973 on a series of booklets aiming to take the university to rural areas. The process of design and elaboration of the material

> is affected by the political and historical situation of the country. There have been occasions in which the booklets have been re-written even six times, because every word had to be thought so that it would not be tergiversated.
> (Valero and Morán, 1978: 19)

In Rhodesia the project for the use of programmed instruction techniques for non-formal education

> ended in 1965, when Rhodesia announced its unilateral declaration of independence forcing many individuals associated with the project to leave the country.
> (Ingle, 1974: 28)

In Peru a project had most of the material printed for courses in mathematics, language, natural science and geo-history but a change in politics stopped the project, and the booklets were not allowed to circulate.

Even if the distance educator is not politically active he has to consider politics when planning a project. In some cases, the life of the project can be assured for a certain period by means of a written agreement with local authorities, and in others the materials must be designed with enough flexibility to adjust to unpredicted changes.

Eloísa Trillo
National Institute of Tele-education
Peru

References

Adams, D. (1971) *Education in National Development.* London: Routledge and Kegan.

Alegria, P. (1978) *Un Sistema de Enseñanza Abierta en México.* Mexico: Centro para el Estudio de Medios y Procedimientos Avanzados de la Educación.

Asheim, L. (1953) Research on the Reading of Adults. *Library Trends.* (University of Illinois) 1, 4, 454-461.

Contreras, L. (1972) *Manual sobre la Preparación de Materiales de Lectura para Adultos.* Caracas: Centro Regional de Educación de Adultos.

Ingle, H. (1974) Communication media and technology: a look at their role in non-formal education programs. *Information Bulletin Number Five.* Washington: The Information Center on Instructional Technology.

Kinsela, H. (1980) *Experiences of Assistance by the New Zealand Technical Correspondence Institute to Developing Countries.* Paper 22 presented at the Open University Conference on The Education of Adults at a Distance.

McBride, J. (1975) Planning for distance education. *Planning.* 4, 5, 2-3.

Schramm, W. (1973) *Big Media, Little Media.* California: Institute for Communication Research, Stanford University.

Searle, B., Friend, J. and Suppes, P. (1976) *The Radio Mathematics Project: Nicaragua 1974-1975.* California: Institute for Mathematical Studies in the Social Sciences, Stanford University.

Spaulding, S. (1953) *An Investigation of Factors Influencing the Effectiveness of Fundamental Reading Materials for Latin American Adults.* Doctoral thesis not published. Columbus: Ohio State University.

Valero, L. and Morán, M. (1978) La Experiencia de una Colección Popular. *Boletín CLEA.* 4, 19-22. Santiago de Chile.

Paper 18

The Fires of Distance Education in Latin America

To develop to its potential as an agent for national and personal development and justice, distance education must be carefully nurtured.

Introduction

Like grassfires on the savannahs or llanos, the flames of distance education have periodically burned across Latin America. The first fires date back several decades, when budding educational technologists and enthusiasts of correspondence courses initiated a variety of schools, institutes, and government efforts in various countries. Like the grassfires, some were superficial and short-lived. But others found fuel to blaze, primarily in the form of commercial or vocational correspondence courses. The courses are mainly in accounting, administration, radio and television repair, etc. As elsewhere in the world, their quality is not uniform. Among the most noteworthy are the Universidad de La Salle in Argentina, the Instituto Universal Brasileiro in Brazil, and radio secondary education of the Radiodifusora Nacional de Colombia, all founded in the 1940s.

Development in the 1970s and 1980s

Periodically since the late 1960s, the publicity associated with the Open University has ignited new fires throughout Latin America. There have been five principal results and recent trends:

1. The older schools have been stimulated and numerous new vocational correspondence schools have been started. They all gained prestige from the publicity about the Open University and distance education methods. The growth has been uneven from region to region. Some new courses have been added, but for the most part the existing methodologies and non-degree course offerings have not changed substantially. Thirty-one such institutes and schools offer 214 courses (nearly half are duplicates) in Brazil. (MEC, 1980). In Spanish there are possibly 150 schools and several hundreds of courses. In the United States there are five schools with correspondence courses in Spanish officially accredited by the National Home Study Council (1979).

2. Three new large, Spanish-language universities have been established exclusively for distance education. The first (founded in 1971) and by far the largest is not Latin American; it is the Universidad Nacional de Educación a Distancia (UNED) of Spain, with 60,000 students in 10 degree programs primarily in engineering, law, chemistry, physics, education, and social sciences. There are 50 study centres throughout Spain. After initial rapid growth it has settled into a period to consolidate and strengthen its program (Ramón-Fernandez, 1979). It has numerous methodological similarities to the OU, as have the two exclusively distance education universities in Latin America, both of which were founded in 1977.

   The Universidad Nacional Abierta (Open) (UNA) of Venezuela has the advantage of an oil exporting nation's budget for building an impressive structure and nation-wide network of over 20 regional tutorial centres. It has over 20,000 students; the principal areas of study are administration, education, and systems/industrial engineering (Villarroel, 1980).

   The Universidad Estatal a Distancia (UNED) of Costa Rica is the smallest of the three, but has had the advantage of concentrating its efforts in a small geographical area with a unique socioeconomic and educational situation. Some of its courses have already been given to the majority of the specific target population (e.g., an extension course on map skills for high school geography teachers). With some minor modifications, these could become the first courses to be widely adopted by distance education programs in other Latin American countries. The program presently focuses on administration and education, with efforts to include various health and rural science degrees and diplomas. There are 19 regional centres throughout Costa Rica to serve approximately 5000 students (UNED-CR, 1980).

3. Numerous (perhaps 50) existing Latin American universities, faculties, and institutes have made serious attempts to enter the field of distance education while maintaining their normal classroom teaching. Most have logically entered the field of teacher training and upgrading, and a few have attempted the laboratory sciences. The vastly predominant mode of instruction is print, not because of lack of interest in radio and television, but because of financial limitations. A quick citation of 19 such universities is in Escotet (1980: 51-53). Their experiences are as varied as the Keller-based program at the Instituto Tecnológico y de Estudios Superiores de Monterrey (Mexico), the national open university being established in Luján (Argentina), and the distance teaching of physics at the Universidad de Chile.

4. Educational technologists have been active in all of these developments. In addition, they have been stimulated since the late 1960s to form professional associations and non-profit foundations. Some of them have substantial financial support from government or private business, especially from the media (publishers and radio and television networks). The larger ones like the Roberto Marinho Foundation and the Editora Abril in Brazil often have truly impressive media productions aimed at mass audiences, but there is some debate about the effectiveness of the materials (because so much depends on the guidance, assessment, and other non-media elements in the educational process). These and others like the "Radio Schools" of Columbia, Ecuador, Nicaragua and almost every country require large audiences; they principally provide primary, secondary, religious, and "home economics" studies.

5. The fifth result of the sweeping fires of the 1970s could be called the "embers", consisting of the "non-starter" universities with attitudes ranging from *interest* to *indifference* to *mild resistance*. The general public has also been made more aware of distance education, but has not participated greatly. Many people are either unconcerned or simply watching what happens to programs started mainly by politicians and educational innovators. Historically, many other fires (e.g., rubber boom in Brazil; Allende's socialism in Chile; agrarian reforms) have burned brightly and then diminished or died out for a variety of reasons. To develop to its potential as an agent for national and personal development and justice, distance education must be carefully nurtured.

Problems and prospects

There are a variety of interrelated issues and problems associated with distance education, especially in the third world: coordination and cooperation; proliferation; duplication; accreditation and acceptance; evaluation and research; application of educational technology. Two are elaborated here with specific examples from Latin America.

Coordination and cooperation

The cultural, historical, and linguistic unity of Latin America is very real and strong, but the region's size, political structures, individualism, and socioeconomic conditions are powerful counterforces making coordination extremely difficult. The ICCE has had a very limited role in Latin America (only 3 individual and 7 institutional members in the 1975-76 directory). Language has been a barrier because ICCE works mainly in English, but since early 1981 more news from ICCE has been distributed in Spanish/Portuguese via the *ED-DIS Bulletin* (edited by Paul S. Anderson in Brazil) and by the ICCE Regional Liaison Officer, Mr. Andrew Joseph in Argentina.

The Lima, Peru, headquarters of the International Solidarity Institute (ISI-FKA) of the Konrad Adenauer Foundation has been particularly active in promoting 9 international conferences for teleducation (Anderson, 1981). The ISI-FKA has directly and indirectly stimulated numerous distance education efforts, both large and small, throughout Latin America. One cooperative effort is the Proyecto Capricornio with nearly 20 universities near the tropic of Capricorn across South America. Each university is preparing teleducation modules to be tested and exchanged with others in the project (Nicolini, 1980). Another project, the Andres Bello agreement, promotes the production and exchange of over 100 cultural television programs for the Andean nations. There are also agreements between the UNA of Venezuela and UNED of Costa Rica that could yield significant results (Escotet, 1980: 60-61). Other cooperative efforts of magnitude will certainly appear as the situation becomes increasingly complex.

Accreditation and acceptance

In Brazil the law prohibits the granting of university credits for courses without compulsory attendance. This was a measure to eliminate the diploma mills, but today it also prohibits degree-granting distance teaching, regardless of quality. A few experimental programs have gained special provisional accreditation, the most notable being the "post-grad" program administered since late 1979 by the ABT (Brazilian Association for Educational Technology) with government funds for the further training of university instructors. Instructors without master's degrees are assigned to a tutor/professor who guides them (by correspondence plus a one-week residential session) through advanced readings and exercises. The enrolment of 350 is distributed in biology, economics, mathematics, psychology, and production administration. Each course lasts approximately 8 months and has an equivalent of 360 class hours. There is no provision for a thesis nor for automatic continuation to a master's degree (details in ABT, 1980). One difficulty has been the professors' lack of experience in distance education. The final evaluations and cost/benefit studies are not yet available.

Apart from accreditation, there is the issue of acceptance. Frankly, most middle and upper class Brazilians appear to be skeptical or without any definite opinion. For most of the lower socioeconomic class, even the primary and secondary school distance education programs have limited interest. Motivation, other than for certificates and diplomas to list on one's curriculum vita, needs careful attention and objective research.

Conclusion

Only a small selection of Latin America's distance education efforts have been mentioned, and all the comments here should be viewed as positive, favourable, and constructive. The final impressions are of newness, diversity, lack of coordination, and fantastic potential. Although not uniformly, the fires of distance education in Latin America are indeed burning, giving warmth and light with increasing brilliance.

Paul S. Anderson
Universidade de Brasilia
Brazil

References

ABT. (1980) Pos-graduação á distancia. *Tecnologia Educacional.* 36 (entire issue) Rio de Janeiro: Associação Brasileira de Tecnologia Educacional.

Anderson, P. (1981) The IX Latin American seminar on university teleducation. *ICCE Newsletter for Distance Education.* (in press), London: International Council for Correspondence Education. (Also published in Portuguese in *ED-DIS.* 2, Brasilia.)

Escotet, M. (1980) *Tendencias de la Educación Superior a Distancia.* San Jose: Editorial Universidad Estatal a Distancia.

MEC (1980) *Ensino por Correspondencia.* Brasilia: Ministério de Educação e Cultura.

National Home Study Council (1979) Directory of accredited home study schools 1979-1980" (pamphlet) Washington: National Home Study Council.

Nicolini, L. (1980) Grupo Capricornio: un programa de cooperación horizontal. *PIUTEC.* 1, 1, 11-18. Londrina, Brazil: Fundação Universidade Estatal de Londrina.

Ramón-Fernandez, T. (1979) La UNED española fué una apuesta en la que pocos creian. *ENLACE.* 2, 6-7, Universidad Estatal a Distancia de Costa Rica.

UNED-CR. (1980) *Información General.* San José: Universidad Estatal a Distancia de Costa Rica.

Villarroel, A. (1980) The Venezuelan National Open University: An Overview. Paper presented at the XXX International Conference of the International Communication Association, in Acapulco, Mexico, May 1980.

Paper 19

The Capricorn Interuniversity Program: An Example of International Cooperation in Distance Education

Institutions in five South American countries are cooperating on distance education.

The Capricorn Interuniversity Program, PIUTEC, is a cooperative venture of universities located in the Capricorn tropic area of Latin America.

Its objectives are to promote and develop distance education among its members through:

– refresher and post-graduate courses

– exchange of teaching staff, technicians and specialists

– educational technology groups and facilities in each of the member universities

– sharing information about courses, fellowships, research results and other activity in distance education

– initial and in-service training of staff

– specialized publications

– development of common standards for design, production and coproduction, and distribution

– a documentation centre and database

– support of activities in the member universities.

The following universities and foundations are members of the program:

Argentina: Universidad Nacional de Salta
Universidad Católica de Salta

Bolivia: Universidad Gabriel René Moreno
Universidad Mayor de San Simón
Universidad San Francisco Xavier de Chuquisaca
Universidad Católica Boliviana

Brazil: Universidade Estadual de Londrina
Universidade Estadual de Maringá
Universidade Estadual de Ponto Grossa

Chile: Universidad de Chile, sede Antofagasta
Universidad Técnica del Estado, sede Antofagasta
Universidad del Norte-Chile

Paraguay: Universidad Nacional de Asunción
Universidad Católica Nuestra Señora de la Asunción

Foundations: Fundación Konrad Adenauer
Fundación Educaciónal Padre Landell de Moura

The program arose from the desire of several countries in the region to pool resources in a cooperative project. There were already successful examples of this approach in industry and tourism. Such mutual assistance, with no direct political connotations, can benefit developing countries without threatening their economic and cultural independence. Once horizontal, or South-South, cooperation is established joint arrangements with developed countries in the northern hemisphere could be added.

This program was launched at the PIUTEC international seminar held at Asunción, Paraguay on August 6, 1979 where by-laws were approved and a board of directors elected.

The principal projects, which began in 1979-80, include:

The network of PIUTEC coordinators

This network has a committee that meets annually in a different location to develop projects and programs, foster relationships between institutions, and monitor progress.

Seminar-workshops in educational technology

The Organization of American States and the Konrad Adenauer Foundation sponsored a workshop on the training of human resources in educational technology at the Universidad Nacional de Salta, Argentina.

Documentation and Information Centre

This centre at the Universidad del Norte-Chile maintains a valuable bibliographic collection on open and distance education.

Latin America through its literature

This project involves the projection of video segments about regional cultural values that are exchanged between institutions.

Capricorn travelling literary exhibition

This exhibition allows the circulation of texts and materials illustrating particular artists and the cultural patrimony of different regions.

Research centre

A research centre for PIUTEC distance education projects is being developed at the Faculty of Communication Sciences, Universidad Católica Boliviana.

Publications and video library

The Universidad Estadual de Londrina, Brazil, publishes PIUTEC's most important research papers and documents. It also operates a video library for the production, copying, storage and distribution of educational and cultural video programs. A network of similar centres in other regions is planned.

Conclusion

PIUTEC is an open, multi-regional distance education system that is helping to promote integration and solidarity in Latin America.

Luis Nicolini
Programa de Integración Universitaria y Teleducación Capricornio (PIUTEC)
Chile

Using Distance Education to Train Business and Government Personnel

ULSA's methods of training focus on individual motivation and the cooperation of the employer.

ULSA and its objectives

ULSA has been engaged for almost 49 years in adult business training by distance education. Its fundamental aim is to cooperate with the in-company training of employees by providing correspondence courses in accounting and business administration.

ULSA serves all of Latin America and Spain. Our clients are not individuals but companies and government departments. Many of our students have a previous knowledge of accounting gained on the job or through training in accounting, finance, or related subjects.

ULSA's training program

– Enrolments result from the visit of an ULSA representative to the appropriate level of the organization. At this visit we explain the training program, the features of the follow-up system, and the effectiveness of the program in other organizations.

Once an agreement has been reached with the client, a meeting is arranged with employees from the accounting, finance, and other administrative departments to give details on courses. To ensure that students register willingly, a sensitivity process takes place: we inform the manager about the convenience of letting his employees listen to our talks and decide for themselves so they will not feel forced by the manager's decision. This is to counteract a tendency on the part of executives to assign students arbitrarily to courses.

— Once the agreement has been signed, student groups are formed and a coordinator is appointed—usually a senior executive or a member of the training director's staff. The coordinator is responsible for handling correspondence between ULSA and the student group, including the delivery of graded assignments. The coordinator's mission is to motivate the student group. ULSA technologists, educators, and psychologists periodically visit the coordinator to help him analyse the progress of the students in his charge. The coordinator has an important role.

One of ULSA's chief aims is to maintain fluid communications with coordinators, and several channels are used to reach this objective, including the publication of ULSA bulletins containing articles on recent developments in distance education.

Follow-up of student progress

An evaluation of the students' progress is made periodically and used as a basis for guidance, as well as ensuring that students do not feel neglected.

If an assignment is below standard, it is returned to be done over, and is accompanied by helpful remarks. If this does not serve to improve the student's work, a new set of materials with simpler language, format, or content is mailed to the student to replace the original.

Daily assignments from 22 countries are promptly taken up by the Teaching Department; most are graded and sent out withing 24 hours. This process demands a highly trained staff and an efficient internal organization.

The problem of motivation

Students' motivation for studying and the reasons for dropping out are strongly influenced by both their working conditions and the learning process itself.

Factors influencing company training

The highest completion rates are attained in companies with a clear understanding of the problem and a high regard for morale as well as respect for employee training.

The fact that a company decides to sponsor a training program, however, is not in itself sufficient to motivate students. It is also necessary that top executives give their whole-hearted support to the program. On the other hand, we have found that when a student is enrolled in a program he has not requested and decides to drop out, the disapproval of superiors has no influence.

Probable causes of drop-outs

Drop-out rates are the consequence of both individual and group criteria. ULSA studies have identified the following causes of drop-outs (group factors prevail):

1. Students enrol because of the influence of their working group to avoid feeling isolated. When their need to belong has been satisfied, their intrinsic motivation to study decreases and they may drop out.

2. Drop-outs result from imitation. When a leading figure in a group drops out, others may follow suit. This is why we do not enrol higher levels together with lower levels in an organization.

3. Students give up studying for fear of failing to meet the requirements set by their superiors or fellow employees. They may fear or resent exposing their inadequacy.

4. Students drop out (some without even starting) because they cannot overcome fears related to the learning process itself (a new experience for them), the fact that they are subject to evaluation, the requirements of independent study, etc.

5. Students who have repeatedly started and interrupted studies tend to follow the same pattern.

6. Students whose motivation for enrolling is to obtain textual materials are apt to drop out quickly, usually submitting few assignments.

7. Dropping out is sometimes due to incompatibility between what students originally expected to achieve and what they subsequently think they can actually achieve.

8. A lack of agreement between what students anticipate from training and the estimate they make of the work required to reach their goals may lead to drop-outs.

9. A delay in obtaining speedy answers to practical problems or to specific points in course content is a frequent cause of drop-outs. It has been proven that drop-out rates are higher in areas with inefficient postal service.

An experience in Brazil: the educational counsellor

To improve motivation and minimize drop-outs, ULSA incorporated a new function: the educational counsellor. The purpose of this new position is to help the coordinator motivate students. Experimentation with this new position began in São Paulo, Brazil, with promising results.

First, the counsellor was trained in adult psychology, motivation resources, and group techniques. His function has been defined as establishing adequate learning situations, fostering proper attitudes towards the learning process, and strengthening the motivation of students. He operates along the following lines:

- keep up the motivation that prompted the student to choose a certain course
- contribute to the acceptance of a non-conventional teaching situation
- implement new study techniques
- stimulate the development of the student's own strategies by establishing a series of goals
- explain ULSA's support services and encourage students to use them
- strengthen the desire to keep on studying by recognizing the efforts already made
- detect individual difficulties that deviate the student's attention from studying.

The only tool the educational counsellor has at his disposal is verbal interaction, but he can aim at creating an atmosphere of harmony and cooperation that stimulates the learning process.

After several years of experience, and in spite of all the efforts made, we have found that results in Brazil have not substantially influenced the drop-out rate. In fact, our statistics show that there was no notable increase in the percentage of graduates, and the time required for completion of studies does not suggest improvement.

Andrew H. Joseph / Susana B. De Milanesi
Universidad la Salle de Sud América (ULSA)
Argentina

National Policies for Distance Education

National policies are required for the efficient development of distance education systems.

Introduction

In such a mixed assembly as the ICCE, with participants from developing as well as industrialized countries, from the private sector as well as the public sector, it is important to state certain assumptions before tackling the controversial subject of national policies for distance education.

One assumption is that whether the state or private organizations provide distance education, there are certain policies that should be decided at the national level, if not by the state itself. The private sector exists because there is a demand for its services. Whatever its faults, it has often pioneered distance education in certain instances where the state was not able to meet public demand. But it is difficult to imagine a distance education system without any form of state involvement.

The need for national policies

At a conference in Addis Ababa in 1978, which brought together distance educators from Africa and Asia, a plea was made for the recognition of distance teaching institutions. I assume that what was meant by "recognition" was equal status with traditional institutions. There was the strong feeling that distance institutions, particularly in the third world, were considered second best, useful only when the traditional institutions could not keep up with demand.

It should be possible to make use of *all* resources available for education. For example, distance students should be able to use facilities in traditional institutions, and there should be a combination of distance methods and traditional face-to-face teaching. The reluctance of traditional institutions to share their resources is based on a number of factors. First, because distance education is regarded by many employers as second best, students prefer conventional courses whenever they are available. Second, there is the perhaps justifiable fear that if distance institutions were fully supported, they would produce an over abundance of skilled labour with consequent demands for jobs and higher salaries, or both. Third, the lack of trained personnel and student support services has made it difficult for distance institutions to inspire confidence. Here we have a vicious circle in which lack of resources makes achievements difficult, which in turn leads to withholding of resources. Finally, there may also be the fear that reducing contact hours between students and tutors might lower standards.

The kinds of policies required

National policies must give distance institutions access to modern educational technology. This means that educational broadcasting, for example, would become not merely an adjunct to the traditional system, but an integral part of distance education. Since extensive use of media is, in most nations, impossible without state involvement, any headway educational programming makes in the face of entertainment requires strong commitment from central authorities.

Distance teaching in general faces the problem of finding skilled personnel, especially in the newly developing field of educational technology. It is in the interest of the country that the state become involved in establishing adequate training programs, even to the extent of providing a centralized system controlling both training and staff transfers among distance and traditional institutions.

The state could also create adequately staffed study centres, making use of existing school facilities where students could not only use expensive equipment, perhaps for a small fee, but also meet student advisors.

All of these measures could be improved by cooperation with private institutions, especially in the area of staff training and the provision of facilities.

A more standardized system of staff training would, of course, lead to questions about the recognition of certificates and diplomas (not only for staff, but also those awarded to students). Proper control of these awards would give staff and students more credibility, and the state could also encourage the creation of professional staff associations that would further increase the value of these awards.

Summary

Whether national policies take the form of those adopted directly by the state, or those arrived at through cooperation between the private and public sectors, they are required to ensure that distance education not be regarded as second best. Appropriate national policies can help distance education make education and training available to the largest number of people.

Kenneth Noyau
Unesco/UNDP
Haiti

Paper 22

Conflict in Distance Education

(Abstract)

Tertiary education in Hong Kong is served mainly by two universities and one polytechnic, hardly sufficient for a population of about 6 million. For example, in the 1980/81 year the polytechnic received 62,495 fully qualified applications for only 11,953 places. In Hong Kong, distance education is more a matter of how far down one is on the list of applicants than how far one lives from a campus.

While this conflict between demand and supply may be rather unique to Hong Kong, the following are other potential conflicts in Hong Kong that may be shared by other distance education systems.

training vs. education

Institutions do not always respond to the legitimate needs of students, and will not be serving students if they offer "pure" education when the real need is for specific training.

means

Institutions must match their own facilities and production methods with the facilities and living conditions of students. In Hong Kong, for example, practically all households have a TV set and free telephone service. But many families live in a one-room flat, so the matching of educational programs supported by telephone tutorials is not as suitable as the combined technology seems to promise. In this situation, a vast institutional expenditure on educational TV programs would likely result in less than desirable results.

language

In Hong Kong, most of the educational materials are delivered in English because of the need to acquire British qualifications. But many subjects could more efficiently be taught in Cantonese.

Such conflicts—potential or actual—should be identified, analysed, and resolved to ensure efficient delivery of distance education.

Barry Hutchinson
Hong Kong Polytechnic
Hong Kong

Correspondence Education: Private Enterprise and Public Responsibility

Because of cooperation between private and public sectors correspondence education has become well established in the education system in Norway.

Introduction

Literature and research on correspondence is rather scanty, and an almost neglected field is the study of correspondence education from the viewpoint of educational policy, especially with respect to private institutes. Recent interest in non-traditional teaching has produced a number of case studies of distance education projects and systems, and in some countries politicians have become interested in correspondence education in relation to consumer protection. But still the place of correspondence education within a country's education system is not often discussed.

In his study of the private sector of correspondence education in Belgium Weinstock (1976) classifies three systems:

- *The liberal system.* Correspondence education exists as a result of private initiative, especially in the commercial sector. This system is found in the Federal Republic of Germany, Great Britain, The United States, and France among others.
- *Private institutions with a public vocation.* This identifies correspondence education in Scandinavia, Finland, and the Netherlands.
- *Distance teaching in socialist countries.* In these countries distance education is incorporated in the state education system.

Perraton (1979) points to the combination of correspondence education with mass media and face-to-face sessions as a development distinct from both the "liberal" model and the "socialist" model.

Karow (1980) gives a thorough discussion of the position of private correspondence education in Western Europe, and describes alternatives for the future in the Federal Republic of Germany. He stresses the point made by Weinstock that in societies with the "liberal" model, state institutions for distance education have often been established (in France, for instance). Private correspondence schools in these countries have often been given only a marginal role.

The position of private correspondence education in Norway is unique. It is unlikely that Norway can be taken as a direct model by other countries, but I hope others can learn something from the Norwegian experience.

Historical factors

This is not the place to describe—or even outline—the history of correspondence education in Norway. But it is necessary to point out some of the history to understand the situation today.

The correspondence schools

Before the Second World War the scene was dominated by one big school: the NKS. It was a sound and serious enterprise. During the 1940s there appeared quite a few rather dubious schools, but they soon disappeared. The main addition after the war has been a number of schools owned by various organizations, and there is one technical college. Today the two biggest schools are organized as non-profit foundations, and the total number of correspondence schools is about 40, most of them very small. Seventeen schools have joined in an association that includes all the big schools (about 5 or 6).

Legislation and control

A law passed in 1949 placed correspondence education under state control. The accreditation of correspondence schools is taken care of by a special advisory body to the Ministry of Education—The State Council on Correspondence Schools. The declared aim of this system is to secure the educational quality of correspondence education.

External examinations

The Norwegian school system is very liberal in offering public examination of candidates who have not received regular teaching at recognized schools. Norwegian students can therefore prepare for most public examinations (at least within general education) on their own or with the help of correspondence tuition. Students are also free to decide how many examinations they want to sit for at a time.

Support system

In 1949 state grants were for the first time given to correspondence study circles, similar to existing grants to study circles in ordinary adult education. From 1961 to 1975 the state refunded course fees for correspondence students who sat for certain public examinations.

In 1975 a radical new system came into effect. A student paid a small fee (US $20-50) at the time of enrolment. All additional costs of course materials and tuition were to be paid by the state. There was a rush of new enrolments for correspondence courses, and an explosion in state subsidies. Parliament demanded that the expenditure be brought under control, and a new system was instituted in 1977. In this system the student pays 50% of the course fee when starting, and on completion the state pays the remaining 50% to the school, and also refunds 35% of the student's initial fee. For correspondence courses used by local school authorities, the authority pays the first 50% on behalf of the student.

Broadcasting institute

The establishment of a state correspondence school was discussed in the late 1940s, but it was never effected. Educational broadcasting has been under deliberation during the 1970s. The outcome was the establishment of a new public institution in 1979, Norsk fjernundervisning (The Norwegian Distance Education Institute). This is meant to be a very small institute, much like a secretariat, that pursues its objectives through cooperation with existing bodies (The Norwegian Broadcasting Corporation, publishing houses, correspondence schools, etc.).

Integration and cooperation

Since the Second World War there has been a growing integration of correspondence education into other forms of study. It began with the expanded use of correspondence courses in study circles. The armed forces have been using correspondence courses from non-military schools since 1947. From 1955 this use has been established by contract between the Ministry of Defense and the main correspondence schools.

Another important development started about 1960 when correspondence study was combined with classroom teaching, in so-called *combined education*. This has been a great success, and correspondence schools cooperate with local organizers of classes all over Norway. Local partners are usually voluntary study organizations or school authorities. Enrolments for "combined courses" almost equals enrolments in traditional correspondence courses.

The present situation

After a rather turbulent intermezzo in 1975-77 the situation has stabilized. Correspondence education is a recognized form of education, used each year by 3-4% of the total population. The revision of the support system in 1977 has proven satisfactory, and has reduced the drop-out rate because of its financial motivation. Cooperation between correspondence schools and voluntary study organizations, school authorities, branches of business and industry, and central and local administration is steadily growing.

We are, however, faced with new problems as well as new challenges. Economic constraints are forced on society as a whole, and education is vulnerable. Grants for adult education are being restrained, and there is an escalating fight for the money available. Conflicting interests are perceived between correspondence and other forms of education, and the teachers' associations view correspondence education with suspicion. Decisions on priorities become more pressing for both local and central school authorities.

The number of public education institutions has been increasing for many years. Vocational training in schools is expanding. The level of general education in society is increasing. Will there be a place for private correspondence education in the future?

There has been almost no correspondence education at the post-secondary level in Norway. Inspired by recent developments in other countries, some post-secondary institutions are experimenting with distance education on a very small scale. Will correspondence schools find a place, independently or in cooperation with other institutions, in post-secondary education?

The Ministry of Education is now preparing a report on correspondence education since 1977. The report will be presented to Parliament in 1982. It is expected to evaluate the control and support systems and possibly suggest amendments. It may also include more general deliberations on the role of correspondence education.

Conclusion

The greatest positive experience in Norway is the broad integration of correspondence education into the whole education system, and especially into adult education. In youth education correspondence courses are used for optional subjects in ordinary schools and in folk high schools. Most correspondence students, however, are participants in adult education programs for school equivalence or non-formal programs, and traditional, individual correspondence students.

The effect of this integration is that many correspondence schools have attained an important role within the education system, and they are trusted with the administration of considerable state grants (about US $10 million in 1981).

The interplay between public authorities and private correspondence schools has on the whole been quite harmonious, but not, of course, entirely free of problems. Some problems we will have to live with; others I hope will be solved. I will point to one of each kind.

Private and public economy work in different ways. The economy of correspondence schools in the Norwegian system has no choice but to be a mixture of the two. The schools will have to accept bureaucratic changes caused by public budgets and new regulations governing public grants. At the same time, they are enterprises operating according to ordinary business laws. This situation may cause some management problems, and necessitates close cooperation with public authorities.

Public authorities face the problem of attaining their own educational objectives through independent correspondence schools. This is not easy, and it is not sufficiently taken care of through the present support system, which is based on two political assumptions:

1. Correspondence education is a good thing, and deserves support.

2. Correspondence education deserves still more support when organized (for example, as combined education) by local school authorities.

    Both statements are of a general nature, and do not have a heavy influence on, for example, the course development policy of correspondence schools. Correspondence schools, on the other hand, will usually base their decisions on estimates of quantitative, not qualitative (or political) demand for courses. So perhaps 10 schools will develop courses in data processing, and there will be no course in Norwegian for immigrant workers.

    The establishment of Norsk fjernundervisning may be *one* step in solving the problem of political influence on correspondence education. But I believe more steps are desirable. School authorities and public administrators ought to consider more deeply how to use correspondence education (in its widest sense) in the future learning society. I hope public authorities in Norway will not leave the initiative solely with the private sector but take on the responsibility and initiate a still more dynamic cooperation with correspondence schools.

Erling Ljoså
Norsk Korrespondanseskole
Norway

References

Weinstock, Nathan, et al (1976) Les cours par correspondence du secteur privé en Belgique. Etude sociologique. Brussel: Editions du Centre National de Sociologie du Droit Social.

Perraton, Hilary. (ed.) (1979) *Alternative Routes to Formal Education: Distance Teaching for School Equivalency.* Washington: The World Bank.

Karow, Willi. (1980) Privater Fernunterricht in der Bundesrepublik Deutschland und im Ausland. Schriften zur Berufsbildungsforschung 58. Hannover: Bundesinstitut für Berufsbildung/Hermann Schroedel Verlag KG.

Continuing Education by Distance Study

Paper 24

The Fernuniversität has achieved success in a short time by applying the techniques of distance study and by integrating traditional with continuing education.

Introduction

In this paper I will deal with a number of implications of continuing education and the role of distance study. I shall refer to the Fernuniversität, a university catering exclusively to distance students. Realizing the difficulty of transferring models from one country to another, I nevertheless hope our experience at the Fernuniversität may help others in analysing problems and recognizing possibilities.

The two goals

Continuing education at the university level in Germany is limited mainly to professional upgrading. A second goal is to offer undergraduate and graduate courses to people working for a living, to open university up to new groups who have not had access to higher education.

    While the first goal dominates, the second is largely regarded as a by-product of the first. The hope is that by taking a wide range of courses, students will become more autonomous, acting in a more rational and tolerant way.

    These two goals are confronted by two main problems. First, our universities are already overcrowded and will remain so for the rest of the eighties. Second, people working for a living are not often willing to leave their work.

    I am convinced that the only remedy is distance study. It enables students to obtain an academic education without overly burdening the universities and without forcing them to give up their jobs.

Special methods and media

Traditional academic teaching is limited by the unity of persons, time, and place, thus excluding many students. Communication media and "prefabricated instruction", however, break down this restrictive unity. The best teachers can instruct, not only a class of 20 or 30 students, but a very great number of students who may study when and where they like.

Students, however, must be willing and able to study on their own. They must be highly motivated learners who plan their studies and who are persistent enough to maintain firm schedules in the face of temptations to be like their fellow-workers and enjoy their leisure.

Four principles

There are four fundamental principles important in developing programs at the Fernuniversität:

- unity of research and teaching
- interdisciplinarity
- practical application
- use of traditional courses.

Unity of research and teaching

When we began planning the Fernuniversität most of our professors stressed the importance of unifying teaching and research, even in continuing education. This means that knowledge presented in courses for continuing studies must be derived from the results of research. Ideally, this calls for the professor who is both researcher and teacher.

Interdisciplinarity

Most of our professors try to integrate more than one discipline in their courses. This is difficult enough in the traditional university but it is even more important and more difficult in continuing studies. You cannot convey knowledge systematically from only one discipline while problems of work and life call for another approach. These problems are often too complex to be solved by any single discipline and require multi-dimensional academic thinking.

Cooperation between professors of different academic disciplines is a most difficult task requiring a change in academic traditions. Although I am unable to relate a success story in this field, interdisciplinarity remains one of the most critical aspects of academic continuing studies.

Practical application

Our laws require that continuing education offered by universities must be oriented to problems of vocational and professional practice. Our professors do not find it easy to teach practical knowledge: often they do not know what current vocational and professional practices are and they consider themselves incompetent in these areas. Also, they feel the danger of a limitless differentiation of knowledge if they apply their knowledge to the many working processes in a highly industrialized society.

We see three possible solutions. First, the Fernuniversität offers courses split up into units and students select the units that seem relevant to their work. They are to apply their new knowledge to their particular work situation. Another approach may be the use of eminent practitioners in the teaching process—in study centres, for example. A third approach is the development of special interdisciplinary projects aimed at special interest groups. This approach seems very promising because the first successful project could be used by a very large number of students.

Use of traditional courses

We are convinced that certain important continuing education results can be reached by offering courses developed originally for traditional undergraduate and graduate students. Professional workers are interested in what universities have been teaching during the years since their graduation. Vocational workers who have never attended university will find it helpful to learn how universities deal with their activities.

The demand for this kind of continuing education is great: more than 10,000 students are enrolled at the Fernuniversität for these reasons. I consider this a first and rather easy approach that can be implemented in the absence of courses devised specially for continuing education.

Implementation

The Fernuniversität has attracted 30,000 students. In its entrance requirements, curriculum, and diplomas it does not differ from traditional universities. But with regard to methods and media it is, indeed, a new and unique institution.

With more than 75% of our students over 25, we have a student population that is older than normal. Nearly 70% have already completed some kind of professional or vocational training, so that a very high proportion are pursuing academic studies for the purpose of continuing their education. Furthermore, 43% are part time, many earning a diploma they could not obtain when they were younger. About 35% of our students are "guest students" (that is, students without university entrance qualifications who are permitted to take courses they like).

In five years the new approach taken by the Fernuniversität has proven successful. The demand has exceeded the first estimates by 100%. It is the only institute of higher learning in Germany that caters in a systematic way to clients wanting continuing education. This could be achieved only by employing the techniques of distance study and by closely integrating undergraduate and graduate studies with continuing studies. The use of distance study material—which had seemed to be dictated by scarce resources—proved to be a great attraction.

Many people working for a living wish to take part in regular academic studies. The Fernuniversität can meet this new demand.

Otto Peters
Fernuniversität
West Germany

The Reform of Adult Education in French-Canada: An Expanded Role for Home Study

A new distance institute is one of the sweeping changes proposed in adult education in the province of Quebec

Introduction

Early in 1980 the Quebec government established the Jean Commission to develop an overall policy for adult education and training. Within the year, the Commission had studied 651 written submissions, held hearings for 245 interest groups, and met over 5000 adults in open meetings in various regions. An interim report issued in May 1981 served as the basis for a final round of hearings before publication of its recommendations in late 1981 (L'éducation des adultes au Québec: hypothèses de solutions, 1981).

A devastating indictment

The interim report was a devastating indictment of current educational practice. In the absence of overall policy, different governments and departments have created a chaotic situation compounded by the multiplicity of institutions trying to attract the adult student. Students complained they had to suffer incompetent teachers and counsellors, bad pedagogy, impractical courses, excessive formalism, discrimination in admissions, poor facilities, inconvenient timetables, insensitive administrators, and self-serving institutions. Less criticism was levelled at home-study courses, although the range of subjects available was considered too limited.

Institutions complained of government bureaucracy—especially about the confusion between the manpower and education departments, poor funding, and the inflexibility of centrally bargained union contracts. Private institutions were convinced that civil servants discriminated against them, while the voluntary sector felt ignored. Unions and management in industry both deplored the acrimonious quarrelling between government departments and institutions, which prevented transfer credit as each sector refused to recognize the other's courses.

Proposed reforms

Having diagnosed adult education in Quebec as a disaster area, the Commission proposed sweeping reforms of policy and organization. Since the energies and resources devoted to educational institutions in Quebec in the last twenty years have been second only to the massive investment in hydro-electric schemes, it was thought unrealistic to ask for more public money.

To promote the de-institutionalization of adult education while improving access and participation, the Commission urged the abolition of distinctions between general, vocational, and sociocultural education and advocated the establishment of a new legal framework. A central element in the new framework would be a Bureau of Adult Education with a key role in funding and policy implementation. Reluctant to place this Bureau in either the education or labour ministries, the Commission suggested its attachment to the prime minister's office or the splitting of the education ministry into two divisions—one for compulsory and the other for post-compulsory education—as is the practice in western Canada.

The Bureau would work through some 25 regional centres responsible for coordinating and publicizing adult education opportunities. Whether these centres would be part of the Bureau (like Saskatchewan's community colleges) or autonomous bodies (like Alberta's further education councils) was left open for discussion. In either case, according to the Commission, existing institutions would provide the actual instruction although the regional centre would decide on course offerings and have a monopoly on publicity.

The report also proposed that firms be required by law to devote 2.5% of their payroll to personnel education and that voluntary associations be given incentives to expand their educational activities. The regional centres would monitor firms' educational expenditures for tax purposes and identify associations eligible for grants. These functions alone would make the centres large and powerful.

Distance education would have an expanded role through the creation of a distance education institute funded by the Bureau. This institute would absorb the existing government correspondence branch and the Télé-université, having a broad adult education mandate similar to that of the British Columbia Open Learning Institute. Existing offerings would be expanded, particularly in study skills training and junior college programs. The Bureau would certify private correspondence colleges and approve their courses whereas conventional public institutions would cease any distance education activities. The report urged that the institute work closely with libraries, and with cable systems and Radio-Québec for media support.

Elsewhere in the report the Commission deplored the small impact of educational TV, blaming the broadcast licensing authorities for defining education too broadly.

Conclusion

The recommendations of the Jean Commission could give Quebec better value for the tax dollars it spends on adult education. They also attack so many vested institutional interests that their likelihood of implementation would, in normal circumstances, have to be rated as small. The style of the current education minister, however, is interventionist, and the possibility of saving money at a time when Quebec's public finances are in a parlous state may clinch the argument in the Commission's favour.

John S. Daniel
Concordia University
Canada

References

L'éducation des adultes au Québec: hypothèses de solutions. (1981) Commission d'étude sur la formation professionnelle et socio-culturelle des adultes, Québec. 389 pages.

Paper 26

Elementary Education of Children at a Distance

Elementary education at a distance faces an uncertain future, but should never lose one of its strongest features: the personal touch.

The beginning of correspondence education for children

In many parts of the world children of elementary school age are isolated from normal schooling by remoteness, illness, or itinerancy. One of the first initiatives to meet the needs of such children was made in 1905 by the Calvert School, a private day school in Baltimore, Maryland, USA. This "tentative and experimental" proposal for "the education of children at home by correspondence" was advertised in publications such as the *National Geographic Magazine* and the first students were enrolled in 1906 (MacKenzie and Christensen, 1971: 35-38).

Pupils followed lesson plans prepared by teachers at the day school for use in class the previous week. The Calvert School still adapts the regular day school curriculum for its external students, and classes serve as an "experimental laboratory" for the preparation of home instruction courses.

Today the Calvert School serves a widely scattered clientele of more than 4500 elementary students living or travelling both within and outside the United States. Increasingly, however, Calvert and other schools are accepting students whose parents view correspondence learning as an alternative or an extension and enrichment of regular schooling (*Time Magazine,* December 4, 1978: 66-67). Calvert charges tuition fees on a non-profit basis for the basic course materials plus an additional fee for the advisory teaching service, thus making it optional for parents to mark the lessons themselves or post them to Baltimore.

Table 1: The establishment of state and provincial correspondence schools in English-speaking countries (1914-1927)

Year	State or Province	Location
1914	Victoria	Melbourne
1916	New South Wales	Sydney
1918	Western Australia	Perth
1919	Tasmania	Hobart
1919	British Columbia	Victoria
1920	South Australia	Adelaide
1922	Queensland	Brisbane
1922	New Zealand	Wellington
1923	Alberta	Edmonton
1925	Saskatchewan	Regina
1926	Ontario	Toronto
1927	Manitoba	Winnipeg

Source: (Jenkins, 1980)

The establishment of education department correspondence schools

Within the next twenty years correspondence schools were established by governments in several other English-speaking countries, especially those in which isolated families lived beyond the reach of small rural schools. In Canada, Australia, and New Zealand most state and provincial governments had, by the mid-1920s, accepted the responsibility of providing free education for children disadvantaged by distance. Most of these schools began by offering primary courses and expanded to include secondary courses.

Correspondence teachers

Unlike the Calvert model, government schools were established exclusively for remote students. Teachers were recruited from state school systems and most were amateurs at designing materials for students they seldom, if ever, met face to face. As their understanding of correspondence teaching deepened, it became apparent that it demanded a specialized and personal approach. At first it was customary merely to transfer classroom procedures onto a printed page. Though it is still accepted that the correspondence curriculum should keep pace with levels in other schools, it is not generally felt that classroom methods are appropriate for isolated children. It also had to be kept in mind that the home supervisor was usually an extraordinarily busy mother who probably had no teaching experience and, especially in the early days, little or no formal education.

Without exception, enrolment in a correspondence school demanded that students correspond with their teacher who is required to develop deft communication skills and an effective way of making the teacher-pupil relationship as personal as possible. By means of assignments the teacher not only initiates corrective teaching but also seeks to guide and encourage the home supervisor and to motivate the student.

In government correspondence schools it became an accepted practice to appoint teachers who had difficulty in coping with classroom teaching. The reputation of these schools among teachers has suffered greatly—with some justification. As the Committee of Enquiry into the Future of the Victoria Correspondence School points out:

> Each year some teachers seek administrative transfer from classroom duties on the grounds of disability. One section of the Department to which some of these teachers have been sent is the Correspondence School, where some have achieved success in their new field whereas others have found no more success or satisfaction than they had in the classroom. The knowledge of this practice and an awareness of its measure of failure have established, in the mind of teachers generally, an image of the Correspondence School which discourages many from participation in its activities.
> (Schruhm, 1978: 25)

In recent years this policy has been discredited in most education systems, although it is accepted as appropriate to appoint disabled teachers if they can do the work.

Pressures for change

For most of their history, education department correspondence schools have been poor relations in the education system: their regular clients have been relatively invisible and politically conservative, and their professional staff have adhered to very traditional teaching methods. These factors were not in themselves detrimental to the service provided, but in Australia at least they prevented correspondence schools from sharing in the expansion of resources in the 1960s and early 1970s. Now that the schools are being staffed with teachers from that era, these teachers are demanding comparable benefits for distance education at a time, unfortunately, when governments are less eager to expand educational services.

The last decade in Australia has seen the formation and rapid growth of the Isolated Children's Parents Association. Its membership is predominantly from the influential, though not necessarily affluent owners and managers of large farming and pastoral properties. Its aims include upgrading correspondence education and providing financial assistance for all isolated families, with particular success in the latter. Assistance takes the form of allowances to compensate for extra expenses and resources involved in educating children at home and to assist in sending secondary-level children to boarding schools.

Several investigations have acknowledged the need to correct the relative imbalance of services provided for "bush" children in Australia. Most prominent is the Report of the Senate Standing Committee on Education of Isolated School Children, which made the following significant recommendations:

- the updating of correspondence courses
- the appointment of itinerant teachers
- special provision for assisting children in need of remedial education
- greater use of audio-visual aids, including the expansion of the School of the Air facilities.

(Davidson et al, 1976: 89-92)

Correspondence courses

Most correspondence schools develop their own lessons. It has often been demonstrated that first-hand knowledge of correspondence teaching is a prerequisite for writing a correspondence course for children. Education departments have found it difficult to accept the specialized nature of the correspondence curriculum. The assumptions underlying policies relating to correspondence schools are now being seriously questioned at adminstrative levels.

These assumptions are summarized by Ross Worthington of the Queensland Department of Education as follows:

1. Distance teaching practices are essentially a translation of oral instruction into written form with only essential omissions and additions to facilitate learning at a distance.

2. Internal courses can be directly translated into relevant and rich external learning experiences through the written word.

3. Teaching/learning activities within distance courses can occur within the same time frame as for internal instruction.

4. Outcomes of distance learners are, and should be, essentially identical to student outcomes from internal courses.

5. Distance learners essentially exhibit the same learning and cognitive processes as do internal learners.

6. No special teaching preparation is required for distance teaching.

7. Teachers who have significant interpersonal problems in constant interaction settings (e.g. classrooms) will not exhibit such problems in the interactional situations demanded by distance education.

(Worthington, 1980: 2)

The first two assumptions have been effectively discredited, and though correspondence course authors must keep in touch with classroom practice, they must adapt (and often drastically rethink) the regular school curriculum.

The next two assumptions are still contentious because, although some correspondence teachers question their validity, most isolated parents view the regular school as the norm, and expect similar outcomes. Only parents seeking an alternative to the regular school system would seriously question these assumptions.

Assumptions (4) and (5) are only beginning to be considered in depth. Correspondence teachers working with primary students have developed ideas and instincts about the way their students learn, but almost no formal research has been done at this level. Those interested in the theory of distance learning must examine writings on the tertiary level. For example, Bååth's analysis (1979) of Gagné's teaching model has been useful in promoting the debate over pure correspondence teaching vs. incorporating face-to-face communication.

With regard to the final two assumptions, the need for developing special skills for correspondence educators has been recognized with the proposal that a Graduate Diploma in Distance Education will be offered by the Adelaide College of Advanced Education, probably beginning in mid-1982.

Today there is greater emphasis on experimentation and consultation in planning and preparing courses. If, as I suspect, the printed page will continue its prominence, despite the tempting predictions of communications technologists, the design, sequential development, and vocabulary of printed assignments will continue to be crucial. When communicating with young children, such factors as the size and style of type, suitability of illustrations, the use of colour for educational and motivational purposes, and the general layout and aesthetic appeal of a page become important educational decisions.

It is accepted that young children are seldom self-motivated. What is not appreciated by people outside correspondence education is the need to motivate the parent-supervisor. (It is debatable whether correspondence teachers teach children or whether they help mothers teach their children.) A course writer must make the task of the parent as straightforward as possible. If instructions are ambiguous or too theoretical or the activities too complicated, learning will suffer.

Itinerant teachers

Most Australian education departments now accept the idea of itinerant teachers. These teachers are based at country centres to provide support to families within about a hundred miles. They are usually expected:

– to act as a link between the student and his correspondence teacher

– to diagnose learning problems and initiate and monitor remedial programs

– to expand the curriculum by adding art, drama, music, and physical education

– to help families arrange contact with other isolated children

– to motivate and advise students and home supervisors

– to spend many hours each week on the rough, dusty roads of the outback.

Remedial programs

Even the best designed courses will not match the interests and abilities of all children. A correspondence course is a basic guide for the so-called "average" student and often requires adapting for the "below" or "above" average child.

Isolated children with serious learning difficulties present almost insurmountable problems. Facilities with staff trained in diagnosing and treating such problems have been established in some states. The most successful are the Chidley Point Special Education Facility for Isolated Children and the Isolated Children's Special Education Unit, both of which include residences for mothers and children.

Schools of the Air

The most uniquely Australian innovation in distance education is the concept of the School of the Air. Since its inception in 1951, the School of the Air has allowed isolated children to participate in daily classes with a teacher and other students over two-way shortwave radio. There are twelve Schools of the Air operating from regions served by the radio networks of the Royal Australian Flying Doctor Service.

At first, Schools of the Air served mainly as a means of breaking down isolation by allowing children to speak with each other without reference to their studies. By 1954 the School of the Air at Alice Springs, the birthplace of the idea, had established close links with the South Australian Correspondence School, and subsequent Schools of the Air followed this model. Today most administer the whole education of their students, using mainly the courses prepared in the state capitals.

In addition to the daily radio link, Schools of the Air, in cooperation with correspondence schools and itinerant teachers, arrange sports days, regional weekend "mini-schools", home supervisors' workshops, and other gatherings.

Conclusion

The future of government-sponsored correspondence schools for elementary children is somewhat uncertain. In most parts of the world, improved roads and expanding community facilities are breaking down geographical isolation. A changing economy has affected traditional occupations in isolated regions, resulting in the exodus of families. Conversely, the same changes have brought about a new and expanding avenue of need—the itinerant family. This phenomenon will force correspondence schools to review their philosophies and strategies.

Improved and expanding educational technology will also demand a review of methods. The South Australian Correspondence School and the Educational Technology Centre are preparing for the launching of Australia's first domestic communications satellite in 1985. The use of the conference telephone, slow scan video, and facsimile transmission will broaden the scope of distance education. Increasingly, schools in remote communities are relying on correspondence schools to supplement their curriculum. More sophisticated communications techniques will expand this demand.

Whatever the future holds, correspondence schools must not lose the attribute they have maintained throughout their sixty-year history—the personal touch. Well designed courses and expanded communication links will only improve the service these schools provide if the children they teach and the home supervisors they assist receive the individualized tuition and understanding encouragement they have come to expect from their correspondence teacher.

John Penberthy
South Australian Correspondence School
Australia

References

Bååth, J.A. (1979) *Correspondence Education in the Light of a Number of Contemporary Teaching Models.* Malmo: LiberHermods.

Davidson, G.S. et al (1976) Australian Senate Standing Committee on Education and the Arts - Report on Education of Isolated School Children. Canberra: Australian Parliament.

Jenkins, J. (1980) *Correspondence Institutions in the Commonwealth 1980.* London: Commonwealth Secretariat.

Mackenzie, O. and Christensen, E.L. (1971) *The Changing World of Correspondence Study.* University Park, Pennsylvania: The Pennsylvania State University Press.

Schruhm, A.E. et al (1978) *Report of the Committee of Enquiry into the Future of the Correspondence School.* Melbourne: Ecucation Department, Victoria.

Teaching children at home. *Time Magazine.* December 4, 1978.

Worthington, R.R. (1980) *Research Paper.* Brisbane: Research Branch, Department of Education, Queensland.

The Process of Learning at a Distance: Recent Research and Developments

Paper 27

Introduction

In his review of research in distance learning Coldeway (paper 6) points out that according to the strictest definition of research, which requires rigourous definition of boundaries and variables, rather little research has been done in distance education. There is, however, no doubt that the work being carried out in many countries to create or develop particular distance learning projects has had a cumulative effect in adding to our know-how and thereby improving day-to-day practice.

Sewart (paper 5) encourages us not to overstress the uniqueness of distance learning but rather to see it as part of the continuum of possibilities open to the adult learner. Waniewicz (paper 28) tells us that institutions of all kinds only account for about 60% of the identifiable learning projects carried out by adults. The decision to learn something new is usually related to a change in an individual's life but the constraints and obstacles set up by institutions cause many to elect to learn informally. Kaye (paper 107) says that promoting the autonomy to learn independently should be a prime aim of multimedia adult education projects. According to Coldeway (paper 29) institutions have not learned the key lessons of educational psychology, namely that adults can learn well provided that the approach used respects individual differences and interprets academic content in terms of tasks facing the student. In paper 26 Penberthy argues that the pedagogical principles of the classroom also require adaptation when children have to learn at a distance.

Helping students develop the special qualities required for learning at a distance is an important task. Singer (paper 49) describes how the student and the institution can create a propitious environment for study and Bååth (paper 7) stresses the importance of encouraging the student to connect new knowledge with his previous experience to produce meaningful verbal learning rather than rote memorization. Marton and Svensson (paper 31) and Morgan et al (paper 32) report that the ability to learn can only be developed in the context of a specific content, a conclusion which has led Forsythe (paper 81) to integrate content chosen by the student into a learning-to-learn course. Penney (paper 34) writes about content analysis in course design and Holmes (paper 35) shows how authors can be helped to write readable materials.

The twin phenomena of drop-out and contact with students have attracted extensive study and comment. Shale (paper 36) shows why valid inter-institutional comparisons of drop-out rates are hard to make and Woodley (37) notes that drop-out rates vary over time for various reasons. Rekkedal (paper 38) has observed a seasonal variation and claims that the fact of studying part time rather than the actual method of learning at a distance is responsible for most drop-outs. Misanchuk (paper 39) agrees that the vagaries of life are usually cited by students as reasons for dropping out rather than problems in the course itself. According to Joseph and De Milanesi (paper 20) peer group influence and the fear of failure are also important. They suggest that fast turn-around of assignments promotes higher completion rates and a similar effect is caused by pacing (Coldeway, paper 6); by computer-assisted assignment correction (Bååth, paper 118; Young, R. and Phillips, paper 114); by reimbursement of fees to successful students (Ljoså, paper 23); and, in the case of children, by better local tutorial support (Tesarowski, paper 40). In the case of adults the situation is doubtless more complex for Coldeway (paper 6) reports that making tutors try harder had no influence on completion rates.

Many authors stress the importance of contact (Finkel, paper 30), mediation (Sewart, paper 5) and communication (Holmberg, paper 97) and most agree with Gitau (paper 10) and Freeman (paper 57) on the importance of counselling. The optimum forms are less clear. Lewis (paper 46) insists on the need to humanize tutoring and this may partly explain the success of schemes involving peer tutors (Coldeway, paper 6), alumni (Smith,K. and Small, paper 47), or training in communication skills (Cochran and Meech, paper 50). Draper (paper 9) stresses the importance of group work in education for social action but according to Coldeway (paper 6) the effects of including seminars at the university level are unclear. In paper 33 Muller suggests that the differences between individual and group work may not be that great.

In the same paper Coldeway urges distance educators to take more notice of Keller's *Personalized System of Instruction* (PSI). This is one of the very few new methods of teaching that have demonstrated their superiority over traditional methods in conventional institutions.

Comparisons between traditional and distance education are made by a number of authors. Paper 41 points out the advantages of links with established universities. Jevons (paper 42) comments on the differences between students in a two-mode institution and White and Taylor (paper 43) have examined the time-effectiveness of learning at a distance. Lefranc (paper 104) analyzes students' media preferences in the light of traditional methods. Griew (paper 68) and Peters (paper 24) advise distance universities to encourage conventional discipline-based research by their staff if they wish to be credible in the academic community.

One conventional discipline that has taken an interest in distance education is economics and Orivel and Jamison (paper 44) have studied the cost-effectiveness of fourteen different projects in nine countries. There seems little doubt that the economics are favourable but, as the results of a survey by David Young (paper 76) indicate, there is still room to improve the public perception of learning at a distance.

The Adult Learners: Who Are They, Why and Where Do They Learn?

Surveys of potential adult learners indicate that there is an enormous market that could be served by the techniques of distance education.

The impact of demographic, social, and technological change on the educational needs of adults is enormous. Technological development and its impact on employment and careers, the rising educational level of the population, the changing role of women in society, leisure time and longevity, changing lifestyles, the rise of "entitlements" among "old" and "new" minorities, all these create a need for delivering new educational opportunities.

Demography and educational attainment

It is worth detailing some current demographic patterns and changes in the educational level of the adult population. (I will be using data mainly from the province of Ontario.) The post-war baby boom, and recent changes in the birth rate are enlarging the proportion of the population aged 25 to 64. While in 1971 this age group constituted 45% of the total population, in 1981 it grew to 50%, and in 1991 it will reach 55% of the population. It will continue to grow well into the twenty-first century, although at a somewhat lower rate.

The level of education of adults is increasing even faster. In 1981, one-third of the Ontario labour force had at least some post-secondary education, while in 1974, less than one-fourth had achieved this level. As we know, the higher a person's educational attainment, the greater his demand for further learning. This growing demand is well reflected in the enrolments at part-time courses in Ontario universities and colleges. In 1980, there were over 40% more part-time students at universities than in 1972, although the population aged 20 and over had increased by less than 20%. Registrations at part-time courses at community colleges rose between 1974 and 1980 by nearly 70%

Unfortunately there are no recent statistics available about adult learning taking place outside traditional educational institutions. Our studies carried out in 1974-75 indicate that 70% of deliberate adult learning takes place outside this system—at work, through trade unions and professional associations, at community and cultural organizations, interest and sports clubs, etc. (Waniewicz, 1976). Observation and partial data lead us to believe that non-formal learning grows at a rate at least equal to the growth rate at universities and colleges.

Future demand

The demand for education leading to formal degrees may become stronger among adults than among young people. Among the latter, this demand may decrease because of an oversupply of post-secondary school leavers in recent years and a growing suspicion that the rate of return on the investment in a university degree is declining.

The situation with adults is different. First, despite the growth in the participation of adults in post-secondary education, adult students constitute only a small proportion of the total adult population and there is, therefore, plenty of room for further growth. Second, the rising level of education of the population will generate a greater demand for post-secondary degrees. For example, the number of labour force members who have incomplete post-secondary education increased by over 45%: from 268,000 in 1974 to 389,000 in 1981; many of these would certainly be interested in completing their education on a part-time basis. An increased demand for formal learning can be expected from those with some or completed secondary education—their numbers increased from 2,028,000 to 2,314,000. The greatest demand for further education, formal as well as continuing, will come from those with completed post-secondary education; their proportion in the total labour force increased from 17% to 23%, and their numbers increased from 600,000 to 1,025,000. Third, many non-participating adults will be encouraged to study further thanks to the better understanding of their needs by traditional universities and colleges, and thanks to the development of distance learning systems.

Educators in the United States predict "realistically but still optimistically" (Cross, 1981) that by 1985, 5% of the adult population 22 years of age or older could be attracted to undergraduate courses for college credit. If the same prediction were true for Ontario, it would mean that in 1985, when the adult population of the same age will be about 6 million, the number of part-time undergraduate students would reach 300,000 (compared with about 75,000 in 1980-81).

Although this projection may seem more optimistic than realistic, there is reason to believe that there exists a large market of part-time learners on the post-secondary level who could be reached if their needs and interest were met. Studies carried out by us in recent years on the needs and interests of the general public (Waniewicz, 1976; Waniewicz, 1979; Waniewicz and Notar, 1979) indicate a growing demand among adults for learning non-traditional subject matter in non-traditional learning situations. Distance from campus, inability to leave home, lack of time, dislike or fear of formal schedules and exams, fears of failure, etc., one on one hand, and on the other, a lack of courses interesting to adults are among the reasons why a considerable proportion of those who feel a need for learning do not register.

The adult learner: who is he?

Who is the adult learner? Who is he going to be in the next 10 years? Before answering this question, we should note the recent tendency to distinguish adult education from adult learning (Cross, 1978; Ziegler, 1977). Adult *education* is related to instruction offered by educational institutions, industry, community agencies, etc., according to accepted programs. Adult *learning* refers mainly to individually planned learning in any area of interest, undertaken for a practical reason or for pleasure or curiosity. Such learning may or may not include organized classes or other established educational resources and facilities. In some cases the learner, while deliberate in his purpose, may not even consider this activity as an educational venture.

The remainder of this paper will deal with the "conscious" rather than the "spontaneous" learner. This is not because of lack of regard for the latter but because meeting the needs of "conscious" learning requires a carefully planned infrastructure that adapts to changing demand.

The conscious adult learner will most often be found in the 21 to 29 age group and to a lesser degree in the 30 to 39 range. The congestion on career ladders caused by members of the post-war baby-boom who in the eighties will swell the 30-39 age group, will boost the need for learning as a means to moving up the ladder or for changing careers. The learner also tends to be better educated, more successful in his past school experience, more achievement oriented, and therefore usually better off financially than the non-learner. The learner will more often than in the past be female.

The prevalence of learning is the highest among professionals. It is also considerably higher among white-collar than blue-collar workers, skilled labourers than non-skilled, and the employed than the under-employed or unemployed.

One of the major issues facing the providers of adult education is, then, how to reach those who are less ready to make a major effort to adapt themselves to the requirements of current learning opportunities.

Why do adults learn?

A recent survey (Aslanian and Bricknell, 1980) of US adult learners found that 83% identified some past, present, or future change in their lives as reasons to learn. This could mean that only 17% learn for the sake of the learning itself, while for the overwhelming majority learning is utilitarian: people want some reward other than the pleasure derived from learning. Career changes were named by 46% as their reasons for deciding to learn, 13% mentioned family concerns, 11% identified problems related to their leisure patterns. These data are very close to our findings in Ontario where the purpose of learning was job-related for 44% In our study 18% related their learning to personal development (the US study did not use such a variable), and a similar proportion (also 18%) referred to recreation interests.

Where do adults learn?

As we have indicated, institutions whose primary objective is education have only a 30% share of the learning activities of adults. It is worth asking whether this low figure is a reflection of insufficient institutional adaptation to the needs of adults in terms of both educational content and the teaching-learning format.

It is true that in the last 10 to 15 years Canada and the United States made a strong effort to make community colleges and universities more accessible to the adult learner. Their image as places for young people who have just left secondary school and are confined to daytime study on campus is gradually changing. Many programs are now being offered in the evenings and during weekends and at off-campus locations. There is also a considerable increase in the number of non-credit and continuing education activities. Still, the changes are rather modest. The content of many courses, even when offered through non-traditional methods, does not sufficiently take into account the enormous variety of needs and desires of adults. And conversely, some courses with content designed specifically for the adult learner are offered in teaching-learning situations suitable to only some of the would-be-learners.

It is interesting to note that in the numerous North American surveys carried out in the seventies on the demand for adult learning, relatively few people (about 20%) mentioned lack of interest as the reason for not continuing their education. The overwhelming majority of non-participants pointed to several major obstacles to learning. Among those mentioned most often are: lack of time, mobility problems (e.g., distance from campus, inability to leave home), costs, and institutional barriers (e.g., the time requirements of programs, attendance requirements, scheduling, various prerequisites, lack of appropriate courses).

One should note, however, a number of new, bold initiatives that may significantly improve the access to adult learning. In Ontario, the University of Waterloo offers a B.A. degree at a distance, providing a sizeable choice of courses that permits majoring in a variety of fields of study. The Télé-université of the University of Quebec, Athabasca University in Alberta, the Knowledge Network and the Open Learning Institute in British Columbia, and the Ryerson Open College in Toronto, specialize in distance education using different combinations of learning media including print, television and radio broadcasting, TV cable, communication satellite, video tape, audio tape, telephone, and face-to-face meetings. The Ontario Educational Communications Authority introduced a new concept in adult non-formal learning, the TVOntario Academy, which combines high-quality television programming, a computer-managed learning system, and specially designed print materials allowing adults to undertake self-directed learning projects. In addition, a number of Canadian universities and colleges offer telecourses in some subjects, usually over cable channels.

Similar important initiatives have been undertaken in the United States on a national scale. The University of Mid-America and its plans to establish an American University, The National University Consortium for Telecommunications in Teaching, the Adult Learning Programming of the Public Broadcasting Service (known as PTV-3), the Annenberg education telecommunications project, are probably the most important, but by no means the only major undertakings.

The main feature of most of these initiatives is a reliance on mass media—broadcasting or cablecasting. The major advantage of mass media is that they can reach vast audiences in the most distant areas (particularly where telecommunication satellites are already available). Reaching individuals at home removes a major obstacle to adult learning—mobility problems.

Summing up

Educators and politicians are gradually becoming aware that individuals in today's world have to engage in continuous learning to be able to cope with life and derive greater satisfaction from it. Lifelong adult education becomes as essential as the education of children and young people. There are, however, a number of characteristics of adult learning that make it immeasurably more complex. The delivery of learning opportunities has to take into account the immense variety of needs, goals, and interests, as well as the immense variety of situations in which adults live. The education of adults at a distance is probably capable of meeting most of these needs and situations, but it is still in its early stages.

Ignacy Waniewicz
TVOntario
Canada

References

Aslanian, Carol B. and Bricknell, Henry M. (1980) *Americans in Transition: Life Changes as Reasons for Adult Learning*. New York: College Entrance Examination Board.

Cross, K. Patricia (1978) *The Missing Link: Connecting Adult Learners to Learning Resources*. New York: College Entrance Examination Board.

Cross, K. Patricia (1981) *Adults as Learners*. San Francisco: Jossey-Bass Publishers.

Waniewicz, I and Notar, T. (1979) A Planning Framework for the Development of OECA Programs in Support of Non-Formal Learning of Adults Through Libraries and YM-YWCAs. Toronto: Office of Planning and Development, The Ontario Educational Communications Authority. (mimeo)

Waniewicz, I. (1976) *Demand for Part-Time Learning in Ontario*. Toronto: Ontario Institute for Studies in Education, for the Ontario Educational Communications Authority.

Waniewicz, I. (1979) Development of Television Series in Support of Distance Learning Courses to be Offered by Some Ontario Universities and Colleges: Progress Report. Toronto: Office of Planning and Development, The Ontario Educational Communications Authority. (mimeo)

Zeigler, Warren L. (1977) *The Future of Adult Education and Learning in the United States*. New York: Educational Policy Research Centre, Syracuse Research Corporation.

Paper 29

What Does Educational Psychology Tell Us About the Adult Learner at a Distance?

Distance education could accept a new order of challenge and increase its impact by using adult learning theory, Instructional Systems Design, and knowledge about individual differences.

Introduction

The definition of educational psychology is itself a problem. More than one writer has claimed that it is not a unified discipline. The difficulty is compounded by the phrase "the adult learner at a distance", which can mean anything from the design of institutions dedicated to distance learning to the specific treatment of adult learners. This paper will assume that any factor influencing the adult learner at a distance, either directly or indirectly, is relevant.

It has been argued that educational psychology has produced little of use in the design of distance learning environments. Looking at educational psychology as a field, this paper will identify the issues and factors that create such an impression. However, particular approaches within educational psychology do have relevance to distance learning and will be described. We will also attempt to describe the commonalities between approaches so as to identify the generic variables that relate to the teaching-learning process and to some of the problems facing distance learning institutions and learners.

The contribution of educational psychology

At a philosophical level educational psychology should remind us that educational goals must ultimately be human in nature and direction. Institutions can get caught up with institutional goals to the detriment of human goals. Getting courses in place, faculty hired (or fired), programs completed, mandates clarified, funding secured, etc., are all necessary for institutional planning but are not sufficient for human learning.

Any dichotomy between educational psychology and the goals of institutions is, however, only partially valid. Much of educational psychology appears of limited value to a clearer understanding of human learning and a large amount of its research literature is also irrelevant. Educational psychologists seem to have a knack for the conceptualization of either trivial or meaningless research. Investigations that assume things like the lecture and type of computer are independent variables and classifications like "adult" are operationally useful reflect this problem. In most research only the superficial aspects of learning situations are identified as important and, once a phenomenon is named on the basis of some trivial aspect, there is a frantic search to justify that distinct title. Factors like the age of the learner, the type of delivery method, the style of print used on the page, are examples of trivial variables that emerge from any examination of educational psychology.

Educational psychology also shares an identity crisis common in social science. It continually strives to be like the more prestigious basic sciences and as a result has produced neither a science of its own, nor procedural guidelines for the large-scale improvement of educational practice. There is a strong propensity for large-scale statistical studies, which have reinforced educational psychologists' self-image of non-individuality and a type of "ex-post-facto" mentality. In a feeble attempt to be "scientific" educational psychologists fail to be prescriptive and manipulative (the strengths of professions like engineering and medicine that face similar practical problems).

Educational psychology has become entrenched in trying to explain phenomenon rather than in creating paradigms using existing data. This encourages hypothetical descriptions of events, many of which are neither operationally defined nor empirically grounded. The recent interest in cognitive models of learning processes reflects this tendency. Although elaborate models purporting to explain learning processes usually generate wide discussion it would take a quantum leap to make them directly relevant to the adult learner at a distance.

In summary, much of traditional educational psychology contributes little to the improvement of individual human learning and to the design of learning environments. Unfortunately, those approaches within educational psychology that do have relevance to individual learning often experience difficulty when they compete with institutional goals.

Contributions from areas within educational psychology that apply to the adult learner at a distance

More recent developments give grounds for hope. These developments are:

    a. adult learning and development

    b. Instructional Systems Design (ISD)

    c. theories of individual differences (often called aptitude x treatment interaction research).

We shall describe each development and attempt to identify the similarities between them.

Adult learning and development

Educational psychologists have always been interested in the stages of human development and have recently extended this interest beyond the formative years to include the later adult years. Since the majority of distance learners are adults this development will undoubtedly improve the understanding of the adult learner at a distance.

Two general philosophical tenets characterizing this field are important to distance learning.

A. Contrary to earlier views that adults' learning capability decreases with age (Thorndike, 1928), more recent evidence suggests that adults of any age are as capable of learning as younger members of society (Sjogren and Knox, 1965).

B. Instructional methods typically used for children and adolescents may not necessarily be effective for adults (Knowles, 1970).

These tenets have a direct bearing on the design of distance learning environments. Many distance education institutions appear to assume that their clientele is capable of learning and that learning should not be restricted by age or some other measure of maturity. In contrast, it is not clear that these institutions have internalized the second position.

Many practices in distance learning appear highly similar to those in traditional forms of education. Concepts like self-directed learning (Knowles, 1975), and life-long learning (Knox, 1978) are not found consistently in distance learning institutions. Although the instructional strategy and methods outlined by many adult learning theories have a firm theoretical and empirical base and appear logical they are often not well implemented.

It is not clear whether the lack of interest in the development of self-directed learners, as one example of an adult learning concept, is due to misunderstanding of the concept or to the pressures on institutions to get courses up rather than promote individual student development.

An important adult learning concept that is widely misunderstood is Knowles' distinction between pedagogy and andragogy (Knowles, 1970). Pedagogy assumes that the learner has a dependent personality, but in andragogy the learner is assumed to be seeking increasing amounts of self-direction. Pedagogy stresses content; andragogy tasks. In the pedagogical model the teacher determines curriculum, teaching methods, and evaluation whereas the andragogical model stresses the importance of the teacher as an agent in helping the learner participate in educational alternatives and make maximum use of all the elements available for teaching and learning.

The processes and procedures that Knowles identifies with andragogy are in fact very similar to those deemed important by instructional designers as effective instructional techniques. Furthermore, these ideas are not particularly new nor are they restricted to adult learners. Years ago, John Dewey called for the development of educational environments that involved children in real world tasks and problems that would capitalize upon the natural curiosity of the learner.

The vast majority of distance learning institutions have, however, never attempted to engage in any type of interaction with learners that could be classified as andragogical. At a theoretical level, there is little excuse for not conducting a systematic test of andragogy. The evidence and logic of the approach demands that it be considered by distance educators. Of course, much of the content of distance learning is taken from traditional campuses and distance learning institutions have never intended to be different from traditional institutions except by doing it "at a distance". The pedagogical models that are at the heart of traditional institutions therefore have a great influence on distance learning institutions.

There is also a problem with the learners. Very few people have had sufficient experience of andragogy to adapt readily to a totally andragogical system. Almost everyone has grown up in a pedagogical system and overcoming this long term indoctrination into pedagogy would require much attention.

Instructional Systems Design

Instructional Systems Design (ISD) is an approach that could assist in the development of all aspects of the distance learning environment. ISD is actually a hybrid made up of concepts in learning theory, systems engineering, instructional technology, and organizational development. It is a systematic attempt to organize procedures and methods of demonstrated effectiveness in the educational context.

Instructional Systems Design rests on several important assumptions:

1. Individual students may differ in:

    a. previous experience

    b. learning style

    c. learning rate

    d. motivation and attention time.

2. The educational system should accept responsibility for overcoming difficulties arising from these differences.

3. Educational methods do not all have the same potential for all objectives and all students.

4. Exposing students to a wide range of subjects, ideas, attitudes, etc., is not a substitute for the identification of relevant content and related skills and competencies.

5. Early hands-on experience and practice on difficult competencies can increase motivation and prevent over-emphasis of low-level objectives.

Instructional systems design models can be produced to apply to almost any educational context. Most begin with an attempt to identify the educational problem at hand and end with the measurement and confirmation that learning has occurred. The steps within the model simply help organize the approach to the general problem of learning and motivation. ISD models are usually cybernetic in orientation (Pratt, 1978), which means they attempt to feed back on themselves and make adjustments as necessary until important objectives and goals are met. Such models are also a direct attempt to increase efficiency and effectiveness in the production of learning materials, in learning systems, and in learner management. This orientation has made ISD an invaluable tool for the business and training world where long training time and poor performance represent losses in dollars and productivity.

ISD and adult learning share many characteristics. One is an interest in the individualization of instruction. Early versions of programmed instruction were attempts to maximize individual success by a design that would accommodate the individual learner. Self-pacing is necessary to effective instruction since learning rate varies widely. It is incorporated in many contemporary approaches to learning including Bloom's mastery learning (Bloom, 1971), Postlethwait's audiotutorial instruction (Postlethwait, et al., 1972), and Keller's Personalized System of Instruction (Keller, 1968). Modern computer technologies offer wide potential for individualized instruction.

With the exception of more recent cognitive models of learning, applied behaviour analysis has been an important basis of ISD. An understanding of basic operant conditioning methods is essential for the design of effective instructional systems. Contingencies of reinforcement are important for adult learners who are volunteer participants in the learning environment. Learner motivation is important in adult learning theory and relates directly to one of the most pressing issues in distance learning: the dropout problem. Unfortunately, many persons espousing ISD have lost track of the importance of motivational concepts. The adult learning literature reminds us of the importance of learner motivation and discusses possible contingencies of reinforcement with methods for integrating them into the design of instruction.

Although the relationship between ISD and adult learning is surprisingly close it has received very little attention in the educational literature and even less in institutions looking for effective instructional methods.

A concern for individual differences

Although our society has adapted extremely well to individual human differences (e.g., most retail businesses supply products to meet the various tastes and preferences of customers), education has progressed rather slowly in this area. Learners are generally treated in roughly the same manner with flexibility afforded mainly through the selection of different courses and programs. A general concern that students may require different instructional treatment has not emerged.

Individual differences have received considerable theoretical attention in educational psychology (Cronbach and Snow, 1977). Recent research has indicated that student aptitude may interact significantly with instructional treatments (i.e., a particular type of student may perform better if presented with a particular type of instructional treatment).

The idea that individual students may require differing treatment has relevance to distance learning for several reasons. First, most distance learning institutions are already flexible in the way they offer courses. The recognition that not all students can attend classes on campus acknowledges the differing requirements of individual adults. Recognizing that students may also require varying instructional treatments would seem to be well within the capabilities of distance learning institutions.

Second, the extreme diversity within the learning population of distance learning institutions calls for differential treatment on a variety of levels. Attempts to individualize courses, provide varying degrees of tutorial support to individual students within courses, present instructional materials using a variety of methods and media, etc., may be viewed as attempts to cope with the large differences that exist between learners even within the same course. The search for effective differential treatment procedures, with an attempt to determine the types of students they are effective for, must continue.

Finally, there appears to be an important relationship between theories of adult learning, ISD models, and individual differences. Moreover, the major concepts in all three areas relate closely to the problems facing distance learning institutions. All three emphasize individual learning and development. All appear to assume that while learning is largely up to the individual and is a function of his participation, it can be facilitated by proper understanding of the learner and of the instructional tools available. Knowles' (1975) attempt to specify self-directed learning as an approach best suited to the adult learning population is a specific recognition of the importance of individual differences. Furthermore, the techniques of self-directed learning start from a model similar to the cybernetic models typical of Instructional Systems Design.

Individual differences, although represented in the educational psychology literature as a specific sub-discipline, are at the heart of both adult learning and ISD and may be the key to understanding the adult distance learner.

Practical considerations

Educators and administrators often claim that although the ideas we have presented may have relevance there is no practical way to make them work. In fact, a quick review of the literature describing the use of recommended methods in adult learning and ISD suggests that:

- almost every major method and technique espoused by adult educators and ISD specialists is accompanied by written guidelines for implementation and management.

- an effective management and administrative system must be designed to fit the methods. For example, it is naive to assume that management and administrative systems for pedagogical systems will work for andragogical systems.

- assuming that new instructional methods must accommodate to traditional management and administrative habits is a direct attempt to impede the improvement of outdated systems. Moreover, it violates the very nature of contemporary management theory that recommends management systems be designed to make other systems and procedures function with maximal effectiveness and efficiency.

- the problem of acceptance of concepts like andragogy and ISD may be based on the reluctance of traditional educators (especially teachers) to change roles. Since almost all methods espoused by adult learning theorists and ISD specialists put teachers in a different role, they may be rejected on personal grounds.

Excuses for ignoring adult learning and ISD theory given by distance learning institutions are just that, excuses. Anyone who isn't particularly interested in reaching every learner and feels that some people should not, or for some genetic reason cannot, learn will have difficulty embracing adult learning theory and ISD models that take such human capabilities for granted. Anyone who feels that learning has to be acquired under the threat of punishment, to be obtained from unclear ideas presented in unclear forms, and to be measured in relationship to the performance of others, will not gravitate toward adult learning theory and ISD for assistance.

Values play an important role in acceptance, much as they did when concepts like programmed instruction were being challenged because of concerns about dehumanization. Then as now these attacks were attempts to defend the role of the teacher rather than being reasoned concerns about the human component in the teaching-learning process.

The very nature of distance learning institutions gives them an opportunity to accept the useful concepts in adult learning and ISD and the importance of individual differences without dramatically increasing stress. Distance learning institutions have accepted the challenge to deliver instruction in a unique way and so have already confronted entrenched traditional values and practices. It is time distance learning accepted a second level of challenge by defending the right of every individual to learn. In facing the challenge it should examine carefully the contribution that educational psychology can make. It is too early to assume that the contribution from fields within educational psychology will be limited. The goal is not to discover when happens when a new method is tried, but to make learning happen using the best methods available.

Dan O. Coldeway
Athabasca University
Canada

References

Bloom, B. (1971) Mastery learning. In Block, J.H. (ed.) *Mastery Learning, Theory & Practice*. New York: Holt, Rinehart & Winston.

Cronbach, L. and R. Snow. (1977) *Aptitudes and Instructional Methods*. New York: Irvington Publishers.

Keller, F. (1968) Goodbye Teacher. *Journal of Applied Behaviour Analysis*, 1, 78-89.

Knowles, M.S. (1970) *The Modern Practice of Adult Education: Andragogy Versus Pedagogy*. New York: Association Press.

Knowles, M.S. (1975) *Self-Directed Learning*. New York: Association Press.

Knox, A.B. (1978) *Adult Development and Learning*. San Francisco: Jossey-Bass.

Postlethwait, S.N. Novak, J. and Murray, H.T. (1972) *The Audio-Tutorial Approach to Learning*. Minneapolis, Minn.: Burgess Publishing Co.

Pratt, D. (1978) *Cybernetic Principles in the Design of Instruction*. Paper presented at the Annual Meeting of AERA, Toronto, Canada, 1978.

Sjogren, B.D and Knox, A.B. (1965) *The Influence of Speed, Attitude and Prior Knowledge on Adult Learning*. Lincoln, Nebraska: Adult Education Research.

Thorndike, Edward L. et al (1928) *Adult Learning*. New York: Macmillan.

Paper 30

Designing Interesting Courses

Treating content imaginatively and phoning students often can increase completion rates dramatically.

Distance learning institutions face a serious challenge when they attempt to achieve course completion rates comparable to those achieved in conventional universities. Most students learning at a distance have far less time than full-time students and many lack the careerist motivations of younger students. Also, when written materials form the bulk of a course package, distance students whose reading comprehension skills are low find themselves at a disadvantage compared to poor readers in a conventional university who get by as a result of attending lectures that cover the major points in the reading.

For all of the above reasons Athabasca University has found that it is more difficult to register course completions than course enrolments. Only one in four Athabasca enrolments results in completion, even discounting students who return their material within one month (although not omitting students who may never begin the course but who fail to return their materials within one month).

Nevertheless, there is a wide variation in course completion rates. One math course had a completion rate of only 2%; popular introductory courses such as accounting, computing, and administrative principles, hover around the 10% mark while an equally popular introductory psychology course has a completion rate of about 35%

Only two areas at Athabasca University have developed several courses with completion rates consistently above 50 per cent: French and history. As the principal author of three Canadian history courses, I would like to offer some reasons why I believe we have succeeded where others have failed.

First, it might be noted that so far, most of the more than 300 students who have taken the Canadian history courses have fewer career reasons for completing their course than do many of the students in the low-completion courses. The history courses also require more reading than any of the low-completion courses in adminstration and social sciences.

Finally, all the assignments and exams in the history courses require the writing of essays, a dreaded ritual that produces course drop-outs even in conventional universities. Why then, with so many odds stacked against them, do these history courses produce more than double the completions of other Athabasca University courses?

One word describes what the history courses contain that many courses lack: imagination. These courses contain materials that are interesting, controversial, and provocative rather than dull, unconnected "facts" that students are expected to digest and regurgitate, or formulae that students are expected to digest and mechanically apply.

Now, this may not sound like an enlightening explanation of why the history courses are successful. As one instructional designer said: "You can't *measure* how interesting materials are" and, as the head of the instructional design unit once commented, in a different context, "What you can't measure doesn't exist." So much of what follows may be of little interest to those who believe that the first step towards solving a problem is to gather quantifiable data, the scientific analysis of which will yield clues leading to a solution of the problem.

It may also appear, even to those who do not believe in a strictly quantitative approach to knowledge, that it is unlikely that only three or four courses among about 60 offered by a university are likely to be interesting. Admitting to a great deal of subjectivity here, my rough guesses about likely completion rates of "AU" courses that I scanned before any completion rates had been published were all correct within five percentage points. My major criterion when I evaluated these courses for likely completion rates was: "If I started this course, and didn't have to finish it for a reason related to career advancement, would I stick it out to the end?"

I might note that a large percentage of the conventional university courses that I had the misfortune to take were also boring. But, like most of my fellow students, almost all of whom were in the 18 to 24 age category, I stuck them through to receive my grades.

Adult students at Athabasca University are too often confronted by courses that outline trivial objectives, such as "to define the following sociological terms", "to list the categories which anthropologists use to describe societies", and "to draw graphs illustrating 32 economic principles". While these courses generally provide endless examples so that even the dullest student who actually completes does indeed "master" the materials, many students no doubt simply yawn themselves out of the course.

Of course, many of these students will politely tell their tutor that they are dropping out because of lack of time. Indeed, who has time to memorize trivia in order to achieve low-level objectives set by instructional designers whose theories of learning are best applied to mice?

To be fair, some of our expensive failures have been produced by teams of academics that kept instructional designers at bay. These courses, while they often contain some interesting ideas, suffer from the opposite problem that the "i-d" courses suffer: they lack any logical development. It is simply assumed that a "serious" student (our academics tend to write off the 74% of students who drop out as being "not serious") is one who has the brain of Einstein and the patience of Job and will first dig up all the necessary background materials that the course fails to provide and then synthesize the unconnected course materials on his own. Unfortunately, many academics wish mainly to impress their colleagues. If the instructional designers are writing for rats, the academics are writing for their colleagues.

In the history courses, an attempt was made to write for the adult student who wished to obtain a general background in Canadian history for interest's sake. While not ignoring the usual materials covered in survey courses in Canadian history, the usual concentration on endless numbers of personalities, events and dates that mark too much of the teaching of history from grade school up was abandoned.

Instead, a set of major issues that characterized the period under study was identified and conflicting approaches to the issue were examined. So, for example, in dealing with the early history of New France, the course materials did not trace the routes of the various "discoverers" of America, list the Jesuits killed by the Indians, or examine the waves of migration to determine from what areas of France the people came. Ignoring these concerns, all of which have bored students of Canadian history from elementary school to graduate studies, we raised two questions: "What were the aims of the Europeans who came to North America and of the native groups who agreed to have economic dealings with them?" and "What impact did each of these groups have upon the other?"

In studying the later history of New France, the course materials do not rhyme off all the bishops, governors, and intendants, indicating the achievements and failures of each. Instead, the social and economic life of the colony was examined, with this question in mind: "What type of society would have developed here had a conquest not occurred in 1760?"

In short, the course authors rejected the type of history that creates a mythology of larger-than-life nation builders, all of whom may best be thought of as long dead and of interest only to statue-builders. Instead, questions about the past that were also of interest in the present were raised: the conditions of native people, and the striving for collective assertion of the Québecois.

Some academic historians reject such an approach on the grounds that it risks the possibility of being overly "present-minded" in one's discussion of the past. But, on pedagogical grounds alone, it seems obvious that the alternative to a "present-minded" approach is to focus on historical trivia and historical problems of interest to a tiny group. Interest in the roots of present-day problems is widespread and the success of Alex Haley's *Roots* both as a book and a television series provides but one example of this interest.

Some would argue, nevertheless, that the scope for imagination that is available in a history course is not available in other disciplines. In an Economics course principles may be laboriously defined and a variety of examples provided followed by problems that require a mechanical copying of the examples with feedback available for those unable to figure out the answer. But students must quickly tire of so many economic principles and graphs. What does it all mean? What does it explain?

A better approach would be to begin with the economic facts that most people know: inflation, unemployment, poverty, wealth, etc., and to raise the ideological or social-value issues that underlie various approaches to economic problems. Students are more likely to get interested in learning economic notions if they realize that there are various approaches both to macroeconomic and microeconomic problems. They can get more involved with the information they are given if they believe they are expected to analyze approaches and reach their own conclusions rather than simply to regurgitate or mechanically apply some textbook author's views.

A similar approach to most courses in social science, humanities, and administration may be used. I would also argue that it applies to the physical sciences.

It is not difficult to combine information that is academically sound and information that is relevant to students. It requires "street smarts" rather than formal degrees, whether in an academic area or in instructional design.

Part of the trick in publishing a course that intrigues the reader without sacrificing academic quality is finding a good editor. Many published academics, unlike authors writing for a general audience, are unaware of the major role played by professional writers in producing popular literature. A good editor is able to pick up the logical inconsistencies, the problems of sequencing, the gaps and the lack of background information in a manuscript, whether in a course or in a book. Because courses tend to deal with far more ideas than any one book and often integrate material from a variety of texts as well as audio and/or visual materials, the role of the editor is even more intricate in a course team than in a publishing house.

While Athabasca University has had a number of good editors, the academics have usually been unwilling to let them alter their mangled prose. Similarly, the "i.d.'s", who wish "to impact behaviour by engaging in criteria definition for learners", while recognizing that editors can translate the gobbledygook they write into English, have been reticent about letting them go beyond copy editing.

The development of the history courses, then, largely involved an author and an editor whose purposes were to determine what issues might best cause students to regard history as alive and exciting and to present these issues in as clear a language as possible. The instructional designer for the history courses largely limited himself to determining whether the indicated objectives of the various units of the course appeared to have been fulfilled. Both the instructional designer and historians external to the university joined the editor in reading the materials for logical problems, historical errors, etc. Each unit of the first two courses went through four drafts (because of experience, it is now done in three drafts) with the second and third drafts representing major modifications of the author's first draft and the final draft being largely a copy edit of the third.

So much for course development. But is a well developed course enough? What role does "delivery strategy" play? The delivery of the history courses diverges in only one significant aspect from most Athabasca University courses: most student-tutor phone contacts are initiated by the tutor. A cross-course survey indicated that 80% of tutor-student phone calls are initiated by students; in the history courses 80% of calls are made by the tutor.

Interestingly, much time has been spent over the past several years by course developers in determining appropriate places to indicate in the Student Guide that the student should call the tutor. This feature has been incorporated into the design for the third Canadian history course.

On the whole, there is no substitute for the tutor-initiated call. Little instruction is provided for the history tutors about what to say; indeed, people who appear sympathetic to the plight of a distance student have been hired as opposed to people whose academic qualifications are superior (in some cases, happily, they are the same people, but this is not always the case).

The only signal given the tutors is that they are expected to be able to tell the coordinator, at any time, how far a particular student has advanced in the course and what problems various students are finding. Some tutors do not attempt to force a discussion of the subject matter if a student says he or she is having no problems; others do begin such a discussion. But the completion rate has varied little between tutors. What has characterized the work of all tutors is that they call their students at least once every two weeks. Student evaluations of the course indicate both the large number of tutor-student contacts and the high level of student satisfaction with this contact.

Unfortunately, the overall statistics for the university indicate that most students are lucky to have any contact, telephone or otherwise, with a tutor more than once a month. Nevertheless, most tutors are conscientious and will spend hours working over a problem or discussing an essay with a student who calls them. The problem appears to be that tutors who report to coordinators with elitist attitudes (the notion of the serious versus the non-serious student) seem to believe that their main job is to act as an academic advisor to good students rather than as a motivator to students who lack self-confidence. In the history courses the two roles have been combined with positive effects on the completion rates.

My own experience as a tutor for a Renaissance course purchased from the Open University and adapted suggests the importance of tutor-initiated contact. When I took the course over, its completion rate over a two-year period was 11% The year I tutored the course, enrolments were equal to those of the two previous years combined, but the completion rate shot up to 38% My tutoring strategy was simple: I called every student every week. I found that many students had difficulty determining what central threads held the course together and was I able, through telephone mini-lectures, to make up for deficiencies in the course package. The drop-out rate nevertheless remained unacceptably high from my point of view, indicating that tutoring alone, while it could dramatically improve completion rates, was not a substitute for a coherent, interesting course. (The Renaissance course, in fairness, is not boring, but it is less coherent than a course studied at a distance, and perhaps a course studied by any method, ought to be.)

I do not wish to exaggerate the success of the history courses. About 60% of the students complete, a rate probably 20-25% lower that in history courses in conventional universities. While certain problems in servicing students contribute to the drop-out rate, I might point to some planned changes that I expect might raise our completion rates even higher: an audio component for the courses, as requested by students (at present the courses are entirely correspondence); more seminars; and a reduction in credit assignments to equal the number expected in conventional university courses (one of our courses requires double the work normally required). The history course team believes that is possible and desirable that distance universities achieve completion rates comparable to those in conventional universities to demonstrate that students need not balance the convenience of learning in their own home against the likelihood of failure if they choose this mode of study.

Alvin Finkel
Athabasca University
Canada

Orientations to Studies, Approaches to Texts: A Relational View of Study Skills Applied to Distance Learning

The content of learning should be the starting point in any analysis of study skills.

The term *study skills* is related to ways of learning and the meaning of learning for the student is related to how he sets about it. There are qualitatively different ways in which learning can be conceptualized and/or experienced. Two such are learning as the acquisition of pieces of knowledge and learning as a change in one's way of conceptualizing a certain aspect of reality. Our own conception of learning corresponds to the second.

A relational view of study skill

In distance learning the student is on his own in dealing with the study task. It is very difficult to give any substantial meaning to study skill generally as we are dealing with a phenomenon dependent both on the task and the individual. We shall focus on two main aspects of study skill; approaches to texts and orientations to studies.

The term *study skill* usually relates to study guides and courses intended to improve the student's study activities. This advice and training is based on systematisation of the treatment of the learning material and the use of memory aids. There have also been attempts to make students aware of their own study activity as a basis for adaptation and change. In the plural form *study skills* refer to a set of activities such as systematic note-taking, use of the surface structure of a text, underlining, making summaries and the use of memory aids like abbreviations, reorganization to aid association, repetition and so on. There is emphasis on the need to concentrate and to study for a purpose. The meaning given to study skills suggests that all these activities are important and each is a skill that will promote learning.

This conflicts with the relational view favoured here. If study skill is dependent both on the task and the individual then one cannot expect the same set of skills to be generally relevant. The skills referred to are described as forms of activities and not in terms of the content treated. Such skills cannot be appropriate irrespective of the content but have to be developed in terms of the purpose and treatment of the content.

Forms of activity like note-taking or relying on the surface structure of a text, using abbreviations and/or vivid associations as memory aids may be either functional or dysfunctional depending on the purpose and the content of the learning. According to the relational view, study skill must concern primarily the approach to the content and the way it is thought about during learning. Activities in the sense described above have an indirect relation to the learning outcome through their impact on the approach to the content. (More extensive presentations of this relational conception of study skill are given by Svensson, 1976, 1977, and 1981.)

The term *skill* refers to the quality of the performance of a task. The learning outcome is crucial to the meaning of study skill. The conception and valuation of different outcomes may vary and with it the meaning of study skill. The conception of learning as a change in quality was mentioned in the introduction as fundamental to the present description of study skill. There are many aspects of this approach to studies of learning which differ from those which are usually a part of a more quantitative approach to the study of learning (cf Marton and Svensson, 1979).

The most common approach to describing the outcome is by labelling it right or wrong. However, this restricted approach does not consider the choice of criteria and the differences in criteria among researchers, teachers and students. Even the fulfillment of the same formal criterion may mean differences in performance of great importance from the point of view of generalization. A more fruitful approach is to describe important qualitative differences in outcome as the basis for study skill.

Qualitative differences in the outcome of learning

A description of study skills should start from the "what" of learning in order to characterize how learning has taken place. Process and outcome belong together and constitute an internal relationship. There are apparent qualitative differences in outcome of learning some of which are more fundamental to the content treated and to a cumulative development of knowledge. We shall specify the qualities and qualitative differences which prove the most fundamental and interesting criteria for describing study skill.

We stated our own idea of learning as a change in one's conception of a certain aspect of reality. A description on this level is necessarily content-specific and has to be phrased in terms of from which conception of aspect X to which other conception of the same aspect X. Lybeck (1981) has, for instance, given a detailed description of how students' thinking about the question "Why do objects sink in water?" changes from

1. "Because they are heavy"
2. "Because they are heavier than water"
3. "Because the quotient between their mass and volume is greater than it is for water."

Since the term *skill* refers to a capability to do something, the skill related to a certain conception of a certain content of learning is the capability to conceptualize that particular content in that particular way.

The three qualitatively different ways of conceptualizing why objects sink in water, discerned by Lybeck, can be described in a less content-specific way as:

1. Absolutist (reasons are given in terms of an inherent quality of a body)
2. Comparative (reasons are given in terms of a relation between the same quality in two bodies)
3. Quantitative (reasons are given in terms of a relation between relations between two different qualities in each of two bodies, expressed in quantitative terms).

These categories can obviously be applied to a far wider range of phenomena. Being structural in character they are to some extent neutral as to content.

Another example is taken from a learning experiment reported by Säljö (1975). The content concerned what is meant by the output of an educational system. In the experiment, 39 students read parts of P.H. Coombs *The World Educational Crisis: A Systems Analysis*. In one chapter the topic is specifically treated and the aim clearly is to promote a particular conception of this phenomenon. The author sees output as a very abstract concept denoting many different qualities which have effects on the individual and on society (Coombs, 1968: 64). The illustration sought here concerns qualitative differences in the conception of this content. Such differences were revealed as answers to the question "What is meant by the output of an educational system?" The answers were found to represent four qualitatively different concepts:

A. the effects of education on society and on individuals through the knowledge, attitudes, etc. which are acquired through schooling
B. those who leave the educational system with or without an examination
C. those who leave the educational system with a completed (in some sense) education
D. what comes out of the educational system.

Only eight of the students expressed the first conception and four the second (which means that they consider the whole impact on all students). Most of the students, twenty-one, expressed the third conception which is actually the opposite of that argued by the author. The fourth conception expressed does not reveal any meaning beyond the abstract general definition of outcome.

The qualitative differences in learning outcome revealed in these two examples may be described generally as a difference in the differentiating and relating of parts of the content treated. In the first example there is a change in the character of the relation between object and water also implying a change in the differentiation of the two parts of the relation. In the first conception the relation is made dependent only upon a quality of the object, in the second upon the relation in the same quality between object and water and in the third conception this relation between object and water is made dependent upon a differentiation and relation within each part of the relation, the object and the water. In the second example the first conception means a differentiation and relation between the immediate outcome of schooling and the subsequent effects of this outcome. The other conceptions do not include this differentiation and relation. The second and third conceptions differ in that they represent different differentiations of the outcome in relation to the system (including all the students or just some of them). The fourth conception represents a lack of specification and differentiation.

Structure

The handling of structural difficulties in learning materials is an important component of the art of studying. One such difficulty is linked with texts based on the principle-example structure. Marton and Wenestam (1979) have used texts in which the main point is a certain principle (such as scientific hypotheses are tested by means of comparing two conditions, on the average equal in all respects but the one which the hypothesis to be tested concerns) illustrated by a single rather comprehensive example (such as Semmelweis' search for the cause of child-bed fever in mid-nineteenth century Vienna). The example is subordinate to the principle it is intended to illuminate. In reality this hierarchical structure is missed by a substantial number of students whose reading of the text lacks the dimension of depth. Instead of understanding it as a main point (a principle) illustrated by one (or several) example(s) they conceive of it as a number of apparently unrelated parts on the same level. In the above example, they think the text is about both the testing of scientific hypotheses and the search for the cause of child-bed fever, without seeing the reason for juxtaposing the two topics. This levelling out of the hierarchical structure of the text has been called horizontalization. In some instances the main point vanishes altogether.

Using horizontalization as a point of departure Brew and Batten (1980) studied how students handle structural difficulties in text materials and television programmes at the Open University. They found that many students have great difficulty in distinguishing between:

a. a theory and that which it is a theory of (e.g. social events and sociological theory) and

b. the main points in a text and the supporting evidence.

Brew and Batten point out that although such capabilities are obviously presupposed by the writers of the course material they are never explicitly addressed.

Svensson (1976 and 1977) found that the main difference between students reading about a proposed reform of an educational system was whether they identified and used the argumentative structure of the texts. The difference between organising the content as arguments and conclusion in relation to each other and treating them as separate units was also indicative of the students' success in their studies in education generally.

Approaches to texts

Differences in study activity closely related to qualitative differences in outcome are differences in organising or structuring activity. An important distinction is between organization of the content into key parts related into a structured whole and an aggregation of particular bits of content. We have called the organising, structuring approach holistic to differentiate it from the other, atomistic approach. The atomistic approach is inferior only in relation to a possible and desired holistic approach.

Another important aspect of thinking during reading and learning is relating the new content to other knowledge. This is the basis for critical assessment of what is understood. Integration and critical thinking are commonly seen as important aims of education. The quality of relating depends on the quality of understanding and may be either atomistic, holistic or both.

In trying to understand the functions behind the differences in approach to content some knowledge of the more general attitude to the learning task is required. This may be described as the overall intention in reading. It cannot be directly inferred from the outcome but has to be revealed by the learner although we may expect a close relation to the outcome. Marton (1975), and Marton and Säljö (1976a) make a distinction between deep and surface approach. In relation to the data used there was an almost perfect correlation between the holistic and deep approaches and the atomistic and surface approaches.

The distinction between deep and surface approach is whether the text is seen as a set of linguistic units to be understood and remembered or as something to go beyond in order to get to know what it is about. The meaning of deep approach and surface is the same from case to case while the meaning of holistic and atomistic is relative to the content in each case. A deep approach is a necessary condition for a holistic approach but not a guarantee, while a surface approach guarantees an atomistic approach. From the point of view of promoting holistic understanding of the content the distinction between deep and holistic approaches is important. Lack of holistic understanding may be due to a surface (and atomistic) approach or to a deep and atomistic approach. These two cases represents quite different pedagogical problems.

A similar distinction is made by Brew and McCormick (1979); they point out that some students view the material presented in lectures

> ..as a framework or skeleton of main ideas on which... (they have) ...to build their own thinking, further reading and experimental work: in terms of the subject as a whole, the lecture (represents) the tip of the iceberg.

while others consider it

> ...as comprising the subject matter to be learnt for examination purposes in its entirety (i.e. the lecture (is) the whole iceberg).

The two different levels of approach present, like the different levels of description of the outcome, an increasing generality. The descriptions on higher levels are less content-specific so the stress shifts from content to form and from outcome to process. Thus the skill, as well as the outcome, may be described on different levels of generality.

Orientations to studies

A third level of description refers to the student's way of conceiving study in general. Taylor, Gibbs, and Morgan (1980) refer to the different ways students relate to their studies as different orientations. Orientations do not assume any psychological trait or state on the part of the student and are of four main kinds: vocational, academic, personal and social. Within each—except the last—we find both an intrinsic and an extrinsic subcategory.

Vocational orientation is of two kinds: qualification and training. Students aiming at gaining qualification are not primarily interested in the content of the course but rather in passing it. Those interested in being trained are more concerned with content though, as this interest is mainly a function of their perception of their future vocational tasks, their orientation is to some extent instrumental.

Extrinsic academic orientation means that the student is primarily interested in getting to the next step on the academic ladder. Intrinsic academic (or intellectual) orientation, on the other hand, reflects the student's interest in the content of his studies. Presumably it is this type of orientation which is most closely linked with the flow experience of learning (Eckblad, 1979) originating from genuine intrinsic motivation. The term *flow experience* was coined by Csikszentmihalyi (1975) and refers to a self-less and time-less state in which the individual is totally absorbed in his own activity, which is its own goal.

Personal orientation has two subcategories; compensation and broadening. Compensation means that the student wants to test his capacity. Broadening stands for the student's goal of developing himself.

The fourth type of orientation, social, is always extrinsic in relation to the content of studies since the main reason for studying is to have a good time.

The orientations are not exclusive in relation to each other but represent differences in emphasis. The relation between orientation to studies and approaches to texts is most apparent as selectivity, i.e. students read some parts but not others. Orientations are also manifested directly in the approaches to the text material. The closest relation could be expected between extrinsic and intrinsic orientations. An example of this has been presented by Taylor, Gibbs and Morgan (1980) concerning adult students at the Open University. We shall focus on the personal orientation.

These authors suggest that the two personal orientations of broadening and compensation seem to be linked to a meaning orientation and a reproducing orientation for approach to studying, respectively. This description seems to parallel the distinction between deep and surface approach. The difference between intrinsic and extrinsic orientation is, however, not identical to the distinction between deep and surface approach. It has different meanings within the different general orientations (vocational, academic, personal and social) and it concerns the orientation towards the whole study task.

The differences between students described in the last three sections can be seen as differences in study skills on various levels if we think of them as differences in the capability to experience and conceptualize the content and process of learning. How a student sets about learning is a function of his idea of learning. In the present context, the student's conception of learning is a more general aspect of orientations to studies.

We have now referred to three increasingly general levels on which students' experience of the content, process, context and phenomenon of learning can be described. Until now, the levels have been dealt with only as categories of description, without any ontological assumptions, and some logical relations between them have been discussed. The discerning of categories and the clarification of the logical relation between them constitute a domain of inquiry which has been labelled phenomenography (Marton, 1981).

The logical relations we have discussed are all of the implicatory kind; a category of description implies another category of description on a higher level of generalizability. A category of the conception-of-content-kind implies a category of the structural kind, which implies a category of the approach kind, which implies a category of the (intrinsic or extrinsic) orientation kind, which implies a category of the conception-of-learning kind. (The hierarchical ordering of the last two levels is, however, somewhat ambiguous.)

A relation between categories of logical nature can be seen as a cause-effect relation from another point of view. Making ontological assumptions about the applicability of the categories opens up opportunites for considering categories belonging to higher levels of generalizability as antecedents to categories belonging to lower levels of generalizability. One would think, for instance, that an accumulation-of-pieces-of-knowledge conception of learning would lead to an external orientation to studies, which would lead to a surface approach to the learning task, which would lead to horizontalization of the text to be read, which would lead to an incorrect understanding of what the author wants to say. The cause-effect relations are, however, not unidirectional. Not only do entities signified by lower order categories reflect (and thereby logically imply) entities signified by higher order categories, they can in fact influence and shape them. The categories do not form a closed system.

The situational context of learning

The demand for qualitites such as deep, holistic approach etc. is not, in most cases, very explicit. Often the examination tasks do not actually demand holistic understanding but the amount of material and the cumulative character of the study task make it almost impossible to manage with an atomistic approach (cf. Svensson, 1976 and 1977). Thus a holistic approach is much more important than the examination tasks suggest.

Hodgson (1980) studies students' experience of relevance in lectures in a conventional university setting. She distinguishes between three different levels: extrinsic, vicarious and intrinsic, with eight subcategories altogether. The experience of relevance comes about, she says, through the assessment system, the lectures and the students' own understanding, knowledge and interest.

Especially interesting is what Hodgson calls vicarious experience of relevance. From a normative point of view, intrinsic experience of relevance is desirable not least because of its being linked with a more desirable approach to the learning task (aiming at understanding rather than regurgitation) and thereby also linked with more desirable outcomes (such as deeper understanding). Vicarious experience of relevance can be seen as a transitional stage between extrinsic and intrinsic experience: it reflects the teacher's effort to bring about relevance. In distance learning, the possibilities of achieving this through the teacher's personal involvement are limited. The second kind of vicarious experience of relevance, the pointing out of the relevance of the content by means of example, can of course be brought about by means of written texts or radio programmes just as it can be done in a lecture. One can of course hardly adapt the choice of the examples to the individual participant. We can operate on the content but there are small margins for a personal and adaptive treatment. As the range of the various modifying factors is more limited in distance learning our hypothesis is that the relation between categories of description for characterizing study skills on different levels of generalizability is stronger than conventional studies.

Brew and McCormick (1979) studied the use of an Open University course in a conventional university. The course had some special characteristics; the text was closely argued, in such a way that the students were forced to follow it in detail. Brew and McCormick say:

> The nature of the text is such that the relationships between concepts are clearly spelled out and links between ideas are drawn. In other words, the course appears implicity to assume that knowledge consists of ideas and concepts in *particular* relationships, and the explanation, and hence learning, has to be effected in terms of such relationships.

Features which may seem to be proof of a high didactic quality obviously raise serious problems for most students. Students differ in their approaches to learning tasks and when a course raises problems for students it does so for different reasons. This is what Brew and McCormick found. Students who considered the content as representing the total amount of knowledge to be learned found the course too extensive. They believed that by adding explanations and illustrations (which was done for didactic reasons) the demands were increased. Students with a more active approach, on the other hand, who aimed at developing their own ideas and building up a structure of their own found themselves constrained by the very explicit structure in the course.

Still, there were some students who benefited from the structure of the course. Brew and McCormick refer to Perry's (1970) work in which the intellectual development during college years is described in terms of a transition from a dualistic conception of knowledge as a collection of right answers through a relativistic stage where the individual realizes that things can be seen in different ways, to commitment to a particular view. Brew and McCormick argue that students on at least the relativistic level profited most from the Open University course. They realized that the course offered them an interrelated system of concepts and ideas and could conceive of developing their own alternative system to be compared to it.

Conclusions

This paper has described students' experience of learning in terms of three main levels of increasing generality. Our hypothesis is that the relationship between study skills described on one level and study skills described on another level is stronger in distance learning. The corollary is that the improvement of study skill is even more important in this context than otherwise. But how can study skills be improved?

The technical interpretation of study skills is irreconcilable with our view of learning as a change in the learner's conceptualization of a certain aspect of his reality. We do not believe in attempts to enable students, by means of all-purpose study technique courses, to deal with any learning tasks irrespective of content.

Another approach is to manipulate the text. If the students lack the capability to discern the main points we can do it for them and make both the basic concepts as well as the relations between them explicit. We pointed out the risks in this approach. Not realizing that the structure represents one way of viewing the particular domain of knowledge students try to learn it instead of trying to understand it and possibly developing an alternative structure of their own. In the students' thinking a means (the structure provided in the text) is transformed into an end (that which has to be learned). A similar means-end reversal has been observed in several experiments in which the aim was to induce a deep approach to a learning task, by means of manipulating questions inserted in the texts and by means of attempts to control the subjects' expectations of the test questions to be given after the reading of the text (Dahigren, 1975; Marton, 1976; Marton and Säljö, 1976b).

The measure we suggest must aim at making the individual more capable of experiencing and conceptualizing aspects of learning in a way which we find more desirable. Gibbs (1978) suggests methods for raising the students' consciousness in order to improve their study skills. His method is to hold sessions during which the participants tell each other about their learning experiences. The phenomenon of learning is thus thematized and participants become aware that learning is something that can be experienced in different ways of which some are better than others.

Gibbs' approach is very general and deals with the total experience of learning. We have tried to demonstrate here that there are several distinguishable levels of generality. We should not only make the students aware of these levels but also of the differences within each. We should point out the qualitatively different ways in which content, structure, learning tasks, studies and learning itself can be experienced and conceptualized.

We consider learning as a transition from one conception of a particular aspect of reality to another. When it comes to study skills we expect the learner to proceed from one way of experiencing or conceptualizing to another and, hopefully, better way. To facilitate the transition we should provide him with the alternative conceptions between which the transition is supposed to take place. In this way, the state that we are aiming at and the states from which we start would be pointed out and the difference between them thematized. We are arguing for the use of what, following Geertz (1973), we might call thick descriptions. By a thick description we mean a complex of alternative interpretative frames in relation to a certain content, structure etc.

The implication of our relational view of study skills is to take the content of learning as as point of departure. We should point out the qualitatively different ways of understanding central concepts, thematize the structures in texts, and discuss the various approaches to texts and orientations to studies. These general aspects should in set in relation to particular contents.

Ference Marton
University of Göteborg

Lennart Svensson
Swedish Council for Research
in the Humanities and Social Sciences

Sweden

References

Brew, A. & McCormick, B. (1979) Student learning and an independent study course. *Higher Education*, 8, 429-442.

Brew, A. and Batten, M.A. (1980) Levels of thinking and Open University students. University Of Essex. (mimeo)

Coombs, P.H. (1968) *The World Educational Crisis: A Systems Analysis*. New York: Oxford University Press.

Csikszentmihalyi, M. (1975) *Beyond Boredom and Anxiety: The Experience of Play in Work and Games*. San Francisco: Jossey-Bass.

Dahlgren, L.O. (1975) *Qualitative Differences as a Function of Content Oriented Guidance*. Göteborg: Acta Universitatis Gothoburgensis.

Eckblad, G. (1979) Spontanmotivasjon - et viktig fenomen for psykologisk teori i dagliglivet? *Nordisk Psykologi*, 31, 30-41. (Spontaneous motivation - an important phenomenon for psychological theory and in daily life?)

Geertz, C. (1973) *The Interpretation of Cultures*. New York: Basic Books.

Gibbs, G. (1978) Intervening in Student Learning - A Particular Strategy. Paper presented at the Fourth International Conference on Higher Education, 29 August - 1 September 1978, Lancaster, Great Britain.

Hodgson, V.E. (1980) Lecturing and Learning: A Study of Students' Experience. Unpublished Ph.D. thesis, Unversity of Surrey.

Lybeck, L. (1981) *Arkimedes i klassen. En amnespedagogisk berattelse*. Göteborg: Acta Universitatis Gothoburgensis. (Archimedes in the class).

Marton, F. (1975) On non-verbatim learning I: level of processing and level of outcome. *Scandinavian Journal of Psychology*, 16, 273-279.

Marton, F. (1976). On non-verbatim learning II: the erosion effect of a task induced learning algorithm. *Scandinavian Journal of Psychology*, 17, 41-48.

Marton, F. (1981) Phenomenography - describing conceptions of the world around us. *Instructional Science*, 10pp. (in press)

Marton, F. and Säljö, R. (1976a) On qualitative differences in learning I: outcome and process. *The British Journal of Educational Psychology*, 46, 4-11.

Marton, F. and Säljö, R. (1976b) On qualitative differences in learning II: outcome as a function of the learner's conception of the task. *The British Journal of Educational Psychology*, 46, 115-127.

Marton, F. and Svensson, L. (1979) Conceptions of research in student learning. *Higher Education*, 8, 471-486.

Marton, F. and Wenestam, C-G (1979) Qualitative differences in the understanding and retention of the main point in some texts based on the principle-example structure. In M.M. Gruneberg, R.E. Morris and R.N. Sykes (eds.) *Practical Aspects of Memory*. London: Academic Press, 644-651.

Perry, W.G. (1970) *Forms of Intellectual and Ethical Development in the College Years: A Scheme*. New York: Holt, Rinehart & Winston.

Säljö, R. (1975) *Qualitative Differences in Learning as a Function of the Learner's Conception of the Task*. Göteborg: Acta Universitatis Gothoburgensis.

Svensson, L. (1976) *Study Skills and Learning*. Göteborg: Acta Universitatis Gothoburgensis.

Svensson, L. (1977) On qualitative differences in learning III: study skill and learning. *The British Journal of Educational Psychology*, 47, 233-243.

Svensson, L. (1981) The concept of study skill (s). Pedagogiska institutionen, Göteborg universitet, 1981:01.

Taylor, E. Gibbs, G. and Morgan, A.R. (1980) The orientations of students studying the Social Science Foundation Course. *Study Methods Group Report No. 7*. Institute of Educational Technology: Open University.

Understanding the Distance Learner as a Whole Person

It is important to understand learning from the student's perspective.

There is a growing body of literature on research and evaluation in education which attempts to describe student learning in natural settings. Entwistle and Hounsell (1979) identified a trend towards qualitative methodologies so as to increase the relevance and usefulness of the findings to course designers. Similarly, Wilson (1977) and Filstead (1979) argue for an ethnographic or qualitative approach to research and evaluation in education so that the complexity of students and their ability to reflect upon experience are recognised. In contrast, mechanistic models of learning ignore the conscious control of learners over their strategies and approaches to studying, and assume students to be passive and easily manipulated by particular teaching devices.

The research group of Ference Marton at the University of Göteborg in Sweden has been particularly influential in developing research which describes learning from the learner's perspective.

Marton and Sevensson (1979) have differentiated between two different research perspectives. The *first-order perspective*, represented by traditional evaluation and psychometrics, is observational whereas the *second-order perspective* is phenomenological and describes learning from the learner's perspective.

This paper will discuss studies grounded in this second-order perspective particularly related to students at the Open University.

Research findings suggest that there are four crucial aspects which influence how students learn: (i) students' orientation to study, (ii) students' development as learners, (iii) students' approaches to studying and the relationship to the learning outcomes and (iv) the demands of the learning materials.

Orientation to study

Orientation is the collection of attitudes, aims and purposes that express a student's relationship with a course and the university. Unlike motivation, which would describe students as more or less motivated, orientation is concerned with the *qualitatively* different ways students view their course. In a study at the Open University, (Taylor, Gibbs and Morgan, 1980) a group of students taking the Social Science Foundation course as their first university course were asked before the course began, a number of key questions, for example "How did you come to be studying with the OU?" and "What do you hope to gain by studying with the OU?" Analysis of the interview transcripts revealed three main types of orientation: *personal, vocational and academic*.

Personal Orientation

This was the most prevalent type of orientation. Two sub-groups could be identified: *compensation* and *broadening*.

Compensation is where students feel cheated of educational opportunities in the past and are using the OU to prove they are capable of getting a degree.

Broadening is where the student wishes to widen horizons and develop inter-personal skills. These students describe a feeling of inadequacy and hope the OU will improve their ability to communicate with people and facilitate their personal development.

Vocational Orientation

In the category of vocational orientation there were two sub-categories of *qualification* and *training*.

Qualification described students who, although they rarely had a particular job in mind, expected that a degree would help them get a better job.

In the case of *training* orientation, OU study was seen as providing knowledge to help with a specific job.

Academic Orientation

In this type of orientation, intrinsic and extrinsic sub-groups were identified.

The intrinsic orientation relates to students who were interested in the topic and wanted to pursue their own interests in the subject area.

In contrast, an extrinsic academic orientation described students who regarded OU study as the next rung on the educational ladder and were primarily concerned to continued studying.

This analysis of orientation suggests that students will want different things out of the course since they have quite different aims and expectations.

Students with a personal orientation and the aims of broadening expect OU study to lead to personal change and development. This broadening orientation and approach to study has similarities with Rogers' (1969) concept of personally meaningful learning.

In contrast students whose aim in studying is towards compensation are concerned to prove their capabilities to themselves and their friends. It seems likely that they will be particularly assessment conscious.

Development as learners

Two similar schemes, developed independently, describe the different ways students perceive learning. In Sweden, Säljö (1979) interviewed a wide range of students to discover the conceptions of learning which exist. In America, Perry (1970) interviewed students at Harvard in order to understand the developments taking place during their careers as students. Both studies showed how students become more sophisticated as learners, by becoming more aware of their study habits, distinguishing between the sorts of learning demanded by different learning tasks, and seeing learning as a personally meaningful activity.

Säljö's (1979) scheme of five *conceptions of learning* is useful in understanding how students actually study.

Conceptions 1, 2 and 3 are concerned with learning as an accumulation of pieces of knowledge. This is a quantitative conception where learning is perceived to involve largely memorisation. In contrast conceptions 4 and 5 describe learning as an abstraction of meaning requiring an active interpretive process by the learner.

A study of OU students (Morgan, Gibbs and Taylor, 1981) at the beginning of their university study identified examples of these five conceptions. Some students whose conceptions of learning matched 1, 2 and 3 realised that the OU would require something different without quite knowing what. One student's description of learning illustrates the point:

> When I do think about learning I'm still very much at school sort of thing and I know it's a very different sort of learning..... I browse through some of the books that I only got last week, the set books, and still at the moment I'm still in the school sort of learning: the facts and dates and names learning rather than content. And if I read something....I have read it and I think "what have I just read?".....at the moment I feel worried about not taking in what I am doing or what I am learning. I still feel very confused about it.

It seems that some students, new to OU study, will have to undergo some sort of *transition* in their conception of learning to cope with the demands.

The first three conceptions essentially describe learning as an increase in information: knowledge is external to the student and the process of learning involves the transfer of knowledge from an external source into the heads of the learners. In contrast, the essence of conceptions 4 and 5 is that knowledge is construed by individuals as a result of an active effort on the part of the learner. The difference between these two broad conceptions is similar to the distinction between the surface and deep level approaches to learning tasks identified by Marton and Säljö, (1976).

The same distinction of approaches to studying has been identified with Open University students studying D101, (Morgan, Gibbs and Taylor, 1981). Broadly, students who adopt a surface approach concentrate on trying to *remember* as much detail as possible rather than on trying to *understand* the overall meaning.

Obviously Open University course materials, although they usually require students to adopt a deep approach, sometimes require them to adopt a surface approach. But for some students, including some of those interviewed on the study reported here, there is little awareness of these different demands.

So, however hard the Open University attempts to encourage students to take a deep-level approach (for example, the student guide "How to Study in the Open University", written by Andrew Northedge (1978), explicity discusses deep and surface approaches), there will be some students who, due to their conceptions of learning, will be oblivious to these attempts and will take a surface approach. It is likely that students whose conceptions of learning were clearly categories 1, 2 or 3 rather than 4 and 5 would be likely to approach studying in this way. As the approaches students adopt towards study tasks have a crucial influence on *what* they learn (Marton and Säljö, 1976), their conceptions of learning are of great significance and concern when we are attempting to improve student learning.

Approaches to studying and the relationship to the learning outcomes

Marton and Säljö (1976) identified two qualitatively different ways in which students approached studying. Students who adopted a *deep-level* approach were looking for the overall meaning and relating ideas together, in contrast to a *surface-level* approach where students were concerned with remembering as much detail as possible.

The approach to study was directly linked to *what* students actually learnt. None of the students whose approach was categorised as surface-level completely understood the arguments. In contrast, none of the students who took a deep-level approach failed to gain a good understanding.

In a study based on the Open University's Social Science Foundation course (Morgan, Gibbs and Taylor, 1981), students were interviewed about how they tackled studying one block of the correspondence text (about four weeks work) and completed the associated essay for assessment. The interview transcripts revealed important differences.

Two examples will be described, which seem to represent the extreme cases of how students studied the correspondence text.

S. "I read through the thing once, either fairly leisurely or fairly quickly depending on time, then I read through it again. In either case more thoroughly, I take notes at that point."

I. "What do you usually do when you go through it the first time?"

S. "Getting the feel for it I suppose. I didn't used to do that before I just used to read the thing and I made notes as I went and found that I was repeating notes because the same topic will crop up in different pages, perhaps the same idea will be expressed much more nicely and I found the notes would wander backwards and forwards on the topic so well as I say I just try and get the feel of the thing and see which ideas are put forward and where."

This student was also describing reading in relation to the material to her personal experiences.

S. "I read the thing pretty quickly and then go through it again and extract things which seem relevant ..... I suppose going back to the bit about applying you know if I can see that they have an application or relevant to life as I see it, you know, they strike a chord perhaps and I take note."

The same student described writing the essay as an activity which crystallised her thoughts and helped her to relate ideas together.

S. "I find the TMAs [Tutor Marked Assignments] actually crystallise ideas a lot you know, I read a block and I end up with lots of what are essentially jumbled thoughts, I am not saying they don't make sense but there is no actual structure to them. You can see that one person says this and one person says that, as to how those different ideas relate to each other in my mind comes clear when I start writing about it. I try and construct a pattern I suppose and then fit different authors' ideas into it and agree or disagree depending on the point I am trying to make."
(Student No. 1)

Here is another student describing his problems with the correspondence text.

"I would have liked some lead up to study. I don't know, I think I do sort of harp back to school and I feel that I would be happy if someone said this is what you do. I can't get out of that thing I don't think......

I might be quite wrong but it's not so much that you are learning a set amount of facts that you have then got to present as an answer to an exam question, isn't it? I assume you are going to be given something—questions on the stuff that you have studied, but argue it around from a different point of view to the questions that you have had for your TMA. Is that sort of basically what's going to happen? I don't know so perhaps it might have done. I just think that I harped back to school days too much and I am surprised that there aren't the facts there presented for me and I don't know. I do find some of the course text. I read it through and I think oh I don't know what an earth I have read there, I read it through page after page."
(Student No. 2)

This student, in contrast to Student No. 1 appears to have problems because the correspondence text does present the "facts" to enable a memorization type approach to be used. Student No. 2 can be described as having a conception of learning represented by Säljö's (1979) conceptions 1, 2 and 3.

In the terms of Marton and Säljö (1976), Student No. 1 and Student No. 2 would be described as taking a deep-level and a surface-level approach, respectively. What is more important, OU students with study methods represented by Student No. 2 *failed* to gain a full understanding of the concept taught in this block.

The demands of the learning materials

In understanding how students learn, one crucial aspect is the design of the teaching and learning materials, in terms of the overall course design and the structure and details of the assessment (e.g. self-assessment questions and inserted-text questions).

Assessment is one of the most powerful influences on students' experiences of learning. As Rowntree (1977) says; "The spirit and style of student assessment defines the de facto curriculum". Similarly, Becker, Greer and Hughes (1968) identified how the pressure to get good grades and meet the assessment requirements determined how students approached their studies.

In correspondence texts for distance teaching instructional designers have always emphasised the importance of inserted-text questions and self-assessment questions, so as to manipulate the learner to become more actively engaged in studying. Although these devices have not been fully evaluated evidence (Dahlgren, 1975) suggests that rather than encouraging a deep-level approach to study, these devices can very easily manipulate students towards taking a surface-level approach because the inserted-text questions focus on the details presented in the correspondence text.

Studies at the Open University indicate that courses which include a project component, where students have some control and responsibility for designing their own learning activities, encourage students to become more actively and personally involved, (Morgan, 1976). Students' descriptions of their experiences of project-based learning fit Rogers' (1969) principles of learning, for example, "learning is facilitated when the student participates responsibly in the process". These studies suggest that the overall context of students' experience of learning must be considered in attempting to improve student learning, besides the influence of specific teaching devices incorporated in the correspondence text.

Conclusions

Attempts to improve learning should have the following goals:

1. The development of students' conceptions of learning, not by didactic teaching on theoretical aspects of learning, but by a student-centered facilitation of students' own awareness.

2. The development of a flexibility in students to adopt learning approaches appropriate to particular study tasks and intentions; by this we do not mean training of specific study techniques out of context of particular subject material.

3. Course design should be based on realistic assumptions of the complexities of the learner and incorporate facilities for students to take some individual responsibility for their learning.

The research we have described shows the importance of understanding learning from the *learner's perspective*. In distance education systems, where research and evaluation into student learning is often conducted predominantly from a first-order perspective, using closed-end questionnnaires, knowledge of the reality of learning as *students* experience it is essential if our efforts to improve student learning are to be effective.

Alistair Morgan / Elizabeth Taylor
Open University

Graham Gibbs
Oxford Polytechnic

United Kingdom

References

Becker, M.S. Greer, B. and Hughes, E.C. (1968) *Making the Grade: The Academic Side of College Life*. New York: Wiley.

Dahlgren, L.O. (1975) Qualitative differences in learning as a function of content-orientated guidance. *Göteborg Studies in Educational Sciences 15*. University of Göteborg.

Entwistle, N. and Hounsell, D. (1979) Student learning in its natural setting. *Higher Education*, 8, 4, 359-363.

Filstead, W.J. (1979) Qualitative methods: a needed perspective in evaluation research. In Cook, T.D. and Reichardt, C.S. (eds.) *Qualitative Methods in Evaluation Research*. Beverley Hills: Sage.

Marton, F. and Svensson, L. (1979) Conceptions of research in student learning. *Higher Education*, 8, (4), 471-486.

Marton, F., and Säljö, R. (1976) On qualitative differences in learning: outcome and process I & II. *British Journal of Educational Psychology*, 46, 4-11 & 115-127.

Morgan, A.R. (1976) The development of project-based learning in the Open University. *Programmed Learning & Educational Technology*, 13, 4, 55-59.

Morgan, A.R. Gibbs, G. and Taylor E. (1981) What do Open University students initially understand about learning? *Study Methods Group Report No.8*. Institute of Educational Technology, Open University.

Northedge, A. (1978) *How to Study: A Guide to Studying at the Open University*. Open University, Milton Keynes.

Perry, W.G. (1970) *Forms of Intellectual and Ethical Development in College Years: A Scheme*. New York: Holt, Rinehart & Wilson.

Rogers, C. (1969) *Freedom to Learn*. Columbus, Ohio: Merrill.

Rowntree, D. (1977) *Assessing Students: How Shall We Know Them*. London: Harper and Row.

Säljö, R. (1979) Learning in the learner's perspective I: some commonsense conceptions of learning. *Reports from the Institute of Education*, No. 76, University of Göteborg.

Taylor, E., Gibbs, G. and Morgan, A.R. (1980) The orientations of students studying the social science foundation course. *Study Methods Group Report No. 7*. Institute of Educational Technology, Open University.

Wilson, S. (1977) The Use of Ethnographic Techniques in Educational Research. *Review of Educational Research*, 47, 1, 245-265.

Paper 33

Individual and Group Work in Distance Studies: Which Process for What Purpose?

(Abstract)

Since there is a broad spectrum of possible processes in both individual and group work it is not easy to identify which parts of a course should be taught by which means. Yet such decisions are made daily by course designers. The literature gives some indication of the didactic potentials and deficits of individual and group work and eight examples of distance education courses are examined in the light of previous writings. In the end individual and group learning are not very different in terms of didactic potential.

Perhaps dialogue is the most important aspect of both work forms. In individual learning dialogue is carried on only with the study material whereas in group work it involves one or more partners.

Klaus Muller
Deutsches Institut für Fernstudien
West Germany

Content Analysis for Course Design

Paper 34

Content analysis, like dancing, combines well known steps and procedures with liberal dashes of creativity and imagination.

I use the term *content analysis* to denote one of the early steps in the systematic design of instruction, usually the third or fourth step, following the identification of *goals and objectives* and before the *planning or designing* of the instructional strategy.

Content analysis refers to the micro-analysis of what is to be learned by the student. It consists of dialogue between a subject matter expert (e.g., a historian, an electrician, a biologist) and an instructional designer (an individual with training and experience in instructional systems design, the psychology of learning and instruction, effective writing and/or audio-visual media design). The deeper exploration of the instructional objectives—the information to be learned, the skill to be acquired, or the attitude to be cultivated—leads to greater understanding on the part of both the subject matter expert and the instructional designer and can ultimately yield more effective instructional strategies and materials.

Why do it?

Among the reasons for doing content analysis are the following:

1. to confirm or revise previously stated objectives
2. to identify enabling objectives
3. to determine the best teaching strategy for a given objective
4. to sequence learning activities.

To confirm or revise previously stated objectives

Sometimes the objectives initially volunteered by a content expert are not the ones she really wants her students to pursue. An original objective of a librarian developing a course designed to teach the skills and procedures involved in acquiring materials for a library was:

> The student will be able to *name* 50 selection tools used in the acquisitions process.

After a closer analysis of the content she wanted to treat, it became clear that her real objective was more like this:

> Given a title, the student will *choose* the most appropriate selection tool from among 50 tools commonly used by librarians.

A *higher level* objective was revealed through content analysis.

To identify enabling objectives

A content expert may identify an appropriate objective but may not be aware of the "stepping stones" or enabling objectives students must achieve before they are ready to tackle the terminal objective. One of my colleagues conducted a workshop to teach how to write instructional objectives. He used all the best learning materials and an appropriate mix of individual, small group, and large group activities, but his participants failed to learn how to write learning objectives because he failed to recognize that before his participants could *compose* their own objectives, they must first learn to distinguish good learning objectives from poor ones. Now, whenever I design a workshop on objective-setting, I always identify as one of my enabling objectives:

> The participants will be able to choose from among a sample of objectives those that most closely meet the criteria for good learning objectives.

To determine the best teaching strategy for a given objective

I am presently working with the staff of one of our nursing programs to develop materials that will allow us to offer this program on a home study basis. One of our objectives was that "students be able to conduct a health history interview" using a particular format we had developed. One of our enabling objectives was that "students be able to recognize poor interviewing skills". It became clear that students had to *hear* an interview in progress in order to identify poor interviewing skills. We then developed a script illustrating good and poor interviewing techniques and an exercise to guide the students through the tape. The final product, an audio tape/print combination, was highly effective.

To sequence learning activities

Sometimes a careful analysis of a terminal objective will reveal the order in which enabling objectives should be learned. One instructor wished to develop a more effective way of teaching student nurses the skill of medication dosage calculation. On the surface, it appears to be a fairly simple procedure but I soon learned that most medications are made up of two components: the active ingredients and the medium. The concentration of drugs available does not always match the concentration of drug ordered by the physician. Therefore, a complex conversion skill is sometimes needed. Our analysis of the skill resulted in the identification of several enabling objectives, one of which surfaced as critical, namely:

Given the information on the label of a drug container, the student will be able to determine how much *active ingredient* is in the container.

Thus, a thorough understanding of the concept *active ingredient* was a *prerequisite* to learning the skill of medication dosage calculation. The instructor designed her teaching strategy accordingly.

If your goal is some combination of the above, for example, to revise objectives, to choose the best teaching strategy, and to sequence the learning activities you will undertake several levels of content analysis, each one yielding a deeper understanding of what is to be taught.

How to do it

Information processing analysis, as described by Gagné (in Briggs, 1977: 116), consists of mentally walking through the capability the student is to acquire, that is, the skill to be learned, the information to be internalized, etc. The role of the instructional designer in such a case is to question constantly the steps the content expert describes, to probe, to seek further clarification, and, by careful questioning, to fill in the missing links, or bring to light all the substeps and decision points that are included in the overall human performance. This is essentially the procedure used in the "medication dosage calculation" example. An information processing analysis yields a diagram or flowchart illustrating the steps and decision points involved in the overall performance.

Task classification is most useful when one wishes to determine strategy for teaching a given objective. The most useful taxonomy seems to be that derived by Gagné (1975: 68) who divides human capabilities, and thus potential learning objectives, into five categories:

1. verbal information
2. intellectual skills
3. cognitive strategies
4. attitudes
5. motor skills.

The category of intellectual skills is further subdivided into concept learning, rule learning, discrimination learning, etc. The conditions, both internal and external to the student, which would be necessary to bring about the learning of each of these types of human capabilities are delineated. The goal of content analysis then, is to classify each objective into one of the five categories. Once this is accomplished, the body of literature most relevant to the teaching of that objective can be accessed and an appropriate teaching/learning strategy can be developed.

Learning task analysis (Gagné, in Briggs, 1977: 129) is the analysis of skills, be they psychomotor or mental. The process begins with the identification of the desired terminal performance. The question "What must the student be able to do before he or she can learn to do this?" is asked repeatedly each time revealing a prerequisite skill until skills are identified at the lowest level of the hierarchy that can be assumed to be among the entry level skills of the student. The process usually yields a hierarchical diagram depicting the skills and sub-skills which make up a complex skill. This type of analysis may reveal enabling objectives not identified earlier, but is most useful for sequencing learning objectives.

Each of these models has its specific applications. If, for example, the goal of content analysis is to sequence learning activities, then the task analysis approach is likely to be most useful. If, on the other hand, one is interested in determining the best teaching strategy for a given objective, the task classification approach is perhaps more appropriate. If, however, one is interested in identifying enabling objectives, the information processing approach or the task analysis approach may be used. Choice of a model depends not only on the goal of the content analysis, but also on the subject matter itself.

Who does it?

Life is a little easier if the content expert can engage in dialogue with another person who may know very little of the content area, but who brings to the situation some objectivity, an analytic framework, and some strategies for analysis. The role of this *process person* is to help the content expert come to grips with the subject matter, to bring to bear on the analysis the procedures, taxonomies and models described earlier.

In addition to having models at his fingertips, this process person (often, but not always, an instructional designer) needs to have tremendous interpersonal communication skills. The process often involves questioning, probing, active listening, verbalizing tentative understandings of given concepts and offering them to the content expert for verification or further clarification. The individual must be able to withhold judgement, to resist the temptation to put his own values on the subject matter being taught, and to assume a facilitating role. The individual must define the role as that of a helper or mentor whose job it is to bring to the surface and give structure to the ideas that are circulating in the heads of others.

In addition to these skills, the facilitator needs patience, flexibility, and the ability to switch from one model to another if the situation demands it. Finally, this process person needs to have an insatiable appetite for learning. Each interaction with a subject matter expert will reveal new domains of knowledge and will require the ability to grasp quickly what that content expert has to offer. The success of the process depends largely on the skills of this facilitator.

Summary

Content analysis, like dancing, combines well known steps and procedures with liberal dashes of creativity and imagination. Properly conceived and properly conducted, content analysis can be a learning experience for the subject matter expert and for the instructional designer. Well done, it results in more effective instructional products and strategies.

Marg Penney
Grant MacEwan Community College
Canada

References

Briggs, L.J. (ed.) (1977) *Instructional Design*. Englewood Cliffs, New Jersey: Educational Technology Publications.

Gagné, R.M. (1975) *Essentials of Learning for Instruction*. Hinsdale, Illinois: Dryden.

The Readability of Study Materials: Recent Research in New Zealand

Analysing extracts of their own work using the Cloze Procedure can alert staff to the importance of readability.

The New Zealand Technical Correspondence Institute is a tertiary institution with a roll of 34,000 students who have a wide range of abilities and educational backgrounds. Many of the 420 tutors have neither taught in a classroom nor written teaching material before their appointment. The Staff Training Department runs compulsory writing courses to encourage tutors to write study materials which the majority of students can read and understand. Both interviews with students attending yearly practical courses (called "block" courses) and readability tests on a sample of assignments suggested that many assignments were written at a level too difficult for correspondence students.

We needed further evidence for this conclusion and information to guide us in designing courses to help tutors write more clearly. Published overseas research did not provide the answers. In 1979, we collaborated with the New Zealand Council for Educational Research to test over 300 students involved in block courses from various departments to see how well they could read and understand randomly selected extracts from their assignments. We used the Cloze Procedure, with a seventh word deletion pattern, on assignments that were familiar in content to the students, but had not been read previously. The students also answered general questionnaires on NZTCI assignments. Analysis of the Cloze Procedure scores and questionnaire responses showed that the extracts tested were too difficult for the majority of students. Fluctuating levels of difficulty in each assignment probably contributed to lower scores.

After discussing these results some tutors asked me to test existing assignments so they could apply the results to re-writing. Some asked for new drafts to be tested so they could eliminate obvious difficulties before production. The aim was to make their writing more readable for the majority of students.

The following steps used for one tutor indicated the testing procedure for all follow-up research:

1. The tutor chose an assignment that he had previously found too difficult for most students taking Horticulture Stage 2. He indicated the five extracts to be tested.

2. I prepared Cloze Procedure tests on these extracts for 67 second year students attending block courses held at various technical institutes in 1980. There were four groups that included all the students expected to study the assignment later in the year.

3. The results from testing the five extracts on Groups 1, 2, 3 and 4 were analysed and discussed with the tutor. Group 1's results are shown in Table 1. Each column shows the individual scores out of 20 for each extract and the individual total percentage scores for the five extracts.

Paper 35

Some readability experts divide Cloze scores into the following three levels of understanding:

a. Cloze scores under 35% show a *frustrational level*. The table shows that 7 students found the extracts beyond them.

b. Cloze scores from 35% to 50% show an *instructional level*. The table shows that 10 students could read and understand the extracts, provided the tutor explained more fully the parts that individuals found difficult.

c. Cloze scores over 50% show an *independent level*. Two students found the extracts readable without needing any help. Table 1 also shows the students' comparative scores for each extract.

The asterisks in Table 1 indicate students with scores under 34% who may need outside help. This is arranged with Adult Literacy tutors, a voluntary group specially trained to work throughout New Zealand.

4. In Table 2, the average scores from Groups 1, 2, 3 and 4 are used to rate the extracts in order of difficulty. All groups tested on the original writing rated Extract C as the most readable, followed by Extracts A, B, E (except Group 2 rated E before B) to the least readable, Extract D.
I compared Extract C with Extract D and concluded that Extract C was more readable because the tutor used fewer polysyllabic words and explanations with short sentences. Extract D had more technical terms,

Table 1

Number of students tested in Group 1: 19
Number of extracts sampled: 5 (A, B, C, D, E) from a Stage 2 Horticulture Assignment
Maximum score for each extract: 20

Students	1*	2*	3*	4	5	6	7	8	9	10	11*	12*	13	14*	15	16	17	18	19	Average Score	Scores range from
Extract A	4	5	4	6	13	11	9	7	8	10	6	5	9	6	7	7	10	7	8	7.47	4-13
Extract B	3	9	3	9	9	12	9	8	7	9	5	4	7	9	9	8	7	7	5	7.32	3-12
Extract C	10	14	8	11	13	15	12	13	15	14	8	7	13	13	13	10	16	12	13	12.11	7-16
Extract D	6	5	6	8	6	8	6	3	6	5	4	2	5	5	8	6	9	7	4	5.74	2-9
Extract E	0	0	6	8	9	8	9	5	12	10	7	2	9	0	13	2	13	10	10	7.00	0-13
Total %	23	33	27	42	50	54	45	36	48	48	30	20	43	33	50	33	55	43	40	Av. % score = 39.63	
SC subjects	2	5	2	5	3	5	5	5	3	4	2		5		5	5	4	2	3		
UE subjects				5		3	4		2				5		2		3				

*Recommended help from outside Adult Literacy tutors.
Replacement words were examined before recommending his help.

Table 2: **Readability ratings of extracts for groups 1, 2, 3 and 4**

Group 1	Group 2	Group 3	Group 4	Group 4 (Rewrites)
C (12.11) Easiest	C (11.94)	C (11.23)	C (12.77)	A (14.00)
A (7.47)	A (8.88)	A (7.69)	A (8.31)	B (10.62)
B (7.32)	E (8.12)	B (6.54)	B (7.54)	E (8.69)
E (7.00)	B (7.47)	E (6.31)	E (6.77)	C (8.46)
*D (5.74) Hardest	*D (6.18)	*D (4.62)	*D (5.46)	*D (4.70)

*D was not rewritten.

Average scores, Group 1 to 4   A (8.09)   B (7.21)   C (12.01)   D (6.25)   E (6.72)

Average scores, Group 4 rewrites except for *D   A (14.00)   B (10.62)   C (8.46)   D (4.70)   E (8.69) some confused sentences, some unnecessary words, and some words unfamiliar to the students.

5. Because I believe that the Cloze Procedure is useful only as a guideline, I prepared a language analysis assessment of each extract for wider interpretation of each student's and each group's performance. This counteracts the rigid classification of understanding outlined in 3(a), (b) and (c). The language analysis of Extract D for the four groups follows on this page and Figure 1. The exact replacements were numbered from 1 to 20 to enable the tutor to refer quickly to the original material. The numbers following the words show how many students gave exact replacements.

Damping-Off Diseases

These diseases may be caused by several fungi, but the most important and common are the water 1. **moulds** (8) *(Phythium and Phytophtora)* and *Rhizoctonia*. Infections 2. **may** (10) cause death of germinating seeds before 3. **seedlings** (0) emerge above ground level (pre-emergence damping-off) 4. **or** (9) death of seedlings after emergence (post-emergence 5. **damping-off** (47)).

The water mould and Rhizoctonia fungi, 6. **which** (12) can exist in the soil as saprophytes on dead organic matter, are not 7. **restricted** (8) to living solely on living plants. 8. **Thus** (0), mycelium of these fungi can continue 9. **to** (56) grow in the soil on crop 10. **debris** (0), weeds, and other organic matter.

Water 11. **mould** (38) fungi are very active in wet 12. **soils** (2) ,whereas Rhizoctonia species are troublesome when 13. **soils** (5) are drier. Damping-off problems from either 14. **of** (51) these fungi are therefore likely to 15. **beset** (0) the horticulturist at any time.

Typical Life Cycle of a Water Mould Fungus

The 16. **full** (0) cycle is summarised in Fig. 4 17. **Water** (40) mould fungi produce zoospores in sporangia 18. **during** (30) favourable periods. The zoospores are released 19. **into** (45) the soil and swim in water 20. **films** (4) around roots and soil particles.

Acceptable replacements from the language analyses of Extracts A, B, C and E were recorded and analysed as for Extract D. (Acceptable replacements are *not* synonyms, but words which, in context, show that the students probably understand the gist of what they are reading.) The tutor agreed to re-write Extracts A, B, C and E, using the language analyses as a guide. He also tested Group 4 with the re-writes first, and the original extracts a week later. The hardest extract, D, was not re-written and was used as a control for all groups.

Readability experts advocate using some general principles as guides to clearer writing. The recorded information helped the tutor to look at these principles to see if he needed to:

a. Use words that were more familiar to students than the original words,

b. Avoid unnecessary clauses starting with which or that,

c. Shorten overlong sentences when students' responses proved they were confused,

d. Use one complex idea instead of several in a sentence,

e. Check the need for three or more syllable words (apart from technical terms),

f. Avoid passive tenses and relate directly to students,

g. Avoid too many prepositions and adverbs,

h. Put action into verbs, and

i. Eliminate unnecessary words and jargon.

6. Group 4 was tested on the re-written Extracts A, B, C, and E, along with the control Extract D. Table 2 shows that Group 4 also found Extract D was the hardest. Group 4 found the re-written Extracts A, B, and E were more readable than the other groups found the original extracts. We thought Extract C was more clearly written, but the adverbs in the deletions had low or zero scores.

The tutor intends to eliminate meaningless adverbs in Extract C. A tabulation of the original material made Extract A much more readable and the weakest students scored 50% or more. A mathematician checked the results from all groups and concluded that Group 4 had a similar range of abilities. We can assume that Groups 1, 2 and 3 would also have gained higher Cloze scores on the re-written extracts.

7. The tutor found the language analysis in Figure 1 helped him to re-write Extract D more clearly. For example:

a. Only 12 out of 67 students gave 'which' as an exact replacement; 8 gave 'that', an acceptable replacement; 26 gave wrong responses; 21 did not respond. Subordinate clauses can confuse many students, so the tutor intends to use two sentences to express the two concepts in the original sentence.

b. No one guessed 'beset'; 44 students gave acceptable replacements (20 used 'trouble', a more familiar word to this group, and a suitable substitute for the tutor to use); 15 gave wrong responses; 8 did not respond.

8. Before the testing was carried out, the tutor had drafted a new assignment for use in 1981 with similar students. He has now used the test results to re-write the draft and feels confident that it will be more read-

Paper 35

Figure 1: Language analysis of the 4 groups' replacement words for extract D

Total number of students: 67

Exact, Replacements	Other Responses—acceptable replacements are in bold type	Nil Responses
1. **moulds** (8)	**mound** (15), **fungi** (25), zoospores (1), spores (2), borne (6), loving (1), content (1), diseases (1), flea (1), swimming (1)	(5)
2. **may** (10)	**can** (43), will (8), often (1), mainly (1), which (1), soon (1), usually (1),	(1)
3. **seedlings** (0)	**shoots** (1), they (63), seeds (1), their (1)	(1)
4. **or** (9)	**and** (22), the (8), is (3), also (2), causes (9), cause (1). sudden (2), causing (1), so (1), even (1)	(8)
5. **damping-off** (47)	**damping** (1), death (1), deaths (1), occurs (2), bot (1), before (1), die (1)	(12)
6. **which** (12)	**that** (8), sometimes (2), mainly (1), these (2), also (4), both (7), often (4), they (2), this (1), has (1), only (1), definitely (1)	(21)
7. **restricted** (8)	**confined** (5), **limited** (2), **orientated** (1), **bound** (1), prone (1), reliant (1), used (3), adapted (9), hazardous (1), taken (1), dependent (7), allowed (1), parasites (1), custom (1), given (1), able (3), subject (1), known (2)	(17)
8. **thus** (0)	**so** (1), **therefore** (1), the (22), however (2), rhizoctonia (1), type (1), some (6), generally (1), often (1), living (1), hyphae (5), saprophytic (1), saprophytes (1)	(22)
9. **to** (56)	and (1)	(10)
10. **debris** (0)	**waste** (5), **wastes** (3), **residue** (1), residues (1), litter (1), remains (7), plants (13), roots (8), grown (2), matter (2), foliage (2), rubbish (1), stubble (1), vegetation (2), material (2), affected (1), ornamental (1), and (1)	(13)
11. **mould** (38)	borne (11), phytophthora (1), spores (1), based (2), activated (1), living (1), swimming (1), producing (1), developing (1), and (1)	(8)
12. **soils** (2)	**conditions** (23), **condition** (1), **soil** (1), **environments** (1), areas (1), weather (29), periods (2), cool (1)	(6)
13. **soils** (5)	**conditions** (30), they (18), leaves (1), areas (2), periods (1), climates (1), weather (1), plants (2),	(6)
14. **of** (51)	one (1), when (1), while (1), the (1)	(12)
15. **beset** (0)	**trouble** (20), **affect** (13), **bother** (3), **strike** (5), **bug** (1), **hinder** (1), **problem** (1), concern (4), emerge on (1), invade (1), fool (1), annoy (2), confuse (1), attack (4), beat (1)	(8)
16. **full** (0)	life (56), **above** (referred to heading) (1), **typical** (2), **water mould** (1), mould (1), water (1), first (1)	(4)
17. **water** (40)	the (11), where (2), most (3), grey (1), un- (1), when (1), on (1), of (1), some (1)	(5)
18. **during** (30)	in (18), region (1), at (2), under (4), and (2), life (1), most (1), create (1)	(7)
19. **into** (45)	in (7), **throughout** (1), **through** (1), to (2), from (3), within (2), onto (1), when (1), released (1)	(3)

20. **films** (4)   **deposits** (1), **film** (1), particles (6), contained (1), pockets (3), (8)
pores (2), ways (1), present (1), trapped (1), in (1), and (4),
down (1), spaces (2), corrected (1), all (4), molecules (4),
droplets (1), areas (1), living (1), held (1), soil (1), drops (1),
currents (1), collected (1), released (1), below (1), ponds (1),
that's (2), mostly (1), solution (1), attaching (1), globules (1),
gathering (1), usually (1), based (1), pools (1)

able. We intend to use the Cloze Procedure to test the new assignment in June 1981.

The Cloze Procedure and the language analyses were useful to the tutor whose attitude changed from being sceptical about readability tenets to accepting that his writing should be tailored to suit the reading capabilities of the majority of his students.

Experts claim that the Cloze Procedure is the best of the readability tests to apply to technical writing. It has provided vital facts for us to use in producing better teaching material.

The main advantages of using the Cloze Procedure have been:

1. Getting some indication of the individual's student's reading ability e.g. the extent of their vocabulary.

2. Providing tutors with useful information about individual and group reading abilities so they can write more clearly for the majority of students taking a course.

3. Showing some students' lack of basic knowledge. Supplementary assignments may be needed.

4. A gradual compiling of lists of familiar words used by particular student groups. Tutors could refer to these lists when writing.

Nola Holmes
New Zealand Technical Correspondence Institute
New Zealand

Attrition: A Case Study

Even relatively benign forms of screening can substantially affect course completion figures.

The problem of drop-outs in higher education has been reviewed by Tinto (1975) and Pantages and Creedon (1978). It is generally accepted as being even more serious in higher distance education although the magnitude is difficult to ascertain. As Connors (1980) observes, "...usually people are very coy about revealing their drop-out rates." The Open University regularly publishes data on drop-outs, Massey University has published an attrition study on extramural students, and some departments of external studies in Australia have either published specific attrition studies (for example, Sheath, 1973) or provided data in annual statistical reports. However, this is not much of a database given the variety of institutions. This paper examines attrition in a Canadian distance education university.

Modelled in part after the British Open University, Athabasca University (AU) specializes in distance education involving a variety of media including television, audio tapes, print, and telephone. AU currently offers baccalaureate degrees in liberal studies and administrative studies. Students are predominantly working adults and a majority are female. The only requirement for admission is that a student be eighteen or older. Students can usually enrol in courses at any point during the year. In general, they proceed through courses at their own pace and complete whenever they feel ready.

The examination of course completions includes the questions: 1) "What proportion of those students who do not complete actually do not make a start at the course and may be classified as 'non-starters' rather than 'non-completers'?" 2) "How far along do those students who are starters, but who do not complete, typically get?"

The answer to the first question is very useful as a basis for an alternative formulation of course completion rates where the number of students who do not start is subtracted from the total enrolments for the course and this reduced number is then used as the denominator in the completion rate calculation (sometimes referred to as the NUEA formula; see Orton, 1977). This formulation of a course completion rate generally results in much higher estimates than the alternative formulation which does not take out "non-starters".

The answer to the second question results in a more refined measure of student activity than the binary "complete-not complete" classification. Noting at what point students typically drop out one might develop a strategy to help them persist.

Definitions

Pantages and Creedon (1978) have summarized the problems of defining attrition and completion in conventional college education. Many of these definitions can be usefully applied in such organizations as the schools of external studies in Australia because the goals and operations of the distance delivery mode of these institutions closely parallel those of the conventional delivery mode. However, students in such institutions as Athabasca University have a number of reasons for undertaking university study—and completion of full degree programs seems to be a relatively minor reason. Since definitions pertaining to dropping out of programs (or a particular year of study) are therefore largely inappropriate, the terms *attrition* and *completion* in this study will pertain to student performance in a course. Specifically, a drop-out is a student who enroled in an AU course but did not successfully complete the entire course (or the portion contracted for).

Methodology

The calculation of completion *rates* is difficult at Athabasca University since students enrol in a course at any time and complete it at any time (within some very general constraints). To calculate a course completion rate, one must know how many people have completed and how many there are who might reasonably be expected to have completed. This latter figure is difficult to determine at AU because of the varying amounts of time students may spend at a course. In a 6-credit course, a student is entitled to a minimum of 12 months and university policy allows students to extend or suspend studies in extenuating circumstances. In such cases, it could be 18-24 months before a student is considered "finished" in a course.

To get around this problem, course completion rates have been estimated using cohorts of enrolments defined by specifying enrolment periods such that all students in the cohort might reasonably be expected to have done all they are going to do in the course in which they were enroled. The cohort definitions are:

1. All enrolments in the period 1978-08-01 to 1978-11-30.

2. All enrolments in the period 1979-01-01 to 1979-03-31.

3. All enrolments in the period 1979-04-01 to 1979-07-31.

4. All enrolments in the period 1979-08-01 to 1979-11-30.

Course and credit completions for these cohorts were counted as of February 28, 1981.

Limitations

A major limitation of estimating course completion rates in this way is that much of the data must necessarily be quite old. This is a problem because: 1) courses may have been revised and changed; 2) it is not possible to estimate completion rates for courses on offer for less than 18 months; and 3) course completion rates may change over time.

These limitations are partially addressed by taking four cohorts. An overall course completion rate can be calculated for each cohort and the stability over time of course completion rates in general. If the completion rate of Cohort 4 is comparable to those of at least the previous two cohorts, then "datedness" is considerably attenuated. The use of four cohorts ensures that the sample on which estimates were based is reasonably large.

There are other problems in treating attrition and completion strictly within the context of single course enrolments. It begs the question of what has happened to students as a result of even a very limited experience in university education at a distance. The criticisms of studies of attrition/completion in conventional institutions are also relevant. What ultimately happens to students as a result of their attempting a distance university course? Do they leave satisfied at having tried something they may have though was beyond their grasp? (There is some evidence that drop-out students do not consider themselves as failures as institutional characterizations do—see Glynne and Jones, 1967). Do they move into higher education later? Do they return to distance study later? Longitudinal studies are needed for a full understanding of the phenomenon of drop-out.

The sample

Only home-study courses offered directly through AU have been included in the study and enrolments for audit were excluded. Also excluded were courses that have been substantially revised or discontinued, and courses that had fewer than 25 students over the three most recent cohorts.

On this basis estimates of course completion rates were obtained for seven 3-credit and fourteen 6-credit courses.

The data

The major indicator of course performance used is the rate of completion. Two formulations of the rate of course completion have been employed:

Formula 1 (Orton's "Total Enrolments Formula"):

$$\text{Rate of Course Completion} = \frac{\text{No. of Course Completions} \times 100}{\text{No. of Course Registrations}}$$

Formula 2 (The NUEA Formula):

$$\text{Rate of Course Completion} = \frac{\text{No. of Course Completions} \times 100}{\text{No. of Course Registrations} - \text{No. of "Non-Starts"}}$$

In this study a "non-start" has been operationally defined as an enrolee who did not complete the first credit block. This definition is reasonable because the cohorts enroled under a now defunct "Introductory Package" policy. Under this policy, AU courses were modularized so a student could undertake a portion of a course on a trial basis and enrol in the remainder after successful completion of this portion and payment of the full course fee. Previous surveys of students who did not complete the Introductory Package (Shale 1979) indicated that these students had done very little work in the course.

For courses which do not allow of partial credits Formula 2 is unsuitable since it is not possible—using the Student Record System—to differentiate between students who did little or no work before dropping out and those students who did a significant amount. Every student not completing the course would be classified as a non-start and by Formula 2 the course completion rate would be a tautological 100%. There were only 4 courses of this type in the study. Including these in the overall completion rate estimates given by Formula 2 causes the estimates to be slightly inflated but this effect should not be significant.

There are two forms a completion may take: either the student successfully completes an entire course or a contract for some specified number of sections/credits. Contracts of this latter sort were very few and these "completers" were added to the number that formed the numerator of the completion ratios. Students who failed the final examination are not considered completers but the number is negligibly small.

Since there may be substantial learning occurring short of a course completion two other indicators have been reported in the study: 1) The proportion of a course done by students who start and earn some credit but do not complete, and; 2) the proportion of "non-starts" to the total enrolments in that course.

It is useful to know how much is done by students who don't complete because it provides an indication of student activity and may indicate how the university could actively encourage students to persist. Knowing what percentage are "non-starts" is also very helpful. It mitigates the harshness of the estimates produced from Formula 1 and may indicate where more needs to be done in matching the expectations of students to what the university can supply.

Course performance data by course and by cohort are displayed in Table 1. As an example the entries for Math 101 would be read in the following manner: for Cohort 1, there were 37 students enroling in the course; 25 of these obtained no credit in the course and are "non-starts"; 5 students started the course but did not complete it, though they did generate a total of 6 (partial) credits; 27 credits were generated in total (the sum of the 6 partial credits and the 21 credits generated by the 7 students who did complete).

Totals down the right hand margin of Table 1 summarize the data for each *cohort,* ignoring distinctions among specific courses. The two sets of totals across the bottom (labelled "ALL COHORTS" and "COHORTS 2, 3, 4 ONLY") are summaries for each course, ignoring distinctions among cohorts. The reason for having a set of data which excluded Cohort 1 was to avoid dealing with information that is very dated.

Table 2 summarizes the course completion rates for each of the four cohorts by 3-credit and 6-credit courses.

Results

1. The course completion rates over all courses and cohorts are 28.8% according to Formula 1 and 58.2% according to Formula 2. For 3-credit courses these rates are 31.9% and 68.6%, respectively; and for 6-credit courses, the rates are 27.0% and 52.8%, respectively. These rates all improve when the data for Cohort 1 is excluded from the analysis.

2. The percentage of "non-starts" to total enrolments for Cohorts 2, 3, and 4 is 51% overall (55% for all 3-credit courses and 49% for all 6-credit courses).

3. Course completion rates may vary substantially within a single subject across cohorts—although the overall course completion rates are quite stable across the cohorts.

4. Those students who actually make a start but do not complete typically do about one-third of the course before dropping out.

Paper 36

Table 1: Estimates of course completion rates for students enroled at Athabasca University

COHORT 1 1978-08-01 To 1978-11-30	Math 101*	French 103	World Ecology 201	Human Communities 202	Computer Science 205	Psychology 206	Sociology 208	Chemistry 209	English 210	Math 212	Math 215	Accounting 216	History 224*	Psychology 228*	Communications 229*	Geology 231	Administration 232*	French 242	Geography 317	History 300*	Administration 319	Totals
Enrolments Generating																						
-Total	37	46	27	17	68	128	43	25	91	20	43	127	0	64	40	19	71	-	-	24	29	919
-No credit	25	21	12	9	29	58	25	13	48	15	23	53	0	27	14	8	41	-	-	17	16	454
-Partial credit	5	N.A.	7	5	30	26	11	2	24	5	12	50	N.A.	12	10	4	13	-	-	N.A.	8	224
Partial credit generated	6	N.A.	15	12	62	57	21	2	45	6	14	85	N.A.	14	15	8	14	-	-	N.A.	20	396
Total credit generated	27	150	64	30	102	315	63	58	159	6	38	229	0	89	63	50	65	-	-	21	48	1577
Course completions	7	25	8	3	9	44	7	10	19	0	8	24	0	25	16	7	17	-	-	7	5	241
COHORT 2 1979-01-01 To 1979-03-31																						
Enrolments Generating																						
-Total	27	21	11	8	47	56	21	2	30	12	17	64	29	29	20	4	170	-	5	5	8	586
-No credit	21	6	3	1	30	29	8	0	21	6	7	36	13	10	3	3	115	-	2	1	4	319
-Partial credit	2	N.A.	4	3	15	8	2	1	5	6	1	23	N.A.	9	5	0	29	-	0	N.A.	3	116
Partial credit generated	2	N.A.	9	5v	26	27	6	1	10	9	1	37	N.A.	10	6	0	32	-	0	N.A.	7	188
Total credit generated	8	90	33	30	33	126	72	7	34	9	28	64	48	40	42	6	108	-	15	12	13	818
Course completions	2	15	4	5	2	19	11	1	4	0	9	5	16	10	12	1	26	-	3	4	1	150
COHORT 3 1979-04-31 To 1979-07-31																						
Enrolments Generating																						
-Total	8	6	15	5	22	14	12	-	23	10	25	29	2	21	19	4	47	-	7	4	4	277
-No credit	6	2	6	2	16	5	4	-	13	7	9	19	0	9	7	2	30	-	3	0	0	140
-Partial credit	1	N.A.	4	2	4	4	3	-	2	2	5	6	N.A.	3	3	0	7	-	1	N.A.	2	49
Partial credit generated	1	N.A.	8	3	4	9	7	-	5	4	6	10	N.A.	5	4	0	8	-	1	N.A.	3	78
Total credit generated	4	24	35	9	11	36	37	-	53	10	39	34	6	32	31	6	38	-	19	0	15	439
Course completions	1	4	5	1	2	5	5	-	8	1	11	4	2	9	9	1	10	-	3	0	2	83
COHORT 4 1979-08-01 To 1979-11-30																						
Enrolments Generating																						
-Total	14	55	13	7	42	84	23	15	55	18	57	97	45	48	24	27	102	47	24	15	32	844
-No credit	12	27	6	6	21	48	5	4	27	13	25	36	21	24	5	14	66	24	9	12	9	414
-Partial credit	0	N.A.	3	0	14	18	10	2	12	3	9	47	N.A.	4	5	4	3	N.A.	2	N.A.	12	148
Partial credit generated	0	N.A.	9	0	35	41	22	2	25	6	9	47	N.A.	6	6	8	5	N.A.	4	N.A.	20	245
Total credit generated	6	168	34	6	60	146	70	55	90	18	76	169	72	66	48	62	102	138	82	9	86	1563
Course completions	2	28	4	1	7	18	8	9	16	2	23	14	24	20	14	9	33	23	13	3	11	282
ALL COHORTS																						
Enrolments Generating																						
-Total	86	128	66	37	179	282	99	42	199	60	142	317	76	162	103	54	390	47	36	48	73	2626
-No credit	64	56	27	18	96	140	42	17	109	41	64	144	34	70	29	27	252	24	14	30	29	1327
-Partial credit	8	N.A.	18	10	63	56	26	5	43	16	27	126	N.A.	28	23	8	52	N.A.	3	N.A.	25	537
Partial credit generated	9	N.A.	41v	20	127	134	56	5	85	25	30	179	N.A.	35	31	16	59	N.A.	5	N.A.	50	907
Total credit generated	45	432	166v	75	206	623	242	120	336	43	181	496	126	227	184	124	313	138	116	42	162	4397
Course completions	12	72	21	10	20	86	31	20	47	3	51	47	42	64	51	18	86	23	19	14	19	756
Course Completion:																						
Formula 1	14	56	32	27	11	30	31	48	24	5	36	15	55	40	50	33	22	49	53	29	26	29
Formula 2	55	100	54	53	24	61	54	80	52	16	65	27	100	70	69	67	62	100	86	78	43	58
Proportion of course done by starters who don't complete:	37	0	38	33	34	40	36	17	33	26	37	24	0	42	45	33	38	0	28	0	33	169
COHORTS 2,3,4 ONLY																						
Enrolments Generating																						
-Total	49	82	39	20	111	154	56	17	108	40	99	190	76	98	63	35	319	47	36	24	44	1707
-No credit	39	35	15	9	67	82	17	4	61	26	41	91	34	43	15	19	211	24	14	13	13	873
-Partial credit	3	N.A.	11	5	33	30	15	3	19	11	15	76	N.A.	16	13	4	39	N.A.	3	N.A.	17	313
Partial credit generated	3	N.A.	26	8	65	77	35	3	40	19	16	94	N.A.	21	16	8	45	N.A.	5	N.A.	30	511
Total credit generated	18	282	102	45	104	308	179	62	177	37	143	267	126	138	121	74	248	138	116	21	114	2820
Course completions	5	47	13	7	11	42	24	10	28	3	43	23	42	39	35	11	69	23	19	7	14	515
Course Completion:																						
Formula 1	10	57	33	35	10	27	43	59	26	7	43	12	55	40	56	31	22	49	53	29	32	30
Formula 2	50	100	54	64	25	58	62	77	60	21	74	23	100	71	73	69	64	100	86	64	45	62
Proportion of course done by starters who don't complete:	33	0	39	27	33	43	39	17	35	29	36	21	0	44	41	33	38	0	28	0	29	163

Prepared by the Office of Institutional Studies, June 1981
Notes: * Designates a 3 credit course
N.A. Designates courses in which it is not possible to earn partial credits
v Designates a number which has been rounded upwards from a value containing a half a credit to the next whole number of credits. This was done to reduce the space required to display the table. However, the actual fractional values were used in all calculations.

Table 2: Course completion rates by cohorts

Formula	COHORT 1		COHORT 2		COHORT 3		COHORT 4		ALL COHORTS		ALL COHORTS EXCLUDING NO. 1	
	1	2	1	2	1	2	1	2	1	2	1	2
3 Credit Courses	28.6	58.4	25.7	61.0	34.4	68.9	40.0	84.7	31.9	68.6	33.1	72.6
6 Credit Courses	25.3	49.4	25.5	52.1	26.5	53.9	30.0	56.7	27.0	52.8	28.1	55.0
All Courses	26.2	51.8	25.6	56.2	30.0	60.6	33.4	65.6	28.8	58.2	30.2	61.8

Discussion

Perhaps the most compelling question that arises is, "How does this compare with how students at other distance universities do?" It is very difficult to address this question directly. Different methods of counting students can imply very different interpretations of completion rates—even though the formulae by which such rates are calculated are ostensibly identical. Interpretations of completion rates may be strongly affected by institutional admission requirements and registration procedures. For example, completion rates of around 70% are frequently cited for OU courses. However, if we examine the situation closely we note the following: 50% of those applying to enter the OU are refused; only 75% of those accepted for a place actually enter the OU; and of this 75% only 70% proceed through provisional enrolment to "finally registered". OU course completion estimates use the number of final registrations as the base figure. This means that there are three screening steps before students are considered true course enrolments. In order for the OU calculations to be comparable to those for AU the OU would have to admit all applicants, and use this figure as the denominator in its course completion estimates.

Clearly we can't make the figures directly comparable—let alone address the issue of whether the two groups of students many reasonably be equated. However, it is useful to approximate the AU calculation using OU figures because it exemplifies the effect that different administrative policies can have on estimates of course completion rate. Using 1978 enrolment and completion data from the OU Digest of Statistics for S100, D222, and M331—and taking the total number of students accepting a position at the OU as the base figure—one obtains a completion rate estimate of 36%. Evidently, even relatively benign forms of screening can substantially affect course completion figures.

The OU experience provides yet another perspective on course completion rates. The reduction of drop-outs has been a central element of the OU's educational philosophy. Sewart (1978) has summarized this philosophy as a "continuity of concern for students in a system of learning at a distance". The University is obliged to strive continually to find ways to "reduce to a minimum the number of students who embark upon courses only to find that they cannot continue with them". The function of estimates of completion rates in this context is simply to keep the institution informed about how effective its strategies are in diminishing student drop-out.

While course completion rates are important indicators of the performance of the university, such indicators are limited representations only of the quality of the full range of educational services provided. In addition, it is important to note that high course completion rates is a goal established by the university and may only be a very imperfect representation of the educational goals of the students.

Why students drop out of university distance education and what institutions might do to address the matter are two vitally important issues not considered directly here. As Pantages and Creedon (1978) have observed, "the goal of attrition research is first to obtain as complete an understanding as possible, and then to apply this knowledge in designing programs aimed at lowering rates of attrition."

Douglas G. Shale
Athabasca University
Canada

References

Connors, B. (1980) Assessment of students in distance teaching. In Armstrong, J.D. and Store, R.E. (eds.) *Evaluation in Distance Teaching*. Townsville, Queensland: Townsville College of Advanced Education.

Glynne, D.R. and Jones, H.A. (1967) Student wastage. *Adult Education*, 40, 3.

Orton, L.J. (1977) Completion and non-start rates in correspondence courses. *Canadian Journal of University Continuing Education*, 4, 21-26.

Pantages, T.J. and Creedon, C.F. (1978) Studies of college attrition: 1950-1975. *Review of Educational Research*, 48, 1, 49-101.

Sewart, D. (1978) Continuity of Concern for Students in a System of Learning at a Distance. Zentrales Institut für Fernstudienforschung Papiere 22, Hagen: Fernuniversität.

Shale, D. (1979) Report on course withdrawals. Report from the Office of Institutional Studies, Athabasca University.

Sheath, H. (1973) *Report on external studies*. University of New England, Armidale, N.S.W.

Tinton, V. (1975) Dropout from higher education: a theoretical synthesis of recent research. *Review of Educational Research*, 45, 1, 89-125.

Paper 37
Reducing the Drop-Out Rate in Advanced Courses
(Abstract)

The drop-out rate, defined as the proportion of finally registered students not sitting final exams, has increased slowly but steadily over the last five years in most of the Open University's third level courses. Drop-out rate does not seem to depend on workload (number of courses taken) but, for a given workload, students do worse the longer they have been enrolled at the University. In general students who pass with a good grade a prior course that is recommended or prerequisite are less likely to drop out of the subsequent course. However this is a relatively weak effect which varies from course to course.

Alan Woodley
The Open University
United Kingdom

Paper 38
The Drop-Out Problem and What To Do About It
Personalizing instruction by integrating teaching and administrative measures will have a positive effect on completion rates.

Why research on drop-out in distance education?

For ten years I have had the privilege of using part of my working time for research in distance education. In the major part of my research, drop-out rates, or to express it positively, completion rates, have been an important aspect, either as the object of the research itself or as the most significant criterion of success for the independent variables examined in some experimental studies. I do not consider statistics on completions and cancellations to be the goal of the research, but I believe that it is important for any institute to disclose and report such figures, because confirmed knowledge is the basis for any serious attempts to develop higher quality teaching systems. Further, higher quality teaching will prove itself—among other things—in lower drop-out rates.

I have often been asked if a high drop-out rate is a more serious problem in distance education than in other forms of education. Meaningful comparisons between drop-out in distance courses and other courses, as well as between distance courses in different educational systems are difficult to make, partly because conflicting definitions of drop-out are presented in the literature and partly because in many studies drop-out is only vaguely defined.

I feel there are good reasons to state that drop-out does not generally seem to be a more serious problem in correspondence or distance education than in other forms of part-time education. In fact, research so far seems to indicate that the main difficulties which cause many distance students to give up their courses stem from the part-time study situation more than from problems of the method itself. Nevertheless, I think that there still are innumerable possibilities for increasing the quality of distance education and improving the situation of the students. Consequently, I still believe that the problem is important and should continue to be given attention by distance educators and researchers.

In my institute, the NKI School, Norway, we have approached the challenge of increasing distance teaching quality and reducing drop-out rates from three different angles:

1. *Professionalization of the staff through participation in external and internal courses, conferences and workshops.*

   Example: A correspondence course (4 study units) for correspondence tutors was developed. The course is compulsory for all distance tutors.

2. *Systematic and continuous development work aimed at increasing the quality of all parts of the distance education system.*

   Example: An author's and writer's guide for the preparation of correspondence course material was developed. Material is developed according to well recognized theories of teaching and learning, particularly Gagné's general teaching model.

3. *Research work.*

   In the rest of this paper I shall describe briefly the research at the NKI School on the drop-out problem and the effect of certain efforts to reduce the rate of non-starters, early withdrawals and drop-outs. This research started in 1970.

The NKI distance program consists mainly of "course compositions" in various branches of technology at different levels. The course compositions vary from smaller ones of about 20 study units to larger ones comprising more than 500 study units and leading to an engineering degree.

Surveys of recruitment, achievements and discontinuation

Our first project was a pilot survey to shed some light on the following areas:

1. Recruitment
2. Persistence and drop-out
3. The students' reasons for discontinuation
4. Correlations between background variables and criteria of success in distance education.

The results of the survey were published some years ago. Here are some of the main findings concerning drop-out. The status of the 1417 students 2.5 years after enrolment was as follows:

– 1085 (76.6%) had discontinued, 283 (20.0%) were still active, while only 49 (3.4%) had completed their courses. We applied a very strict definition of discontinuation: all students who had not submitted assignments during the last three months and had not completed the number of study units for which they had enrolled.

– 168 students (11.9%) did not submit even a single assignment. About 50% of the drop-outs had submitted their last lesson before their 150th day of study, and about 75% had submitted their last work before the lapse of one year.

– The total deviation of the variable "lessons submitted" by the 1085 drop-out students extended from 0 to 165, the median being 8.3 study units (i.e. one half of the drop-outs submitted less than 9 units). The course compositions consist of a number of complete single courses. 65% of all the enrolled students had completed one or more single courses.

During 1972-1978 we completed two other surveys, examining similar problems to see if the findings from the above mentioned study could be generalized. We wanted to elaborate on the problems and find out if efforts to increase completion rates had been successful. Table 1 summarizes some of the findings from these surveys.

Table 1 indicates a small but systematic increase in the amount of work done by the students from year to year. This must be ascribed mainly to a general development in the Institute, but also to education measures introduced on the basis of experimental research.

Some other important findings from the surveys:

1. The seasons of the year appeared to have a significant influence. It seemed to be difficult to

Table 1: Some results from the NKI drop-out surveys

Enrolment year and number of students	*Status 2.5 years after enrolment (%)			Median number of study units completed in the groups			Completed at least 1 course (%)	Median number of courses completed
	Completed	Active	Discontinued	Completed	Active	Discontinued		
1967-68 1417	3.4	20.0	76.6	66	61	8	65	1.5
1968-69 1345	3.8	20.7	75.5	61	62	9	72	2.2
1969-70 1147	5.0	19.2	75.9	61	74	11	76	2.6
1972-73 427	12.2	3.0	84.8	61	125	13	80	3.3

*For the sample enroled 1972-73 the date were collected 4 years after enrolment.

start correspondence studies during the spring months and in December (monthly rates of non-starters varied from 5 to 23%). Discontinuation also showed its peak rates from April to July.

2. Age is positively correlated with persistence; i.e. older students performed better than younger ones (in our surveys "old" means more than 27 years).

3. The level of previous education is positively correlated with all criteria of success in distance education. The single best predictor of success seems to be earlier completion of a correspondence course.

4. It does seem to be a disadvantage if the student has been out of school for some time.

5. The main reasons given for discontinuation seem to be related to circumstances outside the immediate control of the Institute (such as lack of time, job required too much time, changed to other school work or changed career plans, economic reasons, illness, unsatisfactory living or study conditions, personal reasons). However, questionnaires and interviews examining these problems more deeply disclosed study-related reasons as well (such as problems in the method itself, the subject matter or planning/organizing study; dissatisfaction with the study material, the tutors' work and turn-around time of assignments).

Some students reach their goal before the course is completed, but this does not seem to be a very common reason for discontinuation, and should never be used as an excuse for continuing practices which could be changed for the better.

Follow-up of students

During the years following the pilot survey we carried out some experiments on administrative and educational activities. In the first we tried to measure the effect of a sequence of one postcard and two letters, sent to inactive students at one-month intervals to encourage them to resume their studies. The sequence was started automatically when the student had not submitted any assignment for a whole calendar month and stopped when the student made any contact, either by submitting assignments or by communicating with the school's student advisors.

Differences in study activity between an experimental and a control group consisting of about 240 students randomly selected were compared every month. Large and statistically significant differences between the groups were found after the three months. During the third month 46% of the experimental group did submit assignments or made other contacts, while this was the case for only 31% of the control students.

These results initiated another research project involving three experimental and one control group of newly enrolled students where we tried to measure the effect of an introductory course in study techniques as well as a system of encouraging follow-up letters, sent on enrolment and 14, 28 and 42 days thereafter.

Figure 1: Factors making up turn-around time

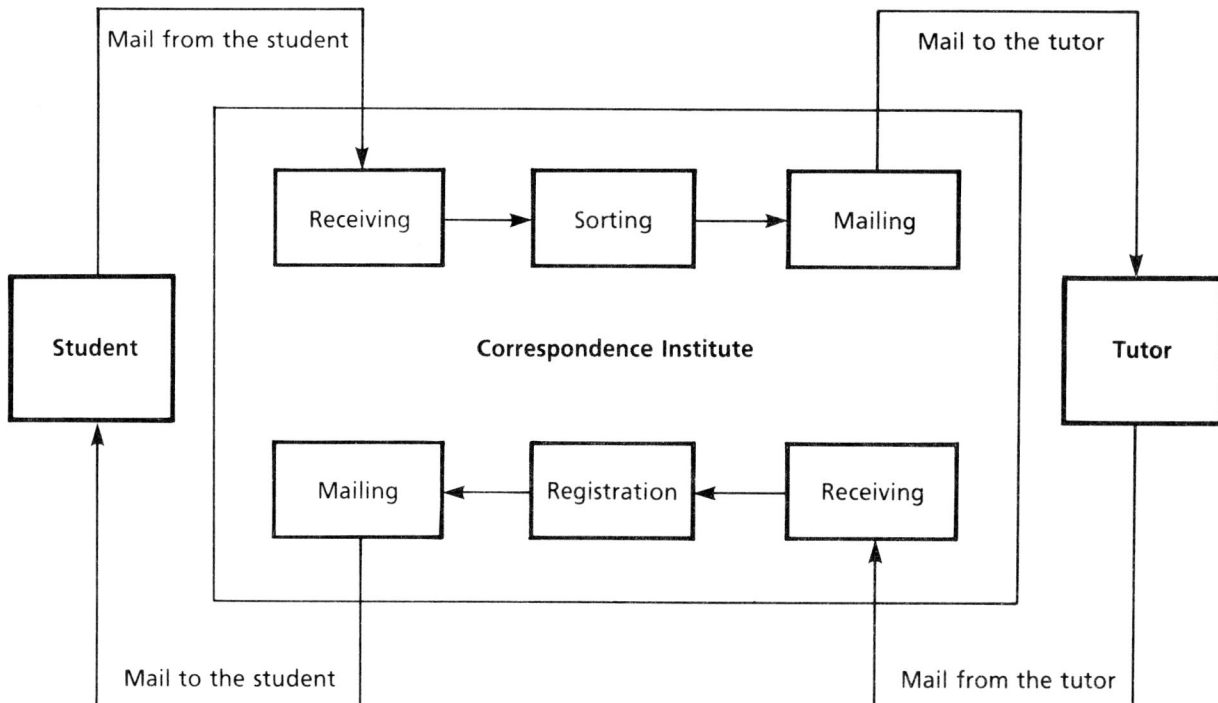

We found that students receiving a personal encouraging letter on enrolment started their studies earlier. (Correlations between lapse of time before submitting the first assignment and completion of studies have been reported earlier).

The data also led us to conclude that the courses in study techniques together with the follow-up letters during the initial phase of the studies may help to reduce the number of early withdrawals. The three experimental groups had submitted a larger number of assignments two and four months after enrolment (not significant differences) and the experimental groups expressed a more favourable attitude towards the school's counselling services.

Turn-around time

One of the problems in correspondence education is that the turn-around time (the time it takes from when the student submits the assignment until he gets it back from the tutor) tends to be relatively long. The turn-around of assignments in many correspondence institutes are illustrated in Figure 1.

Figure 1 shows that the circulation of student papers normally involves four postal and a number of internal operations. At NKI we carried out an experiment where the turn-around time, measured by a student questionnaire, was reduced from a median of 8.3 days in the control group to 5.6 days in the experimental group. The arrangements contributed to an increase in completion rates from 69 to 91%—a statistically significant difference. We also found that the students seemed to accept a turn-around time of a week or less, while a longer period resulted in a considerable number of dissatisfied students. Several measures may be introduced to reduce turn-around time, such as internal rationalization, strict demands on tutors (and control), reduction of the number of postal handlings, etc.

Preproduced tutor's comments

Most correspondence tutors have found that written comments need to be relatively long in order to be educationally efficient, and more or less the same factual content is often written to many students. Thus, it seemed reasonable to examine the effects of intro-

Table 2: Outline of the experimental and control variable in the personal tutor/counsellor project

Aspect	Experimental	Control
1. The tutor	Same tutor during the first 3-11 single courses	Different tutors in the different courses
2. Employment	Working within the institute on a fixed salary	Part-time external working on a per assignment basis
3. Teaching/Counselling	Same person responsible for all student contact	Tutor responsible for written communication through assignments. Student advisors take care of general problems.
4. Turn-around time	All assignments returned the same day	Assignments following the complete circuit as shown in Figure 1
5. Study techniques	Same tutor teaching this course	Separate part-time tutors
6. Initial follow-up	Tutor contacts all students by phone or individualized letters.	Automatic follow-up by printed letters
7. General follow-up	A sequence of 3 individualizd contacts by phone or letters to all inactive students	An automatic sequence of 1 printed card and 2 letters
8. Telephone tutoring	All students are invited to call the tutor during office hours. Tutor calls when needed.	No systematic use of the telephone. Some few tutors invite students to call
9. Tutor's presentation	Personal presentation of the tutor with telephone number and picture is sent with the study material	Presentations of the individual tutors are returned to the student with the first assignment
10. Preproduced comments	Developed for all course. Used when needed	May be used by some tutors

ducing preproduced material in addition to the tutor's written comments. The aim would be to increase the tutor's ability to individualize teaching within the realistic limits set by time and economy. Two parallel experiments have been carried out at NKI and NKS in Norway. Results from such experiments may be even more difficult to generalize than results from the other experiments described in this paper, because courses, contents, and tutors' responsibilities differ a lot from one situation to another.

In fact, the results from the two experiments were not quite compatible. One of the experiments showed a statistically significant increase in completion rates—from 61 to 80% in a 4-unit course—while no significant differences were observed in the other. However, the students in both experimental groups expressed very favourable attitudes towards the additional preproduced comments.

Concluding remarks

In this paper I have tried to show that research can be done within an individual distance teaching institute. We have learned that results from research may help us find ways to improve distance teaching routines. We have also found that internal research stimulates educational thinking among personnel responsible for the day by day functioning of the Institute, and thus aids the overall development of the system.

At present, we are carrying out an experiment to try to integrate educational and administrative measures which have seemed to help distance students to complete their courses. In this experiment, which is part of a cooperative project among correspondence schools in Norway, the experimental students will be in contact with a single personal tutor/counsellor. Table 2 gives an outline of this experiment.

We feel that personalizing the instruction by integrating teaching and administrative measures, which in most distance teaching systems are separated in an effort to rationalize and industrialize the teaching system, will have a positive effect on completion rates. Our preliminary experiences are very positive. We feel that some of these experiments may become important for future developments, even in relatively highly industrialized systems of distance education.

Torstein Rekkedal
Norsk Korrespondanseskole
Norway

Correspondence vs. On-Campus Courses: Some Evaluative Comparisons

Three studies comparing distance with on-campus study resulted in comparisons favourable to distance techniques.

Everyone associated with correspondence education has heard the question: "How can you be sure these independent study courses are of the same quality as regular courses?" The literature is of little help, since it contains very few comparative studies.

This paper summarizes the results of three studies of varying size, scope, method, and rigour. They are not necessarily offered as examples of how to compare independent study courses with on-campus courses, but to illustrate the kind of information that can be collected within the confines of an ongoing program. (A more complete report on the studies is available from the author.)

Before reporting the evaluation studies, we shall describe the courses, and the program of which they are a part.

The independent study program

Although the University of Saskatchewan has been offering correspondence education for more than 50 years, only 25 courses are presently available. Until a couple of years ago formal course development procedures were not used: interested faculty members, in exchange for a very small monetary reward, put together syllabuses for the courses they taught on campus and made them available through the correspondence office. Hence the vast majority of the 25 courses are simply a textbook accompanied by a brief syllabus listing required readings and, usually, essay-type assignments to be mailed in for grading.

The transformation of the correspondence office into the independent study program, and the availability of qualified instructional designers to work on courses, saw the introduction of a quite different model.

In constructing the model, we decided not to be overly structured and regulated. While most of the design features listed below appear in some guise in every independent study course, we recognize that certain courses do not lend themselves to some of these features, and we do not force the structure onto a course or an instructor. For this reason, there is no predetermined number of lessons or units or assignments, nor is there a rigid system of mailing deadlines for assignments for all courses.

A course manual replaces the syllabus, and usually contains the following features for each unit or lesson:

1. An introduction and rationale.
2. A statement of learning expectations.
3. A list of readings.
4. Notes, commentaries, and definitions by the instructor.
5. Audio cassettes.
6. Explicit instructions on the sequence of activities students should follow.
7. A set of self-tests with answers.
8. Periodic mail-in assignments.
9. A good match between objectives, review questions, assignments, and test items.
10. Encouragement for communication with other students and the instructor (who can be called collect).

All three courses studied incorporated the design procedure sketched above, though not all elements appeared in every course.

Overview of studies

Study #1

Study #1 evaluated a pilot project offering a newly developed introductory course in computational science. Nine students completed the course and provided information through course materials questionnaires and a telephone interview with the evaluator. As well, subjective comparisons of student achievement were made by the instructor who designed the course.

Study #2

Study #2, probably the most rigorous and comprehensive of the three, involved offering a modification of the independent study version of a course in quantitative business analysis: it was offered during a summer session on campus, but the instructional load was carried by the materials designed for the independent study course. The instructor met with the class twice a week, but only to conduct brief quizzes and provide some feedback on progress. Hence the on-campus students' experiences were not much different from those of independent study students. A series of course materials questionnaires, telephone interviews by the evaluator, comparison of student achievement and opinion of the course with similar data collected from the regular on-campus class of the preceding spring term, and telephone interviews with drop-outs were used to collect data. Thirty-eight students completed this version of the course.

Study #3

Study #3 used questionnaires with students taking an introductory class in sociology. Most of the information collected was formative in nature (to be used to modify course materials). Nine students provided data. The instructor conducted telephone discussions with students, but only parts of these discussions were evaluative.

What we learned (or re-learned)

— We now have some reason to believe that independent study courses incorporating the design procedure outlined earlier compare very favourably with on-campus courses in terms of student achievement and student satisfaction: in all three cases independent study students performed at least as well as on-campus students on the final examination. With respect to student satisfaction, in all cases again, students were at least as satisfied with the independent study course as they were with other university courses they had taken. (Indeed, we have some indication—but based on so few respondents that we cannot overly rely on the data—that student satisfaction for the courses incorporating instructional design are regarded as superior to on-campus classes, as well as to the previously existing independent study courses lacking those design elements. We are investigating this more completely.)

— Generally, drop-outs are not related to the quality of instruction or to difficulty coping with course content. They have almost always arisen from competing demands for time: family and job demands, illness, moves, deaths and births—in short, life—seem to demand higher priority than education at times and cause learners to drop out of courses.

— There is a tremendous variation among the learners in terms of personal characteristics, time put into the course, perceived difficulty and importance of the course material, background education, etc. In Study #1, for example, students varied in age from 19 to 59 years, and reported a time lapse of from less than 1 to 33 years between the time of taking this course and their previous formal educational experience. (The 33-year person reported being so 'fired up' by the experience, he was determined to enrol in another course straight-away!) In Study #2, learners reported spending anywhere from 3 to 20 hours on each lesson and essay; in Study #1, students reported spending anywhere from 2 to 25 hours a week working on the course. With respect to competing demands for time, Study #3 indicated that learners spent between 9 and 50 hours a week at a job, and there was a high negative correlation between the number of hours devoted to the job and the grade achieved. However, in Study #2, in which more than one-quarter of the class reported no regular activities outside the course, but some individuals indicated as many as 45 hours per week devoted to other regular activities, there was no significant difference on midterm and final examination grades for those having (a) no outside commit-ments, (b) fewer than the average number of out-side commitments, and (c) more than the average number of outside commitments.

— Not surprisingly, students generally found the use of objectives and self-correcting exercises very helpful. In fact, of all the design features, these two prompted the greatest number of spontane-ous favourable comments.

— Simply making provision for having students phone one another or the instructor for assistance has not worked very well in our experience. In the course in Study #3 the instructor deliberately phoned all students two or three times during the course, which seemed to prompt a good deal more discussion than had arisen in either of the other two studies, where students were simply given a phone number and told to call collect. With respect to students contacting students, the general opinion was that aside from a feeling of 'misery loves company', calling another student usually amounted to pooling ignorance and little else. There seems to be a need to build in a task orientation if student-student contacts are really desired.

Conclusion

The three studies indicate that (a) independent study students achieve at least as well as on-campus stu-dents; (b) independent study students are at least as satisfied with their learning experience as on-campus students; (c) the personal and demographic charac-teristics of independent study students are excep-tionally diverse and the influence of these factors on student achievement or satisfaction is difficult to determine; and (d) decisions to drop out of an independent study course apparently are not related to the quality of the learning experiences.

To be sure, a dyed-in-the-wool empiricist may well argue that three studies, two of which were espe-cially small in terms of student numbers, are not a complete answer to the question suggested by the title of this paper. We intend to collect both formal and informal evidence, however, until even the most hardened empiricist is satisfied.

Earl R. Misanchuk
The University of Saskatchewan
Canada

Paper 40

Liaison Between the School System and the Correspondence Branch

(Abstract)

The Manitoba Education Department Correspon-dence Branch was established in 1927 to provide a substitute for classroom instruction and until 1970 two-thirds of its students did not attend regular schools. Since 1970 the situation has reversed and 65% of the correspondence students are now attending school. The Correspondence Branch has undertaken an extensive visitation to schools to develop personal contacts and dissipate misunder-standings about distance education.

Today's students have a much more positive attitude to correspondence study and enrol in courses because of general interest in the subject matter and for reasons of self-fulfillment. Other fac-tors behind the improved perception of distance edu-cation are:

- collaboration between educational agencies and industry to develop technology and materials for individualized instruction
- design of correspondence courses based on current theories of learning
- increased government support for correspondence education
- greater sympathy for correspondence courses among schoolteachers
- parental support for individualized instruction

The Manitoba Correspondence Branch has developed new strategies for the supervision of correspondence students in schools. It has been shown that the supervision of correspondence students by secretaries, paraprofessionals, professionals and senior students results in completion rates of 90% or better. The Branch also attempts to provide 24 hour turn-around for registration and 7 day turn-around for lessons. As a result of these improvements 94% of respondents to a survey rated correspondence school services as 'good' or 'very good'.

Correspondence schools must continue to work with the regular school system while reinforcing the image of distance education as a viable alternative to the classroom. Ruskin's view of education is one we should keep in mind:

> *Education does not mean teaching people what they do not know... It is painful, continual and difficult work to be done by kindness, by watching, by warning, by precept, and by praise, but above all, by example.*

Chet Tesarowski
Manitoba Correspondence Branch
Canada

Characteristics and Attitudes of Correspondence Students

(Abstract)

A mail survey was carried out on a randomly selected sample of 1,283 students in the University of Waterloo's Correspondence Program, one of the largest North American programs of its type. This represents a return rate of 70%. The questionnaire included items on students' demographic characteristics, educational experience and intention, study habits, and general attitudes and opinions concerning correspondence study.

Results show that correspondence students are roughly equally divided by sex, tend to be married, in their thirties, are employed full time in professional or managerial occupations (including 31% who are teachers), and are already well-educated, with 31% holding university degrees. At the same time a major motive for enrolling in correspondence programs is the opportunity to complete a degree.

The great majority (87%) expressed high satisfaction with their experience of correspondence learning, and a major attraction of this type of education appeared to be the opportunity it provided to combine full time employment with study. In this sense correspondence programs can be seen as offering a genuine alternative to conventional university education: in the case of the present sample, most were within commuting distance of a university, with 40% living within ten miles of a campus, and 27% within five miles (the median distance for the total sample was 20 miles).

Other results from the survey indicate that students receive considerable support from their family for correspondence study and that other social support—for example from fellow students—would be regarded as beneficial. Lack of personal contacts with instructors and other students appears to lead to some uncertainties about course requirements, for example what to expect in course examinations. An important factor in selecting this particular program appeared to be the reputation of the University of Waterloo, lending some support to the notion that successful correspondence programs often have firm links with the regular program of an established and well regarded educational institution.

Christopher K. Knapper / Mary Ann Waslycia-Coe
University of Waterloo
Canada

Paper 42
How Different is the Distance Student?

The same materials can be used successfully with on-campus and off-campus students.

The fear is sometimes expressed that if on-campus and off-campus education are combined in a single institution the on-campus component will take precedence and off-campus students will be second-class citizens. At Deakin University we have shown that the combination with on-campus students need not preclude a high standard of provision for off-campus students. This has been done on a relatively small scale: Deakin had about 3000 off-campus and 2000 on-campus students in 1981, the fourth year of the off-campus operation. Possibly there are places elsewhere where existing institutions are seeking to redeploy resources into new areas of activity and some features of the Deakin University experience may be of interest.

With a population of only 14 million in a continent more than 3000 km across, distance is a big factor in Australian life. Distance or external teaching has a long history. The University of Queensland entered the field before the First World War. Since the Second World War the University of New England in New South Wales has become a major provider, and two other universities and a number of colleges of advanced education offer external studies. In each case the institution has on-campus as well as external or off-campus students.

Deakin University originated by amalgamation of an institute of technology and a teacher training college, so inheriting an existing on-campus program and student body. It was given a mandate to offer external studies at university level, serving in the first instance the population of Victoria, the second smallest of the Australian states in area with a population of less than four million. Economies of scale were therefore not available and there was incentive to combine on-campus and off-campus students.

Deakin University policy is to minimize the differences between on-campus and off-campus students. However, we did *not* adapt on-campus courses for off-campus use. On the contrary, we proceeded the other way round. We prepared structured learning materials including plenty of student activities. The materials were prepared by course teams and were professionally edited, designed, and printed in an attractive format. We hoped that if we could solve the educational problems of the off-campus students, those of on-campus students would pose no great difficulties. Indeed, we saw several advantages to this approach.

1. Self-instructional materials provide consistent quality of instruction. Unlike lecturers, learning materials do not have "off" days.

2. The use of self-instructional materials is in theory good educational practice. Staff in the School of Education felt that at last they would be able to practise what they preached. Hitherto they had spent much time standing in front of their classes telling students that they should not just stand in front of their classes telling them things. Now they could encourage learning through activities, just as they wanted their student teachers to do when they got out into schools.

3. Staff radicals saw the new mode as a liberation. Students would be liberated from the constraints of the traditional lecture and tutorial system and staff would be liberated from the lecturing grind and free to teach in more interactive ways.

The open campus program includes not only off-campus courses but also on-campus courses given in the same mode based on self-instructional materials. Three of the six Schools of the University launched the open campus program in 1978. The School of Education offered courses for in-service teachers to upgrade sub-degree qualifications to degree level, the same courses being used on campus as part of the initial training program at second year and third year levels. The School of Humanities and the School of Social Sciences offered a Bachelor of Arts program starting with interdisciplinary foundation courses at the first year level. In 1981 two further off-campus programs were launched—a Master of Business Administration and a Graduate Diploma of Computing. The rest of this paper refers only to the upgrading program for teachers and the Bachelor of Arts program.

Comparative performance of off-campus and on-campus students

Comparisons of students in the same course revealed that off-campus students fare no worse than on-campus students. Indeed, they do slightly better, though the differences are marginal. This conclusion emerged from an investigation of the results of students in nine Humanities and Social Sciences courses with an off-campus enrolment of 100 or more. The students were divided into five groups:

- on-campus, under 21
- on-campus, 21 or older, normal or advanced standing entrant
- on-campus entrant under special mature age scheme
- off-campus, 21 or older, normal or advanced standing entrant
- off-campus entrant under special mature age scheme.

Results for the nine courses showed no consistent differences between any of the sub-groups. Average figures for retention, pass, and good pass (Distinction or High Distinction) are shown in Table 1. The retention is slightly lower for the off-campus groups but the pass rates are somewhat higher and the good pass rates substantially so.

This was for some a rather surprising outcome. A committed distance educator might say he could have predicted it: courses devised with off-campus students in mind work best with off-campus students. From a more traditional viewpoint, however, it represents an inversion of the usual expectations. Off-campus students have usually been thought of as disadvantaged because they lack face-to-face contact with academic staff and the formal and informal support mechanisms available on campus.

With this comparison in mind, I will now discuss some factors that may influence success rates. They are related to content and to the delivery and support mechanisms.

Content

No obvious features of content make the courses more suitable for either group, although some types of content may be more suitable for certain age groups. The distinction between off-campus and on-campus corresponds broadly, but not exactly, to the distinction between school leavers and mature age students. Virtually all our off-campus students are of mature age (defined as over 21) but by no means are all our on-campus students school leavers.

In general the content of the education courses is not more difficult for some age groups than for others. The Humanities and Social Sciences courses are interdisciplinary and draw on life experiences: their protagonists consider them "relevant", in contrast to the "irrelevance" of traditional courses bound to disciplines. Mature students may well have faced moral dilemmas of the kind dealt with by existentialist writers. However, such material is also of interest to school leavers. It opens new areas of experience to them. The grades obtained confirmed the testimony of teaching staff that while mature students do somewhat better the difference between them and school leavers is not at all clear cut.

Delivery and support mechanisms

Delivery and support mechanisms are quite different for the two types of student. Off-campus students get study guides, readers, audio tapes, and informal supplementary material such as newsletters by post. There is no compulsory attendance for any kind of teaching. Optional tutorial support is provided at eleven locations. Those who come greatly appreciate the contact with tutors, but many students do not come. Zealous tutors, delighted at the enthusiasm shown by the students they see, want to pressure others to come. But lack of attendance could be interpreted as a tribute to instructional materials that really do make it possible for a student to study successfully by himself. Although the availability of tutor support is valuable for those who want it, it is clear that attendance is not essential for success.

On-campus students studying in the "open" mode, that is, using self-instructional materials, do not get formal lectures. Typically they have two hours a week contact time used in a variety of ways. Some possible reasons for the failure of on-campus students to do better than off-campus students are as

Table 1: Retention, pass and good pass rates for nine Humanities and Social Sciences courses, 1979

	On Campus			Off Campus	
	Under 21	21 or over (non special entry)	Special Entry	21 or over (non special entry)	Special Entry
% Retention	90	92	94	89	87
% Pass	78	68	67	78	74
% D or HD	13	19	13	29	20

Notes

Retention rates have been calculated as the number receiving a final grade expressed as a percentage of those enrolled at 30 April.

The grade D or HD (Distinction or High Distinction) percentages have been calculated as percentages of the number receiving a final result.

follows. First, there is the simple matter of timing. Off-campus students get their materials a month or more before the start of on-campus teaching in early March. This not only gives them longer to work at the materials, it also gives them longer to change their minds about proceeding with the course before April 30, the date on which enrolments are officially counted.

Second, some on-campus students do not read the materials as thoroughly as they might before the tutorials. In part this is perhaps a function of age: school leavers may be less good at organizing themselves without the help of a structured timetable. Another factor may be a disappointed expectation of a greater measure of spoon-feeding. A few students suggested that because they are not getting two lectures a week they are not "getting their money's worth". Some students seem to want a visible presence to teach them, though it is not clear how far this felt need is an intellectual one and how far it is a social and emotional one. Some students don't much want to be liberated from dependence on teachers. The more radical staff, needless to say, are undismayed by the students' reluctance to seize the opportunity of freedom and want to act more energetically to force them to be free.

A third set of factors concerns the availability of peripheral materials. Although on-campus students get the same study guides and readers, they do not always receive other materials sent to off-campus students. Thus:

1. Off-campus students get newsletters and similar informal communications. The mechanisms on campus for disseminating the same information—announcements in class, notice on bulletin boards or the grapevine—can be more fallible than postal delivery.

2. Off-campus students get a counselling package some months before the start of their first academic year. This is intended mainly to help them decide whether to conform their decision to enrol, but it also includes advice on such things as study skills. It is assumed that on-campus students will just pick up such skills and provision to help them do so is less systematic.

3. Whereas off-campus students each get their own audio tapes, on-campus students are expected to use tapes kept in the library.

So, although on-campus study provides opportunities that off-campus students may envy, it provides them in a way that may be less systematic and more fallible than is often supposed. The contents of a regular mail drop, remote and impersonal as they are, have been devised with a care that may more than make up for the lack of personal contact.

Conclusion

The view that good distance teaching demands recognition of the distinctiveness of distance students has brought great benefits in the last decade. By focusing on the characteristic needs of distance students, distance educators have provided better education. At Deakin University, however, we have shown that it is quite possible to combine a high quality distance teaching operation with on-campus teaching using the same materials. Many details remain to be investigated before we have a good understanding of the factors important for success. It is likely that much depends on elusive details of how students actually use materials and what actually goes on in tutorials.

F.R. Jevons
Deakin University
Australia

Student Achievement as a Function of Study Time: A Comparative Analysis

Forthcoming results will compare the relative importance of study time and entrance qualifications.

Introduction

Large systems of distance education are no less cost-effective and are more cost-efficient than systems based on face-to-face teaching (Laidlaw and Layard, 1974; Rumble, 1981). Might distance education systems also be more "time-effective" than traditional systems? It seems reasonable to suggest that it is more efficient for off-campus (external) students to invest time studying self-instructional packages at their own pace, than it is for on-campus (internal) students to work in groups where they must endeavour to keep pace with the rest. External students can organise their own study time whereas internal students have to attend classes of fixed length at pre-specified times. The flexibility of distance education may engender a more efficient use of time. The main purpose of this study was to investigate the relative time-effectiveness of traditional and distance education systems. Theoretical issues arising from different conceptions of the relationship between time and learning were also examined.

Prior research

Comparative studies of the time-effectiveness of distance education relative to conventional instruction do not figure in the research literature (Gough and Monday, 1979). There is a belief that distance education students suffer from excessive demands on their time by course designers. Connors (1980) in discussing drop-out rates at the Open University suggested that the main cause was student overload. He claimed that students "think that the course material is too difficult for them because they cannot finish it in the ten hours a week that we promised them they ought to be able to finish it in" (p. 15). Similarly, Daniel and Marquis (1979) commented that course designers underestimate the time a typical student will take on a piece of work: "the remote learning course that requires less study time than advertised is a rare phenomenon" (p. 42). In spite of the importance of this issue little effort has been made to collect data that might provide a better basis for ensuring that the credit given is commensurate with the time the student invests.

In the context of classroom instruction there has been a gradual increase in the research effort over the past 20 years. Several recent papers (Berliner, 1979; Fredrick and Walberg, 1980; Rosenshine, 1979) have reaffirmed the promise of time-related variables (Carroll, 1963) in increasing the explanatory power of causal models of student achievement. The value of many of the findings is, however, limited because the majority of researchers ignored pleas to pay more attention to time devoted to learning outside the classroom (Kifer, 1975; Kulik and Kulik, 1979). Nevertheless, several useful conceptual refinements emerged from the research effort.

Conceptions of time

Following Carroll (1963) and Bloom (1974), Anderson (1976) argued that during the time allotted for learning a particular task, the student spends some time working intently on the task and another portion doing things which are not relevant. Anderson defined elapsed time as the "amount of time that the student spends in the presence of the learning task" (p. 226). She divided elapsed time into two parts: "time-on-task", when the student is involved in learning, and "time-off-task", the amount of time not devoted to learning despite being in the presence of the learning task. Similarly, Rosenshine (1979) used the terms "academically engaged time" and "time allocated".

Based on work including Harnischfeger and Wiley (1976), Berliner (1979) developed a variable which focused simultaneously on the student's use of time and the curriculum. He defined academic learning time (ALT) as "the time a student is engaged with instructional materials or activities that are at an easy level of difficulty for that student" (p. 120). Such refinement is symptomatic of the researcher's need to move towards a more precise operational definition of terms. However, the total time spent in the presence of the learning task seems likely to be the student's greatest concern, since the level of difficulty and the associated degree of involvement in study are usually outside his direct control. Apart from dropping out, the student has no alternative but to persevere until the learning task is complete. Elapsed time is an appropriate, if somewhat neglected, focus for the educational researcher.

Theoretical models of time and learning

A recent review of conceptions of time and learning (Fredrick and Walberg, 1980) identified two broad theoretical perspectives—acceleration theory (based on mastery learning) and enrichment theory (based on the normal curve of initial ability). Each starts from a different assumption:

i. acceleration theory is based on the assumption that 95% of all students can attain high levels of achievement, provided that they are given sufficient time under appropriate instructional conditions;

ii. enrichment theory is based on the assumption that little or nothing can be done to improve the level of achievement of individual students, and that the normal curve of achievement is a reflection of the normal curve of initial ability.

The notion of elapsed time (the total amount of time spent in the presence of the learning task) assumes a different importance in each of these frameworks. From the acceleration perspective elapsed time is likely to be a relatively strong predictor of achievement provided the student has the specific knowledge and skills that are prerequisites. Elapsed time spent on an instructional unit such as Accounting B would likely be a relatively strong predictor of achievement for this unit where the student had passed the prerequisite, Accounting A. However, increase in elapsed time would presumably not influence the level of achievement in teaching calculus to a kindergarten class. At the tertiary level such gross mismatches seem unlikely to occur.

According to enrichment theory elapsed time would be at best a relatively modest predictor of achievement. Advocates of enrichment theory believe that differences in achievement are more or less fixed by differences in innate intelligence, and are therefore not significantly altered by increased effort and study time. From this perspective a standardized test of secondary school achievement would be regarded as a relatively strong predictor of achievement in tertiary education.

A study was conducted to determine the support for these two theoretical positions.

Sample

The subjects were enrolled in one of three programs (Associate Diploma in Engineering, Bachelor of Business, Bachelor of Education) at an Australian Regional College of Advanced Education. The sample was stratified in terms of each level of the three programs. Thirty internal and thirty external students were randomly selected from those instructional units with sufficiently high enrolments at each level. The initial sample was therefore 360 students.

Procedure

Internal students were handed a questionnaire which was completed in class. They were given precise instructions on how to calculate their elapsed study time. Some of the sample of external students were given the same questionnaire at their residential school under the same conditions. Those not attending a residential school were sent an identical questionnaire, with the same instructions, through the mail. Regional Liaison Officers were used as a follow up and there was an eighty-five percent return.

Variables measured

The variables required for the initial part of the survey were elapsed study time and tertiary entrance score.

Since tertiary entrance scores were available from student records students were only required to enter their study time for each unit on the questionnaire.

The questionnaire prompted the student to consider all variations of time spent on study in an average week. The difficulty of indicating an average figure when there is often variation in the weekly time spent was acknowledged.

Consideration was given to the advantages of requesting students to self-monitor and record their elapsed study time over a period of weeks. The idea was rejected on the grounds that this could well generate self-correcting procedures (Kazdin, 1975). It was considered that a more accurate estimate would be obtained by seeking the students' general perception of the number of hours at a particular point of time. It was emphasised to students that anonymity would be preserved as the emphasis of the survey was on group data.

It is intended to survey the same students again during the second semester of 1981 to check the reliability of the first survey.

Table 1: **Courses surveyed**

Program	Entry Requirements	Mode of Study	Minimum Duration of Study
Associate Diploma in Engineering	Matriculation or mature age with a trade	Internal External	2 years full-time 4 years part-time
Bachelor of Business (Accountancy)	Matriculation, mature age restricted entry	Internal External	3 years full-time 5 years part-time
Bachelor of Education	Diploma of Education (3 years) plus a minumum of one year's teaching experience	External	1 year full-time 2 years part-time

In this preliminary analysis the following measures were compiled and calculated: the mean, median, mode and standard deviation of elapsed study time and tertiary entrance score.

These were calculated by unit of study, program, and mode of study.

Elapsed study time

Elapsed study time for external students is generally higher than for internal. The one exception in the second level of the Bachelor of Business may be due to a sampling aberration.

Standard deviations of elapsed study time for external students are consistently greater than for internals. Perhaps this is because the study time of internal students is more disciplined since they have set classes to attend.

Tertiary entrance score

Tertiary entrance scores of external students are generally higher than those of internal students and the gap is widening.

The reason is that the mining, refining and power industries in Queensland are expanding rapidly and require an increasing number of para-professional supervisors. The current preference of the firms involved is to offer employment to highly qualified grade twelve students as soon as they matriculate on the condition that they enrol part-time in the engineering diploma. The firms find that the mix of academic study and work experience produces a graduate who is of value to them. The young school leavers also prefer this to enrolling as full-time students and seeking employment after graduation. The net result is that the firms are able to select the better qualified matriculants and the external student profile is changing.

A similar change is taking place in the external student profile in the Bachelor of Business though not quite so rapidly.

The external Bachelor of Education students already have the three year Diploma of Education and are given a nominal tertiary entrance score of 993. Thus an analysis of their scores is not appropriate.

Future developments

Achievement is the main concern of this research project, but at the time of writing students have not been assessed on their year's work. We would expect from the opening discussion that achievement would correlate with either study time (acceleration theory) or tertiary entrance score (enrichment theory).

By the time that the Twelfth World Conference of ICCE is held in June 1982, we will have done two things:

Table 2: Elapsed study time (mean hours per week)

Program and Mode of Study	Level	First	Second	Third	Average of Three Levels
Bachelor of Business					
Internal (N 85)		7.9	8.1	8.1	8.1 (SD = 2.4)
External (N 66)		9.2	6.7	8.5	8.6 (SD = 3.3)
Associate Diploma Engineering					
Internal (N 49)		6.0	6.6		6.3 (SD = 1.8)
External (N 52)		8.0	7.2		8.1 (SD = 2.6)
Bachelor of Education					
External (N 54)		8.2* (SD = 4.5)	12.4* (SD = 5.2)		

* Unequal unit size

Table 3: Tertiary entrance score (range 650 to 990)

Program and Mode of Study	Level	First	Second	Third	Average of three Levels
Bachelor of Business					
Internal (N 85)		880	890	895	899
External (N 66)		900	905	890	900
Associate Diploma Engineering					
Internal (N 49)		845	880		865
External (N 52)		890	910		895

- re-surveyed the same students' perception of their study time. This will give us a check for reliability against the original data.

- carried out linear and non-linear regression analysis between achievement and elapsed study time; and a multiple linear regression analysis between achievement and a number of other variables such as elapsed study time, tertiary entrance score, and age.

We hope our results will be a contribution to the acceleration/enrichment theory controversy. We also hope to provide empirical evidence about time-effectiveness of distance study as compared to its on-campus counterpart.

J.C. Taylor / V.J. White
Darling Downs Institute of Advanced Education
Australia

References

Anderson, L.W. (1976) An empirical investigation of individual differences in time to learn. *Journal of Educational Psychology,* 68, 2, 226-233.

Berliner, D.C. (1979) Tempus Educare. In Peterson, P.L. and Walberg, H.J. (eds.) *Research on Teaching: Concepts, Findings and Implications.* Berkeley, California: McCutchan.

Bloom, B.S. (1974) Time and learning. *American Psychologist,* 8, 682-688.

Carroll, J.B. (1963) A model of school learning. *Teachers College Record,* 64, 723-733.

Connors, B. (1980) Assessment of students in distance teaching. In Armstrong, J.D. and Store, R.E. (eds.) *Evaluation in Distance Teaching.* Townsville, Queensland: Townsville College of Advanced Education.

Daniel, J.S. and Marquis, C. (1979) Interaction and independence: getting the mixture right. *Teaching at a Distance,* 15, 29-44.

Fredrick, W.C. and Walberg, H.D. (1980) Learning as a function of time. *Journal of Educational Research,* 73, 4, 183-194.

Gough, J.E. and Monday, P.R. (1979) Student workloads: an entree to the literature. *Open Campus,* 3, 43-62.

Harnischfeger, A. and Wiley, D.E. (1976) Teaching-learning processes in elementary schools: a synoptic view. *Curriculum Inquiry,* 6, 5-43.

Kazdin, A.W. (1975) *Behaviour Modification in Applied Settings.* Homewood, Illinois: Dorsey.

Kifer, E. (1975) Relationships between academic achievement and personality characteristics: a quasi-longitudinal study. *American Educational Research Journal,* 12, 191-210.

Kulik, J.A. and Kulik, C.C. (1979) College teaching. In Peterson, P.L. and Walberg, H.J. (eds.) *Research on Teaching: Concepts, Findings and Implications.* Berkeley, California: McCutchan.

Laidlaw, B. and Layard, R. (1974) Traditional versus open university teaching methods: a cost comparison. *Higher Education,* 3, 439-468.

Rosenshine, B.V. (1979) Content, Time and Direct Instruction. In Peterson, P.L. and Walberg, H.J. (eds.) *Research on Teaching: Concepts, Findings and Implications.* Berkeley, California: McCutchan.

Rumble, G. (1981) Evaluating autonomous multi-media distance learning systems: a practical approach. *Distance Education,* 2, 1, 64-90.

The Cost-Effectiveness of Distance Teaching for School Equivalency

(Abstract)

Paper **44**

Fourteen distance education projects have been evaluated from an economic perspective, comparing the cost per student and average performance with those of alternative technologies. The projects were split into two categories.

In-school projects

1. Brazil : Minerva madureza
2. Brazil : Bahia Madureza
3. Malawi : Correspondence College
4. Mauritius : College of the Air
5. Brazil: Maranhão FMTVE
6. Brazil : Ceara ETV
7. Mexico : Radioprimaria
8. Mexico : Telesecundaria

These projects maintain a similar teacher-pupil ratio to conventional schooling. The media do not substitute for labour but for skill in labour.

Out-of-school-projects

9. South Korea : Air Correspondence High School
10. Kenya : In-service teacher training
11. Israel : Everyman's University
12. Dominican Republic : Radio Escuela Santa Maria
13. Brazil : Telecurso Secundo Grau
14. China : The Television University

In these projects contacts are less frequent and the bulk of the work is done by students alone with the help of textbooks and electronic media.

Rather than attempting to measure effectiveness in absolute terms each program was compared for effectiveness against the closest alternative. Assessment of impact was based on internal criteria (student performance) and external criteria (improved access). Out-of-school projects are highly cost-effective so long as they enrol sufficient numbers of students to share the fixed costs. The decisive change lies in capital-labour substitution. The in-school projects have a smaller impact on the cost per student but they show that the use of media may improve the performance of the system sufficiently to justify the additional cost. The majority of both types of project are relatively unsophisticated compared to multi-media systems in developed countries and this simplicity has proved a sound choice.

François Orivel / Dean T. Jamison
The World Bank

Student Support and Regional Services

Paper 45
Introduction

The production of course materials is becoming increasingly sophisticated, but as Sewart (paper 5) states, "the production of a standard package through a quasi-industrialized process in no way guarantees learning on the part of a student". This section deals with the difficult relationship between the mass-produced learning package and the diverse student base. The various authors examine methods of encouraging student achievement through improving the quality of their contact with the institution. This contact can be made both from a distance and on a face-to-face basis.

Sewart (paper 5) describes the many options for personal and academic aid available to Open University students. The flexibility of the system ensures that individual needs can be met. Mills and Tait (paper 53) discuss the important ways the development of support for continuing education students has differed from that for regular undergraduate students. Support systems in the community have developed with the assistance of independent volunteer organizations and of professional adult educators.

The Télé-université in Quebec described by Caron (paper 51) has a pluralistic approach to student support including regional workshops, study cells, telephone tutorials, and teleconferencing. Although staff at the Télé-université are currently reassessing their support system, they feel that some student support is essential even though all students do not require the same level of support.

Smith and Small (paper 47) feel strongly that to concentrate on the independence of the learner is to dehumanize the learning process. At the University of New England in Australia, peer support, compulsory residential schools and local support help encourage students towards course completion.

The critical importance of the development of a feeling of warmth and friendliness between student and institution is emphasized by several authors. Lewis (paper 46), in discussing the tutor as friend, teacher and assessor, provides a variety of specific examples for the creation of a friendly dialogue by mail. Singer (paper 49) speaks of the necessity to communicate with warmth to help the student create a successful study routine.

Fritsch (paper 48), on the other hand, discusses the computerization of basic student counselling.

The questions encourage students to examine their own study situations, the computer-generated answers cover areas of common problems, and the counsellors are left free to deal with more urgent problems.

Through a project to develop and increase the communications skills of telephone tutors, Cochran and Meech (paper 50) feel that they have decreased teaching on the part of the tutors, but increased learning on the part of the students.

In Finland, as Kirkinen outlines (paper 52), the *study circle* offers a flexible form of study organization well suited to sparsely populated areas. Organized in adult education centres or folk high schools these circles of students pursue secondary- and university-level programs in a relatively autonomous fashion, aided by local staff who serve as leaders and directors. In Tasmania the response has been the *regional centre* that, as Walker (paper 56) points out, is a departure from the more common Australian approach of institution-specific "study centres". Regional centres have the advantage of being independent of any particular institution, yet accessible to all. Institutions benefit from the arrangement, due to the brokering and educational ombudsman functions performed by such centres.

In British Columbia two open institutions have developed networks of regional centres to give the remote learner face-to-face contact with his institution. North Island College, described by Salter (paper 54), services learners via *learning centres,* which are permanent facilities where enrolments are large, and mobile centres where enrolments are small. The Open Learning Institute, described by Meakin (paper 55), serves the province by means of a number of *regional centres* staffed by advisors who provide students with information and advice in as non-intimidating a manner as possible.

Demographically, the United Kingdom presents a much different picture; however, Freeman (paper 57) reminds us that the distance separating learner and institution is much more than a measurement in kilometres. The National Extension College began as an open institution organized according to the typical model, with course production, student advising, and tuition centralized and with local colleges used in supporting roles. After a decade of limited success the College decided to try to boost student completion rates by turning this system "on its head" and doing *all* the teaching and support locally through local state colleges.

The papers in this section offer an overview of the variety of ways distance education institutions adapt to the physical separation of student and institution, and student and teacher. Even if the distance learner is characterized by a high degree of self-motivation, there is still a place for offering certain services as well as encouragement whether these take the form of a local institutional presence or only assistance in the formation of study groups. It seems assured that mediation of some form between the individual learner and the impersonal study materials will always be an essential ingredient of distance education.

The Role of the Correspondence Tutor *Paper 46*

Friendly tutoring is important and need not conflict with academic standards.

> The courses helped me to plan more efficiently and read more critically—the biggest help has been to give me confidence to work well, on my own. So—many thanks
> (Freda)

The NEC system: the tutor as friend

The National Extension College (NEC) does all that it can to encourage tutors and students to communicate across a distance. Firstly, a student cannot be expected to write warmly to a 'college' or to an unknown, unnamed tutor. So as he enrols each student is sent a personal biography of his tutor. A typical biography is reproduced below:

Your tutor for How to Write Essays/The Arts— A Fresh Approach/Wordpower is:

> Mrs. Elizabeth Maynard,
> 4 Abbots Way,
> Muncaster,
> York. Y03 9LB
>
> Liz Maynard obtained a degree in Sociology from the University of York in 1967, and in 1968 obtained a further degree in Sociology from the same place. At the same time she acquired a husband, who is now a lecturer in Economics, also at York. Three children then followed, which ensured that most activities are home based and that most of her time is taken up with fighting back the sea of toys, sand and old socks which daily threatens to engulf them! However, she has also been a tutor counsellor for the Open University Foundation Course in Social Science since 1971, and as a result has become very interested in the whole field of Adult Education.

At the same time, the student is asked to fill in a 'personal details form' and to send this to the tutor. The form includes space for the student to give his reasons for studying by correspondence, his aspirations and his likely study problems. These forms usually produce rich information:

> Mrs. Donkin aged 40, a Staff Nurse, married to an accountant; 4 children all younger than 16. Hobbies: wine and beer making (and drinking). Reading. Music (Beatles to Bach). Motor cycling. Animal keeping—3 cats, 1 dog, 6 rabbits, 1 guinea pig, 1 fish, 6 chinchillas, 12 ducks. Yoga. Swimming—in winter. Gardening—in summer. Looking after two old ladies referred to as Mrs. C. and Mrs. D.

The tutor will generally write a friendly introduction letter to the student and this kind of contact will continue between assignments. Marked assignments will include questions back to the student, to try to create a written dialogue. Many tutors encourage students to comment on how they *feel* about the work and about studying at a distance. Students generally gain confidence and with the help of tutorial prodding gradually engage in dialogue, often enclosing quite lengthy letters with their assignments:

> I hope the visit to Dortmund was a success....I quite agree with your comments about structure and was aware of the essay's deficiencies when I sent it off. I knew I had the material, it was the ordering of it and using it to its best advantage—which needed more uninterrupted time than I ever had...
> (Margaret)

At NEC in monitoring our part-time tutors' work we look for evidence of personal comment not specifically related to the detail of the assignment along with the more usual criteria of speed of return of script, fullness of teaching comment, tone of comment and explanation of any grade awarded. When recruiting tutors we seek out those candidates who might be expected to deal sympathetically and warmly with students at a distance and we are currently preparing a tape and booklet to encourage tutors to extend this aspect of their work.

This excursion into NEC's view of the tutor's role makes clear the priorities:

1. The tutor is very much more than a 'script marker'. Scripts and related letters are a lifeline for the distant student and in his written comment the tutor is communicating with, supporting and motivating the learner, as well as assessing the work.

2. Tutor-student communication is person-person communication as well. Tutors have as much to learn as students; genuine interest in what he has to say (not just about the course material) shows the student that his experience is respected. Aware of the problem of student 'drop out' the tutor creates for the student the supportive context more usually associated with the informally run conventional class.

The tutor as teacher

The tutor has a crucial role since only he can easily relate the fixed standard product (the course) to the individual student. (Each student is different and students' needs often change as the course progresses.) The tutor acts as a consultant to the student:

> You mention my work being a bit awkward and disjointed at times. Is this the construction of the sentences, or of the structure of the essay as a whole?
> (Paul to Tutor)

> The main problem is the structure of the essay as a whole. You tend to jumble ideas together instead of separating them out to deal with them in clear sections. I suggest a way of doing this at the end of your essay. Have a look, too, at the ideas in Unit 4 Part 3.
> (Tutor to Paul)

Such comment can be very time-consuming. And all the time the tutor works towards the situation in which the student can do without him—i.e., can become an independent learner (though still, hopefully, a friend).

Conclusion

I have outlined two major parts of the role of the correspondence tutor:

- tutor as friend
- tutor as teacher, assessor.

Some readers may wonder whether the general emphasis on friendliness may lessen the discipline and integrity of the learning experience. I should like to end by showing that, in my view, there is no incompatibility at all between friendliness and the successful attainment of the objectives of academic courses. First of all, there is evidence that without friendly accessibility, a tutor may never receive any work from his student and will thus be unable to assume his teaching role:

> I took ages over my first assignment. I felt I couldn't bother a senior academic with high standards with work that was at such a basic level.
> (Ron)

> I was embarrassed—a woman of my age. I felt my tutor would wonder why I hadn't got 'O' level years ago.
> (Veronica)

Secondly, friendliness and discussion of matters other than the narrowly academic will make it more likely that the student will connect course content with his own experience; this is an important learning objective for many courses. Thirdly, it is perfectly possible to comment on inadequacies in a student's work in a friendly and supportive way:

> I try hard never to be utterly negative: there is usually something one can find to praise before suggesting other things could have been improved.
> (History Tutor)

The following example shows this in action. The tutor is not only evaluating his student's work (mentioning strengths as well as weaknesses) he is also communicating enjoyment at having read it. These are in the best sense 'friendly' comments.

> In spite of your pessimistic tone in your letter this was a very good experimental effort. You got some positive results—even if you plot all the results on the graph you will see a relationship—well done. You also got some negative results but even these are important as they still give you information.
>
> Your write-up was chatty and understandable but not in the scientific method. You will have help now with your OU write-up for the moon experiment. Try to separate title, theory, method, results and conclusion; each section is restricted to that particular topic. You had a good basis here but you must practise writing a structured account. This is not as difficult as it seems so don't despair about it. Handling of experimental data from the OU is a great help. Your experimental ideas were very good indeed so be encouraged by that. I disagree with your letter—you show excellent potential as a scientist but need help in the special way we do our writing up. Good luck in the OU.

Postscript

> Thanks so much for your help. I throughly enjoyed the course. I know I have not sent in the completed exercise or form this time. However my excuses are—I have been doing it at very odd moments, son home ill awhile, running a one-woman doll factory and am going abroad on Monday for Christmas. I know I've learned a lot and it really opened up a new world for me. Thank you and a Merry Christmas.
> (Alison)

Roger Lewis
National Extension College
United Kingdom

Student Support: How Much is Enough?

External studies is a form of independent study, not a sentence to solitary confinement.

Even if services are well developed within a system to include such elements as study centres, tutorial groups, telephone tutoring, professional counsellors and other opportunities for interaction on a personal basis, this may still not be sufficient to retain those students who seem to need the moral support of their peers with whom very informal, non-threatening, non-assessable relationships can be developed. To this end, the University of New England has recently embarked upon a project called "UNE Contact" whereby at little cost to the University we are attempting to make better use of one of our most valuable but to date under-utilized resources, our own external graduates, to develop a *graduate advisory network*.

In our view it is unfortunate that some systems are expending vast amounts of time and money trying to devise learning packages which will allow students to become completely independent of teachers and other students. In these systems the notion of learning as a social experience has not received the consideration we believe it warrants.

At the university level the pursuit of this ultimate achievement for instructional designers is not only futile but misdirected because it must lead to dehumanising the learning process. Despite changes to the original concept, the notion of a university as a community of scholars is still important and while it may seem a contradiction in terms to talk about a community of scholars studying as *external* students, no such contradiction need exist at all.

"Getting the right mixture" at the University of New England has always depended to a large extent on compulsory residential schools. The emphasis placed on personal interaction in all its aspects, whether it occurs at residential schools, weekend schools, staff visits to students or in some other form, has increased rather than diminished in recent years. Some critics have suggested that this represents a tacit admission of the failure of independent study as a valid alternative learning mode. However, as an educational alternative for people beset by all manner of personal, family, social and occupational pressures and often in need of a helping hand in human terms, external studies will, by definition, continue to be essentially a form of *independent* study but should never be a sentence to solitary confinement.

In more recent years, as we accept more external students with no or minimal formal educational qualifications under a Mature Age Admission scheme, there has developed an increasing need to provide orientation programs that can help the student to come to terms with the challenge of university study at a distance. In response to this need, we now hold general orientation schools and more specific study skills programs at the University just before the start of each academic year. There still seems, however, to be a need for *local* support and advisory services, no matter how extensive University-based programs may be.

Local support

The development of a comprehensive system of study centres, tutorial classes or regional offices that characterises other distance education systems within Australia and abroad has never been feasible at New England. Offering a wide range of subjects and many courses within subjects to about 6000 students spread across a country as vast as Australia has its own problems, not the least of which is the difficulty of finding viable groups of students enrolled in common courses in any one centre that could justify a more decentralised teaching approach using part-time staff in the regions. We have always invited some of our graduates to do what they can (on a voluntary basis) to act as representatives of the University in calling together students in their area to meet one another early each year so that personal contact can be established and mutual support provided. But this has been a "hit or miss" approach with varying degrees of effectiveness.

Our attempts to develop a more positive approach to self-help techniques that might fill the gaps that our centrally organised system has left are described below.

UNE contact—an advisory network

Agreement to fund a limited pilot advisory scheme for 1981, with the eventual objective of creating the basis of a state-wide network, made it essential that care be exercised in selecting the areas/regions to be covered. It was agreed that total student numbers within specific areas, regardless of enrolment patterns, would be the main criterion to be considered. After the areas/regions were decided upon, selected graduates (many of whom had assisted previously in a voluntary capacity) were contacted to enlist their support. (see Figure 1.)

The letter of invitation suggested that advisers might be able to develop activities along the following lines:

a. Act as a point of contact for enquiries from potential students in the local area.

b. Conduct meetings of enrolled external students, particularly early in each academic year, to discuss mutual problems and assist them in understanding how the system works.

c. Assist in the formation of self-help and tutor-led discussion groups.

d. Establish lists of local resource people who might be willing and able to assist external students in their search for reference material and in developing studying and learning skills.

e. Arrange for second-hand textbook exchanges amongst students.

f. Co-ordinate the sharing of transport for attending residential and weekend schools.

g. Hold social functions to involve students' families so that they feel part of activities associated with the University.

h. Publish a newsletter or circular on a regular basis.

i. Disseminate information relating to facets of external study through personal representation, utilisation of local media and by using local sources known to the adviser, for example, service clubs.

j. Co-ordinate arrangements when the Director or other members of the University staff are visiting the local area by identifying interest groups and arranging meetings.

Figure 1: Distribution of University of New England external students - 1980

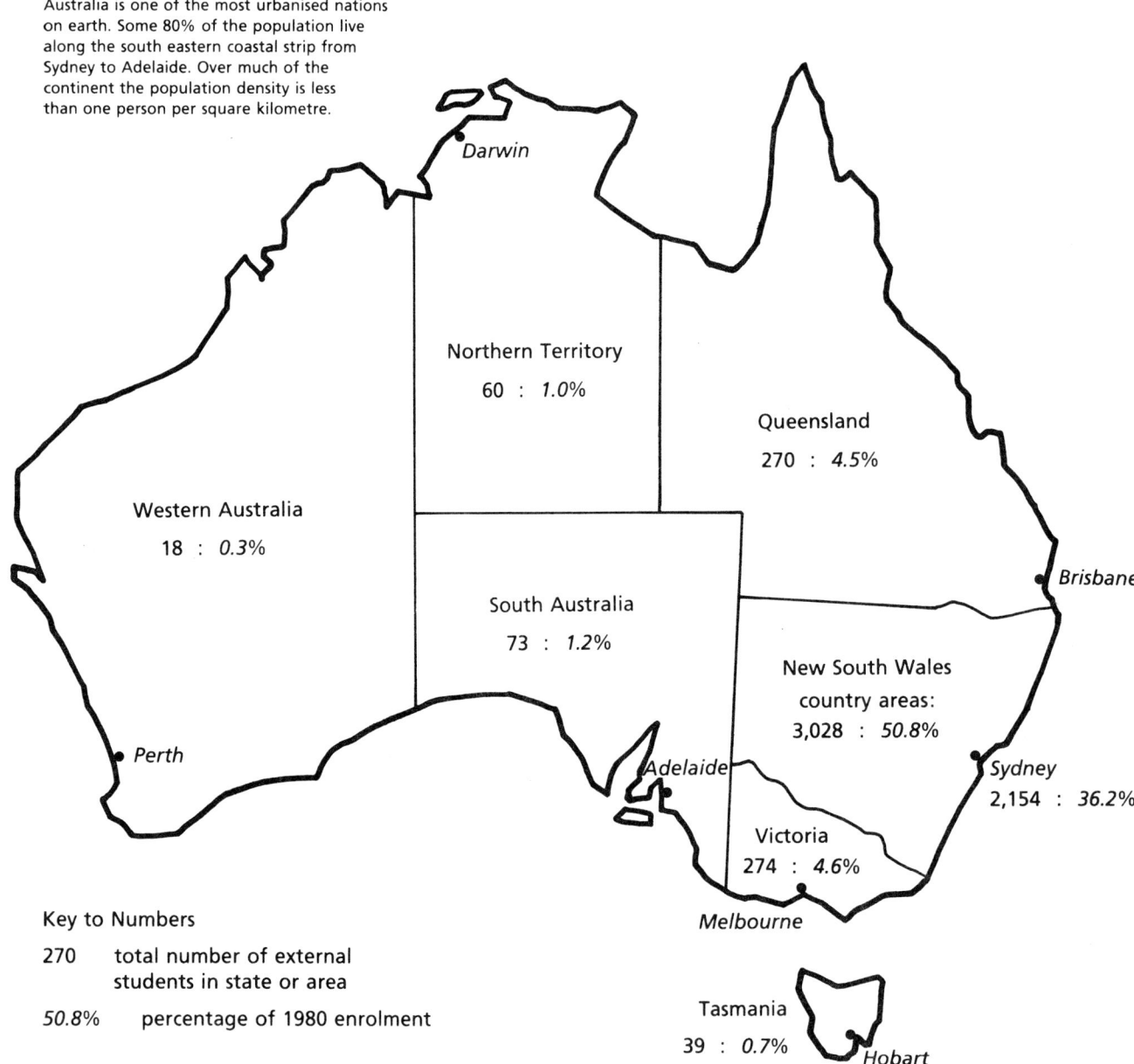

Australia is one of the most urbanised nations on earth. Some 80% of the population live along the south eastern coastal strip from Sydney to Adelaide. Over much of the continent the population density is less than one person per square kilometre.

Key to Numbers

270   total number of external students in state or area

50.8%   percentage of 1980 enrolment

The University agreed to the payment of a small honorarium which would more than defray the costs associated with the adviser's work. At the same time it was made clear that the Department of External Studies would be available to assist with mailing lists, the dissemination of information to students in the adviser's areas and it would meet postage and telephone costs.

Response from those graduates contacted was overwhelming and is further evidence of the high level of affinity that develops between external students and their Alma Mater. It became necessary for financial reasons to restrict the scope of the network initially to 12 regions.

Soon after the academic year began senior staff of the Department of External Studies made personal contact with nine of the twelve appointed advisers. At that time it was emphasised that there was no blueprint that would ensure the success of their efforts. Advisers realised that they would have to establish, perhaps by trial and error, the combination of activities that would best suit the circumstances in their region. They were encouraged to put forward suggestions as to how:

a. contact groups and the University itself might do more to support and encourage external students to persist in their studies when they were faced with difficulties that confront any part-time students attempting to reconcile university commitments with family and occupational obligations.

b. information about external studies might best be disseminated through their local communities.

Different approaches and strategies are already becoming evident. A number of advisers have produced or are in the process of preparing local newsletters to keep students informed of developments. They expect that such newsletters will provide a forum for students to suggest and develop more effective means of helping each other. Efforts are being made by some advisers to involve families of students through social activities and in almost every area there has been an upsurge in the number of self-help and tutor-led study groups. To keep advisers well informed of how the other groups are developing, the Department of External Studies is publishing regular issues of a newsletter called *UNE Contact*. In this way the Department hopes to act as a clearing-house for the ideas and suggestions of advisers.

Initial feedback suggests that most advisers have been effective in developing a stronger sense of community among students in their particular localities and this should provide an excellent basis for further development of the network.

The Sydney Centre

The University of New England draws about 40% (in 1980, 2154) of its external students from the Sydney metropolitan area. In addition, some 20% of internal undergraduate students come from the same area.

In late 1980, the University was able to establish a Sydney Centre through the generosity and co-operation of the Agricultural Societies Council of New South Wales which agreed to the use of its offices, ideally located in the central business district of Sydney.

The Sydney Centre was officially launched in early December, but had been manned from early November, and has proved its worth in acting as an information office for enrolment inquiries, both internal and external. Staff of the Department of External Studies, the Enrolments Office and academic staff members of the Student Liaison Committee shared responsibility for providing advisory services but the main burden fell upon the shoulders of an external graduate representative who volunteered her services for 3 days a week during November and December.

A part-time liaison officer was appointed for 1981 to operate the Centre for an average of three days per week. A recent external graduate, she has already developed a more personal advisory service for Sydney students and is able to provide on-the-spot advice to prospective students. The level of demand generated suggests that the appointment of a full-time Liaison Officer will have to be considered in the near future.

Conclusion

While it is too early yet to conduct a systematic evaluation of the advisory network project, discussions with graduate advisers, our Sydney Liaison Officer and students themselves indicate without doubt that the need for local personal support is being met more effectively now than in the past. The response has been encouraging enough to recommend similar measures for consideration by other institutions facing the challenge of providing better support to off-campus students. The utilisation of the unique qualities and experiences of graduates who have studied externally adds another dimension of support to any distance education system, no matter how sophisticated or professionally staffed its support services may be. In some cases where resources are scarce, it may be the only way that such services can be provided. Clearly, however, the practicality of such an approach depends upon the institution concerned building up a pool of committed graduates whose experiences as external students have been positive ones.

Kevin C. Smith / Ian W. Small
The University of New England
Australia

Paper **48**

Industrialized Counselling

Developing a system that takes care of all pre-known information gives more time for person-to-person contacts.

Counselling may be defined as a form of processing information in order to induce personal change. Processing of information also means matching appropriate information to a specific client-situation. Counsellors take responsibility only for the objective information, leaving the client responsible for any decision that may lead to personal change. The project described below is a form of counselling because objective information is matched to the client's specific situation—the subjective part of the information processing is induced by making the client reflect on his own statements. Our goal was to develop a system of counselling that takes care of all pre-known information needs in order to have more time for person-to-person contacts.

"Industrialized" counselling

A counselling system for mass counselling developed by a small team of counsellors and run with the aid of computer technology can be called "industrialized counselling", not only because of the mass effect (which exists in all forms of advice and counselling given in the mass media) but also because of the aspect of product-variety and division of labour during the process of production of the means of counselling. Yet it is still counselling because of the aspect of individualization and two-way communication. Its major deficit—for any therapeutic goal—is the lack of an authentic person-to-person relationship.

The aim of the activities of this helping agency is not so much to adapt people interested in learning at a distance to the system offered but to leave the responsibility for the encounter with this institution with the client. In order to prevent drop-out it seems to be necessary that people interested in distant study know exactly how the system works. Moreover they should examine their own situation in terms of working habits, time available, style of learning, behaviour towards workloads, motivation, etc.

The following project was developed with two central themes:

– How does the system work?

– What is the client's own learning situation?

STEB (STudienEingangsBeratung)
Counselling at the Beginning of Learning at a Distance

Before enrolling with the Fernuniversität every student-to-be has the chance to order a preliminary course entitled 'How to study' that was developed five years ago and has been revised several times. The assignments are somewhat different from the usual course. We ask the client to answer a set of questions about his life situation, his study motives, learning habits, etc. These questions are a vital step towards our goal of having the client initiate a kind of self-examination with respect to studying. We do not want to judge the clients' motives, we want them to understand their own motives.

We offer a counselling service by mail if the client has answered social, motivational, situational and even practical questions such as "Do you have a cassette-tape recorder?"

Together with the social data, therefore, we have information in crucial fields of interest for motivation counselling and the prevention of early drop-out. The answers are put into our computer and combined with a data bank of counselling texts that are written for each problem area.

By matching the information stored in our data bank with the individual situation we generate:

1. a personal computer-letter

2. a data file of the answer-structures for research purposes.

The computer letter is a very simple but effective procedure to select and to stream information according to a client situation. Within one week the client receives a letter that might consist of 5 to 20 text modules commenting on the answers given in the answer sheet. 96% of the letters are truly individual. Each season we produce some 4000 letters and there are no two letters alike.

The use of such a system only makes sense when there is much information on the university's side—e.g. feedback about a personal situation like fear of dropping-out because of overload—that is difficult to find or easy to forget or not even conscious on the part of the client. The information given in the computer letter is meant to correct the "map" the client has of his future endeavor, or to respond in a positive reinforcing way.

Up to 89% of our clients have found such a letter helpful and would like to see this instrument of counselling continued.

The second effect of the project is twofold: each year at an early stage we get information about the structure of our new clientele and secondly, it can be helpful for system evaluation with longitudinal studies of motivation etc. Currently, we are working on a sub-project to determine differences in personality traits among our students and between our distant-study students and other relevant groups.

The impact of this form of industrialized counselling

There is not much that is totally new about this project—computer technology has had several generations in the field of guidance (Rayman et al, 1978: 349). Systems for interactive communication do exist and have already been evaluated with positive results. Two aspects, however, are worth noting:

1. The institution itself operates this counselling system with the aim of ensuring that clients *do not enroll* unless they really are sure that they want to risk distant study

2. The text modules are developed not with the intention of mere information processing but rather in an attempt to create an understanding climate in order to induce self-examination.

The STEB project might be called a kind of fourth generation (see Rayman et al, 1978: 349) of computerized guidance systems:

1st generation - batch information storage and retrieval systems

2nd generation - on-line information storage and retrieval systems

3rd generation - on-line information systems that deliver significant guidance content beyond career information

4th generation - information retrieval system with guidance and counselling

By 1982 we want to rely in our text modules not only upon information given by the clients but also, in a research part of the project, upon diagnostic information using a learning style inventory (see Kolb, 1976).

Helmut Fritsch
Fernuniversität
West Germany

References

Kolb, D.A. (1976) *Learning Style Inventory*. Self-Scoring Test and Interpretation Booklet. Boston: McBer.

Rayman, J.R. Bryson, D.L. and Bowlsbey, J.H. (1978) The field trial of discover: a new computerized interactive guidance system. *The Vocational Guidance Quarterly*, June 1978, 349-360

Studying at Home

Good study habits and well prepared learning materials are the main elements of successful home study.

William Rainey Harper who is known as the intellectual founder of the University of Chicago initiated a system of instruction by mail which is still emulated throughout the United States.

Emphasis is placed upon the importance of a clearly presented instruction sheet, a lesson plan which is specific in its subject matter and geared to the level of the student. It must be logical in sequence and inspirational in terms of encouraging the student to continue to learn as well as to investigate further avenues of knowledge. It must stress, clarify and simplify unusual, new or difficult problems as the subject unfolds. It must also contain an examination to test the knowledge of the student. Needless to say, the examination will only be successful if the student has properly prepared the lesson. Lessons which refer to technical or manual activities such as agriculture, use or repair of business machines (such as typewriters or computers) must provide either a "hands on" practical article to be returned to the school for analysis or must include additional questions, the answers to which will prove that the student understood the aims of the lesson.

After having completed the examination, the school should require that the student share any procedural problems with the instructor. This can take the form of a one-to-one note or letter in which the student presents questions and the instructor responds on the same paper for immediate reference. It is important, too, that any incorrect responses on the test be noted with reasons and corrections.

The instructor/counsellor must be entirely familiar with both the subject matter of the course and with the problems inherent in its composition. Distance education requires a superior ability to communicate on paper, as contrasted with personal counselling. With communications media coming more and more into use, institutions are finding it expedient to train personnel in the use of computer-education and television and telephonic education techniques. It is extremely important that distance educators familiarize themselves with voice control and speech modulation, and with methods of recording on records or cassettes so that the words come forth with a natural, friendly sound. In some instances, it would be advisable to arrange that cassettes be used to return student lessons and examinations to the school.

The reasons for learning are many. Adult and distance learning, because of their specificity, hold a double responsibility. A challenge must be offered and a need must be fulfilled. How can this be accomplished? The appeal must be dynamic. It must cause the prospective student to want to get information immediately as to how to start studying.

Home study requires complete concentration. It is necessary to set aside a particular area of the home—bedroom, study, basement, or any other place where the student can be completely alone for a specified time. How long and what time depend upon the student's regular daily schedule. If there is no private room available, the family must be introduced to the need for lack of interruption, and must agree to it. No telephone calls, no messages, no company during the study period must be the rule. If possible, the student must set aside a specific time of day (or night) and follow it conscientiously. Among the most important requirements for positive study should be a time for rest and relaxation before starting. Even a short 15 minute period can ensure a rested, alert mind, ready to learn.

A desk or table on which to work, and good light so as not to strain the eyes will be a tremendous assistance. A comfortable bench or chair completes the home study setting.

The first step is to assemble all materials to be used during the lesson. The student should scan the instructions and the lesson to become familiar with the subject matter. Allow, if possible, the same amount of time for each session. Study habits must become so automatic that the student proceeds from one step to the next almost reflexively. The time schedule must be set and followed. After the lesson is completed, the record must be checked. The student should be continually aware of the importance of good reading habits, and should work on improving them. Most important is the new vocabulary, if any, in each lesson. Comprehension of the lesson can only be assured if each term is correctly and completely understood. Notes should be carefully taken and recorded in a convenient notebook.

When the student is sure he has learned the lesson well, he should make a summary of the lesson and include his reactions as well as those of the author. Finally, those notes should be thoroughly reviewed, as well as the vocabulary and the student's reactions to the lesson. At this time, the student is ready to take the test. A well constructed examination will show that the student has mastered the lesson, and will allow for individual thought and interpretation of the facts involved.

The completed test must then be returned to the school for analysis. Upon receiving the corrected examination, the student should go over it carefully, checking for corrections and suggestions from the instructor.

The student is ready to start the next lesson when there are no further doubts about the one just completed. Each succeeding lesson will stimulate its own motivation, and demand increasing initiative and self-discipline. Control of one's own destiny is among the advantages of home study. The ultimate goal, the schedule, the student's own needs are open to his determination.

To those in the less industrialized countries and to smaller schools which have not as yet advanced their equipment to the computer stage, probably the most important part of faculty training is the personal relationship between instructor/counsellor and student. This necessitates the instructor's thorough indoctrination into the aims and objectives of the institution as well as knowledge of the student's needs and requirements both educationally and personally. Counselling must be both direct, cordial and objective.

The quality of counselling can have a tremendous influence upon the reaction of the student, especially because of the distance involved. It is imperative that an atmosphere of warmth be transferred even across great distances. The ability to discuss problems productively whether by mail or phone, or in person where possible is a matter of proper training. While a course is in the process of construction, random sample students will be testing every area. Their responsibility is not only to complete the study involved in the course, but also to return to the author or department questions about unclear or unresolved sections, their responses and suggestions to proposed projects and their reactions to the examinations. It is also helpful to know how much time is required to complete each lesson and each test and how correct the sequence of lessons is in terms of comprehension. With all these basic needs met, the author(s) can revise any areas deemed necessary, and can provide exact details which may be applicable to problems students may present to their instructors later on. With this type of reference sheets readily available, the counsellor should be able to resolve most problems.

Thus the selection of home study courses for personal advancement or professional improvement depends to a certain extent upon the expertise of those constructing the course or revising it, upon the rectitude of the institution of which it will be a part, on the training and application of the instructors and, finally, upon the students. If students have had sincere guidance in making their choices and have applied themselves by employing correct study habits consistently, they will undoubtedly succeed.

Louise Singer
Technical Home Study School
United States

Training Telephone Tutors

A pilot project has had initial success in increasing the communications skills of tutors.

Paper 50

The problem

Three major factors determine the nature of the interaction between Athabasca University learners and their tutors: the dispersion of a relatively small number of learners across a wide geographical area; the enrolment of these learners in a broad range of courses; and an open registration system that allows learners to begin study on the first day of any month. In consequence, there is very little face-to-face meeting of tutors with learners, and very little possibility of dealing with learners as groups since at any given moment few learners are likely to be at the same point in their progress through a course. The tutorial relationship is therefore one-to-one, conducted in writing and by telephone. How can the university ensure that a tutorial relationship conducted through these media is useful to learners and comfortable for tutors?

Types of training for tutors

Part-time tutors are hired by competition according to various criteria, among which the two most important are previous experience with adult students and relevant academic expertise. To ensure that tutors are fully familiar with the courses they will be working with, they are paid a preparation fee after they are hired and before they begin tutorial work. The fee is not paid until the coordinator of the course (i.e., the full-time university staff member in charge) is satisfied that the tutor is adequately prepared.

Tutors are provided with a tutor's manual to the course, with a general handbook of the tutorial philosophies and administrative policies of the university, with marking guides, etc. In the first stages of their employment they have meetings with the course coordinator and the coordinator of tutorial services about academic and administrative matters, respectively. At other times in the course of their employment they meet with other tutors in general meetings and at annual orientations.

Despite the centrality of telephone interaction between tutor and learners, special training in techniques for telephone tutoring has been slow to evolve at the university. Conventional training in interviewing techniques for counsellors, supervisors, etc., is all designed for face-to-face situations. Nevertheless, following upon several recommendations made by a university-wide task force into the roles of tutors that reported in spring of 1979, special application of counselling or helping profession techniques to the telephone tutorial has been attempted. The process has been evolutionary and can be reduced to three stages.

Stage one: the pilot project

A pilot program was organized to develop and increase tutors' communications skills. The material for the workshop had been developed especially for Athabasca University telephone tutors by Carkhuff Associates of Amherst, Massachusetts, and was derived from their general techniques for people working in counselling situations. Two two-day workshops were held (one in November, 1979 and a revised version in January, 1980), followed by a series of analyses of tape-recorded telephone calls between tutors and learners in which tutors attempted to apply the model of problem-solving they had been taught in the workshop.

Although only a small proportion of the university's tutor force did the training—just seven per cent—the reaction was sufficiently enthusiastic to encourage a further evolution of the project. Modifications were suggested: that course coordinators be included; that tutors be paid extra for participation; and that the in-person workshops be shortened to one day plus subsequent follow-ups.

Stage two

As the organizer of the original workshop had moved, a freelance consultant trained in the Carkhuff techniques was engaged to organize the subsequent workshop. Some modification of the original material was made and more emphasis was placed upon the tutor's need to get learners to set their own goals.

Format

Tutors met with the consultant for about seven hours one Saturday. The communications model was explained and demonstrated, then practised by the tutors in small groups. Tutors also brought to this session a tape recording of a conversation with a learner to serve as an example against which their progress could be measured.

Although it was originally planned that tutors would come to university premises to tape conversations with several of their learners while being monitored by the consultant, they found that prospect unsettling and preferred to tape conversations at home in the course of their regular tutoring evenings, and bring the tapes in for feedback. This proved to be less threatening and was very productive.

At the end of the short sequence of tape analyses, the tutors reassembled for another workshop to comment on the process they had gone through, and to practise the techniques they had learned.

The communications model

Most tutors thought of themselves as "teachers" trained for the classroom, and were less comfortable at seeing themselves as facilitators or resource persons who try to stimulate the learner to solve his *own* problem. Changing this perception was the main purpose of the workshop, while another focus was to prepare the tutor to keep the learner motivated and working to schedule.

The Carkhuff model diagrammed below is deceptively simple looking, but is profoundly useful and not at all simple to implement.

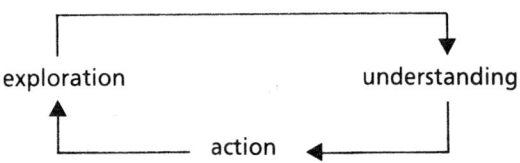

In brief, the more a tutor explores with a learner the problem the learner is encountering with the course material or understands why the learner cannot meet a particular deadline, the better the tutor and learner can together assess the situation and arrive at a suitable formula for action.

Performance

Tutors were to begin by "attending verbally", greeting learners by name, showing consideration for their time constraints and dealing with them as individuals. They did this well, transmitting a feeling of genuineness.

The next step was less easily accomplished. Tutors were to "listen for understanding" and in so doing "reflect both the content and the feeling" of the learner's statements. Tutors had little difficulty in reflecting the content of what learners were saying, but had problems in bringing themselves to try to respond in the prescribed formula for verbalizing the emotional reactions of the learner. They were initially hesitant to use the phrase "you feel x because y", but became more ready to do so after they had listened to several taped conversations in which the formula was used and in which they could recognize the positive effect it had on many learners. Using the formula, tutors found they could convince the learners that they indeed understood the learner's specific situation and problems.

The final step was the most complicated and important, for it stressed working within a limited time frame. After the tutor has established with the learner that he understands what the learner feels and why, the next stage is to identify a proper goal with the learner, and elaborate a sequence of actions to attain that goal. The tutor was encouraged to have the learner define his or her action steps, but if the learner was unable to do so, to offer assistance.

All participants in the workshop agreed that more time could well have been spent practising the last step, which is more difficult than it might seem when one is working within the bounds of two to three short sentences that must transmit proper empathy with the student, and a series of action steps leading to an agreed-upon goal.

Results

Tutors recognized that the end of the formal training was by no means the end of their work at obtaining useful communications skills. They expressed satisfaction with acquiring new skills which they saw helping them relate in an *efficient* and *empathetic* manner with learners. Tutors became more active listeners, *aware* of what they said to the learner, of how they said it, and of the importance of making the learner more responsible for his or her own learning. More learning took place on the student's part; less teaching on the tutor's.

Perhaps the most graphic example was supplied by an accounting tutor who listened to, and solved, his learners' problems as if he were a professional accountant and they clients. Once he became aware of what he was doing—by listening to one of his conversations on tape—the tutor changed tactics. In the next tape that tutor brought in for analysis, there was a much more learner talk, an emphasis upon making the learner explain his problem step by step, and finally, an efficiency in that the tutor had to explain only the small point that tripped up the learner, and not the whole process.

Stage Three

At the time this goes to press, the final phase of the training process is being worked on. The one-day workshop is being omitted, to be replaced by a home-study course designed along the same principles as the university's academic course offerings. Taped conversations will still be required, and they will be analyzed by the tutor and a special tape consultant, working together. Tutors will be paid a flat fee for participating, and from autumn of 1981 participation will be a mandatory part of the terms of employment of new tutors. The home study program will be "field tested" in June, July, and August of 1981 before it is implemented more widely.

This is the only training program of which we know for telephone tutors working in distance education, and we have every reason to expect that the third phase will show increased effectiveness over the previous two. We also expect tutors will find that the skills they attain are effective in helping them provide useful and efficient support to their learners.

Bente Roed Cochran / Alan Meech
Athabasca University
Canada

Student Support at a Crossroads

A student support system has to satisfy the diversity of student preferences which a survey revealed.

Paper 51

Background

The Télé-université now has nine years of experience in serving distance learners. The gradual expansion of its main program—a series of university courses on "Man in his Environment"—has led to a diversity of approaches to student support. In 1978 a new department was established to provide instructional and administrative support to learners and to bring greater order to this important aspect of the Télé-université system. In terms of instructional support, four professionals were responsible for the selection, training, assessment, and counselling of part-time facilitators. The administrative support tasks included setting up group meetings, circulating audio-visual material, and ensuring the availability of space and equipment for regional meetings between students and part-time staff. In 1981 the department had a professional staff of ten whose work also included membership in course teams in order to ensure adequate consideration of student support in the development of new courses.

Types of support

In addition to the course materials package, the Télé-université makes available the services of a facilitator to each student in order to provide help during the learning process. The precise nature of the facilitator's task varies. Student support can take different forms in different courses and within a single course.

The type of support with the longest history is the regional workshop, which was an integral feature of the Télé-université's very first course, "Introduction to the Cooperative Movement". Such workshops are organized for groups of 15-20 students on a regional basis by a part-time local animateur. A three-month course may have between two and six such workshops, which can include viewing audio-visual material, discussion of difficult points, exercises, and question-and-answer sessions.

A second type of support is the local study cell. A study cell is made up of 2-5 students who meet to share experiences and learning activities. Cells may be formed spontaneously by the students or arranged by the Télé-université. They do not involve an animateur, although each group has the name of a resource person who may be contacted by telephone should the need arise. The cell system was first introduced in an advanced French course and proved an excellent innovation since it allowed students to be brought together more easily.

Nevertheless, in some regions of Quebec students are so dispersed that no form of face-to-face group work is possible. In such cases the Télé-université supports students by teleconferences or telephone tutorials. Each teleconference links from 4-8 students with an animateur. Members of the group, who are usually separated by considerable distances, use their home phones. The telephone tutoring system, on the other hand, creates one-to-one contact between a student and a tutor. It does not allow contact between students.

In some courses several of these types of support are used concurrently as Table 1 shows.

Types of support reviewed

Table 1 shows that since the initial support system based on workshops could not be extended to all courses and students, several other types of support were developed. The Télé-université staff now wonder whether certain types of support should not be discontinued. Some would abolish workshops because of their inflexibility and their resemblance to traditional teaching. Others strongly urge the value of workshops since they allow interaction between students and encourage questioning, both important aims of the "Man in his Environment" program. Defenders of workshops admit they cannot be held everywhere, but point out that they are possible in a number of towns and cities.

Telephone tutoring has, according to its supporters, the following advantages:

– flexibility

– encouragement of independent learning

– adaptation to individual student needs

Table 1: Student support in Télé-université courses

Course topic	Workshop	Study Cell	Teleconference	Solo
Management	X		1	
Advertising		0		X
Business	X		1	
English 1 - 4		0		X
Cooperatives	X	2	1	
Economics 1	X	2	1	3
Economics 2		0		X
Environment	X	2	1	
Environment (project)	X	1		2
Spanish 1 - 4		0		X
French (advanced)		X		1
History 1	X	3	1	2
History 2	X	3	1	2
Patrimony	X	1		
Computing	X			
Mathematics	X	2	1	3
Psychology 1	X	1		
Psychology 2	X	1		2
History of science				X
Sex roles	X	0		0
Human biology				X
Human rights	0	X	1	
Personal Health	X	1		

Key
X Main type of support provided
1 First alternative
2 Second alternative
3 Third alternative
0 Combined with main type of support

- uniqueness (compared to other Quebec institutions)
- elimination of travel expenses for students.

The cell also has its particular qualities:
- flexibility
- ease of organization
- group learning, sometimes leading to collaborative group projects
- uniqueness
- provision of the human support needed by some students.

While some staff members recognize the advantages of telephone tutoring and the cell system, they worry that these types of support reduce the quality of the learning experience by lessening the range and intensity of contacts among students and facilitators. The question is not yet settled. Should the Télé-université simplify the types of support it provides in order to make the system more workable, or should other forms of support be developed? The answer must be based on instructional grounds since the objective is to facilitate student learning and academic achievement.

It does at least seem clear that student support helps, for when the Télé-université offered language courses without any formal support, the proportion of drop-outs was higher than in other courses. However, this does not mean all students need the same level of support. Many colleagues urge that the support system be differentiated according to students' academic background and previous experience with distance education. Students would receive more or less intensive support depending on their needs.

This leads to other questions. Should the facilitator and the student be given greater latitude? Should the facilitator be asked to determine the type of support in the light of student needs and the number of students on his list? Do students want to be independent learners, and if so, can they manage it?

These are complex questions that require careful reflection and strategic choices within the institution. As part of this process we conducted a major survey of Télé-université students. They are the people who live the reality of learning at a distance and their views on support services are important.

Survey on student support

Fifty percent of the 1562 Télé-université students surveyed responded. Six areas were covered: student characteristics, time-delays for admission, registration and receipt of course materials, support in language courses, the relation between support and learning, and student services. Some of the aggregate data relating specifically to student support is of interest here.

The typical student is between 30 and 40 years old, married with a child of school age, fully employed, and registered in two Télé-université courses per session with the aim of obtaining credit. Students choose the Télé-université rather than a conventional institution because of: the home-study method (51%); the course topic (21%); the format of instruction and support (14%); convenience of registration and administration (7%).

Most students were satisfied or very satisfied with the information provided about: how to register (97%); course content (92%); learning objectives (93%); support provided (89%); and methods of assessment (86%).

Seventy-nine percent of respondents had a first contact with their facilitator within four weeks of receiving the course materials. Fifteen percent had to wait between four and six weeks, and for 6% it was over six weeks before the first contact was made. In general the shortest delays occur when telephone tutoring or study cells are used, and the longest are associated with teleconferences. This last is not surprising since teleconferences are usually organized as a last resort when it is clear the numbers in a particular region are not sufficient to justify other means of support. Seventy-nine percent of respondents considered the delay before first contact acceptable or very acceptable.

The respondents reported contacts with the facilitator and other students to be mainly of interest because: the exchanges were interesting and stimulating (19%); questions about content were answered (19%); it enabled them to assess their own learning (19%); there were exchanges with other students (15%); they could adjust their own approach (15%). There is a significant relationship between the reason given and the type of support involved. Stimulating exchanges and the assessment of their own learning were the first two reasons given by students in workshops, teleconferences, or combined forms of support. Students in study cells appreciated getting answers to questions and exchanging answers with others. From telephone tutoring, students obtained answers to questions and were also able to adjust their approach.

When the responses to this question are analyzed in terms of students' academic backgrounds, the aim of getting answers to questions is found to be least important for those with a university training. Those with the least previous education look to these exchanges to get feedback on their approach and for stimulation.

In courses with a facilitator, students who did not take part in the contacts scheduled gave as reasons: unpredictable change of circumstances (43%); preference for purely independent study (23%); no feeling of need (18%); lack of interest (10%). However, 38% of respondents had additional contacts with their facilitator over and above those officially scheduled. Their reasons were: to obtain more information (32%); to get details about the approach taken in the course (19%); to give notification of absence from scheduled contacts (16%); to discuss learning difficulties (13%). Those who contacted their facilitator tended to have a stronger academic background and to have taken more Télé-université courses previously.

Most (80%) considered the type of support provided in their course was effective, either rather effective (54%) or very effective (26%). Sixteen percent found the support more or less effective and 4% considered it rather or completely ineffective.

Students were also asked what would have been their three choices (in order of preference) had they been allowed at registration to select a particular type of support for the whole course. The results are shown in Table 2, where the first choice scores three points, the second two points, and the third one point.

Table 2

Type of support	Score	Frequency (%)
Workshops	832	22
Telephone tutoring	757	21
Study Cells	741	20
Solo (language courses)	656	16
Combined format	450	12
Teleconference	284	8
No preference	55	1

Although workshops are the most popular form of support, 78% prefer other types. More than 40% prefer individualized support without group meetings.

Conclusion

The Télé-université has opted for a pluralistic approach to student support that has both advantages and snags. It is now reviewing its policy and will make strategic choices that must take into account foreseeable technological developments. There is no question of abandoning the commitment to student support. The student has the right to support services although support may be provided on a selective basis depending on the student's specific needs. Special care must be taken of those geographically isolated students to whom distance education has a special responsibility.

The results of the survey will be useful in making decisions. Ninety-five percent of students are satisfied with their learning and their courses at the Télé-université. However, 20% feel that there are undue delays and do not appreciate the type of student support provided. The problems they experience are largely due to our present practice and must be solved. Should we move to a fixed semester system or allow continuous enrolment? Do we wish to set up a continuous support system to match a continuous enrolment system? Is it desirable that student support be less interactive and rely more on media?

Student support at the Télé-université is at a crossroads. The staff responsible must come up with new solutions that reflect students' needs, current organizational changes, and a gloomy financial outlook. Fortunately, the track record of the Télé-université provides ground for believing that the challenge will be met successfully.

Simon Caron
Télé-université
Canada

Study Circles

The study circle is a flexible and well adapted form of study organization in sparsely populated areas.

Finland is a large but sparsely populated country with an area of 337,000 km² but a population of only 4.7 million. Half of the population lives in the four southern provinces, the rest in the eight eastern and northern provinces. In the Finnish Lapland the median population density is under 10 persons per square kilometer.

Free studies, offered by different organizations and financed by government, communes, and free associations are very popular. Most extensive is the system of adult education centres maintained by the communes with government help. By the end of 1979 there were 270 adult education centres with about 545,000 registered students. In addition there were 86 folk high schools with about 6500 students. In these institutions a student may obtain free education in many fields of culture, social studies, science, etc., studying either full time or in the evening. Instruction is usually given in classes.

Other forms of free studies include study circles maintained by various organizations that usually receive financial aid from the government. These organizations are united in a "Central Association of Study Activity", which has the responsibility of coordinating and supporting the study activities of its members. At the end of 1979 there were about 20,000 study circles with about 180,000 students. Most of these study circles work at the secondary level.

Free instruction is also offered in the form of open university studies. This began in the 1970s and is still in its first development stage. During the academic year 1979-80 four universities in Finland offered open university studies in cooperation with adult education centres and folk high schools. The statistical situation is shown in Table 1.

The universities of Joensuu and Tampere began experiments in open university teaching in the early 1970s. Turku and Helsinki followed some years later, and recently the Swedish-language university Abo Academi in Turku and the universities of Jyvaskyla and Kuopio have started. The development of an open university in Finland is dependent on financial possibilities, which are quite limited, but the number of students is anticipated to grow during the 1980s.

The Ministry of Education has a commission to coordinate and support open university instruction. Universities are trying to develop dedicated units for open university studies, but because of financial difficulties they are still mostly in an experimental stage. Tampere University has a centre for complementary education, which includes open university activities, and Helsinki University has a centre in Lahti, about 100 km away. Centres are planned for Turku and Joensuu.

In Finland, 22 summer universities offer open university courses from June to August. Summer universities are maintained by towns or special associations with government support. They offer normal academic courses for regular students who continue their studies during the summer, and at the same time offer free open university teaching and organize seminars, conferences and some cultural events. In fact, summer universities are the oldest form of the open university system in Finland. The first was established in 1912, but open university activities did not developed rapidly until the 1960s and 1970s. Today, universities cooperate with summer universities in open university teaching so that open university students can include summer courses in their curriculum and take examinations.

During the regular academic year universities cooperate with adult education centres and folk high schools in organizing open university activities outside the university town. In a centre or a folk high school a qualified teacher is appointed to direct open

Table 1: Open university activities in Finland 1970-80

University	Students	Cooperating with adult education centres	folk high schools
Helsinki University	526	4	
Joensuu University	474	8	3
Tampere University	1409	12	
Turku University	734	4	
Totals	3143	28	3

university studies in cooperation with the university. Usually between 3 and 10 people who wish to study a certain discipline form a study circle, supervised by the director. The circles meet regularly for lectures or seminars, but the members also work individually with the help of books, special audio-visual materials and occasional TV and radio programs. A university teacher visits the study circle regularly to lecture, lead seminars and be available for consultation. He also organizes examinations, which can be held in the local institution. The examinations are graded at the university.

In principle, students cannot obtain regular academic degrees through open university studies. Usually open university students choose a limited program complementary to a particular professional field or science. The student can get a certificate for the program. After a certain number of complementary study courses and programs an open university student can be allowed to register for regular academic studies.

The most popular fields of study in the open university are social sciences, humanities, and education. Little open university teaching is offered in natural sciences and mathematics because these studies are more difficult to organize in study circles without laboratories.

The study circle is a flexible and well adapted form of study organization in sparsely populated areas. The study circle is organized in adult education centres or folk high schools according to the demands of open university studies. Normally these free institutions work at the secondary level, but in cooperation with the neighbouring university they include university-level studies in their program. Each study circle is quite autonomous. It can choose its working hours and methods in accordance with the general program of its home institution. The study circle can work on one or several programs and can arrange the length of studies within certain limits. A study circle can choose different working methods and forms of services like libraries, audio-visual centres, radio, TV and so on. The study circle can include members studying regularly in an adult education centre or in a folk high school, but it can also take outside members so that people of different professions can pursue open university studies during the evenings and holidays.

Naturally there are difficulties in organizing study circles. Long distances limit participation. Limited free time in rural agriculture areas, heavy work, and family responsibilities can be obstacles to open university studies. It is not always easy to find good and experienced directors and leaders. The universities have very little money and personnel available for open university work, and the government has not yet been able to give special posts for open university teaching in the universities. University teachers are not always willing to travel in the country to visit study circles and the number of visits must be limited, especially in sparsely populated areas.

The most difficult problems are the academic level and the lack of teaching materials made specially for the open university. In Finland the open university is technically open to all adults. However, in practice the regional conditions and limited resources restrict offerings. Many students have insufficient basic education and are not able to pursue their studies, dropping out during the first years. Normal study materials prepared for regular university students are less useful in open university studies, where students have to work more individually and in autonomous groups. One of the most urgent tasks for the development of the open university in Finland is the creation of study materials, especially audio-visual materials.

Heikki Kirkinen
University of Joensuu
Finland

Student Support Services in Continuing Education

Study support services form an integral complement to the mass-produced materials of a distance teaching system.

The Open University's commitment to student support services has remained an important and integral part of its multi-media teaching strategy since its inception in 1969 (Open University Planning Committee, HMSO, 1969: 14).

It is convenient to classify courses in the Continuing Education Programme as follows:

a. Courses at degree level: some specifically prepared to cover professional areas, in particular in-service teacher training, and health and social welfare (15 in 1981), and others prepared originally within the Undergraduate Programme but offered as single courses (70 in 1981). These courses are 1 year long.

b. Short courses at sub-degree level: designed to meet educational rather than academic need on topics such as parenthood, consumer affairs, personal health, governing schools, etc. (12 in 1981). These courses are approximately 10 weeks long.

A third element in the Continuing Education Programme lies in the production of "packages" of self-instructional materials. Two have been created to date in the field of microprocessors in industry, and others are planned.

A common factor across all courses in the Continuing Education Programme lies in the commitment of the student for a shorter period of time. The range at present extends from 8 weeks to 1 year (with the exception of the Diploma in Reading Development), as compared with the normal range of 4-8 years for completion of a degree. In these circumstances "continuity of counselling" cannot have the same importance. The advisory and counselling role has a shorter duration and cannot be based on knowledge of a student built up over a number of years. We argue, however, that the same concern must exist for individualising a mass-produced distance teaching system in order to meet the difficulties noted by Sewart (1978) in the undergraduate context: most students, inexperienced in distance education, are not prepared for the demands on verbal skills, the lack of personal contact, or the necessity for careful scheduling of work.

Support for associate students entering degree-level courses

Between 1973 and 1977 the needs of associate students were much neglected. The diversity of their educational and occupational backgrounds, and the implications of their entering on second or third level degree studies through an open admissions policy, were not appreciated. The "post-experience" image of, for example, a confident teacher well able to cope with university-level study, prevailed.

A consequence of this was that the admissions advisory service was rudimentary, on the assumption that those interested in applying could adequately make their decisions on the basis of brief course descriptions. Associate students were placed in the allocation of tutors with undergraduate students, and for counselling were added for a year to the case load of an undergraduate tutor-counsellor.

However, by 1979, the needs of associate students as a separate, albeit heterogeneous group, were much better understood. The views of course tutors in the East Anglian Region on student support needs other than direct subject tuition were collected by Porter and Kelly (1979). The most important factors lay in failure to foresee the intellectual demands of second or third level degree work, the lack of background knowledge (gained in lower level courses by undergraduates), the demands on time and sustained effort required, the lack of developed study skills, the need for reassurance and guidance in resuming academic work after many years, and unfamiliarity with the nature of the OU teaching system.

The identification of these factors has lead to a major revision of associate student services. In particular, support has been developed for the range of decisions in the period leading up to the start of the course (separated into the stages of enquiry, application, admission, preparation, and induction).

Data on the associate student drop-out and failure rate remains difficult to interpret (a student who does not sit the final examination may never have intended to do so, for example). It is conceded, however, that despite the fuller course descriptions, the development of self-diagnostic materials, and access in advance to the course materials themselves, a significant number of students are mismatched in terms of level of difficulty or curriculum content with the course actually being studied. This is a crucial issue, in the light of the view expressed by Moore (1980: 25) that "Adults who work at their real needs are highly motivated, do not drop out, and rarely fail". A more detailed discussion of this issue is given by Kelly (1980).

The introduction of a separate post with training for associate student counsellors has allowed attention to be directed to associate students in their own right, not as "one-year undergraduates". Thus the counsellor involved in admissions advice also introduces the student to the OU system at the beginning of the course and remains his local general adviser throughout the year of study. Each application is treated in an individual manner, regardless of apparent preparedness for a course. Early contact with individual students enables counsellors to make more effective use of induction meetings, with workshop approaches helping students to raise issues of concern. There is also some evidence to suggest that early contact increases the likelihood of students raising issues with their counsellor during the year.

Short courses—three models

Parallel to the degree-level courses for associate students, the OU has, since 1973, produced an array of shorter courses.

The number of students involved to date has been in excess of 50,000 in the period 1973-1980. No tutorial or counselling services in the personal sense have been offered to these students, and where support has been offered it has been in the facilitation of non-tutorial self-help study groups.

However, within this limited development, a number of different models of support for a "course" have emerged. These can be classified in the following way:

i. *Simple despatch:* no organised support is offered locally, and the correspondence course is simply despatched to the student who may watch the accompanying television programmes.
ii. *Independent volunteer support:* independent voluntary organisations organise self-help study groups (the outstanding example is the involvement of the Pre-School Playgroups Association with the writing and mounting of the short course "The Pre-School Child").
iii. *Professionally organised support:* professional adult educators take responsibility for organising local study groups (this has been achieved co-operatively by local Adult Education Services as well as by the OU's own regional staff).

It can be immediately acknowledged that, like all models which abstract from a wide range of concrete examples, this conceptualisation is simpler than the more complex reality. For example, on one course, a mix of models may exist like i) and ii) in different areas. The models provide a useful framework for the examination of the development of short courses. The third and most recent model could provide the most effective basis for comprehensive educational services in the future.

Early prototype

The first short course mounted exemplified the first model. This was a course on the working and impact of the European Economic Community (EEC), mounted prior to the referendum on EEC entry held in Great Britain in 1975, and continuing through 1976. The course comprised written materials despatched to students, together with television and radio programmes.

No responsibility was taken for advice at the stages of application, during study, or on finishing the course. With no examination to pass and no qualification to gain, students made of the course what they wanted. The OU's regional structure, concerned with "mediating" course materials for individual consumption, was not involved at all. This example clearly represented the model of "simple despatch". The model allows for one-directional flow of material to the student (the return of computer-marked assignments on this and other similarly based courses allowed for only a controlled and impersonalised response). The course model is very centralised and in the light of discussion such as Thorpe's article titled "When is a course not a course?" (Thorpe, 1979: 13) represents arguably more of a publishing venture.

Independent volunteer support

The years 1977-1980 have formed an interim and more complex period. In the wake of the establishment of a Centre for Continuing Education within the OU, the major premise of those mounting short courses has been that they are "community" based, influenced from the curricular point of view by the phrase "adult concern". The curricular innovation has been matched by attempts to innovate with systems of student support. Collaboration was initiated by the central course-creating unit with, in the formal sense, non-educational bodies. It was planned that these outside bodies would, through their local networks, set up self-help groups with direction and initiative from the students themselves. The major examples were a course created in collaboration with the Health Education Council (a governmental body), "The First Years of Life", and in collaboration with a voluntary body, the Pre-School Playgroups Association, a course entitled "The Pre-School Child" (both known as the "baby courses"). Evaluation of the local networks has been undertaken centrally (Calder and Lilley, 1978) and notable achievement has been recorded.

This mode has had considerable attention as an alternative to costly professional services organized by the OU's regional structure and can be seen as the major achievement on the student support side of the central course creation unit.

There has been little evaluation of this model locally, although a report produced within the OU East Anglian Region (Davis, 1979) has registered the variability in the organisation of self-help groups and suggests the need for local rather than central organisation, above all in the field of community education.

The successes of the method have tended to mask the fact that for the two "baby courses" in some parts of the country and for a number of other short courses running at the same time, there has been no local network. For these courses, the "simple despatch" model has applied by default rather than by design. Thus limitations can be seen in the "independent volunteer" model.

Professionally organised support

Work by the OU's regional staff (formally charged only with responsibility for degree-level undergraduate and associate student work) began to expand in the short course area and paved the way for present developments. Local adult education and community networks, which were familiar to many of the regional staff, began to be more fully explored for the purposes of student support on short courses. During this period experiments with course creation to meet local rather than national need took place with the Women's Institutes in the East Anglian Region (Calder and Baines, 1978).

Arising out of the increased involvement of regional staff and their local colleagues in adult education comes the "professionally organised support" model. The most pertinent examples lie in the courses "Living with Children 5-10", where regional staff were asked to appoint and brief local coordinators, and "Governing Schools", where regional staff have been asked to find appropriate forums for publicity and networks for student support. Both these requests for regional support were made in the recognition that no relevant outside agency existed with local branches or groups. The model here is analogous to the Adult Literacy Campaign (and subsequently Adult Basic Education) of professionally supported volunteer work (Jones and Charnley, 1978).

Further experimentation is taking place in the East Anglian Region with a counsellor model, based on the associate student counsellor role described earlier. It may be that critical examination of work undertaken by volunteers will lead to greater use of a professional non-tutorial role concerned with facilitation of student learning and progress.

Conclusion

The most important common factor for the majority of both degree-level and short courses for associate students has been that student support services to meet individual need form an integral complement to the mass-produced materials of a distance teaching system. Developments across the range of OU continuing education courses demonstrate the necessity of making specific provision for different educational activities avoiding the unexamined adoption of support models from the Undergraduate Programme.

A. Roger Mills / Alan W. Tait
Open University
United Kingdom

References

Calder, J. and Baines, S. (1978) The Norfolk Experiment. IET, Open University. (mimeo)

Calder, J. and Lilley, A. (1978) Self-help groups and the role of coordinators. Reports 1 and 2. IET, Open University. (mimeo)

Davis, K. (1979) The local impact of short courses. Open University, East Anglian Region. (mimeo)

Jones, H.A. and Charnley, A.H. (1978) Adult literacy, a study of its impact. National Institute of Adult Education Report.

Kelly, P. (1980) How open is the Associate Student Programme? *Teaching at a Distance*, 18, 17-27.

Moore, M. (1980) Continuing education and the assessment of learner needs. *Teaching at a Distance*, 17, 25-29.

Open University Planning Committee, HMSO (1969) Report of the Planning Committee to the Secretary of State for Education and Science.

Porter, E. and Kelly, P. (1979) Unpublished report of survey of tutors' opinions in East Anglian Region of the Open University.

Sewart, D. (1978) Academic support and guidance for individuals in a distance learning system. ICCE, Advanced Papers, 1.

Thorpe, M. (1979) When is a course not a course? *Teaching at a Distance*, 16, 13-18.

Paper 54

Mobile Learning Centres in an Open Learning System

Mobile units are simply portable mini-colleges.

Since 1977, North Island College, on Vancouver Island, British Columbia, has been successful in using mobile learning centres to distribute economically the support components of its open learning system to small, remote communities. In concept, mobile units are simply portable mini-colleges or travelling extensions of the college. While mobile educational facilities are not new, their use in an open learning system is believed to be unique.

Open learning at North Island College

Although sometimes erroneously labelled as a "distance learning" or "correspondence" college, North Island College conducts most of its educational functions through open learning. Mobile units locally enlarge and support the system and stand out as different only by virtue of their mobility.

From its inception, the College was charged with making learning opportunities available to all adults of the population dispersed within the 50,000 square mile region regardless of whether they live in an isolated village or in a large town. A traditional system of instruction was tested initially, but frequent cancellation of classes because of inadequate enrolments confirmed the need for an alternative method. In response the College has evolved its own open learning system and proven its worth by growing in just five years to be the fourth largest college in British Columbia in terms of academic enrolments.

The openness of the system means that a student living anywhere in the region can register for any open course on any day of the year (holidays excepted) and start work on the course immediately. It also means working at a pace chosen by the student and finishing the course (within generous, extendable limits) when it suits the student. There is no requirement to attend any scheduled class because study can be carried out where the student lives and works.

The open approach is permitted by a system comprised of two components. One is a set of completely individualised, self-instructional materials, often a mix of printed and audio-visual components, which are supplied to the student on registration. The materials are designed such that a student could achieve the objectives of the course by contacting the college only for assessment purposes. It is this component, when perceived in isolation, that gives rise to the mislabeling of the College's methodology. However, students rarely opt to work in this lonely but possible way. They prefer the support of the system's second component, the network of tutors available to them on a regular face-to-face basis, or by indirect communication.

The college has learning centres in all the larger towns of the region. Centres consist of one or more rooms, or a building, usually rented in a downtown location central to the surrounding community. Learning centres contain meeting and study spaces, library and audio-visual resources, laboratory facilities and equipment, computers, and other educational hardware and software. Centres are manned by tutors assisted by other non-professional staff. Their total number in any centre reflects the size of the community.

Mobile units are smaller, more compact editions of these static centres, and manned by a single tutor who is also the driver.

Tutor's role

As the sole human resource of a mobile unit (or a small static centre), the tutor works with students taking any of well over one hundred courses, ranging from mathematics through languages to history, and at levels from grade VIII to second year university. A mobile tutor has to perform a generalist role unlike that of a traditional faculty member who is restricted to a single subject area. A mobile tutor is obviously not expected to have a thorough knowledge of all subjects, but has to be familiar with the characteristics of all courses and be able to assist students in every other way. This includes helping a student learn how to learn and to organise and manage course work, supervising examinations, and generally providing the kind of interpersonal communication that demonstrates genuine concern with the student's learning welfare. The ultimate objective of the tutor is to lead the student to the point where the student's learning becomes as independent of the tutor and institution as possible.

In this challenging role, "universal" or local tutors are supported by two other levels of tutor in the college's system. Course assignments brought by students to a learning centre are marked by tutors who possess the required subject expertise for marking, usually at least at the first degree level. Assignments are despatched by the local tutor to the nearest marking tutor with the right subject background. When marked, the work is returned to the student via the local tutor who maintains the academic records. At the third level, each course is backed by a designated course tutor, a graduate degree specialist. On the infrequent occasions when a student confronts a problem that cannot be resolved on the spot, the local tutor telephones the course tutor who provides the solution for the enlightenment of both student and local tutor. If the mobile tutor's discipline happens to be that of the course, then he may be local, marking and course tutor at the same time, which is very convenient! In any event, the academic support is readily available and the mobile tutor has a substantial supporting team to rely on.

Operation of mobile learning centres

Starting with a single unit pioneered by the author to serve the west coast of Vancouver Island, the college now has three units in commission. A fourth is in the process of acquisition. A marine mobile, a ship, which will combine the standard mobile learning centre with a practical marine capability while the vessel is en route between stops, is about to commence operations reaching island and coastal communities inaccessible by road. The distribution of the units is shown in Figure 1.

Vehicular units are of two types. Two of the units include living accommodation for their operators as the vehicles remain overnight in the communities they visit to provide evening access. The other units are termed "daymobiles", containing a washroom for the tutor's use but no other domestic fittings. These daymobiles serve communities within a reasonable distance of a home base so that tutors can return home at night.

The vehicles are constructed on a motor-home chassis or are modifications of a commercial delivery van. Each mobile unit contains study carrels for two to four students, a tutor's station, radiotelephone, storage for files, library resources and audio-visual cassettes, a microcomputer station, and space for laboratory work. Since a third of the courses offered

Figure 1: Map of the College region showing the distribution of learning centres: Areas served by mobile units are indicated by arrows

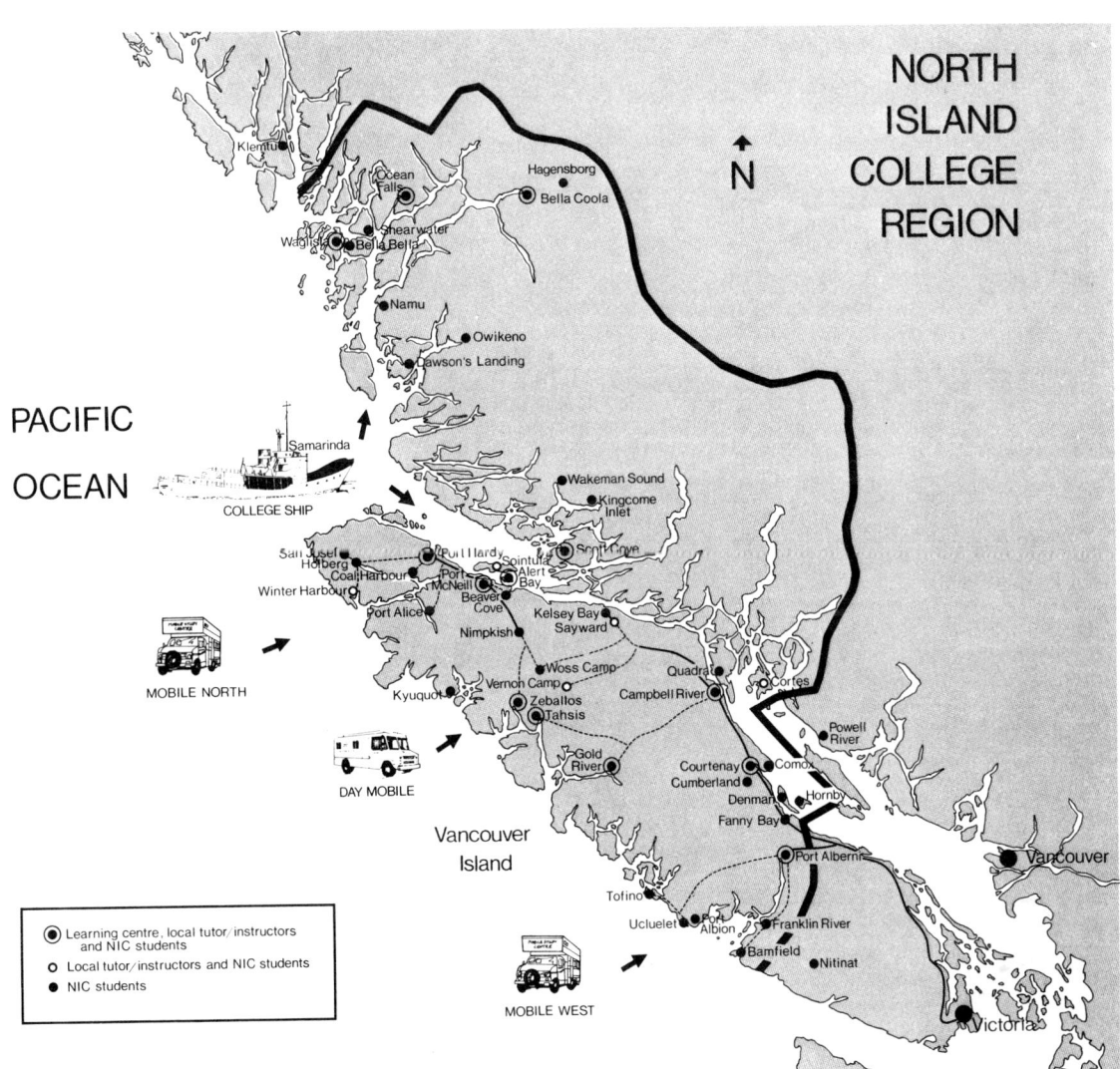

(Reproduced with permission from the 1980-81 North Island College catalogue.)

include a television component, student positions are fitted with individual monitors coupled to playback equipment for multiple viewing of different programmes by different students. A headphone system prevents sound interference.

Mobile units travel to each community on a regular schedule, usually weekly. The vehicles station themselves at locations convenient for their users and adjacent to a plug-in for an AC electrical supply—provided free by the community. Students come by appointment arranged with the mobile tutor the previous week. Students may spend any length of time from a few minutes to several hours, talking individually with the tutor, in discussion with other students, using resources, or writing tests. At any one time there may be three or four students in the vehicle, and prospective students tend to drop in to enquire about the college or seek advice about courses.

The rationale for mobile units, their constraints and future use

The demography of the College region determined the adoption of the open learning system. In turn, it almost inevitably led to the use of mobile centres. Mobility makes these learning centres a very flexible extension to the system as they can be adjusted to suit local student activity. A community currently served by a mobile unit may well grow to the point where enrolment will support a static facility. When that happens, a centre can be established and the mobile unit moved to other places. In a community such as a logging camp where the population seasonally fluctuates, the weekly stay by the mobile can be changed to suit the current need.

Figure 2: The first mobile learning centre

Mobile units are valuable to the college in other ways. Their operators serve the useful function of liaison and distribute materials in support of locally-mounted continuing education activity. Their physical nature makes them a highly visible College "presence" wherever they go. It is probable that the residents of the communities visited are on average better aware of their local community college than people living in the towns with a larger fixed centre.

Mobile operations are successful. Current registrations per unit range from about sixty to more than one hundred during any given month. Enrolment data for the first daymobile unit show an astonishing 19% "penetration", which means that of all the households in the communities served by that unit almost one fifth include a person who is taking a course through the mobile facility.

Some constraints on using mobile learning centres are recognised. One is that their usage is very dependent on the capabilities of their tutors. The nature of the work demands a high level of adaptability, experience and maturity. It is essential for a mobile tutor to approach the instructional situation as an admitted non-expert, willing to work with adults on a more nearly equal level. The mobile tutor's job is demanding, requiring work at night away from home, coping with breakdowns and often difficult driving conditions, and infrequent contact with professional colleagues. Despite these factors, mobile tutors unanimously agree that their job is very rewarding and never dull. It is worth noting that two of the units are manned by husband and wife teams, each sharing the position and alternately taking the vehicle on its weekly run.

A second constraint stems from the fact that it is less easy to offer technical or vocational courses requiring extensive use of equipment and practical training. So far the bulk of courses offered through mobile units are academic. However, it is probable that technological developments in communications and learning materials will soon permit such training to be achieved through a combination of theoretical self-instruction delivered via mobile learning centres and intensive, hands-on training taking place over a short period while a mobile shop or laboratory is temporarily located in a community. North Island College is currently designing a welding training facility mounted on a truck trailer.

The fourth mobile learning centre now being acquired is destined to operate in the same way as the others but with a slight difference. As well as visiting remote villages, it will go to some of the smaller communities within easy reach of the big college centres in the two large towns on the east coast of Vancouver Island. The intent is to ascertain whether a mobile unit is as effective in generating enrolments in a more urban situation as it is in a rural site, and to confirm whether potential students prefer the convenience of the college coming to them and the more personal nature of a mobile centre compared with the necessity of travelling a few more kilometres to a building with its more institutional atmosphere.

Don Salter
North Island College
Canada

The Role of Regional Centres

Educational and institutional access, student support and community liaison are the essential functions of regional centres.

The Open Learning Institute was established in 1978 by the government of the province of British Columbia. Its mandate is very broad, requiring delivery of university degree programs in arts and science, career/technical/vocational programs, adult basic education programs, and continuing education programs, all by distance education methods. In addition, the Universities Act was amended to permit the Institute to offer degrees in its own right.

The first principal of the Institute was appointed in June 1978, with major staff growth starting in early 1979. The first seven courses were offered in September 1979 with 356 students registered to produce a total of 528 course enrolments. Growth has been rapid, with 1981 course enrolments expected to exceed 10,000. (Table 1)

Table 1: Open Learning Institute enrolments, 1981

Semester	Number of Courses	Number of Students	Number of Course Enrolments
Spring 1981	65	2497	3070
Summer 1981	70	2230	2760
Fall 1981	83	3375 (projected)	4185 (projected)

The Institute has in excess of 80 full-time staff, plus more than 120 part-time tutors.

Courses are primarily print-based with audio tape support in some courses. Recently, video support material has been broadcast on the educational television channel; this material has normally been acquired elsewhere, and there are no immediate plans for the Open Learning Institute to move into television production.

Student support

From the beginning, staff accepted the position that strong student support was essential to achieving high completion rates. Particular attention was paid to the successful support systems of the Open University, but significant changes had to be made to produce a workable system for British Columbia, made necessary by the large distances and low population density, and by the less homogeneous student body resulting from the broad spectrum of program offerings.

These considerations resulted in two key decisions:

1. Support would emphasize telephone use, since telephone access is almost universal. Provision would be made for the Institute to pay the costs of calls to avoid financial penalties on remote students.
2. Separate tutoring and advising services would be established to provide subject assistance and general assistance, respectively. No provision would be made for face-to-face contact between students and tutors, but the advising service would be established on a regional basis with expectations of some face-to-face contact.

These decisions were implemented, and after two years of operating the system, it has been found necessary to make only minor changes.

The tutoring service

The role of the tutor is to provide all assistance related to course content, including marking. Tutors are subject specialists comparable to faculty in traditional institutions. Projected enrolments in many courses were such that only a single tutor would be required to service the entire province. Thus face-to-face contact would be impossible or extremely expensive for all but a limited number of students (usually those who could attend a traditional institution anyway) and to avoid discrimination against the rest of the students, no provision was made for such contacts, and tutors were actively discouraged from initiating any.

Since courses at the Open Learning Institute are relatively short and last only four months, students are exposed to numerous tutors as they work through a program.

The advising service and regional centres

To complement the tutoring service, regional centres staffed by advisors were established. Six such centres have been opened in addition to one at the main offices of the Institute. Four main roles have been defined for the centres:

1. **Educational access**

   To provide assistance in selecting suitable vocational and career goals, to advise on selection of suitable programs and courses, to provide information on various educational institutions and their interrelationships, and to assist with admission and registration.

2. **Open Learning Institute access**

   To provide specific information on OLI programs and courses, rules and regulations, and procedures, and to ensure that entry to courses is as easy as possible.

3. **Student support**

   To supplement the tutors by providing to enrolled students support which may include:

   a. all of the student services normally found in a traditional institution (financial aid, study skills, etc.)

   b. functions related to a distance operation (unavailable course materials, examinations, special facilities such as laboratories, etc.)

   Most of all, advisors provide a single point of contact for students with problems, and provide continuity of contact to assist students in identifying with the Institute.

4. **Community liaison**

   To maintain good relations with the community, particularly with the local community college and schools, as well as with the general public.

Staffing of regional centres

Each centre is staffed by an advisor, with half-time or full-time clerical assistance, depending on need. In some cases, the clerical assistance is shared with the local college.

Advisors must be generalists—they have to be prepared to assist students with the entire range of student services, but without the time or resources for in-depth counselling. Referral must be used when very specialized services are needed. For this reason, the term "counsellor" was not used, and there is no requirement that advisors be trained counsellors, although several are. The criteria for selection of advisors are:

- administrative skills
- self-directing
- interpersonal skills
- knowledge of the B.C. educational system
- experience as a mature student.

The educational access function

There was early recognition that OLI students, particularly those in non-degree programs, would be different from students of traditional institutions. It was important to reach potential students who were not being reached by other institutions; this included not only the geographically isolated, but the handicapped, shift workers, single parents who could not afford child care, and—a very important category —

those who for various reasons would not approach a traditional institution. Our typical target was a forty-year old who never went past grade eight, and who was not prepared to expose his perceived ignorance before a class of youngsters. There are reputed to be more than 400,000 adults in B.C. who never completed high school, a significant proportion of whom are functionally illiterate. Access to the Institute had to be simple and non-threatening.

Another problem was credibility. A new institution with an unusual name, a post office box number in a Vancouver suburb, and an innovative approach to education was not exactly designed to inspire confidence. Something visible and tangible was needed for potential students to identify with.

The result of this was the decision to establish regional centres in the major population centres of the province. To provide easy access and visibility, storefront locations in busy shopping areas were considered desirable, and this has generally been achieved.

The educational access function is considered to have two parts:

a. to determine a potential student's program needs and to match him with the most appropriate institution.

b. if the student elects to register at OLI, to assist with all of the necessary processes.

Student support function

There is an ongoing supportive function necessary for the success of many students, especially when terms are short and students are repeatedly exposed to new tutors. The natural feeling of isolation of distance education students is heightened if there is no continuity of contact, or if students don't know where to turn for assistance, or if they have any feeling of being shunted around when they try to make an inquiry. One of the main roles of the advisor is to provide ongoing support to students.

Each student at registration is assigned to an advisor on a regional basis so that there is some opportunity for face-to-face contact. This assignment will be fixed throughout the student's career at OLI. Advisors are charged with providing any assistance the student needs other than that related to course content. In cases where the advisor is not able to assist directly, he is either to obtain information elsewhere, or refer the student to another agency. Specific tasks for advisors include:

a. orientation of new students

b. assistance with learning skills (study techniques, time management, reading and writing skills)

c. assistance in obtaining and using resource materials

d. assistance with financial aid

e. monitoring a student's progress and assisting with selection of appropriate courses

f. organization of regional examination centres or special facilities (e.g. laboratories)

g. assistance with problems such as missing course materials, etc.

h. organization of student peer contacts.

Advisors typically handle 400 to 600 active students. With this student load, and with their other functions, they are not able to reach their full potential in supporting continuing students. However, there can be no doubt of their value—to most students, they are the only "live" part of the Institute ever seen.

The liaison role of regional centres

The announcement of the establishment of the Open Learning Institute generated considerable hostility from the community college system and considerable efforts were expended to develop good working relationships with the colleges. It was decided that, initially at least, regional centres would only be opened with the full agreement of the local college. Of the six centres opened to date, five now have some participation by the college, and negotiations are underway to provide a joint operation in the sixth centre; this would also include one of the provincial universities. This ongoing contact between regional centres and community colleges has provided an excellent channel of communication between institutions, and has done much to develop a growing trust at the operating level. It is now common practice for students to be encouraged to take advantage of courses or services offered by the neighbouring institution. In this way, the Institute is really starting to complement the colleges and to assist them to fulfil their role.

In addition to liaison with community colleges, regional centres are charged with general liaison with the communities in their region. This includes contact with the public school system, government agencies, local media, service agencies, employers, etc. This extensive local contact assists in making the Institute a truly province-wide operation.

Future plans

There is no doubt that existing regional centres are fulfilling an invaluable role in educational access, assisting students complete their studies, and in providing regional liaison. Plans are being made to establish four additional centres over the next two years using essentially the same model. This will complete the primary network of centres.

Since the main regional centres do not provide adequate coverage for some regions of the province (several significant population centres could still be more than 100 miles from a centre), consideration is being given to the establishment of "satellite centres" to service smaller communities. These would be under the control of the main centres with part-time staff perhaps working out of their own home. Use could also be made of school teachers or community librarians.

Denys Meakin
Open Learning Institute
Canada

Local Support for the Local Learner

Establishing a regional centre to provide local support for the local learner enrolled in a course elsewhere requires careful planning and interinstitutional cooperation.

'The tyranny of distance' for Australian education

Northcott (1975: 21) used the phrase 'the tyranny of distance' coined by Blainey (1966) to highlight the unique problems which have always confronted those attempting to provide any public service Australia-wide, education being no exception.

Vaizey (1969: 93) has noted that colonizing powers tend to export their education system to the country being colonized. Certainly the British influence in Australian education is clearly in evidence. However, Britain happened to have a post-secondary education system which had evolved to cater for a large, decentralized population contained in two relatively small islands. The only demographic similarity between the countries is that Australia, too, could be said to comprise two islands.

The two extremes of demography are the

States of Western Australia and Tasmania. Western Australia represents one third the land mass of the larger island: its area is roughly the same as Western Europe, (population 450 million), and yet it has only one city (the capital, Perth) which accounts for over 70% of the State's population of 1 million. Tasmania is about two thirds the size of England (not Great Britain) with a population of 400,000. It is the most decentralized state, with only 40% of the population in the capital, Hobart.

'The tyranny of the campus' for distance education

External study services rarely make concessions to the problems peculiar to the external student in Australia. The whole structure of an external course is almost always a translation of a campus course, rather than a 'de novo' development. This is because in Australia there are no colleges or universities, such as the British Open University, catering *only* to students studying at the tertiary level by a distance education system—thus, as no distinction is made between a qualification gained via the "campus" or "distance" route, the latter is made as similar to the former as possible.

It would be much easier to design appropriate tertiary education systems 'de novo' to suit the appropriate demography. Successful experiments have been carried out in this regard (Walker, 1977: 10) but the campus model is so well established that it is highly unlikely that genuine alternatives will be accepted.

Support for the local learner must therefore take the form of providing analogues for components of the campus system which are not covered by actual teaching materials (the "social" and "ritual" components).

The problem of satellite study centres

A common solution to the problem is the study centre or "institution shop front." These can range from a token presence maintained as a marginal activity by someone employed in another sector of the education system, through to substantial centres with several full-time staff supporting the most heavily subscribed courses.

The main problem with such centres is that they are institute-specific as defined in the Australian Tertiary Education Commission Report for the 1982-4 Triennium (Karmel, 1981: 214). By definition, the more isolated a region, the more likely it is to come within the outer radius of a range of institutions. Inevitably, this leads to competition for a small pool of students. If one institution is supporting a centre, then understandably it will favour its own students first.

The advantages of a regional centre

One logical development of the institute study centre is the regional centre, funded by *the region,* and accessible to *all* institutes. This apparently very obvious development is in fact not made easy by educational funding formulae which are based on numbers of enrolled students at specific institutes. It is therefore easier to fund the institute-specific centres.

The problem has been overcome in Tasmania where the "Office of the Director, North West Council for Community Education" is funded from the state education vote to foster a more effective tertiary education provision in the most isolated region of the smallest state in Australia (Karmel, 1976: 70).

The structure of a regional centre

This will vary somewhat from isolated region to isolated region, but on the basis of the Tasmanian experiment, the centre should have:

- been established in response to regional demand rather than superimposed by government

- tertiary education as its main, but not sole, activity

- a chief executive who is equated in status and salary to a senior position in the tertiary education system

- a clearly defined, *independent* role

- associated with it an advisory committee/council and its own constitution to provide some of the essential "ritual" necessary for credibility

- a full-time staff of at least three

- a guaranteed period in which to become established (3-5 years)

- a locally controlled recurrent budget with built-in flexibility to enable situations to be reacted to quickly, and to seed innovation

- a separate budget which is not seen to be competing with other sectors of education.

Support for the local learner is the ultimate aim of the centre, which must have a physical presence.

Physical presence of the centre

Factors include:

- a quality of building and fittings commensurate with the tertiary campuses

- a location close to the local education system—they will be called upon for cooperation sooner or later

- a location down town—our records indicate that a significant proportion of potential students of all ages are reluctant to contact the providing institution in the first instance.

Strategic functions for the centre

Under this category come those activities which set the overall framework for improved tertiary educational opportunities in the region. They include:

- input to planning and funding bodies to maximize the chances of improved funding (which is never adequate)—this involves establishing and maintaining local data bases of demands/needs/trends for use in such inputs

- acting as catalyst to maximize the incidence of "cross creditation" and "feeder" arrangements between colleges—enabling legislation is often essential to widen the scope of a limited number of external courses

- establishing the centre as the focal point for all matters related to tertiary education in the region via contacts, the media, and promotional activities.

Tactical functions for the centre

- *Educational information:* a comprehensive range of handbooks for potential students to browse through is the first essential. There is scope here for compiling simple directories of similar courses from different institutions, through to use of computer data banks, depending on resources.

  From experience, a quick response to a precise request is the best possible publicity. Further, we have adopted the maxim "If in doubt, the buck stops here" (another good public relations exercise).

- *Educational broker:* once a course has been decided upon, the use of an official broker usually speeds up communication significantly. The centre can also act on behalf of groups seeking to enrol for a course elsewhere, and pressurize for such a course if none exists.

- *Educational ombudsman:* as in brokering the use of an official ombudsman usually speeds up communication significantly. An analogue for dropping in on a range of resource people on campus can be a friendly, approachable centre staff with a liberal telephone budget. Letters can take up to two weeks to turn around in Australia—further, the fact that an expensive long distance telephone call has been made is an additional accelerator to decision making.

- *Listener:* the presence of a sympathetic listener as a problem solving device is too well known to need further amplification.

Mike Walker
North West Council for Community Education
Australia

References

Blainey, G. (1966) *The Tyranny of Distance.* Melbourne: Sun Books.

Karmel, P. (ed.) (1976) *Post Secondary Education in Tasmania.* Canberra: Australian Government Publishing Service.

Karmel, P. (ed.) (1981) *Tertiary Education: Commission Report for 1982-84 Triennium Vol. 1 Part 1 Recommendations on Guidelines.* Canberra: Australian Government Publishing Service.

Northcott, P. (1975) Open tertiary education in Australia: a viewpoint. *Teaching at a Distance,* 4, 21-30.

Vaizey, J. (1969) *Education in the Modern World.* London: Weidenfeld & Nicholson.

Walker, M.N. (1977) Open learning: an Australian experiment in self-paced, personalized, distance education by learning contract. *Australian Journal of Adult Education,* 17, 3, 9-14.

Paper 57

FlexiStudy*

FlexiStudy ensures a student not only high quality, centrally produced course materials, but also a local tutor, local tutorials, and access to college resources.

Origins

The National Extension College was established in 1963 to provide second chance education for adults. The intention was that the new College would offer more than traditional correspondence texts to its remote home students, wherever possible supplementing courses with radio, television, tapes, kits, weekend courses and local seminars.

Such was the policy that the College pursued between 1963 and 1977, but success was limited for two reasons. Firstly, NEC is a self-financing college so that money is always in short supply and every new service is a new cost to the student. Secondly, a distance teaching institution working over a wide area (the UK) from only one centre (Cambridge) is badly placed to provide student support where it is most needed—at the local level. Thus, even when the policy of providing face-to-face support was being pursued most vigorously in 1975 only about 10% of NEC students made use of this service.

At that time, NEC's policy was to arrange weekend residential courses in Oxford—these attracted about 600 students a year—and to encourage local state colleges to run Saturday seminars. In the peak year there were 5 weekend sessions covering about 20 courses and 5 local centres each running 5 or 6 sessions per year. It was at this stage that three things became obvious to us: (a) we did not have the resources to expand the face-to-face work any further; (b) the local state colleges had no great interest in providing further services for the students of another college; (c) unless more NEC students could get face-to-face support, drop-out rates would remain unacceptably high.

Something radical had to be done.

Standing the system on its head

For 14 years NEC had pursued a policy which is common to many distance teaching institutions—to teach and manage distance courses from a central headquarters and to ask local institutions to supplement and support this central teaching. However, if you teach from one centre, of course you find it difficult to provide adequate support for the remote student. So we decided to turn the system on its head and do all the teaching and support locally through the local state colleges which would enrol the students as local students—*not* as NEC students—even though the students would still be distance students. This can best be understood by considering the following diagrams.

In the traditional correspondence teaching system, there is one central college and students are spread out, often over a wide geographical area. The tutors may work in the college or elsewhere but communication between college and student and between tutor and student is usually only by post.

Figure 1: Traditional correspondence course

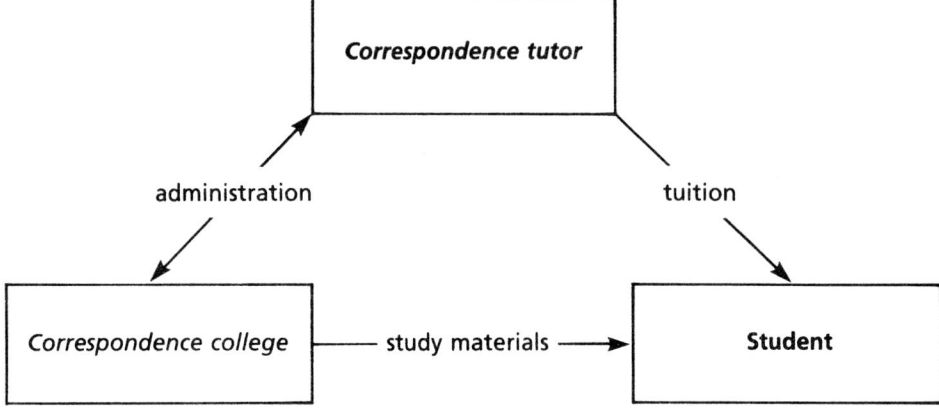

* FlexiStudy is a Registered Trade Mark

In Figure 2 the basic system in Figure 1 is supplemented by local face-to-face teaching. This may well involve a second tutor for the student and there may be no link between the correspondence tutor and the local institution. There are circumstances where this model can work well, particularly where the correspondence college can pay the local institution for the full cost of its services. But it does not always work as the NEC experience shows and did not do so in the early years of the Open University when a similar split between correspondence and face-to-face tutoring occurred.

In the Figure 3 model, the local college takes total responsibility for the student after first obtaining the distance teaching materials from the central correspondence college. So the local college enrols the student, gives him the course materials, provides him with a correspondence tutor, arranges tutorials at the college and provides college facilities such as the library, audio-visual materials and laboratories. This is the FlexiStudy model.

What is special about the FlexiStudy model?

As a diagram, Figure 3 looks absurdly simple—so simple as to suggest that it is not worth a closer study. But on a closer study it actually challenges the way most organisations have run distance education for the last 50 years. The assumption has invariably been that you start with a central college and remote students. This then gives rise to book after book, paper after paper on how to overcome the problems built into the central college model. On the other hand

Figure 2: Traditional correspondence course plus local face-to-face

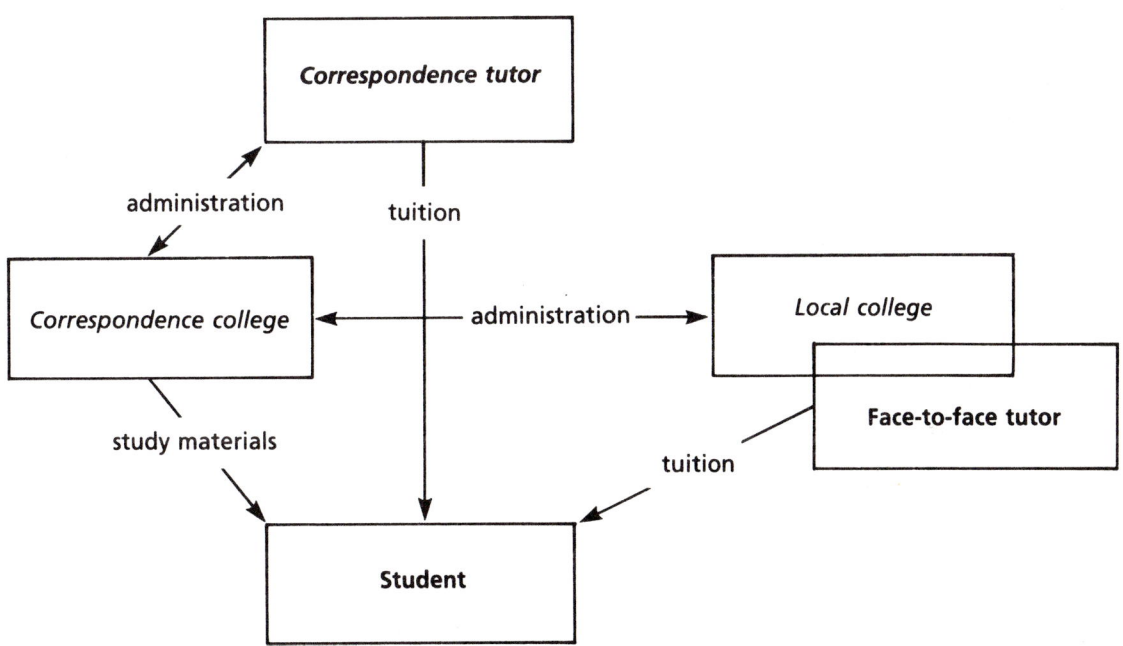

Figure 3: The local distance teaching system

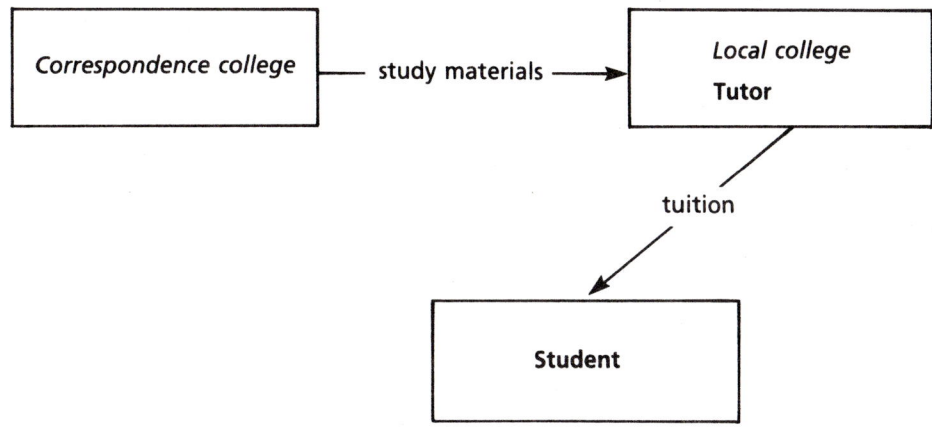

FlexiStudy assumes that the student gets the best course possible when the division of labour is:

Central Activity	Local activity
Production of distance teaching material	Student counselling
Liaison	Student enrolment
Consultancy/advice	Correspondence tuition
	Tutorials/seminars
	Practical work
	Examinations

Now for simplicity, Figures 1-3 have only shown one student, one tutor and so on. In Figure 4 we show the FlexiStudy system for a number of local colleges.

It can now be seen that the FlexiStudy model is not simply an alternative model for running a correspondence college. It is a means of creating a number of separate, local, correspondence colleges.

The present UK FlexiStudy system

What we have presented so far is the modelling that we did in 1976 in our search to find an effective means of supporting distance students at a local level. The model had then to be tested and this was done from September 1977 onwards at Barnet College of Further Education in North London under the direction of Mr G.A. Rowlands. The early stages are described in Sacks (1980). Here we describe FlexiStudy as it now operates in its fourth year of enrolment.

FlexiStudy is a partnership between the National Extension College and, currently (end of 1980) 67 local colleges. NEC already runs around 80 correspondence courses for about 10,000 students a year on the traditional model (see Figure 1) and thus has a range of distance teaching texts available. These it supplies to the local colleges for use in their own autonomous FlexiStudy schemes.

Each local FlexiStudy college plans and runs its own scheme following the guidelines in the system manual produced by NEC. First the local college staff will consult the NEC Publications Catalogue to see what materials are available. Then, taking into account the staff that are available and the needs of the local community, the college will decide what FlexiStudy programme to offer locally. A college will typically start with about 10 courses. The range is from 1 course up to 40 courses.

The range of courses offered at the moment is more a reflection of the materials available from NEC than of potential demand in the community with 52% being General Certificate of Education (GCE) Ordinary level and 27% being GCE Advanced level.

It is more difficult to estimate the number of students on FlexiStudy courses because some of the colleges operate a continuous enrolment system and colleges vary in how they keep their records. However returns from 22 colleges in October 1980 showed a mean of 53.5 enrolments per college during that autumn. Eight colleges had enrolled students in earlier years as well. These colleges had a mean of 55.6 continuing students per college. From these figures

Figure 4: FlexiStudy system with a number of local colleges

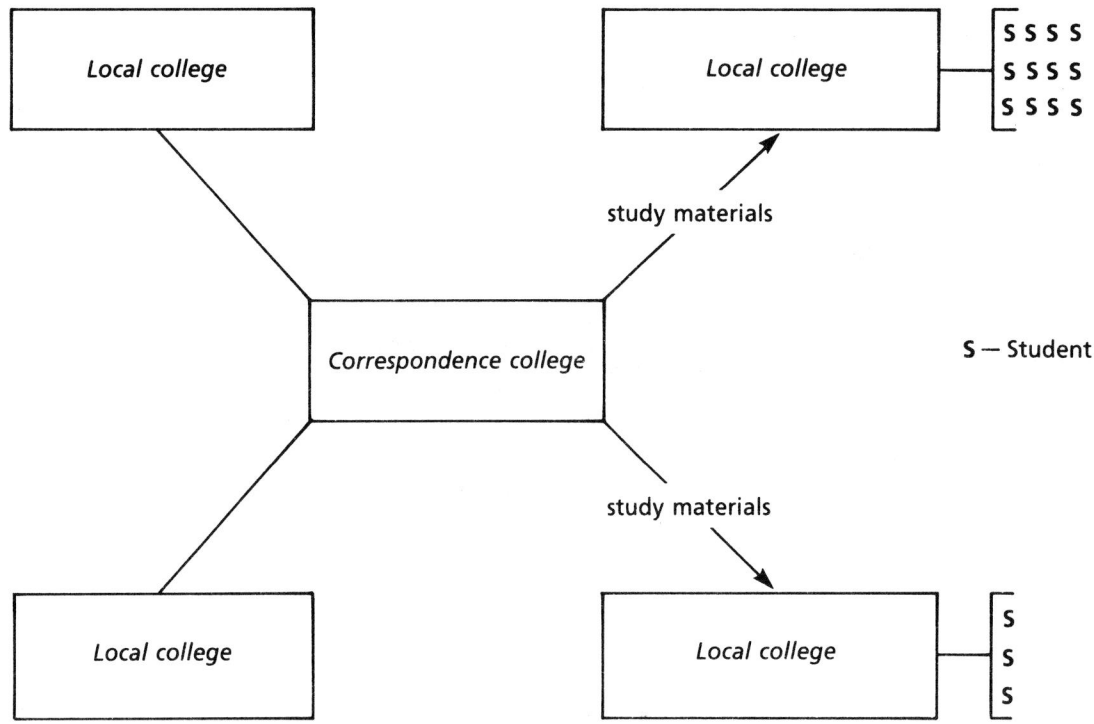

we estimate that there are currently 4500 students in FlexiStudy and that there will be of the order of 8000 FlexiStudy students in September 1981 at 100 centres.

FlexiStudy students

So far only one survey has been carried out on FlexiStudy students. This took place during the pilot year at Barnet College. Students' ages ranged from 16 to 61, with the median age of female students—who outnumbered males by two to one—being 33, that of males 28. Occupational classification showed that there was a heavy emphasis on those with irregular working hours—nurses and other shift-workers, self-employed tradesmen, mobile workers such as drivers and commercial travellers.

Another readily distinguishable group was composed of those whose domestic circumstances made regular class attendance particularly difficult. These included parents of young children whose spouses worked irregular hours, and single parents. There was quite a number of students—mainly, though not solely, housewives—with no unusual personal circumstances, who had simply not studied for 10-20 years and lacked the confidence to contemplate returning to a formal classroom situation after such a long gap (Sacks, 1980). It is important to add that at this college students are admitted to FlexiStudy only if they can demonstrate that they cannot attend ordinary classes. This factor could well bias the student population and make the survey results untypical of FlexiStudy as a whole.

Student performance

Assessment of student performance on FlexiStudy is difficult because each FlexiStudy centre is autonomous and is not therefore obliged to provide information on its courses and students. There are also awkward questions as to (a) what constitutes successful performance on a course—meeting course objectives or the student's own personal criteria? (Lewis, 1980), and (b) what other types of course FlexiStudy should be assessed against. It could be assessed against traditional correspondence courses where Harris estimated drop-out at 35% in professional courses, but he did say that his figures were 'highly speculative' since he was using a retrospective postal survey which is bound to under-represent drop-outs (Harris, 1972). A more likely drop-out figure for correspondence courses might be 60-75%. Alternatively FlexiStudy could be assessed against drop-out and exam success in part-time evening class courses. A recent survey in one college showed that only 18.5% of evening class GCE students passed the examination at the end of the year (Spelthome Adult Education Institute, 1981). Early indications on FlexiStudy are that drop-out runs at a higher rate than in evening courses but that exam pass rates are higher. Overall, therefore, FlexiStudy performance is comparable with evening class study and better than on traditional correspondence courses. Further data on this is awaited.

Conclusions

FlexiStudy has proved a very valuable development in the UK from the of view of all three parties involved. *From NEC's viewpoint* FlexiStudy is proving an effective alternative to the central distance teaching model. It provides a means of giving distance students the local support they need, albeit by NEC having to hand the student over to a local college. *From the student's viewpoint,* he gets a better course. He still gets high quality, centrally produced, course materials but he also gets a local tutor, local tutorials and access to college resources. *From the local college's viewpoint,* FlexiStudy enables them to teach a new group of students—adults who are not able, or who do not wish, to attend regular classes.

Richard Freeman
National Extension College
United Kingdom

References

Harris, W.J. (1972) *Home Study Students.* Manchester: Department of Adult Education, University of Manchester.

Lewis, Roger (1980) *Counselling in Open Learning: A Case Study.* Cambridge: National Extension College.

Sacks, H. (1980) FlexiStudy - an open learning system for further and adult education. *British Journal of Educational Technology,* 2, 11.

Spelthome Adult Education Institute (1981) The Ashford College Study. *Adult Education,* 53, 5. Leicester: National Institute of Adult Education.

Policy-Making and Management

Paper 58
Introduction

"In traditional education a teacher teaches. In distance education an institution teaches. This is a radical difference". This comment by Keegan (1980: 19) underlines the role of the institution in teaching at a distance and implies that management is especially important in this form of education. Not surprisingly most of the articles and this book, and not only those grouped in this section, shed light on the processes of policy-making and management.

A key issue of planning and policy is the size and degree of autonomy of distance education projects. The 1970s saw the creation of a number of large, relatively autonomous institutions, often partly modelled on the Open University of the United Kingdom. Datt (paper 14) and Singh (paper 13) suggest that India still needs a big institution and Daniel (paper 25) reports a proposal to merge into a single organization the projects in French-Canada. Knapper and Wasylycia-Coe (paper 41), Jevons (paper 42), and Penberthy (paper 26) stress the advantages of cross-fertilization between conventional and distance approaches although de Moor (paper 59) reminds us that new projects require considerable autonomy. In his study of Australian two-mode universities Guiton (paper 62) stresses the difference in cost-structure between the modes.

Two trends are clearly identified. Firstly, Bates (paper 2) predicts that a move away from broadcasting will make it easier for conventional institutions to teach at a distance. Secondly, numerous papers explore the growing importance of inter-institutional cooperation. Some new institutions of the early 1980s, like the Japan University of the Air (Sakamoto, paper 60) and the Netherlands Open University (de Moor, paper 59) resemble some of the open university initiatives of the 1970s. More common, however, are projects based on cooperation between a variety of existing agencies. Perhaps the most far-reaching scheme of this kind is Norway's NFU (Rande, paper 63; Ljoså, paper 23) since it involves both public and private agencies. Barnes (paper 106) and Kaye (paper 107) report on collaborative projects involving broadcasters, a type of alliance Perraton (paper 3) sees as particularly important. Rebel (paper 64) describes the success of inter-institutional cooperation involving West Germany's DIFF and Nicolini (paper 19) and Kirkinen (paper 52) give examples of universities working together on a regional basis to expand opportunities for learning at a distance. Holmberg (paper 97) and Sullivan (paper 98) suggest this approach is particularly important at the graduate level. Horlock (paper 95) and Ralph Smith (paper 96) show how existing networks of professionals can provide local support for post-experience courses. Mills and Tait (paper 53) examine various models for such support, including the use of volunteers, a possibility also evoked by Draper (paper 9) and Howell (paper 83).

In the general area of inter-institutional cooperation a particularly interesting model to watch will be the FlexiStudy scheme of the National Extension College explained by Freeman (paper 57). This gives local conventional institutions the major role in course delivery. Walker (paper 56) gives a local perspective on providing support to students learning at a distance with other institutions while Noyau (paper 21) encourages governments to set up networks of local centres for use by adults undertaking any form of study. Meakin (paper 55) and Salter (paper 54) describe different ways in which an institution can organize its own regional presence.

Crawford and Crawford (paper 65) remind us that educational planners place considerable hope in the growth of distance education through inter-institutional cooperation. Although distance education is buoyant (Keegan, paper 8) and cost-effective (Orivel and Jamison, paper 44) creating brand-new institutions is out of fashion in many countries.

If Potter (paper 66) is right that all distance education projects are administered in a rather similar fashion then the controversy about management issues should be of wide concern. Mainusch (paper 67) criticizes the "bloodless centre" of operations while Griew (paper 68) alleges that distance education, especially course production, is tripping over the toes of its over-complexity. Friedman (paper 112) admits that computers tempt planners to create complex systems. Attempts to simplify and render more effective the work of the course team are described by Foks (paper 69) and Bédard (paper 70) while Ansere (paper 12) reminds us that greater reliance on single course writers is a necessity in developing countries. The main criticism of current management in distance education, made forcefully by Coldeway (paper 29) and echoed by Penney (paper 34) and Shobe (paper 71) is that it fails to respect the principles of instructional systems design although these have been clearly spelled out. Rumble (paper 72) reports a tendency to sub-optimize and Dichanz (paper 102) blames the inflexibility of management for the limited use of media. Furthermore, according to such authors as Joseph and De Milanesi (paper 20), Rekkedal (paper 38) and Finkel (paper 30) institutions often fail to be effective in relatively simple matters like turn-around of assignments and maintenance of contact with students, which are known to affect completion rates. Since several authors imply that the management styles of conventional institutions are often misapplied in distance education it will be interesting to see the results of the survey by DeCelles and Marquis (paper 73) that aims to compare managerial functions and behaviour in the two cases.

Other authors are more sanguine about the ability of distance education to manage its affairs although Ansere (paper 12), Trillo (paper 17), Peters (paper 24) and Mugridge (paper 61) stress the complexity of the political environment in which it must be conducted. Mugridge notes, however, that the planners of the Open Learning Institute made correct decisions in important areas such as pacing and course production and there is certainly no lack of research and planning behind a project like the Japan University of the Air (Sakamoto, paper 60).

Staff training is important in any new enterprise. Ellis and Chapman (paper 105), Jenkins (paper 84), and Cochran and Meech (paper 50) report on training techniques for instructors, authors, and tutors. Griew (paper 68) and Peters (paper 24) enter strong pleas that the staff of distance universities be encouraged to pursue discipline-based research lest the academic credibility of such institutions suffer.

The economics of distance education continues to attract interest. Orivel and Jamison (paper 44) have conducted an important study of the cost-effectiveness of projects in many different countries and Guiton (paper 62) examines economic aspects of the Australian two-mode institutions. Rumble (paper 72) recalls that the unit costs of distance education depend mainly on student numbers, program size, and the media mix employed. However, he stresses that although knowledge of institutional cost structures is helpful in times of cutbacks it is not a substitute for financial management.

Recognition of achievement through the accreditation of courses offered at a distance is usually of great importance to students. Ellis and Chapman (paper 105) examine the requirements of accreditation for the distance mode in a two-mode institution and Burcaw (paper 74) and Holbrook (paper 75) describe the accreditation systems in the United States. In other countries, as Ljoså (paper 23) reports for the case of Norway, the state has a key role in the accreditation of distance learning.

Marketing the opportunities for learning at a distance is the subject of several papers. Loudon (paper 93) and Joseph and De Milanesi (paper 20) appear to disagree on the desirability of marketing to employers. Young (paper 76) has conducted a survey to discover how correspondence education is perceived with results that will be useful in the design of publicity campaigns. Brock (paper 77) gives tips on how to conduct such campaigns and Barnes (paper 106) insists on the importance of announcing multi-media adult education projects in plenty of time.

Finally the role of professional associations is examined by Mitchell (paper 78) who describes the evolution of the Australia and South Pacific External Studies Association. Grimwade (paper 79) suggests that this and other regional associations could form the basis for a much stronger international association. The best name for the international association in the field continues to be a topic of controversy. Young (paper 76) argues from the results of his survey that correspondence education should stick to that name but the majority of contributors to this volume appear to find that distance education is now a better term to cover the range of activities discussed at international meetings.

References

Keegan, D.J. (1980) On defining distance education. *Distance Education* 1, 1, 13-36.

Paper 59

Plan to Reality: The Netherlands Open University

A new institution is ready to begin operations although political events could still affect its nature.

History

In March 1977 a white paper entitled 'Nota Open Universiteit in Nederland', promoted the creation of a Netherlands Open University as an independent institution for learning at a distance. The main policy objectives were: greater equality of educational opportunity for adults, a decrease of enrolments in the existing higher education institutions, a reduction of costs per student and innovation in teaching and curricula.

On the day of publication the Minister of Education appointed a planning committee, chaired by the author, to prepare the Open University. The final report, 'De Nederlandse Open Universiteit', dealing with all aspects of the future institution, was presented in March 1979. In October 1979 the Minister issued his proposals—which mostly followed those of the planning committee—in a white paper 'De oprichting van een open universiteit in Nederland', which was discussed in Parliament in June 1980. All political parties agreed on the creation of an Open University as proposed and in the 1981 budget 14 million Dutch guilders were approved for the purpose. May 1981 saw the creation of a corporate body to set it up. Under an Act now in preparation the Open University will become a state university.

It would be wrong to assume from this account that the idea of an Open University and the proposals of the planning committee were unanimously accepted. Objections were raised to both the independent status of the Open University and the use of distant teaching methods.

The Council of Education, a key advisory body to the government, clearly disliked the idea of an independent, new institution. It believed the existing institutions could perform the role intended for the Open University—an opinion shared, unsurprisingly, by some groups in these institutions. The Federation of Dutch Trade Unions also wanted this alternative explored more thoroughly.

The idea of teaching at a distance was sceptically received not only by higher education teachers, but particularly by adult education workers adhering to social and cultural work traditions. They considered the individualized approach developed in emancipatory education to under-privileged adults to be the best approach for all adult education. A more widely shared complaint was that the Open University had been designed too exclusively as a higher education institution, and not specifically as part of adult education.

The increasingly difficult financial situation of the government created fears in both higher and adult education that the financing of the Open University would be at the expense of their own expansion. This argument may explain why the Dutch Labour party and the Federation of Trade Unions are not among the most enthusiastic supporters of the Open University. However, their resistance never became organized and strong whereas the parties most concerned, the Inter-university Council and the Council of Colleges, supported the proposals, although with some reservations.

The Open University as planned: key features

The Netherlands higher education system has separate university and college (vocational) sectors. Government and the planning committee wished to integrate these sectors in the Open University—which was a key reason to opt for a new, independent institution. The Open University is therefore broader than the traditional Dutch university.

Open access

Every applicant over 18 will be admitted irrespective of diplomas acquired and educational attainment. The planning committee had proposed a minimum age of 21 for unrestricted entry but Parliament decided on the age of majority, 18.

The applicant's decision to enrol has to be based on a realistic assessment of his chances of success. The Open University will have an information, advice and guidance department working through 24 study centres all over the country. Orientation courses will also enable students to assess their capability.

Free choice of courses

The Open University will not offer pre-determined programs of study. Students will decide themselves how they will combine courses into programs of differing length, degree of specialization and orientation. For degree programs there are minimum requirements as to the total number of credits and their distribution.

A course is the basic unit and will usually demand 200 hours of study from the "standard student". For each course a certificate can be obtained for 2 credits.

Free pacing of study

Pacing of study by the institution may help student motivation and promote regular effort. It also has organizational advantages for the institution. On the other hand, life and work situations will vary widely among Open University students. Because of this variation students will be free to choose the number of courses they wish to take each year and which of the course examinations, held after each term, they will sit.

Target groups

The target groups may be distinguished by educational career and study goals. In terms of educational career the main groups will be:

- those without normal secondary schooling
- those who could not or did not use their right of access to higher education in the past
- young secondary school leavers who wish to combine study and work
- college graduates who wish to obtain a university degree
- university and college drop-outs who wish to complete a program of higher education
- university and college graduates who wish additional education.

The Open University's educational policy attaches most importance to the first two groups.

Concerning study goals the most important distinction is between those seeking a diploma or degree, and those who only wish to take some courses without aiming at diplomas, degrees, or even course certificates. This latter group might be quite numerous.

A multi-media teaching system

Independent study, supported by a multi-media teaching system, will be the basis of the Open University. The planning committee wished to know more about the specific educational advantages and disadvantages of the various media and their relative costs under various assumptions. The Bureau of Educational Research of Leiden University was commissioned to analyse available literature, research findings and financial data, and published its study under the title 'Onderwijsmiddelen van de Open Universiteit: functies en kosten'.

Preliminary distinctions

Learning objectives may be classified into two main categories: the acquisition of knowledge, and the acquisition of skills. Skills are related to operations *on* knowledge, or operations *with* knowledge. Skills as objectives are often neglected in higher education. Teaching and learning are unduly oriented towards the reproduction of knowledge. The risk of reproductive learning is even greater in distance education. To avoid this risk the planning committee had to choose a media mix which guarantees sufficient training in both types of skills and to decide which types of courses and programs could adequately be provided, taking into account the learning objectives implied and the emphasis on distant teaching methods.

Written materials

Comparing the learning objectives of higher education with the properties of the different distant teaching media made the choice of the primary medium clear. Print is superior to audio-visual media and to the computer. Moreover, at least in the Netherlands, written materials are by far the cheapest medium.

The educational effectiveness of written materials can considerably be increased by a feedback system. Such a system requires that assignments be included in the correspondence courses and responded to either by tutors or by computer.

Computer

The computer will be a supplementary but important teaching medium and terminals will be available in the regional study centres. The important contribution of the computer is increased interaction between student and teacher. Every mistake in a series of cognitive operations can be localized and immediately corrected and remedial teaching can be provided through the computer.

A combination of written materials and computerized instruction could perform the main educational functions in the Open University. The attitudes of both staff and students towards this type of instruction will, however, determine the extent of computer use.

Audio-visual media

Audio-visual media will not play a major role although specific contributions may be needed in some courses. For cost reasons audio-visual media will be mainly used where their specific advantages are important. In language instruction, for example, audio tapes will be used for speaking and listening exercises. Television and radio broadcasting will play only a minor role in distribution. Television broadcasting time is scarce in the Netherlands and one of the disadvantages is that it is strongly time-bound. The emphasis will likely be on the distribution of video tapes or videodiscs to be played in study centres, and, in the long run, at home. This alternative will certainly become more attractive with the connection of tapes and discs to a computer system.

Practical work

The Open University should only offer those fields of study where it can at least equal other institutions in quality at a lower cost per student. Lower costs can only be achieved when classroom work remains supplementary to distant teaching media. Nevertheless, laboratory work, research projects, role-playing, simulation games and conversation lessons will be indispensable. In the regional centres facilities will be provided to meet other students and teachers and for skills training.

Tutorials

Individual support will be needed in case of individual research work, essay writing and thesis writing. Some remedial teaching will be made available in study centres or by telephone. Attendance in the study centres will, as a rule, only be obligatory when learning objectives could not otherwise be achieved.

Co-operation with other institutions

The Open University will have many links with other institutions, especially in the higher education sector.

Course development

For course development a staff of about 130 academics in the steady state is planned. About 40% will be employed by the Open University and the rest will, for one or two years, full time or part time, contribute to course writing under a contract with their institutions. Although not employees, the latter groups will work within the organizational framework of the Open University. It remains to be seen whether this policy will be successful.

A special contribution has to be made to course development and technical production by media experts. The planning committee recommended not to create a department for the production of audio-visual media and their distribution through broadcasting stations. Two existing organizations, *TELEAC* and *Stichting Film en Wetenschap* will contribute their expertise to the course development teams of the Open University.

Tutors

The regional study centres will usually be located in higher education institutions and will, in the study state, have a staff of about 1800 tutors, most of them working 4-6 hours a week for the Open University. The majority will be teachers at other institutions. The government will very likely, for reasons of employment policy, demand that the work for the Open University be done as part of a full-time job. This will probably influence negatively the willingness of other institutions' full-time staff to be tutors.

Policy development

A distinctive organizational feature of the Open University will be the separate organization of the processes of policy development, policy evaluation and policy innovation. This work will be done by groups which will also include experts and "clients" from outside. For example, the working group making policy proposals for the development of courses in economics may include economists from other institutions and experts from industry, banking and the trade unions.

The present reality

The planning committee had unusually close co-operation with the ministry, which explains why the proposals of the committee were adopted by the minister without major modifications. The political decision-making process took a rather long time, but that is usual for parliamentary decisions in the Netherlands which have to be preceded by a consultative process in which a number of advisory bodies are involved.

During this process of consultation and political decision-making the planning committee worked out in detail the organization, information processes and functions in the Open University. The hiring process for the two highest organizational levels has also been prepared.

Hiring will start immediately after the nomination of the Executive Board (3 members) and the Board of Governors (15 members from outside the Open University to be completed with 3 staff representatives) by the Minister of Education. If there is no further delay, the Open University will start teaching in September 1983.

It is still too early to say to what extent the reality differs from the plan. On the day this paper was finished elections took place. It remains to be seen whether a new cabinet and a new Parliament will introduce modifications when definite arrangements have to be laid down in an Open University Act.

Moreover, uncertainty remains when the government has repeatedly to cut public expenditure by billions instead of millions of guilders.

Ruud de Moor
Tilburg University
Netherlands

Plan to Reality: The Japan University of the Air

After nearly twenty years of research and debate the new institution will accept students in 1984.

The establishment of the University of the Air

On June 4th, 1981, after fourteen years of debate, the Act for setting up the University of the Air Foundation was approved by the Diet. Based upon this Act, the University of the Air will be established in 1982. Everyone over 18 years old will be eligible for a degree in liberal arts.

The origin of the project was an inquiry made by the Ministry of Education to the Social Education Commission in 1967, asking them to investigate the possibility of establishing a new broadcasting system for educational television and radio. Afterwards, several committees discussed various aspects of the establishment of the University of the Air. For a list of the reports published by those committees see Sakamoto (1971: 191) and Sakamoto and Fujita (1980: 26).

Preparatory research activities

A variety of research activities have been undertaken in order to prepare the University of the Air.

The first category consisted of field surveys to predict the educational needs for the University of the Air (Sakamoto, 1971: 193). Three large scale surveys were undertaken, the last and most sophisticated survey selecting a random sample of 5000 individuals. Among the results: (1) 45.3% hoped to study in the University of the Air and about one third wanted to get credits or diplomas, (2) courses on health and disease (42%), food, clothing and housing (30%) and education (19%) were most requested (Division of Planning in Higher Education, 1975: 20) The master plan was made to reflect these results.

The second category of research activities involved broadcasting pilot programs and evaluating their effectiveness. There were four stages (Sakamoto and Fujita, 1980: 29).

From August, 1971 to March, 1975, 20 series of fifteen 45-minute radio programs were produced and broadcast by Nippon Shortwave Broadcasting Company (NSB) and 16 series of fifteen 45-minute TV programs were produced and broadcast by NHK UHF in Tokyo and Osaka. Such factors as questions and answers by correspondence, feedback by telephone and small group tutoring were examined.

In the second stage, from May, 1975 to March, 1976, 4 series of TV programs and 3 series of radio programs were rebroadcast. Research on the effectiveness of computer-based correspondence teaching and of instruction on learning by radio and TV was undertaken. The results showed the effectiveness of the methods employed (Sakamoto, Ikeda and Muta, 1978).

In the third stage, from 1976 to 1977, pilot TV and radio programs were produced and broadcast for university extension and correspondence education.

The fourth stage, from October 1978 to March 1982, consisted of more radio and TV broadcasts, evaluations of which are now being undertaken.

The third category of research concerns the use of educational broadcasting in university extension courses (Sakamoto and Fujita,, 1980: 30). Tohoku, Kiroshima, Kanazawa, Osaka and Kumamoto Universities were involved.

The fourth category is related to the development of study methods, including the use of educational radio in the correspondence courses of private universities.

In the first stage from 1958 to 1974, private universities used radio programs for their correspondence courses and conducted their own guidance and evaluation. This was discontinued because NHK became reluctant to ask professors at these private universities to appear on radio and TV.

In the second stage, from October 1976 to February 1978, 7 private universities used 6 series of radio programs through NSB for their courses. Taped audio-instructional materials for foreign languages such as English, German and French were produced cooperatively by university correspondence courses.

From October 1978 to March 1982, 17 series of educational radio programs were produced and utilized in the correspondence courses of private universities. Also, instructional materials for common use have been developed.

The University of the Air in the context of distance education in Japan

In Japan three different types of distance teaching, correspondence, broadcasting and telecommunication technology, are used for formal university teaching, university extension, and social education for adults. This gives nine different possibilities.

Activities at the National Center for Development of Broadcast Education

The Center (Kokuritsu Hoso-Kyoiku Kaihatsu Senta) was established on October 1, 1978, as a cooperative organization of the national universities in order to study and develop university courses and teaching methods through the use of the broadcast media. It has four types of activities.

The first is the production and broadcasting of pilot radio and TV programs for university teaching. Listeners and viewers are supplied with textbooks and are given the opportunity to receive two periods of computer-based correspondence teaching or two sessions of schooling during each course. In 1981, 14 series of TV and 12 series of radio programs are available. In the last half of 1979 a questionnaire was given to monitors who had studied one of six TV pilot programs. The responses of 1,409 of the 2,682 monitors showed that: (1) 19.7% of the monitors viewed all 15 programs in a series and 47.7% viewed them intermittently to the last program; (2) lectures were consistently structured; (3) materials were organized so as to be readily understood; (4) professors on TV spoke comprehensibly; (5) programs were effective in promoting a familiarity with the subject matter, an interest in related areas, the motivation to study and understanding of fundamental principles; (6) correspondence teaching with computer cards was necessary; and (7) interest in the subject matter, successive viewing of the programs and organization of content were important for learning by TV and radio.

The second type of activity is the project on broadcasting in extension courses in five national universities.

The third activity is the experiments in learning methods in the university correspondence courses undertaken in cooperation with the All Japan Association of Private Correspondence Education. In 1979 four series were broadcast: politics, physics, geography and psychology. A survey showed that only 2-2.5% of the respondents viewed the programs from the first to the last. In terms of comprehension, 11.8% reported that the radio lectures were "very well understood", 29.4% "mostly understood", and 35.8% "understood a little". 8.9% answered that they were able to understand the texts after having listened to the radio programs, 14.6% "mostly understood" and 39.3% "understood a little".

As for motivation to study, 9.2% of the students answered that they were "very highly motivated", 21.9% were "highly motivated", and 42.1% were "motivated a little". In the achievement test, there was no significant difference in average scores between those students who had studied by means of radio programs, and those who used the ordinary correspondence methods. However, the rate of drop-out was lower for the former (8.8%) than for the latter (19.0%). These results imply that the use of radio is effective in university correspondence courses (Sakamoto, 1981: 4).

The fourth activity is study meetings of researchers for the use of broadcasting in university teaching.

Through these research activities, the Center will accumulate the knowledge essential to the management of the University of the Air.

The proposed University of the Air

The University of the Air will be established in October 1982, following the establishment of the University of the Air Foundation in 1981. A broadcasting station will be set up in 1982 and lectures will begin in April, 1984. The following is an outline of the University of the Air (Division of Planning in Higher Education, 1981: 1,15).

1. The University of the Air is an innovative education system intended to function as a core institution of life-long education at the university level which will offer effective teaching through broadcasting, with the cooperation of university instructors.

2. The University of the Air is designed as an authorized university where radio and television programs will be utilized effectively in teaching.

3. The University will set up a Faculty of Liberal Arts where students are given not only enriched general education but also specialized education adapted to their various needs, by means of a great variety of subjects including those of an interdisciplinary nature.

4. The University will offer education through radio and television programs, the reading of textbooks and reference materials, and through short papers submitted by students.

5. Tutorials and counselling will also be available at study centers. Study centers will have a principal and teaching staff, and an administrative staff. These centers will be centers of learning in each district. With the cooperation of able people from universities and schools in the district, these centers will offer classes for experiments and practical work. They will also provide individual guidance for students, answer their queries, and handle various administrative services. The University will also consider the possibility of making films and tapes of broadcasts available, by supplying various public facilities with VTR equipment, for the students.

6. The University will administer appropriate examinations through which the performance of students will be assessed and specific credits awarded.

7. The University will not hold entrance examinations but will select applicants by some impartial method such as by lot or on a first-come-first-served basis.

8. A degree of Bachelor of Liberal Arts will be awarded when a student completes a four-year course and earns a required number of credits in specific subjects.

9. In order to meet a great variety of needs for higher education and to offer such education in a flexible way, the University will admit non-regular students who wish to learn a subject or a combination of subjects.

Table 1 shows the curriculum of the University of the Air.

Table 2 presents the first stage plan (Division of Planning in Higher Education, 1981 : 4,5).

Problems in the University of the Air

There will be a lot of problems to be solved in order to make a success of the University of the Air.

First, in order to expand the opportunity for higher education by means of broadcasting and other media and teaching methods, the University of the Air needs to know the needs of students.

Second, in order to implement a multi-media teaching system including broadcasting, textbooks, reference books, study guides, computer-based correspondence teaching, telephone and other communication media, the supporting system must be well equipped and organized.

Table 1: Curriculum

Area of Study	Major	Goal of Education
Science of daily life	Living & Welfare	The necessary knowledge for a wholesome and culturally rewarding family life.
	Child Develoment and Education	Basic knowledge of child rearing and adolescence counselling. Understanding of the role of education.
Industry and society	Society and Economy	Understanding the systems and basic problems of politics, economy and society.
	Industry and Technology	A general knowledge of the trends of industrial technology development and the present state of management.
Humanities and Natural Science	An Inquiry into Human Culture	Inquiring into the characteristics of modern civilization and regional culture. Also further understanding of the trends in mankind's thought, literature and art.
	Understanding Nature	Awareness of the realities of nature. An understanding of mankind's dependence on nature.

Table 2: First Stage Plan

	First Stage Plan	Remarks
Target area	Areas within the range of TV & Radio transmission from Tokyo Tower	A second transmitting station will be built in the Kanto area
Number of student to be admitted each year	17,000 (regular students: 7,000) (students taking selected subjects: 10,000)	First year (1984) 10,000 (regular students: 4,000)
Total number of students	30,000 persons (regular students: 20,000)	
Number of staff	300 persons	
Fixed assets (aggregate)	9,700 million yen	Not including site of headquarters and 6 study centres.
Operational costs (aggregate)	4,700 million yen	

Third, in order to maintain a high quality of teaching, academic staff development should be especially needed in terms of course design, media design, lecturing, tutoring, counselling, and evaluation.

Fourth, it is necessary to set up the cooperative system among universities, especially for the management of study centres, exchange of credits, and exchange of academic staff.

Fifth, the teaching methods in the University of the Air should be models for improving university teaching in general.

When these problems are solved, the University of the Air will be able to provide a better quality of education for a wider range of people.

Takashi Sakamoto
Tokyo Institute of Technology
Japan

References

Division of Planning in Higher Education. (1975) Report on the Survey for Estimating Education Needs for the University of the Air. Tokyo: Ministry of Education, Science and Culture.

Division of Planning in Higher Education. (1981) The Proposed "University of the Air". Tokyo: Ministry of Education, Science and Culture.

Sakamoto, T. (1971) The development of the University of the Air. *Multimedia Systems in Adult Education*. Munchen: Internationales Zentralinstitut für das Jugend-und Bildungsfernsehen.

Sakamoto, T. (1981) *Use of Communication Technology in Distance Teaching at the University and College Level in Japan*. Penang: Regional Symposium on Distance Teaching in Asia.

Sakamoto, T. Ikeda, H. and Muta, H. (1978) The Effect of Radio and TV Experimental Programs in the University of the Air. The Fourth International Conference for Improving University Teaching. Aachen: 1051-1065.

Sakamoto, T. and Fujita, K. (1980) The present state of the University of the Air Project in Japan. *Overseas Universities*. 27, 26-35.

Paper 61

Plan To Reality: The Open Learning Institute

Rapid enrolment growth has vindicated most of the assumptions on which a new institution was based.

The Open Learning Institute (OLI) was set up by the government of British Columbia in the summer of 1978. It had a mandate to provide, throughout the province, programmes in arts and sciences at degree level, in adult basic education (ABE), in career-technical-vocational areas (CTV) and in continuing education. The Institute began to offer courses in September, 1979, and now offers some seventy courses in the three major programme areas, almost all of them developed internally. In the academic year 1980/1981 it has served over 8,000 course enrolments.

OLI has therefore developed very rapidly. It is difficult to separate plan from reality in an institution where what should normally be two distinct phases have frequently occurred at the same time. It is, however, possible to make some comparisons between the Institute's initial views and the developments which have actually taken place.

The Institute has demonstrated very clearly that the original assumption of the Minister of Education was correct: even the sparse population of British Columbia (roughly two and a half million people spread over almost 370,000 square miles with twenty-two other post-secondary institutions) needs a distance learning institution. The mix of students among the three programmes has, however, proved to be somewhat unexpected since the CTV program accounts for roughly half of the total enrolment.

One assumption was that the Institute's programmes were part of an established system so that many potential students would either already have parts of the credentials they wished to complete at OLI or would wish to take OLI courses as preparation for work elsewhere. Grades X and XII completion programmes in ABE had therefore to be acceptable to the provincial Ministry of Education; CTV courses and programmes had to satisfy the requirements for entry to employment; and degree courses had to be readily transferable to the existing universities. Programme directors took considerable trouble to meet these conditions and have gained acceptance for OLI's courses and programmes.

Other assumptions proved less correct. The degree programme emphasized third and fourth year courses so that people could finish degrees through OLI after completing previous university-level study elsewhere. Most students taking an OLI degree have in fact entered the programme with no previous degree work. The other programmes have a similar experience.

A second decision to help OLI programmes fit those of existing agencies was to make the basic period of instruction a semester of four months. This is used at most B.C. colleges and universities; it had the further merit of simplifying the division of subject-matter into units and allowing careful pacing of students. Both factors were regarded as important in the early planning stages.

The decisions to develop courses of manageable size and to pace students carefully have been justified. The former conforms to the expectations of B.C. students and the latter has accumulating evidence in its favour. An examination of completion rates in the same course offered at OLI, North Island College and Athabasca University, paced at OLI but not at the other institutions, showed considerably higher completion rates at OLI.

Semester length, however, is much disputed within the Institute. Apart from the major problems of ensuring that five or six assignments in a semester can be marked and returned in sufficient time, there is growing evidence that the rigid system of three semesters a year is far too restrictive. It does not allow flexibility to students for whom entry in September, January or May is very difficult. Setting examinations at the end of each semester, with a supplementary a month later, is also very difficult for both students and administration. Finally, since it is becoming increasingly clear that some courses cannot be readily fitted into the existing semester, a more flexible system is desirable. The question of semester length is under study at the Institute.

Since most students wish to pursue OLI qualifications, two other early decisions have proved to be particularly fortunate. The first was that it would be impossible for a distance learning institution to offer the broad range of courses and programmes normally offered in traditional institutions. The corollary was to reduce each programme to its most essential components so that students would be able to plan their studies and gain a sound acquaintance with their particular area. The assumption behind this decision seems to have been justified in practice.

The second assumption was the importance of qualified human support for OLI students. Available evidence suggested that students would need extensive support from qualified people, since, however high the quality of OLI course packages, they could not stand alone without tutoring from subject experts. Similarly, an advising service to provide non-academic support to students in such areas as programme planning would be needed. The problem was to provide such services in a province where tutorial centres on the Open University model seemed to be impossible and where, in many areas, library services were inadequate for almost any course. The solution was to provide for regular written comments on assignments and telephone communication between tutors and students to handle academic problems. In addition, a series of advising centres was established to provide an "OLI face" for students and potential students in rural areas. Both decisions have worked well although the tutoring system is undergoing continual refinement in the light of growing experience.

The decisions discussed above were made with good unanimity. In one area of paramount importance, however, there was less initial agreement. The first programmes to begin developing courses in summer 1979 were ABE and the degree programme. They adopted very different approaches, dictated largely by the different requirements of the courses. Beginning with a group of grade X courses, ABE brought in a number of full-time course writers to work cooperatively on courses in different subject areas which would nevertheless fit into a coherent whole. The degree programme, on the other hand, chose to rely on subject experts on short-term contracts as course writers and consultants, supported by a small group of instructional designers, editors and visual designers. When the CTV programme began it tended to follow the second approach. In due course, a new division was set up to provide editorial, instructional design and graphics services to all three programme divisions. One assumption was that instructional designers and editors could profit from working on courses from every programme. The Institute has probably gained from the uniform process of course development made possible by the new division. Problems in copyright, scheduling of development and production, in-house instruction and training have been made simpler. However, the basic assumption may be less valid than it appeared. Course design staff tend to work increasingly on a particular programme because of the practical problems associated with any other approach.

One basic assumption was that there is no universal formula for a successful distance education system. We have found useful the experience and assistance of others but it was not a complete solution to any of our problems. The establishment of tutorial centres is impossible. A new way of providing library services had to be developed. Television was rejected for the early courses because a quarter of the population of B.C. could not be reached, a situation which is rapidly changing, particularly with the recent establishment of the Knowledge Network in B.C. It has often been more reasonable to develop an OLI course than to use a similar course from another institution. Our own experience is beginning to indicate that this may also be applicable to different aspects of the work of the same institution.

Ian Mugridge
Open Learning Institute
Canada

Resource Allocation in the Australian Two-Mode University

Institutions that operate in both classroom and distance modes need a special model for resource allocation.

The economics of distance education systems

Despite any costing formulae resource allocation within universities eventually becomes a political process. Thus, the Australian Universities Commission 6th Report (1975: 261) concedes that:

> relative expenditure incurred in teaching internal and external students is likely to reflect university policy in the allocation of resources as much as any real difference in costs.

This paper examines some aspects of this process in tertiary institutions committed to teaching both on-campus and off-campus students. Such institutions must balance the resource needs of two disparate categories of students within one organisational structure.

The economics of distance education is attracting increasing attention. Institutions established solely for teaching distant students have been ready, perhaps eager, to compare cost-effectiveness with their conventional counterparts. Wagner (1977) drew attention to the vast disparities between fixed and variable costs in the two teaching modes, and argued that the ratio of fixed to variable cost per student is about 2000:1 for the British Open University compared with 8:1 in a typical conventional university. Rumble (1976: 14) developed this theme:

> Where the Open University differs from conventional (campus) universities is that its fixed costs are high and marginal costs low, whereas campus-based universities, by contrast, have low fixed costs but high marginal costs.

By categorising Open University recurrent expenditure, albeit somewhat arbitrarily, as related to students, course production, or overhead, Rumble (1976: 22) argued that even the modest marginal costs can become structurally significant since

> any sizeable increase in student numbers will require additional administrative and academic support....Thus the incremental per capita cost of additional students can be regarded as a step function with intermediate steps of cost between £116 (base marginal cost) and £248 (gross incremental cost) depending on the size of the addition to the student body.

Given the fundamental importance of its fixed (course-related) costs the Open University soon recognised that a staff:student ratio was "clearly inapplicable" as a basis for determining academic staffing. In place of the conventional staff:student ratio a productivity rate which related the input of academic staff time to the output of courses was needed.

Snowden and Daniel (1980) have described the formulation of costing factors for resource management purposes at Athabasca University. They point out that the British Open University analyses assume very large enrolments providing for economies of scale which justify expenditure of up to £450,000 to produce each course. By contrast, Snowden and Daniel focus on small distance education systems serving less than 15,000 part-time students. However, although they reduce the scale of operation they remain in a single mode structure focused only on distant students. This contrasts sharply with the two-mode teaching characteristic of five Australian universities whose combined external enrolments do not reach 15,000.

Acknowledging that the staff:student interface relationship is too broad as a measure of teaching productivity in distance education these authors also recognise that academic staff in small distance education systems are likely to be involved in a complex of activities linking course production (writing) implementation (teaching) and delivery (travelling, counselling). The complex division of labour in the British Open University between specialist course writers, regional academic staff, part-time assignment markers, group tutors and counsellors is unlikely. At Athabasca, the functional distinction is drawn for costing purposes between course development costs (per credit), services delivery costs (per weighted enrolment) and fixed institutional costs.

Reviewing the literature on the economics of distance education indicates that the language and conventional wisdom of resource management in university systems is ill-matched with the organisational requirements of distance education. In both the Open University and Athabasca the concept of staff:student ratio was found to be insufficient and indeed misleading. Yet it is deeply entrenched both in tertiary institutions and government funding agencies in Britain, Australia, Canada and elsewhere. We face a dilemma. On the one hand, those involved in obtaining, allocating and managing resources for distance education need to break through the assertion that academic staffing based on a variable cost measure (staff:student ratio) is appropriate for activities in which a high proportion of the costs are fixed (distance course production). On the other hand as Griew (1980: 74) has reminded us on the basis of his own experience as a senior university administrator:

> the only currency that it is sensible for an individual institution to employ in making decisions about the deployment of its academic staff resources is that used by goverment granting agencies in establishing the recurrent grants to be made available to the institution.

The hazards of doing otherwise are well known to those engaged in managing distance education systems. Snowden and Daniel (1980: 76) express a common problem when they write of

> ...the considerable difficulty we have in describing the institution's operations and its economics to officials in government and funding agencies, to members of other (conventional) institutions and, to some extent, to our counterparts and colleagues in other small distance education systems.

In the political process of resource allocation, others may insist on defining the terms of reference to include concepts such as "contact-hours", even though the significance of this to distance interaction over thousands of miles and through a variety of communication means is manifestly absurd.

Two-mode university teaching for small populations

In 1974 a Committee of Inquiry chaired by Peter Karmel recommended that Australia not adopt the single-mode open university model for tertiary distance education. As a result Australia now has 5 of its 19 universities with distance education operations (External Studies) in them.

No Australian university is entirely dependent on distance teaching but three rely very heavily on off-campus enrolments. All five universities serve the needs of students the throughout vast rural hinterlands of outback Australia and approximately 10% of external enrolments are drawn from outside the home state. Two (Queensland and MacQuarie) currently confine their external enrolments to students resident outside the capital cities in which they are located; two others (New England and Deakin), whilst not located in the capital cities of their States, nevertheless draw large numbers of external enrolments from them. The smallest participating university (Murdoch), located in the Perth, has a significant proportion of students enrolled as "mixed mode" taking different course units on and off campus.

The planning strategies adopted by these five universities are remarkably varied and largely reflect different geographic and demographic contexts. Thus the State of Victoria, with less than a tenth of the Australian land mass but one third of its population, is likely to need a different external studies structure from Western Australia where the proportions are the other way around. The separate universities must determine how far to develop their full degree structure both on and off campus and balance their resources between the needs of their internal and external students. In the small distance education systems described by Snowden and Daniel allocation of teaching resources is complex but directed towards a single mode—distance education. By contrast the two-mode university's resource allocation processes are necessarily more diverse and potentially divisive.

Table 1: Australian Universities 1980

	Total Enrolments	External Enrolments	% External
University of Queensland	18,358	2,724	15
University of New England (New South Wales)	8,461	5,590	66
MacQuarie University (New South Wales)	10,516	1,260	12
Deakin University (Victoria)	4,799	2,645	55
Murdoch University (Western Australia)	2,485	896	36
	44,619	13,115	29%
All Universities	163,156	14,118	9%

Costing the external mode in two-mode universities

Whilst several papers describe the structure of university funding in Australia none appears to address specifically the question of distribution of resources between internal and external teaching. This is understandable because intra-university resource allocation is largely autonomous. However, overall recurrent funding concentrates around a number of variable cost factors:

i. staff:student ratio: as the standard measure of teaching effort

ii. contact hours: as the standard measure of academic staff workload

iii. weighted student units (WSU): as the standard measure of student enrolment.

In Rumble's terms these measures provide valuable indicators of "marginal" cost factors involved in the planning, production and delivery of distance education materials. It is, of course, simply myopic to ignore the fact that academic faculty staff are incurring substantial fixed costs in preparing a separate second mode of their course for delivery to distant students. However, it is scarcely more useful to provide them with any allowance of preparation time against their teaching load if the university's staffing formula recognises only the variable indicator of a staff:student ratio. The fixed preparation time costs incurred in preparing the external mode of a course cannot be expected to vary greatly according to whether 20 or 200 enrolments are projected.

On the basis of the formula developed by Snowden and Daniel, I want to suggest a comparable formula as an initial attempt to establish the recurrent costs of external teaching in a small two-mode university. Three elements are involved:

(i) *Course related costs* (the additional *fixed* costs of external mode course preparation and maintenance)

CRC (external) = $a_1 x_1 + a_2 x_2$

where

a_1 = credit points in development (new course)
a_2 = credit points in maintenance (repeat courses)
x_1 = preparation allowances per credit point
x_2 = maintenance allowances per credit point

(ii) *Student related costs* (the *variable* costs resulting from tutoring of enrollees)

SRC (external) = et

where

e = course unit enrolment in external mode
t = tutoring time allocation per student course unit enrolment

(iii) *Institutional costs* (that share of university services academic services and student services attributable to enrolments in the external mode)

IC (external) = $\left(\dfrac{e}{y}\right)c$

where

e = student course unit enrolments in the external mode
y = total student course unit enrolments
c = total institutional costs

The full equation could therefore be expressed as

External Mode Recurrent Costs = CRC + SRC + IC

or $(a_1 + a_2 x_2) + et + \left(\dfrac{e}{y}\right)c$

Conclusion

The purpose is to define some of the real costs incurred in the external mode and to relate them to the resources earned by the distance education students. In resource allocation processes distance education interests are often severely weakened by unreadiness to define cost factors specific to that teaching mode. We have too readily been drawn into the language and conventional wisdom of a costing structure which assumes that teaching costs will vary directly with enrolments and can be uniformly measured by staff:student ratios which tacitly assume a homogeneous mode of course presentation. Even as we protest about external studies being shortchanged we may get diverted from the central issue of fixed course preparation costs into arguing for special extra resources for the most visible student support facilities such as local study centres. The economic analyses of single-mode open universities have shown that the true costs of distance education can be examined only when the terms of reference are properly defined. In two-mode universities we have a structure which is highly appropriate for small student populations, particularly where students may wish to move between on-campus and off-campus study. But within such a structure resources, like information, rarely flow—they have to be pulled.

Patrick Guiton
Murdoch University
Australia

References

Griew, S. (1980) A model for the allocation and utilisation of academic staff resources. *Canadian Journal of Higher Education*, 10, 2, 73-84.

Rumble, G. (1976) *The economics of the Open University of the United Kingdom*. Paper presented to Anglian Regional Management College/O.E.C.D. Conference.

Sixth Report of the Australian Universities Commission (1975) Canberra: Australian Government Publishing Service.

Snowden, B.L. and Daniel, J.S. (1980) The economics and management of small post-secondary distance education systems. *Distance Education*, 1, 1, 68-91.

Wagner, L. (1977) The economics of the Open University revisited. *Higher Education*, 6, 359-381.

Distance Education by Cooperation

Paper 63

Norway is combining the efforts of correspondence schools, voluntary organisations, and state media agencies to extend distance learning opportunities.

Background

In 1977 the Norwegian Parliament set up a state institution for distance learning, whose primary task was to be the development of educational programmes for adults with limited opportunities for taking advantage of existing educational facilities. It was assumed that the institution's activities would be based as far as possible on the use of resources already available. The institution was given the name *Norsk fjernundervisning (NFU)*—the Norwegian State Institution for Distance Education. It has the task of establishing the *main guidelines* for the academic/technical material, the pedagogical approach and the financial structure. The actual production of teaching aids and the organisation of correspondence teaching and local facilities are to be carried out in cooperation with others. The NFU has often been described as a switchboard for this reason.

Available resources

What resources are available to the institution? NRK (the Norwegian State Broadcasting Corporation) has a monopoly on broadcasting. The entire country is covered by one television channel and one radio channel. A second radio channel will start in 1982. The NRK will sign annual agreements with NFU for the production and transmission of programmes associated with its courses.

Statens Filmsentral (National Film Board), the public institution responsible for the production and distribution of films and other audio-visual aids, has an agreement with NRK to advise on the use of audio-visual media and to undertake production and distribution. The problem of publishing has been solved by an agreement with the University Press which does not preclude the writing and production of other teaching aids. Forty publishing firms are members of the Norwegian Publishing Association, with which NFU negotiates through a special committee.

Distribution of teaching aids will be undertaken not only by the National Film Board and correspondence schools, but also by bookshops and newsstands all over the country. In addition the public libraries are important in ensuring that teaching aids are made available to all. In sparsely populated districts these libraries make every effort to reach people with their own buses or boats.

There are forty correspondence schools in Norway, of which seventeen are members of the Norwegian Association of Correspondence Schools. The first correspondence school was started in 1914, so this form of teaching enjoys a long tradition. A number of correspondence schools combine correspondence with local face-to-face teaching.

It is assumed that local supervision will be carried out in collaboration with voluntary educational organisations in accordance with the special law on adult education passed in 1976. This law, aimed at giving adults equal opportunities for access to knowledge, provides for various forms of adult education and sets out the responsibilities of the parties involved. The state school system at the primary, secondary and advanced level is responsible for qualifying courses, while voluntary organisations provide teaching that does not lead to a qualifying exam. At present there are forty officially recognised voluntary organisations entitled to state grants. These organisations are engaged in extensive teaching activities throughout Norway. In 1980 a total of 95,650 teaching assignments were carried out.

Once priority has been given to a programme, it is the task of NFU to make these considerable resources available in a joint effort to achieve its aims.

Finance

NFU receives a state grant for the production of radio and TV programmes and various other teaching aids. For printed teaching aids NFU covers the basic publishing costs and any additional expenses are financed by sales. In general the actual teaching is financed by the existing system of state grants-in-aid. State grants for adult education rose from approximately 214 million kroner to 466 million kroner from 1975-81 so the activity now enjoys a wide measure of support.

The voluntary organisations receive aid to cover teachers' salaries/fees and administrative expenses related to the scope of the activity. A pupil enrolled in a correspondence course is reimbursed 85% of the fee upon completion. This form of state aid will also apply to the multi-media projects sponsored by NFU.

Activity to date

In the autumn of 1979 the first six members of the NFU staff began planning. The pilot project selected, for offer in the autumn of 1981, is a course dealing with the rights of handicapped persons in the community. Special radio and TV programmes have been produced, as well as a textbook including a correspondence section and tutor training material. Local study activities, supervised by voluntary organisations, have been set up all over the country, so that a start can be made as soon as the first TV programme is broadcast. A correspondence school is ready to handle the correspondence teaching. A number of other projects are also being planned.

Forms of cooperation

Even though the final phase of the pilot project has not yet been completed a provisional description of the working model can be given.

Once the NFU Board has given priority to a project the institution appoints two or three experts charged with submitting proposals for the technical, pedagogical and financial aspects of the project. These guidelines are then submitted to the partners cooperating in the project, enabling them to express their views before it is finalised. Tasks are then allotted to the various partners (broadcasting authorities, publisher, correspondence school, etc.).

To coordinate progress the partners constitute a project group. Representatives of the schools or educational organisations also participate, thus enabling local supervisory measures to be prepared in parallel with the production of teaching aids. Efforts are also made to ensure that information on forthcoming offerings reaches the various local organs.

In planning the interplay between radio, television, different teaching aids and two-way communication, the emphasis is on flexibility so that those participating can as far as possible adapt the method to their special needs. In this way each participant can decide whether he or she would benefit from taking the correspondence portion, making use of local study facilities associated with the course, and so forth.

Evaluation of future prospects

It is important that the experience gained over time from this type of distance learning be capable of systematic collation and future utilisation. NFU will arrange for evaluation of the projects through research institutes.

NFU will be alive to the possible need to adapt its working methods within the general framework laid down. The primary advantage of the model is that existing resources are utilised to the greatest possible extent. On the other hand in a model of this kind it will be difficult to find a satisfactory balance, in the division of tasks and responsibility, between the core institution as a controlling element and the various cooperating partners. In the nature of things most independent institutions and organisations prefer the freedom to make their own decisions whereas the working model calls for the development of teaching aids in accordance with guidelines provided from outside. This is a challenge in cooperation both for the "switchboard" and the individual cooperating partner. So far our experience has been favourable, but certain adjustments will probably have to be made before it can be said that Norway has discovered the best way for state-sponsored distance learning to be planned, produced and implemented.

Hjalmar Rande
Norsk fjernundervisning
Norway

Paper 64

A Cooperative Model for Distance Studies

DIFF cooperates with broadcasters and educational agencies so that thousands of students can benefit from its materials.

West German institutions of higher learning face the following challenges and will have to find answers to them, if necessary in cooperation with radio and television stations, institutions of adult and distance education, etc.:

— To improve the job-placement chances of their graduates they will have to develop profession-oriented programs, especially to provide additional qualifications for students who left university some time ago.

— To cater to these students they will have to develop part-time study programs that allow students to continue their professional or occupational activities.

— To allow people occupational flexibility they will

have to implement the concept of lifelong education, i.e. the possibility of beginning and resuming general, political, or professional/vocational studies at any time.

To create a better balance of job chances among the generations they will have to make access to their programs easier for older people.

— To avoid the scissor-effect between educational and occupational systems and eliminate the bottleneck of one qualification for one job they will have to develop study modules which can be used flexibly to meet new needs within a relatively short time. These study modules should be structured so that they can be combined with other modules, possibly from other institutions, including distance study programs. They have to be recognized by other institutions. Examinations should be of the same standard as conventional ones, although procedures should be adapted to the special situation of the students.

— To take into account changes in the learning habits of the West German population (e.g. the influence of mass media; people accustomed to visual learning; changed motivational structures; orientation to practical needs, etc.) they will have to use modern approaches, including new media, multi-media packages, and a combination of multi-media distance study units with conventional instruction.

The organization of distance studies

The institutions of higher learning cannot rise to these challenges alone. Some unsolved problems cause increasing discontent. For some tasks new methods have been developed, e.g. better structured syllabuses and study materials including modern media. Distance study programmes have been developed and thoroughly evaluated. Modern distance study has proved a suitable and highly effective instrument to meet these challenges. However, much depends on how distance study is organized and integrated into the educational system.

In West Germany there are three main types of organization for distance education at the post-secondary level.

— Students are enrolled full-time at a local college or university. They use the facilities of this institution and are guided by its staff. Distance study materials are used for certain parts of their programs and courses. These materials have either been developed by the staff of this institution (rare) or by DIFF which operates on a national basis.

— Students are enrolled and study at the Fernuniversität mostly on a part-time basis. The Fernuniversität (Distance Study University) caters to these students by sending them study materials (including assignments), offering centralized or decentralized complementary face-to-face instruction and organizing the examinations.

— Students are home-based independent learners, either as part-time students or participants in refresher courses. The distance study materials and most of the audio-visual materials come from DIFF. In some cases they are part of radio or television courses. Agencies like teacher in-service institutes, adult education institutions, church institutes for further education and an increasing number of colleges and universities are partner institutions of DIFF in organizing and running the courses. This pattern is typical of continuing further education by distance study in West Germany.

DIFF: a cooperative model

DIFF was founded in 1967. First financed by the Volkswagen Foundation it now gets its resources from the 11 Länder (especially Baden-Württemberg) and the Federal Government. To date about 120,000 student teachers and teachers have been provided with study materials. Access to these materials is not open to everyone. Usually a partner institution first organizes a course and members of the target groups may then apply to this institution for admission. A second group of DIFF projects is developed with radio and television stations. These courses are open to anybody. About 350,000 students have taken part in them. Finally, Newspaper College projects are a new branch of DIFF. These are launched in cooperation with 120 to 200 newspapers covering the whole of the country. To date about 30,000 people have used the additional study materials besides the weekly articles in the newspapers.

In contrast to the Fernuniversität DIFF is mainly engaged in providing its partner institutions with printed and audio-visual study materials and advice besides doing research. DIFF's partner institutions are almost all at the post-secondary level. They remain fully independent and autonomous in their teaching role. It is up to them whether they integrate DIFF study materials into their courses. DIFF itself does not run the courses and is not responsible for assignments and examinations.

To give a concrete example, Radio College, now 13 years old, begins each year with a new two-term programme. Topics have been taken from various disciplines like philosophy, education, psychology, sociology, politics, economics, history, mathematics, biology and social medicine. More and more an interdisciplinary approach is used.

The Radio College courses are planned, developed, implemented and evaluated under the common responsibility of six radio stations, the ministries of education of 6 Länder, the top coordinating institutions of adult education of 6 Länder, the representatives of the six University Chancellors'/Rectors Conferences, and DIFF.

All partners in the Radio College planning body are equal and share responsibility and costs for the projects as a whole. Each has certain special obliga-

Paper 64

tions and responsibilities: the radio stations for the radio broadcasts; DIFF for the print media, evaluation and research; the ministries of education and the universities for the examinations; the adult education institutions for the tutorials.

The Radio College shows what cooperation among different institutions in West Germany in distance education is like. The key principle is the division of work, costs and responsibility, with the necessary common planning and coordination, and a minimum of institutionalization.

Karlheinz Rebel
Deutsches Institut für Fernstudien (DIFF)
West Germany

Paper 65

From Realities to Plans

Future educational needs will require a uniquely cooperative aproach to the use of technological and human resources.

Economic Realities

Educational funding has recently been defended on the basis of a direct relationship between the educational level and the economic productivity of the work force. Increasingly, as developed nations achieve higher general education levels the marginal cost-marginal benefit of further increasing educational levels becomes questionable.

There is also the increasing cost of traditional education and the new costs of the alternative of correspondence, off-campus, and distance education. Wang (1981) cites higher costs as one of the two major problems confronting higher education today. On what basis can these higher costs be justified? Enrolments? Evidence of students' success? The decline in enrolments is a problem confronting most traditional institutions but less so alternative systems. In Canada, these alternatives are increasing their enrolments. Thus, alternative delivery systems may have more success than their traditional counterparts in defending increasing costs. This may be only a transitory phenomenon if, as Wang (1981) suggests, the second major problem confronting higher education is government interference. On what basis is government likely to interfere in education—perhaps by demanding accountability? To date, most institutions argue for budget allocations primarily in terms of enrolments. If increasing enrolments is a case that distance delivery institutions can make successfully, how well would they fare when asked to demonstrate student accomplishment, student completion, or the economic relevance of their education? It could be argued by governments that educational institutions generally and alternative delivery facilities specifically, have demonstrated neither causal relationships to economic productivity nor the ability to attract, hold, and successfully educate students.

Social realities

Contemporary educational institutions and practices have evolved to serve the needs of Toffler's "Second Wave" industrial citizens (1981). These are people who need to be highly skilled, prepared to assume roles in factory-like environments, and who are expected to adopt fairly similar lifestyles. Educational institutions use classroom instruction, similar curricula, and common expectations for knowledge and skills to serve these citizens.

How are educational institutions adapting to serve the needs of Toffler's "Third Wave" civilization? These citizens are likely to require increasingly individualized and decentralized educational opportunities.

Toffler says:

> More learning will occur outside, rather than inside, the classroom. Despite the pressure from unions, the years of compulsory schooling will grow shorter not longer. Instead of rigid age segregation, young and old will mingle. Education will become more interpersonal and interwoven with work, and more spread out over a lifetime.

(Toffler, 1981: 384)

Two indicators of increasing responsiveness by educators from all over the world to the need for decentralization are the global representation of this conference (i.e., ICCE, 1982) and the proliferation of distance education agencies.

Toffler (1981) describes the new context and the emerging civilization as one in which individualization, personalization, and unique lifestyles are likely to increase. He also describes the emergence of the "prosumer", the person who both produces and consumes. Do our new educational practices accommodate the student as a producer as well as a consumer of education? Do they accommodate new variability in lifestyle? Do they accommodate an "information society" in which most citizens will have access to a wide range of information and databases? Or do they rather re-package classroom-based instruction and classroom-based curricula?

Alternative delivery strategies do increase access to and permit decentralization of educational activities. However, the substance or curriculum delivered in these alternative ways may not be appropriately responsive to the emerging needs of "Third Wave" citizens.

Technological realities

Dramatic developments in information technologies, including microchip-based computers, laser beam videodisc units and videotex, have been well documented. The availability of land and satellite-based transmission and interactive instructional methodologies made possible by these technologies brings nearer the day of Toffler's (1981) "Electronic Cottage" and Godfrey's (1980) NABU's. The advent of environments that permit people to access information, to participate in exchanges of information and ideas, and to participate in instruction at home, at work, or at play puts pressure on educational institutions to understand these technologies and to use them in their educational contexts. While most educators accept the goal of technology, many have difficulty accepting the role of other professionals in preparing courses for delivery by means of electronic-based technologies. Educators are also threatened by potential loss of control of their curriculum during the process of translating their subject matter for delivery by these technologies. Yet, if Toffler's (1981) analysis of the future is valid, both delivery methodologies and curricular substance must change to meet the needs of "Third Wave" civilization.

If traditional campus-based institutions are slow and superficial in their use of emerging technologies, what about the use of these technologies in distance education? In Canada, there is some use of radio and television, teleconferencing, and some explorations with satellite-telephone combinations. Clearly, exploration of alternative technologies is proceeding. Equally clearly, distance education in Canada is characterized by a dependence upon print or audio-based methodologies and reliance upon mail and telephone systems for interaction among students and staff.

Educational institutions thus appear to be somewhat lagging in their response to technological pressures. Some delay in adopting new technologies is legitimate, but some may also be accounted for by the perception of possible loss of control. This perception may be legitimate but the demand of each individual learner for control over learning may be a characteristic of "Third Wave" citizens to which educators will have to adapt.

Responding to the realities

The increase in the number of distance education services is evidence of attempts by educational institutions to meet the emerging diversity of needs of citizens. However, close examination raises questions about the adequacy of the new strategies.

Institutions that convert lectures into prose may find that students who rejected traditional education by "voting with their feet" may also reject this "old wine in new skins" by failing to complete courses, failing to register in other courses, and over time, again "voting with their feet". On the other hand, institutions that adopt the new technologies for the "glamour" and fail to distinguish between technology as a mode of transmission of messages and technology as a set of specific techniques employed in instructional acts (Clark, 1980) may also fall into a trap. Schramm (1977) notes that learning and achievement are affected more by our instructional techniques than by the delivery medium.

Meeting the new need for diversity and decentralization of educational opportunities is therefore likely to require significant effort. In addition to responding to these needs, the educational enterprise must also be able to economically rationalize its activities.

In Canada we already have an excellent array of universities, colleges, and technical institutions. We also have museums, art galleries, libraries, and centres for the performing arts. Further, we have business, industry, and government agencies that are also sources of knowledge, skill, and information. Finally, we have significant economic and technological resources.

These resources should permit us to develop both the decentralized and individualized educational opportunities our citizens are likely to demand. To date, however, most distance education is developed within single institutions and with few exceptions, with neither knowledge of, nor consultation with, other institutions. The pattern is one of competition rather than cooperation. The economic realities that face us make cooperation a prerequisite. It is not possible to provide diverse services unless economies of scale are realized. The technological realities that enable us to deliver services to students almost wherever they live will also force some softening of institutional regional mandates. Further, the costs of preparing serices for delivery using the new technolgies will make cooperation imperative.

The current pattern, then, of institution-specific development in relative isolation is not likely to ensure either an adequate array of programs and services or reasonably equal access to these programs.

Perhaps we can MEND the fabric of the educational coat by initiating a *M*ultipurpose *E*ducational *N*etwork *D*evelopment that would:

- assemble the physical and human components for an interactive educational network
- coordinate the institutions and agencies wishing to use the network in providing educational services
- establish local facilities for interaction among people, technologies, and learning resources
- market existing programs and services and assess needs for new programs and services.

Any institution or agency could provide its programs and services through the network—indeed, some agencies that do not currently provide educational programs might be encouraged to do so. Most "providers" would require additional resources to plan and design programs and services for the network (e.g., course developers, editors, programmers). These resources could be obtained by the institution itself or through a separate wing of the MEND system.

MEND could be funded initially to establish the network, then on a smaller scale to maintain it and provide technical and human services as required.

Initially, each institution might continue to serve students with its own programs and services. Over the longer term, student selection patterns might require alternative mechanisms for credentialling. Students might select courses from college, technical, and university programs; that is, create their own "ladder curriculum". This would bring us directly into the problems Gregor (1979) describes of finding ways to coordinate educational programs across different institutions.

Most of the elements for MEND already exist in Canada. Resistance to such networks seems to be based on:

- the inability or unwillingness of institutions to credential students based on programs from other institutions
- the inability of single institutions to finance system implementation
- the lack of human resources within each institution
- the unwillingness of government to finance the implementation of a network or the human resources within individual institutions.

MEND represents a solution to at least some of these problems. First, by leaving credit-granting and credentialling with the individual institutions it avoids the issue of the relative merits of college versus university versus technical institute courses while still giving students access to the full range of these courses. Second, by implementing a network to be shared by many institutions and agencies MEND makes possible an economically viable arrangement that may receive more government support and funding.

Finally, MEND has the potential of increasing diversity of educational opportunity using the electronic and human technologies in an economically viable way.

MEND does not directly address the problems of educators unable or unwilling to utilize alternative technologies; rather it assumes that these problems can be addressed by providing necessary technical and human resources. Further, MEND does not directly address problems of curriculum adequacy; again, it assumes that if technical and human resources are made available and if students in a relatively free market place are allowed to choose courses and programs, appropriate curriculum changes will result.

Finally, this decription of MEND deliberately does not present detailed organizational and funding strategies. There are a variety of ways of funding and organizing. These are best left to specific provinces and agencies.

In summary, with the complex and diverse educational needs likely to be characteristic of Toffler's "Third Wave" society it is important that we organize our resources so that students can meet their needs. It is important that we not look to individual institutions to address all needs but rather look to mechanisms to increase student access to existing resources and to make all the resources possible for increasing numbers of students.

Perhaps the "multi-coloured coat" of education can be MENDed through a sharing of what we now have and know how to do and what we may build and learn together.

Douglas G. Crawford
Advanced Education and Manpower (Alberta)

Gail C. Crawford
Athabasca University

Canada

References

Clark, R.E. (1980) Issues in the Transfer of Instructional Technology between Nations. Paper presented at the 24th Annual Conference of the Comparative and International Education Society, Vancouver, B.C., 1980.

Godfrey, D. (1980) Introduction. In *Gutenberg Two*. Godfrey, D. and Parkhill, D. (eds.) Toronto: Press Porcepic.

Gregor, A. (1979) The re-alignment of post-secondary education systems in Canada. *Canadian Journal of Higher Education*, 9, 2, 35-79.

Schramm, W. (1977) *Big Media, Little Media*. Beverley Hills, California: Sage Publications.

Toffler, A. (1981) *The Third Wave*. New York: Bantam Books.

Wang, W.K.S. (1981) The dissemination of higher education. *Improving College and University Teaching*, 29, 2, 55-60.

Comparative Models of Distance Education: Institutional Design and Management

The apparent diversity of distance education masks a basic similarity in institutional type and administrative style.

Distance education is becoming a global affair. Its evolution in print form spans a century; in radio form half a century; in video form thirty years; in multimedia form about fifteen years; and in its most recent satellite-based form five years.

Naturally, traditional institutions have had to adapt to the arrival of distance education. Such adaptations have often occurred as responses to local needs and pressures. Although reflecting the uniqueness of each institution and the society it serves, these adaptations, when studied globally, reveal common patterns. There appears to be a certain overall pattern to distance education: common problems; issues that confront everyone; practices in one institution that may resolve the problems of another.

The form of distance education

The type of distance education institution in a particular society depends on:

- government perception of need
- the realisation by individual institutions that satisfying the needs of an adult market may significantly increase programme size
- demand for courses and programmes by people living in remote areas.

Governments and institutions around the world have responded in four basic ways to these developments:

- By establishing autonomous open learning institutions such as Britain's Open University, British Columbia's Open Learning Institute, Alberta's Athabasca University, or Israel's Everyman's University.
- By establishing institutions in which classroom and distance education have equal status and are in fact integrated. New Zealand's Massey University, and Australia's Murdoch University are two examples.
- By establishing extension services within traditional institutions. This is the most common response. Extension services fall into three categories.
  i. The strongest are those with the authority to decide what distance education activities will be undertaken, and to control the design, production and delivery of those activities.
  ii. The most common extension services are those that lack the authority to decide the nature of the distance education programme, but do work closely with on-campus faculty in arranging it.
  iii. The least powerful extension service is the one that may only respond to faculty requests for distance education programmes, and has neither the mandate nor the budget to initiate programmes on its own.

Of these three types there are now few in the third category, and the number in the first category is growing.

- A fourth response is the graduate-studies-only distance education programme. Such programmes appear to emerge directly from institutions that prefer to have undergraduates on campus, and to deliver only advanced courses via a telecommunications medium.

The TAGER system in Texas is an example, utilizing a simple black and white television format to deliver graduate courses to students in some forty institutions, all linked together in a video cable system.

The administration of distance education

How are these various types of distance education institutions managed? The autonomous institution has five principal characteristics:

- clarity of purpose
- high status
- a unique organizational structure
- the opportunity to establish its own reputation
- a clear understanding by faculty members of what is expected of them.

The university whose campus and extension services have equal status is designed to play a very different role from that of an open university. At the open university traditional modes of course delivery are considered just as inappropriate as distance education is felt to be in many traditional institutions. In an institution in which on- and off-campus instruction are of equal status an assumption has been made that it is not fair to exclude qualified students who happen to be unable to attend classes in person. Since the technology to maintain regular contact with such students exists, the public institution is obligated to use it, to explore it and, as with campus-based instruction, to develop effective instructional methods.

Such an expectation makes unique demands upon all who participate in it. The institution's assumptions about the careers of faculty, the role of students, the utilization of communications technology and instructional methodology are considerably different from those of most classical institutions.

Similarity of administrative structure is apparent between the many institutions possessing extension services. Simon Fraser, Queensland, Nairobi, Wisconsin, Delhi, and Maryland are some of the many universities with powerful extension departments that take considerable responsibility for their institution's distance education programme.

The pattern that emerges globally is far from rigid, and certainly not based upon only one or two models. With the exception of the British Open University, most institutions concerned with distance education keep surprisingly little contact with each other. In some places they even appear to be in competition for a slice of what is perceived to be a lucrative adult market. The growth of distance education throughout the world has not been marked by extensive inter-institutional and international cooperation.

It is because the types of style and structure were established in virtual isolation, each a unique response to what was perceived to be a unique set of local conditions, that the emergence of patterns is so interesting.

It is interesting to list issues that distance educators appear to face throughout the world. The external appearance of the attempted solutions to such issues make them appear to be unique although they are not.

A list of issues is:

a. How can the educational needs of people in remote, rural areas be assessed?
   - Are urban academics qualified to judge?
   - Can the poor, the illiterate, the isolated possibly know how to choose, or what they need?

b. How do distance learners learn?
   - Can it be assumed that motivation is enough?
   - What effects do maturity, adulthood, suffering, isolation, skill in surviving, growing up illiterate, poor life-expectancy, mistrust of authority, have upon attitudes towards learning?

c. What are appropriate programmes?
   - Are rural-dwelling adults able to perceive life as divisible into subjects, as urban academics seem able to do?

d. Who is eligible to take a distance course?
   - In view of production and delivery costs, should only the most needy, or the most experienced or the most senior or the ones who can afford it, take courses?
   - Should distance education be directed at adults or children, or both?
   - Should distance education be an extension of school systems, not universities?

e. How will distance educators translate information only available in print-based linear forms to the spontaneous and interactive electro-magnetic media of the telecommunications systems?

f. What is the form and structure of distance education instruction?
   - Should the tutor be at the centre of the process or on the edge?
   - Do the assumptions we make about the validity of our thinking and verbal communication processes in classroom-based instructional institutions hold true for distance education—particularly that which is based upon interactive video?
   - Should we be training distance-education instructors and tutors?
   - Do we understand what happens to the complex process of human communication when a satellite, or radio or correspondence course is wedged between people who are trying to teach and learn?

g. How may institution-based distance educators improve the status of extension services?
   - How will academics be persuaded that teaching off-campus courses will not jeopardize their careers?
   - Can the traditional, campus-oriented regulators of academic career processes be persuaded to give distance education equal status?

h. What support services are required by distance educators?

i. How should distance courses be evaluated?
   - Who is qualified to do it?

Questions such as these are being asked by distance educators the world over.

Concerns are similar. Institutional types and administration styles are similar. Thus does the global distance education network emerge.

Geoffrey Potter
University of Victoria
Canada

How Can the Conventional University Serve the Distant Learner?

Distance educators must be less strident and more rational if the potential of cooperation with traditional institutions is to be realized.

This paper explores some difficulties which arise from the relationship between correspondence courses and traditional university education. As correspondence courses gain recognition and popularity their representatives and supporters must be willing to enter into critical discussion with students and lecturers from traditional universities in order to prevent the foundation of a new ivory tower. The conventional universities watch the successful development of correspondence studies with keen interest. Originally just a means of overcoming geographical distances correspondence courses have developed into an adaptable instrument, especially in the field of further and continuing education.

The sharp distinction between initial training and the long period of professional work has started to dissolve. Nowadays a university degree is more and more regarded as a qualification for further education. This will probably have a strong impact on the traditional universities. The adaptation of the universities to the rapidly changing needs of an industrial society and the increasing importance of general courses which are not oriented towards examinations are significant issues in the future development of the universities. Many traditional universities have programmes of further and continuing education. In the United States the number of students who take part in programmes of further and continuing education has now surpassed the number of traditional students.

Distant learners are no longer simply those people who are geographically distant from a university and who cannot take part in traditional studies for professional or personal reasons. In the contemporary university system there are many distances to be overcome. The limited educational background of many first year students, for instance, calls for the organization of introductory courses. In this case the use of correspondence course material would be just as appropriate as the numerous standard introductory courses. I have never understood why in West Germany, every term, at different universities, more than a hundred courses on "Statistics for psychologists" have to be given. Distance education specialists should have been employed long ago to free their colleagues from routine work.

The increasing interest in PSI in the traditional university also has to do with overcoming distances. PSI is not a parapsychological term but an abbreviation for "Personalized System of Instruction". The most important aspects of this system are the freedom of the individual student to determine the time and speed of learning and to choose from a wealth of material those subjects which match his inclinations and needs.

In the future we must expect increasing cooperation between distance education and traditional universities. However we must recognize that right now correspondence education is far from being popular on the campus. Although the majority of departments for further and continuing education are tacitly accepted on economic grounds they are often looked down upon and their staff members are always eager to be promoted to other departments. In reaction to this, papers dealing with distance education often over-compensate. The qualitative equivalence or even superiority of external studies is heavily stressed and this emphasis serves to instil a feeling of missed opportunities in all those unfortunate enough to have graduated from a traditional Alma Mater.

Communication between traditional university education and distance education has not made much headway recently. Who is responsible? I feel that casual hints about wrongheaded orthodoxy are not a satisfactory answer and that the advocates of distance education have to take part of the blame, since central issues are often discussed with an uncritical and rather superficial missionary enthusiasm. Let me give a few examples. There is no controversy about the importance and indispensability of further and continuing education. But the choir of the apostles of lifelong learning has to do without basses (i.e. without those considerate voices who warn against totalitarian deformations of a new form of learning and against a merciless and inhumane utopianism which confuses the lifelong learner with the lifelong examinee). Albert Einstein is reported to have said in his later years that he now intended to grow sapheaded peacefully. We must learn to accept the decision to content oneself with one's past achievements, to be left alone, and to admire the feats of the younger generation from a safe and serene distance as one of the unalienable rights of man. It is high time for those involved in lifelong learning to rediscover the unpretentiousness, modesty, scepticism and, above all, the sense of fact which have been the hallmarks of science from its very beginning.

A second example. Let us go back to the PSI method aiming at the individualization of studies with the help of correspondence course material. A

Paper 67

commendable approach, no doubt, but how does it mesh with the current definition of distance education as 'the most industrialized form of education', with its innumerable checks and controls, its computerized tests and its inflexible pacing of the learning process. Research papers in this field abound in dubious personality concepts which claim to place the individual student at the centre, but which in fact substitute a bloodless, though highly functional abstraction instead. I do not shrink from applying the term perversion in this context, for there is no other word to characterize a mental attitude which, for example, downplays the personal letter of a tutor in comparison to a computer print-out because of the 'perfect and objective evaluation criteria' of the computer programme and the superior 'decipherability' of its print-outs which save the student from having to grapple with his tutor's illegible handwriting.

Example number three. In the traditional university distance educators often advocate the introduction of new media like self-instructional courses, modules, video-programmes etc. as labour-saving devices. This glosses over the immense and time-consuming difficulties the normal and inexperienced scholar runs into when he is called upon to produce a correspondence course instead of a conventional book on the same topic. In addition, his colleagues in other departments or universities are usually hesitant about adopting his approach, thus limiting the supra-regional distribution of the units produced, which alone would guarantee a reasonable input-output ratio.

Last, university education encompasses more than a narrow range of strictly scientific or technological skills, more than a repertoire of cognitive formulas and easily pigeonholed information. No truly academic socialisation can stop at this. It will forever remain incomplete if it does not stimulate the critical bent of the student's intellect and encourage a sound scepticism which explodes stereotypes, cliches, and pat solutions. This can only be effected through dialogue, debate, and personal interaction.

I am afraid these statements are not too conducive to that atmosphere of reassuring harmony and optimism which seems to be endemic wherever distance educators meet. But controversy and discussion are the heartbeat of science, and sometimes stepping up the blood pressure is known to have salubrious effects. Distance educators must take off their rose-coloured spectacles and give more room to the scientific virtues of soberness, rationality, and self-criticism.

Herbert Mainusch
University of Münster
West Germany

Paper 68

The Neglected Role of Disciplinary Research in the Distance University

Distance educators should avoid some of the more self-congratulatory illusions excusing them from undertaking genuine research.

Introduction

In what follows I intend being purposely very provocative; at times, perhaps, iconoclastic. I do not want to be taken literally in all I say. My purpose by playing Devil's Advocate is to provoke others to defend some of what I have come to regard as the "liturgical superstitions" of distance education. My reason for adopting this purpose devolves on my growing concern that for all our high-sounding talk about our flexible, innovative methods of going about our business, we, in distance education, are beginning to show just as profound a predilection for cant and a new kind of sacred cow as our brethren in more traditional settings.

Let me confess that I have only been involved in distance education for a short time: on and off, perhaps, for ten years or so, but as a major professional commitment for little more than a year. Had I been asked to prepare this piece a year ago, I should probably have declined on the grounds that I knew too little. Although I have a frightening amount still to learn, I am discomfited by a growing conclusion that, at the present point in my education, I probably know more than is good for me. Before swallowing the catechism in its doctrinal entirety, however, I wish to challenge it. At our next meeting I shall probably be one of the faithful. Before faith—and comfort—take over, let me pose a few dirty questions of my own.

A traditional view

When I announced to an old friend and long-time mentor that I had accepted a position as President of a distance university, his response was disturbing. He would have wished for me, he wrote, a different fate. In his experience (and, he added, in the experience of many of those whose judgement he most respected) distance education tended to be the final resting place of those academics who had failed to make (or even were incapable of making) a minimally acceptable mark in research. In the same way as family and community medicine, and preventive medicine (probably the two most important thrusts of modern health care) occupy the lowliest of positions as "also ran's" on the contemporary, medical school totem pole, so, it seems, does distance education in the values of the worldwide system of higher education of which we are a part. Why? And what, if anything, should we be trying to do about it?

No academic, in traditional or innovative educational setting, can by my book jettison what von Humboldt, well over a century ago, termed *wissenshaft:* that attitude that forces the scholar, willy nilly, to engage in research for its own sake, and to bring to bear on all his or her professional activities the most relentless demands of intellectual rigour. I assure you that I believe this fervently, but I believe equally fervently that the view of research in the traditional university is totally out of perspective.

I shall chance my arm and suggest that in many instances research has become so comfortable a way of life that many people have ceased seriously to concern themselves about its value (in principle, or in its specific utility) even to the intellectual community in which it is pursued. When universities bleat about the threats implied by reduced government spending on higher education, too often, I suspect, they are really responding to a different threat: the threat that the comfortable life-styles that their faculties have traditionally enjoyed over the decades may be disrupted. When professors, deans, and presidents pontificate about "excellence", and advise governments that the reduced funding of universities will undermine the very structure upon which civilized society is founded, they also too often, I suggest, reflect the almost atavistic terror of many faculty that the very structures upon which their comfortable lives are founded are likely to be subjected to the indecency of public scrutiny.

It is all ineffably tragic. I have no doubt at all that society will suffer grievously if research and scholarship fail to maintain their preeminent roles in the world's universities. But by over-stating the case, as it is currently being over-stated, nothing but harm will be done to the cause of research and scholarship. Governments are not peopled only by fools. Many cabinet ministers, and most senior officials of civil service departments, are just as capable intellectually as the mass of university professors. They can see through cant and humbug as easily as anyone. They are also quite capable of seeing, with Humboldt himself, that a good researcher will find the means to do his or her research whether encouraged to or not.

But that is as may be. I return to my question. Why is distance education accorded so low a ranking on the academic pole? Well, maybe I am wrong, but such facts as I have been able to tease out since I joined this fraternity suggest to me that the record of distance universities in contributing to the scholarly development of the disciplines they purvey is, by any standards, pretty slim. And it is this kind of disciplinary contribution, let's face it, that carries weight within those traditional cabals that order positions on totem poles. Research into distance education itself, however worthy and useful it may be, is a distinct second-best. As one particularly self-righteous colleague once said to me, "One can always tell when an academic has opted out of real research: It's when he starts studying methods of teaching his subject!"

One perception of distance education, then, is that it gives hospitality to a breed of academics who, at worst, are incapable of "real" research, or who, at best, simply do not share that most crucial of academic values: a commitment to research and scholarship. The perception may be false, but the damaging thing is that it seems to be widespread. And now we arrive at the crux of the problem.

To have to rub shoulders with a group of academics who, apparently uncommitted to one of the most central of university values, seem successful in attracting political and public favour, must surely be a most galling and threatening state of affairs. For all the bland statements of support for distance universities offered by our colleagues in traditional places, their support when it comes to the crunch, is often cavilling and nit-picking. Their discomfort is palpable. Their real feelings are probably at best ambivalent. Our very appearance of being able to achieve some degree of success in what we set out to do without being totally committed to research could so easily be regarded as evidence that universities in general can survive unscathed even if their facilities are jolted out of the comfortable lives that tradition has shaped for them.

Comfort in a distance university

So far I have been engaging in what my old colleagues in Australia would term "rubbishing" the traditional university. Having worked in a handful, I feel sufficient identity with them to be able to do so both with affection and with respect for what they undoubtedly do achieve. Sometimes I confess to wondering whether, however distinguished a contribution distance universities may make to education in the decades ahead, the contributions of the Cambridge's, Harvard's, Uppsala's and McGill's will not outlive them all in their impact on social, moral, intellectual, cultural and even economic development. My effort in this paper is to offer one suggestion as to how we might attempt to build for ourselves an influence that promises a realisation of our undoubted potential for making a lasting impact of significance. To do that, I must start directing a more critical eye inwards, towards our own behaviours.

If one asks (perhaps in the course of tenure or promotion reviews) teachers at a traditional university why they haven't done more research than their records evidence, a common response will be to claim that there simply hasn't been time, what with all the teaching and administrative work that has been thrust at them. I confess that I have always found this to be a rather comic response. A traditional academic year (leaving aside all the devices, like sabbaticals, free trimesters for research, and so on) requires, perhaps, nine or ten hours of contact with students a week, for perhaps 30 weeks of the year. Even given that class preparation demands the commitment of twice as much time again, and that administration eats up another four hours a week on average through the course of the whole year, the average professor can still look forward to having around 22 weeks out of 52 during normal office hours to devote to personal research and scholarship. Further, if our liturgical intonings of the alleged impossibility of treating an academic job as anything but one that commits us 24 hours a day, seven days a week, mean anything at all, there will also be the odd weekend and evening to throw in for good measure. In short, the plea that we have no time doesn't really wash.

Unfortunately, the lore of distance education contains similar elements of humbug. Writing course materials is, we are continually being told, an all-consuming task. Indeed, legitimacy has been given to this view by the often stated warning by authoritative people that if one enters the distance field one should not expect to have much time for personal research. I have some sympathy for the view. At their most distinguished, distance faculty are a most conscientious lot who will strive relentlessly over long periods to create the perfect set of course materials.

But is there not an element in our work of shaping for ourselves a life that is to us just as comfortable as that sought by the traditional university teacher? My view of the distance education enterprise tends at times to the nightmarishly warped. I see dozens of gifted people seeking the most tortuous means of delivering themselves of their wares. They do this in many weird and wonderful ways, of which the following are just a few.

- They'll establish monstrously inefficient course teams, calculated in fact (if not by design) to remove from any one appropriate pair of shoulders responsibility for ensuring that material is produced in adequate form by a specified deadline.

- They'll generate the most cumbrous series of checks and balances in the name of instructional development, ostensibly to ensure that their wares are digestible by their readers.

- They'll establish the most convoluted committee structure designed to ensure that no one can do his job without participation in every decision of every member of the institution; and this will apply, of course, to all matters requiring decision, whether they bear directly on the academic side of the enterprise or not. This, of course, is a habit of all universities, but my perception is that in non-traditional institutions it has reached new levels of lunacy.

- They'll devote themselves conscientiously and devotedly to preparing courses that have been skillfully prepared elsewhere many times, as often as not finding excellent reasons why, in their particular institution, it is quite impossible to use material that has been massaged into optimal effectiveness by people just as qualified as themselves.

My contention—and I offer it with affectionate good nature—is that we probably find these ways of earning our daily bread every bit as comfortable as does our colleague who seeks the life of the researcher in the more traditional institution, and that this search for personal comfort is every bit as hypocritical as his. We accept them, if you like, as "givens", without too much thought as to their utility or necessity, mainly because we simply enjoy the activities they demand of us.

A plea for balance and moderation, and for the re-emergence of disciplinary research in distance universities

In suggesting that we should somehow make more time for disciplinary research in our distance universities, I do so not because I think it necessary that we should ape our more traditional colleagues, but rather because I happen fervently to believe that Humboldt was right in claiming *wissenshaft* as the most important distinguishing characteristic of the academic. We may temporarily attract political, public, even financial favour for being "relevant" in our commitment to increasing access by taking education out to the consumer, but like all fashions, this one cannot be guaranteed a perpetual life. Further, whether we like it or not, traditional universities will increasingly trespass into our territory, and unless we have more than a distance delivery expertise to offer, our longer term future will be sick indeed. Here are three excellent reasons why we remain at our peril indifferent to so major an element of the traditional value system.

The fourth reason is frankly political. We cannot, in my view, afford to rest content at the bottom of the traditional totem pole. For all their flattering comments about the importance of open education, and the wonderful jobs that people such as ourselves are doing, prime ministers and premiers still tend to go to the established, traditional universities for advice. Long-term political clout is rarely exercised by the presidents, faculties, or alumni of new, open universities. Maybe we'll never rise far from the bottom of the academic pole, but let us at least remove one of the major reasons why our placement at the bottom is seen by our traditional colleagues as being so legitimate and proper.

How, then, should we do it? My prescription, written from the viewpoint of self-acknowledged new boy who has lots to learn, is to reassess, if necessary in the most painful of manners, those funny elements of the fast-developing lore of distance education with the object of determining which are really crucial to the success of our mission and which are simply there because we happen to like them. Provocatively, I ask whether course teams are really so crucial to our success; whether distance education warrants so obsessive an attention to instructional perfection; whether we shouldn't allow people more autonomy (even authority) in getting their jobs done; and whether we shouldn't foster the exchange and purchase of courses in a much freer and more aggressive manner so that we do not waste so much invaluable time individually re-inventing the wheel?

If we were to tackle all this sensibly and without intrusion of silly ideology, we should surely free ourselves for a much greater involvement in disciplinary research. And in so doing, I predict, our enterprises would gain in liveliness, and we should start attracting a much higher quality of faculty into them.

Maybe, as well, we should start shedding some of the defensiveness which, in my short experience of distance education, more than anything else tends to characterize the transaction of our business. Finally, I venture to predict that, far from undermining the quality of our products, such a campaign might even improve them. This is a question for empirical study, but until someone demonstrates otherwise, I personally regard the question as entirely open.

Stephen Griew
Athabasca University
Canada

Managing the Course Development Process

Priorities can be clarified and schedules maintained by using simple card-based systems.

Paper 69

This paper deals with two aspects of the course development process in distance education: establishment of priorities and monitoring of schedules. It describes how these two operations are performed by the Victorian TAFE Off-Campus Network (VTOCN) which is responsible for the development and implementation of distance education at the TAFE (Technical and Further Education) level in the state of Victoria, Australia. TAFE courses provide vocational and continuing education at levels ranging from tradesman through to para-professional.

Courses are developed under the auspices of the VTOCN's central co-ordinating authority and delivered through the fifteen local off-campus centres that make up the network. These centres provide a combination of pastoral care, academic support and access to local facilities for students who enrol through the centre most convenient to them.

Establishing priorities

Since the demand for new distance education courses exceeds the VTOCN's capacity to supply, it has been necessary to develop a systematic procedure for establishing priorities amongst the various proposals. The basis for this is the Ratings form shown in Figure 1. This is an attempt to judge proposals within the context of TAFE and VTOCN philosophy and in terms of practicability.

Proposals are arranged in order of priority and slotted into the VTOCN's development program. The priority listing and the development program must be continually updated. The rating system needs ongoing revision and clarification to reflect practical constraints and shifts in philosophy, such as a change in the relative emphases on vocational as opposed to self-development courses.

Considerable emphasis in the implementation of courses is placed upon local, rather than central activity. In order to reflect this in course development an agreed percentage of our effort is devoted to local initiatives where local persons or groups are contracted to develop courses and associated study materials.

One area of TAFE activity is the provision of special purpose short courses for persons returning to study (retraining, new skills, remedial and bridging courses). The VTOCN has allocated a set percentage of its effort to the development of such courses.

Proposals for local initiatives and special short courses go through the rating process but are guaranteed a certain proportion of our development resources.

Figure 1: Ratings form

New subject	Part of course to which we are committed Considerably: 12 Not at all: 0
Existing subject	Change needed because of New law (L) New Syllabus (S), Others (0). Essential: 15 Unnecessary: 0
Vocational subject Part of requirement for:	Skills Licence Essential: 20 Unnecessary: 0 Membership of Occupational Association: Essential: 4 Unnecessary: 0 Promotion or Salary Increment Essential: 6 Unnecessary: 0 Retraining Essential: 20 Unnecessary: 0
Access subject prerequisite for:	TAFE Course Essential: 15 Unnecessary: 0 Tertiary Course Essential: 15 Unnecessary: 0
Self development	Emphasis on self-development: Entirely: 20 Not at all: 0
Alternatives subject Already available	On-campus (Metropolitan) No: 2 Yes 0 On-campus (Non-Metropolitan) No: 3 Yes 0 Off-campus Interstate No: 20 Yes: 0
Development factors	Writers available: Readily: 5 scarcely: 0 Support services available: Readily: 5 Scarcely: 0
Course structure	Is subject: Compulsory: 10; Preferred:5; Optional: 0
Life of Syllabus	Years 5 + : 8 4 : 6 3 : 4 2 : 2 1 : 0
VTOCN enrolment Projected enrolments over next 5 years	100+ :5 70-99:4 40-69:3 10-39:2 1-9:1
Total rating	

Monitoring the development process

It is all very well to determine priorities and design programs around them, but the process does not end there. The projected program must be continually updated, to reflect changing priorities, and schedule changes due to e.g. tardy writers (or for that matter, unexpectedly speedy writers) breakdown of equipment, breakdown of staff, and so on.

To this end we have designed a system of cards which forms the basis for a manual monitoring system and which, it is hoped, will eventually lead to a computerized monitoring system. The manual system uses the card shown in Figure 2.

Each of the 220 subjects we offer has two cards—one is kept centrally with the cards for all the other subjects on a large display area; the other is kept by the VTOCN staff member responsible for the development, re-development or unaltered re-printing of that subject. This course co-ordinator leads a team consisting of a writer(s), consultant(s), curriculum authority(ies) and media expert(s). These teams are brought together for specific development projects. The course co-ordinator acts as a combination of team leader, executive officer, editor, distance education expert and all-round superhuman. The course co-ordinator keeps the subject card up to date on a unit by unit basis, so that, at any moment, the card will indicate the state of development of each unit.

Course co-ordinators' records are transferred to their corresponding cards in the central display area once a week. Here coloured pins are used to indicate the stage of development each unit has reached, so that it is possible to gain an overall visual impression and more readily to identify work which is overdue. This is obviously where a computer would come into its own, producing any sort of exception report much more quickly than a manual card system.

Jack Foks
Victorian TAFE Off-Campus Network
Australia

Figure 2: Subject Monitoring Card

Unit	Old Stock			Writer due	C.D. Edit	Writer, Consultant, Draft Type	Final C.O. Edit C.D.	P.P.	Proof and Correct	Print	New Stock		Desp.	Notes
	Hold	Discard	Clear Issue								Hold	Clear Issue		

PU _____ Subject _____ Due for release _____ Course Development _____ Groups Preferred _____
TL _____ Job cat _____ Emergency _____

Key to Certain Codes
PU - Local subject code number
TL - Local job category identifier
Course Development - Staff member responsible for development of subject
Groups - Combinations of units within Subject to be grouped together for binding

Writer Due - Agreed deadline for submission of copy by writer
C.D. Edit - Preliminary editing by course co-ordinator
Writer, Consultant, Draft Type - To-ing and fro-ing of copy within course development team
PP - Pre-production typing and graphics

Updating the Course Team
(Abstract)

Paper 70

The Télé-université provides higher education at a distance in the Canadian province of Quebec. An important part of its curriculum is two flexible socio-cultural diploma programs. To date each course has been developed by an ad hoc course team. Usually the team is disbanded when the materials are completed and another unit is responsible for delivering the course by providing regional tutorial services and assessing students. Ten years of experience have exposed weaknesses in this system, especially its difficulty in coping with the inevitable academic, instructional or practical problems which arise in any course. The locus of academic responsibility is unclear and it is not easy to find faculty to revise content and prepare exams. This problem is particularly acute when the original authors were on temporary secondment.

In 1981 a committee was struck to update and improve this system. A key recommendation is to keep the course team in being throughout the life of a course even though its dimensions and composition vary with time. Figure 1 summarizes the proposed evolution of the course team and is the basis of the paper.

Roger Bédard
Télé-université
Canada

Figure 1: Schema of the course team variations over the course lifespan with regard to Télé-université's specific needs

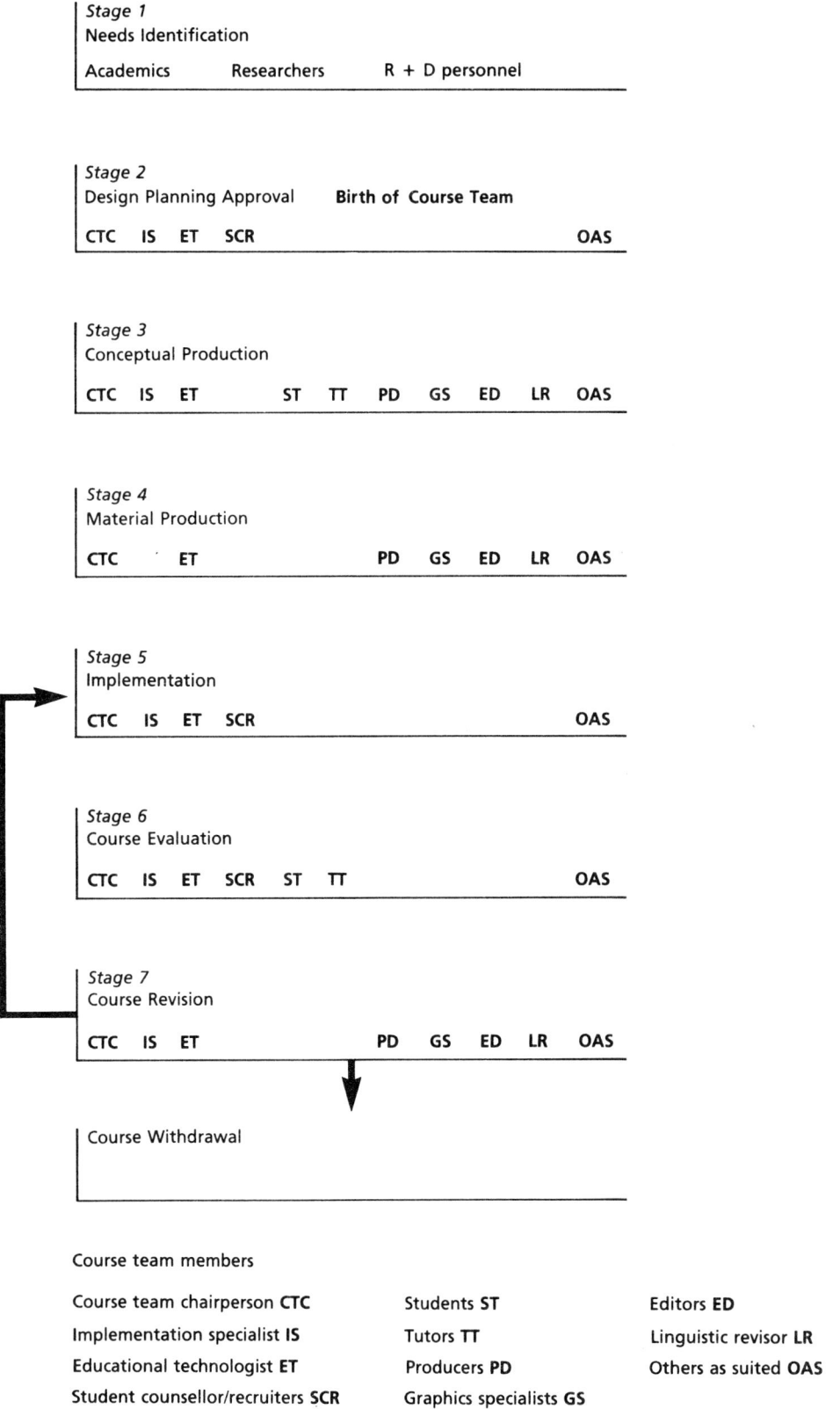

Systems Approaches in Distance Education

Organizations that adopt effective systems analysis/design strategies will succeed best in a changing environment.

Since the late 1950s the "systems approach"—variously described as systems engineering, systems synthesis, and systems analysis—has received considerable attention as an effective strategy for resolving increasingly complex social, cultural, economic, and technological problems (Engstrom, 1957; Jenkins, 1976; Schlager, 1957).

Unfortunately, most of the literature and the more spectacular public successes of systems applications have emphasized technologies such as space vehicles, military hardware and computing systems, or large-scale, profit-oriented industrial projects. As a consequence, the advantages of systems applications have been communicated in terms such as "increased economic viability", "improved competitive advantage", "improved system efficiency", "improved hardware systems" and other equally inanimate—perhaps anti-social—terms. While this growing perception of systems approaches as being necessarily mechanical and impersonal is fundamentally inaccurate, it is nevertheless strongly persistent and will markedly affect the manner in which systems approaches are used to address educational problems in the 1980s.

In recent years, declining post-secondary enrolments, eroding public confidence, inflationary cost increases and restrictive government funding have conspired to force educational institutions into new patterns of operational planning, decision-making and resource allocations. Potentially effective systems analysis strategies have been adopted by governments and educational institutions in their attempts to address these complex problems (Kaufman, 1972), but the introduction of these methodologies has been impeded by the negative connotations noted above. Heavy-handed implementation in some instances (or uninformed resistance in other cases) has accentuated those unfavorable perceptions and further restricted implementation of systems methodologies in conventional educational institutions.

An almost uniform exception to this would appear to be found in the distance education institutions which have been established in recent years. From a growing list of these institutions one can collect an impressive array of policy documents and procedural handbooks which describe course development, production, delivery and student support systems and their regulatory mechanisms. However, while these official documents describe ideal situations, the reality in many institutions is often quite different. Before examining some of those realities, it might be useful first to compare briefly a generalized systems approach described by Jenkins (1976) and a relatively standard distance education systems model such as that adopted by Athabasca University.

Jenkins uses the term "systems engineering" to encompass the four basic steps in the general systems approach: system analysis; system design; system implementation; and system operation. These four steps are further subdivided into 18 operational stages which are identified in Table 1.

The eight basic stages in the instructional systems model adopted by Athabasca University are also identified in Table 1 and the correspondence between the stages of the two models has been indicated. The Athabasca University instructional systems model was patterned on the course development planning and project control model adopted earlier by the British Open University (Lewis, 1971) and on the instructional development models described by Syracuse University (Diamond, et al, 1975), and the Télé-université in Quebec (Bélanger, 1979).

It is interesting to note from Table 1 that the general systems engineering model described by Jenkins—which can be assumed to derive from an engineering/industrial/commercial perspective—places more procedural emphasis on early market analysis, operations modelling, and systems design functions than does Athabasca University. This is not surprising given the "bottom-line" orientation of business and the "cost-effective technical performance" orientation of industrial engineering. In both situations, product orientations and both product and economic performance targets are identified early, and detailed advance planning is essential if there is to be any reasonable guarantee that those performance targets will be achieved.

In this respect, private sector distance education organizations—one of the most notable North American examples being the International Correspondence School—have probably pushed instructional systems methodologies to their qualitative and quantitative limits. These organizations do not publicise their operating methodologies for obvious competitive reasons. Members of public-sector institutions continue to wonder about "dehumanizing, profit-oriented strategies" and to raise questions about the quality of course content and the instructional procedures. In response, these private organizations have simply begun to apply their systems analysis/design procedures—with very considerable success—to the problem of providing profitable, certifiable educational programs via distance education. The certification of ICS to offer degree credit programs is perhaps the most notable example of their success, and one can predict with confidence that other successes will follow in due course. Indeed, most current thinking tends to accept that the coming introduction of high technology instructional/information systems will favour increased involvement of private enterprise in both credit and non-credit educational programming.

In contrast, in the protected environment of publicly supported education, the survival instincts which are so obviously well-honed in the business community have yet to evolve. The response of most conventional institutions to the resource crunch expressed through restricted government funding has been to cry "rape". In many instances a protectionist heritage has been confronted by the overexpansion of the affluent 1950s and 1960s, and these institutions are left with few options other than to request assistance from every quarter.

Having noted that publicly supported distance education institutions have almost universally adopted systems analogous to those of private enterprise, one might speculate that these new educa-

Table 1: A comparison between a general systems model and the Athabasca University instructional systems model

A generalized systems engineering model (adapted from Jenkins, 1976)	Athabasca University instructional systems model
1. System Analysis	1. Long-Range Institutional Planning
1.1 Define the problem	
1.2 Establish the system team	
1.3 Analyze the existing system	
1.4 Analyze the system's context	
1.5 Define the objectives for the wider system (context)	
1.6 Define the objectives for the system itself	2. Program Planning
1.7 Define overall system performance criteria	
1.8 Collect baseline data	
2. System Design	
2.1 Forecast environmental changes	
2.2 Develop models/simulations	3. Course Design
2.3 Optimize system design	
2.4 Develop control systems	
2.5 Assess system reliability	
3. System Implementation	
3.1 Proposal review/approval	
3.2 Production of intended product	4. Course Development
	5. Course Production
4. System Operation	
4.1 Initial use of product	6. Course Delivery
4.2 Evaluation of product performance	7. Course Evaluation
4.3 Modification to improve performance	8. Course Revision

tional organizations are faring better than most in the current harsh economic environment. With very few exceptions one would be wrong. Since, as was noted above, the reality of their internal operations usually bears little or no resemblance to the idealized operating systems described in their literature, neither does their performance approach the output potentials which systems methodologies in private enterprise have achieved.

One should not conclude, however, that their systems analysis and systems design have been faulty; indeed, both in their general features and in their detailed procedures, public distance education instructional systems models mirror their private enterprise counterparts. Instead, it is suggested that the difference between the productivity potential and the operational realities is a function of the internal political processes of public education institutions.

It has been stated that "educational innovations are political processes, severely political, having to do with particular personalities at particular times, doing things and exercising pressure in certain ways" (Hooper, 1977: 337). A review of the histories of most public distance education ventures will bear this out. It is clearly the case, for example, that the British Open University was established through the exercise of political power in support of a radical and largely speculative educational vision (Perry, 1976). Having been created through political will, it was initially staffed by experienced, competent, politically astute educational administrators who designed and very carefully introduced innovative systems models to address the triple challenge of curricular innovation, academic excellence and multi-media publication in a distance education environment. Their first steps involved a meticulous exploration of institutional and environmental concerns such as those identified in Table 1 under "Systems Analysis". This was followed by the establishment of baseline operating parameters (steady-state curriculum projections; course materials development and production procedures, cost guidelines and quality control strategies; and course delivery/student support system configuration)—i.e. system design. The subsequent recruitment, indoctrination and training of staff (and the acquisition of other necessary resources) very obviously proceeded on the assumption that the highly innovative plan as then conceived would be executed more or less as initially stated.

The operational (political) stance which was adopted was that the plan was valid. There being no other institutional benchmarks for comparison, who could say it was not? This stance met (and continues to meet) significant opposition since the staff of the Open University were necessarily recruited from conventional institutions where the length of debates is frequently measured in decades and rates of innovation in centuries. Nevertheless, operations monitoring systems were implemented which assessed success or failure in relation to the previously established operational criteria for the model.

Where necessary, corrective actions were directed at getting things going again in accordance with the established plans except where it was demonstrated that the plan was inadequate (as in certain early Regional and Tutorial Services arrangements) (Sewart, 1980; Keegan, 1981). Such self-regulating (cybernetic) systems are rather foreign to the world of higher education not only because of the precision they impute (a valid concern), but also because of the speed with which adaptation to dissonant feedback is expected to occur (Pratt, 1978), and within the Open University have created tensions. Despite these resistances, when all things are taken into consideration the British Open University provides a clear, relatively well documented (and perhaps unique) example of a public distance education enterprise which through the early application of systems methodologies and the subsequent exercise of political will in support of the adopted system has applied systems approaches effectively and successfully.

In comparison with the relative success at the Open University, the implementation of systems approaches by other public distance education institutions has been restrained by one of two important considerations: many institutions did not carry out a thorough environmental analysis as a basis for systems design appropriate to their own situation; and some institutions which did adopt systems methodologies were unable to sustain them in the face of opposing internal political pressures.

The systems model adopted by Athabasca University has encountered difficulties in both areas. Originally conceived as a conventional, campus-based institution in 1970, it was dissolved before it even got off the planning boards (1971), then re-created as a pilot project in course development for distance education (1972), re-designated as a distance education university (1975), and finally given legislative legitimacy (1978). In 1980 it was directed to relocate to permanent headquarters by 1984 in a small, relatively isolated northern community. Having to fight a ten-year political battle for institutional survival with a doubting, sometimes hostile government, was not conducive to long-range institutional planning. Further, the instability and high uncertainty facing staff who were drawn largely from stable conventional institutions heightened anxieties and predictably increased the resistance of many staff to innovative planning and operating procedures and unfamiliar course design, development and delivery strategies.

Although the Athabasca University instructional systems model was formally adopted in an attempt to provide stability for wavering planning and operating procedures, it was perceived by many to be an attempt to rigidify procedures, to stifle creativity and to restrict the independent exercise of professional judgement by competent academic/professional staff members. Given the unsettling environmental context in which the institution found itself and the inherited perceptions of systems approaches, staff resistance to the model was predictable.

When Bertalanffy first introduced his General Systems Theory in the late 1940s and in his subsequent writings he has consistently argued that systems theory describes a theory of organization—an analytical, integrative problem-solving strategy which is equally appropriate to philosophy and environmental conservation as it is to missile engineering and computer technology.

> This, I believe, is the ultimate precept a theory of organization can give: not a manual for dictators of any denomination more efficiently to subjugate human beings by the scientific application of Iron Laws, but a warning that the leviathan of organization must not swallow the individual without sealing its own inevitable doom.
> (Bertalanffy, 1958: 53)

Bertalanffy thus conceives of the systems approach as combining purposeful activity and rigorous analysis, with creativity in goal-setting, flexibility in problem-solving and human individuality as unifying underlying themes. However, systems approaches have not always been envisaged and implemented with those characteristics in mind.

If systems approaches are to have a future in public distance education it will be necessary for institutional leaders to be more aware of the resistant political/intellectual climate. Systems strategists must incorporate and convey Bertalanffy's concern that such approaches accomodate both purposeful, analytical activity and less empirical, human concerns, and educators must be educated as to the nature of systems approaches—their utility, their flexibility and their strengths—before they can be expected to accept them as powerful tools rather than overpowering constraints.

If systems approaches do not have a future in public distance education, one might predict that the strengths which they give to the private distance educators will enable them to begin to overshadow the public institutions in the not-too-distant future. As the requirement to marry high technology instructional/information systems with the human/social needs of individuals increases, those institutions that are able to analyze, evaluate and respond quickly and efficiently to rapidly changing circumstances will gain the support of an increasingly demanding public. It is suggested that those organizations that have adopted effective systems analysis/design strategies as their fundamental operating mode will succeed best in such an environment.

Charles R. Shobe
Athabasca University
Canada

References

Bélanger, R. et al (1979) *Un Cours a la Tele-Universite: Guide des opérations de conception et de production.* Montreal: The Télé-université.

Bertalanffy, L. von (1958) *General System Theory: Foundations, Development Applications.* New York: George Braziller.

Diamond, R.M. et al (1975) *Instructional Development for Individualized Learning in Higher Education.* Englewood Cliffs, N.J.: Educational Technology Publications.

Engstrom, E.W. (1957). Systems engineering--a growing concept. *Electrical Engineering,* 76.

Hooper, R. (1977) Evaluation Methodology (Animateurs). In *Evaluating Educational Television and Radio.* Bates, T. and Robinson, J. (eds.) Milton Keynes: The Open University Press.

Jenkins, G.M. (1976) The Systems Approach. Chapter 4 in *Systems Behavior.* Beishon, J. and Peters, G. (eds.) London: Harper and Row.

Kaufman, R.A. (1972) *Educational System Planning.* Englewood Cliffs, N.J.: Prentice-Hall.

Keegan, D.J. (1981) The Regional Tutorial Services of the Open University: A Case Study. *Ziff Papiere 36.* Hagen: Fernuniversität.

Lewis, B.N. (1971) Course production at the Open University II: activities and activity networks. *British Journal of Educational Technology,* 2.

Perry, W. (1976) *The Open University.* Milton Keynes: The Open University Press.

Pratt, D. (1978) Cybernetic Principles in the Design of Instruction. Paper presented to the Annual Meeting of the American Educational Research Association, Toronto.

Schlager, K.J. (1957) Organization for effective systems engineering. *Problems and Practices in Engineering Management, American Management Association.* Special Report 224.

Sewart, D. (1980) Creating an information base for an individualized support system in distance education. *Distance Education,* 1.

Responding to Economic Austerity: Can Economic Models of Distance Teaching Help Us?

In reacting to a harsher economic climate the real need is to apply the techniques and approaches of financial management.

Existing economic models of distance teaching systems

A wealth of cost studies of individual distance teaching systems exist, as the bibliography in Unesco (1977: 46-63) shows. An objective of many of these cost analyses was to establish cost functions to identify the main generators of cost within the systems, to relate existing costs to some measure of output, and to study how costs change as key output variables change. Thanks to these studies the general cost structure of distance teaching systems (DTS) is well understood.

In conventional teaching systems the normal measure of output is student related (student numbers, student hours, etc.). DTS incur significant expenses in the preparation of teaching materials (print, television and radio programmes, and other media) and in the establishment of administrative systems (particularly if these are computer based). Moreover, many of the costs of designing and producing a multi-media course or of designing a student administrative system will be incurred before there are any students in the system. Within limits some of the costs (but not all) will be incurred irrespective of the number of students in the system. There are limits because the total number of students to be catered for will determine the overall strategy adopted towards the provision of administrative services.

Course materials themselves represent a significant output of DTS. The absolute costs incurred in their development and production is dependent on the variety of materials (courses) being prepared, the choice of media and, particularly in the case of audio-visual media, the means of distribution or transmission. From the literature Eicher (1978: 8-9) was able to draw certain conclusions about the level of costs incurred in systems using different media and media distribution systems.

The simplest economic models of DTS are expressed in the form

$TC = F + VN$

where TC is the total cost, F is the fixed cost of the system, V is the variable cost per unit of output, and N is the unit of output (normally students, student hours, etc.). More complex models attempt to reflect the cost implications of a number of outputs. Wagner (1977: 367) used a simple equation with two variables to project costs in the British Open University:

$C = a + bx + cy$

where C is the total recurrent expenditure, a are fixed costs, x and y are the number of courses and the number of undergraduate students, and b and c are the unit costs per course and student and are determined for any particular year by dividing the total costs allocated to students and courses by actual student and course numbers in that year. Jamison, Klees and Wells (1978: 93-97) developed a series of generalised cost functions for educational broadcasting systems. Snowden and Daniel (1980: 81) developed a more sophisticated model for forecasting costs in Athabasca University, in which they first identified costs related to three output variables (students, courses in development and courses in delivery) and then took account of the fact that in a developing institution overhead costs were unlikely to be absolutely fixed but rather a fixed proportion of total costs. Rumble (1980, 1981) has developed cost functions for two distance teaching universities which reflect various measures of output (students, courses, broadcasting materials, local academic centres), and the growth of expenditure on overheads in the development period, and the increasing numbers of offices required to coordinate an expanding academic programme.

Uses and limitations of existing economic models of DTS

Such economic models have their uses. One can project global financial requirements given changes in the planned level of output of any of the variables taken into account in the particular model that is being manipulated. Such models are therefore useful both within the institution as broad indicators of likely financial requirements given various levels of future activity, and in discussions with external funding agencies. Their simplicity is a virtue. They are readily understandable both within and outside an institution. They are useful as a means of evaluating major future policy alternatives (as, for example, Snowden and Daniel [1980: 83-86] demonstrate in relation to Athabasca University). They are also useful because they can be rapidly adapted to demonstrate the effect of expansion on average student costs.

Unfortunately, such models have a number of limitations:

- They fail to specify the fundamental variables which affect cost in sufficient detail to be of practical value to those who have to prepare an operating budget. This failure led Rumble, Neil and Tout (1981) to try to identify a whole series of functionally based generalized cost functions formulated in sufficient detail to be of use to those drawing up budgets in multi-media DTS. However, their findings need to be related to academic programmes and cost centres before they can be of practical use within specific institutions.

- They are based on existing expenditure patterns and do not measure cost-efficiency. They cannot help decide how the same level of output (in qualitative and quantitative terms) could be achieved for a smaller level of financial input.

- While they indicate in broad terms the cost involved given a particular level of *future* expansion, their use in periods in financial contraction is dependent on management's willingness to question existing expenditure levels and accept these as variable rather than fixed.

- They do not tell us whether our use of resources is cost-effective. For example, in a multi-media system, they will not show whether the same quality of output of students could be achieved by dropping one of the media.

The more complex cost functions developed by Rumble, Neil and Tout (1981: 250-269), while of greater use in drawing up budgets, are nevertheless abstractions which involve simplifications. By making explicit the relationships between inputs (for example, staff time and equipment), their costs, their production rates and the level of output over time, such cost functions can play a part in planning and budgeting. They can, for example, indicate the financial implications of increasing staff productivity, changing the ratio of junior to senior staff, increasing the number of years during which material will be used prior to remake, and so on.

Cost-cutting in response to budget cuts

The usefulness of budgetary models is thus limited. At best they make explicit the fundamental variables in the budgetary process. At the institutional level the task is to define the total level of resources available in a given year and the constraints to be applied to the system. These constraints may be regulations regarding the use of resources (e.g. the extent to which revenue can be used for capital projects) or targets (e.g. the admission of x new students resulting in a total student population of y). The institution may also establish a target of results. At the departmental level this is likely to be "break-even". At the outset, the managers (department heads) must agree (sign off) their budget as reasonable within the context of given targets. There must be a dialogue between the managers responsible for implementing a plan and those responsible for setting objectives or targets. The managers, having agreed on their allocation as acceptable, must work to budget and be held responsible if there is significant variance (overspending or underspending). However, there must be reasonable and believable financial information if managers are going to operate a system in which budgetary control is exercised. Only if such information exists can the manager have confidence in his ability to project his requirements and then control expenditure.

When an institution has to cut costs it must return to more basic principles of financial management. These are:

- Last year is not relevant for this year (nor this year for next year). Incrementalism, in which the baseline remains unchallenged, is only valid if present activities are to continue unchanged. It does not answer the fundamental question 'should activity z continue?' To achieve savings everything must go into the pot and budget-building must start from scratch. This is the essence of zero-based budgeting.

- While the budget should identify sums that have already been committed (e.g. a continuation of existing staffing costs to termination of contract), this does not necessarily cover unknown but likely future commitments (e.g. a 7% increase in all salaries from the salary review date), nor does it take into account what has to be done in order to achieve a given set of objectives.

- Setting cash limits (in which cash is held to be equivalent to revenue) does not control expenditure because payments by debtors or to creditors can be manipulated, distorting the financial situation greatly. Control, to be effective, must be exercised over the cost-inducing activities themselves, not through the manipulation of cash flows.

- Educational institutions are often large and have a tendency to sub-optimize. The aim is to monitor significant exceptions to plan and to become involved (as controller) only when variance from plan is unacceptable at the institutional level. However, issuing a variance report does not control expenditure unless the individual manager's behaviour changes.

- The first step in modifying behaviour is the identification of those key individuals who exercise responsibility. This can be very difficult, particularly in academic institutions where authority and responsibility is ill-defined. Change (including cost-cutting) can only be effected through people. It is no good getting a budget signed off by someone (whatever his formal position) who cannot influence the outcome.

- Cutting individual budgets should begin immediately. Delay does not help. The aim should be: "destruct test plus one." Budgets should be agreed on the assumption that the budget holder has the minimum necessary to achieve targets. Fat should be taken out, if necessary over a number of years, until the budget is too tight for the manager to achieve his targets without overspending. Only then should a little bit be added.

- Planning and management must be responsive to financial uncertainty. It is generally easier to establish a project and then stop it than to spend late savings at the end of the financial year. In institutions where projects can be delayed, it is probably sensible to aim to overspend a bit, and then cut back to a contingency plan if necessary.

Formula-based budgeting tends to be incremental in its approach. Imposed from above, it denies the manager his role in drawing up, agreeing and operating the budget he has to work to. Accepted without question, it leaves untouched the fat that is in the system, reinforces sub-optimization, and may result in unspent balances at year-end. On the other hand, if variable costs are accepted as such in the contexts of both expansion and contraction positive use can be made of financial models. They must specify the variables involved in sufficient detail to identify them by function, academic programme and cost centre, as required.

Conclusions

Economic models and cost functions are no real substitute for effective financial management which places responsibility for cost control and cost reduction on the individual manager. In reacting to a harsher economic climate, the real need is to apply the techniques and approaches of financial management to distance teaching systems.

Greville Rumble
Open University
United Kingdom

References

Eicher, J.C. (1978) Quelques réflexions sur l'analyse économique des moyens modernes d'enseignement. Paper presented to the International Conference on Economic Analysis for Educational Technology Decisions. University of Dijon, Institut de Recherche sur l'Economie de l'Education, 19-23 June 1978.

Jamison, D.T. Klees, S.J. and Wells, S.J. (1978) *The Costs of Educational Media: Guidelines for Planning and Evaluation*. Beverley Hills and London: Sage Publications.

Rumble, G. (1980) The cost analysis of distance teaching. Venezuela's Universidad Nacional Abierta. (mimeo)

Rumble, G. (1981) The cost analysis of distance teaching. Costa Rica's Universidad Estatal a Distancia. *Higher Education*, 10. (forthcoming)

Rumble, G. Neil, M.W. and Tout, A. (1981) Budgetary and resource forecasting. In Kaye, A. and Rumble, G. (1981) *Distance Teaching for Higher and Adult Education*. London: Croom Helm.

Snowden, B.L. and Daniel, J.S. (1980) The economics and management of small post-secondary distance education systems. *Distance Education*, 1,1, 68-91.

Unesco (1977) *The Economics of New Educational Media*. Paris: Unesco.

Wagner, L. (1977) The economics of the Open University revisited. *Higher Education*, 6, 359-81.

The Administrator's Task: Conventional and Distance Education Compared

(Abstract)

Small but representative groups of administrators in distance education and campus institutions were surveyed in order to find how different were their main tasks. Some tasks are specific to each type of system while others are found in both. Tasks were categorized according to the three traditional functions of universities (teaching, research and public service) and the five administrative functions (planning, organization, leadership, coordination and evaluation). The survey asked administrators to assess their tasks in terms of characteristics such as frequency, difficulty and autonomy of execution.

The results of the survey are used to outline an administrative model for distance education.

Pierre DeCelles / Clément Marquis
Télé-université
Canada

Paper 74

Standards for Independent Study: The American Experience in Higher Education

The NUCEA standards help to ensure that university correspondence courses are at least as good as the classroom equivalent.

Why standards?

The use of standards for independent study programs in post-secondary or higher education in the United States is generally for two purposes—self-study and evaluation by outsiders. Self-study is an evaluation of one's own program to identify strengths and weaknesses and indicate where changes and improvements are needed. Evaluation by outsiders is more complex because it introduces the concept of voluntary accreditation, a specifically American practice.

Accreditation in the USA

Accreditation is a combined process of self-study and outside evaluation conducted in order to ensure that a particular set of minimal standards is being met. The result of this assessment is made available to the public. Although accreditation for educational institutions is voluntary, it does provide these institutions with certain advantages, such as the availability of government aid for their students and the acceptance of their credits and degrees by other institutions and by employers.

In the correspondence study area there are two main sources of accreditation—The National Home Study Council, which evaluates mostly non-credit correspondence study programs in non-collegiate institutions, and the various regional accrediting associations which are responsible for evaluating entire degree-granting institutions (colleges or universities) in particular geographical regions. Although these regional accrediting associations do not look at correspondence study as a separate program, they do review all of the ways in which college credit courses are offered by a particular institution—which includes correspondence study.

Before discussing the standards for correspondence study in collegiate institutions it will be helpful to review the pattern of higher education in America. This may explain why there are no universal standards for higher education, including what should be offered as part of an undergraduate degree program or what a credit course should include. It will also explain why the various accrediting associations have slightly different sets of standards and why there are no nationally accepted standards for correspondence study programs in colleges and universities.

The federal constitution of the United States makes no specific provision for education. Therefore, the individual states have assumed a primary responsibility for this function. Without the direct control of a Ministry of Education, our natural inclination as a nation has been to permit and encourage the growth of a large and diffuse system of higher education. Throughout the history of higher education efforts have been made, with varying degrees of success, to bring some sort of order out of this chaos—to develop some common principles and practices so that degrees and credits will have enough comparability to be used as educational currency. Therefore, by general consensus, a degree and the credits that make up a degree program are based on a mutual understanding that provides some commonality throughout higher education. There are, however, no specific standards to which all institutions must subscribe.

As a result of this considerable diversity, the standards for independent or correspondence study serve only as suggested guidelines for institutions having correspondence study programs. The general tenor of the guidelines is to help ensure that the courses offered for college credit through the correspondence study program are comparable in scope and quality to credit courses offered in the traditional classroom mode. The assumption is that if certain common procedures are followed, quality will result. Thus, these independent study standards, like almost all standards developed for higher education, are based on the process, not the results, of an educational offering. That is, if the right components are present, the educational results are more or less assured. Little has been done to find acceptable ways of developing standards based on educational outcomes.

Guidelines of the NUCEA

The most helpful standards for correspondence study in collegiate institutions are those developed by the National University Continuing Education Association (NUCEA). These were developed in order to assist colleges, universities, and accrediting associations in evaluating independent or correspondence study programs, as well as serving as criteria for membership in the Association. They are guidelines for conducting and improving the quality of programs which also facilitate internal and external program evaluation. They are standards toward which correspondence or independent study programs should strive. They are broad enough to be applicable to all collegiate correspondence study operations regardless of size and scope, yet specific enough to be used in a meaningful evaluation of any program.

The areas covered by these standards include *philosophy, mission, administration, staff, faculty, instruction, services, research,* and *evaluation,* (i.e. the components of any correspondence study program). How correspondence study units meet the standards depends on the particular circumstances and orientation of their institutions.

The following is a broad overview of the standards as developed by the National University Continuing Education Association (National University Continuing Education Association, 1978). Detailed information on the standards and suggestions for their use in an evaluation can be had by contacting the Association's headquarters in Washington, D.C.

Philosophy—The correspondence study program should be operated in accordance with a basic philosophy that recognizes both the right of individuals to improve themselves through education and the importance of providing educational opportunities for all.

Mission—The correspondence study program should be conducted in accordance with the mission of the institution. There should be policies and regulations supporting both the mission and the objectives of the correspondence study program.

Administration—The program should be directed by an administrator who has both authority and responsibility for the program.

Staff—The size and expertise of the staff should be adequate for carrying out the functions and there should be performance reviews, adequate compensation and recognition, and in-service training opportunities.

Faculty—All instructors should have demonstrated competence in the subject they teach and a sympathetic understanding of the correspondence study method of instruction. Instructors of college level courses who are not members of the institution's regular faculty should meet the same standards as regular faculty and be approved by the academic departments whose courses they teach.

Instruction—These are presented in more detail because instruction is the core of any program.

1. Instruction should be related to the objectives of each course, to the unique needs of the students, and to general institutional standards of quality. Maintaining such standards should be the joint responsibility of the academic department and the correspondence study unit.

2. The quality of the instruction should be fully consistent with that maintained in the institution, and the content of a correspondence study course offered for academic credit should be comparable in scope and depth to that of the equivalent course taught in residence.

3. When instructional resources such as books, recordings, and appropriate supplementary materials are required, provision should be made for the student to have ready access to these materials.

4. Course developers should be provided with guidelines, directions, and assistance which encourage creativity and excellence and help maintain consistently high standards for all correspondence study offerings.

5. There should be definite criteria for determining courses to be included in the correspondence study program as well as for a continuous reappraisal of all offerings.

6. Assignments should be evaluated and returned to students within a stated time and with appropriate comments.

7. Special attention should be given to motivating students and assisting students who are having difficulties.

8. Examinations given during and/or at the conclusion of credit courses should be proctored under conditions clearly stated by the correspondence study unit. All possible safeguards must be taken to maintain the integrity of examinations.

Services—Services to students should include information on library and other resources, special resources, counseling and advisement, flexible scheduling of examinations, and special arrangements to meet unusual individual needs, when possible. Complete and secure student records must be kept, the fee structure and refund policy should be fair and well publicized, and all informational and promotional publications should be truthful, clear, and precise.

Research and Evaluation—There should be a planned and ongoing research effort which evaluates and improves the correspondence study program and which includes student input.

From such standards detailed procedures can be developed that will help to assure the higher education community and the public that credits earned through correspondence study will be of at least comparable quality to credits earned in a classroom at the same institution. Furthermore, because of the more individualized approach to learning and the greater emphasis on clarity of presentation, it may be that the educational quality of many correspondence study courses exceeds that of their classroom counterparts.

Susan S. Burcaw
University of California
United States

References

National University Continuing Education Association, Division of Independent Study (1978) *Standards*. One Dupont Circle, Washington, D.C. 20036.

Paper 75

Accreditation: A Workable Option

Accreditation based on peer evaluation is practical and effective.

Introduction

National education systems tend to follow either the French model of a centralized ministry of education or the British system of external examinations to control the quality of education. In every country some variation or combination of the ministry of education or external examination approach has been developed. The one major exception has been the United States. Starting from a belief in the need for a balance of political powers with decentralized authority the United States has developed for educational governance a shifting, dynamic, sometimes uneasy, sharing of authority between the states, the federal government, and voluntary control through accreditation by educators. The concept of accreditation is a product of the American environment and its story is a history of struggles for control and influence over academic standards. Accreditation grew out of a fear of over-centralized government and through the years has counterbalanced state and federal government attempts at increased control. Three entities—the federal government, state departments of education, and voluntary accrediting associations—are frequently referred to as the *triad*. The triad often seems to be an area of combat rather than cooperation but it is successful if it helps to maintain a balance.

Accreditation is the effort of voluntary associations of schools and educators to maintain quality in American education. The term *eligibility* is central to the federal government's interest in education. Since the federal government pours tax monies into schools it has the right to ensure the money goes for its intended purposes in schools eligible to receive it. The third corner of the triad—the state departments of education—use the term *approval* and are concerned that the school is complying with whatever state regulations have been issued. The entire system is confusing, time consuming, controversial, and is probably very much worth all the trouble. While educators sometimes fuss, fume, and fret about the accreditation processes, American school people at all levels seems to prefer accreditation to other systems.

Voluntary accreditation goes back about 200 years to when the University of the State of New York (New York Board of Regents) was required by state law to evaluate the functioning of each college in New York. Late in the 19th century a deep concern developed among American educators that high school students were not being prepared very well for college. Efforts to identify those high schools doing the best job led to the formation of associations of schools. At the turn of this century accreditation began in earnest. In a few years criteria and standards for judging the quality of the schools began to appear. Accrediting associations have developed in several different directions with frequent overlap. There are regional associations that accredit entire institutions in a particular area. There are large numbers of professional associations that accredit schools, and departments training specialists such as physicians, lawyers, architects and ministers. There are nationwide institutional agencies that accredit vocational, trade schools, business schools, and, of course, correspondence schools. A dozen accrediting agencies could be active on a university campus.

Most accrediting associations follow a common pattern. The school or academic department is required to do a careful self-study and produce a self-evaluation report (SER). A team of professional peers then visits the organization, reviews the SER, checks factual information and assesses in a general manner how effectively the educational process is functioning. This team's report is submitted to an accreditation commission which may approve accreditation status, disapprove, remove from accreditation, or put the institution on some kind of probationary status. Accreditation is usually for a specific period of time and accrediting bodies have the right to review the status of the school at any time. A state of "dynamic tension" (meaning a constant struggle over turf) now exists in the field of accreditation. Recently the federal Department of Education began to expand aggressively into controlling and making decisions about the quality of American education. The educational establishment reacted vigorously and rather successfully to this perceived threat to voluntary accreditation.

However, more basic than the struggle over turf is the insistent and still unanswered question—What is a college? Behind it is the eternal struggle between academicians concerned with quality liberal education and the huge world of professional and vocational schools and teachers preparing students to earn a living. Much of the friction in American education revolves around "non-traditional" education including off-campus classes, independent study, weekend courses, special adult degrees, non-credit courses, and a number of degrees that include life experience and work credit toward graduation. Correspondence education is very often classed as non-traditional although it is largely a very traditional activity.

Unless the present trend in America toward less federal control changes, the future probably will see a strengthening of state and voluntary accreditation and a reduction of both federal control and federal tax money.

In an era of declining enrolments, with both public and non-public schools competing for enrolments, the student has an effective voice simply by being able to choose his school. On this basis the private correspondence schools, and to a degree the university-based correspondence schools, have a reasonably bright future in the United States. In a tightening economy correspondence can complete effectively since it tends to be less expensive than on-campus schooling.

Correspondence school accreditation

The independent study division (the correspondence units) of the colleges and universities in the United States are accredited along with the rest of their university by regional accrediting associations. The private, independent, or proprietary correspondence schools may be accredited through the National Home Study Council. The NHSC is recognized both by other accrediting bodies and the federal government as the organization which accredits such correspondence schools. It was organized in 1926 through a cooperative effort of the Carnegie Corporation of New York and the National Better Business Bureau. The NHSC began essentially as a trade association resulting from a study of correspondence education by Dr. John Noffsinger. He found an estimated one million correspondence students in 1926 in the United States. Some of the schools he investigated were ethical; some were not. His recommendation that an association be formed to improve the home study industry and to improve the public image of correspondence education became a reality on November 1, 1926 with Noffsinger as the first executive director. The Accrediting Commission of the National Home Study Council was established in 1955 and 1959 was listed by the U.S. Commissioner of Education as a nationally recognized accrediting agency. The National Home Study Council is a charter member (1975) of the Commission on Post Secondary Accreditation (COPA) which is the umbrella organization of all the recognized accrediting bodies in America.

Correspondence education in the United States began in the late 1800s with Thomas Foster, editor of the *Mining Herald* of Pennsylvania, who developed an independent study course on mining safety based on newspaper columns. A school charter from the State of Pennsylvania to Foster allowed the establishment of what has become the grandfather of both the International Correspondence Schools of Scranton, Pennsylvania and American correspondence education generally. Michael Lambert, Associate Director of NHSC, estimates that in 1981 there were approximately two million active correspondence students in the United States, and an educated guess places at between 55 and 60 million the number of Americans who have studied by correspondence since 1900. The 1981 figures break down to 600,000 correspondence students in private schools; 600,000 in the military; 250,000 studying with universities and colleges; and the rest in both accredited and non-accredited Bible schools or miscellaneous types of schools that are non-accredited. The federal government is by far the largest supplier of correspondence instruction in the United States. Probably half of the total correspondence students study with some organization of the government such as the Air Force, Marine Corps, Coast Guard, Army, Navy, U.S. Office of Personnel Management, Agriculture Department, and a number of other government departments.

Over the past 25 years the Accrediting Commission of the National Home Study Council has developed and refined its evaluative techniques and instruments until it now commands considerable respect in the accrediting community. The NHSC SER asks the school to produce concise and factual answers to a series of questions (samples of some questions follow) that cover the following areas of operation:

Educational objectives

Are they clearly defined and stated?

Are they reasonably attainable?

Are they used in the operation of the school?

Do the school and its courses meet its stated objectives?

Paper 75

Educational materials

How effective, comprehensive, up-to-date are they?

Details such as reading levels, illustrations, study kits, etc. are analyzed.

Educational services

How effectively does the school operate?

How quickly, for example, are examinations handled and returned?

How are students motivated?

Student services

Do students really get what they pay for?

How effectively are students helped with problem areas?

Student success and satisfaction

Samplings of student evaluations are made in each course offered the school, and completion rates are analyzed.

Qualifications of faculty

Do the teachers have the experience and requisite training to do the job effectively?

Admission practices and enrolment agreements

Are they fair to the student and to the school?

Advertising and promotion

Basically the Accrediting Commission wants to know if the school is honest in its advertising.

Financial responsibility

Is the school financially sound?

If the school were suddenly to close, would the students currently enrolled be taken care of appropriately?

Tuition policies

Is the tuition reasonable for the education provided?

Is there a fair refund policy?

Plant and equipment

Is the school plant well organized and a safe place to work?

Are records kept properly and with a reasonable degree of safety?

Research and self-improvement

Does the school actively work toward improving itself and its product?

Over the years a large number of correspondence educators have worked through the self-evaluation reports and have benefited both from the self-study and the subsequent review by a visiting team.

The experience of the National Home Study Council strongly suggests that associations of correspondence schools designed to improve the quality of home study and enhance the public image of correspondence education are useful, practical, and effective. Some form of peer evaluation such as accreditation enhances professional growth and institutional effectiveness.

D.W. Holbrook
Home Study Institute
United States

Paper 76

How Does the Public See Us?

The public sees a role for correspondence education although the level of awareness varies among different groups.

Introduction: description of survey and questionnaire

In December 1980 I was asked to prepare a paper on this topic. I decided to ask the public through a questionnaire mailed to 12 categories of people (see questionnaire and Table 1).

The Questionnaire

1. Have you ever studied a correspondence course? .... YES/NO

2. Amoung your relations and immediate circle of friends have any, to your knowledge (don't ask them!) studied by correspondence? .... YES/NO

3. If you know nothing about correspondence study, please place a tick here- ☐
Then answer only such questions as are relevant for you and still return the questionnaire

4. Have advertisements for correspondence courses caught your eye? .... YES/NO

5. If YES - Have they or would they induce you, given an educational need, to enquire for details? .... YES/NO

6. To describe your impression of correspondence colleges please tick one of the following five lines-
   (a) They are all in it for the money regardless of the student .... ☐
   (b) Most colleges provide only a mediocre service .... ☐
   (c) They vary between providing a mediocre and a good service .... ☐
   (d) Most colleges provide a good service .... ☐
   (e) They all provide excellent service to their students .... ☐

7. Correspondence study is variously termed - (a) home study .... ——
   (b) extension study .... ——
   (c) distance education .... ——
   (d) open learning .... ——
   (e) correspondence education .... ——

   Which term is most likely to encourage a student to pursue studies by correspondence? Indicate your order of preference by numbers after each of the above 5 terms (1 = most likely; 5 = least likely).

8. Did you know that most United Kingdom correspondence colleges are accredited (i.e. inspected and officially approved)? .... YES/NO

9. If YES do you set store by such accreditation in the UK or in your own country (if similar inspection exists)? .... YES/NO

10. Do you regard correspondence study as a necessary part of the education system in modern society? .... YES/NO

11. Would you accept that there are situations in which teaching by correspondence is preferable to teaching by word of mouth? .... YES/NO

12. Do you regard correspondence study as a method of study that is (tick one) -
    (a) A first class way of study .... ☐
    (b) Educationally equal to evening, or part-time, classes .... ☐
    (c) Providing only a second chance for those who can't study elsewhere .... ☐
    (d) A means to be used only in the last resort .... ☐

13. Do you believe the student who qualified by correspondence education while working (as opposed to full time study at a university or polytechnic) is - (a) better equipped .... ☐
    (b) equally equipped ..... ☐
    (c) less equipped .... ☐
    to serve his employer (tick one of the three).

14. In the next few lines please make, if you wish, any general comment about correspondence college or correspondence education.

It is up to you whether you give below your name and address or remain anonymous, but please be so good as to state here your profession or occupation

Name _____ Profession or occupation _____

Table 1: The questionnaire mailing list and response details

Categories Mailed	Numbers Sent	Numbers Returned	Percentage Returned
(1) Students of UK Accredited Correspondence Colleges	1850	378	20.4
(2) Secretaries of Professional Institutes and of General Certificate of Education Boards	102	27	26.5
(3) Random Names from London Telephone Directory	321	18	5.6
(4) Students who enquired but did not enrol for courses of The Rapid Results College	200	21	10.5
(5) Personnel Officers of large companies	731	118	16.1
(6) Bank Managers	211	43	20.4
(7) Building Society Branch Managers	101	22	21.8
(8) Senior Local Authority Officers	110	25	22.7
(9) Education Correspondents of the media (press & TV)	67	11	16.4
(10) Principals of Colleges of Further Education	123	40	32.5
(11) Ministers of Education in the Commonwealth	36	3	8.3
(12) Students of English-speaking members of ICCE	2875	369	12.8
Totals	6727	1075	16.0

The addresses of (2) to (10) are all within the UK

The response

Although a response rate of 16% might appear low, a low rate was expected because:

- a postal questionnaire is easily ignored
- many approached would have matters of greater interest to attend to
- some questionnaires may have gone to out-of-date addresses.

Survey results

i. Overall response

The Total Column of Table 2 gives full details of the overall response. I comment on the main features of these results in question number order.

1. 77% of respondents had studied by correspondence. This high percentage reflects the greater interest in the survey shown by those with prior acquaintance with correspondence courses.

2. 66% knew friends or relations who had studied by correspondence.

3. 7% of respondents claimed to know nothing about correspondence study.

4. 77% of the respondents said they were familiar with advertisements of correspondence colleges.

5. 71% of *all* respondents agreed that given an educational need the advertisements would stimulate them to enquire for course details. This implies that 92% of *those familiar with the advertisements* would enquire for course details given an educational need, suggesting that those who are aware of correspondence education have a positive attitude towards it.

6. 2% of responses took the view that correspondence colleges were just in it for the money.
5% believed that colleges provided a mediocre service only.
36% suggested that the service varied between mediocre and good.
40% regarded the service provided by colleges as good.
10% regarded it as excellent.
Thus 50% of all responses indicated service was good or above.

7. The field in which ICCE members work is variously termed and there is a continuing debate about changing or retaining the name of the Council. With this background it was felt important to include a question asking respondents to indicate which term was most likely to encourage a student to pursue studies by correspondence. The question was phrased so that each respondent had to

Table 2: The overall response

Question Number	Answer Category	Total Column	A	B	C
		1075	829	171	75
1	Yes	77	100	-	-
	No	23	-	100	100
2	Yes	66	70	57	39
	No	33	29	43	57
	X*	1	1	0	4
3		7	-	-	100
4	Yes	77	78	77	64
	No	21	21	20	31
	X	2	1	3	5
5	Yes	71	73	64	55
	No	8	7	13	14
	X	21	2	23	31
6	a	2	1	2	4
	b	5	4	4	12
	c	36	38	39	17
	d	40	42	40	20
	e	10	10	9	9
	X	7	5	6	38
7	a	2.02	2.04	1.99	1.92
	b	3.12	3.10	3.21	3.08
	c	4.04	4.05	3.97	4.04
	d	3.52	3.55	3.44	3.37
	e	2.30	2.26	2.39	2.59
	X	170	121	23	26
8	Yes	38	38	47	19
	No	61	61	52	79
	X	1	1	1	2
9	Yes	38	39	43	20
	No	10	10	10	8
	X	52	51	47	72
10	Yes	86	90	80	67
	No	12	10	16	27
	X	2	0	4	6
11	Yes	72	74	64	71
	No	26	25	32	24
	X	2	1	4	5
12	a	18	20	11	12
	b	38	40	37	28
	c	33	31	36	43
	d	7	6	10	13
	X	4	3	6	4
13	a	26	28	18	20
	b	56	57	60	44
	c	15	13	17	31
	X	3	2	5	5
14	C*	65	70	51	47
	R*	34	30	20	29

Column **A** is responses from those who had studied by correspondence

Column **B** is responses from those who had not studied by correspondence

Column **C** is responses from those with no knowledge of correspondence education

Notes

All figures are percentages except for
- the first line and 7X, which are numbers
- 7 a-e, which give average votes

*X = Unclassified
*C = General comment made
*R = Copy of Research Report requested

give an order of preference for the five terms. 170 replies without a clear order of preference could not be analysed. 905 respondents had clearly put one against their first choice, two against the second and so on. Thus each effectively cast 15 votes, and the term with the least votes is the most preferred. The result of the count is:

	Total Votes	Average Vote (Total ÷ 905)
Home Study	1833	2.03
Correspondence Education	2080	2.30
Open Learning	2820	3.12
Extention Study	3185	3.52
Distance Education	3657	4.04
		15.01

Thus 'Home Study' is most popular with 'Correspondence Education' coming in a close second. 'Distance Education' was the least liked.

8 38% knew that UK correspondence colleges are accredited—a disappointingly low percentage, even allowing that over a third of the responses came from overseas.

9 This question was to be answered only by those who were aware of accreditation and, as 38% set store by accreditation, the answer seems to indicate that those who know about accreditation were satisfied with it.

10 86% regarded correspondence study as a necessary part of the education system in modern society.

11 72% accepted that there are situations in which teaching by correspondence is preferable to teaching by word of mouth.

12 18% regarded correspondence study as a first class way of study.
38% took the view that it was educationally equal to evening or part-time classes.
33% regarded it as providing only a second chance for those who cannot study elsewhere.
7% saw it as a means of study to be used only in the last resort.

13 26% reckon that the student qualifying by correspondence education while working is better equipped than the student studying full time at university or polytechnic.
56% reckon that the CE student is equally equipped.
15% regard him as less equipped.

14 65% took the trouble to enter general comments in their questionnaire.

ii. **Comparison of responses from those who had studied by correspondence and those who had not**

In Table 2 we can sub-divide the overall responses into those who:

A had studied by CE

B had not studied by CE

C had no knowledge of CE.

(**A, B, C** are now used to identify the three groups.)

While the general pattern of response varies little, some groups do throw up a different emphasis in certain questions.

2 **A** had more friends and relations who had studied by CE.

4 As 20% of **A** were not familiar with advertisements, did they become CE students on recommendation?

6 Of **A** 52% rated service good or above. Was it from lack of knowledge or from prejudice that only 29% of **C** rated it so highly?

7 For the terms used to encourage students to use our field of study, the pattern of responses in the groups is constant. With **A** 'Correspondence Education' increases its popularity, but does not overtake 'Home Study'.

8 **B** are almost entirely UK respondents, so their greater, but still not sufficient, knowledge of accreditation is explained.

10 With **A** the proportion who regard CE as a necessary part of the education system in modern society increases to as high as 90%.

11
12 ⎫ Not surprisingly the percentages from **A** improve in favour of CE.
13 ⎭

iii. **Comparison of responses from the different categories of the mailing list**

  - see Table 3

Numbers of responses in some categories are small and must be interpreted with caution. The interesting features of Table 3 for each question are:

2 The high percentage of Local Authority Officers (8) with friends and relations who have studied by CE probably indicates that many study for their profession by correspondence.

4 Several categories have a greater awareness of advertisements, most noticeably the Secretaries of Examining Bodies (2).

5 (2) would also respond well to CE advertisements, but (3) Random Names and (10) Principals of CFEs show above average negative ratings (25% and 20%).

6 Adding the good and the excellent ratings for service, gives the following 'league table':

(12) Students of ICCE members 59%
 (4) Enquirers who did not enrol 57%
 (1) Students of UK accredited colleges 55%
 (8) Senior Local Authority Officers 53%
      (Overall mean point) ....(52%)
 (6) Bank Managers 49%
 (5) Personnel Officers 36%
 (2) Secretaries of Professional Institutes
      & GCE Boards 34%
 (7) Building Society Branch Managers 28%
 (3) Random Names 25%
(10) Principals of Colleges of Further Education ..24%

Table 3: Responses from those who had studied by correspondence
(broken down into category of respondent as per the questionnaire mailing list, Table 1)

Question Number	Answer Category	Total Column	(1)	(2)	(3)	(4)	(5)	(6)	(7)	(8)	(9)	(10)	(11)	(12)
		829	332	12	8	14	77	33	18	17	2	25	2	289
1	Yes	100	100	100	100	100	100	100	100	100	100	100	100	100
	No	-	-	-	-	-	-	-	-	-	-	-	-	-
2	Yes	70	63	50	50	64	79	70	72	94	50	68	100	75
	No	29	36	50	50	36	20	30	28	6	50	28	0	24
	X*	1	1	0	0	0	1	0	0	0	0	4	0	1
3	-	-	-	-	-	-	-	-	-	-	-	-	-	-
4	Yes	78	82	100	88	86	84	73	67	88	100	84	50	71
	No	21	17	0	12	14	16	21	33	12	0	16	0	27
	X	1	1	0	0	0	0	6	0	0	0	0	50	2
5	Yes	73	80	100	75	79	74	67	61	82	100	64	50	66
	No	7	5	0	25	14	10	6	6	6	0	20	0	7
	X	20	15	0	0	7	16	27	33	12	0	16	50	27
6	a	1	1	8	0	0	3	0	0	0	0	0	0	3
	b	4	4	8	0	7	3	12	11	0	50	4	0	3
	c	38	36	50	75	36	52	36	61	41	50	60	50	31
	d	42	44	34	25	57	35	46	28	47	0	24	50	43
	e	10	11	0	0	0	1	3	0	6	0	0	0	15
	X	5	4	0	0	0	6	3	0	6	0	12	0	5
7	a	2.04	1.81	1.75	1.37	1.42	1.76	1.66	1.88	1.86	1.00	1.78	1.00	2.56
	b	3.10	3.25	3.75	3.25	3.42	3.13	3.16	3.19	2.86	3.00	3.26	4.00	2.84
	c	4.05	4.29	3.25	4.25	4.58	4.09	4.31	4.63	4.57	4.00	3.70	5.00	3.68
	d	3.55	3.40	4.00	3.88	3.58	3.81	3.44	3.37	4.14	5.00	3.48	2.00	3.62
	e	2.26	2.25	2.25	2.25	2.00	2.21	2.43	1.93	1.57	2.00	2.78	3.00	2.30
	X	121	44	4	0	2	14	1	2	3	0	2	1	48
8	Yes	38	43	83	25	64	55	48	61	29	0	88	50	19
	No	61	56	17	63	36	45	52	39	71	100	12	50	80
	X	1	1	0	12	0	0	0	0	0	0	0	0	1
9	Yes	39	41	75	37	29	48	39	50	47	0	72	50	29
	No	10	8	8	37	29	12	18	6	12	0	20	50	9
	X	51	51	17	26	42	40	43	44	41	100	8	0	62
10	Yes	90	90	100	88	93	86	70	89	94	100	80	50	93
	No	10	10	0	12	7	14	27	11	6	0	20	50	6
	X	0	0	0	0	0	0	3	0	0	0	0	0	1

11	Yes	74	74	75	75	64	65	45	44	82	100	76	50	81
	No	25	25	25	25	36	34	52	56	18	0	24	0	18
	X	1	1	0	0	0	1	3	0	0	0	0	50	1
12	a	20	25	0	12	21	16	9	11	29	0	4	0	19
	b	40	40	33	50	29	26	36	11	35	50	28	100	46
	c	31	29	42	38	50	36	43	61	18	50	48	0	28
	d	6	4	0	0	0	14	12	11	6	0	12	0	5
	X	3	2	25	0	0	8	0	6	12	0	8	0	2
13	a	28	31	25	63	21	19	27	39	41	0	20	0	27
	b	57	55	42	25	58	55	55	56	35	100	32	50	63
	c	13	12	25	12	21	22	15	5	24	0	36	50	9
	X	2	2	8	0	0	4	3	0	0	0	12	0	1
14	C*	70	75	67	75	79	69	39	44	59	50	72	50	69
	R*	30	33	33	38	43	19	12	6	29	50	24	50	50

Notes

All figures are percentages except for
-the first line and 7X, which are numbers
-7 a-e, which give average votes

*X = Unclassified
*C = General comment made
*R = Copy of Research Report requested

7 Some differences among the responses of the categories are revealed:

- The Secretaries of Examining Bodies (2) give 'Distance Education' its best rating, but it overtakes only 'Open Learning' and 'Extension Study'.
- 'Correspondence Education' tops the list with: Local Authority Officers; and students of English-speaking ICCE members.
- 'Home Study' generally remains the favourite term.

8 The two groups of 'educators', Secretaries of Examining Bodies (2) and Principals of CFEs (10), show the greatest awareness of accreditation. Excluding non-UK respondents (12), the rest show a 49% awareness of accreditation.

9 'Yes' answers rate significantly higher proportions than 'no' answers except for Random Names (3) and Students who did not enrol (4). A hint of scepticism about accreditation, or just failure to interpret the question correctly?

10 Again CE as a necessary part of modern education receives high ratings. Secretaries of Examining Bodies (2) are 100% positive. Principals of CFEs (10), who might view CE as a competitive form of education, are 80% positive.

11 Responding to the view that there are situations in which teaching by correspondence is preferable, positive answers from Bank Managers (6) and Building Society Branch Managers (7) dropped from the norm of 74% to 45% and 44% respectively, which is surprising since they are well familiar with CE, as many of their staff study by correspondence, as they probably did themselves.

12 CE as a method of study is more easily evaluated if the positive percentages (a & b) and negative (c & d) are compared:

(a) + (b)

Total	(1)	(2)	(3)	(4)	(5)	(6)	(7)	(8)	(10)	(12)
60	65	33	62	50	42	45	22	64	32	65

(c) + (d)

Total	(1)	(2)	(3)	(4)	(5)	(6)	(7)	(8)	(10)	(12)
37	33	42	38	50	50	55	77	24	60	33

(a) + (b) loses it majority with Secretaries of Examining Bodies (2), Personnel Officers (5), Bank Managers (6), Building Society Managers (7) and Principals of CFEs (10). Among students both in the UK (1) and overseas (12) positive responses are double negative.

13 Random Names (3) give a clear majority for CE qualified students being 'better equipped'. Principals of CFEs (10) are less convinced. Most chose the middle answer, (b).

14 Why, in both comments made and reports requested, did Bank Managers (6) and Building Society Managers (7) rate at the bottom of the league?

Summary

Respondents with experience of CE give very positive answers, but the general public needs greater knowledge of our method of study. While service to students is reasonable, improvement is still needed.

'Home study' and 'correspondence education' will recruit students to correspondence education more effectively than the term 'distance education'. Accreditation is not adequately understood and needs more publicity. Correspondence education is needed in modern society.

David M. Young
Rapid Results College
United Kingdom

The Use of Media in Public Relations and Advertising for Correspondence Courses

Keep in mind that your own gut feelings and experience count as much as those of the advertising professional.

Correspondence schools are unique institutions. The schoolroom is a mailbox. Without campuses, ivy-covered halls or baton twirling cheerleaders they have only one commodity to promote—education. The plus side of this situation is obvious: no peripheral distractions. The minus side is overwhelming: how to bring your only commodity to the attention of the public in such a way as to attract qualified potential applicants into your fold. Also, once they are enrolled as members of your student body, how to maintain a positive image which they can relate to with pride. The concept of school image is determined at two levels, internal—how the student sees the school from his standpoint as a student; and external—how the student relates to the public image of the school. Both are inherent in maintaining the level of motivation necessary for retention. Internal public relations should motivate and infuse confidence in your staff so as to create a contagious enthusiasm about their individual and departmental responsibilities. One element of internal public relations is your staff's reaction to the outside world's perception of your organization. Creating and maintaining a positive image in the minds and hearts of the general public can be a problem because you do not have an overwhelming physical facility.

The most immediate solution is the use of mass media. Properly used, mass media can disseminate information about your school and any new courses it is offering to large numbers of target potential students. This can also influence legislation concerning your organization and the industry in general. It can make you many friends in the fields of endeavor which are the ultimate goal of your graduates, so

assisting you in placement. And, when effectively and intelligently coordinated, mass media can create lasting positive impressions which pay dividends long after the medium or the specific message has left the level of consciousness.

Media include local, regional and national newspapers, general and special interest magazines, television and radio as primary carriers. Internal publications, flyers and special interest publications in a variety of related fields are secondary carriers.

The internal public relations staff can create a press kit about the school and follow it up with a monthly press release to publications which have conjunctive interests. The cultivation of specific editorial personnel and writers at these publications is often well worth the time and effort required. Newspapers have space to fill. If, by maintaining contact with important publications in your area, you can be aware of upcoming editorial requirements, changing legislation, and special educational editions, you can structure newsworthy articles they will use. They are grateful to you for making their job easier and you have developed a public relations avenue to obtain what is known in the trade as "free ink"—mass exposure highlighting your school positively at little cost.

Advertising, on the other hand, can be quite costly. Most correspondence schools are not set up to handle the complexities inherent in creating and effecting a viable advertising plan of action. The creation of cost-effective advertising to establish a positive public image of your school and motivate inquiries resulting in enrollments can be a convoluted and complex procedure.

Many organizations use outside advertising

agencies whose expertise includes writing copy, making up print ads, producing radio and television commercials and designing brochures or flyers. Beyond that, advertising professionals have a grounding in research and media selection. The important point to remember is that an advertising agency is employed by *you* and no plan proposed to you is inviolate. Ad agencies are not infallible, regardless of what they would have you believe. In the structure, planning and placement of your advertising keep in mind that your own experience and gut feelings do count at least as much as the recommendations of the advertising professionals. You have the ultimate right of veto, since your money is being spent.

Some organizations use an in-house advertising agency. The advantages are immediate access to the ad people and total control of the way advertising is to be structured. Familiarity with the day-to-day functioning of the organization can be invaluable in advertising planning and placement and only an in-house department can have this. Part of the cost of an in-house agency can be defrayed by taking the agency discounts offered to ad agencies.

Television and radio are time-framed advertising media. You are exposed to the public for only a very short period, usually 30 seconds or 1 minute. In order to make this expensive time count you must be selective as to the time of day, the format of the medium (programming) and the message. Researching the likes and dislikes of your student body will give you an indication of the words, phrases and images most likely to be suitable. Every medium trumpets its specific demographics. Study them to see if what you need and what they purport to deliver match. Monitor response. If it isn't what you anticipated try to analyze why. It could be that *they* overestimated their pulling power or that you misjudged the way to approach your target audience. The variables are numerous but try to isolate as many as possible and weigh each one carefully. The more you isolate and give proper weight to variables (such as time of day, weather, type of programming, location in the programming, words in your ads) the easier it will be to rectify flaws.

In print advertising you have slightly more control over your message and its exposure. Although your audience is not as captive as in broadcasting (people may just read one section of the paper, or they may just flip through a magazine, ignoring all the ads) a reader who spots your ad and is even perfunctorily interested will tend to spend more time with it than someone who happens to catch your 30 second radio or television ad. Print advertising is not as time-framed as broadcast, but it also tends to be more expensive.

The primary consideration in any advertising must be the number of qualified inquiries it attracts. By using this as your criterion you will soon be able to establish the medium and the approach best suited to attract your target audience.

Columbia School of Broadcasting, being a training school for broadcasters, announcers, copy writers, engineers and time-sales people, uses mostly television and radio advertising. We write and produce our own commercials and even have an in-house advertising agency consultant to buy time and place our ads. In addition, we advertise in print when a special section dealing with education is scheduled to be published in a locale in which one of our communication centers is established.

In addition, we have a staff public relations person whose function is to write and disseminate press releases as well as various internal publications (known as house organs) of interest not only to our students but to the broadcasting industry as a whole. This dovetails with our placement assistance service department, working toward getting our graduates employment.

It's all a part of cohesive whole, of which the education itself is the centerpiece. Our efforts in education would have very little chance of achieving the enormous success and recognition which Columbia School of Broadcasting has achieved without the use of mass media to help us find our qualified enrollee, to maintain contact with the industry which will eventually corroborate our faith in our students' ability to complete the course, and finally to be receptive to our graduates as working members of the broadcasting fraternity.

Marcia Brock
Columbia School of Broadcasting
United States

How Can Regional Associations Be Useful? The Example of ASPESA

Regional association can be an effective way of promoting professionalism and cooperation in distance education.

Local institutions and associations may be limited in their access to world-wide resources. On the other hand world conferences are held infrequently, are costly to attend, and embrace a wide range of interests. The regional association may be a satisfactory half-way house, having access to wide resources and also a knowledge of local situations. This has been the experience of ASPESA.

Beginnings

ASPESA stands for the Australian and South Pacific External Studies Association, which was formed in 1972-73. When it was formed some eleven higher education institutions were already operating in external studies in Australia and New Zealand. Some had a long history (e.g. Massey University in New Zealand and the University of New England in Australia), with the oldest, such as the University of Queensland and the University of Western Australia, going back over sixty years. The number of higher education institutions operating in external studies in Australia alone increased to forty by 1980.

The technical education programmes mounted by the Royal Melbourne Institute of Technology, the West Australian Institute of Technology and the New Zealand Technical Correspondence Institute also had a long history. The Correspondence Schools and Schools of the Air had also established world-wide reputations reaching back to 1909 for the Victoria Correspondence School and to the 1920s in the case of the New Zealand operations.

Many of these institutions had also offered services to South-East Asia, Papua New Guinea and the South Pacific communities.

Smith describes the beginnings of ASPESA as follows:

> Initially, the Forum (1972) was to be held for the benefit of universities and colleges of advanced education already engaged in offering degree and diploma courses externally within Australia but such was the interest shown by the time the final programme was arranged that some 24 institutions from five Australian States, from Papua and New Guinea, New Zealand and Fiji had arranged to send representatives. So successful was the Forum in providing an exchange of views and personal contact with others in the same field of interest and endeavour that the members present resolved that efforts should be made at the next Forum in 1973 to create a permanent organization in the form of a national or wider regional association for the promotion of external studies at the tertiary level. At the 1973 Forum held at the University of Queensland the resolution was put into effect and ASPESA was born.
> (Smith, 1974: 1).

Membership: profile and problems

The Association's membership embraces both institutions and individuals. Among its individual members are those who are active in ICCE and those who research, teach or contribute to government policy-making on distance education. They are involved in formal and informal education at all levels for students of all ages in both public and commercial institutions.

The students served by distance education live predominantly on islands of the Pacific or in isolated towns and outposts in the Australian semi-arid deserts, the farmlands or the northern tropical coastal regions. They are of many nations and speak many dialects.

There are problems in having such a diverse membership although goodwill helps minimize them. Some of the difficulties are:

— our region covers many nations and we are still getting to know each other

— our region is 6,000 miles from east to west

— Australia itself is 2,500 miles from east to west; travel is costly over these distances

— members from commercial schools have difficulty in ensuring their interests are considered since they are easily outnumbered by members from public institutions

— there are divergent approaches to distance education between universities and correspondence schools (Keegan, 1977)

— there are many interest groups other than those mentioned above, e.g. teachers, administrators, audio-visual technical staff, counsellors, office staff, researchers, publishers, etc.

— some instutations seem to have plenty of money and others have little, with enrolments expanding in some and contracting in others

— while goodwill prevails among members, their institutional employers may be in direct competition and fighting for survival

- the individual member, while dedicated to servicing isolated students, can himself feel isolated in his association with ASPESA.

Programmes and activities

To enable all members to participate fully and pursue their interests within ASPESA it:

- conducts a forum, at a different major centre, every two years
- conducts at least three sub-regional workshops between each forum
- encourages local institutions to host workshops/conferences on specific themes
- arranges for visiting scholars to attend forums and make tours through the various countries, states and institutions where there are members
- publishes a regular newsletter
- sponsors the international journal, *Distance Education*
- encourages institutions to release and exchange specialist staff to meet particular needs
- provides information to enable students to change institutions as their needs change.

Role of the executive

The executive is elected at each forum. Its structure is designed to give representation to the different educational sectors and to the editors of the newsletter and *Distance Education*. The executive is empowered to act for ASPESA between forums. In that role it either develops and implements policy or prepares proposals for decision by the membership at the forums.

This delegation of authority to the executive has been important since it enables implementation of policy without undue delay. Its initiatives include striking a committee on the use of satellites, advertising an annual research scholarship, and establishing an annual Visiting Fellow programme.

Because of the wide geographical scatter of its members the executive meets by teleconference.

ASPESA and the future

Don Bewley (1980) listed several issues which demand the attention of ASPESA in his paper to the 1981 forum in Fiji. Some of the questions he raised were:

- How 'pan-Pacific' is ASPESA's outlook?
- Are we still middle-distance, state-wide thinkers? What immense-distance strategies do we have for pan-Pacific or even Austalia-wide teaching?
- What provision do/can distance education organizations make (i) in Australia for its Aboriginal, settler and recent non-English speaking immigrant inhabitants and, (ii) elsewhere for ethnic variety or transferring communities?
- What role, if any, do distance education systems have in the development and maintenance of nationhood in new (and the older) Pacific states?
- Should distance eduation be confined to major world languages? What contribution can it make to teaching English (or another language) as a second language?
- What are the courses that can be offered 'across cultures'? By what means can their teaching be adapted to the needs of overseas students?
- In regional co-operation, who has what to offer? Who can benefit and on what terms? How can ASPESA assist?

Conclusion

In his foreword to the papers of the 1972 forum Howard Sheath (1972), then Director of External Studies at the University of New England, described the event as a watershed and the list of forum members as bearing "testimony to the widespread and rapidly increasing interest in external studies". As funds have become available the growth has substantiated his claim. An over-riding problem now is that government educational funds are evaporating and many institutions face hardship. Just as ASPESA acted as patron to growth, it may now have a new role as comforter of the disinherited.

ASPESA was formed to meet needs for professional interaction among those attempting to serve rapidly-growing populations of external students. Growth and demand are still present but decreased funding, changing technology, and the academic development of the discipline of distance education have altered the environment. Many pressing issues need resolution.

ASPESA provides a context for problem-solving. It provides an element of objectivity not available to the local institution or association together with an immediacy and intimacy not available from ICCE. It satisfies an evident need and we believe other regional associations could fulfill a similar function.

Ian McD. Mitchell
Adelaide College of the Arts and Education
Australia

References

Bewley, D. (1980) Dimensions of distance: distance education in a South Pacific setting. Theme paper for 1981 ASPESA Forum, Massey University, N.Z.

Keegan, D.J. (1977) Distance education at primary and secondary levels. *ASPESA Newsletter*, 3, 4, 12-17.

Sheath, H.C. (ed.) (1972) *Proceedings of a Forum on External Studies*. Armidale: University of New England.

Smith, K.C. (1974) President's message: introducing ASPESA. *ASPESA Newsletter*, 1, 1, 1-3.

A Regional Basis for an International Organization for Distance Education

Distance education has grown substantially in the last decade throughout the world. A significant aspect of this growth is the increasing recognition by prestigious educational institutions that distance education is legitimate and acceptable. Another is the widespread use of distance education by the developing countries to accelerate the provision of educational opportunities for their people.

The need for an international organization to promote communication and cooperation in the development of distance education is self-evident. The paper examines alternative models for such an organization and argues for its having a regional basis so as to provide economically for the differing situations around the world. ICCE could develop the framework for the international organization.

Jerry Grimwade
Royal Melbourne Institute of Technology
Australia

Diverse Subjects, Diverse Approaches

Paper 80

Introduction

An increasingly wide range of subjects is being learned at a distance. The papers in this section describe the approaches needed to provide instruction in topics varying from music to affective relationships. Papers elsewhere in this volume also contain references to the application of distance education to specific subject areas.

Even those who agree with Griew (paper 68) that the process of course development in distance education has reached lunatic levels of complexity and expense in some institutions, accept that it is an inherently costly process. This restraint on the multiplication of course offerings should oblige institutions to concentrate on priorities. Foks (paper 69) describes how priorities can be established and Mugridge (paper 61) recommends that each program be reduced to its essential components.

Recognizing that learning at a distance makes special demands, many have wondered whether there is not a set of skills that can be taught to new students to help them in any course they may take. Schimeck (paper 103) notes that visual literacy is now an important skill. However, researchers such as Marton and Svensson (paper 31) and Morgan et al (paper 32) have warned that study habits cannot be learned outside the context of a particular content. This has led Forsythe (paper 81) to try and combine a "learning-to-learn" course with a specific project of interest to the individual student.

Writing is a particularly important skill for both teachers and learners. Howell (paper 83) reports on the development of a language skills course for adult Polynesians that she claims could be a model for low-cost projects in developing countries. Cumming and Mackay (paper 82) outline a method whereby the learner takes over many of the tasks of the teacher in assessing and improving writing proficiency. Jenkins (paper 84) and Holmes (paper 35) suggest how institutions can help their course authors to write better. It is a sign of the success of distance education that authors now accept the need for training. Readability analyses are a useful tool in helping them reflect critically on the suitability of their writing for particular groups of students.

Foreign languages have long been a popular subject to study at home and the four language skills of listening, speaking, reading, and writing lend themselves naturally to the use of media. Stephens (paper 85) examines the problem posed by the diversity of objectives that lead students to learn languages and urges that courses include useful applications and show something of the culture behind the language. Stringer (paper 87) stresses that the student who wishes to add a new language to his repertoire of skills must avail himself of every opportunity to practise using it. To facilitate this the BBC, as Innes (paper 88) reports, links its multi-media courses to classes held around the United Kingdom. One interesting technique she describes is the use of television to help students become accustomed to a new alphabet. Abrioux (paper 86) describes the characteristics of students learning French at a distance. Particularly noteworthy is the high success rate of students over 65-years old in advanced courses.

The training of teachers is the most powerful motor and multiplier of educational development. In-service training via distance education is, according to Ansere (paper 12) a particularly effective technique. Nashif (paper 89) points out the irony of training people at a distance for the task of classroom teaching. However, the UNRWA/Unesco project for Palestinian teachers shows that in-service training at a distance can be highly successful provided appropriate face-to-face sessions are included. In the project described by Boulianne (paper 91) video cassette material is used as the focus for group meetings of second-language teachers receiving in-service training in the Canadian north.

Datt (paper 14) criticizes the academicians who would limit distance learning to bookish subjects with no practical component. In fact, history shows that distance education has often risen successfully to challenges that conventional techniques were unable to handle. Penberthy (paper 26) provides an interesting review of the development of correspondence education for children in remote areas and Bonani (paper 4) argues that only distance learning will enable large numbers of high school drop-outs to achieve their potential. Echoing a complaint heard often from educators in developing countries Gitau (paper 10) talks of the obstacle placed by the existing examination system in the way of vocational education. In Africa it is difficult to wean both school drop-outs and their parents from a colonial model of education. Yet, according to Draper (paper 9) the developing countries are now the leaders in non-formal education. Community and social action is really a process of individual learning that must combine anticipation (the ability to deal with the future) and participation (involvement in creating the future). In the industrialized world media-based distance education is also being used to attack social problems as Kaye (paper 107) reports in his guide to recent projects in Europe. Similar aims are behind the new "TV academies" in Canada described by Waniewicz (paper 108). Music was the subject of one academy and the challenges of distance education in music are explored in an engaging paper by Ottem (paper 92). "How do you communicate a communication?" he asks in drawing the lessons from his experience in northern Norway.

The rapid changes of the contemporary world are behind many current developments in distance education. A pioneer use of videodiscs is for technical and sale training (Ruggles and Blackmore, paper 111). For Loudon (paper 93) all business education must now be education for change. Developments in agriculture create educational needs among farmers (Shah, paper 16) and, as Penney (paper 34) insists, the complexity of modern medicine requires a highly rigourous approach to skill training for nurses. In some countries changes in legislation and social attitudes create specific educational needs. Rande (paper 63) tells of a course on the rights of the handicapped and Marchand (paper 94) describes the challenge of providing affective education at a distance.

Singh (paper 13) reminds us that technical education has always been an important thrust of distance education in Russia and the United States. Since no initial training can completely equip an individual for a lifetime of work in today's world, post-experience education in new technologies is everywhere a growing need. de Moor (paper 59) forecasts that skills will be a major focus of the Netherlands Open University and Horlock (paper 95) examines the opportunities for continuing technological education in the United Kingdom. Ralph Smith (paper 96) reports on the success of a post-experience course on microprocessors at the Open University and shows how the organization of such courses differs from that of the regular degree program. Teaching students to handle real-world problems can be done through case studies, as Weaver describes (paper 90).

Finally Holmberg (paper 97) and Sullivan (paper 98) discuss the requirements of graduate study at a distance. At this level, communication between student and advisor is particularly crucial. Collaboration between a number of institutions can do much to ensure the quality of graduate education and enrich the students' experience.

Learning to Learn

A course in study skills can be adapted to help a student explore his own way of learning.

Almost all distance learning systems have recognized that people need help in learning how to study at a distance.

Study skills resources almost all suffer from the fact that they are not integrated with the content or structure of the knowledge to be learned. Study habits are developed early and are not easily changed: such habits cannot be learned outside the context of the content of the subject. Improvement in learning comes from the change from surface-level understanding of a subject to deep-level understanding.

Gordon Pask (1978) argues convincingly for the need at this time in history for skills in general problem-solving which he describes as "learning to learn".

With the increasing ability to contain both knowledge and knowledge structures by electronic means, we must learn how to learn if we are to see technology as an extension of mindpower and not our master and to see that the *process* and skills of using knowledge to solve problems and thus create new knowledge *is* the root of all learning endeavours.

Concomitant with these more philosophical approaches to the idea of learning to learn is the literal explosion in new knowledge about the human brain, in particular, the discovery of the existence of man's two brain hemispheres, which essentially function as two minds that work independently and in concert with one another, each containing distinct strategies and talents for performing both the same and different functions.

The implications of this new understanding of brain function for education are dramatic and support Wittrock's (1977: 203) view that learning be reconceived as a generative cognitive process, and that the art of teaching needs to devise sophisticated ways to facilitate the multiple processing systems of the brain. Recent research on the lateralization processes of the human brain provides scientific evidence to indicate that learning and memory are processes that often involve constructing representations in both brain hemispheres.

With our new knowledge of the brain, our awareness of individual differences in learning style, and our differentiation of surface and deep-level knowledge structures, "study skills" seem an inadequate palliative to the age-old educational question of how to help each other learn. "Learning to learn" is a conceptual way to describe this change from a superficial treatment offered to the student, to a process designed to educate—to draw forth what is potential—by having a student explore his own way of learning through introspection and new knowledge of the skills attendant in communicating, processing information and problem-solving in order to transfer this learning ability to whatever change demands.

The Learn to Learn Project

From exploring many approaches to the idea of improving "learning", "study skills", and "learning to learn", the author attempted to identify a resource which seemed to address all sides of the problem.

The resource decided upon was *Use Your Head*, a ten-part television series produced by the BBC in 1974 based on the work of Tony Buzan. The series was supported by a short book by Tony Buzan, published by the BBC in 1974.

Tony Buzan's work grew from his experience as a speed reading specialist and his work on memory and mnemonics. His ideas are most often presented by two-and three-day workshops given by teachers trained in the Buzan method. The author participated in two of these workshops which contained new content on the brain but essentially followed the same pattern as the TV show. The difference seemed to be that there was a very sophisticated guide who led the participants through a group experience in a rather controlled path. To explore this idea further, the author decided to develop a written guide for the television and text which might retrace the path and be used in conjunction with a human instructional agent to replicate this guiding process. Just as one cannot learn to read without having something to read, so one cannot learn to learn without having something to learn. A number of student-centred exercises were integrated with the process.

Use Your Head is a resource that purports to address learning to learn by methodology. The Learn to Learn Project was not intended, however, to validate the research upon which *Use Your Head* is based but rather to test its usefulness in a real setting and to develop this new element, the student workbook, to integrate the existing television programmes and the text and make the course suitable for use in an open learning system.

The Learn to Learn Project was conducted from January to June, 1980. A prototype workbook was prepared in January and used with students from February to May 1980 and revised in July 1980. The fieldwork was done in the Campbell River Learning Centre of North Island College and also involved students who lived in remote logging communities.

Characteristics of the project

It seemed that what the existing *Use Your Head* course lacked was a contextually related experience and a personal guide to the individual's exploration of the learning process.

The introduction to the course sets the new exploratory mood.

WHAT IS USE YOUR HEAD?

Use Your Head is a course with a difference! Rather than learning about a set subject, this course is about learning itself.

By using the **Use Your Head** resources you will be exploring your own learning, finding out how you can improve upon what you already know, how you can improve your ability to read, to remember, to think and to create and to solve problems.

Use Your Head is not a prescription for instant success. You probably already know a great deal about how you learn best. Because of your individual life experience and your attitudes, your learning will always be unqiue to you. We expect you to be critical about this course. Think about and try what seems comfortable to you. Perhaps you will find that you are a much more efficient learner than you think you are!

At the end of this course you should:

1. be able to read more efficiently
2. be able to remember more

3. be able to use notes for recall and for creative purposes
4. be more aware of how you think and how you learn

Use Your Head is designed to be a self-help resource. This means that most people will be using the resource on their own. You should ask your tutor if you need help. A good idea would be to involve a family member or friend in taking the course with you so that you have someone to discuss it with.

Instead of merely creating 10 units from the existing resource, five functional and developmental changes were identified. Indeed, the order of the units was changed as experience had found that many students were turned off by the early introduction of high speed reading training. Throughout the workbook a conscious effort was made to present ideas symbolically or visually as well as to write them.

The workbook was designed to be interactive, i.e., to pose very student-centred questions and to encourage a great deal of response. This was done to attempt to have the student question the information given in relation to his own experiences.

The true innovation, however, was the integration of the learning project with the *Use Your Head* resource which meant that each individual's reason for taking the course was unique. Reasons ranged from wishing to improve essay-writing and grades, to preparation for entry into vocational programs or to graduate school, to use as a literacy tool, or for the study of advanced electronics, as a personal reading structure and to prepare for the adoption of a disturbed adolescent.

The basic idea behind the Learning to Learn Project is that students choose to learn something *they* want to learn—and that the *Use Your Head* course is applied to the learning project. In this way, the student should be in charge of his own learning, using the *Use Your Head* resources as they are needed. The intent of *Use Your Head* was to change habits, as well as to give information. The course was presented as a series of infinite possibilities combined within a finite structure in order to explore that structure.

Clearly the act of independent study requires the ability to learn for survival as a student. What the concept "learning to learn" suggests is that this need not necessarily be a hit and miss process. It is a *process*, a process of discovery that by its nature is individual. The work reported in this paper suggests that a generic structure or a meta-model might be applied to that process in order for an individual to explore structure itself by his own pursuit of it. Experiencing one such in-depth exploration of deep knowledge topology may be a powerful way to *begin* a learning endeavour such as an open learning degree, allowing adult part-time students to optimize the limited time and personal energy available to them.

Another important potential impact of the learning to learn construct is in the area of curriculum and instructional design and teaching/learning methods, i.e., the roots of education.

If we are to avoid indoctrinal education then we must attend to the process of thinking, problem-solving and creativity. Attending to these as both prerequisite process and generic structure in open learning might well overcome many of the self-generated problems we are now facing in open learning. Our course materials might become less structured, and less expensive; the use of visual elements might well be optimized to enhance hemisphericity and learning style, tutors might find this human problem more potentially challenging and accept this new professional role with more enthusiasm.

This project had no conclusive results to indicate that the resources in questions were powerful enough to effect such learning to learn. However, the author is pursuing this area of research into the application of learning methods in open learning systems and welcomes advice, information and criticism.

Kathleen Forsythe
Knowledge Network of the West
Canada

References

Buzan, T. (1974) *Use Your Head*. BBC Publications.
Pask, G. (1978) New methods of assessment and stronger methods of curriculum design. Final report, Vol. I, IET, Open University.
Wittrock, M.C. (ed.) (1977) *The Human Brain*. Englewood Cliffs, H. J.: Prentice Hall.

Paper 82

Increasing Study Involvement, Minimizing Teacher Dominance: The Assessment and Practice of Writing Improvement

Extensive use of self-assessment helps students learn to write and has significant economic advantages.

Introduction

This paper outlines an approach to the instruction of writing wherein the learner participates in many of the processes of assessing and improving his writing proficiency which would normally be performed by a teacher. Most of the learning and practice can occur without the presence of a teacher. The procedures, ideas and materials described here have been tried out and found to be successful with university students who find it necessary to improve their writing skills.

The principal characteristics of this approach are:

- realistic writing tasks which involve reading and employing information obtained from reading

- clearly specified purposes for the writing of each task

- emphasis on the cumulative development of skills

- a system of self-assessment and self-monitoring to promote learner involvement

- criteria for self-assessment which are specific, relevant and comprehensible to the student and accessible to students of a wide variety of writing proficiency levels, as well as to individuals using English as a second language.

Writing tasks

The materials consist of series of tasks. Each task includes source materials—usually a text or a text plus tabular or diagrammatic material, and a set of instructions which specify a written assignment based on these materials. The tasks are similar to those an educated adult is likely to be required to perform in formal, academic, or professional circumstances. The face validity of the tasks is therefore high (to the student and to the teacher) because they engage the writer in realistic, contextualized, and non-trivial production of written work.

The tasks are designed to be both "fail-safe" and sequenced. The nature of each task requires the learner to produce writing which adheres to conventional or rhetorical forms. The form employed arises naturally from the requirements of the task and so involves him in the regular employment and practice of such written forms. The sequence of the tasks, in turn, promotes the learner's cumulative development of specific types of skills which contribute to proficient writing. Initial tasks call simply for the organization of information. Subsequent tasks require the student to exemplify concepts or principles, make comparisons, classify and finally synthesize information presented in the texts and diagrams.

The successful performance of each consecutive group of tasks requires the student not only to use the new rhetorical form demanded by the new task, but also the skills and form learned and mastered in the preceding tasks. After offering the student adequate practice in each of these types of skills, the final tasks ask that he respond to diverse points of view presented in the source materials by synthesizing the skills of organization, exemplification, comparison and classification practised in earlier tasks. Examples of tasks involving organization and a final task which we call synthesis, requiring the employment of various rhetorical conventions, are given in Appendix A.

The self-assessment instrument

The instrument for self-assessment removes students from the position of being dominated by a teacher, where only the teacher corrects and evaluates written work, and creates instead criticism and self-monitoring. Criteria to guide the learner in evaluating his own work are clearly formulated, comprehensible to the student and teacher, and largely usable by the student. The result is that the student either by himself, in discussion with other students, or in consultation with a teacher can:

- identify weaknesses in his own work

- perceive a number of specific areas where he could improve his written performance

- focus on the mastery of specifics which contribute to the effectiveness of his overall proficiency

- revise and improve subsequent drafts of his own work

— exert a conscious effort on areas in his future work where he is likely to experience failings.

The criteria for the student's assessment of his work are a set of questions. They cover the following important features of effective writing:

- size of written sample
- the speed with which it was written
- degree of conformity to the goals set in a task
- quality of ideas
- organization
- correctness of syntax, lexis, punctuation, spelling
- complexity of language structures
- breadth of vocabulary
- conviction expressed
- interest value.

Each question represents a query that a critical, proficient reader might pose in regard to his own writing. The questions are applied to written work in an ordered fashion, from numbers 1 to 30. A sequence of negative responses to the questions places a student's work at a certain point on the scale. The scale is grouped into bands which represent 5 levels of proficiency.

See Appendix B for an example of the evaluation criteria.

Application of the criteria

With work diagnosed in this way characteristics of the student's writing are identified and the student can see what aspects need improvement. He then refers to sample compositions offered for each set of tasks in each band. The sample essays are accompanied by detailed answers to criteria—questions whose purpose is to expose and exemplify the features of writing which justify placement of the writing sample in a particular band. Working from comparison of his writing with the sample composition, the student is able to check for similar features in his own work and set about correcting or revising them.

Effectiveness

The effectiveness of this approach has been demonstrated by teacher agreement on its operability and student satisfaction with its results. Estimates of the amount of agreement between teachers trained to use the grading system indicate an 80% level. Compare this to a typical factor of reliability of test grades of around 67%. Despite satisfaction over the evident communicability of the grading criteria, a greater source of achievement has been the fact that students have demonstrated that they can use the approach and benefit from the self-assessment procedure. This increases the confidence of students in their own abilities, nurturing their independence as language users and reducing the burden traditionally carried by the writing teacher.

Advantages

This approach has advantages for both student and teacher. The student is more actively involved in determining the effects of his learning process. This results in increased motivation. His weaknesses and means of improving on them are clarified and specified. His progress is readily measurable on an appointed scale. Hence the distance between student and teacher becomes irrelevant.

The teacher is released from spending large amounts of time marking or grading written work, and is thus able to devote attention, when in contact with the student, to more critical points of instruction, such as persistent mistakes whose recurrence detracts from the student's performance. The teacher's workload is further reduced by the element of guided instruction inherent in the nature of the writing tasks, which to a certain degree precludes the need for extended explanation or lectures on rhetorical forms. The teacher is also helped by the specification of grading criteria which are clear, easily employable, and objectively defensible.

This approach to the practice and improvement of writing skills described makes possible instruction in which (1) a teacher-to-student ratio is considerably higher than is normally practised, (2) writing programmes for literacy and second language purposes could be implemented on large yet standardized scales, (3) tutors, rather than highly (formally) qualified professionals, can be employed as teachers since the learner requires only occasional consultation with an instructor, (4) the necessity for a high number of contact hours between instructor and students is greatly diminished.

Alister Cumming / Ronald Mackay
Concordia University
Canada

Appendix A
Sample of Two Writing Tasks

Sample 1: Synthesize

Writing Task: Read the two following paragraphs which present an argument and a counter-argument for the same topic. Select one point of view and write an essay of not less than 500 words which supports the point of view you have adopted and which responds to both the argument and counter-argument.

Topic: Should People Be Required By Law To Use Bicycles In Cities?

Point of View A

The law exists to defend individuals from both their own irresponsibility and that of others. One of the greatest acts of irresponsibility demonstrated by members of present day society is the use of automobiles in the city. Automobile accidents are responsible for the death or injury of hundreds of thousands of people each year. The pollution resulting from automobile use in the city is the cause of countless instances of respiratory illness every year. To observe the pollution caused by automobiles in cities, you only have to climb the hills around Los Angeles, Mexico City, or Buenos Aires. Moreover, the use of automobiles is responsible for deteriorating physical health due to lack of exercise. Finally, the irresponsibility of using automobiles in cities is demonstrated by the anti-social procedure of using every available open space as a parking lot, thus depriving citizens of numerous parks, gardens and recreation areas. The use of the bicycle on the other hand would have none of the above disadvantages and yet allow people to travel to their destinations rapidly. There is no doubt, therefore, that to defend individuals from their own and others' irresponsibility, a law should be passed obliging people to use bicycles in the city.

Point of View B

A law requiring people to use only bicycles as a mode of transportation in cities no doubt conforms to the best of all idealistic plans for our ecological and physical well-being. But it is stupid. We might as well institute similar laws which would require each of us to wear orthopedic shoes because they are best for our feet, which would ban the wearing of tight-fitting clothing as it restricts our movements, or which would demand that all of us wear only the most efficient sort of wristwatch so that we would all know the exact time. People have a right to choose and use what forms of commodities they prefer, and this is especially true for means of transportation. Imagine moving furniture or machine parts on a bicycle. Think of riding a bike to work in the morning during a snowstorm. Consider what it would be like offering "to double" a prospective business client to an elegant restaurant for lunch. How would parents transport children? Or how could older people get about? The list of absurd situations which would arise if such a law were implemented are innumerable when you think about this in light of contemporary civilized existence. Today, we use our cars or trucks or buses as the circumstances demand. Nevertheless we are still free to ride bicycles, even unicycles or tricycles, should we so choose.

Sample 2: Organize

Explosion at Blue Stone Mine

Writing Task: Carefully examine the diagram and the 5 statements. Then as a responsible journalist write a newspaper report which describes the most significant details about the explosion at Blue Stone Mine.

Statement by Job Jackson, May 10, president of the local Association of Miners:

"On May 2nd we had issued a warning to the Chief of Operations at Blue Stone mine that the atmosphere in the mine contained excessive quantities of methane gas. The conditions in the mine shaft were far from those prescribed by government regulations. Up to this point federal authorities have refused to comment on this statement."

Statement by Louis Candellina, May 9, survivor of the explosion:

"It was like hurricane. You know, it seemed as if someone had taken a handful of gravel and thrown it in my neck. I could hardly breathe. The force of the explosion was so strong I thought for sure I was going to die. Thank God I'm still here."

Statement by the Head of Emergency Rescue Operations at Blue Stone Mine, John Oborsky, May 9:

"For the past 20 hours a team of rescue workers has been working furiously to rescue survivors and recover the bodies of the dead after an explosion of toxic gas at Blue Stone Mine. We have had to work with extreme caution in the mine shaft as pockets of methane gas still remain in the area.

Yesterday afternoon our team was called to an explosion which had trapped 15 miners in the main shaft. We have thus far discovered the bodies of 10 miners who were caught by the gas at the level of approximately 2,500 metres below ground level. I regret to inform you that all of these men are dead. At the level of about 2,000 metres below ground level 5 other miners were found wounded and these men have been taken to hospital. Twelve other men who were working near the opening to the shaft of the mine all escaped without injury. The rescue team will continue to look for other bodies which may have been trapped in a secondary shaft of the mine, but up to this point, no reports have been received concerning missing persons or workers who may have been on duty at the time of the explosion."

Statement by Michael Richards, May 10, Regional Inspector of Mines:

"The Blue Stone mine was perhaps the most dangerous and gaseous of mines in the area. This is the third such accident which has occurred in this mine in the past 3 years. We plan to launch an immediate investigation into the causes of this explosion and we hope to find a good explanation of how such a tragedy could have happened. Thus far the directors of the mine have refused to comment on the situation, but I plan to seek answers.

Methane is a particularly dangerous gas because it is colorless and odourless. I'm only glad that none of the rescue workers were injured in the blast, as it is a highly toxic and tricky substance to work near."

Statement by Helen Bradshaw, May 9, wife of one of the miners killed in the explosion:

"This is horrible, horrible. There is no other way to describe it. My worst fears, since we came here. I've been waiting outside the mine shaft for 15 hours now with a few of the other families of miners. We plan to stay here until there is some official word on what happened. I just can't go home."

Appendix B
Example of Evaluation Criteria

Band C - Restricted Writer

10. Does the writer carefully mix references from the source materials with his own writing and acknowledge his references?
11. Are there fewer than 2 grammatical errors per sentence?
12. Is the writer's perspective on the information presented consistently and clearly?
13. Are there smooth connectives between all units of thought?
14. Is the material presented in logical sequence?
15. Has only essential material been selected for presentation?
16. Does the writer employ punctuation conventions successfully?
17. Does the writer effectively introduce and close the writing?

If 'yes' to a majority of questions 10 - 17, continue.
If 'no' to a majority of questions 10 - 17, place the composition in Band C.

Appendix C
Sample of Student Writing
(Response to Sample 2 in Appendix A)
with Answers to Evaluation Questions

Band C

1   A HORRIBLE EXPLOSION IN THE BLUE STONE MINE

    May 8 - A horrible explosion in the
    Blue Stone Mine, today, killing ten miners
    and wounding five miners.
5   It is no doubt that the survivors of the
    explosion would get a terrible experience in
    that accident. "It was like a hurricane"
    Mr. Louis Candellina, survivor of the explosion,
    went on "You know, it seemed as if someone

10 had taken a handful of gravel and thrown
    it in my neck. I could hardly breathe. The
    force of the explosion was so strong I thought
    for sure I was going to die. Thank God I'm
    still here."

15 Since there still have methane gas
    remain in the area of the explosion, a team
    of rescue workers had been working furiously
    to rescue survivors and recover the bodies
    of dead. after the explosion in about 20 hours.

20 The head of the Emergency Rescue Operations,
    Blue Stone Mine, John Oborsky said that their
    team was called to an explosion which had
    trapped 15 miners in the shaft. He regretted
    to inform the fact that their team discovered
25 ten of the dead miners who were caught by
    the gas - at the level of about 2,500 metres
    below the ground level. Another five miners were
    found at the level of 2,000 metres below the
    ground level; they were wounded and had been
30 delivered to the hospital. Forturnately, twelve
    men who were working near the opening to the
    shaft of the mine all escaped without injury.

    "The rescue team will continue to look
    for other bodies which may have been trapped
35 in a secondary shaft of the mine, but up to
    this point, no reports have been received concerning
    missing persons or workers who may have been on

duty at the time of the explosion". said by Mr. John Oborsky.

40 This sudden accident made the families of the dead miners very upset and wanted a faire official statement from the related authorities. Helen Bradshaw, wife of one of the miners killed in the exposion, said "This is horrible,
45 horrible. There is no other way to describe it. My worst fears, since we came here. I've been waiting outside the mine shaft for 20 hours now with a few of the other families of the miners. We plan to stay here until there is some
50 official word of what happened. I just can't go home."

What caused the accident? Is there any inspection provided by the government? Mr. Job Jackson, president of the local Association
55 of Miners, said "On May 2nd we had issued a warning to the Chief of Operations at Blue Stone Mine that the atmosphere in the mine contained excessive quantities of methane gas. The conditions in the mine shaft were far
60 from those prescribed by government regulations. Up to this point federal authorities have refused to comment on this statement." By the way, we want to know more about the explosion. There are some informations
65 came from Mr. Michael Richards, Regional Inspector of Mines. He said that the Blue Stone Mine was perhaps the most dangerous and geseous of miners in the area. The methane
70 gas is colorless and odourless, and is a dange gas. "IM only glad that none of the rescue workers were injured in the blast, as it is a highly toxic and trickly substance to work near." This was the third accident in the past three years, but the directors of the mine refused
75 comment on the situation.

Answers to Evaluation Questions

10. No. The writer has not worked quotations into his own writing. Large chunks of indirect quotation are presented where they would normally be summarized.

11. No. The writer averages 2 grammatical or lexical errors per sentence.

12. No. It is difficult to determine the writer's perspective on the events because of the awkwardness of the quotations presented. The writer shifts perspective on the events from his initial viewpoint of reporting to an investigative and argumentative pose in lines 63-64.

13. No. Many connectives (such as "and" in line 41 or "It is no doubt" in line 5) are used inaccurately.

14. No. Most of the important details concerning what happened in the explosion are not presented until lines 23-30. Also, the information is not extensively reworked from the source format.

15. No. There are excessive amounts of unnecessary quotations (i.e. "you know" in line 9). The writer has not been selective enough in choosing important details.

16. No. Commas or colons are not used to introduce quotations.

17. No. The introductory paragraph is sparse and there is no concluding structure.

Read and Write Better

(Abstract)

Paper 83

The New Zealand Technical Correspondence Institute found that adult Polynesians enrolled in trade and technician courses were seriously handicapped by their inadequate English skills. In 1978 the Department of Education authorised the writing of English teaching modules that would overcome the problem. Dr. Brenda Howell, a curriculum designer with Unesco service in the Pacific, was asked to co-ordinate the project.

At Todd Motors, a large vehicle assembly plant, 60 of the staff (mainly Polynesian) enrolled as volunteers to test a pilot correspondence course written at a variety of levels of English use. Data from the volunteers' response during the pilot research year (1979) enabled a student profile to be made and the target group of improvers to be identified.

The "Read and Write Better" course (1980-81) is the outcome and is the first of its kind in Australasia. It is designed for Maori and Pacific Islands adults who have learned English for 2 to 4 years at high school but who realise later that they have not mastered English language skills at a level which enables them to manage tertiary studies or effective and confident communication in other areas of life. (Maori and Pacific Islands people together form 12% of the total New Zealand population.)

A special feature of the course is the contribution of ideas and materials from the community, both Polynesian and non-Polynesian. More than 500 people from 76 organisations have helped to make the course which has been put together by a small team of two writers—the co-ordinator and one part-timer, a specialist in reading—and voluntary unpaid help from an artist and a technician. All the taped reading and dialogues that accompany the printed study units have been performed by Polynesian volunteers. This enthusiastic contribution has made possible a low-cost learning package tailored to the community's needs.

Another significant feature is the use of audio tapes as a bridge and complement to the printed units. Tapes and units extend language practice in tandem. The Todd research clearly demonstrated the value of this educational aid in overcoming the inherent difficulties of improving language skills through the correspondence mode.

The results of the Todd experiment, other research, and the special teaching language and strategies used in the course have been fully documented during the 2-year project by the co-ordinator. Outcomes of the project so far suggest that further development of the work begun could effect improvements in distance education in other subjects, and could benefit majority as well as minority groups. It also suggests that models along similar lines could be constructed for rural low-cost education projects in developing countries.

The "Read and Write Better" course will be available, early 1982, in a kit package of 14 Units and 6 audio tapes, offering a year's study for adults.

Brenda Howell
New Zealand Technical Correspondence Institute
New Zealand

Tell Me How to Write

Paper 84

The variety of attitudes and experience course writers bring to their task requires a flexible training program.

Course writers today demand training. Gone are the days when the novice writer would confidently set about the task of writing with only minimal guidance. Gone are the days of experiment, when the enthusiastic writer would, unaided, become aware of the problems of teaching by correspondence and creatively adapt his or her classroom techniques to teaching at a distance. Gone are the days when the intervention of an editor or educational technologist was considered a wrongful intrusion into the preserve of the teacher.

Ten or more years ago, at least in my experience then at the National Extension College, writers did not expect to be trained. With better writers this was not a problem. They would produce good lesson drafts to start with, and tended to welcome discussion of their work. With weaker writers, the only acceptable form of training was tactful suggestion and quite often, such advice was not followed.

This experience was, I suspect, typical in any country where people were only just beginning to take distance teaching seriously. That time is now past. Today, distance teaching is an acceptable form of education. Those without experience do not attempt to struggle alone. They look to institutions or people with experience to provide advice and training.

How does a new writer feel?

First, there are the confident writers: "Just tell me all about the techniques I need and I'll have no trouble in applying them." They assume there are a few simple rules to be learned. They are shocked and surprised when they are presented with a challenge to their assumptions about teaching. They are forced to rethink how they should present their subject. This process contains an implicit questioning of the effectiveness of all their teaching. What they *want* is a quick guide to the theory and practice of distance teaching. What they *need* is to learn to think very carefully about what they teach and how they do it.

Any good teacher is, of course, prepared to do this. The shock to the course writer comes because a mystique has built up around the idea of distance teaching. Writers expect, and look for, a new kind of challenge. They discover instead that the major requirement is a familiar one, the hard slog of teaching to a high standard; and, worse, their teaching no longer takes place in the privacy of the classroom or lecture hall, but is open to the scrutiny of their peers and a variety of course development personnel. Their initial confidence is often severely shaken. Their training must, indeed, bring about this disruption, but it must also go on to restore confidence.

Second, there are writers who lack confidence: "I've never done any writing and I'm worried about it." The ones who admit to this worry are easy to help, with encouragement and constructive criticism. The difficult ones—and there are plenty of them—are those who don't like to acknowledge that they are worried. If a college provides only informal training, the problem may come to light when the deadline for submitting lessons arrives, and nothing has been written.

Third, there are those who resist training. There are still a few who believe it is quite unnecessary. If you've ever attended a writer's workshop, you may have met the sulky-faced person who sleeps ostentatiously in the back row. Others pay lip-service: "Give me the right books, I'll read them and get on with it." They are nevertheless determined to do things their own way. Sometimes, with patience and luck, they become more receptive; in other cases, the production of a course becomes a stormy and unpleasant experience for all involved.

There are, of course, other attitudes, but these three are typical and each presents training difficulties. The problem for the trainer is to build on the writer's initial receptivity; and to do so without destroying enthusiasm. In those cases where the writer has a negative attitude, the trainer has to attempt to break through the barrier.

What kind of training?

I have dwelt on the question of attitudes because I believe it crucially affects the content and conduct of training. Institutions can only provide limited training, and a training programme should therefore be designed to train writers in essentials. Opportunities for training may be limited for many practical reasons; a course may be needed in a hurry, money may be short, or trainers may be unavailable. But perhaps the most serious constraint is the one imposed by the writers themselves: they are seldom prepared to devote much time to training.

However, we must accept that, particularly for part-time writers, time is important. People want to get on with the job. This implies that a training programme should be efficient and selective. Our objective should be pragmatic rather than perfectionist: that is, to train writers to be competent. And the training needs to be built round the writers' experience and to take into account their attitudes.

A minimum curriculum for training

A typical new course writer has considerable experience of teaching in class but will know little about distance education, and have little or no experience of writing. For such people, a minimum curriculum should cover the following 6 topics:

1. What it is like to learn at a distance. In particular, the writer must consider the study environment, motivation and the needs of the group of students he is to teach.

2. Planning and writing by objectives. Most teachers have only a vague notion of objectives and their use. They need to clarify their ideas and, in particular, learn to write precise objectives.

3. Relating activities to objectives. The next step after writing objectives is to provide activities to test that they have been achieved. This is not obvious to those who are unfamiliar with teaching by objectives.

4. Providing constant feedback. Teachers need to learn to translate into print the normal classroom interaction. They need to be shown why frequent self-assessment questions are necessary, and need guidance on devising a variety of such questions.

5. Writing clearly. First attempts at writing are often unnecessarily heavy and complex. Writers need to learn to write simply and clearly. They also need to learn to write thorough but clear instructions.

6. How the course will work. Writers, particularly external ones, cannot be expected to understand the administration of a course. They need to know exactly what kind of support services are available to students, and how they operate. In particular, they need to understand how best to use a tutor's assessment skills, if a tutor is provided.

In addition to these six essentials, training should include some writing, either part of the writer's actual course or a lesson written as an exercise. The temptation to cover more topics must be resisted, if as a result writing is postponed. Any delay in starting to write increases the fears of writers with little confidence. Others immediately see the relevance of their subsequent training, as they can apply what they learn directly to their own drafts. They learn, too, that a writer must be prepared to redraft his work several times. The International Extension College has produced a training manual, *Writing for Distance Education* (1979), which starts by asking people to use some given information to write a few pages. Only then does it begin to look at techniques. We have used the manual in several workshops and find it is effective in helping all writers, even reluctant ones, develop their competence.

There is also the problem of time. Writers need to feel they are achieving something, and doing so quickly. It is tempting to introduce more topics into a training programme, but if time is limited, training should kept to the basics and to helping writers get started.

How can we train writers?

A number of training methods can be used to suit different circumstances.

Training by correspondence

Some years ago the International Extension College produced a correspondence course for correspondence course writers. It consisted of nine units, some of which were related to teaching particular subjects at a distance. It proved less than satisfactory. The problem was time. Although people began to write their courses as they worked through the units, they wanted to proceed faster than the course allowed. The delay while assignments were marked and returned was, for most, a severe handicap. This method of training has its uses, and other institutions may have found it more satisfactory; but I prefer other methods.

Self-tuition

There are now a number of training manuals available. It is difficult to assess their effectiveness, as feedback from users is lacking. My impression is that they are much better than nothing, but are more effective if used with some tutorial support, such as occasional seminars or a trainer who will answer queries. One institution, which asked its writers to use the International Extension College manual on their own, found that the trainees needed an opportunity to discuss their work.

Workshops

In my experience, intensive training and writing workshops are the best form of training. In a workshop of 2 or 3 weeks, trainee writers both learn the job and produce some finished lessons. Training manuals come into their own, forming the basis for seminars. Writers get feedback from trainers and other writers, which builds their confidence. Even a workshop of 1 week can be satisfactory, especially if it is followed by support from an editor.

In-service training

This is the best term to describe training which involves an editor and a writer working closely together. Such training can be individualised, and can take place face-to-face and by correspondence. Training manuals can be used, on the advice of the editor. This method has many advantages: in particular, the problems of teaching specific subjects at a distance can be closely examined. However, there is a risk that it will not be systematic enough, and writers will lack the benefits gained from group work in a workshop.

Given the choice, I would prefer to train writers in workshops. But, clearly, different methods are appropriate in different cases. Whatever the method, it is important to give writers the satisfaction of achieving results soon. And this means that a writer needs to get at least one lesson written quite quickly. Once a writer has written a lesson or section and revised it, or knows how to do so, he should be able to continue with confidence. Formal training can stop here, to be supplemented with informal advice.

Conclusions

This paper has looked at the sort of training writers require, what that training should include, and different training methods. I've suggested that, since training must be selective, training programmes should be designed to take into account writers' attitudes. Dominant attitudes today are largely due to the mystique that has grown round the concept of distance teaching. Writers are misled into thinking either that the whole business is very difficult, or that there is a simple system which will provide them with infallible guidance. I've suggested that, to overcome these difficulties, actual writing of lessons should form part of a training programme.

Janet Jenkins
International Extension College
United Kingdom

References

International Extension College (1979) *Writing for Distance Education*. Cambridge: International Extension College.

Paper 85

Learning Spanish at a Distance

As global interdependence becomes a reality we must learn to communicate with people of different languages and cultures.

Since at least fifteen million Hispanics live in the United States making it the fourth largest Spanish-speaking nation in the world, the potential market for elementary Spanish courses is tremendous. The main emphasis of this paper will be on courses which rely primarily on written communication.

Distance education language programs are attractive to full-time students who have schedule conflicts or who need to accelerate their progress in order to meet graduation or other deadlines, and to individuals who simply enjoy learning for its own sake. Of those who choose to study by this method, some may want oral skills for travel-related reasons or for more effective communication with friends or colleagues. Others seek writing skills in order to carry out business or personal correspondence, and still others hope to learn how to read foreign literature for research or pleasure. The main problem confronting the correspondence educator is deciding the goal of a foreign language course.

While on-campus courses generally emphasize the four skills related to language learning (i.e., speaking, listening, writing, and reading), distance education must be flexible in order to meet diverse needs. Ideally correspondence departments should offer courses combined with radio, television, telephone, computers, or other media, which make acquiring the four skills possible. A survey of language teaching at a distance conducted in October, 1979, by Muriel Stringer at Athabasca University, however, revealed very little use of radio and television programs, or even of cassette tapes. Radio and television delivery can be particularly effective in language learning, as Abrioux (1981: 12) notes, because the student can be presented a variety of native voices and real-life situations.

More media usage in distance language courses is imperative, not only because many students want and expect it, but also because traditional methods of teaching both in the classroom and by correspondence are rapidly becoming obsolete as a result of modern technology. Samuel L. Dunn (1979: 389) predicts that education will move from the campus to the living room with improvements in cable television, the computer and other modern delivery systems. Thus, correspondence study combined with these systems could well be the primary method of education in the future, and distance education language teachers should be heading in that direction now.

The desirability of offering language courses through newer media does not reduce the value of programs which rely on written communication, provided they are flexible enough to fulfill the different desires of adult learners. One option is to offer courses geared to specific needs such as "Spanish for the Traveller" or "Businessmen's Spanish", in which different skills can be emphasized. When this approach is not feasible, a general course can be organized in two separate parts: one mandatory for all students and another consisting of four tracts, one of which would be selected by each student. The four tracts may be designated as follows: Tract A—Speaking; Tract B—Listening; Tract C—Writing; and Tract D—Reading. At the time of enrollment, the student must indicate the tract he wishes to pursue. He then will be sent, in addition to the syllabus, the appropriate packet of materials for that particular tract.

Each lesson in the syllabus should have an assignment from the textbook, when used, or basic grammatical explanations and vocabulary to be studied by all the students. The packet must also contain an additional assignment for each student. Tract A and B students, for example, would be required to purchase tapes on which dialogues and oral exercises are recorded. Tract A students would also be given blank cassettes and instructions for recording lessons. Tract B students might listen to recorded stories or anecdotes and then be asked to summarize them in English. Tract C students could have exercises for translation from English to Spanish or paragraph topics on which to write. Tract D students would be provided with reading selections and asked to summarize or answer questions. With the provision of optional tracts, the student will be able to concentrate on the skills most compatible with his goals.

Motivating the student

Once the student is enrolled, his motivation must be maintained through an attractive, carefully developed syllabus. Technical considerations are very important since the student's first impressions are based on the syllabus cover and the arrangement of the printed matter on the page. To involve the student immediately the cover should reflect some aspect of Spanish culture; for example, Indiana University's beginning Spanish course for high school students, which won an NUEA Distinguished Course Award in 1979-80, has a deep red cover with a black ink sketch of Don Quixote and Sancho Panza. As the student moves from the cover and glances through his syllabus, he should see things which cause him to pause for a second look: maps of various Spanish-speaking countries (in color if possible), cartoons in Spanish, crossword puzzles, Spanish recipes, charts, grammar points and vocabulary explained through graphics, Spanish songs (possibly with the music) and other eye-catching materials.

When the student begins reading the introduction, he should be confronted right away with the target language in the form of a greeting followed by the translation. The introductory paragraphs ought to stimulate interest in the Spanish-speaking world through the use of cultural materials or through questions that give information, such as "Did you know that the United States is the fourth largest Spanish-speaking nation in the world?"

Also necessary in these beginning paragraphs is what Holmberg (1974: 78) calls the "link-up with experience and interests." The student might be shown how much Spanish he already knows in names of foods *(chocolate)* or names of states *(Colorado)*. He can be reminded of terms learned through Westerns *(hombre, amigo)*. To build his confidence, he could be given a simple reading with many cognates or a short paragraph in English with Spanish words interspersed to show him how much can be learned from context.

After the student is properly motivated, matters pertaining to the course itself should be addressed. An explanation of good study techniques is essential. Information on dictionaries, vocabulary cards, end vocabularies, irregular verb charts and idioms should be given. In addition, the student should be told the estimated time the lessons will normally take for complete mastery since beginning lessons are often deceptively simple. He should also be provided with an optional timetable for turning in assignments.

Setting the tone

While the content of the introduction is important, the style and tone of writing also deserve careful attention. A personal tone can be established partly by using phrases in Spanish such as "Isn't that right?" "Do you agree?" or "What do you think?" Not only are key phrases reinforced, but the student will get the feel of two-way communication.

A personal touch can be maintained throughout the course by means of periodic telephone calls to the student, an occasional greeting card in Spanish, an evaluation on cassette tape of the student's progress, humorous interjections in the syllabus, and by comments or questions on the evaluation sheet. These comments, in the target language when possible, can be based on specific information the grader has about the student's job or family, or on general topics such as the weather or current events, particularly those relating to Spanish-speaking countries. Newspaper or magazine clippings, which would help the student relate his language experience to the real world and thereby avoid the feeling of learning in a vacuum, can be mailed periodically. The student may, in turn, be asked for his reaction.

While a good introduction is essential, no less care should be given to the first lesson. A good way to begin is to provide the student with a packet of slides showing interesting features of various Spanish-speaking countries. A script with explanations of the slides should include not only factual material about the individual pictures but also Spanish vocabulary and possibly some of the elementary rules of pronunciation with names of places used as examples. The first written assignment may be an encyclopedia report on a certain cultural topic or a list of questions to be answered from the slide script. This kind of lesson will help motivate the student to learn the language of the people and places to which he has been introduced.

Helping students complete

Just as the introduction and the first lesson must be carefully constructed to maintain student interest, the remaining assignments should have several key elements to assure a successful completion of the course. One of these is thorough explanatory material. When a textbook is used, adequate discussion of idioms and unusual vocabulary, elaborations on grammar points, study tips, definitions of terms and concrete examples must still be given. The basics of English grammar should also be provided when appropriate since instructors cannot assume that students understand the rules of their own language.

Another key element is review. Each assignment must begin with a summary of the material covered in the previous lesson. To make the student aware of his weaknesses, a short self-check quiz should be included as part of the opening section of each assignment. A review of structures previously introduced must also be incorporated into the explanations of new grammatical concepts. These new concepts need to be presented gradually using the concentric method, an effective technique for language learning whereby the teacher introduces a small part of the difficult material at a time, supports it with secondary material and checks the student's knowledge before bringing in additional difficult material (Holmberg, 1974: 25). Also as part of the review process, three or four self-check tests which use the same format and grading scale as the final exam should be spaced evenly throughout the course. The graded exam should be sent to the instructor, who would determine weak areas and make suggestions for further study.

A third key element of success is variety. Whereas the initial review helps to reorient the student into thinking Spanish and to give him confidence, the remaining part of the assignment should have some surprises. Knowing exactly what is

Paper 85

involved before he begins the lesson often causes the student to procrastinate. Variety can be achieved through the length and difficulty of the assignments and through visuals and enrichment materials. Verb charts, crossword puzzles and other graphics mentioned previously should not be gimmicks merely to entertain the student but teaching aids for vocabulary building and recall or for spelling skills. Short anecdotes in Spanish break the monotony of grammar and also give the student a feeling of accomplishment when he sees rules and vocabulary used in a meaningful way. A cassette tape with simple Spanish songs and the script may be sent at some point in the course. Information on free materials available—for example, Spanish aviation packets* or a Spanish cookbook**—should be provided. Optional assignments for extra credit such as preparing a Spanish dish, attending a play or film relating to Spanish-speaking countries, or reading a Spanish novel in translation and then reporting the event to the teacher will encourage the student to make Spanish a part of his everyday world, thereby creating a more valuable learning experience which will provide the basis for continued enrichment of his life even after the course is completed.

A final key to the success of the course is sensitivity to student problems since studying a foreign language for the first time can be very frustrating. A brief questionnaire should be sent after three or four lessons to determine any difficulties. At the end of the course a more complete survey form, which elicits specific responses about course content, oral work, and taped or written exercises, should also be filled out by each student. Changes should always be made in response to frequent complaints.

In conclusion, as global interdependence becomes an increasing reality, contemporary man must be able to communicate with peoples of different languages and different cultures. Correspondence educators should be aware now, as never before, of the need for many stimulating courses in foreign languages at all levels, which use newer media as well as traditional systems of delivery. These courses, if carefully organized, can help adult learners obtain the necessary skills to live and work effectively in the modern world, which is continually becoming smaller and smaller as a result of improvements in transportation and communications technologies.

Doris T. Stephens
University of Tennessee
United States

References

Abrioux, D (1981) Studying French at a distance: a captive Canadian audience. *ICCE Newsletter,*. 10, 4, 12-13.
Dunn, S.L. (1979) The case of the vanishing colleges. *The Futurist,* October, 385-393.
Holmberg, B. (1974) *Distance Education: A Short Handbook.* Malmo,: Hermods.

---

* The Federal Aviation Administration offers a free packet of materials, including a set of ditto masters in Spanish/English entitled: *Un Viaje al Aeropuerto.* Write: Federal Aviation Administration, United States DOT, Facilities Management Branch TAD-443, Washington, DC 20590; request the Bilingual Aviation Materials (No. Ga-300-120).

** *Best Spanish Cuisine (Cocina Española)* can be ordered from the Instituto del Olivo, Españoleto 19, Madrid, Spain.

Paper 86

Teaching University French from a Distance: The Student Population Examined

French courses attract students who do not wish to enrol in a complete university program.

Should course development in non-traditional universities be aimed at the traditional university student or at the individual who is motivated by personal reasons? The success of a program must depend upon the aims it sets out to achieve. Nowhere is this more true, at Athabasca University, than in the French language program. Initiated only in September of 1978, the course offerings now allow a student to enrol in a B.A. with a concentration (major) in French.

Moreover, the first three courses developed are directly transferable to other (traditional) universities. Significant also are the high enrolments the individual courses have attracted, their acceptable completion rate, and the percentage of completers who re-enrol in a subsequent course.

It must be admitted that our striking success not result from careful planning and market studies to assess either the need for a distance-delivered French (second language) program, or the form it should take. The venture was truly a shot in the dark. When first retained as the subject matter expert to package an introductory French language course and coordinate its delivery, I was faced with the following situation: the BBC multi-media general interest course *Ensemble* had already been selected; this had been made not by an expert in second-language instruction, but by an instructional designer whose knowledge of French was limited to the first year university level; within two months, I not only had to adapt this purchased course to the Athabasca University model (with which I was not familiar) but also to modify it to ensure its acceptance for transfer by other Alberta universities. That these aims were achieved at all, never mind on schedule, is evidence that the team approach to course development is essential. It must be stressed, however, that the instructional designer's primary role was that of course team manager, which proved an essential link between the conceptualization and production of the course.

With two years of data we can now analyze the demographic make-up of the students who enrolled. Such a study helps us to define the prospective students who can be attracted to distance-delivered university language courses.

We have restricted ourselves to data on students enrolled in three courses: *Ensemble* (Beginners), *Sur le vif* (First Year University), and *Allez France* (Second Year University). These courses all use the BBC series of the same names, and are supplemented in varying degrees by other instructional components. The *Ensemble* group comprises students who registered between September 1978 and October 1980, for *Sur le vif* between September 1979 and October 1980, and for *Allez France* during September and October 1980. As the level of the course increases, the number of students decreases.

The accompanying tables cast light on two fundamental questions: why do certain adults choose to study French at a distance and who are these individuals? Table 1 indicates the program students selected.

It is of particular note that 70% of the students in the beginners course were non-program students. While the more advanced courses attracted fewer students in this category (61% in *Sur le vif*, 57% in *Allez France*), a clear majority of students enrolled in these courses for non-program related reasons.

Two conclusions emerge from Table 1. First, all three courses attracted considerably more non-program than program students. Second, whereas enrolments decline as the level of the course increases, the percentage of program students increases.

In this context, the information provided in Table 2 follows logically.

Students selected one reason from each of two categories. In the first, which asks whether the student is enrolling for career, educational, or personal reasons, over 50% indicated a personal motivation. The career category attracted nearly half of the remaining selections from each group.

The conclusions to be drawn from the second category are less tangible. "Time" indicates a student's perception that this mode of course delivery fits his lifestyle better than regular classroom instruction. More students selected Athabasca University for this reason than for any other, but the percentage motivated by this factor diminished as the course level increased.

The reasons that attract adults to learn French at Athabasca University help to explain the sex and age distribution of the samples. (See Table 3)

Table 1: Program choices of students

	Ensemble		Sur le vif		Allez France	
	N	%	N	%	N	%
Non-program	184	70	77	61	16	57
Bachelor of General Studies	13	5	8	6	2	7
Bachelor of Arts	14	5	15	11	6	22
Bachelor of Administration	6	2	3	2		
Transfer/Visiting	44	17	24	19	4	14
No response	3	1	-	-	-	-
Total	264	100%	127	99%	28	100%

Whereas 70% of the *Ensemble* sample was female, for both *Sur le vif* and *Allez France* this figure rose to 79%. This is significantly higher than the university-wide average of 62%, which can be attributed in part to the comparatively high percentage of women who usually register in second language courses. The figures on average ages are also higher than the university average. The age range narrowed as the course became more advanced; however, the most advanced course had 25% of its students over 60.

The broad age range for the beginners course results from the course's level of difficulty: like matriculation it attracts a handful of secondary school students who require an individualized, self-paced program. In turn, *Allez France,* drew nobody under the age of 20 and thereby had the narrowest age range.

The fact that adults who have attained the age of 65 do not pay tuition fees may initially lead them to register in university courses. However, this does not account for their selection of distance learning nor for their remarkable success rate. Given the difficulties of learning a language at this mature age and the lack of a financial commitment, one would expect this group to be less successful than others. This is not the case, and six of the seven (85%) from this age bracket to register in *Allez France* had successfully completed both *Ensemble* and *Sur le vif.*

The final table presents the residential distribution of the samples.

The three cities identified in the table house traditional universities. These cities supply more than 65% of the student body. This is particularly noteworthy since urban centres of their size offer numerous alternatives to adults desiring to learn French: other university courses, extension classes, continuing education programs, profit-making business organizations, French or French-Canadian associations and church groups, to name but a few. We have seen that the choice of Athabasca University was motivated by the time advantages of learning at a distance. The ability to complete the course and to continue learning a language through this medium depends upon students' assessment of the course.

Athabasca University's initial good fortune in adapting an existing course to serve both the adult in search of a university education and the adult motivated by some other reason, cannot be overemphasized. The first year's enrolment in *Ensemble* was found to be predominantly non-traditional. This fact, together with the institution's paranoia about approval and recognition from traditional universities, led to a unique multi-media approach to the distance delivery of second language courses.

Dominique A.M.X. Abrioux
Athabasca University
Canada

Table 2: Reasons for Attending Athabasca University

Category 1	Ensemble		Sur le vif		Allez France	
	N	%	N	%	N	%
Career	44	17	22	17	7	25
Educational	31	12	21	17	5	18
Personal	153	58	72	57	11	39
No response	36	13	12	9	5	18
Total	264	100	127	100	28	100

Category 2	Ensemble		Sur le vif		Allez France	
	N	%	N	%	N	%
Time	127	48	49	39	7	25
Distance	42	16	32	25	8	29
Educational	44	17	22	17	6	21
Financial	13	5	7	6	2	7
No response	38	14	17	13	5	18
Total	264	100	127	100	28	100

Table 3: Sex/age distribution

Sex	Ensemble		Sur le vif		Allez France	
	N	%	N	%	N	%
Male	78	30	27	21	6	21
Female	186	70	100	79	22	79
No response	-	-	-	-	-	-
Totals	264	100	127	100	28	100

Age	Ensemble		Sur le vif		Allez France	
	N	%	N	%	N	%
-20	5	2	5	4	-	-
21-29	60	23	28	22	6	21
30-39	87	33	36	28	7	25
40-49	51	19	29	23	6	21
50-59	18	7	13	10	2	7
+60	43	16	16	12	7	25
Total	264	100	127	99	28	99
Average	41 years		40 years		45 years	
Range	67 years		57 years		49 years	

Table 4: Residence distribution

	Ensemble		Sur le vif		Allez France	
	N	%	N	%	N	%
Greater Edmonton	164	64	68	54	15	52
Calgary	21	8	19	15	4	14
Lethbridge	6	2	3	2	0	0
Elsewhere	64	25	37	29	10	34
Total	255	99	127	100	29	100

Paper 87

Learning French at a Distance: The Student's Perspective

Students can learn at a distance to speak a new language provided they make use of opportunities for practice outside the course.

The home-based course always presents difficulties to the student. Some of these are course-specific and stem from the nature of the content and the way it is communicated; others are more general problems of home-study, such as failure to sustain motivation and discipline, and inability to schedule time and to cope with conflicting demands.

Athabasca University began offering French language courses in October, 1978 through mixed media systems involving television, radio, and telephone tutoring as well as print materials.

A survey carried out in other institutions teaching languages at a distance showed that this is a considerably richer mixture than is generally used. At

Table 1: Course components[1]

Course materials[2]	Beginner (French 103)	Intermediate (French 242)	Advanced (French 361)
Television (BBC)	24		
Radio (BBC)	24	20	20
Audio cassettes (BBC)	2	2	2
Language laboratory (non-monitored)	20	11	0
Textbooks (BBC)	2	2	1
Textbooks (Other)	0	2	2
Study guide/workbooks	1	1	1
Student manual	1	1	1
Tutorial Support			
Oral-telephone (bi-weekly)	11	15	15
Oral-seminar (bi-weekly)	12	16	5
Written-exercises	12	10	15
-essays	—	4	8
Assessment			
Written - exams	2	2	2
Oral - exams	2	2	2

[1] The figures opposite each type of component represent numbers of television or radio programs, workbooks, etc. With respect to the tutorial support, the figures indicate the number of times the student has contact with the tutor.

[2] The BBC series *Ensemble, Sur le Vif* and *Allez France* are integrated into the respective courses. In the intermediate and advanced courses, however, they are utilized primarily as oral components, and are supplemented with grammar and literature units.

Athabasca, the product of the recipe seems to be palatable since the language program is considered one of the University's more successful ventures, with an average completion rate across courses of about 60%.

Evaluation has been a continuing process since the courses were first offered, most of the data being collected through questionnaires. Course designers are not usually willing to sample the instructional smorgasbord they have concocted for consumption by others but in this case, having acted as designer/manager for the two years when the foundation courses in the French program were being prepared, I then enrolled as a student in two of the courses consecutively. To gain a broader sample of the student's perspective of language learning, I also carried out a telephone survey among forty-three students across the three core courses. The composition of the sample is shown in Table 2.

In all three courses, the greatest deficiency seemed to be in the lack of conversation practice. In the intermediate and advanced courses, difficulties with grammar were also experienced by a number of students.

Perceptions of the usefulness of radio and television in helping the development of verbal skills varied a good deal, but most students seemed to believe that the cassette tapes provided for home use were a valuable part of the package.

None of the components listed in Table 4 requires the student to respond verbally in any way, and none provides feedback on the students' attempts to speak the language.

Two possibilities for live conversation formed part of the instructional system: a province-wide telephone tutoring service, and, in Edmonton, a discussion group or bi-weekly seminar.

Through the telephone tutorial system, the student has access to a French-speaking tutor at specified times, usually during the evening. Tutor calls may be made to ask for help on grammar or vocabulary problems, to take oral exams, or simply to speak French and to check pronunciation. The calls may be initiated by the student or by a tutor concerned about apparent lack of progress of one of his charges. Reactions of students to telephone tutoring were mixed.

Table 2: Structure of student sample

Course Number	Number of Students in Sample Taking Course For Interest	Number of Students in Sample Taking Course For A Degree	Total
103 (Beginner)	9	6	15
242 (Intermediate)	7	5	12
361 (Advanced)	10	6	16

Table 3: Major problems identified by students

Course Number	Number of Students With Conversation Problems	Number of Students With Grammar Problems
103 (Beginner)	8	1
242 (Intermediate)	10	4
361 (Advanced)	11	5

Table 4: Reactions to non-interactive components

Course Number	Radio			Television			Audio and Cassettes		
	+ve	−ve	Neutral	+ve	−ve	Neutral	+ve	−ve	Neutral
103 (Beginner)	3	6	6	3	8	4	10	3	2
242 (Intermediate)	2	7	3	NA	NA	NA	9	1	2
361 (Advanced)	4	6	5	NA	NA	NA	10	2	4

Table 5: Reactions to telephone tutoring

Course Number	+Ve	−Ve	Neutral
103 (Beginner)	4	6	7
242 (Intermediate)	9	3	0
361 (Advanced)	5	4	7

In the beginner course, where the learner had very little command of the spoken word, there was a marked reluctance to attempt to converse over the phone. Some students disliked talking to a disembodied voice, others complained of poor quality of sound on the line, and a few confessed to feeling embarrassed and inhibited even before members of their own families who might overhear the conversation. Talking by telephone seemed less threatening to students in the more advanced courses, presumably because of an increased ability to speak the language and a concomitant growth in confidence.

Seminars, while considered very useful by those who participated, were poorly attended and were regarded in general as an unanticipated inconvenience.

Almost without exception, convenience and flexibility were the features that attracted students to the Athabasca courses as opposed to other options, such as campus day classes or evening courses. Any requirement or even option to leave home to attend a conversation group at a specified time tended to be difficult for most students to accommodate, and discussion groups thus served only a small proportion.

Interestingly, several students appeared to be pursuing a policy of self-help and were attempting to improve their verbal and comprehension skills by use of people and other resources not provided as parts of the courses.

Problems with grammar stemmed from two sources: a poor grasp of the fundamental principles of English grammar; and the use in the advanced course of a grammar book written entirely in French.

Substitution of explanations of grammar rules in English seems a straightforward solution to this last problem. A variety of strategies might be used to help the student overcome deficiencies in English grammar, such as pre-testing, and provision of remedial materials, or the interpolation into the package of a series of remedial loops based on materials illustrating particular grammatical principles.

Coping with conversation is, however, a much more difficult task, the suggestions from students and from my own experience falling essentially into two groups, viz (i) radical changes in the commitment the University makes to teach language skills, and (ii) changes in the communication systems used and their importance in the total delivery system.

Simplest—but probably least palatable from the University's point of view—is to cease trying to teach the student to speak the language and to concentrate on teaching him to read and write it well. Alternatively, the institution may choose to offer a separate, campus-based conversation component much like the widely used immersion course. In this case, it would consist of a session designed to follow rather than to be integrated with a course on the non-verbal elements. Collaboration with other organizations

Table 6: Attendance at seminars

Course Number	Number of Sample Students Attending	Number of Sample Students Not Attending Available Seminars	Number of Students To Whom No Seminar Was Available
103 (Beginner)	4	8	3
242 (Intermediate)	4	6	2
361 (Advanced)	5	6	5

Table 7: Use of outside resources

Course Number	Numbers in Sample Conversing with People Other Than Tutor	Watching TV Other Than AU Programs	Listening To Radio Other Than AU Programs	Reading Materials Other Than AU Course Books
103 (Beginner)	9	5	2	3
242 (Intermediate)	6	7	3	5
361 (Advanced)	9	8	6	8

better equipped to cope with the spoken aspects is also possible, and indeed some Athabasca students are already exploring such options to improve their conversation skills.

While the majority of the students seemed to accept with good grace that "the penalty of convenience is a cut in conversation", it may be premature to abandon attempts to teach students to speak a second language through distance delivery systems. It is true that increased one-to-one tutoring by telephone would become prohibitively expensive if every student had an adequate amount of conversation time. Reticence and distaste for conversing with an unknown individual could not, in any case, be overcome by increasing telephone time. But there are other electronic systems that may well be worth exploring. Teleconferencing offers the student the comfort of the support of his peers in much the same way as a discussion group without the inconveniences of travelling to a major centre. Such larger-scale telephone tutoring may, in fact, be one answer to the rising costs of personal service. Satellite link-ups may provide an even more attractive feature, with video as well as audio communication helping the student overcome his inhibitions.

One experiment which has not been found effective for the language student at Athabasca is the "study buddy" system whereby students wishing a telephone partner to talk with could have their names put on a list. None of the students in the survey sample had a "buddy" although some said they would very much like to.

It would be unfair, however, to give the impression that one cannot learn to speak a language through a distance teaching system such as that offered by Athabasca. It is possible, but only if the student avails himself of every opportunity both formally through the University and informally elsewhere. The language, if it is to become a part of the student's repertoire of skills, must be looked on not as a course to be taken as a discrete entity but as a part of the fabric of his life.

Muriel H.L. Stringer
Athabasca University
Canada

Teaching Languages Through Broadcasting

Broadcasting should be part of a learning strategy that gives the student a range of options.

Paper 88

There are many kinds of broadcast language provision, from structured courses broadcast to motivated students in off-peak times, to stimulatory programmes in which the cultural element is more important than the linguistic, transmitted in prime time on a national network. Between these extremes lie enrichment series, such as *Télé-Journal* and *Heute Direkt,* which show the evening news programs from French- and German-speaking countries with special explanations of cultural and linguistic differences and difficulties. The aim is to increase understanding of people and language and reduce the well-known British insularity which once made the Times of London report: 'Fog in Channel: Europe Isolated'.

Designers of multi-media language courses, while keen to offer the student a flexible learning system, need to be aware that too complex a package can be positively alienating. Such a system demands a high degree of commitment from the student in time and effort. The most effective multi-media courses are not necessarily those which use the largest number of components. To ensure that the course has the user very much in mind the following checklist of questions is helpful:

- Is it consciously designed to diminish anxiety?
- Is there as little reliance as possible on short-term memory?
- Is learning based on activity by the learner?
- Can the learner control the pace at which he works?
- Is the learner likely to achieve success at every stage?
- Can the learner find out whether he has learnt correctly?
- Is the material interesting, stimulating and relevant?
- Does it take account of the adult learner's existing experience?
- Are opportunities for constant practice built in?
- Can learners participate in learning with others?

In 1975 BBC Education broadcast a beginners course in German called 'Kontakte'. This was a milestone in broadcast language teaching. It was with this course that 'actuality'—real people speaking real language—came into its own. One innovatory aspect was that it first combined radio and television with joint support materials.

Other 'firsts' for the 'Kontakte' course were:

- the television programmes were entirely in German
- there were very close links with classes up and down the country
- flexible support materials including three film strips were usable at a variety of levels by teachers not necessarily using the 'Kontakte' course
- at the end of the course there was an optional achievement test devised and processed by the University of Cambridge Local Examinations Syndicate
- Bursaries were provided by the Federal Republic of Germany for six deserving students to spend a fortnight trying out their newly acquired 'Kontakte' Deutsch where it really mattered.

Most teachers and experts felt that combined radio and television courses marked a major step forward. Support materials were considered to be about right in quantity. The content and presentation of the course books came in for much praise, although more solid reference grammars were occasionally asked for—a possibility that the BBC is currently pursuing. Teachers' notes were welcomed but sometimes thought to be a little thin. There were requests too for in-service training provision on television which would assist teachers in exploiting the broadcast materials more fully. This suggestion was taken up with a series of programmes 'Modern Language Teaching' on television and 'Teaching Languages' on radio.

For the distant student following a broadcast course the importance of face-to-face counselling and the value of being able to practise speech in groups cannot be overemphasised. We have experimented with regional day clinics, where students can go for help, and a tutorial service by telephone. The latter has proved somewhat complex to organise. Over the years linked classes have proliferated and there has been enthusiastic support for residential summer schools.

Over the years there has been support for the policy of offering two showings and two hearings each week for a combined radio/television course. Busy people welcome the flexibility of alternative transmission times. For the motivated, there is no doubt that a pattern of watching the television programme, listening to the radio programme, using the recorded material and the course book, attending a linked class and then viewing and listening to the repeat transmissions is enormously beneficial, but it takes more time than many followers of broadcast language courses are ready or able to give.

In our consultations it has been made apparent over and over again that there is a powerful need to build students' confidence in a system that is new to them. Adult attitudes are notoriously difficult to shift. They have a healthy scepticism of new ideas. Letters and surveys have revealed that plenty of guidance is needed to show students how a package of broadcasts, print and recorded material works and what is the role of the various components. More discussion of different ways of combining the components and more sympathy and understanding for the fact that many students have little time to spare is needed. More guidance on how to plan study and, at a more basic level, how to return to study can be given both on television and in books. Radio phone-ins can enable students to share their experiences and problems. Those who attend classes have this exchange of views and discussion of learning difficulties built in, but for those studying on their own constant reassurance is essential. It is therefore important to try to build into a broadcast course at frequent intervals some form of monitoring or self-assessment.

A Russian course

The reactions of tutors who are using the materials are of particular interest and their evaluative comments have brought a number of profound changes to the style and approach of BBC language courses over the past decade. So has the emergence of new transmission times. The most recent multi-media course, 'Russian—Language and People' managed to win a peak-time placing on BBC-2. The programme needed, therefore, to be accessible to the widest possible audience and to be lively in style and presentation and strictly limited in linguistic scope.

The course avoided grammatical terminology and tried to provide a learning experience which, although it progressed to a useful level, was accessible to an audience of very limited linguistic sophistication. The television programmes were so constructed that a potential viewer would not reject them at any stage because of his lack of language. The intention was to provide enough in each unit to entertain and interest him in the Soviet Union and to keep him engaged. Because of the nature of the Russian alphabet and the difficulties of the language, the established hierarchy of language learning skills was changed. Putting reading comprehension first, followed by listening comprehension, speaking and writing reflected the importance of the alphabet as an obstacle to be overcome in the early stages—the real-life situation of visitors to the Soviet Union. Social sight word recognition on a word shape basis was used to teach the Russian alphabet, including film of such words in their realistic contexts inside and outside Moscow shops, cinemas, hotels, cafes, etc.

Television is clearly the medium best equipped to provide the widespread stimulus needed, if only in terms of sheer numbers reached. In pedagogical terms its visual strength is ideally suited to presenting an unfamiliar alphabet and the BBC's computer played a major creative role during the series, as did specially taken photographs of shop and street signs in Moscow and Leningrad. Perhaps most importantly, television can portray something of how ordinary Russians talk, look, dress, behave and live their everyday lives. A central feature of the series, therefore, was the use of film interviews with ordinary Russians in a variety of situations.

The support materials—book and audio cassettes—go into the language in more depth, both within each unit and in the very full grammar section; the page margins of the book and chapter summaries form a continual reference system and a progress check. The support materials, though following the same themes as the television programmes, have a different content. They deliberately do not merely reproduce the material in the programmes but are designed to be used independently and to have a longer life than the transmission period. The book contains many exercises based on stimulation and understanding by means of word games, recognition of sounds, survival exercises of various kinds, and also provides systematic grammar for those interested in taking the study of Russian further.

The book and the cassettes are designed to be used in very close conjunction, particularly as far as the alphabet is concerned, relating the look of the characters to the sound of the letters. Some exercises can only be done by using book and cassettes together.

The methodology of the whole course is heavily biased towards recognition and comprehension, with the support materials involving the learner more actively in developing these skills. It is a distinctive learning package with the stimulus and cultural context on television and a large amount of practice material in the course book and on cassettes. The Russian course book was reprinted after only one month and early programmes in the series reached an audience of 1 1/4 million—the highest for any BBC language series to date.

Nevertheless, for most adults who lead busy lives, 20 weeks is a long commitment. The drop-out rate is high and personal factors of family, health and work intervene. Reasons for drop-out are overwhelmingly personal rather than course-based. But there may be gentler and more enticing ways of presenting materials with plenty of revision and overlap built in at all stages, so that the challenge is a series of shorter bursts of activity that the student can opt in or out of, mastering a bit at a time. Recent research has pointed to the importance of a variety of forms of learner support—a broadly based learning strategy, the core of which is the BBC course book and the broadcasts. This implies a set of options for flexible use by the learner, who can choose between different forms of support according to his needs and inclinations. Classes exist up and down the country; self-help groups are growing; a course newspaper has proved popular linked to a major language course; a correspondence course was voted by 65% of learners in one research study to be highly desirable and residential courses and weekends, ideally in the country of the target language, provide excellent ways of keeping in touch with like-minded students and sustaining momentum and motivation. Television, radio, cassettes and print are powerful aids to language learning. But broadcasters must always remember that they cannot operate effectively in a vacuum.

Sheila Innes
British Broadcasting Corporation
United Kingdom

Distance Education for the In-Service Training of Teachers

Paper 89

In-service teacher education requires a special combination of media and face-to-face meetings.

Introduction

The UNRWA/Unesco* Institute of Education is responsible for the in-service training of widely spread Palestinian teachers serving in UNRWA/Unesco schools in five areas: Jordan, Syria, Lebanon, West Bank and Gaza Strip.

* UNRWA is the acronym for "United Nations Relief and Works Agency for Palestine Refugees".

In the early years of UNRWA's existence, the vast majority of teachers in UNRWA schools had little experience and no professional training. Despite summer vacation courses, teachers' individual studies, and the newly established teacher training centres, efforts to remedy the situation were largely lost owing to the constant influx of new and untrained teachers to meet the natural growth in enrolment, and the steady drift of experienced teachers towards better paid jobs in the Gulf States and elsewhere.

By 1963, an estimated 90 per cent of the UNRWA/Unesco school teachers were professionally unqualified, which was a major obstacle in the way of developing a satisfactory education programme. The UNRWA/Unesco Department of Education recognized that an innovative approach to teacher training was needed, since the traditional method of withdrawing teachers from their classrooms and placing them in teacher training centres would temporarily deplete the ranks of UNRWA/Unesco teachers and be too expensive and time-consuming because of the numbers involved. Instead, the UNRWA/Unesco Institute of Education, a specialized institution for in-service training which has focussed on introducing modern teaching methods on a wide scale throughout the UNRWA/Unesco educational programme, was created and began operating in 1964, with the aim of improving the quality of education in UNRWA/Unesco schools through in-service training.

The methodology developed and used by the Institute is a multi-media approach which depends on the integration of various educational media within the framework of systematic in-service courses, with adequate provision for follow-up throughout each course. Indirect methods comprising self-study assignments, reference material, audio-visual media including closed circuit television, and a limited amount of programmed instruction are combined with direct methods of weekly seminars, tutorial guidance and practical training carried out by the field tutors and subject supervisors in the five fields. The direct methods are complemented by action research projects and intensive summer courses, which are normally held in UNRWA teacher training centres on a residential basis.

In the first stage of its operation, the Institute devoted most of its efforts to the upgrading of professionally unqualified elementary school teachers. Later, in-service courses were organized for preparatory school teachers. With the decline in the number of unqualified teachers in UNRWA/Unesco schools, it was possible to diversify the activities of the Institute to include courses for head teachers and other key educational personnel, refresher courses for qualified teachers, *ad hoc* courses and courses to meet curricular changes.

Distance education in in-service teacher training

For the in-service training of UNRWA/Unesco teachers, distance education takes a different approach from that of correspondence schools, open universities or external studies departments of traditional universities. To be successful in in-service teacher training distance education should:

- include face-to-face teaching

- ensure full integration of the various components of the multi-media approach

- include communication media as an integral part of the teacher training curriculum

- make extensive use of individualized and task-oriented instructional material

- rely heavily on evaluation and feedback for the continuous improvement of instructional material.

Face-to-face teaching

Is face-to-face teaching in distance education courses an optional extra, a compulsory element or merely a return to traditional methods of teaching?

In certain academic courses, the combination of face-to-face teaching with distant indirect methods may be desirable but not essential. In in-service teacher training, however, this combination is essential because it is dictated by the nature of many of the competencies with which the teacher/trainees should be provided. Teacher/trainees for example, are expected to put the theory they learn in assignments into practice in the classroom, and to give practical demonstration of the desired performance skills. Here are a few examples of the long list of competencies which graduates should possess:

- applying methods of teaching effectively, not as conveyors of knowledge, but as organizers, facilitators and promoters of their pupils' learning

- applying suitable motivation techniques

- maintaining an active teaching situation which reflects students' involvement and participation

- producing improvised AV media from materials available in the local environment

- employing various types of questions in the classroom, according to the objectives of the learning situation, including questions which stimulate students' interests and participation.

All these competencies necessitate the employment of face-to-face teaching which involves direct confrontation and interaction between teacher and learner. The absence of face-to-face teaching may defeat the main purposes of the in-service teacher education programme.

Integration of media

Practically every distance education expert calls for integration of media. Although intriguing and desirable, the term *integration* has remained vague and mystifying in many of the distance education courses organized for the tertiary cycle because it is not easy to give a practical application of the desired integration. In in-service teacher training, however, there is ample room for the achievement of integration between the media. The teacher/trainee is asked to read self-study assignment No. S/M/4 on the teaching of history through the use of source texts. This is followed by a seminar where difficulties are explained and where implications for teaching history based on source texts are discussed. In the same seminar participants are shown videogramme VT/St 10, dealing with the same subject, with the illustration of a demonstration lesson. Since the trainees are practising teachers, they will have the immediate opportunity to apply the theory in practice under the guidance of tutors. In summer courses they can also watch and discuss live demonstration lessons.

Media—an integral part of the curriculum

In a distance education curriculum communication media should not be conceived as additive frills and furbelows whose purpose is just to extend the range of experiences. They should be built into the curriculum in an integrative and inseparable fashion because of the nature of the target population. Being heterogeneous adults employed as teachers in remote places, the target population is, to a great extent, deprived of the face-to-face confrontation which normally exists between teacher and learner. Communication media are required to play an integrative role to replace the normal teacher/learner relationship and provide for the varying needs of the learners.

Learning objectives

In the selection of an approach medium the learning objectives must be one of the deciding factors. If the objective is affective, as in dramatic performance, TV or radio with complementary activities may be the most suitable. But if the objective is cognitive, involving analysis as in philosophy, the printed word will probably be more effective. For the presentation of skills, direct confrontation or TV viewing with supporting home kits are called for.

Forms of knowledge

When selecting distance media the form of the knowledge to be imparted must be considered. Forms of knowledge differ in the practical and intellectual skills they entail. Each has its unique concepts, logical structure, methods of enquiry and thought, and criteria of truth. The historical method of enquiry is based on the availability and interpretation of evidence. The structure of mathematics is logical and deals with concepts which are derived in terms of other concepts; the ability to deduce a result within its axiom system is its criterion of truth. The physical sciences require the observation of phenomena, curiosity or wonder, questioning, hypotheses, experimentation and confirmation or rejection. Language may be divided into symbolic and aesthetic aspects. The former requires methods related to reception (listening and reading) and production (speaking and writing), whereas the latter requires methods related to literary appreciation and criticism.

Importance of dialogue

In these days of electronic magic it is sometimes forgotten that learning is a conversational process (dialogue). Learning involves progressive interaction between originator and receiver, or teacher and learner. Thus, dialogue is essential to all communication media. Naturally, the extent to which dialogue can be active depends upon the nature of the subject being communicated. The radio and TV teaching and information programmes, in their present form, have limited impact because of their one-way non-interactive function and the speed at which they are presented. Although teaching by these media is recommended from all sides, this limitation must be taken into account. Any audio-visual electronic programme used must be complemented by other media to ensure dialogue, such as telephone conversation, or written answers or direct confrontation methods like seminars, workshops and tutorial meetings.

Cultural and language background of learners

Another important factor is the cultural and language background of the adult learners. If the learners are adults with academic qualifications lower than full secondary, they may need simple language and publications in the form of leaflets and flipcharts. Many teachers may not respond actively to sophisticated modern media, like computer-based information systems. They may prefer seminars or tutorial work or social symposia which are called in Arabic *Madafa* or *Diwaniyya*.

Individualization of learning

Although the teachers enrolled in a particular course are roughly homogeneous in terms of paper qualifications they are really a heterogeneous group for several reasons. They obtained their qualifications at different times and in varying contexts, and they differ widely in their conditions of life and work, their study pace and their readiness to respond to the various media.

For a long time self-study work assignments were the backbone and master medium of the instructional materials addressed to teacher/trainees. It has been realized recently that more extensive attempts should be made to individualize instruction and use other media as the master medium. Programmed learning was used to a very limited extent (topics on programmed instruction, mathematics, cartography). Recently individualized materials were produced for:

— Teacher as change agent in the Palestine community (module)
— Nutrition and nutrition education (module)
— Prevention of accidents (learning package)
— Concepts and methods of teaching (learning package).

In several cases the master medium is no longer the work assignment but closed circuit TV videogrammes, films and slides, which are complemented by activities presented in the form of print.

The teachers also learn to individualize instruction through the use of job sheets, exercise cards, and elaborative thinking cards.

Feedback

Experience has indicated the need for the development of regular feedback devices to ensure that the instructional materials are effectively accomplishing their objectives and to acquire information to be used for continuous revision.

Teaching training needs

Teaching training needs should always be consulted to determine the content and methodology of the in-service training programme. The Institute used to rely on the subjective impressions and judgements of supervisors. Recently, a questionnaire has been developed to seek the views of the teachers themselves.

Pre-service and in-service teacher education used to be attached to two different divisions. Arguments arose about which of the two types of training was more effective. Its sponsors argued that pre-service training had better facilities, and the student/teachers dedicated themselves completely to study and application. Sponsors of in-service training argued that their trainees lived the reality of their schools, had better and closer understanding of their children and were immediately able to apply in classroom teaching the theories they had learned in the seminars.

About three years ago the two divisions were amalgamated in order to establish and develop integration and complementarity between the two kinds of training. It was felt that pre-service education could be no more than an initial foundation and could not provide for all the changing demands of a school system. Studies are now underway for the introduction of the induction year whose main objective is to help new teachers who graduated from UNRWA/Unesco teacher training centres in the preceding summer to overcome the difficulties and troubles they may face in their first year of teaching.

If the aim of training is to qualify untrained teachers, pre-service teacher education and in-service teacher education may be identical in terms of general objectives and competencies. In-service teacher education may, however, differ with respect to methodology and content because its target population is adults already employed as teachers and in close touch with their children.

Continuity of in-service training

From the point of view of the UNRWA/Unesco school system, in-service education and training of teachers is necessary for the upgrading of untrained teachers and for solving the problems of curricular change which are now frequent and considerable in the Arab World. But even without these pressures the retention of in-service training would be imperative. The role of the teacher will continue to change and expand. He should be made aware of the new patterns of his responsibilities and provided with training to perform them.

A.M. Nashif
UNRWA/Unesco
Jordan

Uses of Case Studies in Self-Learning Texts

Paper 90

(Abstract)

The essential difficulty in teaching technology is handling complexity. Real-world problems are solved by application of several models, often stemming from academic disciplines that would traditionally be regarded as distinct. The conventional development of the skills for attacking such problems has been by integration of separately mastered techniques—e.g., economics, mathematics, science.

Encouraged by the spur of teaching adult part-time students who from experience realize the need for coordinating disparate knowledge but who lack the knowledge itself, the Faculty of Technology at Open University has made much use of case studies. Case studies describe the real world with sufficient complexity to provoke the need to master particular branches of knowledge, which are then taught.

This paper enunciates the pedagogical principles of this style of teaching and explores, with examples, some of its advantages and snags for both author and student. The structural variety of courses using case studies is displayed. Conclusions are drawn in the form of criteria for the selection of case study topics.

Graham H. Weaver
Open University
United Kingdom

The Training of Teachers of Second Languages at a Distance

Paper 91

Courses centred on video tape have satisfied an important need quickly and successfully.

Canada is a large country with two official languages, English and French, and in one of its ten provinces, Quebec, French is the official language. In addition, there is a native population of Indians and Inuit who speak a multiplicity of languages and dialects and immigration has brought to Canada large numbers of people whose first language is neither French nor English. Clearly, in Canada second language teaching warrants considerable attention.

The great majority of French-speaking Canadians is concentrated in Quebec. In the province's total population of approximately 6,000,000 (27% of Canada's population), about 4,800,000 speak French, 800,000 speak English, 18,000 use native languages and dialects, and some 250,000 speak other languages, the dominant one being Italian (100,000). Because of this diverse population, Quebec's need for teachers of French and English as second languages is great. Both French and English are compulsory subjects in the elementary and secondary schools where, in addition to regular instruction, there is a growing number of immersion programs. Furthermore, school boards, community colleges, and universities all offer language courses, mostly in the evening, to the adult population.

The university programs in Quebec to train specialists for this work cannot meet the demand. Therefore, many teachers with little or no training in second language teaching must be assigned this task in the public schools. The evening programs for adults fare even worse. Many teachers hold no qualifications whatever, let alone training in second languages, and because their employment is essentially part time, there is a high staff turnover. This high turnover makes it difficult to establish any kind of substantial training program.

To meet this need for trained second language teachers, the universities must continue to train specialists through their regular and part-time programs. However, the most urgent need is for emergency measures to help those who are teaching second languages with little or no training. There is a need for courses in basic second language instruction, going beyond survival skills, that could be offered virtually anywhere in Quebec.

Such courses should meet the following criteria:

1. high quality, combining a judicious mix of theory, demonstration and practice;

2. readily accessible to a population scattered over a large territory;

3. flexible and easily administered and capable of being put into operation quickly in response to demands;

4. personnel-effective since university resources are limited and largely committed to the regular programs;

5. cost-effective since only regular university funding is available.

To meet this challenge, McGill University's Faculty of Education designed two multi-media courses as portable units to be offered anywhere off-campus.

The first was an adaptation of *Teaching English as a Second Language—Secondary Schools,* a course given to regular students. The production was done entirely by the University's Instructional Communication Centre. The course consisted of twenty-two modules, each focussed on a half-hour video tape and supplemented by printed student instructions, notes, a textbook, and a travelling library. Content and procedures for workshops were designed to be conducted by animators, generally language consultants employed by school boards. A telephone service was made available for students needing additional assistance.

The course went through a pilot phase with the evaluation monitored by McGill's Centre for Learning and Development. It was offered on cable television in the Montreal area and in two off-campus locations, Arvida and Schefferville. The course was administered by the Faculty of Education's Office of Part-Time Studies which was responsible for registering students; supplying materials, directives, notes, textbooks, tapes, travelling library; collecting assignments, tests, mark reports; processing contracts, and payrolls.

The evaluation by the Centre for Learning and Development was most positive and coincided closely with the independent evaluation made by school board consultants. The teachers felt they had learned a great deal that was immediately applicable. There were no drop-outs and all received a passing grade. However, this achievement did not come easily since most of the teachers felt they had had to work very hard to meet the course requirements.

Administratively, the course was also a success. It was truly portable and it could be mounted virtually anywhere in the province within weeks of a request. It was effective in the use of personnel since no faculty member was needed to teach these additional sections. Because the course was modularized and taped, the student contact work (workshops, discussions and practical assignments) could be handled by local personnel—language consultants from school boards. The only responsibility left to faculty was the grading of assignments and final examinations, and this could be done by graduate students under faculty supervision.

The financial aspects of this course were most rewarding. The initial production costs were relatively low since McGill personnel, equipment and studios had been used, and other costs were minimal since the administration of the course was handled through the existing Office of Part-Time Studies. Tapes could be reused, and the cost of notes, textbooks, and other materials was recoverable through sale to students. Personnel costs for teaching were low also. Only a modest stipend was paid to local animators since their academic involvement and preparation was minimal. Finally, since this was a credit course, the University received full time equivalent student grants from the Ministry of Education.

Following this successful pilot phase the course underwent a number of minor revisions and adaptations to make it useful not only to secondary school teachers but also to those teaching in elementary schools and teaching adults. At this stage the Faculty felt it had met its objective of preparing and offering a course in the basic skills of teaching English as a second language.

Because of this success, the Faculty was requested to produce a similar course for the teaching of French as a second language. The need was described as urgent and the Ministry gave McGill a grant toward the production of this new course.

The production of the second course, *Didactique du Français pour adultes non-francophones,* proceeded very differently. This course was a team effort of five members. The course consisted of twelve modules centred on half-hour video tapes supported by audio tapes, printed directives, notes, a textbook, a travelling library, reading assignments, activities and tests. In terms of teaching and learning and administration, it followed a pattern similar to that of the English course. It sought to achieve the same objectives, training language teachers in basic skills at a distance.

This course will serve as an example of their basic pedagogical structure. Each of the 12 modules is divided into three parts totalling nine activities connected to the central activity of viewing the video tape.

A. Prior to Viewing the Video Tape
   1. Read
      a. the objectives of the module
      b. the plan of the video program;
   2. Read assigned sections of notes and other texts and write a comprehension test;
   3. Work on practical assignments specific to the module;
   4. Read the instructions accompanying the video tape.

B. Viewing the Video Tape

C. Post-Viewing of the Video Tape
   1. Participate in the discussion outlined in the module with an animator;
   2. Listen to the audio tape of the module to complete notes;
   3. Read complementary assignments from the textbook and travelling library, followed by a comprehension test;
   4. Work on a practical assignment outlined in the module.

All except two of the phases, viewing the tape and the discussion, can be done by the student alone, on his own time. The final evaluation is done by means of a computer-marked objective test.

This distance training of language teachers has continued from the 1977-78 academic year to the present (1981). These two courses were offered as twenty-two independent course sections in fifteen locations from Northern Quebec and the Arctic (some 1,500 kilometers away), to the Gaspé coast in the Gulf of St. Lawrence, to the Eastern Townships, and to Western Quebec, to a total of 371 teachers.

Evaluations have indicated that these courses have been successful and we have received numerous requests from school boards where these courses were given to continue the training process by offering teachers the complete 30 credit Certificate in Second Language Teaching. Hundreds of teachers have registered in this program which has created a demand for services that is stretching our resources to their limits. Since there are only two portable courses available, meeting this sudden influx of teachers has meant hiring numerous sessional lecturers to fly to many parts of the province to deliver courses in the traditional manner. However, it has produced also a considerable amount of activity in the preparation of other modular courses.

Réal G. Boulianne
McGill University
Canada

Music in Distance Education: Possibilities and Limitations

Music is communication, distance education is communication—how do you communicate a communication?

Introduction

Ten years ago if anyone had tried to convince me that distance education could be applied to music studies, I would probably have asked them whether they ever would consider flying with a pilot trained through correspondence courses. The reason for my attitude was the belief that music is a subject closely connected with skills, and skills are best learned when an experienced craftsman shows you how to execute them, directly and without the help of other means than his person and his instrument.

When the Northern Norwegian Music Conservatory four years ago started its interest in music as a subject for distance education, the school knew quite a lot about music, but nothing at all about distance education. During the first years, we did not even have the wit to ask those who did know. We still have not been able to ask all the questions we need answers to. What we know we have learned the hard way, by trial and error. Although our failures have been numerous, it still seems as if we are at the very beginning. We recognize music as a possible subject for distance education, but we still do not know how to go about it.

I am scared stiff at the thought of writing this article. My only reason for accepting the invitation is the welcome opportunity to pose questions in the hope that someone can supply the answers.

What are the reasons which prompted the youngest music conservatory in Norway, situated well above the Arctic Circle, to develop an interest in distance education?

Needs

In Northern Norway we have half the area, but only one tenth the population of the country. That means we have to cope with a scattered population—people living far apart, often in small communities. *Distance* is, in fact, one of our major problems. Living in Northern Norway one has the impression that Oslo is comparatively close, this because of our natural dependency on the central government. However, looked at from the south Tromso, for example, appears as remote as the North Pole.

This has resulted in political demands that even this part of the country should have the right to live and prosper, not only the big centers in the south. The political slogan deriving from this is "decentralisation", and we have during the last ten years begun to see a new development that will possibly reduce the second big problem in our area, *economy*.

Our musical life has recently exploded—if you can call it an explosion when it starts from practically nothing except the nostalgia of male voice choirs and school brass bands. Whatever it is called, it has produced activities in most areas of music and—more important—in even the smallest communities. But the communities are faced with a third serious problem, *lack of music instructors of all kinds*. The Conservatory wanted to help by educating local people in music at different levels. We thought this could be achieved by enabling students to live at home and work part time during their studies by using educational aids that reduced the need for local instructors. Thus we suddenly found ourselves with the need to provide the necessary materials for distance education.

Through the years we have been able to define other and more specific needs. We have seen possibilities where music education could be very successful with proper methods and materials of distance education. To mention a few:

1. Shorter subject-courses (evening courses, usually between 15 and 25 lessons, mostly for adults).

2. Instructors' courses for those working with music in small communities (choirs, brass bands, orchestras, ensembles, etc.).

3. Courses covering subjects required for entrance examinations to higher musical education.

4. Courses used to supplement institutional education in music.

5. Combined courses giving a career education.

A credo

What's so special about music? Can't music be treated just like every other subject which has been used in distance education?

I suppose there are areas within music that can be paralleled with other subjects—at least if we consider only its theoretical aspect. But it is important to underline that music is sounds and silence—and only this. We ought to concentrate on this essence, not only on the words, explanations or symbols whose sole mission is to try to help us reach into the heart of the subject.

Music is a way of communication—universal, yet unable to state opinions in clear text. Distance education is also a way of communication. How do you communicate a communication?

Music is often a matter of emotional, religious and/or social entanglement. In this sense, music becomes a highly private and subjective matter. How do we convey these inner feelings through distance education?

The reason for my mentioning this is not to conclude that DEM (Distance Education in Music) is impossible—but to try to bring down my expectations and those of others to a more realistic level. We must not fool ourselves with the belief that is possible to lock oneself away in solitude and experience the vast realms of music through distance education only. On the other hand, it is possible to believe that DEM can be a valuable supplement—in some respects even a small substitute—to other means of music education.

Adjusting to subjects

In spite of my scepticism, much *can* be learned about music, through the very imperfect tools of words, music symbols, graphic symbols and recorded examples. I propose to begin the discussion here—trying to find out what can be done instead of dwelling on what is impossible.

Every subject has its own specifics and educational possibilities, often established as a result of decades—even centuries—of experimentation. So we have to find a way to integrate these specifics with those of distance education. Theoretical matters like music appreciation (history, analysis, etc.), theory (ear-training, harmony, counterpoint) and even educational theory (psychology, didactics, etc.) can probably very easily be transformed into materials for distance education. We could form most of these subjects into nice, theoretical correspondence courses. But theory alone will never get the student into real contact with music, so we have to think of methods of bringing the music to them—all those sounds and silences. Considering the potential of our media, this should not be too difficult.

To play an instrument you have to:

– know the symbols of musical notation

– transfer that knowledge to the instrument and know how to make the instrument "speak" correctly

– interpret the music, to play in a way that is in accordance with the composer's intentions and the stylistic rules

– very often play with others and submit your egoistic opinions to a common ideal

– put something into the music if you want to say something through it.

In playing, you have to combine your intellect and your understanding with emotion and technical skills if you hope to express something. Some of these factors can grow through DEM, but others most certainly can't.

Can you learn to be a music teacher through DEM? To teach is also complicated for you must know your subject and be able to communicate this knowledge to your students. To teach is a skill, and skills are best learned by practice, but before you start to practise you must know the character of the materials and tools you can use, the reason for choosing a certain material or tool for a certain situation, etc.

Again, I am certain that it is impossible to get a full training as a music teacher through distance education, but I am equally convinced that many aspects of this education can successfully use such techniques.

Adjusting to media

The media used in distance education are:

- spoken words, direct demonstrations (the teacher)
- written words (books, correspondence texts, etc.)
- printed music (scores, compositions, etc.)
- still pictures (photos, drawings, etc.)
- recorded sound (cassette recorder, grammophones)
- recorded sound and pictures (films, video)
- transmitted sound (radio, telephone)
- transmitted words (teletext, data)
- transmitted sound and pictures (television).

Learning music is often based on direct communication between teacher and student. If you separate the two, you would achieve the best learning results through media with two-way communication. For music we then are left with the written word/music and the cassette recorder. The latter requires some extra comment.

Use of technical instruments is dependent on whether you can afford to buy them and whether you can manage to operate them. The cassette recorder is very simple to use and is now in the possession of most families. In this respect distance education already has an "instrument" to "play" on. All we have to do is to learn to play it skillfully.

There are many different aspects of musical information needed in the communication between teacher and student:

The music itself (listening examples of theoretical subjects, recorded examples of the teacher's and the student's playing, recorded accompaniments, etc.).

Verbal comments (between musical examples, covering technical matters, etc.).

Recordings of musical experiences (concerts, playing experiences, etc.).

There are, of course, several problems in the use of cassette recorders yet to be resolved. The production of master cassettes probably needs a studio. You need ways to copy the cassettes in sufficient numbers and you need permission to use recorded examples (i.e. from gramophone records) in the cassette program. (I sincerely wish that record companies could see what investment they would place in future buyers by making it easier for educators to use examples from their productions.)

The video recorder has in principle the same advantages as the cassette recorders and can carry living pictures out to the students. Developments in this field will almost certainly lead to still cheaper and more easy-to-use equipment. And we need video in DEM. It can show the student how to play an instrument, not merely how it sounds when properly played.

On organising

Having tried to organise DEM our conservatory has acquired a renewed respect for the difficulties involved in getting things done in the right order and at the right time. You also need to raise funds for developing the material and for channelling it into its proper use.

In developing materials for DEM, you have to mix—in the right proportion—expert knowledge on the subject, teaching the subject, sound production, printing, and distance education.

You have to bring the people involved through all the different phases in the process: discussions on aims and target-groups, discussion on use of media, subject discussions, construction of the material, testing of the material, revision, and final production.

Having got the materials ready for use, don't think your problems are over. You then have to make the materials function by advertising the project, distributing the materials, teaching students to use them and establishing the proper means of communication between teacher and students.

Conclusion

Music is a young subject within distance education, but valuable experiments have been undertaken and have shown that the subject has great possibilities if we do not try to hide its limitations.

If we get the means to develop the methods of DEM, we could get results that

- reduce or remove the disadvantages of a scattered population
- offer a musical education to people who can't undertake an institutional education
- give us materials which also help the institutional student
- increase the possibilities of music education without solely relying on direct communication between teacher and student
- create equal possibilities for people to develop their skills and interests in music, without regard to where they live, local music milieu, economic ability, etc.

Paper 92

Distance Education in Music is an area worth developing. As music is an international (so-called) language, perhaps ICCE could give a lead in this area.

Bernt J. Ottem
Northern Norway Conservatory of Music
Norway

Paper 93

Business Education: Our Major Challenge

'More of the same' is not a sufficient response to the changes ahead.

A strange title, surely! There are enormous challenges across the whole range of correspondence teaching: why should business education present the *most* significant one?

Business education is education in change

To one whose first "business machine" in 1946 was a wax cylinder dictaphone, the acceleration of the rate of business change since the mid-70s has outdated great areas of conventional business teaching. The computer increasingly handles information storage and retrieval, addressing and stock-keeping, accounting and budgeting, payroll preparation and credit management. Word processors, facsimile transmitters, and real-time banking techniques have altered the whole face of clerical work today.

What conclusions follow?

1. Enormous numbers of employees will have to adapt, while still in employment, to new skills. Since their currently more routine tasks will be eliminated or performed electronically, many will have to be upgraded and re-educated rather than merely retrained.

2. This process may happen, in the working life of tomorrow's employee, not once, but perhaps two or three times. Education for tomorrow's business must be education for change.

3. The world of business, the secondary and tertiary sectors, is flooding into the less developed countries, where vast numbers of people will have to learn new ways of looking at life.

4. In this accelerating continuum of change, the traditional class teacher of commerce will not even barely suffice. Teachers with drive are already being lured into business employment where opportunities for advancement are better. The less ambitious don't keep up with change. Both are in any event handicapped by the reluctance of business employees to go back to school, and to subject themselves to visible social competition in class.

Business education needs new methods

It is no longer enough to look on correspondence training as a means of spreading the coverage a good teacher can give, for few trained teachers stay in the forefront of this hurricane of change. Increasingly, each course is the joint product of a business systems expert and a skilled course rewriter/editor, the latter fashioning into teaching form the raw materials of fact, practice, and theory described by the former. The vital element is the effective use of the simplest and most widely understood language. Business—even in its most technical forms—*can* be explained without jargon or buzz-words.

I believe that the pressures developed by these changes will reverse the present tendency to create easier and more memorable study units. The need will be for more general understanding. Two examples will suffice:

Travel Agents have learnt skills involving airfare calculations and ticket writing—both complex procedures. Today on-line computer terminals and printers can perform both functions. The travel clerk must now become a travel consultant able to interpret clients' needs, give advice and service, promote sales of peripheral products, and monitor client reactions.

Bank staff have routinely been taught skills involving monetary transmission, document security, credit evaluation, and foreign currency techniques. Great areas of this work are now computerised, and employees are being re-educated in the marketing of bank services and in the interpretation of trends to customers.

Both examples involve upgrading the mental agility and understanding of staff and call for innovative teaching material. Since the rate of change will increase the businessman of tomorrow must be able to read faster, to skim scientifically, and to analyse and learn more effectively. Correspondence courses develop these skills.

Can we adapt?

The adaptability of business must be matched by the reaction speed of our teaching. We are no longer producing academic courses to last us for years with only minor face-lifts! We shall be handling changes in income tax rates and methods, in statute law, in computer programming, in leasing practices, with a frequency and unexpectedness that challenge the college's ability to respond. But respond it must, for the student who receives dated material is the student whose confidence fails and whose progress stops.

Note that we are *not* producing definitive texts, largely obsolete before the final footnote has been pencilled in. We are working "live" with experts, daily engaged in the skills they set down for our editors to fashion into effective teaching documents. Call it, if you like, "real-time" teaching, a vital concept, for the student is also involved daily in the same real business world.

Can we resist temptation?

Look round the marketplace today: two short-cuts to student numbers are enormously tempting.

item: sell to the employers. They, or the state, are after all the ones who seek this skilled staff. Why not sell *them* courses, in bulk, with no credit risk, to hand over to their staff for in-service study? Simply because it doesn't work! The employee will study if self-motivated—the horse who takes himself to the water will drink! It is the rare exception among employers who can so motivate and encourage study among his staff that at the end of the day he will say, in chorus with them all:— "Correspondence training works!" All too often sponsored study fails because the student who is supposed to be studying puts in little effort.

item: create own-course diplomas. As a quick-return marketing device, this brings in *this* year's business—and probably destroys most of next year's, for a diploma is valuable, persuasive, and useful only to the extent that employers accord it recognition. This grows only where they have themselves had a role in supervising the standards set and the scope of knowledge demanded, where there is evidence of modernity and effectiveness, and where sheer multiplicity of diplomas has not muddied the waters beyond recognition!

Our major challenge as business educators is to fashion the accelerating changes into educative courses for great numbers of students without being diverted into byways by the lure of too facile a marketing policy. What we *should* be doing is clear enough: *can* we?

J. Grant Loudon
Rapid Results College (Durban)
South Africa

Affective Education at a Distance: An Extensive Experiment

Paper 94

Provided the course team is creative, affective education at a distance can be highly successful.

Emotions and distance being generally considered antagonistic, elaborating courses at a distance in affective education was for the course team involved an almost impossible challenge. Since 1977, the calendar of the Télé-université, a unit of the University of Quebec, includes two distance courses on affective education. *Affectivity and Sexuality* and *Sexuality and Relationships.* More than 12,000 adults have taken these courses which suggests the chal- lenge was worth taking up.

Writing these courses was a team effort of 3 men and 2 women with backgrounds in adult education, creativity and sexology. Essentially, the team members avoided criticising each other's proposals so as to promote the flow of ideas. It is a principle of creativity that quantity brings quality, as it is better to have many ideas to choose from.

Various techniques were used such as brainstorming, synectic, creative imagery and role-playing. The team was essentially creative, implying that the participants were using both brain hemispheres, and made maximum use of sensorial and affective, as well as cognitive abilities.

In writing these courses we tried to apply the theory of andragogy which holds that the adult learner:

- has immediate purposes and objectives
- has registered in a course as part of a search for a solution to a personal problem
- is a better learner when the activity follows his own tempo, without competition and with documentation related to his own experience
- has in himself the potential needed for self-actualization, development and orientation.

Finally, as these courses were to be given at a distance, they also had to respect the principles of distance education including:

- the creation of an appropriate learning climate by the written material supplied
- the maintenance of contact by keeping in touch in various ways such as mail, phone or occasional meetings, providing opportunities to submit concerns and to engage in self-diagnostic exercises
- the opportunity for the participants to express their emotions, as emotion might encourage or discourage pursuit of the activity.

Although at first writing distance courses on affective education appeared an almost impossible challenge, it soon turned out that by relying on the principles of andragogy and distance education, it was not only possible but the course generated a more broadly based demand than originally anticipated and the interest of the participants was sustained.

Louise Marchand
University of Montreal
Canada

The Future of Teaching Technological Subjects at a Distance

Distance learning in technology will develop as an important area of continuing education.

Introduction

The future of technological education is under discussion in many countries at the time of writing. In the UK in particular, a substantial report on the engineering profession was submitted to government by the Finniston Committee of Enquiry into the Engineering Profession. Finniston was particularly concerned with new forms of education for professional engineers, although the original terms of reference of the committee required it also to report on education for technicians.

Figure 1 shows the various elements in technological education and training for three levels of professional engineer or technologist—the professional, the technician, and the craft worker. The elements shown are academic education, conventional training (if any), and a new area of particular interest, post-experience study.

There are four areas where distance learning may be particularly important. *Firstly,* the Open University has found that most of those studying for its technological subjects are either interested in a general academic qualification, which includes some introduction to technology, or *secondly* are technicians who wish to improve on the academic qualifications they already hold (usually diplomas or certificates) by the addition of a full university degree. (However a substantial minority of students use the OU to obtain conventional first degrees in engineering. The University does not at present play much part in providing the academic education and conventional training for technical qualifications, or in the conventional training of the craft apprentice).

Thirdly, the use of distance learning in updating or retreading the professional is gaining a new emphasis, and it is this role which has been strongly emphasised by the Finniston Committee. Recommendations numbers 55 and 57 of their report were as follows:

All registered engineers should be required to commit themselves to maintaining their expertise as a condition of remaining on the register, and demonstrable failure to uphold this commitment should be grounds for deregistration.

The Engineering Authority, working with engineering departments, companies and institutions should evaluate, promote and where necessary fund the initial trial and expansion of 'distance learning' methods as vehicles for continuing formation for engineers.

Fourthly and finally there is much interest in the UK at the present time in the introduction of distance learning for the technician who has to retrain within his company later on in his career, or experiences redundancy and has to acquire new training to get another job. We describe these four particular areas in more detail below.

The teaching of technology within a general distance learning technology degree

The Open University's foundation courses in technology (T100, later replaced by T101) have tried to put the introductory teaching of engineering and technology into a social context. Experience with the first course showed that a good deal of general teaching at foundation level was needed in addition to the more technological, mathematical and scientific topics dealt with. T101 now has a broader set of educational aims and deals with five technological issues which have implications for society, such as the question of introducing combined heat and power stations rather than conventional electricity generating stations.

The new course has attracted a large number of students. There is no doubt that many people take the course who have no intention of becoming professional engineers. At the same time, however, the course provides an important introduction to the study of "The Engineer in Society", a mandatory topic for those wishing to become professional engineers.

Improvement of existing qualifications

The conversion of the technician who holds a diploma or certificate into a professional technologist is an important challenge for the Open University. After the foundation courses students can select from a range of courses and obtain a good education in materials, electronic engineering and most branches of mechanical engineering. They do not have the opportunity to study civil engineering over such a wide range of subjects. One difficulty in providing professional engineering education through distance learning lies in the provision of laboratory courses, although several courses provide quite advanced home kits and many students do practical work at OU summer schools. It appears that although the Open University degree can provide the academic education for professional engineering "formation", further evidence of practical experience will be requested for professional recognition. However, many technicians taking OU engineering courses have obtained extensive practical experience during their working lives and recently one of our graduates obtained professional recognition from the Institution of Electrical Engineers and the Council of Engineering Institutions. This is an important breakthrough for Open University engineering students, who may in future be able to submit individual profiles of course studied, together with records of their own practical experience, to obtain such recognition.

Figure 1: Elements of technological education

Level/Element	Academic Qualification	Conventional Training (if any)	Post-Experience Formation
Professional	First Degree B.Sc., B. Eng)	Post-Graduate Apprenticeship	Higher Degree (taught master's) Research Updating or retreading
Technician	Diploma Certificate B. Tech.	Traineeship/ Apprenticeship	First degree Higher Degree (taught master's) Updating or retreading
Craft		Apprenticeship	Training for new skill
General education (with some technology)	General Degree		

Continuing education for engineers

The newest development in technological education at the Open University is in the post-experience (or continuing education) field. The conventional taught master's degree in engineering has not been a success in the United Kingdom. Few experienced UK engineers go back to university to follow the full-time courses offered by universities and polytechnics, although some success has been obtained with part-time modular courses for the master's degree (for example, a very successful venture in civil engineering at Strathclyde University).

Most industrial companies will not spare a good engineer for a whole year, in order for him to take a full-time master's course. They may allow him time for a short course of two or three weeks (and there are many such short courses which are well attended by practising engineers in both the UK and the United States).

A new approach lies in the post-experience distance learning courses that the Open University is now building up. Most successful has been the first course in microprocessors for managers—a packaged course of 60 hours with no television or radio and no marked assignments—simply a package of written material together with experimental equipment. This course is marketed for $350 and several thousand packages have been sold. It is estimated that those reading the course number five times as many as those buying the course, so we estimate that some 20,000 people have already been reached with this first updating course in technology. A second course, microprocessors for engineers—more ambitious in technical content and experimental equipment—followed in summer 1981 and expected a comparable market.

The University is in discussion with other bodies—particularly the UK Science and Engineering Research Council—about further continuing education courses for professional engineers and managers. These new updating courses may include manufacturing processes, including polymer technology, computer systems, and management studies. But many students in industry already take advantage of a wide range of existing OU courses in science, mathematics and technology through our Associate Student programme.

The Open University cannot pretend that it will be able to supply technical expertise in the many areas which are being proposed for these updating courses for engineers. We have to place the emphasis on cooperation with other universities, polytechnics and industries who will supply much of the expertise, with the OU ensuring coherence of subject matter and academic standard, and providing its experience in distance education and production of material.

As with all distance learning courses a large amount of up-front money is required. For example, the microprocessor courses required an underwriting of over £400,000, particularly to cover the initial expense of experimental kits; in practice the deficit on current account did not exceed £150,000. Income from sales of the course has exceeded the initial cost by several times and money is being refunded to the Department of Industry which provided the pump-priming. The first course was prepared in just over a year.

Continuing education for technicians

There is a current proposal for an "Open Tech" in the United Kingdom, a collaborative venture in which a central government agency (the Manpower Services Commission) would place contracts with several outside agencies for the production of distance learning material. This proposal is under discussion at the time of writing and it will probably be 1982 before any major decision to go ahead is made; however, I make some comments here.

My *first* and main concern is that the central educational thrust, and the control of academic standards, is at present lacking in the proposal. It is vital that the educational foundation of any Open Tech be sound; if the basis is weak then the benefits of an open learning system will be diluted. A *second* point is that it may be artificial to separate professional engineers from technician engineers in the post-experience area. For example, we are under considerable pressure to start courses in management for those of junior managerial status. We have two courses being planned—"The Effective Manager" and "Finance for the Non-Financial Manager" (two of several subjects suggested to us for industry and commerce in general); it may be artificial to require the student taking these distance learning management courses to have a degree. So it may well be that the "Open Tech" is not a sharply defined entity, and that the required material could come from an extension of the Open University.

Thirdly, I am by no means convinced that distance learning can be the main means of teaching craft skills. In general the further down the professional scale, the narrower is the required education and training, and the less opportunity there is for distance learning. This may be too definite a conclusion, but I feel that it is probable that conventional craft skills will generally have to be taught locally, primarily on a face-to-face basis. However, it must be remembered that the individual may well adapt to what is on offer, and select from a mixture of face-to-face and distance study, if it is available.

Fourthly, we observe that in our rapid expansion in continuing education at the Open University our tutorial system for first degrees (which even at this higher level is an essential part of the overall instruction and is based on hiring of individual tutors by our regional staff) will not necessarily be applicable for the professional updating courses. We may have to accept that tutorial groups responsible to other educational or or training agencies should be used—those already existing in technical colleges, in industrial design offices, in teaching hospitals and a variety of places. Further in order to achieve the openness of which we are so proud, it may be necessary to devise new ways of bringing educational material to students (e.g. development of computer-aided learning) and of bringing them into contact with the appropriate specialist experts (e.g. by using telephone conferencing etc.).

Conclusions

Distance learning in technology is still in its infancy in the UK, but it appears that a major expansion will occur in the continuing education area. Engineers and technologists will be provided with updating courses by distance teaching institutions, in collaboration with conventional universities and polytechnics, and with industry itself.

John H. Horlock
Open University
United Kingdom

Providing Continuing Education for Special Professional Groups

The Open University's programming now includes updating courses for professional groups.

Development of a continuing education at the Open University

At its inception the Open University saw its first priority as the creation of an undergraduate programme, though it always felt that its particular expertise would have wide application in the post-experience field.

In 1976, the University undertook a major study through a Committee on Continuing Education which produced a major policy document. The Senate approved the major recommendations and there was created a Centre for Continuing Education, a Delegacy for Continuing Education with a significant number of externals as the policy-making body, and a special Pro-Vice-Chancellorial post with responsibility for its development. It was envisaged that there would need to be extensive collaboration with external bodies, both in course creation and local support networks.

In the continuing education programme, the emphasis is more on the needs of specified target groups than on academic coherence *per se*. These target groups are envisaged to be:

a. those who want courses for personal development (which tend to be at undergraduate level);

b. those who want courses for social development (which are usually below degree level and attract large numbers);

c. those who want courses for occupational professional development (which tend to be at undergraduate and postgraduate levels).

The programme is self-financing though the University continually makes a case to the Department of Education and Science for support grants. In one year only, 1980, the University was awarded a grant of a pump-priming nature. The expenditure in that year was covered approximately 65% by student fees, 25% by special project grants and 10% as an overall grant from the DES. In 1979 and 1980 the financial situation was sufficiently pressing for there to be an overall rule that we could not launch any new projects unless external financing was available to provide the initiation costs.

Stimuli for development

The stimuli for developments in self-financing continuing education are a mixture of educational needs and financial realities. External concerns can be expressed either through interpreters of these needs—a Government department or a professional institution—or through surveys.

In the first case, the microprocessor course, the major stimulus was government concern that the UK was lagging behind in microchip investment programmes and in awareness of the import of these new developments. One outcome was the launching of a substantial Microprocessor Awareness Programme by the Department of Industry. The Open University became involved because of its recognised capacity to reach large numbers of people with high quality educational materials in a relatively short time: its activity was to be complementary to that of the technical college sector and take the education to the home or workplace.

In the second case, the drug therapeutics course, the stimuli were mixed. A national council concerned with postgraduate medical education was the prime mover though, at a later stage, the medical general practitioners, through their professional body, approached the University to set up a Primary Health Care Unit with a wider remit. The national government was also concerned about the full and effective use of the drug bill.

In the third case, the course for dairy farmers, the prime mover was the Royal Veterinary College. Subsequently the proposal has been tested with the agricultural ministry, advisory services and training board (who have provided some finance to back their judgements). At the time of writing (May 1981) we are considering what survey to undertake.

Target audiences

For the microprocessor course the main aim was to give managers in industry an understanding of how the process of developing a product is affected by the introduction of a microprocessor. Previous knowledge of microprocessors was to be neither required nor assumed. In addition to this, the course was to look at some of the personnel, financial and other effects in industry of introducing microprocessors and the effects on the products themselves. The main target audience was therefore those who had to make decisions about new products: technical, financial, personnel, product-planning and marketing managers; and managers concerned about how the incorporation of a microprocessor into their product or their competitors' products will affect their organisation and its competitive position. A special concern of the Department of Industry was that the course should attract those in small to medium-sized companies.

For the medical course, the potential audience was regarded as the 60,000 practising doctors in the country whereas, for the diary farming course, it is the 120,000 or so dairy farmers and herdsmen.

Course design and production

The standard method of designing courses at the Open University is a team approach involving, typically, academics, external consultants, educational technologists, editors and designers, and BBC producers. The course evolves by a series of feedback loops involving developmental testing, external assessing and criticism by fellow team members. Courses can take over two years to prepare.

The microprocessor course is for managers, and since the Department of Industry was keen to have the materials available soon a target development time of one year was agreed. This required several important decisions. The first was not to use television or audio-visual materials. Experience has shown these can be time-consuming to produce and, although there would be a considerable benefit in having part of the course presented on television to arouse interest, there was also the disadvantage that it would tend to restrict the usage of the course to a particular time of year. The second was that the course team chairman would need to have more executive authority in order to shorten timescales where possible, and to provide incentives to externals by the commercial encouragement of bonuses when timetables were met. The team consisted basically of three internal academics, only one full-time, and nine external consultants who were nearly all individuals currently working in both industry and education. In this case, the core subject expertise lay within the University, in the Faculty of Technology.

The process of designing the course to meet the needs of the target audience was similar to that undertaken by any manufacturer entering a new market. The course team chairman was familiar with microelectronics and microprocessors and had considerable contacts in industry. By visiting different industries and examining case studies, some of which were provided by the Department of Industry, an assessment was made of what was needed. As is often the case, the product needed to be a judicious mixture of what people said they needed and what their needs really were, to make the outcome sufficiently attractive on the first count and sufficiently useful on the second.

One important design feature included despite the difficulty of developing it with the time and resources available, was a small kit to go with each learning pack. Although it was not intended that managers should become adept at using microprocessors themselves, it was felt vital for them to have some hands-on experience to obtain a greater conceptual grasp of what a microprocessor looked like, and what it could do, as well as to reinforce their familiarity with the jargon.

The drug therapeutics course is to be launched in May 1982. The course team is breaking new ground in the Open University which has no faculty staff in the medical field. One external member of the course team has been appointed from a London Teaching Hospital as academic course team chairman responsible for the academic excellence of the course. An internal executive course team chairman has overall responsibility for the educational nature of the material and for piloting the course through the production sequence. The issue of the extent of social context material has caused tension between some members of the University and some of the medical educators but the realisation that this was indeed an ongoing debate in the medical profession itself, and that the Open University did not consist only of sociologists, has somewhat lessened this. In the microprocessor course, there was no audio-visual component and no tutorial support network; in the medical course both were considered vital with the latter organised through a collaboration network of the Postgraduate Medical Centres in major British hospitals. These have Deans and clinical tutors who run regular courses throughout the academic year.

They are the front line of provision of group opportunities for audio-visual viewing and follow-up group discussion. The initiation of the programme is local.

The dairy farmer's course is at present (May 1981) at an early design stage and various options are still being considered. There are several issues still to be resolved. The first is the nature of the initiation course team. Whilst the Royal Veterinary College is the centre of academic excellence and the Open University the base for distance learning expertise, the Agricultural Training Board is also involved in producing training materials and agricultural colleges have had their own role to play. These are typical problems in the setting up of course teams and will be relatively straightforward to resolve. More difficult and less certain at the moment is the tutorial support network. Often, for continuing education courses, a pre-existing tutorial network is an important component, as with the drug therapeutics course, and it is unnecessary and wasteful to create a separate Open University network in each case, like that for the undergraduate courses. In this case, several possibilities exist, none of which is completely satisfactory on its own. The first is to use the vets themselves in their own localities. This could imply a patchiness of provision in quantity and quality with pre-existing professional relationships between vets and farmers sometimes being an obstacle. The Agricultural Training Board has its own network, as do the agricultural colleges though the support provided could be patchy.

Promoting the courses

The microprocessor course

The Department of Industry itself was, and is, involved in a major publicity campaign to ensure that Great Britain remains with the frontrunners in microprocessor developments. This involved seminars and distribution of information throughout the country and, as part of its general advice about training to accompany the revolution, it drew attention to the availability of the Open University course for home and work study as well as to the provisions at the local colleges. During the spring/summer 1981, for example, the Department of Industry hired a special train to travel all over the UK to promote awareness of microprocessors and the course was displayed and explained.

The second means of promotion was advertising and articles in professional journals and a third was direct national advertising through Sunday and daily newspapers.

Expenditure over the first year was:

National newspapers:	17,700
Professional journals:	4,400
Leaflets:	14,500
	£36,600

This activity generated about 10,000 enquiries in the first twelve months of which over 2,900 bought the course.

Finally, we are using our own regional network to make industry more aware of the provision. The Open University has thirteen regional offices in which there are academic staff from all the faculties, counsellors and regional staff. We have allocated £500 to each region, both to stimulate new interest in the course and to follow up some of the enquirers who had not subsequently purchased the course. A range of different activities has arisen: for example, seminars to which local industry and staff from the further education sector were invited, and personal approaches by members of the Open University staff.

The other two courses are both at an early stage but some general ideas are emerging. First, the course for doctors depends almost entirely on local stimulus through the specific and individual updating plans in over 100 Postgraduate Medical Centres. It is hoped that each will arrange for a minimum of 30 local doctors (who would be provided with the materials free of charge) per annum to participate in the course. The materials—booklets, video tapes and audio cassettes—would be distributed through these centres.

In the case of the dairy farmers' course, it is felt less likely that national advertising will be the key. Rather, there are suggestions that the Milk Marketing Board might be prepared to send information about the course with the monthly pay cheque; that regular broadcast farming programmes might incorporate a reference to the course as well as the medium of normal farming journals.

Impact of the microprocessor course

Under the auspices of Ms. J. Calder a survey was undertaken of the first 1900 or so buyers of the course which produced a response rate of 68%. This showed that the course had been successful in reaching the specified target audience.

The buyers came from all sectors of industry with 61% from manufacturing and engineering. Over 40% came from companies with fewer than 250 employees. 70% of the buyers held management status within their companies. About a third read about the course in newspapers and a third in professional journals. The majority of buyers (86%) had never previously studied with the Open University and 80% had bought no other course about microprocessors. They bought the Open University course because they felt it was written at the right level for them (29%); because of the Open University's reputation (26%); good value for money (21%).

As might be expected, users outnumber buyers by a significant factor—four or five to one—as several companies bought the course for in-company training plans. Though the majority of users were still managers, they also included engineers (15%) and foremen and inspectors (6%).

Paper 96

There was considerable praise for the lucidity of the prose and how it had enabled the reader to obtain a mastery of computer jargon. There were many positive remarks about the microcomputer and the practical work, and the extent to which it had boosted confidence about or removed the mystique from microcomputers.

Ralph C. Smith
Open University
United Kingdom

Paper 97

Distance Study at the Post-Graduate Level

Graduate study at a distance requires greater attention to communication with the student.

Introduction

Post-graduate study implies either *widening* or *deepening* of knowledge and insights based on previous study which has led to a degree. Post-graduate study of the widening type has a long history. British professional bodies have examined distant students during the whole of this century. Distance study methods have also been used since the 1930s in industrial training, public administration, teacher training and in the further training of hospital staff.

Comparatively few programs of post-graduate study of the highly specialised type preparing students for research and higher degrees are offered. There are some master's and doctoral programmes available on an external degree basis, for instance in the USA, but most require some time on campus, for instance, at Brigham Young University in Utah, the University of Oklahoma and Nova University in Florida.

Australia has considerable experience of a somewhat less advanced type of post-graduate distance study. In 1979, 50 different post-graduate courses were offered, 28 of which "were in the area of education" (Kings 1980: 7). The Australian graduate diploma (i.e. post-graduate) award "will usually require one year's full-time study, or its equivalent" following the completion of a basic university degree or diploma (according to nomenclature guidelines for awards in advanced education: Section 17 as quoted by Kings 1980: 1).

Distance study (Fernstudium) on the East German model (largely substituting consultation hours and seminars for non-contiguous communication and adhering to rather strict timetables) plays a considerable part in post-graduate study in the German Democratic Republic (Möhle 1980).

The need for post-graduate distance study

Listing further training needs as well as known wishes and needs for research opportunities would seem to be a suitable way to start any consideration of how to organise post-graduate distance study. Questions of the following type will have to be asked:

- Are facilities available for distant research students to prepare themselves for and acquire research degrees?

- Are opportunities of graduates in various occupations to update, widen and deepen their knowledge and proficiency properly provided?

- Should society, in its own interest, actively promote activities of this kind? If so, in limited areas only? Or, does a generous liberal policy better agree with the educational principles of the countries concerned?

- Should individuals be offered unlimited opportunities for leisure-time post-graduate distance study? If so, at whose cost?

- Should certain groups of post-graduate students be offered paid leave of absence from their jobs for certain periods, wholly or part time? If so, what groups?

258

Arguments in favour of post-graduate distance study

Post-graduate distance study of the 'widening' type (as well as distance study at the undergraduate and secondary levels) are favoured by:

- the well known effectiveness of the method (Childs 1965 and 1971; Granholm 1971)
- the possibilities for individualisation of study pace
- the student's assumedly habit-forming experience of work on his own which is felt to develop independence and lead to greater autonomy than other types of study
- the applicability of distance education to large groups of students as a kind of mass communication
- the economy both of the large-group approach and of the facts that the need for residential teaching is eliminated or diminished and that study can take place during leisure time and anywhere
- the feasibility for large-scale projects to enlist the services of the very best subject specialist and educationists (Peters 1971).

Considerations for teaching practice

The methods and media of distance education at lower levels can well be adapted to post-graduate distance study (cf. Handal et al 1973; Holmberg 1977a, 1981; and Sparkes 1980). Nevertheless there are special conditions and requirements influencing the mode of presentation in post-graduate study.

Distance courses are—in principle—of two kinds, *self-contained courses* and *study-guide courses*. The former contain all the learning material and the basis for communication that is necessary and have proved particularly valuable where the content is fairly elementary and does not call for a study of different sources. The latter guide and supplement scientific and scholarly literature and establish communication between students and supervisors.

In post-graduate study—and often in other types of study—students must be made to see a complicated picture of the study object with conflicting theories and views, to learn how to trace facts and arguments from different presentations, and to study various sources critically. In such cases the study-guide causes students to read and/or listen to presentations of various kinds, to compare and criticize them and to try to come to conclusions of their own (Holmberg 1977b; Ljoså 1975; Ljoså and Sandvold 1979; Weltner 1977).

In post-graduate study it is usually felt to be proper that students should be offered a choice of what units of a course are to be regarded as relevant in each individual case. Such an approach leads to each unit or each small set of units being separate and providing a sufficient treatment of a limited, and strictly defined, part of the subject. When that is the case, students can build their own curricula from units or sets of units belonging to different courses.

Communication methods

In my experience it is important for the students' motivation and success to establish a personal relationship between the supporting organisation, represented by authors, tutors and counsellors, and the students. Any post-graduate distance study must have a truly communicative character if more is meant than merely providing reading lists and odd comments on students' work. This applies to the guidance of project work and research as well as to traditional learning (cf. Graff 1977 on correspondence seminars and Cross and Ransome 1977 and Henry 1977 on project work).

For some kinds of learning (surgery, for instance) non-contiguous communication alone is not enough. The value of supplementing distance study by residential courses is evident in such cases. A question under debate, however, is to what extent face-to-face sessions should also be used for the purpose of securing cognitive learning by discussion and application of the knowledge acquired to themes brought up in direct contacts with tutors and fellow students. Whereas one school of thinking finds face-to-face sessions essential, another finds them unnecessary and even in some cases harmful as they may encroach on students' independence if tutors act as teachers rather than as resource persons (cf. Holmberg 1977c).

However successful pure distance study has proved to be, traditionalists still insist that face-to-face sessions represent something indispensable. Even during the 1970s the value of post-graduate distance study was occasionally judged on the basis of the amount of supplementary resident study it was combined with. Thus non-traditional doctoral study was considered to be of low quality mainly because it waives "requirements for full-time study, for residence on campus" (Ashworth 1979: 174). It should be—but apparently is not—self-evident that post-graduate distance study and other forms of non-traditional teaching and learning should be judged on the basis of their results, i.e. their academic standards. The amount of face-to-face communication can be no criterion for the assessment of academic standards.

Organisational aspects

It is, of course, perfectly possible to leave the possible introduction of post-graduate distance study to individual or institutional initiatives. Such a laisser-faire policy may be conducive to high quality on certain points where the enthusiasm of devoted workers in the field exerts a dominating influence, but it makes provision neither for an economical wide offer of study opportunities, nor for consistent use of the most advantageous procedures. If that is what is desired some kind of planning is required. There can be little doubt that a central organisation that can afford specialists for the different parts of the work paves the way for professional quality. A small central institution for distance study with a very limited staff of its own but relying on external experts for a great number of tasks is another possibility. As long as there is a basic, responsible organisation it has proved practicable and useful to engage various external specialists as ad hoc members of work teams.

A decentralised approach relying on traditional universities offering distance study as a parallel of their traditional programmes is imaginable and, in fact, occurs in various parts of the world, particularly at undergraduate level. Australia, Canada, the USA and lately also Sweden (although a country with very favourable experiences of centralised distance study) are nations where examples can be found. Considering the somewhat limited but necessarily very personal interaction between highly specialised postgraduate students and their supervisors as well as the advantages of author and tutor being the same person this decentralised approach may be particularly suitable for this stage.

Looking further into the advantages and drawbacks of centralised and decentralised organisations is something that is inevitable for post-graduate distance study of the two types discussed. Maybe a realistic answer for the highly advanced study leading to research is on one hand to create skeleton organisations which give educational, administrative and possibly financial service to institutes and professors of traditional universities supervising doctoral and similar students, and on the other hand to rely on the established distance study universities. These are also most suitable for the 'widening' type of postgraduate study, in which—to some extent at least—the existing course offerings can be profitably used.

Börje Holmberg
Fernuniversität
West Germany

References

Ashworth, K.H. (1979) Why I have not changed my position. *Phi Delta Kappan*, April, 1979.

Childs, G.B. (1965) Research in the correspondence instruction field. *Proceedings of the seventh ICEE conference*, 79-84, Stockholm: ICCE.

Childs, G.B. (1971) Recent research developments in correspondence instruction. In: MacKenzie, O. and Christensen, E.L. (eds.) *The Changing World of Correspondence Study*. University Park: Pennsylvania State University Press.

Cross, N. and Ransome, S. (1977) Survey of a project-based course. *Teaching at a Distance*, 8, 59-61.

Graff, K. (1977) Diskussionsvorschläge zum wirtschaftswissenschaftlichen Hauptstudium an der Fernuniversität. *ZIFF-HINWEISE*. Hagen: Fernuniversität.

Granholm, G. (1971) Classroom teaching or home study--a summary of research on relative efficiency. *Epistolodidaktika*, 2, 9-14.

Handal, G. et al (1973) *The Selection of Relevant Media/Methods for Defined Educational Purposes within Distance Education*. EHSC. Oslo: NKI.

Henry, J. (1977) The course tutor and project work. *Teaching at a Distance*, 9, 1-12.

Holmberg, B. (1977a) Models and principles of course design. *Epistolodidaktika*, 1, 65-74.

Holmberg, B. (1977b) Das Leitprogramm im Fernstudium. *ZIFF Papiere 17*. Hagen: Fernuniversität.

Holmberg, B. (1977c) Die Ergänzung des Fernstudiums durch Nahstudium. *ZIFF Papiere 15*. Hagen: Fernuniversität.

Holmberg, B. (1981) *Status and Trends of Distance Education*. London: Kogan Page.

Kings, C.B. (1980) An Analysis of Graduate Diploma Courses in Australia: Some Implications for Planning. Unpublished paper given at the Jubilee ANZAAS Congress in Adelaide, 12-16 May 1980.

Ljoså, E. (1975) Why do we make commentary courses? In Granholm, G. (ed.) *The System of Distance Education*, 112-118. Malmo: Hermods.

Ljoså, E. and Sandvold, K. (1979) Hvorfor og hvordan be kommentarkurs? *Mellom oss*, 10. Oslo: NKS.

Möhle, H. (1980) *Post-Graduate Further Education by Means of Distance Education in the GDR*. Leipzig: Karl Marx University, Department of Pedagogics.

Peters, O. (1971) Theoretical aspects of correspondence instruction. In Mackenzie, D. and Christensen, E.L. (eds.) *The Changing World of Correspondence Study*. University Park: Pennsylvania State University Press.

Sparkes, J.J. (1980) Matching Educational Aims to the Characteristics of Different Communication Methods. Madrid: Unesco Symposium Document. (mimeo)

Weltner, K. (1977) Die Unterstützung autonomen Lernens im Fernstudium durch integrierende Leitprogramme. *ZIFF-Papiere 17*. Hagen: Fernuniversität.

Open Access Study

Post-graduate studies on an individualized basis are made possible by institutions working together.

The Open Access Study Plan (OASP) was developed to complement and supplement the programming offered by other institutions in the Atlantic region of Canada. Students are allowed to pursue graduate studies in academic areas not normally offered in these institutions. This is accomplished by coordinating the resources (e.g., professors) of institutions to bring together the expertise required.

OASP provides a blend of traditional and non-traditional graduate programming. On one hand, students have individually designed programs, no residency requirement, and the flexibility of pursuing courses at many institutions and in many forms other than normal course work. On the other hand, students have supervisors, supervisory committees, programs of study, orals, candidacy exams, theses and dissertations, and external examiners.

Program objectives

The aims of the Open Access Study Plan are:

a. to provide those in the Atlantic region who wish advanced study in education, broader opportunities for learning, even if they live and work far from university centres;

b. to more fully utilize the resources for learning available in the Atlantic region;

c. to widen the opportunities for further education by offering teachers the possibility of pursuing organized and systematic programs of study on a part-time basis;

d. to enable teachers to pursue programs of study in fields not at present offered in existing institutions;

e. to contribute to the in-service education of teachers by encouraging advanced study of the educational sciences;

f. to provide, through independent study opportunities, methods of learning which cannot easily be pursued through university courses.

Intended clientele

The clientele for OASP are all educators in Atlantic Canada wishing to pursue advanced graduate studies. The Plan has been designed to accommodate many varieties of educators in many educational disciplines. The clientele usually have normal graduate academic entrance requirements of a university, but application may be made for exemption from ordinary entrance requirements, normally through possession of recognized alternative academic experience.

Planning process

The planning process followed by the Open Access Study Plan was similar to most of the major projects of the Atlantic Institute of Education. The need for such a program was determined by surveying the present programs to ascertain if it was possible to pursue graduate studies in all areas of education at both the master's and doctoral levels in the Atlantic provinces. After determining that there were many areas in which it was impossible to complete a degree in education in Atlantic Canada, a plan was devised to mount graduate programs in the areas of deficiency. This plan was presented to the Atlantic Institute's Academic Council for their direction and approval. It is important to note that this Council is composed of representatives from all organizations in teacher education in Nova Scotia as well as the School Boards' Association and Teachers' Union.

Subject matter

After the student has submitted an application to the Committee on Admissions and has been accepted, he is assigned a program advisor to assist with the design of his program. The student and advisor work closely together to design a detailed program proposal describing the courses, the institutions, and the instructors involved. Each program is specifically designed for the individual student.

The program is sent to an external evaluator for appraisal. It is then scrutinized by the members of the Committee on Programs and Degrees (a standing committee of the Academic Council) for final approval. After the program of studies has been approved, the student proceeds at his own pace (with a minimum requirement of three credit hours per semester) until the course work is completed. All programs, both master's and doctoral, carry with them a thesis and dissertation (respectively). The general requirements for the Master of Education are a minimum of 30 credit hours and a thesis. The Doctor of Philosophy requirements are a minimum of 30 credit hours of approved study beyond the master's level and a doctoral dissertation.

Instructional and/or learning strategies

Open Access Study Plan students are encouraged to take regular university courses, independently designed courses and internships. In addition, all of these activities can be pursued virtually at any location in the world as long as the unit of study has been approved before the student enrolls. However, the Institute does maintain a policy of having at least one half of the course work completed in Atlantic Canada.

The supervisor and supervisory committee members for the students must all be residents of Atlantic Canada and, although most of these people are university professors, this is not a necessary requirement. Some of the instructors are highly qualified individuals not employed in a higher education institution.

Outcome

The Open Access Study Plan has been in existence since late 1975. Since that time, four master's degree and two doctoral degree students have graduated. There are presently 42 students enrolled in the program, 31 of whom are doctoral students. The anticipated graduation rate is three to four students per year.

Those familiar with education in Atlantic Canada will know that there are numerous small education faculties throughout these provinces. Two of the most positive aspects of OASP are the opportunities for professors in small faculties to work with graduate students, and professors from separate institutions with similar interests to work together on supervisory committees. Well over 100 faculty members from Atlantic universities are presently involved with OASP students either as instructors or supervisory committee members. Inter-institutional cooperation seems to be expanding rapidly.

Keith C. Sullivan
Atlantic Institute of Education
Canada

The Contribution of Media and Technology to Learning at a Distance

Introduction
Paper 99

Distance education is a land of contrasts. Nowhere are these more evident than in the technology used by institutions in different countries. Although this section contains articles with communications media or computer technology as their main focus many other papers in this book also address, directly or indirectly, the role of these developments in distance education.

Shah (paper 16) argues that since radio and television are expensive and of questionable effectiveness, developing countries should stick to simple correspondence education. Other writers from these countries are less categorical. Datt (paper 14), Singh (paper 13), and Anderson (paper 18), among others, suggest that in some regions lack of central coordination and undue duplication of offerings prevent any single institution from attaining the critical mass necessary to use media effectively. Datt and Singh also draw attention to a frustrating chicken-and-egg problem: those subjects that can use media particularly effectively, such as science and technology, are not offered at a distance in some countries because academics there still believe they cannot be taught effectively in this way.

Yet Orivel and Jamison (paper 44), after examining 14 media-based distance education projects in nine different developing countries, concluded that they were generally more cost-effective than in-school instruction. They found that these projects used media in a simple and unsophisticated manner and hold that this is the best approach for such countries. Speaking of the case of Ghana, Ansere (paper 12) strongly supports the idea that projects be of modest size and complexity so as to adapt better to unforeseeable circumstances. One relatively simple medium is radio. Perraton (paper 3) reports on the successful use of radio in countries such as Tanzania, and Draper (9) sees an important future for this medium in the developing world.

Contrary to the simplistic notion that distance education in the industrialized world is richer in technology than projects elsewhere Dichanz (paper 102) argues that the role of audio-visual media is often marginal. He suggests that institutions have not developed the organizational effectiveness distance education requires. Course design tends to drift towards a lowest common denominator based essentially on print and this format then perpetuates itself in an increasingly inflexible manner. Institutions follow this line of least resistance because, as Bates (paper 2) and Schimeck (paper 103) point out, almost none of their staff have received any training in the use of media. Lefranc (paper 104) and Ellis and Chapman (paper 105) describe how the conservatism of students and pressures of academic tradition in two-mode institutions also constrain the use of media.

The year 1964, when plans for a "University of the Air" began to develop in Britain, is an important date in the history of media applications in distance education. That project became, of course, the Open University. After the fourteen years of debate and research described by Sakamoto (paper 60) Japan has now created a University of the Air. The use of this name is particularly interesting in view of Bates's (paper 2) observation that the use of broadcasting is declining in the twelve distance learning systems he studied in 1980. In the Open University the decline began because the institution's appetite for air time grew too large for the BBC to satisfy. In most other cases, however, the decline seems due to inadequacies of staff and organization. Perraton (paper 3) notes that there are examples going back fifty years of projects that once used broadcasting but no longer do. He suggests that since the world's massive educational needs require the use of mass media, it is urgent for educators to broadcast more.

TV broadcasting is playing a larger role in non-formal education. Although Barnes (paper 106) fears the increasing number of options available to the home viewer will dilute the impact of this type of programming there is a growth of mass adult education projects in which a broadcasting organization joins with national or regional special interest groups to address topical issues. Kaye (paper 107) has studied a number of such projects in the European Economic Community and gives a list of the qualities that make for success. Superb central organization must be combined with great flexibility at the local level. In an interesting example of this type of project Waniewicz (paper 108) describes how the TVOntario Academies provide students with individualized feedback by computer.

In formal education Bates (paper 2) forecasts considerable development of non-broadcast media and reports on the dramatic success of audio cassettes at the Open University. The humble cassette, now that it is used to do much more than package radio programs, has become the first instructional medium, after print, to be uniformly popular with students, academics, educational technologists, and financial comptrollers. Will video cassettes or videodiscs—whichever first conquers the mass market—enjoy the same popularity? D'Antoni (paper 109) and Ruggles and Blackmore (paper 111) examine the characteristics and applications of videodiscs and de Moor (paper 59) reports that the Netherlands Open University is waiting to see how this technology develops before incorporating television into its teaching strategy. Lewis (paper 116), after surveying 70 distance education projects in the United States also detects a trend towards the use of simpler and less expensive technologies. In paper 91 Boulianne describes how video cassettes play a central role in the in-service training of second-language teachers in outlying areas. Indeed, to judge by the papers of Abrioux (86), Innes (88), Stephens (85) and Stringer (87) language teaching appears to be in the vanguard of media use.

Computers are already an important technology in distance education. Central mainframes can provide the keystone of a student administration system and the direct use of microcomputers by students is growing rapidly. Friedman (paper 112) analyzes the stages in the development of data processing at the Open University and warns that computers encourage institutions to create complexity since new systems can be added to cope with it. There comes a point at which the integration of systems becomes necessary and Lampikoski (paper 113) reports how numerous sub-functions can be driven by a unified data base. An increasingly important sub-function for many institutions is the text processing facility described by Cowper and Thompson (paper 117).

One of the sub-functions first noticed by students is the marking of assignments by computer. Bååth (paper 118) describes how this application has been developed into a system of computer-assisted tuition that is more popular with students than correction and comment by a tutor. Success with a similar system is reported by Phillips and Young (paper 114) and Fritsch (paper 48) has applied the same principle to the provision of counselling and guidance. This application of technology in the interactive component of learning at a distance is undoubtedly a breakthrough. Educators will have to decide for themselves whether it is a welcome development or, as Mainusch (paper 67) argues, a perversion.

A less controversial technology for interaction with students is the telephone. Its use is steadily expanding although Finkel (paper 30) and Misanchuk (paper 39) remind us that it is still best for the tutor to take the initiative in making telephone calls to individual students. Realizing that good telephone tutorials require specific communication skills, Cochran and Meech (paper 50) have developed a special training program for tutors.

As we move into the mid-1980s it will be increasingly difficult to discuss an individual medium in isolation. Television, telephone, and computer are merging into a single technology called either *compunications* or *telematics* depending on where one lives. Madden (paper 101) suggests that this fusion of technologies is better described as an "intelligence revolution" than an "information revolution". He believes that home-based learning will be transformed by the combination of videotex (see papers 109 and 110) and personal computers. Boyd (paper 100) agrees that these technologies have great potential but stresses that the manner in which they are used is crucial. His important contribution warns that, if we are to avoid promoting further alienation and social turbulence, compunications must be used to create cooperative electronic communities among teachers and learners. One step in this direction is the CYCLOPS system described by McConnell (paper 115), which was developed to increase the versatility of telephone tutorials.

It is gratifying to see distance educators both pioneering new developments themselves and playing a key role in helping other people master new technologies. Ralph Smith (paper 96) reports the success of a course designed to introduce managers to the potential of microprocessors and Horlock (paper 95) examines the opportunities for continuing education in various technologies.

Taken together, the papers on developments in media and technology presage fundamental changes in distance education during the 1980s. Present technologies of communication require institutions to operate a rather complex delivery system of broadcasts and mailings in order to take advantage of the various devices in the student's home (TV set, radio, telephone, cassette player, etc.). If the advance of technology integrates these devices into a single domestic terminal it will greatly simplify the delivery system needed. Ultimately a course could become a consumer item. The learner would need to buy only a single plastic disc to have access to a whole program of media-rich courses in his own home. Should distance education indeed become a consumer industry then private enterprise, which is better than the public sector at designing, producing, marketing, and distributing consumer goods, will recover the important position it held in the earlier days of correspondence instruction. The growth of multinational distance education companies may help to cure some of the duplication and parochialism in the public sector.

As Bates (paper 2) points out, however, these new developments in media also provide opportunities for local conventional institutions. Such institutions may not be able to compete in the production of packages for the independent learner but they can be of great service in allowing him to interact and cooperate with a wider community of learners.

In one of the earliest descriptions of an academic the poet Chaucer wrote, "And gladly would he learn and gladly teach". Perhaps the age of compunications will enable institutions to create, at a distance, the ideal of a mutually dependent community of teachers and learners.

Three Ways of Providing Computer-Assisted Learning at a Distance and Their Probable Impacts on Various Classes of Clients

Paper 100

Since some of the computer and communications facilities that can be employed to deliver pre-packaged computer-assisted instruction are totally unsuited to collectively elaborative computer-assisted learning it is important which facilities we choose.

Notes on the approach

My categorization of three modes of computer-assisted learning is based on my own experiments in computer-assisted learning, my observations of the National Development Program on Computer Assisted Learning in the United Kingdom, my involvement with the PLATO system with CAN and the Concordia version of CAN, CITCAN, and my familiarity with the OISE/CAN/CAL development project. This approach to classifying CAL modes reflects about ten years' observation of this field. The notion of the "client dimension" is borrowed from the Boyd and Apps (1980) three-dimensional adult education model: transactions, clients, systems. Another basis for this analysis is Anton Zijderfeld's *Abstract Society* (1970), which points out that the one real unifying mechanism of modern society is bureaucracy. The division of labour and the limited scope for choice in a heavily bureaucratized society have as their counterparts the privatization and alienation of life. Hence the community today is not a traditional but a bureaucratic community, and the individual is not a whole individual but a schizoid union of bureaucratic operative and private person. Not being satisfied with this state of affairs one looks for alternatives. I have investigated the "New Age network", and twice visited the Findhorn "New Age" community in Scotland. An alternative to the bureaucratic mode based on affiliation among New Age communities seems possible although such affiliated communities are totally unsuited to the conduct of major operations such as global airlines and space programs. Some bureaucracies remain indispensable.

Making the bureaucracies work better requires networks of skilled amateurs cutting across their boundaries. The great strength of some CAL programs and organizations such as the (UK) NDPCAL and the (US) Association for the Development of Computer-Based Systems (ADCIS) is that they have indeed served to form affiliative networks of competent, mutually trusting professionals cutting across bureaucratic boundaries.

Romiszowski (1981) has shown that virtually all planned learning activities can be classified as either expositional (e.g., RULEG) or experiential (e.g., operant conditioning) or a mixture of the two. Pure exposition is most suited to teaching facts and algorithms where retention and reproductive skills are the main objectives, while experiential learning activities are best suited to teaching principles and heuristic strategies that are to be transferred and generalized. In this context pre-packaged CAI provides a wide range of expositions but a rather narrow range of discovery experience whereas auto-elaborative CAL allows a wide range of discovery experience with concepts and images.

Cooperatively elaborative CAL adds the capability of interpersonal experiential learning and is therefore the most complete mode for learning at a distance.

CAL provision modes

Computer-assisted learning may be provided in many different ways. I have grouped these together in three main modes because, by and large, they require different facilities and offer different possibilities to the learner and to other beneficiaries. To some extent I have ignored conventional classifications. The field is usually divided between computer-assisted instruction (CAI) and computer-managed instruction (CMI) on one side, and simulation and gaming, the computer as a laboratory tool, and the computer as a means for preparing instructional materials on the other. For this analysis, I have taken a different perspective.

The provision modes are:

1. pre-packaged CAI/CMI,
2. open-access auto-elaborative CAL, and
3. gated-access collectively elaborative CAL.

Pre-packaged CAI/CMI

The bulk of current activity, particularly in North America, tends to come under this heading. Examples are: the commercial CAI studyware sold for Apple and TRS80 computers, the TICCIT and CANVI courseware and the software distributed by CONDUIT.

This sort of pre-packaged CAI/CMI does work; it enables people from an appropriate population to develop particular knowledge and skills. A key feature is that it is possible to separate the delivery and use of the materials from their authoring and development. It is possible to talk of development systems and delivery systems separately. The materials may be packaged on floppy disks, perhaps with an instruction book, and sold for use on personal computer, or they may be put on a cable television videotex system where a small keypad may be enough for doing multiple-choice questions, branching, and so on. Pre-packaged CAI/CMI is quite well suited to distance learning, and is often cost-effective if learners' time is a cost.

Auto-elaborative CAL

Seymour Papert's book, *Mindstorms* (1980), describes an altogether different approach. Papert advocates, and has provided, small computer systems that are a powerful tool kit enabling learners to build and experiment with abstract structures, procedures, iteration, recursions, and so on. The object is not so much to learn particular facts or skills but to learn the general skills of problem-solving, abstract thinking, and organizing one's own learning.

Another example of the auto-elaborative mode will be Ted Nelson's Xanadu® network (Nelson, 1981). This should not normally be thought of as CAL. An open "Docuverse" is a public library, a laboratory, and a communication medium all at once. It can therefore support all three of Alfred North Whitehead's phases of learning: "Romance, Definition, and Generalization".

In the auto-elaborative mode the main question is what kind of, and how much, guidance needs to be provided to the learner. A system such as Xanadu® provides minimal guidance in the form of certain protocols that must be followed to record, edit, and examine, and a language that makes this possible. The Turtle/LOGO computer systems, which Papert favors, provide no built-in guidance to the learner. The guidance has to be provided by a teacher or other mentor, and will vary, of course, depending on who owns the system and whether it is in a school, a home, or a library.

Gated-access cooperatively elaborated CAL

An example of the gated-access cooperatively elaborated mode was the college level physics computer-assisted learning project at the University of Surrey, where students themselves worked in BASIC to produce instructional packages used by other students in the same course. I call this sort of thing *gated* because, unless one has passed prerequisite courses and satisfied the people running the project that one can be a contributor, one is not given the opportunity to produce instruction. The gates may be transparent to allow unqualified persons to look in or they may be opaque to keep people from harm (e.g., some medical areas should be closed to hypochondriacs and poisoners).

At present, the third mode also occurs, in a sense, among many of the professors and teachers who produce CAL materials. Here the people playing the game are not so much students as other developers of CAL materials, so affiliative organizations like ADCIS and the British CAL81 series of conferences enable people to share the materials they have produced and to build on each other's work—someone facetiously said "stand on each other's shoulders rather than stepping on each other's toes".

I think these three categories constitute an exhaustive categorization of the modes through which computer-assisted learning can be provided. The three categories are not necessarily mutually exclusive, although I have put the term *open-access* in the second category and the term *gated-access* in the third to emphasize the important distinction between these two approaches.

The client dimension

Robert Boyd and Jerrold Apps, in their book *Redefining the Discipline of Adult Education* (1980) put forth a model of adult education with three basic dimensions; the transactional dimension, the client dimension, and what they call the "system" dimension. For the purpose of this analysis, the client dimension is the most interesting one. They divide it into three categories. The first category of autonomous client is the *individual* learner, learning for himself. The second is the *group,* learning for its own satisfaction and development. From this standpoint, the group is a "being" going through a life cycle. The third form of autonomous client is the *community* client. The community may need to know how to improve its health care or how to reschedule work or how to rearrange transportation. I have reservations about this categorization, which I think applied to a simpler world than ours.

It seems to me that the most useful and illuminating client divisions are four: first the private *individual* learning for his avocational life; second the obverse, namely the *bureaucratic* client. The *bureaucracy* may send either operatives, managers, or administrators to study various facts, skills, etc., and in this case it is not the individuals who are the prime clients of the program but the employing bureaucratic organization itself. Often such organizations are the providers of the distance learning, too, which can make for an invidious kind of circularity. The third category is that of *affiliative groups and networks* of people with a common interest in a particular puzzle or problem area. (For example, mathematicians all over the world who are interested in certain problems in point-set topology read each other's papers and communicate to form a teaching/learning group for each other.) The fourth category, that of locally dense *lifestyle networks,* includes ethnic groups, religious communes and New Age communities, etc.

On the analysis of Henry Jacoby in the *Bureaucratization of the World* (1973), or of Zijderfeld in *Abstract Society* (1970), one would have only the first two client categories—merely subjective autonomous individuals and objectively autonomous bureaucratic organizations. But, in fact, we also have the various affiliative networks and groups such as ethnic churches on the one hand and scientific societies on the other.

The puzzle and problem networks can and do provide links between the lifestyle networks and the bureaucratic "autonomata" and the private learners. The third and fourth categories are to me what give room for optimism. (See also Strassmann: 1980)

Implications of modes of CAL for each category of client

The most straightforward way to show the relationships between forms of computer-assisted learning and the needs of various clients for distance learning is by a table. (See Table 1.) Such a table is necessarily an over-simplification because in trying to give a global view it is necessary to gloss over many of the complexities of the relationships.

In general, pre-packaged CAI is of substantial value to novices in all four client groups. It may also be of some value to journeymen and occasionally to leaders in each group. The auto-elaborative mode is of most value to individuals who are either ambitiously climbing in the bureaucratic structure or involved in puzzle or problem networks and need specialized skills and knowledge. If the right guidance is available, auto-elaborative computer-assisted learning may also be the most powerful education tool for the young, as Seymour Papert has pointed out in his book, *Mindstorms* (1980).

The gated-access positive-sum-game for collectively elaborating and employing computer-assisted learning is precisely what is required for both novices and journeymen and perhaps to some extent for leaders in affiliative groups and networks. In the table I have used a code of two pluses for a highly beneficial mode, a single plus for a moderately beneficial mode, a plus-minus combination for a mode with some advantages but some disadvantages for the client.

The table represents plausible conjecture rather than the results of controlled research. It is programmatic, in that if you doubt some of the relationships then it may be worthwhile conducting experiments to see whether the implications I draw are valid.

Conclusion

Computer-assisted learning at a distance is just beginning to play a significant role in distance educa-

Table 1: Relations among CAL modes

Cal Provision Mode	Necessary Computer Communications Facilities	Learning Types Supported	Clients Supported
1. Pre-packed CAI/CMI	A + C + − B +	E − F +	I + − K − J + + L −
2. Auto-elaborative CAL	A + − C + + B −	E + + F −	I + + K − + J − − L − +
3. Collectively-elaborative CAL	C + +	E + + F + +	I + + K + + J − L + +

Key to codes

+ + highly beneficial
+ moderately beneficial
+ − advantages and disadvantages

A Tape or disc
B Broadcast or narrowcast
C Packet data or telephone

E Experiential
F Expositional

I Individual
J Bureaucratic organizations
K Problem group networks
L Lifestyle group networks

Paper 100

tion, particularly in adult education (Bramer, 1980; Prisk, 1981). This is not because its value had not been realized before but rather because the costs were too great. With the advent of the cheap personal computer and of various videotex systems it is now economically feasible to provide
assisted learning at a distance for fairly large numbers of adults. If computer-assisted learning at a distance is merely CAI, or CAI with a CMI framework to manage it, and if the computer and telecommunications arrangements that carry the bulk of adult learning at a distance are chosen with the CAI paradigm in mind, then, if my analysis is correct, its introduction will tend to reinforce schizoid entrapment in bureaucratic entities and alienated private lives. If the second, amoral, form of computer-assisted learning advocated by Seymour Papert, and in a different way by Ted Nelson, is espoused we shall see more and more opportunistic turbulence in our society. If, on the other hand, we make provisions for supporting gated cooperatively elaborated CAL at a distance we should be able to reinforce and extend those cultural groups and their networks that can provide some real hope for the future.

Gary M. Boyd
Concordia University
Canada

References

Boyd, R.D. and Apps, J.W. (1980) *Redefining the Discipline of Adult Education.* Washington: Jossey-Bass.

Bramer, M. (1980) Using computers in distance education: the first ten years of the British Open University. *Computers and Education,* 4, 4, 293-301.

Jacoby, H. (1973) *The Bureaucratization of the World.* Translated from the German by Evelyn Kanes. Berkeley: University of California Press.

Nelson, T.H. (1981) *Literary Machines.* Swarthmore: Ted Nelson, Pub.

Papert, Seymour (1980) *Mindstorms.* New York: Basic Books.

Prisk, D.P. (1981) A central communication network in continuing studies for a university system: a needs assessment. *T.H.E. Journal,* 8, 4, 48-51.

Romiszowski, Alex J. (1981) *Designing Instructional Systems.* London: Kogan Page.

Strassmann, Paul A. (1980) The office of the future. *Technology Review,* 82, 3, 54-65.

Zijderfeld, Anton C. (1970) *The Abstract Society.* New York: Doubleday Anchor.

Paper 101

Distance Education and the Information Revolution

The arrival of videotex systems is of great importance to distance educators since it will make computer-assisted learning economical and efficient.

Introduction

An important difference between distance educators and conventional educators is that distance educators are forced by circumstance to educate in the literal sense of the Latin root of the word, i.e., *to lead* their students *out* towards greater knowledge and understanding. Traditional teachers are able to succumb to the temptation of bashing knowledge into the student.

For this reason the so-called information revolution will favour distance educators, though it may change their tasks beyond all recognition. Sleepy afternoons spent marking correspondence course tests and suggesting further reading or exercises will be replaced by urgent questions from students requesting immediate advice, explanation or clarification via return electronic mail. Good teachers will be hard pressed to keep current with a bewildering variety of new course material.

The term "information revolution" is not particularly to my taste, for what is actually happening is a revolution of greater significance. We are launched into nothing less than an "intelligence revolution", where much more than the mere sifting of data to yield information is involved. Microelectronics are making possible the intelligent application of information to perform tasks of ever increasing complexity. In the military sphere we hear of cruise missiles that are capable of navigating and piloting themselves over thousands of miles at low altitude. In industry robots are ceasing to be seen as heroes of science fiction and are becoming instead fast and reliable production workers.

About 50% of the work in Canada and the United States is information work—that is, work related to the sifting, sorting, transmitting, promulgation or assimilation of information. The productivity of this group has changed remarkably little over the years. One recent estimate suggests that information productivity has increased by only 4% during the last decade, while industrial productivity in the same period grew by 90%. Normally the wages of information workers are roughly coupled to those of industrial workers, suggesting that the lack of an increase in productivity by information workers may be a major cause of inflation. So we are now seeing increasing focus on improving office productivity under the catch-all phrase "Office of the Future". However, although educators too are information workers, there seems to be much less emphasis on the "School of the Future".

While military, industrial, and office requirements appear to be the driving forces behind microelectronics innovations, education, and particularly distance education, could be the greatest beneficiary.

One-way and two-way systems

What can a marriage of some new and old technology do in the field of distance education? It is useful to make a distinction between one-way (or broadcast) educational systems and two-way (or interactive) systems. The best known one-way system is television, which is already performing yeoman service in distance education. It allows first class educational material to be encapsulated for viewing by many people. Moreover, the video tape and the videodisc are freeing this medium from the constraint of viewing the material at a set time in the broadcast schedule. Another major constraint of one-way educational material is that viewer feedback, which evokes an immediate response from the educator, is almost impossible although this form of feedback on educational TV is now being used in British Columbia and elsewhere.

Broadcast educational systems are already familiar to many. I shall focus here on two-way systems where a computer is used to augment or replace the teacher in the question, answer, and discussion process that is so important to learning. To illustrate the potential of computer-assisted learning I have resorted to a layman's dream about the properties of an ideal learning aid. The properties I would look for are: suitability, quality, understanding, availability, responsiveness, and depth—and of course, low cost.

Suitability

Having decided that I want to learn I need assistance appropriate to the topic, to what I already know, and to my temperament and learning skills. If I simply want to learn to do what my mother or father do already, computers, books, and professional teachers may all be redundant. Assuming more ambitious objectives, computer-assisted learning routines share with books the property of being amenable to compilation in great variety by experts and to dissemination at a unit cost that decreases with volume. As with books, it is useful to have access to a learning facilitator who can give advice about the most appropriate instructional material. Computer-assisted learning has the disadvantage relative to books of being presently more expensive and requiring a communications network.

On the other hand, computer-assisted learning has a much greater capacity to adapt to the learner's requirements by calling in extra material where learning is proceeding slowly and by moving along faster for those who find the material easy. Furthermore, by using both voice and visual display and by forcing active learner participation, computer-assisted learning can hold the attention of the average user longer. Once speech recognition systems become commonplace, thus permitting the learner to reply verbally to questions, computer-assisted learning will become even more convivial.

Quality

It will be many years before totally automatic learning routines are better than human instruction of premier quality. Indeed, it may never happen. However, we cannot all have access to such instructors unless their expertise is encapsulated and made accessible.

Of course the computer cannot be programmed to replace the instructor completely; but some properties of his instruction can be replicated—namely his approach and his knowledge of the subject. The more personal attributes such as his sympathy, understanding, and adaptability can to some degree be taken on by a human educator who need not be a subject expert. Where distances are involved the use of the telephone, teleconferencing, and electronic mail can do much to give the student a feeling of human contact.

Understanding

While human beings have much in common there are still substantial differences between us. As a learner, I want my teacher to understand my peculiarities, even to impose discipline if it is needed. For most of us, understanding is a human and not a microelectronic property.

Even if we look to humans rather than to computers for understanding, it would be a mistake to dismiss the computers too peremptorily on this score. There have been many cases, particularly with young children, where the learner has found the encouraging and friendly responses given by the computer much more "human" than the responses of their everyday teachers. Good computer-assisted learning routines can be responsive and understanding.

Availability

There are many millions of people with a thirst for education, but neither teachers nor books are in limitless supply. Nor are TV sets and computer terminals. However, once the basic TV and computer equipment has been acquired it can be used for learning in a wide variety of subjects. Furthermore, although broadcast TV restricts the subjects under simultaneous viewing to one per channel, computer-assisted learning systems can in theory be called in to assist learning on any subject at any time. Where the terminal has two-way communication with a central store of instructional material then the ideal of education available at the flick of a switch comes very close to reality.

Responsiveness

In a one-on-one teaching situation with an understanding teacher I can ask questions almost at will and expect immediate and direct responses. This ideal is harder to realize in a large class, by mail, or when using a computer-assisted learning system. The latter, however, will become more and more responsive. There are now computerized data bases where access to information is gained through the use of logical combinations of key words. Such systems can search through large bodies of information. For some time however, access to a human facilitator who knows both the learner and the data base will be the most efficient way of ensuring responsiveness.

Depth

It can be extremely frustrating to find a particular avenue of enquiry closed because of lack of suitable information. The importance of well stocked libraries is familiar to all of us, and we are aware of their high cost. Yet a very large fraction of new printed material is available in computer readable form at some time in its production process. In principle, therefore, it is amenable to access by phone from any place in the world.

Computer-assisted learning routines are rapidly increasing in both number and variety while improving in sophistication. The arrival of videotex systems on the scene will, in my view, lend enormous impetus to this trend. It is already possible to access a large variety of computer-stored information and learning programs over a telephone line. Hence the depth of knowledge accessible to those visiting the British Museum or the Library of Congress will be equally accessible electronically to people in Tuktoyaktuk in the Canadian Arctic, Alice in Central Australia, or Zanzibar.

Cost

Can these desirable goals be achieved economically? After all, relatively expensive computer-assisted learning systems have been with us for some time. The major new elements today are microelectronics and communications transmission technologies that are pulling down the critical cost barriers so as to make an explosion in computer-assisted learning possible. This explosion will be accompanied by an explosion in the depth and sophistication of learning material.

Order of magnitude improvements in the communications infrastructure are being made by satellites, optical fibres, and the application of digital techniques to switching and transmission systems. The same developments that brought the price of electronic calculators from several hundred to just a few dollars in less than a decade are making it possible to convert a simple TV set into a computer terminal or even into a stand-alone computer for considerably less than the cost of a holiday in Hawaii. The cost of this conversion will probably halve several times before this decade is over.

The key factor in microelectronics price decline is volume, which is why the arrival of videotex systems is of such great importance to distance educators. Videotex, simply defined, is just a conversion of a TV set to permit it to become a vehicle for interactively accessing computers anywhere over an ordinary telephone line or a suitably modified cable TV system. Its value as an educational tool, particularly when augmented with sound—a capability that will surely not be long in coming—is immediately obvious.

Telidon

In the world of emerging videotex systems, Britain is known for its Prestel system, France for Antiope, and Canada for Telidon. We believe that Telidon, which was the last to appear on the scene before the UN-sponsored telecommunications standards organization known as CCITT defined, at least for the next four years, the recognized world standards, has some tremendously important advantages over its competitors insofar as educational applications are concerned.

In May of 1981, AT&T announced that it had chosen its (and very possibly by extension the North American) videotex standard. While providing the capability (after suitable translation) for users to access Prestel and Antiope data bases, the AT&T standard is essentially a creative extension of Telidon that provides a greatly enhanced animation capability. I thus look forward to much more creative use of the animation capabilities of Telidon.

The most obvious of these advantages is the superior graphic image possible on what has come to be thought of as an essentially graphic medium (i.e., TV). And there are other more subtle characteristics that have excited educators in Canada and elsewhere. The ability to provide animated sequences of graphics is thought to be of great importance, though as yet this ability has hardly been exploited. Perhaps of equal importance is the adaptability of the Telidon protocol to a wide range of terminals of substantially differing capabilities and costs. For example, medical education may demand the use of relatively expensive terminals that can show very detailed graphics while most residential users would probably opt for a lower resolution display at lower cost. Yet both devices would be capable of displaying the same information, though of course such things as X-ray photographs would appear in much less detail on the less expensive system. Since most of the investment in videotex in the future will be in program material (sometimes called serviceware), rather than in hardware, the ability of a wide range of terminals of different capabilities to access the same information is an important feature.

Conclusions

Rapid change imposes stress on individuals and on society as a whole. Much of this stress is caused by a sense of helplessness before seemingly threatening and uncontrollable change. Whether or not we can control the rate of change is a debate I leave for others. I suggest, however, that these rapid changes have, in computer-assisted learning, engendered a tool that can greatly assist us both in understanding what is happening and in adapting to change. These developments would appear to be of relatively greater benefit to the distance educator than to his conventional counterpart. I believe that these changes present an opportunity we cannot afford to ignore.

John C. Madden
Microtel Pacific Research
Canada

Reflections on the Use of Media in Distance Education

Paper 102

(Abstract)

For at least a generation, educators have believed that media can help to individualize instruction, objectify content, and promote variety in programming. Such a belief in the potential of media was and is an important component of the political support for institutions like the Fernuniversität. In addition to absorbing some of the enrolment pressure on the higher education system, planners hoped this institution could play a coordinating role in the development of continuing education and be a guarantor of quality.

Home study makes new demands on students, teachers and institutions. The strains of these demands cause distance education systems to become rather inflexible and there is a tendency for media to be squeezed out of the teaching strategy or, at least, reduced to an enrichment function. The political and legal difficulties that often accompany an attempt to use media do not help.

The use of media in conventional education in West Germany is rather patchy but it is more surprising to learn that 90% of all study materials at the Fernuniversität are printed materials and that there is little variety in the use of media. Since the volume of media use in education is less than was anticipated when educational technologists began theorizing about media didactics, many of the theories and hypotheses remain untested. While it does appear that media have helped to objectify subject matter there is less evidence that it has had a substantial impact in the individualization and differentiation of programming.

Horst Dichanz
Fernuniversität
West Germany

Paper 103
Television in Distance Education
The educational use of TV is still hampered by difficulties of instructional design and program distribution.

Introduction

At present, virtually every industrialized state, and quite a number of developing nations, have made some form of investment in educational television. An honest evaluation would indicate that the results have seldom matched the expectations.

The three links in the chain of communication between teacher and student are the viewer, the medium, and the development/production/distribution system. In the classroom the teacher is able to monitor and partially control the interaction with the system. In distance education this is not possible and the viewer must face problems of scheduling, integrating print and audio-visual media, and receiving programs.

A visual medium

The major thrust of Western education over the past century has been to produce a print-literate populace. The introduction of television into the educational process has created the need for visual literacy. Film and television communicate by means of an audio-visual language which, while related to spoken and written language, possesses a grammar and vocabulary of its own. The average viewer is only subconsciously aware of the subtleties of meaning created by the interaction of the elements of motion, picture, and sound. The language of television is extremely rich, expressive, and powerful, but without the acquisition of visual literacy skills, viewers cannot obtain more than a shallow understanding of content. The correspondence student needs to be assisted in developing visual literacy skills, or television programs will never be able to carry the core content of a course.

Television has limitations that make it unsuitable for certain applications. It has a voracious appetite for visual information. Without a steady supply of pictures, the potential to involve the viewer through motion is lost. Those involved in distance education should bear in mind that television is only one of the tools at their disposal. Because of its costs television should only be used in educational situations that make effective use of its strengths.

Working with TV

The development, production, and distribution of educational television programs present major challenges.

The first concerns personnel. Few commercial television stations are involved in content research or instructional design. It takes a number of years for an educational television agency to develop the skilled manpower necessary for striking a balance between the requirements of TV production and the objectives of the educators. The research and development phase of educational television is often more time-consuming than the actual production. Educators have attempted to short-circuit this rather lengthy process, either by scrimping on content or by producing the program first and then developing the objectives. Such cost-cutting is usually very obvious in the final product. Lessons must be learned from the producers of industrial training films in which the objectives are usually very specific and the visual treatment follows directly from them.

Television programs can seldom convey all the information required and are most successfully used in an integrated package with print, non-print, and human components. Every effort should be made to ensure that the television program complements rather than duplicates the other materials. Otherwise the viewers, who tend to be more conscious of time than are their teachers, will not watch more than one or two programs before abandoning them for textbooks that cover the same ground.

Production techniques for educational television deserve an entire volume. On the technical level every effort should be made to compete with the best of commercial television although such competition should seldom extend to the production style. Production style also depends on the intended method of distribution. Educational television agencies have made the greatest number of mistakes in the distribution of programs. One senses that such agencies feel their work is done when a program is completed when, in fact, it has only begun. This is especially true in distance education.

Broadcast distribution is not adequate for program distribution since it forces the learner to adapt to a schedule that may have been drawn up thousands of miles away. The viewer has no control over the speed of presentation. Some programs may require a second or even a third viewing for full comprehension, which is usually impossible with broadcasting. Video tape and videodisc distribution is superior from a pedagogical standpoint but since very few students own playback equipment most have to make do with an inferior means of distribution. Some institutions have set up learning centres with video equipment and a program library, but the time and travel required for using such centres can be insurmountable obstacles for students.

Television has proven to be a highly effective educational resource. However, attempts to use television to expand, rather than augment, existing educational facilities have generally been unsuccessful. The use of television in distance education has been hampered by lack of an effective distribution system and by an unwillingness on the part of course designers to allow TV programs to carry core content. Until these difficulties are overcome, the cost-effectiveness of television for distance education will continue to be highly questionable.

Wolfgang Schimeck
ACCESS Alberta
Canada

Student Perceptions of Media in French University Distance Education Systems

Students like a balanced media mix, and the preferred components vary between disciplines.

Introduction

The first university distance education systems in France were created in 1963/64 for the arts and humanities faculties of 5 universities, under the name of Radio-Propédeutiques. In 1964/65, 5 other faculties acquired such systems, and the name was changed to Radio Universités. Radio was the main medium and most universities had up to 18 hours (36 broadcasts of 1/2 hour each) of radio time a week on the corresponding regional network. (In 1963/64, the Conservatoire National des Arts et Métiers - CNAM - created Télé-CNAM, now discontinued, which had 8 hours of TV on the second national network). In the following years, 9 new projects were created and all 19 systems were renamed Centres de Télé-Enseignement Universitaire. The prefix "Télé" was used in its Greek meaning "at distance" and did not imply the use of TV.

At the beginning these systems relied mainly on radio broadcasts and correspondence but slowly the role of radio diminished. Now all systems have become multi-media and include a more balanced set of components in three categories:

a. audio-visual components

 - radio
 - audio cassettes
 - television
 - telephone

At present, for financial reasons, radio broadcasts have been reduced to about 4 per university and have been partly replaced by audio cassettes and printed materials. Broadcast TV is used only occasionally.

b. printed components

 - books
 - mimeographed materials
 - correspondence (including exercises)

c. face-to-face contact

 - residential courses (optional)
 - seminars
 - workshops
 - student/teacher meetings

At the beginning, except for Télé-CNAM, courses were offered only in arts and humanities for the first two years of university. Later, courses were offered to first degree level and in many cases to the master's level. In addition 6 universities in Paris and Grenoble now provide distance education programs for degrees in law and economics.

Student population

Our latest national survey of the student population (1976/77) gave the figures in Table 1.

Table 1: Student population survey

age	20 and under	5%
	21 to 25	38%
	26 to 30	30%
	31 to 40	19%
	41 and over	8%
sex	male	47%
	female	53%
occupation	full-time job	76%
	part-time job	8%
	full-time student	8%
	miscellaneous	8%
distance of residence from university	less than 50 km	52%
	between 50 and 200 km	26%
	more than 200 km	22%

The percentage of students living far from a university is really greater because the above data include students from universities situated in Paris or in large cities such as Marseilles. For example, 47% of the students of the University of Rheims live more than 100 km away. This proportion increases to 67% for Nancy and 76% for Dijon.

The study

Our distance education research group has conducted a number of studies on student population, pedagogical methods and many other areas since 1963. This paper is based on a study made in 1976/77 of the students in eight universities in three disciplines:

– law and economics (Grenoble II, Paris I)

– arts and humanities (French, foreign languages, history, geography, philosophy, etc.) (Rennes II, Nancy I, Paris III, Paris X, Dijon)

– technology (CNAM).

We have tried to measure the difference between the actual use by the students of eight components of the teaching system and their expectations of their potential usefulness. We have analysed the ways in which the students use the various components and compared this to traditional teaching. A definition of the optimal conditions of use from both practical and psychological standpoints has been attempted. We present here some general results as well as a breakdown by discipline.

Each student was asked to rate a list of components from 1 to 5 according to their importance (1 being minimum importance, 5 maximum importance) first by considering the components actually used in the university, and then by expressing an ideal rating if the media mix could be varied at will.

The ratings in the two tables are the score for each component as a percentage of the total score for all eight components.

Results

Table 2 shows that as far as the actual use of the components is concerned, the students rate them as follows in decreasing order of importance: books, mimeographed materials, audio cassettes, workshops, radio broadcasts, one-day seminars, TV broadcasts, residential courses.

Table 2: Global comparison between the actual use of the pedagogical components and the wishes of the students

	Actual use	Wishes
Radio broadcasts	12.3	11
TV broadcasts	7.9	10.7
Audio cassettes	13.4	12.5
Books	15.15	13
Mimeographed materials	15.6	14.5
One-day seminars	11	11.5
Workshops	12.8	14
Residential courses	11.8	12.8

The student ratings correspond fairly closely to the present situation in the French distance education systems in humanities and law/economics since:

– the systems are based primarily on printed and mimeographed materials

– the number of hours of radio has been greatly reduced and radio broadcasts have been replaced by other media

– residential courses and seminars are rare in most systems

– 3 universities have no TV and others broadcast only a few programs.

Bearing in mind that some students are from systems that do not use radio or TV it is interesting to examine their ideal preferences among media. Components were ranked as follows: mimeographed materials, workshops, books, residential courses, audio cassettes, one-day seminars, radio broadcasts, TV broadcasts.

We can readily detect the desire of distance students to experience the same media mix as traditional students. Should we conclude that they ask for audio cassettes, one-day seminars, radio and TV broadcasts only as a last resort, a stop-gap for want of something better? Certainly not. In fact, the students have little knowledge of the real pedagogical value of these other media.

We should note that the difference between the extreme scores is much smaller in the case of the expectations (10.7 to 14.5) than in the case of the real situation (7.9 to 15.6). For the ideal preferences the ratings are more homogeneous.

The data suggest that students want more TV broadcasts, residential courses, one-day seminars, and workshops. They seem to want fewer radio programs, books and textbooks, mimeographed materials, and audio cassettes. If we reflect that the components of which students want less are the main components of the existing systems, we can see that students want more of the missing components: TV broadcasts, residential course, seminars, and workshops.

Table 3 shows that the data concerning use of media in humanities and law/economics are similar: the trilogy books/mimeographed materials/audio cassettes is predominant; radio is important; the role of residential courses or TV broadcasts is small and seminars are rare.

The only major difference concerns workshops, which are rare in humanities, and important in law/economics.

In terms of preferences there is again some consensus among students in humanities and law/economics: an increased demand for the trilogy books/mimeographed materials/audio cassettes; and important role for radio and one-day seminars; requests for workshops; little demand for residential courses; the wish to see TV play a greater part, even at the expense of radio.

The data for technology students reveals major differences. Indeed, the only real consensus between the three branches of instruction is the constant request for workshops. Whatever the branch of instruction, students always request more workshops. Is not this a revealing sign of a pedagogical evolution and of the psychological evolution of students in all disciplines?

Conclusion

This study revealed the flexibility of multi-media systems in which media and pedagogical components are adapted to the discipline and are chosen according to the student population, the objectives and the different conditions of teaching. It also showed that students seek a better balance between media, with no single component predominating.

Robert Lefranc
Ecole Normale Supérieure de St-Cloud
France

Table 3: Comparison between the actual use of the pedagogical components and the wishes of the students according to the different branches of instruction

	Actual use			Wishes		
	Law Economics	Humanities	Technology	Law Economics	Humanities	Technology
Radio broadcasts	13.9	13.4	7	12.3	11	7.5
TV broadcasts	5.15	7.7	13.1	9.2	10.4	13
Audio cassettes	13.65	15.4	6.3	12.5	14.1	7.9
Books	16.25	15	14	14.2	13	12.5
Mimeographed materials	16.05	17.8	13.4	14.5	15.2	12.8
One-day seminars	8.6	11.1	11.4	11.25	11	13.4
Workshops	15.9	9.25	18.65	14.2	13	17.3
Residential courses	10.4	10.3	16	11.75	12.1	15.3

Paper 105

Academic Equivalency of Credit Courses by Teleconference

The political problem of academic equivalency can be resolved by addressing the specific areas of concern.

Introduction

Despite the implementation of educational technology in open learning institutions, many traditional universities have difficulty accommodating the changes necessary. Such universities must make substantial changes in their regulations and ways of dealing with remote adult students before credit students using a technological delivery system can be accepted as having received an academically equivalent course.

Current trends will require institutions of higher education to adapt to the adult learner, in terms of both administration and access. Loring (1978: 2) stated that institutions must adapt in six ways:

- making deadlines, timing and schedules more flexible
- creating a supportive and compatible environment for learners
- establishing special admission and retention policies
- developing interdisciplinary degrees and programs to accommodate adult lifestyles and interests
- employing educational technology to deliver knowledge to distant learners
- modifying budget structures to realize benefits suitable to the implementation of technology.

Loring (1978: 3) also identifies barriers to the use of educational innovation, the most significant being the desire to protect the academic excellence of the university. This desire is essentially positive since everyone wants to maintain quality and high standards, but it does generate strong resistance to change and innovation. Thus, when a teleconferencing system is proposed concerns are raised about:

- ability of the system to deliver the same quality instruction as face-to-face methods
- preparation and ability of the professors to utilize the system adequately
- lack of control over grading, testing and educational measurement
- "level" of the innovative course compared to the campus-based version
- access to library, research and resource learning materials during the courses
- lack of student access to instructors
- actual number of contact hours of instruction and student "on-air" class time versus live classroom interaction.

We have addressed these concerns in implementing an educational teleconferencing network at the University of Calgary and offering some twenty courses by this means (Ellis, 1981: 18).

Ability of the system

There have been a number of studies on the effectiveness of audio teleconferencing from the point of view of student learning. Short, (1974: 62) concluded that the telephone has never been found worse than face-to-face and sometimes there was better recall of content by communication on the telephone.

A University of Calgary educational statistics professor (Black, 1981) observed that upper-level undergraduate statistics students on teleconferences did as well as or better than most campus-based classes and had a drop-out rate of zero. Traditional correspondence instruction averages 40-60% drop-out rates. Satisfaction was high and remote learners thought the course did not lack rigor or suitable content.

Hugdahl (1978:7) indicates that many studies have reported the effectiveness of educational teleconferencing and a complete literature review has been published by Parker and Monson (1980).

Professor preparation

Training instructors to use the system has received major emphasis at Calgary. The University would understandably be uneasy about the equivalency and value of credit courses if professors were unprepared to handle the technical aspects of the system. The curriculum developer needed to provide training to potential users without threatening their academic freedom. The experience has been positive since most professors had sufficient anxiety in approaching teleconferencing to accept help in the spirit intended.

Five kinds of instructional assistance are given:

- visits to current credit teleconferencing courses

- sample models of materials from successful teleconferencing classes
- formal in-service instruction from specialists
- literature on teaching technologies and methodologies
- hands-on demonstration of the functioning of the technical system.

Those who took advantage of these opportunities appeared to have the most successful classes, both academically and logistically. One instructor commented that the preparation for teaching by teleconferencing was so useful that his on-campus course was going to be appreciably better.

Grading

Student assessment and examinations are the sacred cows of higher education. This is one area where deviation from the accepted practices is unwise and sometimes unnecessary. Administrators are correctly concerned about such issues as:

- security of answer and test materials
- avoidance of unfair advantage to students
- ethical examination conduct
- equivalency of examinations for comparative norms
- privacy in writing, correcting, and reporting.

The exact duplication of campus examination conditions is obviously impossible in remote towns, but major breaches of accepted examination practices could invalidate a course. Many approaches have been used to avoid abuses of the distance delivery mechanism. Key solutions have been remote proctoring by other educational agencies, requiring students to take examinations at the University during a face-to-face seminar, and replacement of the written examination by an oral examination over the telephone.

Difficulty has been experienced in receiving examinations back due to mailing and shipping problems. Procedures such as the 48-hour deadline for submitting grades to a campus office are impossible to meet. Campus grades are usually posted, which is difficult at a distance.

Similarity of distance and on-campus courses

The fear that remote learners might receive a watered-down version of a campus course is a serious problem. Cases have been reported of departments refusing to allow distance courses as credit when the student came to study on campus.

Academic departments police their course offerings to ensure they do not deviate significantly from accepted standards. Some departments require course outlines and syllabuses to be filed with the department head for approval. However, many would argue that only the professor, who may be the sole specialist in an area of study, can decide if a course is acceptable. Those responsible for distance courses must tread with care in this touchy area.

Access to learning resources

Higher education has traditionally used the quality of the library as a measure of the greatness of an institution. It is axiomatic that students who are to receive a quality education must have access to this resource. But how do remote learners get an equivalent education without access to the academic library? It is not a fair answer to say that many rural communities have good town libraries. Academic libraries specialize in professional fields and rural libraries do not have these specialized collections. A partial solution is to have a set of guidelines for the types of courses offered on the system.

The higher the level of the course, the more necessary is access to research literature, periodicals, theses, and books. The following strategies are helpful:

- instructors provide copies of periodicals for students as part of their learning materials
- students are required to attend seminars periodically and part of this time is to be spent in the library (preferably on campus)
- the University sends reference sets by interlibrary loan to rural libraries
- students check out books from the main library to take to their rural setting for the duration of the course
- instructors use large numbers of texts to give greater breadth of learning resources.

Library access is more significant problem if an entire program is delivered by teleconferencing.

Access to instructors

In the classical higher education model the student learns under the wing of the scholar. The distance learner is isolated.

Many open learning institutions have telephone tutorials for individuals and groups of learners to give periodic feedback. Short (1974: 65) indicates that:

> ... regular face-to-face meetings were not held because of a perceived lack of effectiveness of the system (in the sense that some activities had to be kept for face-to-face meeting) but simply because of the perceived need to maintain personal contact.

He determined that face-to-face meetings were regarded as a very important component of user satisfaction.

Many instructors organize their courses so that each lesson originates at a different location thus giv-

Paper 105

ing learners periodic face-to-face interaction. Combined with telephone availability on scheduled days and times this makes distance education professors as accessible as most busy campus-based professors. Other instructors have chosen to start and finish their course with a face-to-face seminar that establishes personal contact.

Contact hours

Courses at the University of Calgary are officially assigned a number of hours of contact in a classroom. A specific amount of laboratory time is also stipulated. Inherent in this policy is the notion that a specific number of hours of contact be required before an off-campus course can be equivalent. One could argue that highly planned, technology-based educational experiences use fewer hours to achieve the same result, but the need to justify the equivalent number of hours is a very real force.

Where possible, the live teleconference class time combined with face-to-face presentations and campus seminars must equal the approved contact hours for the course.

Summary

The administrator delivering credit higher education courses to remote learners must be aware of the components of academic equivalency. Each will have its challenges but ample proof exists that all can be accommodated.

Academic equivalency can be as much a political as a physical problem. Even though all the above issues may be suitably addressed, educational teleconferencing may still be criticized by academics. The research, however, stands as a testimony to the diligence of educational teleconference course specialists in addressing the reasonable and real concerns of the academic community.

G. Barry Ellis / Robert S. Chapman
University of Calgary
Canada

References

Black, D. (1981) Department of Educational Psychology Report on the Comparison of Measurements of Class Learning: Teleconferencing Compared to the Norms for Regular On-Campus Classes. An unpublished report, The University of Calgary.

Ellis, G. Barry (1981) University of Calgary's new educational teleconferencing system. *Journal of the Alberta Association for Continuing Education*, 9, 1, 18-24.

Hugdahl, E.O. (1978) Distance Learning in Music Through the Teleconferencing Principle: A Six Year Experience in Wisconsin on State-Wide Basis. ERIC ED 168534, 2-15.

Loring, R.K. (1978) Adapting institutions to the adult learner: experiments in progress. *Current Issues in Higher Education*. American Association for Higher Education, ERIC, ED 177285, 2-4.

Parker, L.A. and Monson, M.K. (1980) *More Than Meets the Eye*. University of Wisconsin-Extension.

Short, J. (1974) Teaching by telephone: the problems of teaching without the visual channel. *Teaching at a Distance*, 1, 61-69.

Paper 106

The Contribution of Broadcasting to Adult and Continuing Education

The growing range of options available to the TV viewer will likely cause the BBC to change the emphasis of its adult education programming in the next decade.

Background

The British Broadcasting Corporation (BBC) is an independent organization distinct and separate from government. It is funded not by taxation but by a licence fee paid by each person owning a television receiver. Its educational broadcasting output is wholly financed from this licence fee and is an integral part of the BBC's regular provision on radio and television.

Programs produced by the education departments of the BBC are transmitted on the main channels and networks, none of which are specifically dedicated to educational broadcasting.

The BBC broadcasts nationally on two television channels (BBC-1 and BBC-2). At the time of writing there is one other channel, the responsibility of the Independent Broadcasting Authority, and this is the medium for a number of regionally based commercial television companies. The BBC has four national radio networks and twenty or more local radio stations: there are also at present twenty commercially operated local radio stations, again the responsibility of the IBA.

The BBC's provision of broadcasts specifically designed for use as educational material dates back to the very start of the BBC in the early 1920s. Radio programs for use by schools were first transmitted in 1924 and this provision has grown and continued uninterrupted ever since, joined in 1957 by a parallel national provision on television. Adult education series on radio also began in the earliest days of the BBC and there has been a regular and sizeable output first of radio and, since 1964, of television series designed specifically with adult educational aims.

Additionally, not a direct part of this operation, the BBC produces and broadcasts radio and television programs linked to courses run by the Open University. This contractual arrangement, which started in 1971, is in addition to the BBC's own commitment to educational broadcasting. The independent television network also provides a substantial range of series for schools as well as educational series designed for adult audiences.

BBC education broadcasting for adults

While is is relatively easy to define and describe what is meant by BBC school broadcasts it is very difficult to describe, even to a member of the British public, what are the essential characteristics of the BBC continuing education television and radio output. This is chiefly because most of the programs are transmitted without any special identification within the regular broadcast hours of the BBC network.

It is necessary first perhaps to state what the educational output is *not*. It is not material linked to any form of credit courses (as these are understood in North America), nor, in most cases, is it linked to any specific syllabuses nor designed for use in an institutional setting.

The basic tradition within which the departments operate is the long established one of providing the public in their own homes with a range of broadcast material designed to stretch the imagination or intellect and to encourage subsequent more systematic study. Extensive learning *solely* by means of radio and television programs is not what is sought. The emphasis is on the need for the individual to take things further. What, then, marks off the output of the continuing education departments from the remainder of the BBC's public service oriented output?

In the first place, the overall shape of the output of the BBC continuing education departments (radio and television) does not just happen by chance. It reflects priorities in the world of post-school education—formal and non-formal, vocational and recreational. Evidence of these priorities is chiefly gained through the activities of the small staff of BBC education officers and also by eliciting the views of the BBC's Continuing Education Advisory Council. BBC education sees its output in terms of a total national strategy with the balance between different kinds of output shifting in the light of general trends, sometimes reflecting change, at other times attempting to anticipate it.

Secondly, the BBC education department has always recognized the need to give early and dependable advance information about its plans. The prime element of educational broadcasting has from the outset been to plan the major part of the year's output in one piece and to publicize it at least six months before the start of the academic year. An elaborate sequence of annual programs and other advance publicity items pour in a regular flow to institutions in all parts of the country via an extensive mailing list of tens of thousands of addresses. This system was built on the pattern of BBC publicity to schools and assumes that, like school teachers, adult education tutors and others who receive this advance information will take action to incorporate BBC material into their teaching schemes.

Just as important a justification for the BBC's involvement in educational broadcasting has been its intention and ability to reach the general public at home, and provide them with attractively designed materials—foreign language courses and craft and domestic skills, for example. So the third distinguishing characteristic of educational broadcasting is that for the general listener or viewer it has also provided specially created books, kits, address lists, etc., to enable the individual to move on to more intensive forms of learning. These three characteristics have been constant factors in the BBC's educational broadcasting for adults. What has changed over recent years is the perception by both broadcasters and adult educators of what it might be possible to achieve by carefully linking audiences with appropriate sources of learning, information, and advice. Increasingly ambitious and complex arrangements have been attempted and found to be workable.

Current developments

The fact that most of BBC output on radio is simultaneously networked throughout the UK has been of great significance in the development of education broadcasting. As a result BBC education projects have been able to be developed as 'national' schemes and consequently attract the cooperation of national bodies involved in mass adult education as well as the support of agencies at the local or regional level. During the 1970s the particular strengths of networked and of regionally broadcast educational programs, set within a wider scheme of collaboration between educational providers, were seen increasingly clearly. The BBC's involvement in the UK Adult Literacy Campaign (1975-1978) is often quoted as if it were the only example of its kind. It is not, but that collaborative project represented in a highly developed and effective way a wide range of forms of collaboration—between broadcasters, local authorities, central government, voluntary bodies, etc. It was able to develop because there had been a sequence of earlier collaborative schemes where the parties involved had worked alongside the BBC on an equal footing in the erection of national educational ventures. The number and sophistication of such projects has increased since the time of the adult literacy project and the forms of collaboration that have been developed are now perhaps the most significant characteristic distinguishing BBC educational broadcasting from other programs. What follows is a brief outline of some current projects illustrating the key role now played by the BBC.

Health education

The BBC has been collaborating for the last three or four years with the Health Education Council and the Scottish Health Education Group. As a result a number of broadcast series have formed the basis of UK national health education campaigns with specially designed logos and the mass distribution of hundreds of thousands of free booklets. For example, accident prevention organizations throughout the country are being brought together in 1981/82 by a ten-program television series on child safety, 'Play It Safe', with the intention of coordinating all efforts, previously dissipated, into a major educational campaign to coincide with the start of the series. The BBC has thus been able to bring together for the first time agencies concerned with such separate but similar concerns as road safety, home safety, community health and medical services.

International Year of Disabled People

BBC education has been collaborating with agencies concerned with the care of various disabled groups for several years in the production of radio and television series. In 1981 we redoubled our efforts and produced, for example, a new series to encourage the learning of social skills by young mentally handicapped people, "Let's Go", and a series for those caring for handicapped dependents in the home. In each case informational literature is made available to professional specialist teachers and to the general public in association with the agencies most concerned. This provision is being given a greater cohesion by the special development of the telephone referral system developed on a national basis for the BBC's Adult Literacy Campaign. Each of these series is linked to 'Line 81' by which information and advice is available via a central telephone number.

Technical training and updating

BBC Education has for many years provided resource material for use in the vocationally oriented Further Education Colleges. Such program series are transmitted during the day to be recorded off-air and used as learning resources material by lecturers. Surveys suggest that the vast majority of these colleges regularly use BBC material in this way. A ten-program series of this kind on engineering science was based on the syllabus requirements of a nationally approved vocational training scheme designed by the Technician Education Council. Professional and technical updating series are also produced: in 1981 a television series on supervisory management was used in hundreds of colleges and training establishments as the basis of training and seminars.

The microchip revolution

An area of social concern is the likely impact of the microcomputer on work and leisure. A major BBC project is aimed at improving computer literacy amongst the general public. "Hands on Micros" aims to teach people how to operate a machine and to understand its potential uses. The BBC has been closely cooperating with the UK Government Department of Industry and as a result the broadcasts have been linked to other educational activity promoted by the department. But most important and significant, the BBC has commissioned the creation of its own microcomputer, which it has put on sale to the public. This computer is one of two selected by the Department of Education as eligible for a major subsidy by purchasing schools.

Ethnic minorities

Building on the long tradition of foreign language courses, BBC education is currently involved in a major long-term project initially involving a twenty-part television series designed to encourage those for whom English is a second language to improve their English language skills. But "Speak for Yourself" is designed to be more than simply a language course, for the appropriate social skills are stressed at every point. This series has become the focal point for activity on a national scale. Every public library in the country has become a local distribution centre for learning materials linked to the programs and language classes are recruiting increased numbers of students drawn in by seeing the logo shown on the program or referred via a nationally operated telephone referral scheme. A second such series is planned for 1982/83.

Conclusion

These examples demonstrate that the BBC is recognized by other educational and quasi-educational agencies as having a key position both in providing specifically educational material and in being the focal point for coordinated strategy.

This is possible because of the small number of available television channels (a fourth channel opens at the end of 1982). Because the size of the UK and the organization of broadcasting allows for simultaneous networking and because the education system is essentially a devolved rather than a centralized one, initiatives rely on cooperation rather than command.

The development of European television satellite transmissions in the mid 1980s and the inevitable rise in the range of options available to the television viewer at home must inevitably cast a shadow over the indefinite continuation of the sort of educational activities outlined above. For the use of broadcast television to be effective in this way there must be a reasonable chance of reaching a significant proportion of the target population.

So, while the BBC's contribution to adult education in the UK in the past decade has been one of increasing significance, its role in the next decade may require a change in emphasis.

Neil H. Barnes
British Broadcasting Corporation
United Kingdom

Multi-Media Methods for Adult Basic Education

Basic education programs should be designed in terms of real-life situations and need strong face-to-face support locally.

Introduction

This paper summarizes a study carried out by the Open University's Distance Education Research Group for the Commission of the European Communities. The principal objectives of the study were:

— to collect data on initiatives within the European Community using multi-media methods for adult basic education, and on organizations with an interest in this field

— to explore the conditions under which these methods can be effectively used for providing adult basic education

— to examine the circumstances in which a distance learning model or a system can be used for adult basic education

— to identify any major themes and issues concerning the use of multi-media and distance methods for adult basic education

— to identify needs for further information and research in the Community

— where appropriate, to formulate specific proposals to the Commission of the European Communities for initiatives and action.

The interest of the European Commission is related to the adoption of social and educational measures by member states in reaction to:

— increasing evidence of educational and social disadvantage in the adult population

— the needs of immigrants and migrant workers for basic education in the language and customs of their host country

— the rapidly increasing levels of unemployment in the Community

— the needs for re-training associated with a changing employment structure.

What is adult basic education?

It is perhaps easier to start by describing what it is *not*. It is not the academic education that forms the bulk of current teaching in secondary schools, colleges, and universities. Nor is it strictly professional or vocational training in specific fields. Nor is it only a second chance for groups and individuals to use existing opportunities in these areas—through full-time or part-time study—to achieve upwards social mobility. The notion of adult basic education should encompass that of education for, *and by,* the groups involved—not merely the opening of new channels to forms of knowledge and culture designed by the privileged for the less privileged. Adult basic education should encompass not only the development of a "toolkit" of special skills, but also its application to the acquisition, use, and production of knowledge to bring about changes in society itself.

What comprises this toolkit of basic education skills? The following areas are important:

— *functional literacy and numeracy skills* related to practical needs (reading newspapers, following instructions, filling in forms, keeping account of household expenditures, shopping etc.)

- *social coping skills* for the complexities of modern society (seeking employment, obtaining housing, social services, health care)
- *parental and family education:* the importance of family milieu and parental attitudes in childhood development is well established
- *consumer education* to help people learn how to get the "best buy"; the problem is to make consumer information available to the groups who are often the most easily exploited
- *domestic economy:* guidance on balancing a housekeeping budget, carrying out basic repair and maintenance tasks in the home, etc.
- *community education:* provision of help and information to enable members of a community to take group action to improve their situation (e.g., obtaining improved health, education, and employment)
- *the raising of awareness about existing opportunities* for education and vocational training, and how to make use of them.

The study is concerned with multi-media projects with such aims directed at the disadvantaged.

Disadvantaged can be defined broadly to refer to those groups and individuals unable—for whatever reason—to use the existing educational system to satisfy their needs.

Outcomes

The study was carried out by a team from the Open University's Distance Education Research Group, with contributions from a network of practitioners and policy-makers from all the existing and future member states of the European Community, over the period March 1980 - May 1981. The study involved five principal phases:

1. identification of relevant initiatives
2. preparation of detailed case studies of twelve particularly interesting projects, by appropriate personnel from each project
3. preparation of special reports on relevant issues and topics (e.g., organizational and collaborative frameworks, community media)
4. identification of major themes and issues in the use of multi-media and distance methods for adult basic education

Table 1: Case Study Projects

Country	Project Title	Target Audience	Scale	Principal Media/Method
Belgium	Canal-Emploi, Liège	urban unemployed	local	Cable TV and group instruction
	Charleroi, Collective Action	urban unemployed	local	group work; planned TV
Denmark	Danish for Adults	adults needing literacy	national	TV, radio, distance, face-to-face
France	Télé-Promotion-Rurale	agriculturalists	regional	TV, press, group meetings
	CNEC French courses	adults needing literacy	national	correspondence tuition, TV
W. Germany	DIFF/Zeitungskolleg	community at large	national	newspapers, group meetings
Netherlands	Open School	adults needing basic education	national	group work, print, radio, TV
Portugal	Popular Adult Education	adults needing basic education	national	local groups, some central materials
Spain	Radio ECCA	adults needing basic education	regional/national	radio, print, tutorials
U.K.	Adult Literacy Campaign	adults needing literacy	national	TV, radio, print, volunteer tutors
	UKOU Comunity Education	community at large	national	TV, radio, print, local groups
	"Just the Job"	rural unemployed youth	regional	TV, radio, print, counsellors

5. preparation of recommendations for action by the European Commission in this area (e.g., information exchange (dissemination, co-planning workshops, etc.)).

Table 1 lists the projects chosen for case studies and some of their principal characteristics.

The principal outcomes of the study are the reports and documents listed in the Appendix. In addition there is an extensive report to the European Commission, and a forthcoming book on using the media for adult basic education.

Some conclusions

Some of the main *prescriptive* elements that have emerged are:

1. Adult basic education projects—particularly functional projects—aimed at disadvantaged groups, should help create conditions that encourage participants to help themselves, to become autonomous, and to take on responsibility for their own situations.

2. Programs should be of immediate relevance in terms of objectives, style, content, and approach to the real needs of the participants; they should provide the information, knowledge, and skills needed to bring about concrete changes.

3. Key questions that need answering at the early stages of planning include the following:
   - will the *primary* learning mode be through self study or through face-to-face tuition on a group/individual basis (i.e., will it be a media-based project or a media-supported project)?
   - will the project encompass *variants* in learning methods (e.g., an independent study option, a distance learning option, a class-based option)?
   - what will be the primary *result* or *output* of the project (achievement of personally set, functional objectives, delivery of a diploma or certificate, action at local level)?
   - will the project include elements designed *specifically* to favour the disadvantaged groups and individuals who do not spontaneously seek adult education?

4. Functional basic education programs should where feasible be designed in terms of real issues (e.g., finding employment, organizing a tenants' association, managing a household budget) rather than in terms of basic "disciplines" such as literacy, numeracy, economics, etc.

5. Disadvantaged groups and individuals do not generally articulate their objective needs for educational resources; objective needs must generally be determined through an analysis of problems, and through discussion of subjective needs with eventual participants.

6. Provision of an educational resource relevant to subjective needs and able to meet objective needs will stimulate a demand if publicized through appropriate channels.

7. Multi-media education projects—whether functional or examination-oriented—should exploit to a maximum the popular communication styles of radio, television and the press, thus removing possible psychological barriers to access.

8. Participation levels in multi-media programs will be enhanced if:
   - the procedures for enquiry and enrolment are as simple as possible (e.g., telephone referral, a "drop-in" shop)
   - the provision itself is as flexible as possible in terms of timing, location, pace and methods of learning
   - there is redundancy among the different elements in the project (i.e., a participant who misses a broadcast or a tutorial class can obtain the information through another channel—for example, a self-teaching text)
   - very close integration between the different media used (leading to an imposition of a relatively rigid study sequence) is avoided.

9. Clear functions should be assigned to each medium. These functions will include: publicity, awareness-raising, recruitment, instruction, resolving learning problems, providing feedback, and so on.

10. For publicity and recruitment, as wide a range as possible of information channels should be used: broadcasts, press, posters, personal and institutional contacts, leaflets, etc. Specific information channels (e.g., particular radio or TV programs and broadcast times, specialist newspapers/magazines) should be used to get through to specific sub-groups of the target population.

11. Multi-media basic education programs intended to reach disadvantaged groups will need to place strong reliance on face-to-face tuition and counselling in both group and individual situations, with the media probably playing a supporting role.

12. Recruitment and training of staff to work at the local level is of major importance in any multi-media project aimed at disadvantaged groups; development of specific skills in working with adults in the following situations is required:
    - pre-enrolment counselling
    - group counselling during the project
    - one-to-one tuition
    - group tuition
    - group leadership and "animation".

13. Distance learning methods based essentially on home-based, independent study, with minimal tuition and group work, will usually be appropriate only for individuals who are strongly motivated and have previous successful experience of learning at a distance. Educationally disadvantaged groups and individuals will likely need some form of guidance and preparation.

14. Learning materials suitable for adults in skills such as numeracy and literacy will need to be developed from scratch, as few suitable materials exist in these areas, and those used at the school level are not appropriate for mature students.

15. Centrally produced materials (broadcasts, print materials) should be designed for flexible use in a variety of situations ranging from independent, home-based learning to supported group study.

16. Learning materials for basic education programs should be extensively piloted, both with representative members of the target group and with adult educators familiar with their needs, before they are finalized.

17. Procedures for obtaining regular feedback from participants and local animateurs and tutors on the effectiveness of centrally produced materials should be built into the design of any multi-media project; likewise, resources should be allocated for the revision and updating of materials in the light of this feedback.

18. Projects lacking automatic monitoring of learners' progress through assessment/examination procedures should include procedures for monitoring participants' progress in other ways to ascertain participation and drop-out rates.

19. A team structure, with close working relationships between members with different specialist skills, is generally the most appropriate one for the production of multi-media materials; where feasible, every effort should be made to involve eventual project participants (learners and tutors/animateurs) in the process of materials creation.

20. Projects involving collaboration among a number of different agencies in preparing materials and in providing local publicity and support, should be based on a clear allocation of functions, responsibilities, and resources among the different agencies; regular opportunities for monitoring and comparing progress need to be built into the project brief.

21. Projects using central resources (such as broadcasting), that create a demand for local resources (such as evening classes) should be planned from the start in close collaboration with the agencies responsible for local provision; extreme care should be given to scheduling to ensure the necessary meshing of local and central provision when the project starts, as the time required for booking local resources may vary widely between one agency and another.

22. In designing projects, every effort should be made to keep a record of the actual costs of each component, regardless of the source of financing; standard procedures for describing, analysing, and projecting costs should be devised.

23. Evaluation procedures for assessing the effectiveness of the components should be incorporated into the design of any new multi-media project; particular care should be given to devising methods for evaluating the effectiveness of non-assessed, functional projects where participants can set their own learning objectives and levels of participation.

Anthony R. Kaye
The Open University
United Kingdom

Appendix: Major Outcomes of the Study

Listed below are the main documents produced as part of the study.

A. Project Case Studies

(available in mimeo from DERG, UKOU)

Cepeda, L.E. (1980) *Structure and Educational Technology of Radio EECA* (in English and Spanish)

Farnes, N. and **Calder**, J. (1980) *A Distance Learning Contribution to Community Education (UKOU).*

Girardin, M. (1980) *L'Expérience de Télé-Promotion Rurale* (in French and English)

Jacquet, F. (1980) *Canal Emploi: Presentation d'une Expérience: Perspectives d'un Projet Intégré de Formation Permanente* (French)

Jones, H.A. and **Charnley**, A.H. (1980) *A Case Study of the Adult Literacy Initiative in the United Kingdom 1974-1979.*

Looms, P.O. (1980) *Danish for Adults: A Case Study.*

Melo, A. (1980) *The Mass Media and Distance Teaching for Basic Education: A Case Study on Portugal.*

Reischmann, J. (1980) *Zeitungskolleg: A Mass Media and Distance Learning Project for Open Learning.*

Vabre, H. (1980) *The Pre-Training Scheme of the French National Centre for Correspondence Education* (in French and English).

Vellekoop, L. (1981) *The Dutch Open School Project: A Case Study.*

Verniers, C. (1981) *Presentation de l'Action Collective de Formation de Charleroi et Reflexion sur le Rôle que les Mass Media Peuvent y Jouer* (in French)

Reeves, B. (1980) *National Extension College/Westward TV 'Just the Job' Project.*

B. Special Reports

(available in mimeo from DERG, UKOU)

Berrigan, F. (1980) *Access to Broadcast Media and Community Use of Media in Respect of Adult Basic Education Programmes.*

Cain, J. (1980) *A Personal Report on the British Experience of the Use of Mass Media for Basic Adult Education.*

Doglio, D. (1980) *A Report on the Current Situation in Italy as Regards the Use of Mass Media for Adult Basic Education.*

Robinson, J. (1980) *Organisational and Collaborative Frameworks for the Provision of Adult Basic Education using Multi Media Methods.*

C. Study Report to the European Commission

Available as a monograph from DERG/UKOU

Harry, K., **Kaye**, A.R. and **Wilson**, K. (1981) *A Report on the European Experience of the Use of Mass Media and Distance Methods for Adult Basic Education.* (This reports presents the main findings of the Study, and includes appendices of:

– summaries of the various case studies
– a Directory of relevant projects and initiatives in Europe
– an annotated Bibliography).

D. A book based on the Study

Kaye, A.R. and **Harry**, K. (eds.) (1982) *Using the Media for Adult Basic Education,* Croom Helm, London.
(this book includes seven of the case studies—those which represent national or regional projects using broadcasting, print, and local provision in an integrated manner; it also includes a Directory of European projects and initiatives, and an annotated Bibliography).

The TVOntario Academy

The combination of television broadcasting and computer-managed learning has proven a popular success.

Paper 108

Introduction

In January 1980, TVOntario began the use of computer-managed learning (CML) in support of television broadcasting. The three projects that have been carried out are very promising for the future.

The TVOntario Academy consists of a combination of high-quality television programming, a computer-managed learning system, and courseware designed to encourage TVOntario viewers towards self-directed learning projects on subjects related to the television series. Viewers who express an interest in undertaking this type of learning are provided with guidance and advice in formulating their learning goals and interests. Learners are given the opportunity to respond to frequent sets of exercises designed to provide further clarification of concepts, intellectual stimulation, and an opportunity for self-evaluation. The CML system lets learners receive individualized feedback to their responses.

The three projects to date are: a 14-week *Health and the Environment Academy,* an 8-week *Music of Man Academy,* and a 12-week *Parents' Academy.*

How does the Academy work? The basic component of a TVOntario Academy is a carefully selected series of television programs that cover a well-defined body of knowledge. As the clients of TVOntario Academy are individual viewers in their homes who might not otherwise have studied that subject, the television series has to be an attractive production of professional quality. The *Health and the Environment Academy* is based on a series produced by TVOntario in cooperation with the inter-university Education Council on Health and the Environment. The 14 half-hour documentaries focus on health concerns ranging from processed food to species survival. The issues are discussed from an environmental and interactional perspective, which stresses the increasing demands that modern technology has placed on the human body and the role lay people play in health matters. The *Music of Man Academy* is based on 8 one-hour programs produced by the Canadian Broadcasting Corporation, in association with the OECA, written and narrated by Yehudi Menuhin. The programs provide a unique panorama of the world of sound, and present the musical traditions of five continents, with performances by many of the world's distinguished artists. The *Parents' Academy* programs were selected from several series produced by TVOntario in the last two years and deal with the development of normal and atypical children.

The television series is the initial stimulus for learning. When the plans to broadcast the series are announced, we make the public aware that this could be a good opportunity for many individuals to learn on their own, and gain considerably more from watching television.

The major components of an Academy, in addition to the television series, are: a Learner's Guide, describing the educational objectives of each unit of learning; reading materials, usually in the form of essays from 2-15 pages in length written to accompany each program; and multiple-choice questions for each learning unit designed to involve the participants intellectually, to stimulate their curiosity, and to sustain their interest.

The most dynamic element is the computerized system of feedback or, as we call it, prescriptions to the responses the participants send in. We use the prescriptions as an important channel of information. We use them also to clarify particular concepts, to stimulate further inquiry, to advise on related activities, and to help participants contact each other for possible group meetings and discussions. This feedback is presented in the form of letters to the participants.

The CML system used by the Academy allows considerable individualization of the letters. Each participant can receive comments and suggestions that take into account not only his choice of alternative in each question, but also his personal learning goals and interests, as stated in his registration form, his educational background, occupation, geographic location, etc. These individualized letters are one of the main features of the Academy providing personalized contact.

Highlights of evaluations

The findings of an evaluation of the *Health and the Environment Academy* and the *Music of Man Academy* provide interesting information about the motivations of participants, as well as their perceptions of the learning process and effects. Here are some highlights:

- the geographic distribution of the participants reflected closely the actual population distribution
- among reasons for enrolling in the Academies, over 40% of the participants indicated that the idea of a television-based learning experience appealed to them
- when asked about the reason for participating in a television-based learning activity rather than another type of course, the largest number of respondents chose the replies "It is a convenient way to learn" and "I wanted to try a course using television"
- participants found the registration process very simple
- the overwhelming majority, around 90% of respondents, enjoyed receiving the computer-generated letters, found that the comments were helpful and that they related directly to their needs and interests; the majority was satisfied with the language and style of the letters; they indicated that the responses stimulated reflection and discussion of the television programs
- when asked to evaluate each component of the Academies, nearly 90% of respondents considered the main components of the Academies (the television programs, the learning guide, the questionnaire sets, and the computer-generated responses) as "very useful" or "somewhat useful."

Similar results were achieved by the *Parents' Academy,* which operated in the first quarter of 1981, and achieved its goal of 2000 paid participants. Nielsen estimates indicate that the programs were watched on Wednesday evenings by nearly 40,000 viewers and on Saturday afternoons by 18,000 viewers. Such audiences are rarely reached by TVOntario programs in these time slots.

The type of contact and rapport between the Academies and a substantial proportion of the participants strongly confirms the viability of the project and its method, and the significant meaning it has for many people.

One of the most important results is the development of a new type of courseware. This *new* educational design encourages a systematic effort by the learner to be spread over a number of weeks; it provides guidance and pacing; and it feeds and enriches the learning process. And most importantly, it gives the person who is learning alone—and most home learners do learn alone—a desirable channel for expression. We have now strong evidence that a substantial portion of the Academy participants understand the opportunities the system provides and take full advantage of them.

The numerous comments, even those criticizing certain aspects of the Academies, express acceptance and appreciation. The individualization of the replies is easily recognized by participants and appreciated by them.

The Academies are, in our conditions, a significant achievement in two important respects. Firstly, they are successful examples of the educational and instructional capabilities of television broadcasting; in all the Academies the broadcasts were the main stimulus for the learning projects and a significant part of the resource material. Secondly, the Academies are a form of truly interactive television made available without capital investment in hardware by both the broadcaster and the viewer. Interaction does not always need immediacy, as we are proving with the Academy projects.

Our further plans include an Academy on computing, designed in principle for teachers of elementary and secondary schools but also expected to attract a considerable number of people from the general public. This Academy, which is now in preparation, will be a good example of the further development of the Academy concept. Not only will it meet a need felt urgently by an important target audience towards whom TVOntario has a particularly strong commitment, but unlike the earlier Academies that had mainly a motivational character, this Academy will be aimed at a more rigorous course of learning, and will enable its participants to achieve a set of specific proficiencies. We expect that each participant will receive at the completion of the course a certificate containing a detailed evaluation of the results achieved for each unit of learning selected. This would be made possible through the computer-managed evaluations made available to each participant each week on a voluntary basis.

Ignacy Waniewicz
TVOntario
Canada

Videodisc and Videotex: New Media for Distance Education

The programs developed for them will determine whether these new systems succeed or fail.

Introduction

Videodisc and videotex are two new media that increase the capacity of the television set. Videodisc is a system similar to the long-playing record except that it carries both audio and video through a conventional television set. Videotex allows the home television set to function like a computer terminal and retrieve text information and graphics from a remote database. The importance of both technologies is the power they can bring into the home at a reasonable cost.

In Canada there is an increasing demand for continuing education that can be satisfied in two ways: the student can come to the institution, or the institution can make educational opportunities available in the workplace or the home. Telecommunications will make learning at a distance more feasible. Distance education has always been well suited to the adult learner and those with special needs such as the handicapped. Videodisc and videotex offer the promise of more sophisticated teaching techniques and are important new tools for educators in general and "distance educators" in particular.

Videodisc Technology

> The world has spent more than a decade and nearly $1 billion arming for the coming battle over videodiscs. By the end of next year [1981], three technologies and at least twice that many giant companies will be pitted against one another, each with the same goal: to win the lion's share of a lucrative new U.S. consumer market... *The impact of videodiscs will go far beyond the consumer marketplace, however.* Coupled with a little computer power, they promise to change the way that employees are trained, equipment is maintained, students are taught.
>
> (*Business Week*, 1980: 72)

A videodisc looks like an irridescent space-age, long-playing record. It rotates on the turntable of the videodisc player at a high speed and is read by a stylus or a laser. Information on the disc is contained in microscopic pits of varying length and density. The pits are in tracks or grooves. The information read from these pits is displayed on a regular television set.

There are two major types of videodisc systems. In the capacitance system discs are read by a stylus in contact with the disc, which may be grooved or grooveless. The optical videodisc player uses a low powered laser beam to read the information on the disc, which may be either reflective or transmissive. Reflective discs are covered with a coating that causes the laser beam to bounce off the surface, while transmissive discs are transparent, allowing the beam to shine through the disc.

A second distinction concerns the intended usage of the machine. Consumer models are intended for use in the home and do not support interaction. Educational/industrial players are more rugged and derive greater versatility and capability from a built-in microprocessor. They are also more costly.

The videodisc, particularly the optical disc, has exciting potential for educators. It has enormous storage capacity; optical discs can store 108,000 tracks, 54,000 on each side. The information recorded in each track consists of a video image or frame for display on the television set. Each of the 54,000 frames on a side is addressable with a five-digit number and can be randomly accessed in 5 seconds or less. The entire Encyclopedia Britannica could be stored on a single videodisc with room to spare.

The disc plays uninterruptedly for thirty minutes on each side and individual images can be displayed indefinitely in a freeze frame mode without wear on the disc since there is no mechanical contact. The system is also capable of fast forward, fast reverse, slow motion and step frame movement. The two discrete audio channels available on optical discs permit stereophonic sound or two different sound tracks for visual sequences. Sound is currently available only in the normal playing mode and cannot be used in the freeze frame mode. The intelligent videodisc system, which is particularly useful for educators, consists of a videodisc player under the direct control of a computer.

> This system permits interactive instruction using both alphanumeric and graphic stimuli generated by the computer, and audio and video information stored on the videodisc. The logic for branching to appropriate text or audio-video segments is stored in the computer program which can also carry out sizable calculations. Players with a built-in microprocessor and external interface are specifically designed for such instructional applications and known generally as educational/industrial players.
>
> (Sustik, 1980: 9)

The players can also be programmed through the keypad or other controls and it is possible to encode automatic stops directly on the disc. Hence the industrial/educational model is a powerful, stand-alone educational tool. The combination of videodisc and microcomputer creates media capabilities previously limited to large, expensive systems. It has been called an omnibus medium since it can record virtually all other communications media—film, television programs, filmstrips, slides, microfilm, video tapes, transparencies, computer data, and printed text.

Such a broad range of capabilities is a challenge for the educator.

> ...we need to reassess our basic paradigms to insure that we look at the whole phenomenon of instructional design. The added capability afforded by the videodisc/computer system in the way of storage of digital and ionic symbols, retrieval speed, memory and access presents the designer with a set of resource and constant variables that are much different from those assumed in the past. Our current models no longer fulfill the requirements of representing all of the structural parts, process elements, and possibilities available, and if we persist in using them, we may very well hamper future instructional theorization.
>
> (DeBloois, 1979: 35)

Videodisc applications

US videodisc projects reveal a broad range of potential applications in elementary, secondary and post-secondary education, continuing education, special education, and training.

Figure 1: Videodisc systems and their parent companies

Optical Transmissive

Thompson CSF (France)

Optical Reflective

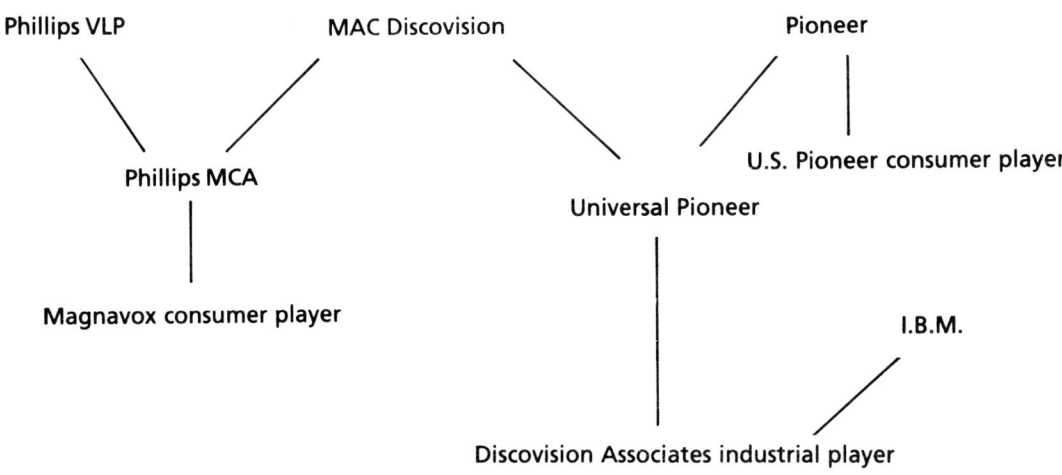

Capacitance Grooveless

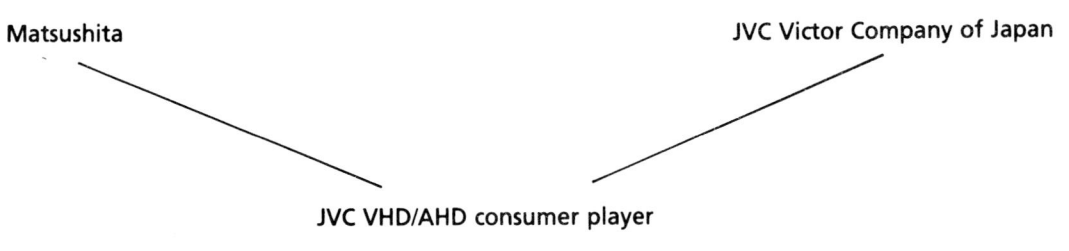

Capacitance Grooved

RCA Selectavision

Source: (Sustik, 1980: 9)

One notable development in elementary school programming is the Schooldisc Program announced in 1980 by the National Education Association and the American Broadcasting Corporation. This is an unprecedented joint venture of classroom teachers and television. A series of 20 one-hour programs is being developed for grades four through six. Distribution is scheduled for the fall of 1981 to between 5,000 and 10,000 schools. This example highlights a key economic feature of videodisc production: economics are achieved with large numbers.

In post-secondary education a disc was developed for individualized instruction in biology. The project was funded by McGraw-Hill and developed by WICAT Incorporated. An evaluation of student performance revealed that when compared with traditional classroom students, those who had studied material on videodisc reduced their study time by as much as 30% and outscored their peers by 15% to 20%.

Videodisc technology could significantly change the delivery of special education programs—for the handicapped as well as the non-handicapped learner. A videodisc computer-assisted instruction system allows self-paced, individualized instruction and frees the teachers to attend to the students' special problems. The University of Nebraska has developed programs for the deaf. Discs include a captioned Encyclopedia Britannica film, finger-spelling skills for adults, a visual textbook for high school literature, and a program for parents of hearing impaired children. Videodiscs may help learning impaired students reach their full potential.

General Motors Corporation is the largest and possibly best known user of videodiscs, with 10,000 players distributed among its dealerships. Initially installed to spur car sales, they now also guide mechanics through complicated repairs and train sales staff. The educational/industrial Discovision model was chosen because its program branching capability permits interactive instruction. A field test compared videodisc with other media and found it very effective.

Videodisc facilitates individualized instruction. Dr. Leo Leveridge, who has been active with new technology for the *American Medical Association,* suggested that:

> Since the discs themselves are inexpensive when mass-produced, and require little storage room, it is likely that the individual will accumulate a rather extensive library of courses on discs for his particular field. This will allow easy and timely review of material whenever necessary. Thus the user will have a wide range of educational and reference materials at his fingertips... Because the videodisc/computer combination is well suited to self-instruction, it will meet the educational needs of the mature audiences in the professions who should be allowed to learn at their own individual paces and at the times and places that suit their own convenience.
>
> (Leveridge, 1979: 38)

If videodisc is widely accepted by the consumer there will be a large new market for distance education institutions. Videodisc probably addresses the adult learner's need for flexibility better than any other medium.

Videotex technology

Videotex uses television and the telephone to allow access to computerized information. A hand-held numeric keypad is used to request pages or "screenfuls" of information from a remote computer to which a modified TV set is connected by telephone.

Videotex turns the home television set into a terminal. Just because it used devices already present in many homes it promises broad social utility.

> Perhaps the greatest social significance of videotex is the possibility it offers for much wider access to information and conversely, the much greater ease with which new concepts and ideas can be transmitted.
>
> (Madden, 1979: 16)

There are two systems that deliver words and graphics to a modified television set. *Videotex,* as used in this paper, uses the telephone to connect the user to the database. It was originally called *Viewdata* by the British and is also known as *two-way* or *interactive videotex. Teletext* operates on a different basis. Information is piggy-backed on an ordinary television signal using two spare lines. Pages of teletext information are broadcast in a cycle, usually of no more than 400 pages, and when the requested page comes up in the cycle, it is "grabbed" and displayed on the screen. This system is also called *broadcast videotex, one-way* or *non-interactive videotex.* Videotex is sometimes used as a generic term to denote both types of systems.

There are now three international standards for videotex: British (Prestel), French (Antiope) and Canadian (Telidon). Field trials are bing conducted around the world.

To understand videotex it is necessary to examine the hardware. The user terminal is a "dumb terminal" that allows access to the database. It has three components: a conventional colour or black and white television set modified for Red Green Blue (RGB) input or radio frequency (RF) input, which serves as a display; an external control unit that couples the television set with regular telephone lines; and a hand-held keypad that allows the user to interact with the system. The keypad has ten numeric and ten control keys and uses infrared remote control or a wired connection. A full alpha-numeric keyboard is also available as an alternative.

Information for the Telidon system is prepared by the information provider using the Information Preparation System (IPS) terminal. The IPS is a stand-alone intelligent graphics terminal providing off-line processing independent of the host computer and page storage on a floppy disc. All page creation and editing takes place on this terminal. Pages and information concerning their placement in the database are stored on local memory on the floppy disc that is transported to the host computer for entry during low usage hours.

The database is central to the Telidon system and allows information to be stored and retrieved in a logical and systematic fashion. It is organized in a hierarchical tree-structure permitting rapid subject selection and retrieval of the desired information. This structure is also economical of computer processing time.

In the database there are two categories of pages: index pages and document pages. Index pages divide a category into sub-categories that lead the user through the levels of the tree, requiring him to make a choice at each level, thereby leading him to the appropriate document page.

The first page in the Telidon tree-structure is a general index page (or "menu") numbered page 0. It is followed by nine more levels of pages with nine choices at each level. At any branch in the tree there can be a sequential file of 1000 pages.

Any page may be reached in two ways. It may be accessed directly if the page number is known. A printed directory is sometimes used to give the user an overview of the database structure and to facilitate searching. Alternatively a page may be accessed as a result of a search through the index pages.

The simple system of organizing the database in a tree-structure will allow any user to access information without having to learn new skills. This presumably facilitates the introduction of a new technology.

Videotex applications

It is too early to predict the eventual context and operation of videotex systems. A videotex market may develop in two phases. The first will be the saturation of the business market as businesses become aware of the importance of information and willing to pay for a system that serves their needs. With a high level of usage, the cost of the hardware and software will be brought down to a suitable level for the consumer market.

Services proposed for the home are many and varied. They include financial transactions, electronic newspapers, computer-assisted instruction, shopping, electronic mail, computer tutor, special sales information, travel information and reservations, calendar of events, correspondence courses, personal daily calendar, consumers' advisory service, weather bureau, restaurant and entertainment guide, and library access.

The education sector has shown considerable interest in videotex and a number of applications are being tested. Sigel (1980: 54) reports that in Britain educational word games have been developed as well as programs for learning a second language. Two educational experiments have been carried out, one with 19 schools and technical colleges, the other with primary schools. Two schools for the deaf were involved. The Open University is exploring the potential of videotex for distance education.

In distance education three different types of uses come to mind: the transmission of general or specific information; the transmission of courses; two-way interaction.

A videotex system would be very useful in disseminating general information about courses and programs available through distance education. It could raise the level of awareness of potential students about all the educational opportunities available, regardless of geographic location. The system could be equally useful, given a substantial database, in allowing students in remote locations access to the kind of information currently available only to students in areas with large libraries.

Courses, portions of courses, or supplementary print information for telecourses could be distributed to students on videotex. Since the size of the screen and therefore the number of words on a page is limited, the most appropriate applications must be determined. For this use, videotex offers the advantage over other communications media like radio, television, and the telephone of being free from a time schedule. With the addition of a keyboard to the user terminal it is possible to offer computer-assisted instruction.

Two-way interaction between student and tutor is also possible with a keyboard. This application resembles electronic mail with the student able to address questions to the tutor and receive immediate feedback. The advantage over the post for this kind of interaction is faster turn-around. It has an advantage over the telephone if there is any difficulty in establishing a mutually convenient time for the discussion. It may also prove to be more cost effective.

Standards and development

Although there is currently a problem of standards for both videodisc and videotex, these must not prevent exploration and development to test each medium. The hardware problem will no doubt be solved long before a good range of software and courseware is available. Similarly, although videotex is still at the field trial stage in most countries and videodisc has not yet achieved a significant level of use within the general population, it must not be assumed that there is no need to consider development of programs yet. Without programs, neither technology will appeal to either the general public or the potential learner. It is the programming and information available for these systems that will ultimately determine their acceptance or rejection. The education sector has a responsibility to ensure that both media offer more than entertainment.

Susan G. D'Antoni
Ryerson Polytechnical Institute
Canada

References

DeBloois, M. (1979) Exploring new design models. *Educational and Industrial Television.*

Leveridge, L. (1979) The potential of interactive optical videodisc systems for continuing education. *Educational and Industrial Television.*

Madden, J. (1979) *Videotex in Canada.* Ottawa: Ministry of Supply and Services.

Sigel, E. (ed.) (1980) *Videotext: The Coming Revolution in Home/Office Information Retrieval.* White Plains, N.Y.: Knowledge Industry Publications, Inc.

Sustik, Joan M. (1980) Videodisc: A Technical Description. *Pipeline,* Fall.

Videodiscs, A Three-Way Race for a Billion Dollar Jackpot. (1980) *Business Week,* July 7.

Using Videotex in Distance Education
(Abstract)

Paper 110

The University of Manitoba correspondence program has depended on print for fifty years although it has experimented with new media—audio tape, video tape, teleconferencing, radio—as a means of enhancing student-instructor interaction and enriching the instructional process. The most recent media project involved the evaluation of Telidon, Canada's version of videotex.

The Manitoba Telephone System initiated Canada's first domestic field trials of videotex with 180 Telidon terminals in two communities. The University accepted an invitation to be an information provider for these trials. Roughly 400 "pages" or "frames" of information were created including course advertising, program registration information, public service announcements, and two short courses.

Our limited testing of Telidon videotext technology indicates the following:

1. Telidon can produce high quality text and graphic images.

2. Videotex could be an effective educational tool if home users had a full alphanumeric (typewriter style) keyboard. Most current Telidon units use a numeric keypad and a non-random access memory, severely limiting freedom of access and flexibility.

3. Use should reflect graphic design techniques from television and film as well as educational research.

4. The application of videotex in correspondence education should:

    - use systematic instructional design techniques
    - reflect the unique attributes of the medium (it is a suitable adjunct to printed correspondence lessons, and useful for tutorial functions)
    - recognize that computer-assisted instruction is best for simulation and modelling, and less effective as a surrogate teacher
    - solicit political support for the long-term amortization of high capital start-up costs
    - employ highly skilled staff, including in-house computer specialists
    - optimize program size so that courseware is cost-effective and varied
    - ensure that access costs are reasonable
    - benefit from the experience gained in the educational application of other media.

5. Educators should promote the development of home videotex terminals with off-line data processing capabilities (RAM and ROM microprocessors), third-party access, and the use of methods such as packet switching that lower transmission costs.

Videotex can help overcome some of the limitations of traditional correspondence study. The experience gained in Canada since 1979 shows the advantages to the educational sector of becoming involved early in any government plan to use videotex. One major shortcoming has been insufficient funds to support the development and evaluation of the videotex database.

Educators should also appraise other forms of computer-telecommunications systems. Specialized videotex databases and products may well give way to microcomputers that can plug into any adapted television set, use a variety of mass storage I/O devices, and access either broadcast or transmitted data (videotex) telecommunications.

Paul Hurly / Denis Hlynka
University of Manitoba
Canada

Paper 111

Videodiscs: Will Laser Technology Help Light the Way for Learning at a Distance?

(Abstract)

Videodiscs can store tremendous amounts of information (a 54,000 frame capacity) in the form of textual material, slides, photos, tape or film. A single frame of the disc can store one page of written material and thus it becomes theoretically possible to store the equivalent of a small encyclopedia on one side of a disc. Each frame can be accessed individually by the user and consequently the videodisc educational model, which includes a microprocessor, becomes a new learner-centred tool for providing individualized instruction. Because of the dual audio track capacity, it also becomes possible to provide bilingual discs.

The paper provides a brief historical background to the development of videodiscs. The various types of videodisc technology (optical or laser; capacitance; and mechanical) are described and some of their advantages and disadvantages noted.

Current videodisc applications in education and training are reviewed. This includes references to the ABC/National Education Association School Disc project in the United States; the use of videodiscs for technical and sales training in industry, for example, at General Motors and Ford; medical and health training projects; native cultural applications and bilingual discs; and military and other simulation exercises.

Having noted some of the principal features of videodisc technology and a few of their current applications in education and training, the authors speculate as to their possible use for distance education programs and the advantage offered by this technology.

R. Ruggles / D.E. Blackmore
Educational Research Institute of British Columbia
Canada

Paper 112

The Contribution of Data Processing to Student Administration at the Open University

Data processing was crucial to the success of the Open University where use of the computer has already evolved through three stages.

Introduction

By the time that the United Kingdom Open University (UKOU) was established in 1969, data processing was widely used in the administration of conventional universities. Such use, however, tended to be restricted to applications such as financial management, inventory control, staff and payroll systems, and to shared use of computers whose primary duties were academic. Experience within distance teaching was likewise insubstantial (Sorensen, 1969: 107).

The decision of UKOU's planners, then, to set the computer in the centre of administrative activities (Perry, 1972: 95) while not being revolutionary, was certainly bold, particularly given the academic's traditional mistrust of bureaucracy and the belief that computers, except in their role as research tools, represent bureaucracy. That decision had a profound influence on the nature of the institution that has grown up over the last decade. Was that influence benign or otherwise?

UKOU chose a highly centralized model for its administration. Although the regional offices have always enjoyed substantial autonomy, it has been at the centre where policies have been determined, strategies adopted and where the computer has remained custodian of the central resource of student data. Arguably, it has been this last factor that has contributed most in practice to centralization.

Data processing applications

To set the context for this discussion I will fall back on a diagram I used in an analysis of student administration in Kaye and Rumble (1981: 124). This diagram analyses student administration into three systems of admissions, student records and assessment and certification, and shows how the student record created during the admission process becomes the central resource for subsequent processes.

Such a diagram would have seemed very futuristic when in 1970 as my first task for my new employer I was asked to design an admission system. The system began by accumulating a file of applicants from which the first cohort of students would be selected once admission policy had been agreed. Here is a good example of how the computer made certain policies possible. With an admission period some six months in length it would have been possible, and certainly simpler, to have admitted students to the undergraduate program on a continuing basis. Instead, UKOU chose to allocate places all in one go. Each year the file of undergraduate applicants grows to some 40,000. When selection operates half of these receive direct offers of a place, some 5,000 are put on reserve, and 15,000 refused admission. Place offers are made on the permutations of course, area of residence, occupation and sex, a matrix of some 1800 cells. Considering only this one process, of setting selection parameters after repeated analysis of the file, of distributing 40,000 records in 1800 cells, the whole process iterated several times

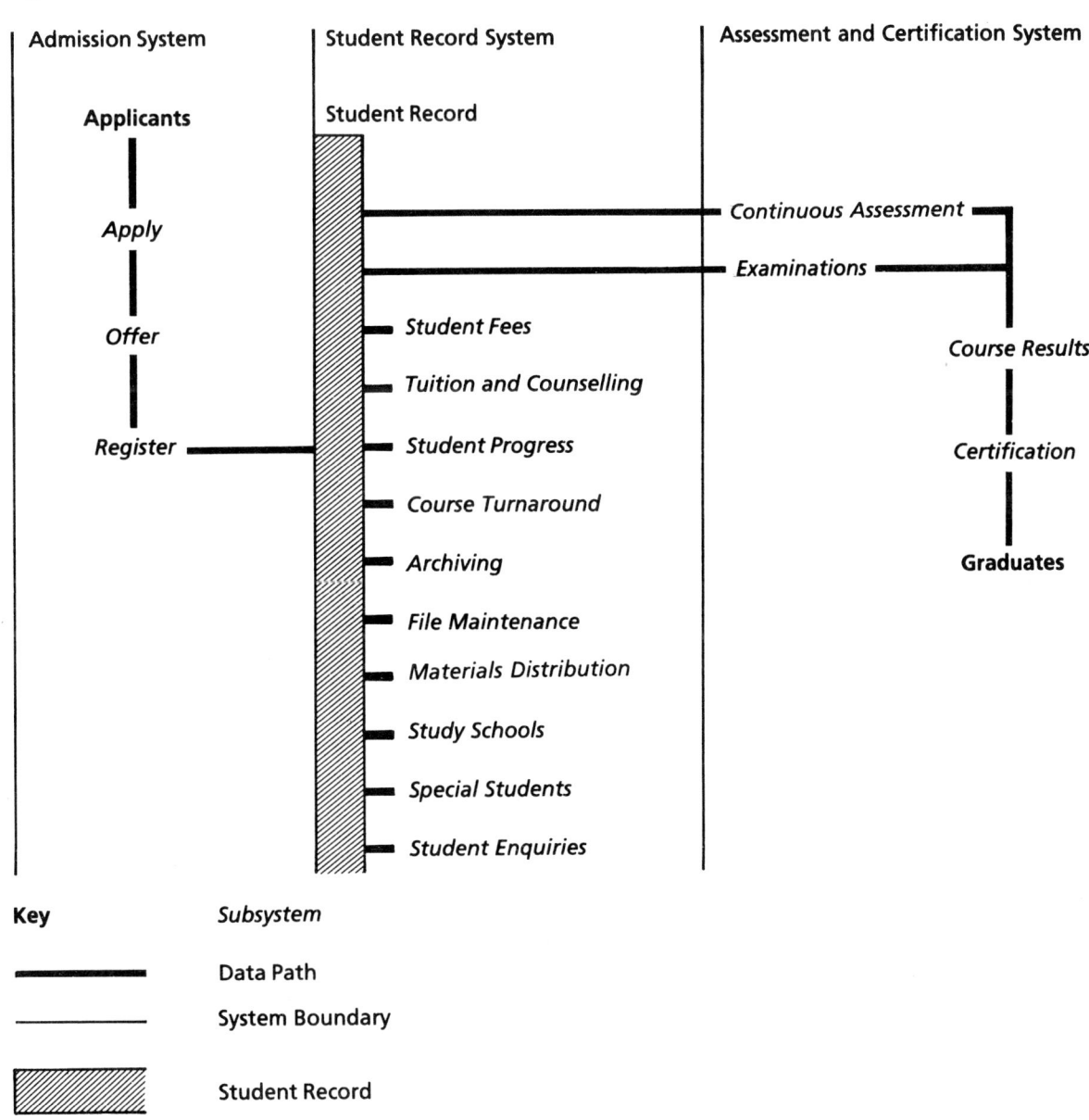

Figure 1: The student operating system and subsystems

to optimise the outcome, and all within two or three days, then it is difficult to imagine that this could be accomplished without a high level of mechanization. This sort of selection gives much greater control of the overall entrant population than continuous admission.

Most of UKOU's characteristic components were in operation right from its first year, and the student record file was soon called upon to provide a central data resource for a wide variety of processes. It was the basis for the mailing of course materials and of home experiment kits to the student. Indeed, selecting a great range of mailing labels across a variety of courses and students became one of the chief occupations of the computer, which is at the centre of a continual series of communications from the institution, asking for fee payments, informing of allocation of summer school or exam, requesting return of the home experiment kit, prompting course choices for the next year, and so on. Not all mailings were premeditated. We were obliged to send out corrections, afterthoughts or apologies more frequently than we would care to admit. Stories abound of instances where simple errors created simultaneous bewilderment across the nation.

The evolution of data processing at UKOU

Stage 1: 1970-1975

The evolution of data processing at UKOU appears to be falling into three stages. During stage 1, the years 1970 to 1975, we developed systems as we needed them—the normal response of any new organization. It was clear that to follow the admissions system, a system of student records was the next step. Then, as the institution developed its strategies, we found the need for systems to maintain records of the growing number of part-time staff becoming tutors and counsellors, and systems to process students' assignments. As is now generally known, the University adopted a dual assignment policy, using traditional tutor-marked assignments allied to objective testing marked by computer. This computer-marked assignment (CMA) system brought together a greater variety of objective testing techniques than, in all probability, had previously been combined into a single assessment system. It is almost inconceivable that such complexity would have been attempted had it not been for the computer and its document reader, able to process two thousand assignments an hour.

Year-end procedures provide perhaps the most noteworthy example of using data processing to achieve results impossible by less sophisticated means. All undergraduate students start and finish their courses at the same time. The consequence of this audacious simplicity of academic planning is an administrative problem of outstanding magnitude. A nationwide campaign of examinations culminates in the recording by the computer of a hundred thousand examination scores, their analysis and standardization, and their combination in various ways with the results of over half a million assignments. This, again, must be accomplished in days rather than weeks, so that reallocation to the next year's courses can go ahead on schedule.

Stage 2: 1975 to the present

During 1975 UKOU changed its batch processing computer using magnetic tape for a more advanced model using direct assess disks, and with a database and terminal network. This machine could be seen as the apotheosis of the central data resource philosophy. With the earlier machine, the physical expression of this philosophy was a very large serial file on six reels of tape; an efficient file if you were transferring to it fifty thousand course results, but very clumsy if you wanted to immediately update it with student Bloggs' latest address. The order of the new computer, incidentally, resulted from a strategy review as early as 1972 (Perry, 1976: 7). Initially we simply converted our stock of systems to the new computer—that is if you can describe as simple a task that consumed 30 man-years of work! Then, in 1975, began the work of redesigning systems to take advantage of the new facilities. If I now say that the first of this second generation of student systems came into operation last year (1980) you will get some idea of the gestation period of large-scale computer systems. However, that gives a rather false impression unless qualified by adding that this period was also occupied by simultaneously setting up the new database and telecommunications environment.

Lessons from experience

Back in 1969, as well as planners who declared the whole venture impossible without data processing, there were those who argued that to give prominence to the computer would unacceptably constrain academic policy. Now, more than a decade on, we may ask who was right. As always, of course, they were both right. First, though, one should say that data processing is expensive. The administrative computer has regularly cost UKOU between five and six per cent of its recurrent expenditure, a proportion that may well cover the entire administrative overhead of many a less complex teaching institution. You may say that to do what is being done using an army of clerks instead would be even more expensive, but then one would not attempt to land on the moon without a moon rocket. The very power of the computer to create systems of great complexity is, I feel, the most difficult of gifts to use well.

There were, and indeed still are, a class of problems arising from the interaction of academic traditions with the demands of operational data processing. Academics are not good at meeting deadlines. Apart from the headaches this gives to editors and printers of course materials, the failure to deliver assignment marking parameters on time means delay to operational schedules. More seriously, parameters are sometimes wrong. The computer will contentedly wrongly score thousands of assignments and send off thousands of letters before anyone notices the error. With highly integrated automated systems, small errors can be greatly magnified.

Then there is the problem of deciding what data to maintain. Coming from a commercial computing background, I tended to resist the attempts of academic colleagues to burden, as I saw it, the admissions system with a range of social and educational data without operational relevance. Clearly it is difficult to decide which burdens will eventually yield meaningful results, and which will remain simply burdens, but in retrospect I was perhaps wrong to scorn intuitive arguments. With manual systems this is a non-problem—manual systems rarely indulge in keeping data other than that essential to their operation.

As well as making many policies strategically possible, the administrative computer is accused of constraining innovation and restricting academic freedom. It takes several years from conception to implementation of a major computer system. Given the need to set and honour deadlines, there are absolute constraints over second thoughts and late inspirations. Several times in those early years, we scrapped a system representing some man-years of work after a very short operational life. At times this was because of bad design, but more usually it was because system development had run too far ahead of policy development. The computer did at times win a battle, but I think that policy always won the wars.

UKOU is still a highly innovatory institution, although our general direction of travel is naturally clearer now than it was ten years ago. However, the problem of reconciling academic innovation with the detailed long-term planning demanded by the computer remains far from solution. If anything, the growing sophistication of the data processing system has increased gestation periods, so the problem of asking policy makers and strategy implementers what sort of systems they would like in four or five years time remains. They may not be absolutely certain what sort of system they ought to be operating right now, and, besides, the inheritors of their prognostications in years to come may see the whole thing quite differently.

Stage 3: where to from here?

Earlier I mentioned a three-stage evolution. Our second generation of administrative data processing systems will be complete by 1984. By that time we shall be some way into stage three, which I see as the incorporation of management information systems into our stock. Not that our systems do not at present produce great quantities of information, much of it directed towards the higher management function. However, a true management information system can result only from a prior identification of management requirements and a recognition of the need to integrate data derived from both operations and research (Erdos, 1975: 11). This take a lot of experience.

There are those who see in the computer a means to advance directly to the level of management information systems without the intermediate frustrations of learning by experience. They are sadly mistaken. The computer has no inherent ability to solve our major problems for us. It simply enables us to use our experience to greater effect.

H. Zvi Friedman
Open University
United Kingdom

References

Erdos, R (1975) The system of distance education in terms of sub-systems and characteristic functions. Papers to the *10th ICCE International Conference.* Malmo: ICCE.

Kaye, A. and Rumble, G. (1981) *Distance Teaching for Higher and Adult Education.* London: Croom Helm.

Perry, W. (1972) *The Early Development of the Open University.* (Report of the Vice-Chancellor January 1969 - December 1970). Milton Keynes: Open University Press.

Perry, W. (1976) *Report of the Vice-Chancellor 1975.* Milton Keynes: Open University Press.

Sorensen, L. (1969) Electronic data processing in the administration of correspondence education. *Proceedings of the Eighth International Conference of the ICCE.* Paris: ICCE.

Paper 113

Towards the Integrated Use of the Computer in Distance Education

The key to economy in using computers lies in handling many subfunctions in an integrated fashion.

Introduction

The computer can be used as a teaching medium, a learning tool and a manager of learning (Edmonds, 1980: 98). The computer is also an aid to administration. In distance teaching institutions the computer has generally been applied initially to the latter function. The shift to computerized processing means both a large financial investment and sizable organizational changes for the correspondence school. Accordingly, in the institution's strategic planning careful consideration must be given to determining what functions are to be computerized. An interesting goal is the integrated computer system.

What does integration mean?

Integration means making a whole out of parts. It requires that the unit in charge of planning and developing computer functions should have a sufficiently defined view of:

— the largest possible number of subfunctions that can in principle be handled with the aid of a computer

— the criteria for making recommendations and decisions about the subfunctions that are to be handled this way.

A central decision criterion is whether computer functions can be integrated into a single well functioning totality where different functions support each other. Such totality of functions is economical in comparison with a manual system. At the technical level integration means a method of operation in which the fewest possible information inputs are used to obtain simultaneous reactions in different subsystems and automatically produce different outputs as desired.

Factors influencing the use of computers in distance education

Increasing numbers of students and the rationalization of functions

In distance education the use of the computer reflects the large numbers of students and teachers that give rise to a continual and large flow of events to be recorded.

Economic planning and monitoring

The institution must be able to make efficient and purposeful use of its economic, intellectual, and material resources. Investments should be carried out at the right time and answer specific needs. With the aid of the computer the planning and monitoring of economic activity becomes more efficient. Budgeting and billing are speeded up, comparison of the profitability of different courses is facilitated, the need for loans and the form in which they are to be taken can better be appraised, the planning and follow-up of investment decisions is made easier, etc.

Developing the guidance function

Counselling and guidance for students can be rendered more efficient as monitoring of study progress keeps better track of the situation and as study counsellors are better able to allocate their time for contacts with students. It can be assumed that the increased efficiency of guidance and monitoring will reduce lagging and interrupted studies.

Guidance and course planning can also be made more efficient with improved initial knowledge and statistics. Course planning can be modernized on the basis of an ADP (administrative data processing) system (Lampikoski, 1980) and guidance and monitoring of the production of study materials improves the quality of the materials produced.

What functions can be handled by the computer at a distance education institution?

Teaching applications*

Applications marked with an asterisk (*) are already in use at the Institute of Marketing and those marked with an (o) are in the planning or test stage.

Teaching applications can be roughly divided into on-line and off-line categories (Bååth, 1980: 41). On-line applications are used chiefly to familiarize students with questions about data processing, training in programming occupying a key role. They are also used in handling data when solving problems in statistics, physics etc. In an on-line setup the computer terminal is either part of the equipment of the face-to-face teaching institution (Lovis, 1975; Pengelly, 1974) or is located in the student's home or firm as part of a so-called tel-set system (e.g., Viewdata and Prestel); in addition, micro-computers can be provided for students (Zorkoczy, 1974).

At a number of distance teaching institutions off-line setups based on multiple-choice homework assignments are used. At the Institute of Marketing we have used a form of multiple-choice test since 1975 and as of 1978, multiple-choice tests based on probability and matrix principles. The marking of and commenting on these tests is handled by computer (Lampikoski and Mantere, 1978: 181-206).

Other applications that can facilitate teaching are computer-performed pretesting of students' knowledge on enrolment (o), planning (o) and printing an individualized study program, monitoring the progress of studies (*) and the automatic guidance of studies required (*), the writing of certificates and compiling of tests using a computer terminal and storing them in a test bank (o) as well as the selection of tests from the test bank (o). Further applications include computer-based information access for the needs of course planning and production of study materials (*) and the monitoring of the quality of materials and teaching.

A number of data files used in teaching and guidance can also be stored in the computer (e.g., language glossaries (*)), automatic data files for information services (e.g., dial access to course information).

A wide range of applications can also be found for face-to-face teaching linked with distance teaching (e.g., teaching with the aid of corporate games and microgames (*) and the use of files of information stored in data banks external to the institutions (*)). In the long run testing of the comprehensibility of a text will be feasible with the aid of a computer (Siegel and Wolf, 1975). A range of potential uses lies in hooking up computers to word processing systems (o).

Administrative applications

A number of administrative applications for computers are:

- budgeting and monitoring of finances (*)
- statistics (*)
- student billing (*)
- payroll (*)
- bills and debts ledger (*)
- mailing of test scores (o)
- materials production monitoring (o)
- registrar routines (*)

What are the criteria for making selection decisions?

Zorkoczy (1974: 47) considers the key criteria to be educational desirableness, economy, and organizational feasibility. These are used at the Institute of Marketing for making practical decisions about the functions to be handled by ADP. We have, for example, observed it to be economically and organizationally efficient to carry out quality control (through student feedback) of study material and teaching using the semi-automatic Otamatic machine.

The writing of certificates is another example of screening. Although the marks on the course

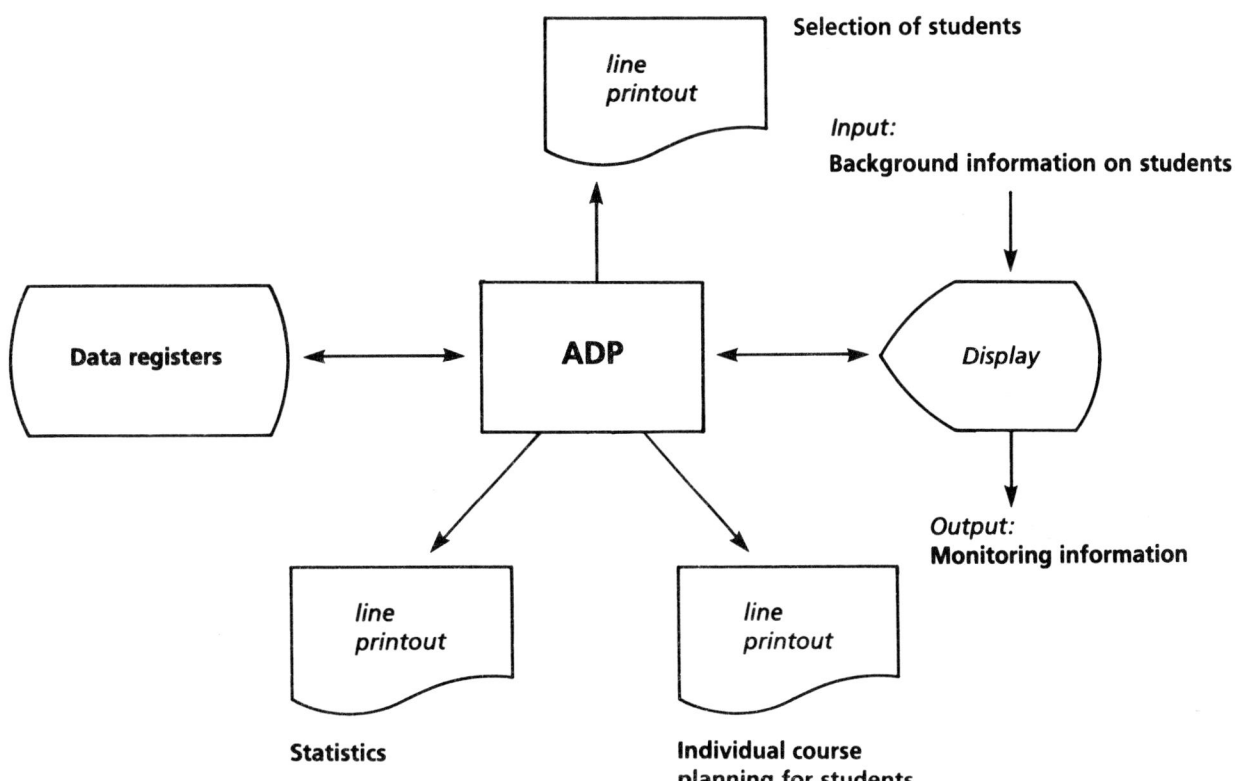

certificate are handled by computer, the certificate is prepared by a printer and signed by hand for human reasons.

To Zorkoczy's criteria can be added the requirement of integration. The economy of using a computer derives precisely from the fact that it handles the largest possible number of subfunctions in an integrated fashion. Although the advantages of integration are most in evidence in economic and administrative applications, teaching also becomes more efficient through the integration of functions. For example, by feeding in students' level of knowledge at enrolment we can simultaneously guide their course selection (the screening function) and the planning of their study career (the function of course planning). In addition, initial data make it possible to process statistics automatically to be sent to state authorities (the statistical function) and to mobilize study guidance (the monitoring and guidance function).

Another example of integration is ordering multiple-choice texts in matrix form from a test bank used in a teaching situation. We may also envision a way of using computer-corrected assignments completed at a distance by having a classroom teacher access them on-line.

The study monitoring system is in itself a highly integrated system in which the student is automatically furnished with instructions and information regarding his studies on the basis of preliminary information and accumulated course credits and test results. Information is reported in the form of a computer printout supplied in a mailable envelope. At the same time this information goes to the teachers in charge of guidance and to the study counsellor, serving such functions as payment, billing, and payroll orders, etc. This system enables the institution to bill the student automatically through his bank's computer. The institution's computer converses with the computer at the student's bank without the need for human intervention (*).

Choosing a system

There is a wide variety of computer options. Procurement may take the form of use of an ADP service, leasing of a computer, purchase of an office unit, purchase of the services of a small computer firm, off-line or on-line setups etc. It is essential to weigh carefully the advantages and drawbacks of each alternative. The most important criteria are cost, flexibility and reliability of use, provision for updating functions, and the need to train staff.

Kari Lampikoski
Institute of Marketing
Finland

References

Bååth, J.A. (1980) *Postal Two-Way Communication in Correspondence Education.* Malmo: LiberHermods.

Edmonds, E. (1980) What next in computer aided learning? *British Journal of Educational Technology,* 11, 2, 98-104.

Lampikoski, K. (1980) The development of new information acquisition in correspondence schools. EHSC workshop paper, Bled.

Lampikoski, K. and Mantere, P. (1978) *Final Report of the Distance Education Development Project.* Report 3, The Institute of Marketing, Helsinki.

Lovis, F.B. (1975) The Open University's approach to computer education. In *Computers in Education.* (eds.) Lecarme, O. and Lewis, R. New York: North-Holland Pub. Co.

Pengelly, R.M. (1974) The student computing service and its future development. *1974 International Conference on Frontiers in Education.* London: The Instituter of Electrical Engineers.

Siegel, A.I. and Wolf, J.J. (1975) Computer analysis of comprehensibility. In *Computers in Education.* (eds.) Lecarme, O. and Lewis, R. New York: North-Holland Pub. Co.

Zorkoczy, P.I. (1974) The computer and the distant learner. *1974 International Conference on Frontiers in Education.* London: The Institute of Electrical Engineers.

Paper 114

Increasing Completion Rates with Computer-Assisted Lessons

(Abstract)

In 1973 the University of Missouri began to develop a computer-assisted lesson service (CALS) for its correspondence courses using a system developed by the United States Armed Forces Institute. The first CALS course was offered in 1975 and more than 160 such courses were available by 1980. In CALS courses students submit standardized answer sheets based on objective items. These are processed by optical scanner and the information is copied onto a computer tape from which the CALS program generates a lesson or exam report.

The lesson reports consist of instructional comments on the student's responses to the lessons. For each incorrect response and for some correct responses an instructional comment is provided. These comments are written by the authors of the courses when they develop the items. Since they select the reading assignment and design the objective items, they should be completely familiar with the sources of information needed to respond correctly to all the items, and can include references to these sources in their comments. Comments can be extensive or brief. At a minimum, the comments refer students to the pages in the assigned reading to enable them to determine the correct answers. Authors are encouraged to include enriching information in the comments whenever appropriate. Generally, the comments for incorrect responses do not themselves give the correct answers to the items. We believe the information will be more meaningful to students if they use it to discover the right answer themselves.

The advantages of CALS are:

1. In university CALS courses completions are 16% higher than in our instructor-scored correspondence courses.
2. In high school CALS courses completions are 30% higher.
3. Lesson turn-around time is typically 2 days.
4. There are significant cost savings in courses with substantial enrolments.
5. Students appreciate the fast response and consistent feedback of CALS courses.
6. Since implementing the first CALS course at the University of Missouri in 1975, enrolments have grown approximately 235%.

C. Alex Phillips / Roger G. Young
University of Missouri
United States

Tutoring by CYCLOPS
(Abstract)

Paper 115

The Open University has seen a change from small numbers of courses with high student populations to large numbers of courses with small student populations usually widely scattered throughout the country. This scattering makes face-to-face tutorial support difficult.

Alternatives are being used, of which telephone tuition (teleconferencing) is the main example. Despite its usefulness and success, many tutors and students comment on the lack of visual support during teleconferencing. Diagrams and charts can be circulated to students in advance, but they are difficult and tedious to use during the tutorial.

CYCLOPS is an interactive audio-visual aid that enables students and tutors to write electronically to each other over the telephone and have their words and pictures reproduced at the other end on a TV screen.

As part of a trial project, the Open University (in conjunction with British Telecom and Aregon International) is currently using CYCLOPS to tutor some three hundred students in twenty courses from all parts of the curriculum in the Nottinghamshire Region. With the use of a public conference bridge, up to nine different groups of students scattered hundreds of miles apart can be tutored simultaneously, sharing a common picture display and linked by voice through loudspeaking telephones. Peripheral aids such as a light pen and bit pad for writing and creat-

ing drawings and diagrams, and the facility of prerecording complex visuals on ordinary audio cassettes for replay, enhance the quality of teaching and learning.

The effectiveness of CYCLOPS is being evaluated. Preliminary findings point to several areas of concern, namely:

— the need to train tutors and students in the effective use of the system (including overcoming user resistance, and facilitation of group interaction)

— the provision of efficient back-up facilities

Paper 115

- problems with the public teleconferencing service—we are considering investing in our own conference bridges
- means of linking CYCLOPS to the use of video cassettes and Optel.

As well as helping to overcome the problem of tutoring low enrolment courses the interactive nature of CYCLOPS suggests a future in which the various technological adaptations to teaching could be linked together to provide an integrated, multi-media approach to learning at a distance within the Open University.

David McConnell
Open University
United Kingdom

Paper 116
Reaching Learners Through Telecommunications
(Abstract)

Opportunities for individuals in the United States to learn at a distance from a university campus were, until recently, limited primarily to traditional correspondence programs. However, changing conditions in post-secondary education and developments in electronic communications have combined to produce a diverse array of delivery systems capable of serving learners at a distance. Programs employing some form of television, radio, telephone, or computer technology to serve distance learners are gradually changing higher education in the United States.

To assess these developments, the Center for Learning and Telecommunications (CLT) was established in 1980 within the American Association for Higher Education. Its objectives are to systematize information about programs serving learners at a distance via telecommunications and to improve practice. The Center conducts research on current programs and publishes materials written in layman's language to assist educators.

In addition to publishing a bi-monthly digest of current literature and developments called *TELESCAN*, the Center is conducting a survey of 70 educational programs in the United States that use telecommunications. The Center will publish two comprehensive volumes in the spring of 1982, based on in-depth interviews of staff at each of these programs. The first will be a reference book including 3-5 page descriptions of each program. These descriptions divide the information into 16 categories, including: curriculum, technologies, delivery system, faculty roles, finances, noteworthy aspects, problems encountered, future plans, contact person. The title is *Meeting Learner Needs Through Telecommunications: A Directory of Programs.*

The second volume will offer a systematic overview of current practice in these 70 programs. This volume is entitled *Meeting Learner Needs Through Telecommunications: A Guide to Current Practice.* While both volumes focus only on programs that use telecommunications they do not encourage the use of electronic technologies for their own sake or as a replacement for print. Rather, they emphasize the educational problems of serving learners at a distance and describe various programmatic responses to them. The 70 programs included in the survey span undergraduate, graduate, and professional continuing education. Most programs offer instruction for credit, but some offer certificate and non-credit programming. Organizations surveyed include two-year colleges, four-year colleges, universities, consortia, broadcast and cable facilities, governmental agencies and professional associations, as well as non-profit and profit-making organizations.

Though most of the programs evolved out of a tradition other than correspondence study, they share many similarities with correspondence education. This is particularly evident at colleges and universities that also offer correspondence education. There is also a trend among many educators toward the use of less complex and expensive technologies, a departure from past practices in this country.

Raymond J. Lewis
American Association for Higher Education
United States

Text Processing: The Revolution in Word Manipulation

Text processing offers a powerful tool to authors and editors for creating and editing documents.

Introduction

Despite a strong interest in electronic technology Athabasca University is essentially a publishing house. As a result a decision was made early in our development to employ the latest computer text processing tools to handle efficiently the course manuscript production process. The text processing system we use today has proven eminently suitable to the demands made on it—it would be the envy of some publishing houses—and we feel it is flexible enough to adapt to changes in the foreseeable future.

Text processing

What is text processing? At AU the component parts are: a mini computer, software especially designed for manipulating text, a line printer, text entry and editing personnel, and an on-line interface with a typesetter. (For the technically minded, we use a VAX 11/780 computer with a UNIX operating system, and a Linotron 202 typesetter.) The basic steps are as follows:

1. text entry personnel: initial input of text with embedded formatting commands (input is handwritten, dictated or typed). The text is run through the formatting program (Nroff) using a "macro" package designed for line printer output and copies are generated.
2. course team: editing, rewriting of manuscript.
3. text entry personnel: change the computer files as per course team editing instructions. Run copies of corrected manuscript. (Steps 2 and 3 can recur several times.)
4. course team: final proof of manuscript.
5. text entry personnel: final changes to file.
6. typesetter: runs the text file through the typesetting program (Troff) using a different "macro" package that meets the visual designer's markup specifications to produce "repro". The text file with embedded commands remains unaltered by this process.
7. course team: checks visuals and tables in pasteup.

What is notable here is the lack of a final proof of the text in pasteup--except for handset items like visuals and complex tables, it isn't required. Computerized typesetting allows us to avoid this common (and laborious) step in publishing.

Berkeley VAX/UNIX version 4.1 (our operating system) contains a number of powerful commands for manipulating words, thus saving time and energy while simultaneously increasing accuracy.

Spell

The "spell" program, for example, allows an automatic verification of the spelling of every word in a file simply by entering

spell *filename*

The "spell" program rapidly scans the file to check every word against the dictionary stored in computer memory. Unfamiliar words are printed out and the operator can identify errors and correct them. (Either US or British spelling can be selected.)

This does not mean, however, that the proofing step can be eliminated since the program will not recognize legitimate words in the wrong context (e.g., "form - from", "to-too", "experiential - experimental", "retain - retrain").

Grep

Other commands, especially when the editor is doing his own editing, offer even more time-saving devices for ensuring accuracy. Suppose you are editing a long document held in a number of files all beginning with the word "part". This document contains several direct quotations. You have chosen the spelling "behaviour", and you want to check if there are any instances of the alternate "behavior". You would enter

grep behavior part.*

If there were instances of the alternate spelling, the name of the file, the line number, and the line of text containing the word "behavior" would be printed out. If such a line were part of a direct quotation, you would leave it as it is; if it were part of your own prose you would change it.

On the other hand, if there are no direct quotations, you can "swap" all instances of the alternate spelling for the one you want by running an editor and entering

g/behavior/s;;behaviour;

Since this global command can "swap" virtually any string of text (or any command) for another, an editor is able to make sweeping changes without having to find each occurrence and make the change individually.

In editing this book, for example, it was decided that the hyphenated noun "drop-out" was preferable to "drop out" or "dropout". The editor entered grep drop out paper.*

then

grep dropout paper.*

to find all instances requiring change. Since there are nearly 120 papers by authors from widely varied linguistic backgrounds, there were many instances of the two variants. Correcting the variants took less than 30 minutes. The time it would take to do this manually (there are nearly 250,000 words in the combined papers) points dramatically to the time one can save by having such utilities.

Yes, it true that an editor could prepare a style sheet beforehand, edit the papers before they are entered, and thus save the trouble of "grepping" and "swapping" things that could have been corrected in the first place. But anyone who has prepared an initial style sheet and then had to proof a manuscript not only for inconsistencies but also for errors in entering will agree that the scope for controlling text and for increasing accuracy is greatly improved by having these kinds of commands at one's disposal.

In our system extensive use is make of "visual editors", which allow the user to put up a page of text and modify it by moving the cursor and executing simple keyboard commands. These editors are excellent tools for authors who want to create documents "on-line". This paper was written in just this way.

Diff

When final editing is being done on a file it is important to be sure that only the desired changes are made. This can be easily accomplished by making a copy of the file before editing and comparing it to the edited file with the "diff" command. Lines that differ in the two files are printed out so that a quick visual check is possible.

Diction

For writers with basic problems in wordiness there is a program called "diction". If you enter

diction *filename*

the program identifies every instance it defines as an example of wordiness. If you go on to query the correction, the program prescribes rules that, if adopted with due attention to the demands of rhetoric, would go a long way in curing some of the worst excesses. Some samples of the rules are:

use "each" for "each and every"

use "unimportant" for "of very minor importance"

use "doubtless" for "there is very little doubt that".

Style

For those with a technical interest in style there is a program called "style", which can be activated by entering

style *filename*

To illustrate, we have run the "style" program for the introduction to the section titled "Learning at a Distance and National Development" (paper 11). The results are as follows:

Style: Paper 11

readability grades:

(Kincaid) 18.6 (auto) 18.5 (Coleman-Liau) 14.5 (Flesch) 17.0 (14.6)

sentence info:

no. sent 37 no. wds 1096
av sent leng 29.6 av word leng 5.32
no. questions 0 no. imperatives 0
no. nonfunc wds 681 62.1% av leng 6.80
short sent (<25) 32% (12) long sent (>40) 16% (6)
longest sent 62 wds at sent 15; shortest sent 7 wds at sent 28

sentence types:

simple 38% (14) complex 46% (17)
compound 3% (1) compound-complex 14% (5)

word usage:

verb types as % of total verbs
to be 41% (39) aux 16% (15) inf 20% (19)
passives as % of non-inf verbs 18% (14)
types as % of total
prep 13.4% (147) conj 4.1% (45) adv 3.1% (34)
noun 33.1% (363) adj 18.7% (205) pron 3.0% (33)
nominalizations 6 % (62)

sentence beginnings:

subject opener: noun (18) pron (2) pos (1) adj (4) art (5) tot 81%
prep 5% (2) adv 5% (2)
verb 0% (0) sub_conj 5% (2) conj 0% (0)
expletives 3% (1)

Even without an explanation of the numbers and scores, one can see that this program permits users to analyse their documents according to measurable criteria, and make changes to improve readability.

Conclusion

The text processing system at Athabasca University offers a powerful tool for manipulating words. It is relatively easy to use while at the same time presenting authors and editors with an unusually efficient means of creating and editing documents.

Don W. Cowper / John R. Thompson
Athabasca University
Canada

Experimental Research on Computer-Assisted Distance Education

Students were more satisfied with computer-assisted tuition than with the tutor's manual correction and commenting.

Introduction

Distance education can be designed in many different ways. In my book, *Correspondence Education in the Light of a Number of Contemporary Teaching Models* (Bååth, 1979), I analysed one major form of distance education—correspondence education—starting from seven different approaches to learning and teaching. Each of these models is applicable to correspondence education although the practical designs will vary considerably . Nevertheless, all may very well include a sub-system for computer-assisted two-way communication at a distance.

The CADE System

A paper to the Eleventh World Conference of ICCE described a system for such computer-assisted two-way communication, called CADE (Bååth and Månsson, 1978). The system was developed by Hermods in Sweden, in collaboration with the Norwegian correspondence school NKS. In CADE, the correspondence tutor's work is to a great extent taken over by the computer. The system analyses the students' answers to carefully designed multiple-choice questions. Personalized letters to the students are printed by the computer.

Within the framework of the EHSC research project (Flinck, 1975) interesting new data on the effects of the system have been generated (Bååth, 1980).

The two experimental studies

In experiments carried out at the University of Lund, Sweden, two different versions of the same correspondence course were compared with regard to a number of outcome variables. One version of each course had traditional correspondence tuition by a tutor, whereas the other version used CADE.

Courses and students involved

Two LiberHermods courses were involved in the investigation. **YES 1** is an elementary English course for adults. The course material comprises audio as well as printed components. Most students are over 30 and have a low level education. They are evenly distributed with regard to sex. Their motivation for studying is largely knowledge-oriented (as opposed to career advancement, etc.).

Psychology, General Course is an upper secondary level course for adults. The students are younger and have a somewhat higher level of formal education. Two thirds are women. Their motivation is markedly knowledge-oriented.

Experimental design

Students applying for either course over a period of about two years were included in the investigation. Students enrolling during the first year were allocated to one group, students applying during the second year to the other. A statistical analysis of the similarity revealed no essential difference between the experimental groups in each course.

Outcome variables

In order to compare the two experimental versions of each course the following outcome variables were used:

1. start (*starter* = a student who has submitted at least the first assignment for correction and comments)
2. completion (*completer* = a student who has submitted all the assignments for correction and comments)
3. attitudes to various aspects of the course (data collected by means of a final questionnaire)
4. final test results (in each course, the final test consisted of an equal share of free-answer and multiple-choice questions, in order that the design of the test should not favour any of the experimental groups)
5. study time (defined as the total time elapsed from enrolment to completion).

Since a large proportion of students did not complete their course, there is little data on outcome variables 3 - 5. However, separate analyses indicate that this has probably not affected experimental results.

Experimental Results

The experimental outcome is summarized in Table 1.

In all, 20 statistical tests of significance were performed. Seven significant differences were found. This is considerably more than could be expected by mere chance, as a result of testings on the 5% level.

In six cases out of seven, the significant differences point in the same direction. Students with computer-assisted two-way communication:

Paper 118

Table 1: Survey of experimental results

Significant differences: on the **5%** level, on the **1%** level, and on the **0.1%** level.

Course	Outcome variables									
	Start	Completion	Attitude						Final test	Study time
			1	2	3	4	5	6		
YES 1	5%				0.1%	1%				
Pscyhology, G.C.	0.1%	0.1%				1%				1%

Altitude 1: Attitude to the course and the teaching
       2: Attitude to the assignments for submission
       3: Attitude to the type of assignment questions
       4: Attitude to the correction of and commenting on student's assignments
       5: Feeling of isolation in the study situation
       6: The wish for other kinds of support in the studies than can be provided by means of pure correspondence education

- started submitting assignments to a greater extent than students with traditional correspondence tuition (both courses)
- completed their course to a greater extent than students with traditional tuition (*Psychology, General Course*)
- adopted more favourable attitudes to the correction of and commenting on their submitted assignments than did students with traditional tuition (both courses)
- completed their course within a shorter time (study time) than did students with traditional two-way communication (*Psychology, General Course*).

The outcome is in accordance with reports from previous investigations, mostly non-experimental, (e.g., Brittain (1973), Lambert (1977), and Schümer (1979)). It decisively confirms the favourable students' attitudes found in the evaluation studies of the CADE system (Bååth and Månsson, 1977, 1978).

The remaining significant difference refers to the attitudes to the type of assignment questions (**YES 1**). Here students who had worked with free-answer questions stated that they prefer this type, whereas students having multiple-choice questions apparently prefer that type. This finding is consistent with what could be expected from previous (non-experimental) studies (e.g., Grahm (1969) and Bååth and Månsson (1977)).

Discussion

Computerization as a feature of an industralized form of teaching

Peters (1973) has analysed distance education as an *industrialized* form of teaching, distinguished by—among other things—rationalization, careful planning, considerable division of labour, mechanization of certain functions, mass production, and an assembly line principle for certain functions. Although this analysis does not apply to all types of distance education—in certain cases of distance education at the university level, an analogy with handicraft activities would be more adequate—it is rather illuminating with regard to all fairly large correspondence schools, as well as the British Open University and the West German Fernuniversität. It might, therefore, appear logical to try to proceed one step further, automating those highly repetitive correspondence tutor functions that can be handed over to a computer.

Multiple-choice questions

As a rule, computer-assisted two-way communication off-line is coupled to multiple-choice questions (or the like). This is not necessarily a disadvantage. It is possible to design multiple-choice questions for most kinds of cognitive objectives. (e.g., Coffman, 1969, Bloom et al., 1971). Moreover students "spend most of their time in thinking and writing when taking an essay test. They spend most of their time in reading and thinking when taking an objective test." (Ebel, 1965: 90)

Reading is normally a considerably quicker task than writing. Consequently, students get more time for thinking when taking a multiple-choice test. (Alternatively, they save time for other activities!) It is interesting to note that cognitive learning psychologists like Ausubel (1968: 300-301, 583-585) and Bruner (1960: 30) adopt a favourable attitude towards multiple-choice questions, whereas an extreme behaviourist like Skinner (1968: 216-217) rather takes the opposite position.

Functions of computer-assisted two-way communication as compared with functions of traditional postal tuition

Feedback and motivation functions could, in principle, be served by means of computerized comments, whereas the contact function would probably be more difficult to fulfil this way.

It is even possible that the *feedback function* could be better served in computer-assisted than in traditional two-way communication. Among facts supporting such an assumption are the almost unlimited capacity of the computer to store and to utilize data about the students and their previous achievements, and, further, the possibility in computer-assisted tuition consistently to provide extensive, carefully planned comments, which—in addition—are always legible.

As concerns the *motivational function,* multiple-choice questions can be at least as stimulating as assignment questions of other kinds, judging from students' reactions (Bååth and Månsson, 1977: 29). Computer-mediated tutor comments also have the advantage over comments by tutors in traditional postal communication that they can always be made in a friendly, patient, encouraging spirit. The computer does not suffer from human weaknesses such as getting tired or irritated. On the other hand, the computer does not possess the potential of a human tutor to improvise, to adapt to unexpected situations, to give something new in a personal dialogue.

It may be possible to achieve faster turn-around of assignments using the computer.

Implications

The experimental outcome favours the computer-assisted system. Particularly remarkable are the students' attitudes. In both courses, the students were more satisfied with the computer-assisted tuition than with the tutor's manual correction and commenting. This supports the assumptions about the instructional and motivational functions of computer-assisted two-way communication.

Not even the *contact function* was experienced less favourably in the computer-assisted versions than in the traditional ones, judging from the answers to the questionnaire questions about feelings of isolation and need of simultaneous contacts.

The original aim of the CADE project was practical—to search for new ways to render correspondence education more effective and to improve its instructional quality (Bååth, 1972). The outcome of the two field experiments has clear practical implications. Correspondence education with computer-assisted two-way communication off-line, arranged as in these experiments, appears to yield educational effects that are in several respects more favourable than those of traditional correspondence education.

CADE has already been tried in a considerable number of different subjects at varying levels. The experience indicates that the computer constitutes a very useful addition to the educational aids of correspondence tuition.

John A. Bååth
University of Lund
Sweden

References

Ausubel, D.P. (1968) *Educational Psychology. A Cognitive View.* New York: Holt, Rinehart & Winston.

Bååth, J.A. (1972) Improving correspondence instruction by means of electronics. *Convergence,* 5, 2, 64-75

Bååth, J.A. (1979) *Correspondence Education in the Light of a Number of Contemporary Teaching Models.* Malmo: LiberHermods.

Bååth, J.A. (1980) *Postal Two-Way Communication in Correspondence Education.* Malmo: LiberHermods.

Bååth, J.A. and Månsson, N.O. (1977) *CADE - A System for Computer-Assisted Distance Education.* Malmo: Hermods Skola.

Bååth, J.A. and Månsson, N.O. (1978) Our computer corrects student papers and writes individual personal letters to each student. In Wentworth, R.B. (ed.) (1978) *Correspondence Education: Dynamic and Diversified.* Volume 1, The Advance Papers. ICCE. 167-174

Bloom, B.S. Hastings, J. T. and Madaus, G.F. (1971) *Handbook on Formative and Summative Evaluation of Student Learning.* New York: McGraw-Hill.

Brittain, C. (1973) Computer Assisted Lesson Service at USAFI: An Interim Report. Paper presented at the Annual Meeting of the American Educational Research Association, Feb. 25 - March 1. New Orleans, Louisiana. (stencil)

Bruner, J.S. (1960) *The Process of Education.* Cambridge, Mass.: Harvard University Press.

Coffman, W.E. (1969) Achievement tests. In Ebel, R.L. (ed.) (1969) *Encyclopedia of Educational Research.* 4th ed. New York: Macmillan.

Ebel, R.L. (1965) *Measuring Educational Achievement.* Englewood Cliffs, N.J.: Prentice-Hall.

Flinck, R. (1975) Two-way communication in distance education - an evaluation of various models. *Pedagogical Bulletin,* No. 2. Lund: Department of Education, University of Lund.

Grahm, A. (1969) *Vad tycker eleverna om insändningsuppgifter?* (With an English summary: What students think of assignments in correspondence education). Malmo: Hermods. (stencil)

Lambert, M.P. (ed.) (1977). Workable data processing for home study schools. *NHSC News,* Summer 1977, NHSC News Supplement.

Peters, O. (1973) *Die didaktische Struktur des Fernunterrichts, Untersuchungen zu einer industrialisierten Form des Lehrens und Lernens.* Weinheim: Beltz.

Schümer, R. (1979) *ZIFF-Projekt: CMA-Rechnungswesen. Meinungen von Fernstudenten zum maschinellen Korrekturdienst für den Kurs 'Buchhaltung' im Studienjahr 77/78.* Hagen: Zentrales Institut für Ferstudienforschung, Fernuniversität.

Skinner, B.F. (1968) *The Technology of Teaching.* New York: Appleton-Century-Crofts.

Appendix

Distance Education - A Musical Revue

A Coarse Proposal for an ICCE Musical Revue

Editor's Note: The following course proposal has been received from Dr. R.H. Paul, Vice-President of Learning Services at Athabasca University. While only Athabasca would even contemplate the development of such a course, Dr. Paul has agreed to deliver it "live" (pardon the heresay) as a field study test at the I.C.C.E. conference in Vancouver on June 14, 1982.

A. Course Demographics

Title: "Difficult Delivery—A Musical Revue"

Level: 1—Lowest Common Denominator

Prerequisites: Alcoholic audience, polluted cast, much goodwill

Credits: No one will take credit for this

Enrolments: None so far, but completely open admissions policy. (Free to adults under 12.)

Estimated Completion Rates: (100%) unless there are enrolments. Then only the pianist, author and hotel bouncer will be around at the end.

B. Course Materials

The student's home-study package consists of the following course materials:

1. Course Manual: A guide to the in-jokes, the non-sequiturs, or alternatively, instructions as to how to get the course to self-destruct by blowing up the cast.

2. Learning Units: No learning will take place during the performance

3. Text: Derivative

4. Costs: Whatever the pianist can drink in an evening or $4.00, whichever is less.

5. Copyright: Unnecessary—no one has ever shown interest in it.

6. Delivery Method: Forceps and local anesthetic. (Song: "Leaping Into the Breech.")

7. Course Outline: The course provides an introduction to distance education, spanning its long history (since 1957) for the only people really interested in distance education—those who got stuck with jobs in institutions of distance education.

It is divided into three acts à la Christmas Carol—the ghosts of distance education past, present and future.

Prologue

In the beginning, God created the heavens and the earth, but they weren't the same thing, so God created distance to set them apart. And God created man, but took a ribbing for that mistake so He created woman, thus increasing the distance between heaven and earth. So God, in one last attempt, created "education" but, instead of creating heaven on earth, this made man think he was God. And, lo, man tried to be God and created "distance education" and while this was obviously no better than "education", at least it was cheaper, or so man thought (but God knew better).....

Act I: Distance Education Past

This section includes:

1. The origins of distance education are explained with an impartial presentation of both the Darwinian and ludicrous Creationist explanations of this development.

2. Distance education around the world is presented mainly to justify the expensive sabbatical of the course team which has had to visit Tahiti, Fiji, Martinique, New Zealand, London, Milton Keynes, Shakespeare Lenin, and the town of Athabasca, Alberta.

3. The jargon of distance education is traced throughout history, starting with the classic "Let's take education to the remote areas and the isolated students" to the more modern "The needs assessment paradigm impacts on inhabiting the head space of dislocated student situations via accessed interface multimediated delivery systems."

4. Live interviews are presented with the nine students who have successfully completed their degrees via distance education, including the two who didn't cheat.

Act Two: Distance Education Present—"Cacauphonous Cooperation"

1. A musical presentation of the strange harmonics of the course team—editor, instructional designer, visual designer, etc.
2. Who's Who in Distance Education—(incidentally, they've all written articles in this book). Includes:

    Buckminster "Slipped" Videodisc—Believes output variance can be modulated by the injection of satellite-based microfibric technology and he has just the hardware ($6.5 million) for you.

    Jerome B. Penpal III—Has been in correspondence education since 1927. Has a mail-order degree from Foreign Correspondence University, likes to write letters and resents those who have jumped on the distance education bandwagon.

    Dr. P.S.I. Skinnerbox—Objectifies and behaviorizes all learning so as to maximize and impact world education.

    Dr. Ivor E. Tower—Doesn't really believe in distance education but couldn't get a job at Oxford. Is against all technology, although may use phone to call for taxi.

    Mr. Ramesh Sharma (MA,failed)—Has just completed tour of North American institutions with an average of 75 staff producing courses for some 6000 course enrolments to see how he can improve his own university at which 47 staff produce courses for 81,234 course enrolments.

    Prof. Marco Magellan—A leading exponent of distance education, he has visited 47 countries on 26 grants and produced 173 articles on setting up regional offices over the past five years. Has never written or delivered an actual course, but his advice is valued around the world. (His university would appreciate his forwarding address from anyone who happens to bump into him).

Act Three: Distance Education Future—"Technology's The Answer"

1. Since to deliver all courses face-to-face, commonly assumed to be the most effective mode of presentation, would belie the whole raison d'être of distance education (ie, to get as far away from the student as possible), the next best answer to all problems is to "go technological". This unit presents this utopia, featuring such songs as:

Teleconferencing Bridge Over Troubled Waters

Technology's the Answer (The show-stopper, sample lyrics follow):

In distance education, it is so very rare
That you ever see a student (I wonder if they're there)
From Canada to South Africa, they're so very far away
But there's one great magic answer that's always on display.

Chorus:

YES...technology's the answer, it gives you good vibrations
You never have to worry about humanistic relations
Technology's the answer, it's the latest thing today,
Technology's the answer when you're far away.

Face-to-face interaction makes students so uptight
Sit them all at home instead and transmit by satellite
And if the students pressure you in their search for the Holy Grail,
You can slow the whole thing down, using the royal mail.

Chorus:

There's no worry about discipline or students talking back
A little bit of computerese will absorb any flak.
So if you're short of tutors and student record clerks
Just put it all on Telidon and let the machines do all the work.

Chorus:

At this point the course automatically comes to a halt.

R.H.P./R.I.P.
Revue

Glossary

Advisor/Counsellor
Person who assists learners by helping to build self-confidence, improve study habits, set up work schedules, guide course choice, establish career goals, etc.

Andragogy
Theory for the design of instruction for adults. It identifies areas where instructional principles applicable to children (pedagogy) need modification.

Animator—see Facilitator

Aptitude Treatment Interaction (ATI)
Field of educational research based on the interaction of individual learning style with a particular instructional treatment. The aim is to provide guidelines for the design of instruction.

Broadcasting
Transmission of radio/television to a geographically dispersed audience via terrestrial airwaves or satellites. Sometimes also used of cable television systems.

Combined Education
The combination in a single course of face-to-face and distance methods.

Computer-Aided Learning (CAL)
Learning mediated by computer. This mode emphasizes the acquisition of general problem-solving skills, abstract thinking, and self-organized learning. Emphasis is on a process of discovery and the system's output can be guided by the direction of the learner's discovery process.

Computer-Assisted Instruction (CAI)
Instruction mediated by computer. The most common application is teaching facts and algorithmic processes through structured questions and answers. CAI focuses on student mastery of subject material. The system allows for remediation based on answers but not for a change in the underlying program structure.

Computer-Managed Instruction (CMI)
The use of computers for management of instruction by the processing of information on student performance, assessment, progress, and final grades. It can also include test analysis.

Content Analysis
A formal process of investigation and assessment of information relevant to the objectives of a course. The purpose is to choose and sequence information for presentation.

Correspondence Education
A form of distance education that emphasizes independent study without extensive support systems. It features an almost exclusive use of print material and postal communication.

Counsellor—see Advisor

Course Design
Process of choosing and sequencing course content and activities. The aim is to organize material in a form most learners find understandable, compatible with their learning style, and feasible to process within the set time frame.

Cybernetics
The science of communication and control. It incorporates invariant laws governing the growth and stability, adaptation and evolution of any system. It is concerned with information transfer between the system and its environment and also among the parts of the system.

Distance Education
An educational approach in which the learner is separated from the institution by time and/or space. Communication in distance education is non-contiguous but interactive. Courses involve various media rather than face-to-face teaching.

Distance Learning
Study involving an educational institution but not requiring regular face-to-face contact with a teacher.

Educational Technology
An approach to producing and maintaining stable educational outcomes based on the principles of cybernetics and systems theory. It is primarily concerned with planned intervention aimed at changing individual ability, the design of instructional material and communication, the management of educational resources, and the planning of educational systems.

Evaluation
The choice of criteria, measurement methods, and assessment tools for judging students' work. Sometimes used to describe the assessment of a course or program.

External Studies
A combination of independent and interactive learning undertaken within the context of a university program. Term in common use for distance education in Australasia.

Facilitator/Animator
Manager or catalyst of learning activities who helps the student to maximize change and adapts courses to local needs. Contrasts with the traditional teacher who is the arbiter of the learning process.

Feedback
A mechanism by which information as output is fed back into the same system as input so that this information regulates the information to come. Feedback controls the present system state by amplifying (posi-

tive) or limiting (negative) deviations from the previous state. Feedback is a key principle of cybernetics.

Home Study
Independent learning carried on without extensive support services and characterized by reliance on print.

Independent Study
Learning that is almost entirely self-directed. The purpose of independent study is to free learners from constraints inappropriate to their learning styles or aims.

Individualized Learning
A system with the flexibility necessary to satisfy diverse learning styles.

Instructional Systems Design
The application of a systems approach to the design of instruction. (see Systems Approach) This approach entails the operationalization of the instructional process. The use of systems principles and tools allows the designer to analyze and plan the content and structure of the course and evaluate its effectiveness prior to implementation.

Interactive System
Systems of instruction that allow for two-way communication between the learner and the institution. Communication need not be simultaneous nor involve face-to-face contact.

Media
Means by which information is communicated. Covers all forms of communication but usually designates audio-visual and computer communications.

Meta-Model
A representation of a system by means that are superordinate to the system and thus allow the description of its underlying assumptions and implications (e.g., the grammatical or semantic structure of a language itself).

Microprocessors
Integrated circuits permitting both an increase in computing power and a decrease in costs. Microprocessors are part of the hardware of the computer as opposed to the software or programs.

Model
A representation of a system designed for the purpose of understanding its dynamic nature and purpose. There are two types: prescriptive (simulation of change in a system under certain specified conditions) and descriptive (accurate depiction of the system components and their interrelationships).

Needs Analysis
A preliminary stage of instructional systems design for determining the gap between the learners' current states and required or desired states.

Open Learning
Learning is accessible and available to all, usually characterized by an absence of entrance requirements and a clear statement of learning objectives. It may also entail learner participation in designing and evaluating the program.

Study Skills
Strategies of effective learning. Includes the ability to discriminate among strategies appropriate to the particular learning activity. Includes note-taking, speed-reading, and time management.

Support Services
Ancillary systems providing student needs not supplied by course materials. These include access to advisors, tutors, group meetings for peer contact, regional centres for study, equipment, and other resources.

System
Any organizational whole (a set of elements and their interrelationships) that is viable, continues in a steady state, and is subject to continual change.

Systems Approach
A holistic methodology that includes non-algorithmic procedures for analyzing and synthesizing ideas. It is a flexible tool incorporating systems analysis, design, implementation, and reappraisal. Systems analysis involves isolating and defining a problem so as to allow a rational approach to solution. Systems design entails building a model of relevant sub-systems and appraising its effectiveness. Implementation involves applying the model and appraising changes. Reappraisal involves changes to the model required to alter further the system's output.

Task Analysis
Task analysis involves examining what skills and concepts are required for the performance of a task. It includes consideration of the time necessary for task completion, tools, physical requirements, prior skills and knowledge, and the relation of a particular task to others.

Teleconferencing
A telephonic communication network linking more than two individuals or stations. It may provide contact between a tutor and a group of learners or among a group of learners.

Telephone Tutoring
Use of the telephone for discussion between a tutor and an individual learner.

Tutor
Person who mediates between learner and course materials. The tutor's role includes helping the learner organize the course work, providing feedback, marking assignments, and maintaining personal contact with the learner.

Videodisc
Playback system similar to a record player that transmits both audio and video signals through a conventional television receiver.

Glossary

Videotex

System for the retrieval of text information and graphics from a remote computer. Information is transmitted via an interface of computer/television technology to a home television receiver. Data can be transmitted in a broadcast signal (teletext) or by telephone/cable (viewdata).

Visual Literacy

The ability to decode effectively information presented visually as actions, objects, or symbols. It includes the ability to interpret correctly the different forms of media and their conventions such as the use of zooms, pans, cuts, and flashbacks.

Glossary compiled by

Mary Lee Brassard
Concordia University
Canada

Bibliography

This section lists those references that relate directly to the field of distance education. The number at the end of each entry identifies the paper (or papers) containing the reference. For convenience, the entries are grouped under the major sections of the book.

International Trends

Ahlm, M. (1972) Telephone instruction in correspondence education. *Epistolodidaktika*, 2, 49-64. **7**

Anderson, N. (1979) *Strategies and Applications for Correspondence Course Development*. Rome: Accademia (EHSC Autumn Workshop). **4**

Anderson, T.H. and Tippy, P.H. (1971) An exploratory study of correspondence students. *ERIC Report Number 70960*. **6**

Aspy, D. (1969) The relationshop between teacher functioning and facilitated dimensions and student performance on intellectual indices. *Florida Journal of Educational Research*. **6**

Ausubel, D.P. (1963) *The Psychology of Meaningful Verbal Learning*. New York: Grune & Stratton. **7**

Ausubel, D.P. (1968) *Educational Psychcology: A Cognitive View*. New York: Holt, Rinehart & Winston. **7**

Bååth, J.A. (1976) Postal contacts and some other means of two-way communication: practices and opinions at a number of European correspondence schools. *Pedagogical Reports*. Number 5. University of Lund: Department of Education. **6**

Bååth, J.A. (1978) Research in development work correspondence education. *ICCE Newsletter*. 8, 4, 9-15. **6**

Bååth, J.A. and Wangdahl, A. (1976) The tutor as an agent of motivation in correspondence Education. *Pedagogical Reports*. University of Lund: Department of Education. **6**

Barratt-Brown, J. (1976) Courses for disadvantaged adults. *Teaching at a Distance*, 6. **4**

Bates, A.W. (1981) The unique educational characteristics of television and some consequences for teaching and learning. Submitted to: *Journal of Educational Television and Other Media*, 1981. **2**

Bates, A.W. (1981) *The Planning and Management of Audio-Visual Media in Distance Learning Institutions*. Paris: Unesco. **2, 8**

Beck, P. (1978) Peer tutoring at a community college: training and using peer tutors. *College English*. 40, 437-439. **6**

Bloom, B.S. (1968) Learning for mastering. *Evaluation Comment Number 1*. **6**

Bonani, G. (1978) *The Slow Demise of the Work Ethic*. Rome: Society of International Development. **4**

Bonani, G. (1979) *L'Insegnamento per Corrispondenza e il suo Pubblic*. Rome: Accademia. **4**

Bonani, G. Sauda E. (1980) *Gli studenti della Scuola Accademia*. Rome: CISID. **4**

Born, D.G. and Whelan, P. (1973) Some descriptive characteristics of student performance in PSI in lecture courses. *Psychological Record*. 23, 145-152. **6**

Boshier, R. (1978) Relationship between motives for participation in and drop-out from adult education. *Psychological Reports*. 43, 23-26. **6**

Botkin, J.W. Elmandjra, M. and Malitza, M. (1979) *No Limits to Learning: Bridging the Human Gap*. (A report to the Club of Rome). Toronto: Pergamon Press. **9**

Bowles, S. and Gintis, H. (1976) *Schooling in Capitalist America*. New York: Basic Books. **4**

Bradley, A.P. and Lehman, T. (1975) Attrition at a non-traditional Institute. Saratoga Springs: State University of New York, Empire State College. **6**

Brown, M.A. and Copeland, H. G. (1979) *Attracting Able Instructors of Adults*. San Francisco: Jossey Bass. **6**

Butler, R.E. (1979) World communication network. *Transactional Perspectives*, 5, 3, 114. **9**

Carp, A. Peterson, R. and Roelfs, P. (1973) Learning Interests and Experiences of Adult American. Berkeley, California: Educational Testing Services. **6**

Childs, G.D. (1971) Recent Research Developments in Correspondence Instruction. In *The Changing World of Correspondence Study: International Readings*. MacKenzie and Christensen (eds.) University Park: Pennsylvania State University Press. **6**

Coldeway, D.O. (1980) An Examination of Tutor Management Strategies for use in Distance Education. *REDEAL Research Report #2*. Project REDEAL Athabasca University. **6**

Coldeway, D.O. (1980) Exploring the Effects of Peer Tutoring in Distance Education. *REDEAL Research report #3*. Project REDEAL. Athabasca University. **6**

Coldeway, D.O. and Schiller, W.J. (1974) Training Proctors for the Personalized System of Instruction. In R.S. Ruskin and S.F. Bono (eds). *Proceedings of First National Conference on Personalized Instruction in Higher Education.* Washington, D.C.: Centre for Personalized Instruction, Georgetown University. *6*

Coldeway, D.O. and Spencer, R. (1980) Distance Education: Interaction between Learner Attributes and Learner Course Performance. *REDEAL Research Report #9. 6*

Coldeway, D.O. and Spencer, R.E. (1980) The Measurement of Attrition and Completion in Distance Learning Courses. *REDEAL Technical Report #8.* Project REDEAL. Athabasca University. *6*

Coldeway, D.O., McKrury, K. and Spencer, R. (1980) Distance Education from the Learner's Perspective: The Results of Individual Learner Tracking at Athabasca University. *REDEAL Research Report #10.* Project REDEAL. Athabasca University. *6*

Council of Europe (1978) *Permanent Education-Final Report.* Strasbourg. *4*

Crawford, G. (1980) Student Completion Rates under Three Different Pacing Conditions. *REDEAL Technical Report #11.* Project REDEAL. Athabasca University. *6*

Crawford, J. (1977) Interactions of learner characteristics with a difficulty level of instruction. Paper presented at the Annual Meeting of American Education Research Association, New York. *6*

Creaner, R.C. and Dubé, N.S. (1978) Administration of Personalized Instruction Programs in the Middle School. In J.G. Sherman, R.S. Ruskin, and R.M. Lazer (eds.). *Personalized Instruction in Education Today: Selected Papers from the Third and Fourth National Conferences on Personalized Instruction.* San Francisco: San Francisco Press. *6*

Cronbach, L. and Snow, R. (1977) *Aptitudes and Instructional Methods.* New York: Irvington Publishers. *6*

Cropley, A. (1977) *Lifelong Education.* New York: Pergamon Press. *4*

Daniel, J. Marquis C. (1979) Interaction and independence: getting the mixture right. *Teaching at a Distance,* 14. *4*

Daniel, J. and Stroud, M. (1981) Distance education: a reassessment for the 1980s. *Distance Education,* 2, 2, 201-220. *8*

Davies, E. (1976/1977) The role of self-paced study in undergraduate science teaching. *British Journal of Educational Technology,* 7, 3/8, 2. *4*

Davies, W. (1979) Open learning or open access? *British Journal of Educational Technology,* 10, 2. *4*

Dei, M. Rossi M. (1978) *Sociologia Della Scuola Italiana.* Bologna: Il Mulino. *4*

Dick, W. and Gallagher, P. (1972) Systems concepts in computer-managed instruction: an implementation and validation study. *Educational Technology.* 12, 33-39. *6*

Donehower, J.M. (1968) Variables Associated with Correspondence Study Enrolments at the University of Nevada, 1963-1965. unpublished Master's thesis. *6*

Draper, J.A. (1973) Universities and the challenge of an illiterate population: A research question. *New Frontiers in Education,* 3, 1, 27-35. *9*

Dubin, R. and Taveggia, T. (1968) The Teaching Learning Paradox. Center for the Advanced Study of Education Administration, University of Oregon, Eugene, Oregon. *6*

Duby, P.B. and Giltrow, D.R. (1978) Predicting student withdrawals in open learning courses. *Educational Technology.* February, 43-47. *6*

Elton, L.R.B. (1980) Can the Keller Plan help in our understanding of the problems of distance learning. *Journal of Personalized Instruction.* 4, 2, 94-99. *6*

Entwistle, N. Thompson, J. and Wilson, J. (1974) Motivation and study habits. *Higher Education,* 3,4. *4*

Erdos, R. (1976) *La Mise en Place d'une Institution d'enseignement par Correspondance.* Paris: Unesco. *4*

Essex, D.L. And Anderson, T.H. (1972) Some Correlates of Success in Correspondence Study. *ERIC Report Number 70952.* 1972. *6*

Fakes, J. (ed) (1973) *Technical Education at a Distance.* Cambridge: IEC. *4*

Falkenberg, E. (1976) Journey of a thousand miles. *Learning,* 1, 1. *9*

Fawcett, S.B. Matthews, M.R. Fletcher, R.K. Morrow, R. and Stokes, T.F. (1976) Personalized instruction in the community: teaching helping skills to low-income neighborhood residents. *Journal of Personalized Instruction.* 2, 86-90. *6*

Feather, F. (ed.) (1980) *Through the '80s: Thinking Globally, Acting Locally.* Washington, D.C.: World Future Society. *9*

Feather, F. and Mayur, R. (1980) The co-optimistic solution. *Futures Focus,* 1, 1. *9*

Flammer, G.H. (1971) Learning as the constant and time as the variable. *Engineering Education.* 61, 511-514. *6*

Freeman, R. (1975) Preparatory studies and adult education. *Teaching at a Distance,* 4, 31-44. *4*

Gaff, J.G. (1975) *Faculty Renewal.* San Francisco: Jossey-Bass. *6*

Gagné, R.M. (1977) *The Conditions of Learning.* (3rd ed.) New York: Holt, Rinehart & Winston. *7*

Gall, M.D. and Gall, J.P. (1976) The discussion method. In N.L. Gage (ed.). *The Psychology of Teaching Methods.* The 75th Yearbook of the National Society for the Study of Education. Chicago: University of Chicago Press. *6*

Gattullo, M. (1976) *L'Andamento della Selezione Scolastica.* Bologna: Il Mulino. *4*

Geis, G.L. (1980) Research: Use, Abuse and Refuse. Paper presented at the Annual Meeting of the American Educational Research Association in Boston, April 8th, 1980. *6*

Gibbs, G. Durbridge, N. (1976) Characteristics of the Open University Tutors. *Teaching at a Distance,* 6, 96-102 and 7, 7-22. *4*

Glatter, R. and Wedell, E.G. (1971) *Study by Correspondence.* London: Longmans. *6*

Glick, D.M. and Semb, G. (1978) Effects of pacing contingencies on personalized instruction. a review of the evidence. *Journal of Personalized Instruction.* 3, 36-42. *6*

Gowin, B. (1972) Is education research distinctive? In Thomas, L.G. (ed.) (1972)*Philosophical Redirection of Education Research.* Chicago, Ill.: The University of Chicago Press. pp. 9-25 *7*

Gozzer, G. (1977) *La Scolarizzazione di Massa.* Rome: Accademia. *4*

Graff, K. (1965) Exercises and tests in correspondence education. *Home Study Review.* 6, 1, 22-29. *6*

Graff, K. Saxe, B. and Ostlyngen, E. (1966) Correspondence education in Europe today. In *CEC Yearbook.* Lincoln: CEC. 42-77. *6*

Grahm, A. (1969) *What Students Think of Assignments in Correspondence Education.* Malmo: Hermods. *6*

Granholm, G.W. And Ljoså, E. (1977) ICCE Research Survey 1976. *ICCE Newsletter.* 7, 4, 3-30. *6*

Grant, D.A. (1962) Testing the null hypothesis and the strategy and tactics of investigating theoretical models. *Psychological Review.* 69, 1, 54-61. *6*

Hakemulder, J. (ed.) (1979) *Distance Education for Development.* Bonn: German Foundation for International Development. *8*

Harper, W.R. (1971) A system of correspondence. In Mackenzie, O. and Christensen, E.L. (eds.) *The Changing World of Correspondence Study.* University Park: Pennsylvania State University Press. 7-13. *6*

Harrington, F.A. (1977) *The Future of Adult Education.* San Francisco: Jossey Bass Publishing. *6*

Harrington, F.H. (1979) *The Future of Adult Education.* Washington, D.C.: Jossey-Bass Publishers. *9*

Harris, W. Williams, J. (1977) *A Handbook on Distance Education.* Manchester: Department of Adult Education. *4*

Harris, W.J.A. (1975) *The Distance Tutor.* Bournemouth: Department of Adult Education, University of Manchester. *6, 4*

Hays, R.A. (1978) Implementation of a Peer Tutoring Program. Introductory Practicum, Nova University. *6*

Henneberry, J.K. (1976) Initial progress rates as related to performance in a personalized system of instruction. *Teaching of Psychology.* 3, 178-181. *6*

Holmberg, B. (1974) *Distance Education.* Malmo: Hermods. *6*

Bibliography

Holmberg, B. (1977) *Distance Education*. London: Kogan Page. *4*

Holmberg, B. (1977) *Distance Education: Survey and Bibliography*. London: Kogan Page. *6*

Hornik, R.C. (1976) Useful evaluation designs for evaluating the impact of distance learning systems: methodology. *Educational Broadcasting International*. 9, 6-10. *6*

Husen, T. (1974) *Talent, Equality and Meritocracy*. The Hague: Martinus Nijhoff. *4*

International Labour Office. (1972) *Employment,* incomes and equality: a strategy for increasing employment in Kenya. (4th ed., 1977) Geneva: ILO. *10*

Jencks, C. (1972) *Inequality*. New York: Harper-Colophon. *4*

Johnson, K.R. (1975) An Evaluative Review of the Proctor Component of Personalized Instruction. Paper presented at the American Psychological Association, New Orleans, 1975. *6*

Joyce, B. and Weil, M. (1972) *Models of Teaching*. Englewood Cliffs, N.J.: Prentice-Hall. *7*

Karow, W. Storm, U. (1977) *Wie kann Fernunterricht zur Verbesserung der Beruflichen Bildung Beitragen?* Berlin: BIBB. *4*

Karow, W. (1977) *Privaten Fernunterricht in 16 Ländern. Übersicht und Vergleich*. Berlin: BIBB. *4*

Karow, W. (1979) How to find the right work in distance education. *Epistolodidaktika*, 2, 3-9. *8*

Karow, W. (1979) *A Survey of 16 Countries' Private Correspondence Education*. Rome: Atti Convegno Accademia. *4*

Kaye, A. and Rumble, G. (1981) *Distance Teaching for Higher and Adult Education*. London: Croom Helm. *8*

Keegan, D. (1980) On defining distance education. *Distance Education*, 1, 1, 13-26. *8*

Keller, F.S. (1968) Goodbye teacher. *Journal of Applied Behavior Analysis*. 1, 78-89. *6*

Kelly, H. (1963) From the editor's notebook. *Home Study Review*. 4, 3, 1-3; 43-49. *6*

Kennedy, D. Powell, R. (1976) Student progress and withdrawal. *Teaching at a Distance*, 7, 61-75. *4*

Kersteins, G. (1976) Report on the Peer Tutoring Program: 1973-1975 School Years. El Camino College, Torrence, California. *6*

Knowles, M. (1975) *Self-Directed Learning: A Guide for Learners and Teachers*. Chicago: Associated Press, Follett Publishing Company. *6*

Knowles, M.J. (1966) The Role of the Instructor in Correspondence Study. In Wedemeyer, C. (ed.) 100-106. *6*

Kulik, J.A. Kulik, C.C. and Colin, P.A. (1979) Meta-analysis of outcome studies of Keller's Personalized System of Instruction. *American Psychologist*. 34, 307-318. *6*

Lampikoski, K. and Mantere, P. (1976) *Didactic Principles as Tools in Analysing and Developing a Guidance System for Distance Education*. Helsinki: The Institute of Marketing. *7*

Larson, A. (1929) A Study of the Relative Ability and Achievement of Class Extension Correspondence and Residence Students at the University of Kentucky. University of Kentucky, Lexington, Master's Thesis. *6*

Larson, A. (1936) Comparative quality of work done by students in residence in correspondence work. *Journal of Educational Research*. 25, 105-109. *6*

Lee, G.E. (1976) An experiment in communications and adult education for Newfoundland and Labrador. *Learning*, 1, 1. *9*

Lewis, R. (1975) The place of face-to-face tuition in the Open University system. *Teaching at a Distance*. 3, 26-31. *6*

Ljoså, E. (1978) Trends and priorities in distance education research. *ICCE Newsletter*. 8, 4, 4-8. *6*

Lloyd, K.E. and Knutzen, N.J. (1969) A self-paced program undergraduate course in experimental analysis of behavior. *Journal of Applied Behavior Analysis*. , 2, 125-133. *6*

MacIntosh, N. and Morrison, V. (1968) Student demand progress and withdrawal: the Open University's first four years. *Higher Education Review*. 7, 37-66. *6*

MacKenzie, O. Christensen, E.L. and Rigby, P.H. (1968) *Correspondence Instruction in the United States*. New York: McGraw-Hill. *6*

Mackenzie, N. Postgate, R. Scupham, J. (1977) *Open Learning*. Paris: Unesco Press. *4*

Malley, J.I. Brown, A.P. and Williams, J.W. (1976) Drop-outs from external studies: a case study of the investigation process. *Epistolodidaktika*. 2, 170-179. *6*

Mathieson, D.E. (1971) Correspondence Study: A Summary Review of the Research and Development Literature. ERIC Clearinghouse on Adult Education. Syracruse University, New York, March 1971. *6*

Mathis, B.C. and McGaghie, W.G. (1974) From theories for learning to theories for teaching. In Stiles, L.J. (ed.) (1974) *Theories for Teaching*. New York: Dodd, Mead & Company. pp. 30-50 *7*

McClusky, H. (1970) *An Approach to the Differential Psychology of the Adult Potential*. Washington: Adult Education Association. *4*

McConnell, D. and Sharples, M. (1981) *Distance Teaching by CYCLOPS: Tutor Handbook*. Nottingham: Open University. *2*

McDonald, R. Knights, S. (1979) Returning to study: the mature-age student. *Programmed Learning and Educational Technology*, 16, 2. *4*

McKeachie, W.J. (1975) *Teaching Tips*. Lexington: D.C. Heath. *6*

Menal, J. (1977) *La Relacíon Alumno-Tutor en al Enseñanza para Correspondenica*. Copenhagen: CEC. *4*

Merrill, P.F. (1974) Computer-Managed Instruction at Florida State University. In H.E. Mitzell (ed.) An Examination of the Short-Range Potential of Computer-Managed Instruction. Conference Proceedings, November 6-8, 1974. National Institute of Education. *6*

Monstain, B.R. (1974) Students who desire independent study: some distinguishing characteristics. *College Student Journal*. 8, 85-92. *6*

Moore, M.G. (1977) A model of independent study. *Epistolodidaktika*, 1, 6-40. *7*

National Christian Council of Kenya. (1965) *After school what?* Nairobi: NCCK. *10*

Nicholson, N. (1977) Counselling the adult learner at the Open University. *Teaching at a Distance*, 8. *4*

Northcott, P. (1975) The Keller Plan in external studies. *ASPESA Newsletter*. 2, 4. *6*

Orton, L.J. (1977) Completion and non-starts rates in correspondence courses. *Canadian Journal of University Continuing Education*. 4. *6*

Page, E.B. (1958) Teacher comments and student performance: a seventy-four classroom experiment in school motivation. *Journal of Educational Psychology*. 49, 1, 173-181. *6*

Pagney, B. (1977) *L'Enseignement a Distance et la Formation Professionelle*. Berlin: BIBB. *4*

Pantages, T.J. and Creedon, C.F. (1978) Studies of college attrition: 1950 to 1975. *Review of Education Research*. 48, 1, 49-101. *6*

Patterson, R.T. (1976) Planning and Implementing a Peer Tutoring Approach to Individualized Instruction to Improve Reading Achievement. *Max II Report*. Nova University. *6*

Perraton H. (1981) *Basic Education and Mass Media* (mimeo) (unpublished report to the World Bank, IEC Cambridge) *3*

Perraton, H. ed. (1979) *Alternative Routes to Formal Education: Distance Teaching for School Equivalency* (World Bank, mimeo) (also John Hopkins University Press, forthcoming) *3*

Peruniak, G. (1980) Seminars as an Instructional Strategy in Distance Education. *REDEAL Research Report #6*. Project REDEAL. Athabasca University. *6*

Peruniak, G., Spencer, R.E. and Coldeway, D.O. (1980) Interface of the Host Institution, Athabasca University. *REDEAL Technical Report #6*. Project REDEAL. Athabasca University. *6*

Peters, O. (1971) Theoretical aspects of correspondence instruction. In Mackenzie, O.and Christensen, E.L. (eds.) *The Changing World of Correspondence Study*. University Park: Pennsylvania State University Press. 223-228. *6*

Peters, O. (1965) *Der Fernunterricht. Materialien zur Diskussion einer neuen Unterrichtsform*. Weinheim: Beltz. *5, 8*

Peters, O. (1973) *Die didaktische Struktur des Fernunterrichts. Untersuchungen zu einer industrialisierten Form des Lehrens und Lernens.* Weinheim: Beltz. *5, 8*

Petrusa, E.R. (1978) Opthalmocscopy: a self-paced unit for physician assistants. In J.G. Sherman, R.S. Ruskin and M.R. Lazer (eds.). *Personalized Instruction Education Today: Selected Papers for the Third and Fourth National Conferences on Personalized Instruction.* San Francisco, San Francisco Press. *6*

Project REDEAL, (1980) Athabasca University. *6*

Redmond, M. (1977) Aspects of adult learning. *Teaching at a Distance,* 8. *4*

Richardson, M. (1975) Who are preparatory studies for? *Teaching at a Distance,* 4, 35-37. *4*

Robinson, B. (1979) *Telephone Teaching: A Handbook for Tutors.* Nottingham: Open University. *2*

Sarramona, J. (1975) *La Enseñanza a Distancia.* Barcelona: CEAC. *4*

Savins, D. Pfeiffer, J.W. and Ragsdale, J.P. (1972) Effective letters and postcards of encouragement on the submission of lessons in correspondence study. *Journal of Experimental Education.* 41, 87-90. *6*

Schreve, B. Majer, K. and Hedges, L. (1976) The OASIS Peer Tutoring Program: A Model for Academic Support. LaJolla, California. University of California, San Diego. *6*

Schwartz, G.E. (1976) What is doing the teaching in PSI courses? In L.E. Fraley and E.A. Vargas (eds.). *Behavior Research and Technology in Higher Education.* Gainsville, Florida: University of Florida, Society for Behavioral Technology and Engineering. 35-40. *6*

Sewart, D. (1976) A new look at the preparation of Open University students. *Teaching at a Distance,* 15. *4*

Sewart, D. (1978) Continuity of concern for students in a system of learning at a distance. Hagen: *ZIFF Papiere* 22. *5*

Sewart, D. (1980) Creating an information base for an individualised support system in distance education. *Distance Education,* 1, 2. *5*

Sewart, D. (1981) Distance teaching: a contradiction in terms. *Teaching at a Distance,* 19. *5*

Shale, D. (1980) Course completion rates. Edmonton: Athabasca University, Office of Institutional Studies. August 1980. *6*

Shapovalenko, G. (1963) *Polytechnical Education in the USSR.* Paris: Unesco. *4*

Sjogren, D.D. (1963) The influence of varied teacher behavior on performance in correspondence study. *Journal of Experimental Education.* 32, 81-83. *6*

Smith, P.J. (1976) Some factors contributing to the rate of student withdrawal from part-time correspondence courses. *Epistolodidaktika.* 1, 26-33. *6*

Snow, R.E. (1977) Individual differences and instructional theory. *Educational Researcher.* 6, 11-15. *6*

Spencer, R.E. (1980) Investigating the Use of the Personalized System of Instruction in Distance Education. *REDEAL Research Report #1.* Project REDEAL. Athabasca University. *6*

Spencer, R.E. (1980) The Effects of Computer-Generated Schedules on the Performance of Athabasca University Learners. *REDEAL Research Report #5.* Project REDEAL. Athabasca University. *6*

Spencer, R.E. Peruniak, G. and Coldeway, D.O. (1980) A Comparison between Pace-Package and Home-Study Courses with Respect to Completion Data. *REDEAL Research Report #11.* Project REDEAL. Athabasca University. *6*

Stein, L.S. (1960) Design of a correspondence course. *Adult Education.* 10, 161-166. *6*

Thitu, P.N. (1980) Analytical and evaluation study of Muguga-wa-Gatonye distance education pilot project. Diploma dissertation, University of Nairobi. *10*

Tobias, S. (1976) Achievement treatment interactions. *Review of Educational Research.* 46, 61-74. *6*

Toft, R. (1975) College TV: A New Approach. In J.M. Johnston (ed.). *Research and Technology in College and University Teaching.* Gainsville, Florida: Department of Psychology, University of Florida. *6*

Tosti, D. and Wilson, S. (1972) *Learning is Getting Easier.* San Raphael: Individual Learning Systems. *6*

Tough, A. (1978) Major learning efforts: recent research and future directions. *Adult Education.* 28, 4, 250-263. *6*

Trivellato, U. (1979) Instruzione ed economia. In *Quindicinale di Note e Commenti.* Rome: CENSIS. *4*

Trivellato, U. (1979) *Sociologia Della Scuola Secondaria.* Rome: Accademia. *4*

Van Eck, E. Houtkoop, W. (1979) *Educational Careers of Participants in Correspondence Courses at General Secondary School Level.* Amsterdam: Kohnstamm Instituut. *4*

Wagner, L. (1972) The economics of the Open University. *Higher Education,* 1, 2, 158-183. *3*

Wagner, L. (1977) The economics of the Open University revisited. *Higher Education,* 6, 3, 359-381. *3*

Wagner, L. (1980) Costs and effectiveness of distance learning at the post-secondary level. In Unesco (1980) *The Economics of New Educational Media* vol. 2 Paris: Unesco. *3*

Wangdahl, A. (1977) Types of Face-to-Face Contact in Combination with Correspondence Education. A Survey of the Literature. *Pedagogical Report Number 10.* Lund, Sweden: University of Lund, Department of Education. *6*

Watts, G. (1979) Personal counselling at the Open University. *Teaching at a Distance,* 15. *4*

Wedemeyer, C. (1974) Theory of Learning By Correspondence - Some Theoretical Propostions. Keynote Address to the N.H.S.C. Conference in South Bend, Indianna, October 7th, 1974. *6*

Weinstock, N. (1978) *Les Cours par Correspondance du Secteur Privé en Belique.* Brussels: Centre National de Sociologie du Droit Social. *4*

Wentworth, R. (ed.) (1978-79) *Correspondence Education: Dynamic and Diversified.* London: Tuition House. *8*

White, R. (1976a) *An Alternative Pattern of Basic Education: Radio Santa Maria.* Paris: Unesco. *3*

White, R. (1976b) *Mass Communications and the Popular Promotion Strategy of Rural Development in Honduras.* Stanford: Institute for Communication Research. *3*

White, M.A. (1976) Reflections on research into higher education by external study in Asutralia. *Epistolodidaktika.* 2. *6*

Wiedhaup, C.J.J. (1976) Dutch research on correspondence education: KISO Project. *Epistolodidaktika.* 1. *6*

Williams, E. and Holloway, S. and Hammond, S. (1975) Student reactions to tutoring by telephone in Britain's Open University. *Educational Technology.* 15, 42-46. *6*

Williams, V. (1980) Research and Evaluation of Tutor Skills Training Project. *REDEAL Research Report #4.* Project REDEAL. Athabasca University. *6*

Williams, V. (1980) Communications Skills Workshop for Tutors: The Manual. *REDEAL Technical Report #7.* Project REDEAL. Athabasca University. *6*

Wilson, J.A. (1978) Johnny Gets Personalized. In J.G. Sherman, R.S. Ruskin and M.R. Lazer (eds.). *Personalized Instruction Education Today: Selected Papers for the Third and Fourth National Conferences on Personalized Instruction.* San Francisco: San Francisco Press. *6*

Wilson, W.R. and Miller, H. (1964) A note on the inconclusiveness of accepting the null hypothesis. *Psychological Review.* 1, 3, 238-242. *6*

World Bank (1980) *Education: Sector Policy Paper.* Washington, D.C.: World Bank. *9*

Young M. et al (1980) *Distance Teaching for the Third World: The Lion and the Clockwork Mouse.* London: Routledge and Kegan Paul. *3*

Young, M. Perraton, H. Jenkins, J. and Dodds, T. (1980). Distance Teaching for the Third World. The Lion and the Clockwork Mouse. London: Routledge and Kegan Paul. *8*

Ziegel, W.H. (1924) The Relation of Extra-Mural Study to Residents Enrolment and Scholastic Standing. George Peabody College for Teachers, Nashville, Tennessee. Ph.D. Thesis. *6*

Bibliography

Learning at a Distance and National Development

ABT (1980) Pos-graduação á distancia. *Tecnologia Educacional.* 36 (entire issue) Rio de Janeiro: Associação Brasileira de Tecnologia Educacional. *18*

Adams, D. (1971) *Education in National Development.* London: Routledge and Kegan. *17*

Ahmed, M. (1975) *The Economics of Nonformal Education: Resources, Costs and Benefits,* New York: Praeger Publishers. *12*

Anderson, P. (1981) The IX Latin American seminar on university teleducation. *ICCE Newsletter,* (in press), London: International Council for Correspondence Education. (Also published in Portuguese in *ED-DIS,* 2, Brasilia.) *18*

Ansere, J.K. (1979) The development of correspondence education in Ghana. *Kenya Journal of Adult Education,* 7, 3, 12-18. *12*

Asheim, L. (1953) Research on the Reading of Adults. *Library Trends,* (University of Illinois) 1, 4, 454-461. *17*

Bååth, J.A. (1979) *Correspondence Education in the Light of a Number of Contemporary Teaching Models.* Malmo: LiberHermods. *26*

Contreras, L. (1972) *Manual sobre la Preparacion de Materiales de Lectura para Adultos.* Caracas: Centro Regional de Educacion de Adultos. *17*

Coombs, P.H. (1968) *The World Education Crisis: A Systems Analysis.* London: Oxford University Press. *12*

Escotet, M. (1980) *Tendenicas de la Educacion Superior a Distancia.* San José: Editorial Universidad Estatal a Distancia. *18*

Illich, I. (1970) *De-Schooling Society.* New York: Harper and Row. *12*

Ingle, H. (1974) Communication media and technology: a look at their role in non-formal education programs. *Information Bulletin Number Five.* Washington: The Information Center on Instructional Technology. *17*

Jenkins, J. (1980) *Correspondence Institutions in the Commonwealth 1980.* London: Commonwealth Secretariat. *26*

Karow, Willi. (1980) Privater Fernunterricht in der Bundesrepublik Deutschland und im Ausland. Schriften zur Berufsbildungsforschung 58. Hannover: Bundesinstitut für Berufsbildung/Hermann Schroedel Verlag KG. *23*

Kaye, A.R. (1973) The design and evaluation of science courses at the Open University. *Instructional Science,* 2. *12*

Kinsela, H. (1980) *Experiences of Assistance by the New Zealand Technical Correspondence Institute to Developing Countries.* Paper 22 presented at the Open University Conference on The Education of Adults at a Distance. *17*

Laidlaw, B and Layard, R. (1974) Traditional versus Open University teaching methods, a cost comparison. *Higher Education,* 3. *12*

Mackenzie, O. and Christensen, E.L. (1971) *The Changing World of Correspondence Study.* University Park, Pennsylvania: The Pennsylvania State University Press. *26*

McBride, J. (1975) Planning for distance education. *Planning,* 4, 5, 2-3. *17*

Nicolini, L. (1980) Grupo Capricornio: un programa de cooperacion horizontal. *PIUTEC.* 1, 1, 11-18. Londrina, Brazil: Fundação Universidade Estatal de Londrina. *18*

Perraton, Hilary. (ed.) (1979) *Alternative Routes to Formal Education: Distance Teaching for School Equivalency.* Washington: The World Bank. *23*

Ramón-Fernandez, T. (1979) La UNED española fué una apuesta en la que pocos crei'an. *ENLACE,* 2, 6-7, Universidad Estatal a Distancia de Costa Rica. *18*

Reimer, E. (1972) *School is Dead: Alternatives in Education.* New York: Doubleday. *12*

Robertson, C. The nature and effects of differential access to education in Ga society. *Africa,* 47, 2, 208-219. *12*

Schramm, W. (1973) *Big Media, Little Media.* California: Institute for Communication Research, Stanford University. *17*

Searle, B., Friend, J. and Suppes, P. (1976) *The Radio Mathematics Project: Nicaragua 1974-1975.* California: Institute for Mathematical Studies in the Social Sciences, Stanford University. *17*

Spaulding, S. (1953) *An Investigation of Factors Influencing the Effectiveness of Fundamental Reading Materials for Latin American Adults.* Doctoral thesis not published. Columbus: Ohio State University. *17*

UNED-CR (1980) *Informacion General.* San José: Universidad Estatal a Distancia de Costa Rica. *18*

Unesco (1961) Conference of African States on the Development of Education in Africa. Addis Ababa, 15-25 May, 1961, Final Report. *12*

Unesco (1962) The Development of Higher Education in Africa. Report of the Conference held at Tananarive, 3-12 September, 1962. *12*

Valero, L. and Morán, M. (1978) La Experiencia de una Colección Popular. *Boletin CLEA.* 4, 19-22. Santiago de Chile. *17*

Villarroel, A. (1980) The Venezuelan National Open University: An Overview. Paper presented at the XXX International Conference of the International Communication Association, in Acapulco, Mexico, May 1980. *18*

Wagner, L. (1977) The economics of the Open University revisited. *Higher Education,* 6, 359-381. *12*

Weinstock, Nathan, et al (1976) Les cours par correspondence du secteur privé en Belgique. Etude sociologique. Brussel: Editions du Centre National de Sociologie du Droit Social. *23*

The Process of Learning at a Distance: Recent Research and Developments

Anderson, L.W. (1976) An empirical investigation of individual differences in time to learn. *Journal of Educational Psychology,* 68, 2, 226-233. *43*

Aslanian, Carol B. and Bricknell, Henry M. (1980) *Americans in Transition: Life Changes as Reasons for Adult Learning.* New York: College Entrance Examination Board. *28*

Becker, M.S. Greer, B. and Hughes, E.C. (1968) *Making the Grade: The Academic Side of College Life.* New York: Wiley. *32*

Berliner, D.C. (1979) Tempus Educare. In Peterson, P.L. and Walberg, H.J. (eds.) *Research on Teaching: Concepts, Findings and Implications.* Berkeley, California: McCutchan. *43*

Bloom, B. (1971) Mastery learning. In Block, J.H. (ed.) *Mastery Learning: Theory & Practice.* New York: Holt, Rinehart & Winston. *29*

Bloom, B.S. (1974) Time and learning. *American Psychologist,* 8, 682-688. *43*

Brew, A. and McCormick, B. (1979) Student learning and an independent study course. *Higher Education,* 8, 429-442. *31*

Briggs, L.J. (ed.) (1977) *Instructional Design.* Englewood Cliffs, New Jersey: Educational Technology Publications. *34*

Carroll, J.B. (1963) A model of school learning. *Teachers College Record,* 64, 723-733. *43*

Connors, B. (1980) Assessment of students in distance teaching. In Armstrong, J.D. and Store, R.E. (eds.) *Evaluation in Distance Teaching.* Townsville, Queensland: Townsville College of Advanced Education. *36, 43*

Coombs, P.H. (1968) *The World Educational Crisis: A Systems Analysis.* New York: Oxford University Press. *31*

Cronbach, L. and R. Snow. (1977) *Aptitudes and Instructional Methods.* New York: Irvington Publishers. *29*

Cross, K. Patricia (1978) *The Missing Link: Connecting Adult Learners to Learning Resources.* New York: College Entrance Examination Board. *28*

Cross, K. Patricia (1981) *Adults as Learners.* San Francisco: Jossey-Bass Publishers. *28*

Csikszentmihalyi, M. (1975) *Beyond Boredom and Anxiety: The Experience of Play in Work and Games.* San Francisco: Jossey-Bass. *31*

Dahlgren, L.O. (1975) Qualitative differences in learning as a function of content-orientated guidance. *Göteborg Studies in Educational Sciences 15.* University of Göteborg. *31, 32*

Daniel, J.S. and Marquis, C. (1979) Interaction and independence: getting the mixture right. *Teaching at a Distance,* 15, 29-44. *43*

Eckblad, G. (1979) Spontanmotivasjon - et viktig fenomen for psykologisk teori i dagliglivet? *Nordisk Psykologi,* 31, 30-41. (Spontaneous motivation - an important phenomenon for psychological theory and in daily life?) *31*

Entwistle, N. and Hounsell, D. (1979) Student learning in its natural setting. *Higher Education,* 8, 4, 359-363. *32*

Filstead, W.J. (1979) Qualitative methods: a needed perspective in evaluation research. In Cook, T.D. and Reichardt, C.S. (eds.) *Qualitative Methods in Evaluation Research.* Beverley Hills: Sage. *32*

Fredrick, W.C. and Walberg, H.D. (1980) Learning as a function of time. *Journal of Educational Research,* 73, 4, 183-194. *43*

Gagné, R.M. (1975) *Essentials of Learning for Instruction.* Hinsdale, Illinois: Dryden. *34*

Geertz, C. (1973) *The Interpretation of Cultures.* New York: Basic Books. *31*

Gibbs, G. (1978) Intervening in Student Learning - A Particular Strategy. Paper presented at the Fourth International Conference on Higher Education, 29 August - 1 September 1978, Lancaster, Great Britain. *31*

Glynne, D.R. and Jones, H.A. (1967) Student wastage. *Adult Education,* 40, 3. *36*

Gough, J.E. and Monday, P.R. (1979) Student workloads: an entree to the literature. *Open Campus,* 3, 43-62. *43*

Harnischfeger, A. and Wiley, D.E. (1976) Teaching-learning processes in elementary schools: a synoptic view. *Curriculum Inquiry,* 6, 5-43. *43*

Kazdin, A.W. (1975) *Behaviour Modification in Applied Settings.* Homewood, Illinois: Dorsey. *43*

Keller, F. (1968) Goodbye Teacher. *Journal of Applied Behaviour Analysis,* 1, 78-89. *29*

Kifer, E. (1975) Relationships between academic achievement and personality characteristics: a quasi-longitudinal study. *American Educational Research Journal,* 12, 191-210. *43*

Knowles, M.S. (1970) *The Modern Practice of Adult Education: Andragogy Versus Pedagogy.* New York: Association Press. *29*

Knowles, M.S. (1975) *Self-Directed Learning.* New York: Association Press. *29*

Knox, A.B. (1978) *Adult Development and Learning.* San Francisco: Jossey-Bass. *29*

Kulik, J.A. and Kulik, C.C. (1979) College teaching. In Peterson, P.L. and Walberg, H.J. (eds.) *Research on Teaching: Concepts, Findings and Implications.* Berkeley, California: McCutchan. *43*

Laidlaw, B. and Layard, R. (1974) Traditional versus open university teaching methods: a cost comparison. *Higher Education,* 3, 439-468. *43*

Lybeck, L. (1981) *Arkimedes i klassen. En amnespedagogisk berattelse.* Göteborg: Acta Universitatis Gothoburgensis. (Archimedes in the class). *31*

Marton, F. (1975) On non-verbatim learning I: level of processing and level of outcome. *Scandinavian Journal of Psychology,* 16, 273-279. *31*

Marton, F. (1976) On non-verbatim learning II: the erosion effect of a task induced learning algorithm. *Scandinavian Journal of Psychology,* 17, 41-48. *31*

Marton, F. (1981) Phenomenography - describing conceptions of the world around us. *Instructional Science,* 10pp. (in press) *31*

Marton, F. and Säljö, R. (1976) On qualitative differences in learning I: outcome and process. *The British Journal of Educational Psychology,* 46, 4-11. *31, 32*

Marton, F. and Säljö, R. (1976) On qualitative differences in learning II: outcome as a function of the learner's conception of the task. *The British Journal of Educational Psychology,* 46, 115-127. *31, 32*

Marton, F. and Svensson, L. (1979) Conceptions of research in student learning. *Higher Education,* 8, 4, 471-486. *31, 32*

Marton, F. and Wenestam, C-G (1979) Qualitative differences in the understanding and retention of the main point in some texts based on the principle-example structure. In M.M. Gruneberg, R.E. Morris and R.N. Sykes (eds.) *Practical Aspects of Memory.* London: Academic Press, 644-651. *31*

Morgan, A.R. (1976) The development of project-based learning in the Open University. *Programmed Learning & Educational Technology,* 13, 4, 55-59. *32*

Morgan, A.R. Gibbs, G. and Taylor E. (1981) What do Open University students initially understand about learning? *Study Methods Group Report No.8.* Institute of Educational Technology, Open University. *32*

Northedge, A. (1978) *How to Study: A Guide to Studying at the Open University.* Milton Keynes: Open University. *32*

Orton, L.J. (1977) Completion and non-start rates in correspondence courses. *Canadian Journal of University Continuing Education,* 4, 21-26. *36*

Pantages, T.J. and Creedon, C.F. (1978) Studies of college attrition: 1950-1975. *Review of Educational Research,* 48, 1, 49-101. *36*

Perry, W.G. (1970) *Forms of Intellectual and Ethical Development in the College Years: A Scheme.* New York: Holt, Rinehart & Winston. *31, 32*

Postlethwait, S.N. Novak, J. and Murray, H.T. (1972) *The Audio-Tutorial Approach to Learning.* Minneapolis, Minn.: Burgess Publishing Co. *29*

Pratt, D. (1978) *Cybernetic Principles in the Design of Instruction.* Paper presented at the Annual Meeting of AERA, Toronto, Canada, 1978. *29*

Rogers, C. (1969) *Freedom to Learn.* Columbus, Ohio: Merrill. *32*

Rosenshine, B.V. (1979) Content, time and direct instruction. In Peterson, P.L. and Walberg, H.J. (eds.) *Research on Teaching: Concepts, Findings and Implications.* Berkeley, California: McCutchan. *43*

Rowntree, D. (1977) *Assessing Students: How Shall We Know Them.* London: Harper and Row. *32*

Rumble, G. (1981) Evaluating autonomous multi-media distance learning systems: a practical approach. *Distance Education,* 2, 1, 64-90. *43*

Säljö, R. (1975) *Qualitative Differences in Learning as a Function of the Learner's Conception of the Task.* Göteborg: Acta Universitatis Gothoburgensis. *31*

Säljö, R. (1979) Learning in the learner's perspective I: some commonsense conceptions of learning. *Reports from the Institute of Education,* No. 76, University of Göteborg. *32*

Sewart, D. (1978) Continuity of Concern for Students in a System of Learning at a Distance. Zentrales Institut für Fernstudienforschung Papiere 22, Hagen: Fernuniversität. *36*

Sjogren, B.D and Knox, A.B. (1965) *The Influence of Speed, Attitude and Prior Knowledge on Adult Learning.* Lincoln, Nebraska: Adult Education Research. *29*

Svensson, L. (1976) *Study Skills and Learning.* Göteborg: Acta Universitatis Gothoburgensis. *31*

Svensson, L. (1977) On qualitative differences in learning III: study skill and learning. *The British Journal of Educational Psychology,* 47, 233-243. *31*

Svensson, L. (1981) The concept of study skill (s). Pedagogiska institutionen, Göteborg universitet, 1981:01. *31*

Taylor, E., Gibbs, G. and Morgan, A.R. (1980) The orientations of students studying the Social Science Foundation Course. *Study Methods Group Report No. 7.* Institute of Educational Technology, Open University. *31, 32*

Thorndike, Edward L. et al (1928) *Adult Learning.* New York: Macmillan. *29*

Tinton, V. (1975) Dropout from higher education: a theoretical synthesis of recent research. *Review of Educational Research,* 45, 1, 89-125. *36*

Waniewicz, I. (1976) *Demand for Part-Time Learning in Ontario.* Toronto: Ontario Institute for Studies in Education, for the Ontario Educational Communications Authority. *28*

Bibliography

Wilson, S. (1977) The use of ethnographic techniques in educational research. *Review of Educational Research*, 47, 1, 245-265. **32**

Zeigler, Warren L. (1977) *The Future of Adult Education and Learning in the United States*. New York: Educational Policy Research Centre, Syracuse Research Corporation. **28**

Student Support and Regional Services

Blainey, G. (1966) *The Tyranny of Distance*. Melbourne: Sun Books. **56**

Harris, W.J. (1972) *Home Study Students*. Manchester: Department of Adult Education, University of Manchester. **57**

Jones, H.A. and Charnley, A.H. (1978) Adult literacy, a study of its impact. National Institute of Adult Education Report. **53**

Karmel, P. (ed.) (1976) *Post Secondary Education in Tasmania*. Canberra: Australian Government Publishing Service. **56**

Karmel, P. (ed.) (1981) *Tertiary Education: Commission Report for 1982-84 Triennium Vol. 1 Part 1 Recommendations on Guidelines*. Canberra: Australian Government Publishing Service. **56**

Kelly, P. (1980) How open is the Associate Student Programme? *Teaching at a Distance*, 18, 17-27. **53**

Kolb, D.A. (1976) *Learning Style Inventory*. Self-Scoring Test and Interpretation Booklet. Boston: McBer. **48**

Lewis, Roger (1980) *Counselling in Open Learning: A Case Study*. Cambridge: National Extension College. **57**

Moore, M. (1980) Continuing education and the assessment of learner needs. *Teaching at a Distance*, 17, 25-29. **53**

Northcott, P. (1975) Open tertiary education in Australia: a viewpoint. *Teaching at a Distance*, 4, 21-30. **56**

Rayman, J.R. Bryson, D.L. and Bowlsbey, J.H. (1978) The field trial of discover: a new computerized interactive guidance system. *The Vocational Guidance Quarterly*, June 1978, 349-360. **48**

Sacks, H. (1980) FlexiStudy - an open learning system for further and adult education. *British Journal of Educational Technology*, 2, 11. **57**

Sewart, D. (1978) Academic support and guidance for individuals in a distance learning system. ICCE, Advanced Papers, 1. **53**

Spelthome Adult Education Institute (1981) The Ashford College Study. *Adult Education*, 53, 5. Leicester: National Institute of Adult Education. **57**

Thorpe, M. (1979) When is a course not a course? *Teaching at a Distance*, 16, 13-18. **53**

Vaizey, J. (1969) *Education in the Modern World*. London: Weidenfeld & Nicholson. **56**

Walker, M.N. (1977) Open learning: an Australian experiment in self-paced, personalized, distance education by learning contract. *Australian Journal of Adult Education*, 17, 3, 9-14. **56**

Policy-Making and Management

Bélanger, R. et al (1979) *Un Cours a la Tele-Universite: Guide des opérations de conception et de production*. Montreal: The Télé-université. **71**

Clark, R.E. (1980) Issues in the Transfer of Instructional Technology between Nations. Paper presented at the 24th Annual Conference of the Comparative and International Education Society, Vancouver, B.C., 1980. **65**

Diamond, R.M. et al (1975) *Instructional Development for Individualized Learning in Higher Education*. Englewood Cliffs, N.J.: Educational Technology Publications. **71**

Godfrey, D. (1980) Introduction. In *Gutenberg Two*. Godfrey, D. and Parkhill, D. (eds.) Toronto: Press Porcepic. **65**

Gregor, A. (1979) The re-alignment of post-secondary education systems in Canada. *Canadian Journal of Higher Education*, 9, 2, 35-79. **65**

Griew, S. (1980) A model for the allocation and utilisation of academic staff resources. *Canadian Journal of Higher Education*, 10, 2, 73-84. **62**

Hooper, R. (1977) Evaluation Methodology (Animateurs). In *Evaluating Educational Television and Radio*. Bates, T. and Robinson, J. (eds.) Milton Keynes: The Open University Press. **71**

Jamison, D.T. Klees, S.J. and Wells, S.J. (1978) *The Costs of Educational Media: Guidelines for Planning and Evaluation*. Beverley Hills and London: Sage Publications. **72**

Kaufman, R.A. (1972) *Educational System Planning*. Englewood Cliffs, N.J.: Prentice-Hall. **71**

Keegan, D.J. (1977) Distance education at primary and secondary levels. *ASPESA Newsletter*, 3, 4, 12-17. **78**

Keegan, D.J. (1980) On defining distance education. *Distance Education*, 1, 1, 13-36. **58**

Keegan, D.J. (1981) The Regional Tutorial Services of the Open University: A Case Study. *Ziff Papiere 36*. Hagen: Fernuniversität. **71**

Lewis, B.N. (1971) Course production at the Open University II: activities and activity networks. *British Journal of Educational Technology*, 2. **71**

Perry, W. (1976) *The Open University*. Milton Keynes: The Open University Press. **71**

Pratt, D. (1978) Cybernetic Principles in the Design of Instruction. Paper presented to the Annual Meeting of the American Educational Research Association, Toronto. **71**

Rumble, G. (1976) *The economics of the Open University of the United Kingdom*. Paper presented to Anglian Regional Management College/O.E.C.D. Conference. **62**

Rumble, G. (1981) The cost analysis of distance teaching. Costa Rica's Universidad Estatal a Distancia. *Higher Education*, 10. (forthcoming) **72**

Rumble, G. Neil, M.W. and Tout, A. (1981) Budgetary and resource forecasting. In Kaye, A. and Rumble, G. (1981) *Distance Teaching for Higher and Adult Education*. London: Croom Helm. **72**

Sakamoto, T. (1971) The development of the University of the Air. *Multimedia Systems in Adult Education*. Munchen: Internationales Zentralinstitut für das Jugend-und Bildungsfernsehen. **60**

Sakamoto, T. (1981) *Use of Communication Technology in Distance Teaching at the University and College Level in Japan*. Penang: Regional Symposium on Distance Teaching in Asia. **60**

Sakamoto, T. Ikeda, H. and Muta, H. (1978) The Effect of Radio and TV Experimental Programs in the University of the Air. The Fourth International Conference for Improving University Teaching. Aachen: 1051-1065. **60**

Sakamoto, T. and Fujita, K. (1980) The present state of the University of the Air Project in Japan. *Overseas Universities*, 27, 26-35. **60**

Schramm, W. (1977) *Big Media, Little Media*. Beverley Hills, California: Sage Publications. **65**

Sewart, D. (1980) Creating an information base for an individualized support system in distance education. *Distance Education*, 1. **71**

Sheath, H.C. (ed.) (1972) *Proceedings of a Forum on External Studies*. Armidale: University of New England. **78**

Smith, K.C. (1974) President's message: introducing ASPESA. *ASPESA Newsletter*, 1, 1, 1-3. **78**

Snowden, B.L. and Daniel, J.S. (1980) The economics and management of small post-secondary distance education systems. *Distance Education*, 1, 1, 68-91. **62, 72**

Toffler, A. (1981) *The Third Wave*. New York: Bantam Books. **65**

Unesco (1977) *The Economics of New Educational Media*. Paris: Unesco. **72**

Wagner, L. (1977) The economics of the Open University revisited. *Higher Education*, 6, 359-381. **62, 72**

Wang, W.K.S. (1981) The dissemination of higher education. *Improving College and University Teaching*, 29, 2, 55-60. **65**

Diverse Subjects, Diverse Approaches

Abrioux, D. (1981) Studying French at a distance: a captive Canadian audience. *ICCE Newsletter*, 10, 4, 12-13. *85*

Ashworth, K.H. (1979) Why I have not changed my position. *Phi Delta Kappan*, April, 1979. *97*

Childs, G.B. (1965) Research in the correspondence instruction field. *Proceedings of the Seventh ICEE Conference*, 79-84, Stockholm: ICCE. *97*

Childs, G.B. (1971) Recent research developments in correspondence instruction. In: MacKenzie, O. and Christensen, E.L. (eds.) *The Changing World of Correspondence Study*. University Park: Pennsylvania State University Press. *97*

Cross, N. and Ransome, S. (1977) Survey of a project-based course. *Teaching at a Distance*, 8, 59-61. *97*

Dunn, S.L. (1979) The case of the vanishing colleges. *The Futurist*, October, 385-393. *85*

Graff, K. (1977) Diskussionsvorschläge zum wirtschaftswissenschaftlichen Hauptstudium an der Fernuniversität. *ZIFF-HINWEISE*. Hagen: Fernuniversität. *97*

Granholm, G. (1971) Classroom teaching or home study--a summary of research on relative efficiency. *Epistolodidaktika*, 2, 9-14. *97*

Handal, G. et al (1973) *The Selection of Relevant Media/Methods for Defined Educational Purposes within Distance Education*. EHSC. Oslo: NKI. *97*

Henry, J. (1977) The course tutor and project work. *Teaching at a Distance*, 9, 1-12. *97*

Holmberg, B. (1974) *Distance Education: A Short Handbook*. Malmo,: Hermods. *85*

Holmberg, B. (1977) Das Leitprogramm im Fernstudium. *ZIFF Papiere 17*. Hagen: Fernuniversität. *97*

Holmberg, B. (1977) Die Ergänzung des Fernstudiums durch Nahstudium. *ZIFF Papiere 15*. Hagen: Fernuniversität. *97*

Holmberg, B. (1977) Models and principles of course design. *Epistolodidaktika*, 1, 65-74. *97*

Holmberg, B. (1981) *Status and Trends of Distance Education*. London: Kogan Page. *97*

Ljoså, E. (1975) Why do we make commentary courses? In Granholm, G. (ed.) *The System of Distance Education*, 112-118. Malmo: Hermods. *97*

Ljoså, E. and Sandvold, K. (1979) Hvorfor og hvordan bør vi lage kommentarkurs? *Mellom oss*, 10. Oslo: NKS. *97*

Möhle, H. (1980) *Post-Graduate Further Education by Means of Distance Education in the GDR*. Leipzig: Karl Marx University, Department of Pedagogics. *97*

Pask, G. (1978) New methods of assessment and stronger methods of curriculum design. Final report, Vol. I, IET, Open University. *81*

Peters, O. (1971) Theoretical aspects of correspondence instruction. In Mackenzie, D. and Christensen, E.L. (eds.) *The Changing World of Correspondence Study*. University Park: Pennsylvania State University Press. *97*

Weltner, K. (1977) Die Unterstützung autonomen Lernens im Fernstudium durch integrierende Leitprogramme. *ZIFF-Papiere 17*. Hagen: Fernuniversität. *97*

Wittrock, M.C. (ed.) (1977) *The Human Brain*. Englewood Cliffs, N. J.: Prentice Hall. *81*

The Contribution of Media and Technology to Learning at a Distance

Ausubel, D.P. (1968) *Educational Psychology. A Cognitive View*. New York: Holt, Rinehart & Winston. *118*

Bååth, J.A. (1972) Improving correspondence instruction by means of electronics. *Convergence*, 5, 2, 64-75 *118*

Bååth, J.A. (1979) *Correspondence Education in the Light of a Number of Contemporary Teaching Models*. Malmo: LiberHermods. *118*

Bååth, J.A. (1980) *Postal Two-Way Communication in Correspondence Education*. Malmo: LiberHermods. *113, 118*

Bååth, J.A. and Månsson, N.O. (1977) *CADE - A System for Computer-Assisted Distance Education*. Malmo: Hermods Skola. *118*

Bååth, J.A. and Månsson, N.O. (1978) Our computer corrects student papers and writes individual personal letters to each student. In Wentworth, R.B. (ed.) *Correspondence Education: Dynamic and Diversified*. Volume 1, The Advance Papers. ICCE. 167-174 *118*

Bloom, B.S. Hastings, J. T. and Madaus, G.F. (1971) *Handbook on Formative and Summative Evaluation of Student Learning*. New York: McGraw-Hill. *118*

Boyd, R.D. and Apps, J.W. (1980) *Redefining the Discipline of Adult Education*. Washington: Jossey-Bass. *100*

Bramer, M. (1980) Using computers in distance education: the first ten years of the British Open University. *Computers and Education*, 4, 4, 293-301. *100*

Bruner, J.S. (1960) *The Process of Education*. Cambridge, Mass.: Harvard University Press. *118*

Coffman, W.E. (1969) Achievement tests. In Ebel, R.L. (ed.) (1969) *Encyclopedia of Educational Research*. 4th ed. New York: Macmillan. *118*

DeBloois, M. (1979) Exploring new design models. *Educational and Industrial Television*. *109*

Ebel, R.L. (1965) *Measuring Educational Achievement*. Englewood Cliffs, N.J.: Prentice-Hall. *118*

Edmonds, E. (1980) What next in computer aided learning? *British Journal of Educational Technology*, 11, 2, 98-104. *113*

Flinck, R. (1975) Two-way communication in distance education - an evaluation of various models. *Pedagogical Bulletin*, No. 2. Lund: Department of Education, University of Lund. *118*

Jacoby, H. (1973) *The Bureaucratization of the World*. Translated from the German by Evelyn Kanes. Berkeley: University of California Press. *100*

Lambert, M.P. (ed.) (1977). Workable data processing for home study schools. *NHSC News*, Summer 1977, NHSC News Supplement. *118*

Lampikoski, K. and Mantere, P. (1978) *Final Report of the Distance Education Development Project*. Report 3, The Institute of Marketing, Helsinki. *113*

Leveridge, L. (1979) The potential of interactive optical videodisc systems for continuing education. *Educational and Industrial Television*. *109*

Lovis, F.B. (1975) The Open University's approach to computer education. In *Computers in Education*. (eds.) Lecarme, O. and Lewis, R. New York: North-Holland Pub. Co. *113*

Madden, J. (1979) *Videotex in Canada*. Ottawa: Ministry of Supply and Services. *109*

Nelson, T.H. (1981) *Literary Machines*. Swarthmore: Ted Nelson, Pub. *100*

Papert, Seymour (1980) *Mindstorms*. New York: Basic Books. *100*

Pengelly, R.M. (1974) The student computing service and its future development. *1974 International Conference on Frontiers in Education*. London: The Instituter of Electrical Engineers. *113*

Peters, O. (1973) *Die didaktische Struktur des Fernunterrichts, Untersuchungen zu einer industrialisierten Form des Lehrens und Lernens*. Weinheim: Beltz. *118*

Prisk, D.P. (1981) A central communication network in continuing studies for a university system: a needs assessment. *T.H.E. Journal*, 8, 4, 48-51. *100*

Romiszowski, Alex J. (1981) *Designing Instructional Systems*. London: Kogan Page. *100*

Bibliography

Schümer, R. (1979) *ZIFF-Projekt: CMA-Rechnungswesen. Meinungen von Fernstudenten zum maschinellen Korrekturdienst für den Kurs 'Buchhaltung' im Studienjahr 77/78.* Hagen: Zentrales Institut für Ferstudienforschung, Fernuniversität. *118*

Siegel, A.I. and Wolf, J.J. (1975) Computer analysis of comprehensibility. In *Computers in Education.* (eds.) Lecarme, O. and Lewis, R. New York: North-Holland Pub. Co. *113*

Sigel, E. (ed.) (1980) *Videotext: The Coming Revolution in Home/Office Information Retrieval.* White Plains, N.Y.: Knowledge Industry Publications, Inc. *109*

Skinner, B.F. (1968) *The Technology of Teaching.* New York: Appleton-Century-Crofts. *118*

Strassmann, Paul A. (1980) The office of the future. *Technology Review,* 82, 3, 54-65. *100*

Sustik, Joan M. (1980) Videodisc: A Technical Description. *Pipeline,* Fall. *109*

Zijderfeld, Anton C. (1970) *The Abstract Society.* New York: Doubleday Anchor. *100*

Zorkoczy, P.I. (1974) The computer and the distant learner. *1974 International Conference on Frontiers in Education.* London: The Institute of Electrical Engineers. *113*

Notes on the Contributors

Abrioux, Dominique A.M.X. pioneered the development of French language instruction at a distance in western Canada and is Director of Liberal Studies, Athabasca University, 15015-123 Avenue, Edmonton, Alberta, Canada T5V 1J7.

Anderson, Paul S. is editor of the *ED-DIS Bulletin* published in Spanish and Portuguese. Formerly with the University of New England in Australia he is now professor of geography, Universidade de Brasilia, Brasilia, D.F. 70910, Brasil.

Ansere, Joe K. acquired his own early education by correspondence and is now Vice-Chairman of the African Association for Correspondence Education. He produces courses himself in addition to his duties as Head, Correspondence Education Unit, University of Ghana, P.O. Box 31, Legon, Ghana.

Bååth, John A. is a leading researcher and writer on correspondence education. From 1973 to 1980 he took part in the European Home Study Council's research on two-way communication while continuing his twenty-year association with LiberHermods, 20510 Malmo, Sweden.

Barnes, Neil H. was a part-time adult education lecturer and tutor before joining the BBC in 1965. He is now Senior Education Officer (Continuing Education), Broadcasting House, Portland Place London W1A 1AA, United Kingdom.

Bates, Tony W. joined the Open University at its creation in 1969 and has published extensively on the use of media in that institution. He has been consulted by institutions in Norway, Thailand, India, Philippines, Iran, and Afghanistan and is currently Head, Audio-Visual Media Research Group, Institute of Educational Technology, Open University, Milton Keynes MK7 6AA, United Kingdom.

Bédard, Roger holds a doctorate in education from Laval University. He is currently Director, Social and Cultural Programs, Télé-université, 214 Ave. St-Sacrement, Quebec, Canada G1N 4M6.

Blackmore, D. E. is with the Educational Research Institute of British Columbia, Suite 400, 515 West 10th Ave., Vancouver, B.C., Canada V5Z 4A8.

Bonani, Giampaolo has previously worked with the Accademia Scuola. He is now a consultant with Istituto Teologico per Corrispondenza, via Antonino Pio, 75 Roma, Italy.

Boulianne, Réal G. spent a period of leave in 1981-82 studying educational technology at the University of Montreal. He is with the Office of Part-time Studies, Faculty of Education, McGill University, 3700 McTavish, Montreal, Quebec, Canada H3A 1Y2.

Boyd, Gary M. helped to develop the CAL language NATAL and spent a period of leave with the UK National Development Program in CAL. His original studies were in physics, English and philosophy and he now teaches educational cybernetics as Professor, Graduate Programme in Educational Technology, Concordia University, Montreal, Quebec, Canada H3G 1M8.

Brassard, Mary Lee is a teacher of English who is currently working towards a master's degree in the Graduate Programme in Educational Technology, Concordia University, 1455 de Maisonneuve West, Montreal, Quebec, Canada H3G 1M8.

Brock, Marcia J. trained as a dancer for 16 years and joined the Columbia School of Broadcasting as a file clerk in 1968. In 1980 she was elected President, Columbia School of Broadcasting, P.O. Box 1970, Hollywood, California 90028, U.S.A.

Burcaw, Susan S. was formerly director of University Continuing Education at the University of Idaho and State Coordinator of Correspondence Study. She is now Executive Assistant to the Chancellor, University of California, Santa Cruz, California 95064, U.S.A.

Notes on the Contributors

Caron, Simon trained as a public administrator at the Ecole Nationale d'Administration Publique. Since 1978 he has been Director of Regional Support Services, Télé-université, 214 Ave. St-Sacrement, Quebec, Canada G1N 4M6.

Chapman, Robert S. has a special interest in the continuing education of professionals, having worked in management development in the petroleum industry before entering academic life. He is now Dean, Faculty of Continuing Education, University of Calgary, Calgary, Alberta, Canada T2N 1N4.

Cochran, Bente Roed is a native of Denmark now resident in Canada. She is an active reviewer and critic of the visual arts in addition to her work of recruiting and training telephone tutors at Athabasca University, 15015-123 Ave., Edmonton, Alberta, Canada T5V 1J7.

Coldeway, Dan O. is on the executive of the post-secondary education division of the American Educational Research Association. Holder of a doctorate in psychology he is Director, Instructional Design, Athabasca University, 15015-123 Ave., Edmonton, Alberta, Canada T5V 1J7.

Cowper, Don W. is the Director of Computing Services at Athabasca University. Before coming to the University as an instructional designer, Don worked extensively with text processing and computer-assisted instruction. Current projects include upgrading computer mail and a Telidon field trial at Athabasca University, 15015-123 Avenue, Edmonton, Alberta, Canada T5V 1J7.

Crawford, Douglas G. studied and taught at the University of Toronto before joining Athabasca University as the first head of Instructional Development. He is now responsible for policies to infuse educational technology at the post-secondary level as Director, Learning Systems Branch, Alberta Advanced Education and Manpower, 11160 Jasper Ave., Edmonton, Alberta, Canada T5K 0L1.

Crawford, Gail C. originally trained as a nurse before continuing her studies to the doctoral level at the Universities of Toronto and Alberta. She has designed learning systems and materials in business and medicine and is currently Instructional Developer, Athabasca University, 15015-123 Ave., Edmonton, Alberta, Canada T5V 1J7.

Cumming, Alister has worked on the testing of reading and writing skills for students in academic settings since 1979. Joint author of *Informed Writing*, he teaches at Carleton University and in the TESL Department, Concordia University, 1455 de Maisonneuve West, Montreal, Quebec, Canada H3G 1M8.

Daniel, John S. is program chairman of ICCE. A graduate of the Universities of Oxford and Paris he gained experience at the Open University, the Télé-université and Athabasca University before becoming, in 1980, Vice-Rector, Academic, Concordia University, 1455 de Maisonneuve West, Montreal, Quebec, Canada H3G 1M8.

D'Antoni, Susan G. held appointments at the Ontario Institute for Studies in Education and the Ontario Correspondence Branch before becoming Coordinator, Distance Education, Ryerson Polytechnical Institute, 50 Gould St. Toronto, Ontario, Canada M5B 1E8.

Datt, Ruddar has taught economics at the Universities of Punjab and Delhi for over three decades. He is currently Principal, School of Correspondence Courses and Continuing Education, University of Delhi, 5 Cavalry Lines, Delhi 110007, India.

DeCelles, Pierre is a mathematician who has worked at Laval University and the University of Quebec at Trois Rivières. He was administrator of the Télé-université in 1980-81 and is now Vice-President, Planning and Communications, University of Quebec, 2875 Laurier Bd., Ste-Foy, Quebec, Canada G1V 2M3.

De Milanesi, Susana Buigues has taught and conducted research at several Argentinian universities. After a period with ULSA, she is now an educational counsellor at various institutions in Argentina. ULSA, Independenica 388, Casilla de Correo 9, 1653 Villa Ballester, Buenos Aires, Argentina.

de Moor, Ruud chaired the Royal Commission for the Development of Higher Education and the Open University Planning Committee. He is a member of the Netherlands Academy of Letters and Sciences and professor of sociology at Tilburg University, Delmerweg 23, 5035 Ex Tilburg, Netherlands.

Dichanz, Horst taught in public schools before becoming science advisor at DIFF and then professor at the Fernuniversität, Am Mühlenbach 4, 4403 Senden, West Germany.

Draper, James A. has worked in India and the Caribbean specializing in third world studies, literacy and cross-cultural communication. He is now at the Ontario Institute for Studies in Education, 252 Bloor St. West, Toronto, Ontario, Canada M5S 1V6.

Ellis, G. Barry has spent the last five years developing technology-based continuing education, including a teleconferencing network, as Associate Professor in Distance Education, University of Calgary, Calgary, Alberta, Canada T2N 1N4.

Finkel, Alvin holds a doctorate in history from the University of Toronto and has taught at universities in three Canadian provinces. Since 1978 he has been responsible for the development of history courses at Athabasca University, 15015-123 Ave., Edmonton, Alberta, Canada T5V 1J7.

Foks, Jack G. is an Australian of Swiss origin who taught for twelve years before becoming, in 1978, Head, Victorian TAFE Off-Campus Study Network, RMIT, 167 Franklin Street, Melbourne, Australia.

Forsythe, Kathleen graduated from the Open University in 1974 and was later closely involved with the development of North Island College in British Columbia. She is a part-time graduate student at the Open

Notes on the Contributors

University in addition to her responsibilities as Manager, Learning Systems Development, Knowledge Network of the West, Box 3200, Victoria, B.C., Canada V8W 3H4.

Freeman, Richard is a member of the BBC Continuing Education Advisory Council and the UK Advisory Council on Adult and Continuing Education. He is Executive Director, National Extension College, 18 Brooklands Ave., Cambridge, CB2 2MN, United Kingdom.

Friedman, Zvi is currently investigating the use of microcomputers in the administration of the Open University where he designed several of the early student data systems. He is Senior Systems Analyst, Open University, Milton Keynes, MK7 6AA, United Kingdom.

Fritsch, Helmut is editor of ZIFF-Papiere at the Fernuniversität. After working as a radio journalist he was with DIFF from 1970-75 before taking up his present position as Senior Lecturer, ZIFF, Fernuniversität, Postfach 940 D. 5800 Hagen, West Germany.

Gibbs, Graham was a research fellow at the Open University before becoming Head, Educational Methods Unit, Oxford Polytechnic, Oxford, United Kingdom.

Gitau, Ben K. joined the Correspondence Course Unit of the University of Nairobi in 1974 and specialized in distance education during graduate work at Manchester University. Currently he is Assistant Director, Correspondence Course Unit, University of Nairobi, P.O. Box 30688, Nairobi, Kenya.

Griew, Stephen trained as a psychologist and was Vice-Chancellor of Murdoch University, Australia from 1972-77. After a period at the University of Toronto he became, in 1980, President, Athabasca University, 12352-149 St., Edmonton, Alberta, Canada T5V 1G9.

Grimwade, Jerry E. was President of the Australia and South Pacific External Studies Association for 1981. He is Director of External Studies, Royal Melbourne Institute of Technology, 167 Franklin St., Melbourne, Australia.

Guiton, Patrick is in charge of a coordinating unit with both academic and administrative responsibilities as Director of External Studies, Murdoch University, South Street, Murdoch, 6150 Australia.

Gupta, Arun Kumar is editor of the *Indian Journal of Educational Research* and has published many research papers himself as Director, Research and Training, Model Institute of Education and Research, B.C. Road, Jammu 180001, India.

Hlynka, Denis has co-authored several articles on Telidon and videotex and is an associate professor in the Faculty of Education at the University of Manitoba, Winnipeg, Manitoba, Canada R3T 2N2.

Holbrook, D.W. has conducted school evaluations in 26 countries. Active in both the National Home Study Council and the National University Continuing Education Association he has been, since 1965, President, Home Study Institute, 6940 Carroll Ave., Takoma Park, Washington, D.C. 20012, U.S.A.

Holmberg, Börje was Director General of Hermods, Sweden, before assuming direction of the Fernuniversität Institute for Research into Distance Study. President of ICCE from 1972-1975, Börje is widely acclaimed for his writings on distance learning. Fernuniversität ZIFF, Postfach 940 D 5800 Hagen, West Germany.

Holmes, Nola has taught at primary and pre-school levels and served on various educational committees. She has spent the last three years as Staff Training and Research Officer, New Zealand Technical Correspondence Institute, Private Bag, Lower Hutt, New Zealand.

Horlock, John H. was elected to the Royal Society in 1976. He held professorships at Liverpool University and Cambridge University before his appointment as Vice-Chancellor of Salford University in 1974. In 1980 he became Vice-Chancellor, Open University, Milton Keynes, MK7 6AA, United Kingdom.

Howell, Brenda holds a doctorate from London University. After experience in teaching and journalism she carried out a number of assignments for Unesco before joining the New Zealand Technical Correspondence Institute, Private Bag, Lower Hutt, New Zealand.

Hurly, Paul has published widely in the field of videotex and is currently editing a book on the social impact of computer technology. Coordinator of the Telidon field trial for the University of Manitoba, Paul is an assistant professor in the Continuing Education Division, University of Manitoba, Winnipeg, Manitoba, Canada R3T 2N2.

Hutchinson, Barry is a physicist who has published three textbooks on building science. After teaching at colleges and schools in the UK, he is now Coordinator of Educational Technology, Hong Kong Polytechnic, Hong Kong.

Innes, Sheila is a Governor of the Centre for Information on Language Teaching. A graduate of Oxford University, she joined the BBC World Service in 1953 and is now Head, BBC Further Education, Villiers House, Ealing Broadway, Ealing, London W5, United Kingdom.

Jamison, Dean T. holds degrees in philosophy and engineering from Stanford University and a doctorate in economics from Harvard. He undertakes research on the role of education and communication in development at the World Bank, DEDPH, 1818 H. St. N.W., Washington, D.C. 20433 U.S.A.

Jenkins, Janet is editor of the *ICCE Newsletter.* She worked at the National Extension College until 1975 when she became research and training officer at the International Extension College, 18 Brooklands Ave. Cambridge, CB2 2HN, United Kingdom.

Jevons, Frederic R. became first Vice-Chancellor of Deakin University in 1976. He has published extensively on the philosophy and sociology of science. Deakin University, Victoria 3217, Australia.

Joséph, Andrew H. is the ICCE liaison officer for Latin America. A co-founder and former president of ULSA, he is now educational counsellor at its Argentine headquarters. ULSA, Independenica 388, Casilli de Correo 9, 1653 Villa Ballester, Buenos Aires, Argentina.

Kaye, Anthony R. has wide experience of distance education around the world, including two years directing the evaluation of the Ivory Coast ETV project. Joint editor and contributing author to two recent books on distance education, he is Senior Lecturer in Educational Technology, Open University, Milton Keynes MK7 6AA, United Kingdom.

Keegan, Desmond J. is a member of the ICCE program committee and visited 62 distance education institutions on four continents in 1978-79. He is joint executive editor of *Distance Education* and Head, School of General Studies, Open College of Further Education, 208 Currie St., Adelaide, 5000 Australia.

Kirkinen, Heikki obtained his doctorate from the University of Helsinki and taught for four years at the University of Paris. He joined the University of Joensuu in 1970 and became in 1971 Rector, University of Joensuu, P.O. Box 111, SF-80101 Joensuu 10, Finland.

Knapper, Christopher K. combines the role of teaching resource person with his appointment as Professor of Environmental Studies, University of Waterloo, Waterloo, Ontario Canada N2L 3G1.

Lampikoski, Kari heads the design and implementation of distance teaching projects as Director of Research and Development, Institute of Marketing, Töölöntullinkatu 6, 00250 Helsinki 25, Finland.

Lefranc, Robert has studied at Columbia University and obtained his doctorate from the University of Paris. For thirty-five years he has played a key role in the development of educational technology in France as Director, Centre Audio-Visuel, Ecole Normale Supérieure de Saint-Cloud, Grille d'honneur, Parc de St-Cloud, 92210 St-Cloud, France.

Lewis, Raymond J. did research in Sierra Leone for his doctorate in political science. He is now Director of Research, Center for Learning and Telecommunications, American Association for Higher Education, 1 Dupont Circle, Washington, D.C. 20036, U.S.A.

Lewis, Roger has extensive experience of teaching at all levels and has published a number of articles on distance learning. He has been a staff tutor at the Open University and is now Assistant Director, National Extension College, 18 Brooklands Avenue, Cambridge CB2 2MN, United Kingdom.

Ljoså, Erling was editor of the *ICCE Newsletter* from 1975-78 and was elected Vice-President in 1978. He is Principal, Norsk Korrespondanseskole, Industrigt 41, Oslo 3, Norway.

Loudon, J. Grant saw wartime service in Italy and the Western Desert. He has twice been President of the Association of Correspondence Colleges in South Africa and since 1948 Joint Principal of the Rapid Results College, P.O. Box 1809, Durban, South Africa.

Mackay, Ronald is a graduate of the Universities of Edinburgh and Aberdeen. Joint author of *Informed Writing* he is director of proficiency testing in English (Second Language), Concordia University, 1455 de Maisonneuve West, Montreal, Quebec, Canada H3G 1M8.

Madden, John C. has been involved in the development of Telidon since its early beginnings in a Canadian government laboratory. Co-author of *Gutenberg Two: The New Electronics and Social Change,* he is now President, Microtel Pacific Research Limited, 105-4664 Lougheed Highway, Burnaby, B.C., Canada V5C 5T5.

Mainusch, Herbert chaired a national committee on the continuing education of teachers in West Germany in 1972 and is now chairman of a DIFF advisory committee. He is Professor of English, University of Münster, Johannisstrasse 12-20, 4400 Münster, West Germany.

Marchand, Louise worked as a consultant for the Téléuniversité from 1976 to 1978. She is a Professor of Andragogy in the Department of Education, University of Montreal, Montreal, Quebec, Canada H3C 3J7.

Marquis, Clément worked as a teacher before joining the Télé-université. After heading its office of institutional studies he is now Educational Technologist, Télé-université, 214 Ave. St-Sacrement, Quebec, Quebec, Canada G1N 4M6.

Marton, Ference has, for over twelve years, been engaged in research on learning seen from the learner's perspective. He has published over 50 papers and books and lectured in countries around the world. Currently he is Professor of Education, University of Göteborg, Box 1010, 5-43126 Mölndal, Sweden.

McConnell, David is interested in student learning from media and qualitative approaches to research. Recently he has worked on the CYCLOPS project as Research Fellow, Institute of Educational Technology, Open University, Milton Keynes MK7 6AA, United Kingdom.

Meakin, Denys was the first registrar at the College of the Bahamas and director of admissions at Simon Fraser University before becoming responsible for planning student support systems as Director of Student Services and Registrar, Open Learning Institute, 7671 Alderbridge Way, Richmond, B.C., Canada V6X 1Z9.

Meech, Alan studied oriental languages and history in the United Kingdom and Japan before returning home to his native Canada. Since 1975 he has been responsible for tutorial and regional services at Athabasca University, 15015-123 Ave., Edmonton, Alberta, Canada T5V 1J7.

Notes on the Contributors

Mills, A. Roger first joined the Open University as a part-time tutor in 1971. He has been closely involved with the development of student support services for associate students in his capacity as Senior Counsellor, East Anglia Region, Open University, Cintra House, Hills Rd., Cambridge, United Kingdom.

Misanchuk, Earl R. specialized in instructional development while completing his doctorate at Indiana University. After teaching at universities in Ontario and Alberta he is now Associate Professor, Division of Extension and Community Relations, University of Saskatchewan, Saskatoon, Saskatchewan, Canada S7N 0W0.

Mitchell, Ian McDowall has been on the executive of the Australia and South Pacific External Studies Association since 1975 and is joint executive editor of *Distance Education*. After obtaining broad experience in research, teaching, and chaplaincy in institutions at different levels he is now Head of External Studies, Adelaide College, 46 Kintore Ave., Adelaide 5000, Australia.

Morgan, Alistair holds a doctorate in chemistry. He joined the Open University in 1972 and in 1979 founded the Study Methods Group. He is Lecturer, Institute of Educational Technology, Open University, Milton Keynes MK7 6AA, United Kingdom.

Mugridge, Ian holds degrees from Oxford University and the University of California. He was Chairman of History and Assistant Vice-President (Academic) at Simon Fraser University before taking up his appointment as Dean of Academic Affairs, Open Learning Institute, 7671 Alderbridge Way, Richmond, B.C., Canada V6X 1Z9.

Müller, Klaus began research on the role of face-to-face contact in distance learning while working as a school teacher and later joined DIFF to develop an in-service training program for the academic staff. Konrad-Adenauer-Str. 46, 7407 Rottenburg 1, West Germany.

Nashif, Abdul Malik is responsible for pre-service and in-service teacher education in Jordan, Lebanon, Syria, West Bank, and the Gaza Strip as Chief, Teacher and Higher Education Division, UNRWA/Unesco Department of Education, P.O. Box 484 Amman, Jordan.

Nicolini, Luis has published extensively on video technology and university ETV and organized the first international seminar held in South America on this topic in 1972. Currently he is Executive Secretary of PIUTEC, Casilla 380, Quilpue, Chile.

Noyau, Kenneth has produced and directed educational programs in radio, television and film and worked as a Unesco advisor in Haiti. A native of Mauritius, he joined the Mauritius College of the Air in 1972 and became director in 1974. Unesco/UNDP, B.P. 557, Port-au-Prince, Haiti.

Orivel, François specializes in the economics of human resources at the French National Centre for Scientific Research. He has worked as a consultant to the World Bank and Unesco. 67, rue Vannerie, 21000 Dijon, France.

Ottem, Bernt Johan has played an important role in coordinating musical resources in northern Norway and working with amateur musicians. He joined the North Norwegian Conservatory of Music in 1971 and has been its headmaster since 1976. Gammelgardveien 34, N-9020 Tromsdalen, Norway.

Paul, Ross has taught at all levels in the public school system and university, and has been a senior administrator at Dawson College in Montreal. Ross pursues his hobby of writing musical revues while fulfilling his duties as Vice-President (Learning Services), Athabasca University, 15015-123 Avenue, Edmonton, Alberta, Canada T5V 1J7.

Penberthy, John has taught at a number of elementary schools in rural Australia and at Schools of the Air in Ceduna and Alice Springs. He is Deputy Principal, South Australian Correspondence School, 64 Pennington Terrace, North Adelaide 5006, Australia.

Penney, Marg has been interested in content analysis since she experimented with PSI in an introductory course and studied instructional design at McGill University. She has been instrumental in the redevelopment of an off-campus nursing program as Coordinator of Instructional Development, Grant MacEwan Community College, 7319-29 Ave., Edmonton, Alberta, Canada T6K 2P1.

Perraton, Hilary has worked in distance education since 1964 with the National Extension College and, since 1971, as co-director, International Extension College, 18 Brooklands Ave., Cambridge CB2 2HN, United Kingdom.

Peters, Otto is a member of the executive committee of ICCE. After a distinguished career as professor of education he became, in 1975, Founding Rector of the Fernuniversität, Feithstr. 152, 58 Hagen, West Germany.

Phillips, C. Alex was a teacher and administrator before becoming, in 1966, Assistant Director, Centre for Independent Study, University of Missouri, 515 South Fifth St., Columbia, Missouri 65211, U.S.A.

Potter, Geoffrey is interested in the social effects of mass communication systems. He is Faculty Coordinator of Distance Education, University of Victoria, P.O. Box 1700, Victoria, B.C., Canada V8W 2Y2.

Rande, Hjalmar was secretary of the interim board that planned the Norwegian State Institution for Distance Education (NFU) and has been managing director of the new institution since its creation in 1979. Norsk Fjernundervisning Prinsens gt. 6, Oslo 1, Norway.

Rebel, Karlheinz is professor of education, University of Tübingen and Managing Director of DIFF, 74 Tübingen, Wohrdstr. 8, West Germany.

Rekkedal, Torstein is a graduate of the University of Oslo. He has been, since 1972, Director of Research and Development, NKI Skolen, P.O. Box 10, N-1321 Stabekk, Norway.

Ruggles, Robin is International Projects Officer with the Educational Research Institute of British Columbia, Suite 400, 515 West 10th Ave., Vancouver, B.C., Canada V5Z 4A8.

Rumble, Greville has worked and advised on distance education projects in Columbia, Costa Rica, Iran, Nicaragua, and Venezuela as a member of the Centre for International Cooperation and Services, Open University, Milton Keynes MK7 6AA, United Kingdom.

Sakamoto, Takashi has authored numerous papers on educational technology and learning psychology. He is a professor at the National Centre for the Development of Broadcast Education and Professor of Educational Methods, Tokyo Institute of Technology, 2-12-1 Ohokayama, Meguro-Ku, Tokyo 152, Japan.

Salter, Don L. has prospected for diamonds in Tanzania and sailed his own yacht across the Atlantic. A university teacher of geology for ten years he joined North Island College in 1976 and operated mobile units before his appointment as Coordinator of Research and Development, North Island College, 156 Manor Drive, Comox, B.C., Canada V9N 6P7.

Schimeck, Wolfgang taught high school in southern Alberta before joining ACCESS in 1976. He is now Associate Director, Field Services, ACCESS Alberta, 16930-114 Ave., Edmonton, Alberta, Canada T5M 3S2.

Sewart, David is a member of the program committee of ICCE. After training in classics at the University of Hull he joined the Open University in 1972 and played a key role in the development and coordination of student support services. He is now Regional Director, North West Region, Open University, 70 Manchester Rd., Chorlton-cum-Hardy, Manchester MZ1 1PQ, United Kingdom.

Shah, Gunvant B. is President of the Indian Association for Educational Technology and writes lyrical essays, novels and poems in addition to his responsibilities as Head, Department of Education, South Gujarat University, Surat 395 007, India.

Shale, Douglas G. is a specialist in evaluation who has been with Athabasca University since 1976. He is now Head, Institutional Studies, Athabasca University, 12352-149 St., Edmonton, Alberta, Canada T5V 1G9

Shobe, Charles R. holds a doctorate in biochemistry. Since 1975 he has held a number of appointments at Athabasca University where he is now Associate Director, Regional and Tutorial Services, Athabasca University, 15015-123 Ave., Edmonton, Alberta, Canada T5V 1G7.

Singer, Louise is Treasurer of ICCE and active in the National Home Study Council as well as several community organizations. She is Secretary, Treasurer and Director of Education, National Home Study Schools, 60 Brandon Ave., Wayne, New Jersey 07470, U.S.A.

Singh, Bakhshish is President of ICCE. Active on various committees of the University Grants Commission he was founding President of the National Council for Correspondence Education in India. He is Director, Correspondence Courses, Punjabi University, Patiala, India.

Small, Ian W. was himself an external student and taught for eleven years in secondary schools. After joining as a graduate assistant in 1972 he is now Student Services Coordinator, Department of External Studies, University of New England, Armidale N.S.W. 2351, Australia.

Smith, Kevin C. was the Founding President of the Australia and South Pacific External Studies Association, and chosen by ICCE as the 1982 Broady Lecturer. He has been with the University of New England for nearly twenty years and is now Director, Department of External Studies, University of New England, Armidale, N.S.W. 2351, Australia.

Smith, Ralph C. is a member of the Council for National Academic Awards (UK). He joined the Open University as professor of mathematics in 1969 and became Pro-Vice-Chancellor (Planning) in 1971. He is now Pro-Vice-Chancellor (Continuing Education), Open University, P.O. Box 188, Milton Keynes MK3 6HW, United Kingdom.

Stephens, Doris T. has published a book on Latin American poetry as well as book reviews and journal articles. After teaching French and Spanish at secondary and university levels she is now Resident Instructor, Division of Continuing Education, University of Tennessee, Knoxville, Tennessee 37916, U.S.A.

Stringer, Muriel H.L. has been closely involved in the design and evaluation of French courses as Instructional Developer, Athabasca University, 15015-123 Ave., Edmonton, Alberta, Canada T5V 1J7.

Stroud, Martha A. is a member of the editorial committee of ICCE. She worked at Athabasca University before moving to Calgary where she is raising a family and holding a part-time appointment in the Office of the Vice-President (Academic) University of Calgary, Calgary, Alberta, Canada T2N 1N4.

Sullivan, Keith C. is Coordinator, Continuing Education, Atlantic Institute of Education, 5244 South St., Halifax, N.S., Canada B3J 1A4.

Svensson, Lennart has conducted empirical research on the learning and study activity of university students. Formerly with the University of Göteborg he is now Senior Research Fellow, Swedish Council for Research in the Humanities and Social Sciences, Stockholm, Sweden.

Tait, Alan W. worked at the headquarters of the Open University before moving to a regional office. He has been active in the creation of continuing education courses for local need as Senior Counsellor, East Anglia Region, Open University, Cintra House, Hills Rd., Cambridge, United Kingdom.

Taylor, Elizabeth trained as a sociologist and is working on her doctorate as Research Assistant, Institute of Educational Technology, Open University, Milton Keynes MK7 6AA, United Kingdom.

Taylor, James C. heads a team of twelve instructional designers and course assistants as Senior Lecturer, Darling Downs Institute of Advanced Education, Toowomba, Queensland 4350, Australia.

Tesarowski, Chet has taught in schools in Canada and Malaysia. Since 1972 he has been responsible for various important developments at the Correspondence School Branch, Department of Education, 528 St. James St., Winnipeg, Manitoba, Canada R3G 3J4.

Thompson, John R. has a background in conventional university teaching in English literature and is currently an editor at Athabasca University, 15015-123 Ave., Edmonton, Alberta, Canada T5V 1J7.

Trillo, Eloísa has training in mathematics and educational technology. She is particularly interested in audience research and materials evaluation as Chief, Evaluation Unit, National Institute of Tele-education, San Eugenio H 103, Lima 14, Peru.

Walker, Mike trained as a biologist and worked for a number of years at the Western Australia Institute of Technology. His interest in the development of appropriate learning systems for small isolated communities is pursued in his capacity as Director, North West Council for Community Education, P.O. Box 447 Burnie, Tasmania 7320, Australia.

Waniewicz, Ignacy was the founder and head of educational programming of the Polish National Television Network before moving to Canada in 1969. He has published numerous works in print, film and television and is now Director, Office of Development Research, Ontario Educational Communications Authority, Box 200, Station Q, Toronto, Ontario, Canada M4T 2T1.

Wasylycia-Coe, Mary Ann trained as a sociologist and works as tutor, marker and research consultant, Teaching Resource Office, University of Waterloo, Waterloo, Ontario Canada, N2L 3G1.

Weaver, Graham H. has been involved in the development of a number of courses on materials and technology. He is Senior Lecturer, Faculty of Technology, Open University, Milton Keynes MK7 6AA, United Kingdom.

White, Vernon J. worked as an economist before becoming Head, Department of External and Continuing Education, Darling Downs Institute of Advanced Education, Toowomba, Queensland 4350, Australia.

Woodley, Alan has evaluated the appropriateness of distance learning for school-leavers and investigated student drop-out in the context of his wider interest in mature students. He is Research Fellow, Survey Research Department, Open University, Milton Keynes MK7 6AA, United Kingdom.

Young, David M. is Past President of ICCE and is active in the European Home Study Council. He studied by correspondence himself and has spent over 30 years managing and developing the Rapid Results College. He is now Principal, Rapid Results College, Tuition House, London SW19 4DS, United Kingdom.

Young, Roger G. directed correspondence units at the Universities of Nebraska and Minnesota before becoming, in 1979, Director, Centre for Independent Study, University of Missouri, 515 South Fifth St., Columbia, Missouri 65211, U.S.A.

Author Index

Authors mentioned in papers and introductions to sections are listed alphabetically below. The paper numbers are given in boldface.

A

A'Aeth, R. *12*
Abrioux, D. *80, 85, 99*
Adams, D. *17*
Ahlm, M. *7*
Ahmed, M. *12*
Akuffo, F. *12*
Alegria, P. *17*
Anderson, L. *43*
Anderson, N. *4*
Anderson, P. *11, 18, 99*
Anderson, T. *6*
Ansere, J. *11, 12, 58, 80, 99*
Asheim, L. *17*
Ashworth, K. *97*
Aslanian, C. *28*
Aspy, D. *6*
Ausubel, D. *7, 118*

B

Bååth, J. *1, 6, 7, 26, 27, 99, 113, 118*
Bacsich, P. *2*
Barnes, N. *58, 99*
Barratt-Brown, J. *4*
Bates, A. *1, 2, 8, 58, 99*
Beck, P. *6*
Becker, M. *32*
Bédard, R. *58*
Bekoe, D. *12*
Bélanger, R. *71*
Berliner, D. *43*
Bertalanffy, L. *71*
Bewley, D. *78*
Black, D. *105*
Blainey, G. *56*
Bleed, W. *12*
Bloom, B. *6, 29, 43, 118*
Bonani, G. *1, 4, 11, 80*
Born, D. *6*

Boshier, R. *6*
Botkin, J. *9*
Boulianne, R. *80, 99*
Bowles, S. *4*
Boyd, G. *99*
Boyd, R. *100*
Bradley, A. *6*
Bramer, M. *100*
Brew, A. *31*
Briggs, L. *34*
Brittain, C. *118*
Brock, M. *58*
Brown, M. *6*
Bruner, J. *7, 118*
Burcaw, S. *58*
Butler, R. *9*
Buzan, T. *81*

C

Calder, J. *53*
Campbell-Platt, K. *12*
Caron, S. *45*
Carp, A. *6*
Carroll, J. *43*
Chaucer, G. *99*
Childs, G. *6*
Childs, G. *97*
Clark, R. *65*
Clennell, S. *5*
Cochran, B. *27, 45, 99*
Coffman, W. *118*
Coldeway, D. *1, 6, 27, 58*
Connors, B. *36, 43*
Contreras, L. *17*
Coombs, P. *12, 31*
Cowper, D. *99*
Crawford, D. *58*
Crawford, G. *6*
Crawford, J. *6*

Creaner, R. *6*
Cronbach, L. *6, 29*
Cropley, A. *4*
Cross, N. *97*
Cross, P. *28*
Csikszentmihalyi, M. *31*
Cumming, A. *80*

D

D'Antoni, S. *99*
Dahlgren, L. *31, 32*
Daniel, J. *4, 8, 11, 43, 58*
Datt, R. *11, 58, 80, 99*
Davidson, G. *26*
Davies, E. *4*
Davies, W. *4*
Davis, K. *53*
DeBloois, M. *109*
DeCelles, P. *58*
Dei, M. *4*
de Moor, R. *11, 58, 80, 99*
Dewey, J. *29*
Diamond, R. *71*
Dichanz, H. *58, 99*
Dick, W. *6*
Dodds, T. *10*
Donehower, J. *6*
Draper, J. *1, 9, 11, 27, 58, 80, 99*
Dubin, R. *6*
Dunn, S. *85*
Durbridge, N. *2*

E

Ebel, R. *118*
Eckblad, G. *31*
Edmonds, E. *113*
Egan,. *7*
Eicher, J. *72*
Ellis, G. *58, 99*

325

Author Index

Ellis, G. *105*
Elton, L. *6*
Engstrom, E. *71*
Entwistle, N. *4, 32*
Erdos, R. *4, 112*
Escotet, M. *18*
Essex, D. *6*

F

Fakes, J. *4*
Falkenberg, E. *9*
Faure, E. *4*
Fawcett, S. *6*
Feather, F. *9*
Filstead, W. *32*
Finkel, A. *27, 58, 99*
Flammer, G. *6*
Flinck, R. *118*
Foks, J. *58, 80*
Forsythe, K. *27, 80*
Foster, T. *75*
Fredrick, W. *43*
Freeman, R. *4, 11, 27, 45, 58*
Friedman, Z. *58, 99*
Fritsch, H. *45, 99*

G

Gaff, J. *6*
Gagné, R. *7, 26, 34, 38*
Gall, M. *6*
Gattulo, M. *4*
Geertz, C. *31*
Geis, G. *6*
Gibbs, G. *4, 31*
Gitau, B. *1, 11, 27, 80*
Glatter, R. *6*
Glick, D. *6*
Glynne, D. *36*
Godfrey, D. *65*
Gough, J. *43*
Gowin, B. *7*
Gozzer, G. *4*
Graff, K. *6, 97*
Grahm, A. *6, 118*
Granholm, G. *6, 97*
Grant, D. *6*

Gregor, A. *65*
Griew, S. *27, 58, 62, 80*
Grimwade, J. *58*
Guiton, P. *58*
Gupta, A. *11*

H

Hakemulder, J. *8*
Haley, A. *30*
Handal, G. *97*
Harnischfeger, A. *43*
Harper, W. *6, 49*
Harrington, F. *6, 9*
Harris, W. *4*
Harris, W. *6*
Harris, W. *57*
Hays, R. *6*
Henneberry, J. *6*
Henry, J. *97*
Hodgson, V. *31*
Hoffsinger, J. *75*
Holbrook, D. *58*
Holmberg, B. *4, 6, 27, 58, 80, 85, 97*
Holmes, N. *27, 80*
Hooper, R. *71*
Horlock, J. *58, 58, 80, 99*
Hornick, R. *6*
Howell, B. *58, 80*
Hugdahl, E. *105*
Hurly, P. *99*
Husen, T. *4*
Hutchinson, B. *11*

I

Illich, I. *12*
Ingle, H. *17*
Innes, S. *80, 99*

J

Jacoby, H. *100*
Jamison, D. *72*
Jenkins, G. *71*
Jenkins, J. *26, 58, 80*
Jevons, F. *27, 58*
Johnson, K. *6*
Jolly, R. *12*

Jones, H. *53*
Joséph, A. *11, 27, 58*
Joyce, B. *7*

K

Karmel, P. *56*
Karow, W. *4, 8, 23*
Kaufman, R. *71*
Kaye, A. *8, 12, 27, 58, 80, 99, 112*
Kazdin, A. *43*
Keegan, D. *1, 8, 58, 71, 78*
Keller, F. *6, 29*
Kelly, H. *6*
Kelly, P. *53*
Kennedy, D. *4*
Kersteins, G. *6*
Kifer, E. *43*
Kings, C. *97*
Kinsela, H. *17*
Kirkinen, H. *45, 58*
Knapper, C. *27, 58*
Knowles, M. *6, 29*
Knox, A. *29*
Kolb, D. *48*
Kulik, J. *6, 43*

L

Laidlaw, B. *12, 43*
Lambert, M. *118*
Lampikoski, K. *7, 99, 113*
Larson, A. *6*
Lee, G. *9*
Lefranc, R. *27, 99*
Leveridge, L. *109*
Lewis, B. *71*
Lewis, R.J. *99*
Lewis, R. *6, 27, 45, 57*
Ljoså, E. *6, 11, 27, 58, 97*
Lloyd, K. *6*
Loring, R. *105*
Loudon, J. *58, 80*
Lovis, F. *113*
Lybeck, L. *31*

M

MacIntosh, N. *6*
Mackenzie, N. *4*
Mackenzie, O. *6, 26*
Madden, J. *99, 109*
Mainusch, H. *58, 99*
Malley, J. *6*
Marchand, L. *80*
Marton, F. *27, 31, 32, 80*
Matheison, D. *6*
Mathis, B. *7*
Maturi, I. *10*
McBride, J. *17*
McClusky, H. *4*
McConnell, D. *2, 99*
McDonald, R. *4*
McKeachie, W. *6*
Meakin, D. *45, 58*
Menal, J. *4*
Merrill, P. *6*
Mills, A. *45, 58*
Misanchuk, E. *27, 99*
Mitchell, I. *58*
Möhle, H. *97*
Monstain, B. *6*
Moore, M. *7, 53*
Morgan, A. *27, 32, 80*
Mugridge, I. *58, 80*
Muller, K. *27*
Mungai, J. *10*

N

Nashif, A. *80*
Nelson, T. *100*
Nicolini, L. *11, 18, 58*
Nicolson, N. *4*
Noffsinger, J. *75*
Northcott, P. *6, 56*
Northedge, A. *32*
Noyau, K. *11, 58*

O

Orivel, F. *27, 58, 99*
Orton, L. *6, 36*
Ottem, B. *80*

P

Page, E. *6*
Pagney, B. *4, 8*
Pantages, T. *6, 36*
Papert, S. *100*
Parker, L. *105*
Pask, G. *81*
Patterson, R. *6*
Penberthy, J. *11, 27, 58, 80*
Pengelly, R. *113*
Penney, M. *27, 58, 80*
Perraton, H. *1, 3, 32, 58, 99*
Perry, W. *31, 32, 71, 112*
Peruniak, G. *6*
Peters, O. *5, 6, 8, 11, 27, 58, 97, 118*
Petrussa, E. *6*
Porter, E. *53*
Postlethwait, S. *29*
Potter, G. *58*
Pratt, D. *29, 71*
Prisk, D. *100*

R

Ramón-Fernandez, T. *18*
Rande, H. *58, 80*
Rayman, J. *48*
Rebel, K. *58*
Redmond, M. *4*
Reimer, E. *12*
Rekkedal, T. *27, 58*
Richardson, M. *4*
Robertson, C. *12*
Robinson, B. *2*
Rogers, C. *7, 32*
Romiszowski, A. *100*
Rosenshine, B. *43*
Rothkopf, E. *7*
Rowntree, D. *32*
Ruggles, R. *80, 99*
Rumble, G. *12, 43, 58, 62, 72*
Ruskin, J. *40*

S

Sacks, H. *57*
Sakamoto, T. *58, 60, 99*
Säljö, R. *31, 32*
Salter, D. *45, 58*
Sarramona, J. *4*
Savins, D. *6*
Schimeck, W. *80, 99*
Schlager, K. *71*
Schramm, W. *17, 65*
Schreve, B. *6*
Schruhm, A. *26*
Schümer, R. *118*
Schwartz, G. *6*
Searle, B. *17*
Sewart, D. *1, 4, 5, 27, 36, 45, 53, 71*
Shah, G. *80, 99*
Shale, D. *6, 27, 36*
Shapovalenko, G. *4*
Sheath, H. *36, 78*
Shobe, C. *58*
Short, J. *105*
Siegel, A. *113*
Sigel, E. *109*
Singer, L. *27, 45*
Singh, B. *11, 58, 80, 99*
Sjogren, D. *6*
Sjogren, B. *29*
Skinner, B. *7, 118*
Smith, K. *27, 45, 78*
Smith, P. *6*
Smith, R. *58, 80, 99*
Smock, A. *12*
Snow, R. *6*
Snowden, B. *62, 72*
Sorensen, L. *112*
Sparkes, J. *97*
Spaulding, S. *17*
Spencer, R. *6*
Stein, L. *6*
Stephens, D. *80, 99*
Stone, G. *4*
Strassmann, P. *100*
Stringer, M. *80, 99*
Sullivan, K. *58, 80*
Sustik, J. *109*
Svensson, L. *31*

Author Index

T

Taylor, E. *31, 32*
Tesarowski, C. *27*
Thitu, P. *10*
Thorndike, E. *29*
Thorpe, M. *53*
Tinton, V. *36*
Tobias, S. *6*
Toffler, A. *65*
Toft, R. *6*
Tosti, T. *6*
Tough, A. *6*
Trillo, E. *11, 58*
Trivellato, U. *4*

V

Vaizey, J. *56*
Valero, L. *17*
Van Eck, E. *4*
Villarroel, A. *18*
Von Humboldt, F. *68*

W

Wagner, L. *3, 12, 62, 72*
Walker, M. *45, 56, 58*
Wang, W. *65*
Wangdahl, A. *6*
Waniewicz, I. *27, 28, 80, 99*
Watts, G. *4*
Weaver, G. *80*
Wedemeyer, C. *6*
Weinstock, N. *4, 23*
Weltner, K. *97*
Wentworth, R. *8*
White, M. *6*
White, R. *3*
White, V. *27*
Whitehead, A. *100*
Wiedhaup, C. *6*
Williams, E. *6*
Williams, V. *6*
Wilson, J. *6*
Wilson, S. *32*
Wilson, W. *6*
Wittrock, M. *81*
Woodley, A. *27*
Worthington, R. *26*

Y

Young, D. *27, 58*
Young, M. *3, 8*
Young, R. *27, 99*

Z

Ziegel, W. *6*
Ziegler, W. *28*
Zijderfeld, A. *100*
Zorkoczy, P. *113*

Subject Index

The items in this index are listed alphabetically with the number(s) of the paper in which they appear.

A

Abo Academi: *52*
ABT (Brazilian Association for Education Technology): *18*
academic equivalency: *105*
Accademia: *11*
Accelerated Primary and Open High School (Mexico): *17*
acceleration theory: *43*
access to education: *12, 22, 24, 25, 59*
accountancy: *20, 43*
accreditation: *18, 58, 74, 75, 76, 95*
Achimota Secondary School (Ghana): *12*
ACPH: *3*
ACPO: *3*
ADCIS (see Association for the Development of Computer-Based Systems)
Addis Ababa: *12, 21*
Adelaide College of Advanced Education: *26*
administration: *57, 58, 66, 73, 74*
administration, :
    computer applications 112, 113
administrative data processing: *112, 113*
administrators: *71*
admission: *36, 112*
adult basic education: *61, 107*
adult education, :
    models 100
adult education theory: *94*
adult illiteracy: *9*
adult learning theory: *29*
advance organizer: *7*
advertising: *58, 76, 77*
affective education: *80, 94*
Africa: *1, 4, 12, 21, 80*
African Association for Correspondence Education: *8*
agrarian reform: *18*
Air Correspondence High School (South Korea): *44*
Akita University: *60*
Alberta: *9, 25, 86*
Alice Springs: *26*
All Japan Association of Private Correspondence Education: *60*
alumni, :
    role of 47
American Association for Higher Education: *116*
American Broadcasting Corporation: *111*
American Telephone and Telegraph: *101*
andragogy: *29, 94*
Andres Bello: *18*
animateurs: *10, 51*
Antiope: *101, 109*

aptitude-treatment interaction: *6, 29*
Arctic: *91*
Aregon International: *115*
Argentina: *18, 19, 20*
Asia: *4, 21*
ASPESA (see Australian and South Pacific External Studies Association):
assessment criteria: *82*
assessment of students: *6, 32, 105*
assignments: *74*
assignments, :
    marking 15
    computer-marked 53
Association for the Development of Computer-Based Systems: *100*
Athabasca University: *2, 6, 8, 28, 30, 36, 50, 61, 62, 66, 71, 72, 85, 86, 87, 117*
Atlantic Institute of Education: *98*
AT&T (see American Telephone and Telegraph):
attrition: *6, 36, 37, 38*
audio cassettes: *2, 9, 15, 49, 50, 60, 83, 87, 88, 92, 104, 115*
audio cassettess: *99*
audio-visual media: *1, 2, 26, 52, 54, 59, 99*
Australasia: *83*
Australia: *1, 5, 8, 12, 26, 42, 43, 45, 56, 58, 59, 62, 68, 69, 78, 97, 101*
Australian and South Pacific External Studies Association: *58, 78*
Australian Universities Commission: *62*
authors: *58*
authors, :
    training of 80, 84

B

Bachelor of Arts Degree: *42*
Bahia Madureza (Brazil): *44*
Baltimore: *26*
bank employees: *93*
banking industry: *16*
Barnet College of Further Education: *57*
behaviourism: *7*
Belgium: *4, 107*
billing: *113*
Bolivia: *19*
Brazil: *11, 18, 19, 20, 44*
Brigham Young University: *97*
British Broadcasting Corporation: *80, 81, 86, 88, 96, 99, 106*
British Columbia: *45, 54, 55, 61, 101*
British Telecom: *115*
broadcasting: *1, 3, 9, 58, 60, 72, 99, 101, 103, 106, 108*

Subject Index

broadcasting, :
  audience use *2*
  organizations *2*
  times of *2*
  radio *5*
  television *5*
budgetary models: *72*
bureaucracy: *100*
bureaucracy, :
  as societal mechanism *100*
business education: *20, 80, 93*

C

cable television: *2, 91*
Calvert School: *26*
Cambridge: *57*
Cambridge University: *68, 88*
Canada: *8, 25, 26, 28, 51, 54, 58, 61, 65, 70, 73, 80, 91, 94, 97, 98, 100, 109, 110*
Canadian Broadcasting Corporation: *108*
Cantonese: *22*
Capricorn Interuniversity Program: *11, 18, 19*
Carkhuff Associates: *50*
Carnegie Corporation: *75*
case studies: *90*
cash limits: *72*
Ceara ETV (Brazil): *44*
Ceefax: *2*
Centre National de Télé-enseignement: *4, 8*
Centres de Télé-enseignement Universitaire: *104*
certification of staff: *21*
certification of students: *21*
children, :
  education of *11, 27*
Chile: *18, 19*
China: *9, 44*
Cloze Procedure: *35*
cognitivism: *7*
Colombia: *18*
Columbia School of Broadcasting: *77*
combined education: *21, 23, 95*
communication, :
  two-way *7, 101, 108, 109*
communication skills: *34*
communities: *100*
community education: *107*
community liaison: *55*
completion rates: *3, 6, 30, 36, 37, 38, 40, 55, 61, 85, 86, 87, 114, 118*
compulsory school attendance: *4*
computer literacy: *106*
computer marking: *27, 113, 114*
computer-assisted instruction: *60, 95, 99, 100, 101, 110, 118*
computer-assisted learning: *100*
computer-assisted lesson service: *114*
computer-generated letter: *67, 108*
computerized instruction: *59*
computer-managed instruction: *100*

computer-managed learning: *108*
computer-marked assignment: *112*
computers: *65, 99, 109, 117*
computers, :
  administrative uses *112, 113*
  integrated uses *113*
  personal *2*
  effect in business *93*
computing, :
  costs *112*
  teaching of *42*
concentric method: *85*
conceptions of learning: *32*
concepts, :
  differentiation *31*
Concordia University: *100*
Conservatoire National des Arts et Mètiers: *104*
consumer education: *107*
consumer legislation: *8*
content analysis: *34*
content structure, :
  atomistic *31*
  deep *31, 32*
  holistic *31*
  surface *31, 32*
continuing education: *95*
conversation: *89*
conversational skills: *87*
cooperation: *64, 65, 67, 106*
cooperation, :
  inter-institutional *58*
cooperative movement: *51*
cooperative projects: *2, 18, 19*
Correspondence College (Malawi): *44*
correspondence courses, :
  enrolment reasons *40*
  in schools *40*
  perceptions *40*
correspondence study, :
  terminology *76*
cost function: *72*
cost study: *72*
Costa Rica: *8, 17, 18*
cost-effectiveness: *12, 21, 27, 44, 58, 109*
costs: *3*
costs, :
  capital *12*
  recurrent *12*
  institutional *2*
  student *2*
  distance vs. conventional *27*
  fixed and variable *62*
  traditional vs. distance *65*
counselling: *4, 6, 20, 27, 49, 53, 55, 61*
counselling, :
  computerized *45, 48*
  postal *48*
counsellors: *5, 10, 50*
counsellors, :
  training *20*
course authors: *15*

course design: *30, 34, 49, 85*
course development: *12, 13, 15, 26, 42, 45, 52, 53, 59, 61, 69, 70*
course production: *58, 65, 68, 84, 117*
course revision: *15*
course teams: *58, 68, 69, 70, 94, 96, 107, 117*
courses, :
    duration 15
courses by newspaper: *8*
craft skills, :
    teaching of 95
creativity: *94*
credit system: *59*
credit transfer: *61*
Cuba: *9*
curriculum: *1, 60*
cybernetic models: *29*
CYCLOPS: *2, 99, 115*

D

Dag Hammarskjold Foundation: *12*
data processing: *112, 113*
Deakin University: *42, 62*
democratization of education: *4, 11*
demographic patterns: *28*
Denmark: *107*
Deutsches Institut für Fernstudien: *8, 33, 58, 64*
Developing Countries Farm Radio Network: *9*
developing nations: *1, 11, 12, 14, 17, 21, 78, 80, 99*
dialogue: *89*
DIFF (see Deutsches Institut für Fernstudien)
differentiation of concepts: *31*
disabilities, :
    education 106
disadvantaged populations: *107*
discovery learning: *7*
distance education, :
    centralization 13
    graduate study 18
    professional associations 21
    status 21
    integration with traditional 23
    interdisciplinarity 24
    history 26
    models 57
    methodology 6
    public image 76
    international organization 79
    characteristics 8
distance educators, :
    self-image 15
Dominican Republic: *44*
drop-out rates, :
    effect of age 38
    seasonal effects 38
drop-outs: *1, 4, 6, 10, 11, 14, 20, 27, 30, 36, 37, 39, 48, 53, 57, 80, 88, 91*

E

East Europe: *4*
East Germany: *4, 97*
economic model: *72*
Ecuador: *18*
editing: *117*
Editora Abril: *18*
editors, :
    role 30
education, :
    traditional vs. distance 5, 6, 12, 13, 14, 15, 39, 43, 97, 105
    cooperation 11, 18, 19
    democratization of 4, 11, 13
    levels 12
    standard of living 12
    state role 21, 25
    access to 22, 24, 25
    conflict 22
    language of instruction 22
    training vs. pure education 22
    models 23
    funding 25
educational access: *55*
educational attainment: *28*
educational discrimination: *4*
educational funding: *65, 68, 71, 75*
educational hardware: *16*
educational network: *65*
educational policy: *25*
educational policy: *23*
educational psychology: *27, 29*
educational research: *6*
educational technology: *9, 11, 18, 19, 21, 22, 26, 65, 99*
educational technology, :
    survey 116
El Salvador: *11, 17*
electronic community: *99*
electronic mail: *101, 109*
elementary education: *80*
elementary students: *4, 26*
employers,:
    selling courses to 93
Encyclopedia Britannica: *109*
engineering: *43*
engineering, :
    teaching 90
engineers: *95, 96*
enrichment theory: *43*
enrolment: *15*
environmentally based education: *10*
ETV Maranhão: *2*
Europe: *4, 17, 80*
European Economic Community: *53, 99, 107*
European Home Study Council: *8, 118*
evaluation: *74*
evauation: *108*
Everyman's University: *8, 44, 66*
examinations: *15, 105*
experimental kit: *96*

Subject Index

extension service: *66*
extrinsic orientation: *31, 32*

F
face-to-face contact: *4, 5, 6, 10, 45, 54, 55, 89, 95, 97, 105, 115, 118*
facilitator: *51*
facilities, :
    sharing 21
facsimile: *26*
faculty: *74*
family education: *107*
farmer education: *16*
farmers: *96*
fee policy: *74*
feedback: *5, 6, 84, 85, 89, 101, 108, 114, 118*
Fernuniversität: *11, 24, 33, 48, 64, 102, 118*
fibre optics: *9*
Fiji: *78*
film: *9*
financial management: *72*
Findhorn: *100*
Finland: *45, 52, 113*
Finniston Committee: *95*
FlexiStudy: *57, 58*
flow experience: *31*
folk high schools: *52*
Ford Foundation: *12*
Ford Motors: *111*
foreign aid: *12*
formal education: *4*
France: *4, 8, 23, 75, 101, 104, 107*
French, :
    teaching of 51
French courses: *86, 87*
Fundacíon Educacíonal Padre Landell de Moura: *19*
funding, :
    educational 65, 68, 71, 75

G
Gaza Strip: *89*
General Motors: *109, 111*
Germany: *4*
Ghana: *11, 12*
governance: *59*
grading: *105*
graduate studies: *58, 66, 80, 97, 98*
grants to students: *63*
Great Britain: *4, 53, 56, 75, 88, 97, 101, 109*
Grenoble: *104*
group meetings: *6, 33, 60, 87*
group support: *9, 10*
group viewing: *2*
guidance: *6, 48, 88, 113*
Gujarat Agricultural University: *16*

H
handicapped, :
    education of 63
    rights of 80
Harvard University: *68*
Hawaii: *101*
health education: *106*
Helsinki University: *52*
Hermods: *118*
Hiroshima University: *60*
history courses: *30*
Hobart: *56*
Holland: *4*
Hong Kong: *11, 22*
horizontalization: *31*
human factors: *2*

I
ICCE (see International Council for Correspondence Education)
IIEP: *2*
India: *11, 12, 13, 14, 16, 58*
Indiana University: *85*
individualized learning: *111*
industrialized teaching: *5*
inflation, :
    cause of 101
information revolution: *101*
initiation of students: *4*
input: *72*
in-service training: *13, 16, 44, 80, 88, 89*
Institute of Marketing: *113*
institution, :
    classification of 66
    types of 66
institutional access: *55*
institutional autonomy: *58*
institutional image: *77*
institutional size: *58*
institutions, :
    funding 13
    models 8
Instituto Tecnologico y de Estudios Superiores de Monterrey: *18*
Instituto Universal Brasileiro: *18*
instruction, :
    models 7
instructional design: *30, 32, 34, 39, 81, 85, 103*
instructional systems design: *29, 58*
instructional theory: *1*
instructor training: *105*
integration of media: *89*
integration of work and education: *4, 10*
intelligence revolution: *101*
interactive media: *101*
inter-institutional cooperation: *59, 63, 65, 95, 98*
inter-institutional relations: *55*
International Correspondence School: *71, 75*

Subject Index

International Council for Correspondence Education: *8, 15, 18, 23, 58, 76, 78, 92, 118*
International Extension College: *84*
International Labour Office: *10*
interpersonal skills: *6*
intrinsic orientation: *31, 32*
Iran: *2, 8*
ISI-FKA (Internation Solidarity Institute): *18*
isolation: *9*
Israel: *44, 89*
Isreal: *8*
Italy: *4, 11*
Ivory Coast: *12*

J

Japan: *2, 60*
Japan University of the Air: *58*
Jean Commission: *25*
Jordan: *89*
Jyvaskyla University: *52*

K

Kanazawa University: *60*
Karmel Commission: *62*
Kenya: *10, 11, 44*
Kirigu Project: *10*
Knowledge Network of the West: *28, 61*
Konrad Adenauer Foundation: *18, 19*
Kumamoto University: *60*
Kuopio University: *52*

L

Labrador: *9*
language learning skills: *88*
language teaching: *51, 60, 80, 83, 85, 86, 87, 88, 99, 106*
Latin America: *4*
learner characteristics : *27*
learner-treatment interaction: *6*
learning, :
    models 100
    non-formal 28
    obstacles to 28
    reasons for 28
    effect of age 29
    models 32
learning centres, :
    mobile 54
learning objectives: *34*
learning outcome: *31*
learning projects: *81*
learning theory: *9*
learning-to-learn: *27, 81*
Lebanon: *89*
Leiden University: *59*
Leningrad: *88*
libraries, :
    access to 109
life insurance industry: *16*
life-long learning: *9, 67*

literacy: *107*
literacy campaign: *106*
local centres: *59, 69*
local support: *56, 58, 59*
Lund University: *4*

M

MacQuarrie University: *62*
Malawi: *44*
management: *58, 73*
management studies: *95*
Manitoba: *40*
Manitoba Telephone System: *110*
manpower development: *12*
Maori : *83*
Maranhão FMTVE (Brazil): *44*
marker reliability: *82*
marketing: *58*
marking: *46*
Marseilles: *104*
mass education: *4*
mass media: *77*
Massey University: *36, 66, 78*
Master of Business Administration: *42*
mathemagenic activities: *7*
Mauritius: *44*
Mauritius College of the Air: *2, 12, 44*
McGill University: *68, 91*
McGraw-Hill: *109*
media: *21, 24, 49, 67, 92, 99, 102, 105*
media, :
    broadcast 101
    interactive 101
    student preferences 104
    accessibility of 2
    control of 2
    convenience of 2
    theory of 2
    costs 72
    in language teaching 85
medical education: *96, 101*
Memorial University: *2, 9*
Mexico: *17, 18, 44*
microcomputers: *9, 54, 99, 100, 110, 113*
microelectronics: *101*
microprocessors: *2, 53, 80, 95, 96, 99*
Minerva Madureza (Brazil): *44*
minicomputers: *100, 117*
mobile learning centres: *54*
Moscow: *88*
Muguga Project: *10*
multi-media: *4, 8, 9, 12, 64, 80, 86, 87, 88, 89, 96, 104, 107, 109, 110, 115, 116*
Murdoch University: *62, 66*
music teaching: *80, 92*

Subject Index

N

Nairobi: *10*
National Better Business Bureau (USA): *75*
National Center for Development of Broadcast Education: *60*
National Centre of Sociology of Social Legislation (Brussels): *4*
National Council for Correspondence Education (India): *15*
national development: *11*
National Education Association: *109, 111*
National Extension College: *11, 45, 57, 58, 84*
National Home Study Council: *18, 74, 75*
National University Continuing Education Association: *74*
needs analysis: *96*
needs assessment: *9*
needs survey: *60*
Netherlands: *8, 59, 107*
Netherlands Open University: *8, 11, 58, 59, 80, 99*
networks: *100, 101, 106*
New Age Community: *100*
New Guinea: *78*
New South Wales: *59*
New Zealand: *26, 78, 83*
New Zealand Council for Educational Research: *35*
New Zealand Technical Correspondence Institute: *4, 17, 35, 78, 83*
Newfoundland: *9*
newspaper: *88*
Newspaper College: *64*
NFU (see Norsk fjernundervisning)
Nicaragua: *9, 18*
Niger: *12*
NKS (see Norsk Korrespondanseskole)
non-starts: *36*
Norsk fjernundervisning: *58, 63*
Norsk Korrespondanseskole: *23, 38, 118*
North America: *100, 106*
North Island College: *6, 45, 54, 61, 81*
North Pole: *92*
Northern Norway Music Conservatory: *92*
Norway: *2, 11, 23, 38, 58, 63, 80, 92*
Norwegian Distance Education Institute: *23*
Norwegian Film Board: *63*
Norwegian State Broadcasting Corporation: *63*
Nova Scotia: *98*
Nova University: *97*
NUEA Formula: *6*
numeracy: *107*
nursing training: *34, 80*
NURT Poland: *2*

O

objectives: *6*
office of the future: *101*
OISE (see Ontario Institute for Studies in Education)
Ontario: *28*
Ontario Educational Communications Authority: *28, 108*
Ontario Institute for Studies in Education: *100*
Open Access Study Plan: *98*
open admission: *15, 60*
Open Learning Institute: *6, 25, 28, 45, 55, 58, 61, 66*
Open School of India: *3*
Open University: *2, 3, 4, 5, 6, 8, 12, 17, 18, 31, 32, 36, 37, 45, 53, 56, 58, 62, 66, 71, 72, 80, 90, 95, 96, 99, 106, 107, 109, 112, 115, 118*
operating budget: *72*
Optel: *2, 115*
Oracle: *2*
Organization of American States: *19*
orientation to study: *32*
Osaka University: *60*
Oslo: *92*
output: *72*
Oxford: *57*

P

paced-package course: *6*
pacing: *6, 36, 58, 59, 61*
Pakistan: *8*
Palestine: *80, 89*
Papua: *78*
Paraguay: *19*
parallel education: *10*
parallel school: *4*
Paris: *12, 104*
payment of tutors: *6*
pedagogy: *29*
peer evaluation (of institutions): *75*
peer tutors: *6*
Personalized System of Instruction: *6, 27, 29, 67*
Perth: *56*
Peru: *11, 17, 18*
phenomenography: *31*
Phillipines: *2*
philosophy: *74*
PIUTEC (see Capricorn Interuniversity Program)
planning: *59, 60, 71, 113*
PLATO: *2, 8, 100*
policies, :
    national *21*
policy: *58*
political changes: *17*
political environment: *58*
polymer technology: *95*
Polynesia: *17*
Polynesian: *83*
Polytechnic Institute (Poland): *4*
Portugal: *4, 107*
postal communication: *7, 45, 48, 57, 65*
poverty: *9, 14*
pre-service training: *89*
Prestel: *2, 101, 109, 113*
primary school leavers: *10, 12*
print: *2, 17, 88*
priorities: *80*
priorities in development: *69*

private institutions: *1, 4, 10, 11, 21, 23, 25*
private sector: *8, 21, 99*
private sector education: *71*
productivity, :
    in information jobs 101
professional education: *58*
professional programs: *14*
professional updating: *95*
programmed instruction: *17*
programmed texts: *16*
Public Broadcasting Service (USA): *28*
public examinations: *23*
public relations: *77*
public sector education: *71*
publicity: *58, 74, 77, 96*

Q
Quebec: *11, 25, 45, 51, 70, 73, 91, 94*

R
radio: *2, 8, 9, 10, 12, 15, 25, 52, 57, 60, 65, 87, 88, 99, 104, 106, 109, 116*
radio, :
    shortwave 26
Radio College: *64*
Radio Escuela Santa Maria (Dominican Republic): *44*
Radio Santa Maria: *3*
radio schools: *18*
Radio Universites: *104*
Radioifusora Nacíonal de Columbia: *18*
Radioprimaria (Mexico): *44*
Radio-Propedeutiques: *104*
Rashtriya Chemicals and Fertilizer: *16*
readability: *35, 80*
reading skills: *17*
reception learning: *7*
record-keeping: *6, 92*
REDEAL: *6*
regional centres: *25, 45, 55, 56, 59*
regional tutorial services: *70*
regionalization: *56*
registration: *36*
reminder letters: *38*
research: *1, 6, 9, 13, 19, 27, 32, 38, 60, 68, 76, 97, 118*
research, :
    integrated with teaching 24
residential courses: *104*
Rhodesia: *11, 17*
Roberto Marinho Foundation: *18*
robots: *101*
Rockefeller Foundation: *12*
Royal Australian Flying Doctor Service: *26*
Royal Melbourne Institute of Technology: *8, 78*
Royal Veterinary College: *96*
rural development: *10, 12*
Ryerson Polytechnical Institute: *28*

S
Saskatchewan: *25*
satellites: *2, 9, 26, 65, 66, 78, 106*
Scandinavia: *4*
scholarship: *68*
scholastic recuperation: *4*
School of the Air (Australia): *26, 78*
school of the future: *101*
science: *67*
science education: *13, 14*
screening of entrants: *48*
second language teaching: *82, 91*
secondary school leavers: *12*
secondary students: *4, 26*
self-assessment: *82*
self-directed learning: *29*
self-evaluation (of institutions): *75*
self-financing courses: *96*
self-instruction: *17*
self-pacing: *6*
self-study: *74*
self-study centres: *10*
semester length: *61*
seminars: *6, 51, 104*
Senegal: *12*
services: *74*
sexuality: *94*
shortwave radio: *26*
Simon Fraser University: *66*
software, :
    compatibility 2
South Africa: *8*
South America: *11, 18, 19, 20*
South Korea: *44*
South Pacific: *78, 83*
Soviet Union: *4, 8, 12, 13, 80, 88*
Soviet Union, :
    distance education and work 3
    radio schools 3
Spain: *4, 8, 18, 20, 107*
Spanish courses: *85*
speech recognition: *101*
Sri Lanka: *8*
staff training: *1, 21, 35, 38, 58, 99*
staff/student ratio: *62*
standards: *74*
state institutions: *21*
structural communication: *7*
structure of texts: *31*
student achievement: *6*
student advising: *45*
student assistance: *14*
student contact: *15*
student data: *112*
student failure: *4*
student motivation: *45*

Subject Index

student motivation, :
    isolation 10
    low prestige 10
    parental attitudes 10
    peer influence 10, 27
student performance: *6, 43*
student support: *1, 4, 42, 52, 55, 56, 59*
student support, :
    contact programs 14
    libraries 14
    peer support 45
    professional 45
    regional workshops 45, 51
    residential schools 45
    study cells 45, 51
    teleconferencing 45, 51
    telephone 45, 51
    volunteer 45, 53
    continuity 5, 53
    individualized 5
    mediation 5
    professional 53
    study groups 53
    workshops 53
student tracking: *113*
students, :
    occupations of 104
    deaf 109
    disabled 109
    motivation 6, 20, 26, 48, 85, 86
    funding 13, 23, 63
    preparation 17
    assessment 20
    financial motivation 23
    military 23
    characteristics 24, 27, 51, 55, 57, 86
    elementary 26
    isolation 26
    remediation 26
    initiation of 4
    geographic distribution 41, 52, 104
    reasons for studying 41
    social support 41
    ages 42, 104
    distance vs. traditional 42
    relationship with institution 45
    skills 53
    management of 6
student/teacher ratio: *82*
study, :
    orientation 31
    orientations 32
study buddy: *87*
study centres: *2, 14, 24, 45, 56, 57, 60*
study circles: *23, 45, 52*
study groups: *52, 59*
study guides: *7*
study habits: *49*
study schedule: *6*
study skills: *27, 31, 32, 55, 80, 81, 88*
study time: *43, 109, 118*
sub-optimization: *72*
summer school: *88, 89*
Sweden: *97, 118*

Syracuse University: *71*
Syria: *89*
systems analysis: *71*
systems design: *71*
systems theory: *71*

T

TAGER system: *66*
Tampere University: *52*
Tananarive: *12*
Tanzania: *2, 9, 99*
target populations: *59*
task analysis: *82*
Tasmania: *45, 56*
teacher training: *42, 80, 89, 91, 98*
teachers: *16*
teachers, :
    training 12, 15, 26
    graduate study 26, 98
    itinerant 26
    qualifications 26
    role 26, 101
teaching methods: *6*
technical education: *13*
technical training: *106*
technicians: *95*
technological education: *95*
technology: *95*
technology teaching: *80, 90*
telecommunications: *101, 109, 116*
teleconferencing: *2, 26, 65, 87, 95, 105, 115*
teleconferencing, :
    research 105
Telecurso Secundo Grau (Brazil): *44*
Telekolleg: *4*
telephone: *2, 5, 9, 22, 30, 50, 51, 54, 55, 65 87, 99, 109, 116*
telephone tutoring: *7, 60, 88*
Telesecundaria (Mexico): *44*
Teletel: *109*
teletext: *2, 109*
Télé-université: *8, 25, 28 45, 51, 70, 71, 73, 94*
television: *2, 8, 9, 12, 22, 25, 52, 54, 57, 60, 61, 65, 81, 87, 88, 99, 101, 104, 106, 108, 109, 111, 116*
television, :
    distribution 103
    production 103
Telidon: *2, 9, 101, 109, 110*
text processing: *99, 117*
texts, :
    structure 31
Tezukayama Gakuin University: *60*
Thailand: *2*
The Television University (China): *44*
Third World: *9*
time-effectiveness: *43*
Tohoku University: *60*
Tokai University: *60*
Tokyo Institute of Technology: *60*

Subject Index

Total Enrolment Formula: *6*
trade unions: *59*
training, :
    need for 2
travel agents: *93*
Tromso: *92*
tuition fees: *14*
Tuktoyaktuk: *101*
Turku University: *52*
turn-around time: *20, 27, 38, 40, 58, 109, 114*
tutor comments: *38*
tutor letter: *67*
tutor training: *50, 99*
tutorials: *42, 57, 105*
tutoring: *1, 4, 6, 27, 46, 50, 53, 61, 87, 109, 115*
tutoring skills: *6*
tutor-marked exercises: *10*
tutors: *5, 7, 10, 17, 51, 57, 58, 59*
tutors, :
    role 45, 54
    training 45
    interaction with students 46
    skills 54
tutor-student relationship: *6*
TVOntario: *28, 99, 108*
two-mode institutions: *27, 42, 58, 99, 105*
two-mode operation: *62*
two-way communication: *7, 108*
two-way comunication: *109*
typesetting, :
    computerized 117

U

ULSA (see Universidad la Salle de Sud America)
UNA (see Universidad Nacional Abierta):
UNED (see Universidad Nacional de Educacíona Distancia)
unemployment: *10, 14*
Unesco: *4, 12*
United Kingdom: *2, 8, 11, 45, 57, 76, 80, 95, 96, 100, 106, 107*
United States: *4, 8, 13, 26, 28, 58, 74, 75, 80, 85, 95, 97, 99, 101, 109, 114, 116*
Universidad Abierta: *4*
Universidad Católica Boliviana: *19*
Universidad Católica de Salta: *19*
Universidad Católica Nuestra Señora Asunción: *19*
Universidad Centroamericana: *17*
Universidad de Chile: *18*
Universidad de Chile, sede Antofagasta: *19*
Universidad de La Salle: *18*
Universidad del Norte-Chile: *19*
Universidad Estadual de Londrina: *19*
Universidad Estadual de Maringá: *19*
Universidad Estadual de Ponta Grossa: *19*
Universidad Gabriel René Moreno: *19*
Universidad la Salle de Sud America: *20*
Universidad Mayor San Simón: *19*
Universidad Nacional Abierta: *18*

Universidad Nacional de Asunción: *19*
Universidad Nacional de Educacíona Distancia: *18*
Universidad Nacional de Salta: *19*
Universidad San Francisco Xavier de Chuquisaca: *19*
Universidad Tecnica del Estado, sede Antofagasta: *19*
university extension: *60*
University Grants Commission (India): *13*
University of Calgary: *105*
University of California (San Diego): *8*
University of Delhi: *14, 66*
University of Electro-Communications: *60*
University of Ghana: *12*
University of Joensuu: *52*
University of Lagos: *12*
University of Lund: *118*
University of Manitoba: *110*
University of Maryland: *66*
University of Mid-America: *28*
University of Missouri: *114*
University of Nairobi: *10, 66*
University of New England: *42, 45, 59*
University of Oklahoma: *97*
University of Quebec: *51*
University of Queensland: *42, 62, 66, 78*
University of Rheims: *104*
University of Saskatchewan: *39*
University of the Air (Japan): *60, 99*
University of the Air (UK): *99*
University of the State of New York: *75*
University of Waterloo: *41*
University of Western Australia: *78*
University of Wisconsin: *12, 66*
urban migration: *10*

V

Vancouver Island: *54*
Venezuela: *8, 18*
veterinary education: *96*
Victoria: *69*
Victoria Correspondence School: *78*
Victorian TAFE Off-Campus Network: *69*
video: *2, 19, 26, 99*
video cassettes: *2, 3, 80, 89, 92, 99, 115*
video tape: *9, 91, 101, 103*
videodisc: *2, 65, 80, 99, 101, 103, 111*
videodisc, :
    capacitance 109
    evaluation of 109
    optical 109
    bilingual capability 111
videodisc players: *109*
videotex: *2, 65, 99, 100, 101, 109, 110, 113*
viewdata: *2, 109*
village polytechnic: *10*
visual literacy: *80, 103*
vocational education: *10, 61*
vocational subjects: *80*

Subject Index

vocational training: *13*
Volkswagen Foundation: *64*

W
West Bank: *89*
West Germany: *8, 11, 23, 33, 58, 64, 67, 88, 97, 102, 107*
Western Australian Institute of Technology: *78*
Western Europe: *23, 56*
WICAT Inc.: *109*
Wisconsin: *2*
work, :
    integration with education **4, 10**
workshops: *104*
World Bank: *9*
writing, :
    improvement of **35**
    teaching **80, 82, 84**

X
Xanadu network: *100*

Y
Yugoslavia: *4, 8*

Z
Zambia: *12*
Zanzibar: *101*

Notes